LIVERPOOL FC
THE OFFICIAL GUIDE
2007

Sport Media
A Trinity Mirror Business

HONOURS

LEAGUE CHAMPIONSHIP
1900-01, 1905-06, 1921-22,
1922-23, 1946-47,
1963-64, 1965-66, 1972-73, 1975-76,
1976-77, 1978-79, 1979-80, 1981-82,
1982-83, 1983-84, 1985-86,
1987-88, 1989-90

DIVISION TWO WINNERS
1893-94, 1895-96, 1904-05, 1961-62

LANCASHIRE LEAGUE WINNERS
1892-93

FA CUP WINNERS
1964-65, 1973-74, 1985-86, 1988-89,
1991-92, 2000-01, 2005-06

LEAGUE CUP WINNERS
1980-81, 1981-82, 1982-83, 1983-84,
1994-95, 2000-01, 2002-03

FA CHARITY SHIELD WINNERS
(FA COMMUNITY SHIELD)
1966, 1974, 1976, 1979, 1980,
1982, 1988, 1989, 2001
(SHARED)
1964, 1965, 1977, 1986, 1990

EUROPEAN CUP
(UEFA CHAMPIONS LEAGUE)
1976-77, 1977-78, 1980-81, 1983-84, 2004-05

UEFA CUP WINNERS
1972-73, 1975-76, 2000-01

EUROPEAN SUPER CUP WINNERS
1977, 2001, 2005

SUPER CUP WINNERS
1985-86

INTRODUCTION

Liverpool FC The Official Guide 2007 is the bible of club information for Reds fans everywhere. From contact numbers to essential club information, player profiles to club records, everything and more is included in this invaluable publication.

Following in the tradition of its debut release last year, the Guide is again packed full of facts and stats about the famous Mersey Reds. To achieve this we have again utilised the finest statisticians and club experts to provide as much up-to-date information as possible that deadlines have allowed, prior to the new campaign.

New for this year is a key section on Liverpool's exploits in European competition and the Club World Championship, with comprehensive information about former opponents and famous games, up to and including the final game of the 2005/06 season, a certain FA Cup final clash against West Ham United.

A full Premier League section documenting our record since 1992/93 has been updated, as have sections including the definitive guide to the club's FA Cup history. There is also a fascinating insight into the first two seasons of each of the club's managers from Shankly onwards, while new features include a record of Robbie Fowler's goals for the club, a list of the Reds' records created in 2005/06 and a history of Liverpool in penalty shootouts. In addition, with the summer of 2006 having witnessed the World Cup, there will also be a focus on Liverpool players to have played for their country in the finals.

All of the 2005/06 playing stats again come as standard, and we continue to strive to make this series the kind of book that you will take down from your bookshelf time and again as a source of reference. To complete an outstanding package, it features some of the finest pictures from matches involving the Reds from the past year, not least the sensational Millennium Stadium triumph and the remarkable run all the way to that final.

We pride ourselves on our accuracy and reflecting the constant changes in and around the club. We hope you continue to enjoy it.

CONTRIBUTORS

Ged Rea and Dave Ball are Liverpool FC's official statisticians. Ged's Liverpool FC records are second-to-none, while Dave is a key researcher for long-running BBC TV show 'A Question of Sport'. James Cleary has also played a major role in researching and writing key information.

Sport Media

A Trinity Mirror Business

Executive Editor: KEN ROGERS Editor: STEVE HANRAHAN

Art Editor: RICK COOKE Production Editor: PAUL DOVE

Sales and Marketing Manager: ELIZABETH MORGAN

Writers: JAMES CLEARY, ALAN JEWELL, GAVIN KIRK, DAVID RANDLES, CHRIS McLOUGHLIN,
JOHN HYNES, WILLIAM HUGHES

Designers: BARRY PARKER, GLEN HIND, COLIN SUMPTER, LEE ASHUN, ALISON GILLILAND

ISBN 1 9052 6611 1

978 1 9052 6611 1

Printed and finished by Scotprint, Haddington, Scotland

CLUB TELEPHONE NUMBERS

Main Switchboard	0151 263 2361
Customer Services	0870 220 2345

Ticket Office

Credit Card Booking Line	0870 220 2151
UEFA Booking Line	0870 220 0034
League/FA Cup Booking Line	0870 220 0056
Priority Booking Line (Priority Ticket Scheme members only)	0870 220 0408
24-hour match ticket information line	0870 444 4949
Mail Order Hotline (UK)	0870 6000532
International Mail Order Hotline	+ 44 1386 852035
Club Store (Anfield)	0151 263 1760
Club Store (City Centre)	0151 330 3077
Conference and Banqueting (for your events at Anfield)	0151 263 7744
Corporate Sales	0151 263 9199
Development Association	0151 263 6391
Community Department	0151 264 2316
Museum & Tour Centre	0151 260 6677
Membership Department	0151 261 1444
Public Relations (including all charity requests)	0151 260 1433

BECOME A MEMBER OF THE OFFICIAL LIVERPOOL SUPPORTERS CLUB
To join, please call: 08707 02 02 07
International: +44 151 261 1444

SUBSCRIBE TO THE OFFICIAL LFC PROGRAMME AND WEEKLY MAGAZINE
To take out a subscription please call: 0845 1430001

OFFICIAL LFC SMS ALERTS - Keep up to date with the Reds wherever you are!
For news, team sheet, goals and results to your mobile simply text LFC 4U to:
87058 (UK)/53235 (ROI)
For ticket alerts, text LFC TIX. For news only, text LFC NEWS. For goals, text LFC GOAL.
Full range of packages and T&Cs at www.liverpoolfc.tv.

Show your true colours and get LFC on your mobile by visiting www.liverpoolfc.tv/mobilezone and
choosing from LFC Wallpapers, Ringtones, Commentary Realtones and much, much more.

Sign up for an e Season Ticket to see Premier League goals & highlights, on-line TV channels and
follow the team live through Turnstile.
To sign up go to www.liverpoolfc.tv

LFC Save & Support Account with Britannia
For more information visit www.britannia.co.uk/lfc, call 0800 915 0503 or visit any Britannia branch

Liverpool FC Credit Card in Association with MBNA
For more information call 0800 776 262

CONTENTS

	Pages
Liverpool honours list	4
Introduction	5
Club telephone numbers	6
Foreword: Rick Parry	9
Key dates 06/07	10-11
Fixture list 06/07	12-13
Anfield past and present	14-15

THE BOSS 16-27
An overview of Rafa Benitez's two seasons in charge of Liverpool, while also comparing his success over that period with that of the Reds' previous managers, from Shankly onwards.

THE PLAYERS 06/07 28-45
A definitive guide to this season's squad, including appearances and goals for the club. Reserve, academy and ladies statistics are also present, including fixture lists for the new campaign - plus a nod to the club's FA Youth Cup-winning squad.

THE TOP 10 MOMENTS 05/06 46-53
A pictorial reminder of the highs of the last campaign, culminating in another unforgettable final success - this time in Cardiff.

EUROPE AND BEYOND 54-85
From TNS in July to Cardiff in May - plus every Reds result in Europe and Japan.

THE 05/06 PREMIERSHIP CAMPAIGN 86-109
A look back at the domestic season, documenting the results, quotes, Liverpool's league progress and gems of wisdom from Reds boss Rafa Benitez.

THE PREMIERSHIP 110-119
Liverpool's Premiership record, record appearance holders and goalscorers since 1992/93 are documented together with other facts and statistics.

THE CUPS 120-151
From the Club World Championship to every domestic cup competition, each game is listed including the Reds' FA Charity Shield/FA Community Shield record. There is also a feature on Liverpool's seven FA Cup triumphs.

THE RECORDS 152-179
Section containing appearance and goalscoring records, with new features including a celebration of the new records created in 2005/06; an evaluation of Robbie Fowler's Liverpool record; Liverpool's penalty shootout record and, in World Cup year, a look at Reds players who have played in the biggest tournament in international football.

PREMIERSHIP OPPONENTS 180-191
A look at who the Reds will be facing in the 2006/07 season, with useful information including how to get to the different stadiums and Liverpool's recent record against each team.

ESSENTIALS AND ENTERTAINMENT 192-208
From ticket details and how to join the Reds' supporters club, to travel information and other Liverpool products, essential info for following the Reds.

FOREWORD

RICK PARRY
CHIEF EXECUTIVE

Welcome to our second highly comprehensive Liverpool FC Guide. We go into the 2006-07 campaign as FA Cup holders and our ambitions remain stronger than ever.
This Guide takes you to the heart of our famous club and should satisfy your hunger for all things Liverpool - alongside some of our other mediums.

* Our magazine – "LFC" – is the ONLY official weekly club publication in the country. This in itself demonstrates your insatiable appetite for exclusive interviews and features from the heart of Melwood and Anfield.
* Our website – liverpoolfc.tv – provides all of the breaking news coming out of the club and much more. Our e-Season ticket package, available through liverpoolfc.tv, strives to bring the match experience right into your home, even enabling you to view the manager's big match press conferences.
* We have a quarterly Official Liverpool Poster Magazine for younger fans and our award-winning This Is Anfield matchday programme is rated as one of the best in the country.
* We even have exclusive quarterly glossy magazines for both our junior and senior Official Liverpool Supporters' Club members. The content focus in these publications looks at every angle of club life, from what the ground staff do to how our world-class Melwood training facility operates.

We hope this Guide will remain a constant companion for our fans, with a specific focus in this edition on our FA Cup statistics in the wake of our superb final victory over West Ham United.

Thanks for your passionate and loyal support.

Rick Parry

KEY DATES 2006-07

(Dates are subject to change)

August

9	UEFA Champions League 3rd qualifying round, 1st leg
13	FA Community Shield (Millennium Stadium, Cardiff)
19	Premiership kick-off
22/23	UEFA Champions League 3rd qualifying round, 2nd leg
24	UEFA Champions League group stage draw
25	UEFA Cup first-round draw
31	Transfer window closes (5pm)

September

12/13	UEFA Champions League group stage matchday 1
14	UEFA Cup 1st round, 1st leg
26/27	UEFA Champions League group stage matchday 2
28	UEFA Cup 1st round, 2nd leg

October

3	UEFA Cup group stage draw
17/18	UEFA Champions League group stage matchday 3
19	UEFA Cup group stage matchday 1
24/25	Carling Cup third round
31	UEFA Champions League group stage matchday 4

November

1	UEFA Champions League group stage matchday 4
2	UEFA Cup group stage matchday 2
7/8	Carling Cup fourth round
21/22	UEFA Champions League group stage matchday 5
23	UEFA Cup group stage matchday 3
29/30	UEFA Cup group stage matchday 4

December

5/6	UEFA Champions League group stage matchday 6
13/14	UEFA Cup group stage matchday 5
15	UEFA Champions League first knockout stage draw
15	UEFA Cup round of 32, round of 16 draw
19/20	Carling Cup quarter-final
31	Transfer window re-opens

January

6/7	FA Cup third round
9/10	Carling Cup semi-final 1st leg

KEY DATES 2006-07

(Dates are subject to change)

January

23/24	Carling Cup semi-final 2nd leg
27/28	FA Cup fourth round
31	Transfer window closes (5pm)

February

14/15	UEFA Cup round of 32 1st leg
17/18	FA Cup fifth round
20/21	UEFA Champions League first knockout round 1st leg
22	UEFA Cup round of 32 2nd leg
25	Carling Cup final (Wembley Stadium, London - TBC)

March

6/7	UEFA Champions League first knockout round, 2nd leg
8	UEFA Cup round of 16 1st leg
9	UEFA Champions League quarter-finals, semi-finals and final draw
10	FA Cup 6th round
14/15	UEFA Cup round of 16 2nd leg
16	UEFA Cup quarter-finals, semi-finals and final draw

April

3/4	UEFA Champions League quarter-finals 1st leg
5	UEFA Cup quarter-finals 1st leg
10/11	UEFA Champions League quarter-finals 2nd leg
12	UEFA Cup quarter-finals 2nd leg
14/15	FA Cup semi-finals
24/25	UEFA Champions League semi-finals 1st leg
26	UEFA Cup semi-finals 1st leg

May

1/2	UEFA Champions League semi-finals 2nd leg
3	UEFA Cup semi-finals 2nd leg
13	Premiership final day
16	UEFA Cup final (Hampden Park, Glasgow, Scotland)
19	FA Cup final (Wembley Stadium, London - TBC)
23	UEFA Champions League final (Olympic Stadium, Athens, Greece)

FIXTURE LIST 2006-07

August

9	UEFA Champions League 3rd qualifying round 1st leg		
13	Chelsea (FA Community Shield)	(N)	
19	Sheffield United	(A)	– 12.45pm kick-off
22/23	UEFA Champions League 3rd qualifying round 2nd leg		
26	West Ham United	(H)	– 12.45pm kick-off

September

9	Everton	(A)	– 12.45pm kick-off
12/13	UEFA Champions League group stage matchday 1		
17	Chelsea	(A)	– 1.30pm kick-off
20	Newcastle United	(H)	– 8pm kick-off
23	Tottenham Hotspur	(H)	– 12.45pm kick-off
26/27	UEFA Champions League group stage matchday 2		
30	Bolton Wanderers	(A)	– 12.45pm kick-off

October

14	Blackburn Rovers	(H)	
17/18	UEFA Champions League group stage matchday 3		
22	Manchester United	(A)	– 1pm kick-off
24/25	Carling Cup 3rd round		
28	Aston Villa	(H)	
31	UEFA Champions League group stage matchday 4		

November

1	UEFA Champions League group stage matchday 4		
4	Reading	(H)	
12	Arsenal	(A)	– 4pm kick-off
18	Middlesbrough	(A)	– 5.15pm kick-off
21/22	UEFA Champions League group stage matchday 5		
25	Manchester City	(H)	
29	Portsmouth	(H)	– 8pm kick-off

December

2	Wigan Athletic	(A)	
5/6	UEFA Champions League group stage matchday 6		
9	Fulham	(H)	
16	Charlton Athletic	(A)	– 12.45pm kick-off

FIXTURE LIST 2006-07

December

23	Watford	(H)
26	Blackburn Rovers	(A)
30	Tottenham Hotspur	(A)

January 2007

1	Bolton Wanderers	(H)
6	FA Cup 3rd round	
13	Watford	(A)
20	Chelsea	(H)
27	FA Cup 4th round	
30	West Ham United	(A) - 7.45pm kick-off

February

3	Everton	(H)
10	Newcastle United	(A)
17	FA Cup 5th round	
24	Sheffield United	(H)
25	Carling Cup final	

March

3	Manchester United	(H)
10	FA Cup 6th round	
17	Aston Villa	(A)
31	Arsenal	(H)

April

7	Reading	(A)
9	Middlesbrough	(H)
14	Manchester City	(A)
	(FA Cup semi-final)	
21	Wigan Athletic	(H)
28	Portsmouth	(A)

May

5	Fulham	(A)
13	Charlton Athletic	(H)
16	UEFA Cup final	
19	FA Cup final	
23	UEFA Champions League final	

ANFIELD PAST AND PRESENT

Since Liverpool's formation in 1892, there have been a host of changes to the stadium which now resides on Anfield Road. From an original capacity of 20,000, extensive redevelopment, beginning particularly in the Bill Shankly era, has seen Anfield host upwards of 60,000. The ground, which hosted European Championship games in 1996 and whose most recent showpiece match was England's friendly with Uruguay in March 2006, currently holds 45,522 – with this figure taking into account the Press and disabled areas and all seating, some of which is not used due to segregation at the Anfield Road end.

THE KOP - Capacity 12,409

Built in 1906 after the Reds won the league championship for a second time. It was, of course, named 'Spion Kop' after a South African hill which was the scene of a bloody Boer War battle. In 1928 it was rebuilt and a roof was added with the capacity reaching close to 30,000 - the largest covered terrace in the Football League at that time. It was rebuilt in 1994 to its current splendour after an emotional 'last stand' against Norwich City.

CENTENARY STAND - Capacity 11,414

The original Kemlyn Road Stand incorporated a barrel roof and was fronted by an uncovered paddock. It was demolished in 1963 to make way for a new cantilever stand. In 1992 a second tier was added and the stand was renamed to mark the club's 100th anniversary.

MAIN STAND/PADDOCK - Capacity 12,277

The original structure was erected in the late 19th century, a 3,000-capacity stand with a distinctive red and white tudor style with the club's name in the centre. In 1973 it was redeveloped with a new roof and opened by HRH the Duke of Kent. Seats were added to the Paddock seven years later.

ANFIELD ROAD - Capacity 9,045

In 1903 the first Anfield Road stand was built. Once a simple one-tier stand which contained a covered standing enclosure (1965), it was demolished to make way for a two-tier development in 1998 - the stand having been altered to accomodate seating in the early 1980s.

RECORD ANFIELD ATTENDANCES (Highs)

Overall:	61,905 v Wolves, 02/02/1952, FA Cup 4th round
League:	58,757 v Chelsea, 27/12/1949, Division 1
League Cup:	50,880 v Nottingham Forest, 12/02/1980, semi-final 2nd leg
Europe:	55,104 v Barcelona, 14/04/1976, Uefa Cup semi-final 2nd leg

RECORD ANFIELD ATTENDANCES (Lows)

Overall:	1,000 v Loughborough Town, 07/12/1895, Division 2
Record (post-war):	11,976 v Scunthorpe United, 22/04/1959, Division 2
FA Cup:	4,000 v Newton, 29/10/1892, 2nd Qualifying Round
FA Cup (post-war):	11,207 v Chester City, 09/01/1946, 3rd round 2nd leg
League Cup:	9,902 v Brentford, 25/10/1983, 2nd round, 2nd leg
Europe:	12,021 v Dundalk, 28/09/1982, European Cup 1st round, 1st leg

The Kop (top) and the Anfield Road end (bottom), full to capacity of a matchday at Anfield

The F

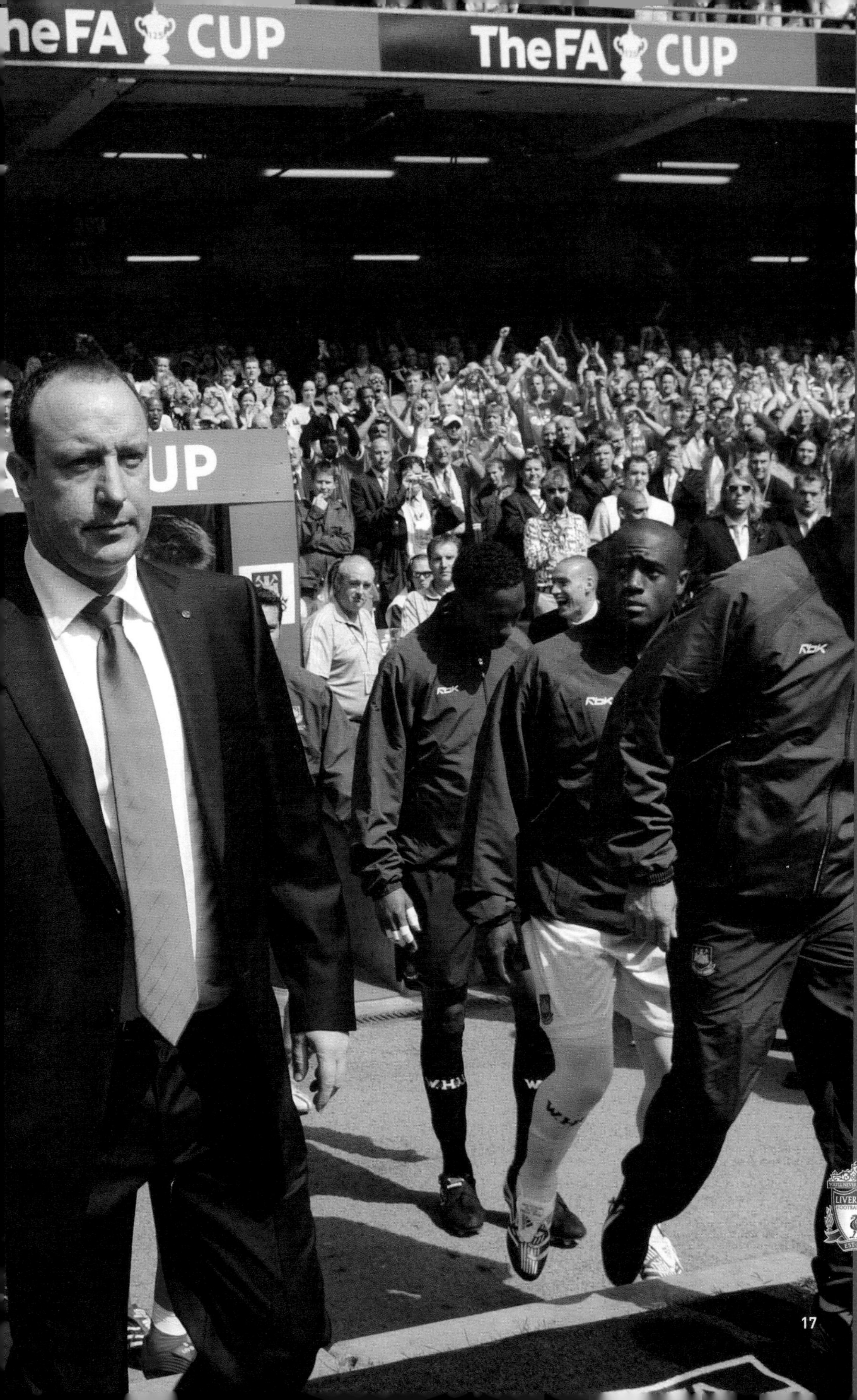
TheFA CUP
TheFA CUP
UP

LIVERPOOL'S MANAGERS

Of Liverpool's 16 full-time managers, there are only a select few who were able to record firsts in the top job at Anfield. Tom Watson oversaw the Reds' first championship success in 1900-01, Bill Shankly the first FA Cup triumph (1965), Bob Paisley the first League Cup success (1981) and European Cup win (1977) while Phil Taylor is the only Liverpool manager to have managed the club in Division 2 throughout his time in charge. Bob Paisley is the most successful in terms of silverware won, an impressive haul of 14 major trophies in nine seasons, although Kenny Dalglish, Liverpool's first player-manager, has the best win ratio - 60.91%. That said, the current man in charge is the only boss to collect silverware in each of his first two seasons in charge.

Incidentally, the following list does not take into account W.E. Barclay (1892-1896), who was the secretary-manager of Liverpool while John McKenna was seen as the man in charge despite not holding down the official title of manager - in reality he performed many of the duties of the role.

RAFAEL BENITEZ	June 2004-Present
GERARD HOULLIER	November 1998-May 2004
ROY EVANS (joint manager with Gerard Houllier)	July 1998-November 1998
ROY EVANS	January 1994-November 1998
GRAEME SOUNESS	April 1991-January 1994
RONNIE MORAN (caretaker)	February 1991-April 1991
KENNY DALGLISH	May 1985-February 1991
JOE FAGAN	May 1983-May 1985
BOB PAISLEY	July 1974-May 1983
BILL SHANKLY	December 1959-July 1974
PHIL TAYLOR	May 1956-November 1959
DON WELSH	March 1951-May 1956
GEORGE KAY	May 1936-February 1951
GEORGE PATTERSON	February 1928-May 1936
MATT McQUEEN	February 1923-February 1928
DAVID ASHWORTH	December 1919-February 1923
TOM WATSON	August 1896-May 1915
JOHN McKENNA	August 1892-August 1896

RAFAEL BENITEZ'S RECORD

Such were the highs created by Liverpool's UEFA Champions League exploits in Istanbul at the end of Rafa Benitez's first season in charge, that it was always expected to be a tall order to repeat the feat in 2005-2006. But despite the holders (who were forced to begin their campaign on July 13th, their earliest start to a season ever) bowing out in the last 16 to Benfica, the overall impact made by the Spaniard, which culminated in another dramatic Cup-winning finale in May, has continued to set new ground.

That FA Cup victory over West Ham ensured Benitez became the first Reds manager to win a major trophy in his first two seasons. In terms of who came before him, that in itself is a remarkable achievement. It was the icing on the cake of a season that, amongst other records, saw the following feats:

A club-record 11 consecutive clean sheets, a total of 1040 minutes
The third best-ever home goals conceded record
Most home wins since 1987-1988 (15)
Most goals ever scored by substitutes (21)
Liverpool going 10 games at Anfield without conceding
Most Premiership points in a season (82)
Most consecutive wins (12 - another club record)

In terms of domestic improvement, aside from an early exit in the Carling Cup to Crystal Palace, Liverpool's Premiership record surpassed all other campaigns since the formation of the current top flight in 1992. The haul of 82 points was their best ever, and highest since the Championship was won in 1987-1988. This also saw an Anfield record which yielded 15 out of 19 wins and with successes at Manchester City and Wigan Athletic, it meant the Reds have now won at every current Premiership stadium - apart from this season's newcomers Sheffield United and Reading.

It would not do the Reds justice too if their other success was overlooked - namely the European Super Cup victory over CSKA Moscow. That 3-1 triumph completed a hat-trick in the competition, while the Club World Championship in December saw Liverpool see three goals disallowed in the final, a 1-0 defeat to Brazilian side Sao Paulo in Yokohama, Japan.

The following statistics are a breakdown of Rafa Benitez's record in charge following his second campaign. Incidentally, the FA Cup final victory, like the previous season's European Cup final triumph (despite the 3-3 scorelines before Liverpool took the trophy on penalties), are both recorded as an away win in the overall table, and a win in the other tables.

2005-2006 SEASON													
		HOME					AWAY						
	Pld	W	D	L	F	A	W	D	L	F	A	GD	Pts
LEAGUE	38	15	3	1	32	8	10	4	5	25	17	32	82
FA CUP	6	1	0	0	1	0	5	0	0	19	8	-	-
LEAGUE CUP	1	-	-	-	-	-	0	0	1	1	2	-	-
CHAMPIONS LEAGUE	14	3	2	2	8	3	5	1	1	12	4	-	-
EUROPEAN SUPER CUP	1	-	-	-	-	-	1	0	0	3	1	-	-
CLUB WORLD C'SHIP	2	-	-	-	-	-	1	0	1	3	1	-	-
TOTAL	62	19	5	3	41	11	22	5	8	63	33	-	-

Season total:(all comps)					
Pld	W	D	L	F	A
62	41	10	11	104	44

RECORD IN ALL GAMES						
	Pld	W	D	L	F	A	Pts
LEAGUE	76	42	14	20	109	66	140
FA CUP	7	6	0	1	20	9	-
LEAGUE CUP	7	5	0	2	11	6	-
CHAMPIONS LEAGUE	29	17	6	6	40	17	-
EUROPEAN SUPER CUP	1	1	0	0	3	1	-
CLUB WORLD C'SHIP	2	1	0	1	3	1	-
TOTAL	122	72	20	30	186	100	-

Up to and including May 13th 2006

TWO-SEASON WONDER

In recognition of a second successive trophy-winning campaign for Rafa Benitez, it is worth noting the respective records of Liverpool's last 8 managers, including Benitez, in their first two seasons in charge in order to recognise the relative success of the Spaniard's Anfield reign thus far.

Apart from Bill Shankly, whose 2 seasons were in Division Two, each boss took charge in the top flight and each tasted some success. Statistics are noted for each of the two campaigns plus the overall record, whilst our level of rating is taken on account of the percentage wins.

RAFA BENITEZ

BENITEZ 2004-2005   **(Premiership, three points for a win)**
TROPHIES WON   **European Cup**

RECORD									
	Pld	W	D	L	F	A	Pts	Pos	% Wins
LEAGUE	38	17	7	14	52	41	58	5th	44.74
FA CUP	1	0	0	1	0	1	-	-	00.00
LGE CUP	6	5	0	1	10	4	-	-	83.33
EUROPE	15	9	3	3	20	10	-	-	60.00
OVERALL	60	31	10	19	82	56	-	-	51.67

Despite one of the lowest percentage of wins in the league and an early exit from the FA Cup, a run to the final of the League Cup boosted Benitez's overall record - while success in Europe ensured a trophy in his first season.

BENITEZ 2005-2006   **(Premiership, three points for a win)**
TROPHIES WON   **FA Cup, European Super Cup**

RECORD									
	Pld	W	D	L	F	A	Pts	Pos	% Wins
LEAGUE	38	25	7	6	57	25	82	3rd	65.79
FA CUP	6	6	0	0	20	8	-	-	100.00
LGE CUP	1	0	0	1	1	2	-	-	0.00
EUROPE	14	8	3	3	20	7	-	-	57.14
SUPER CUP	1	1	0	0	3	1	-	-	100.00
C. WORLD	2	1	0	1	3	1	-	-	50.00
OVERALL	62	41	10	11	104	44	-	-	66.13

From one of the worst to the best, Benitez's second season in charge yielded the greatest win percentage of all managers. The improvement in the league saw a turnaround of 8 defeats = 8 wins and 24 extra points to the previous season, while FA Cup success was also obtained with a 100% record from 6 games. The only downside was an early exit in the League Cup, although having been forced to enter the Champions League in the first qualifying round, the Reds' run to the last 16 was achieved by playing just one game less than the previous season.

BENITEZ TWO-SEASON TOTAL								
	Pld	W	D	L	F	A	Pts	% Wins
LEAGUE	76	42	14	20	109	66	140	55.26
FA CUP	7	6	0	1	20	9	-	85.71
LGE CUP	7	5	0	2	11	6	-	71.43
EUROPE	30	18	6	6	43	18	-	60.00
C. WORLD	2	1	0	1	3	1	-	50.00
OVERALL	122	72	20	30	186	100	-	59.02

GERARD HOULLIER

Initially joining the club in the summer of 1998 as joint manager alongside Roy Evans, Gerard Houllier was handed overall control in November of that year. The following statistics take into account the first two full seasons in charge of the Reds' first overseas manager - and former Liverpool schoolteacher.

HOULLIER 1999-2000 (Premiership, three points for a win)
TROPHIES WON   None

RECORD									
	Pld	W	D	L	F	A	Pts	Pos	% Wins
LEAGUE	38	19	10	9	51	30	67	4th	50.00
FA CUP	2	1	0	1	2	1	-	-	50.00
LGE CUP	3	2	0	1	10	5	-	-	66.67
OVERALL	43	22	10	11	63	36	-	-	51.16

Winning exactly half his league games, Houllier achieved UEFA Cup qualification having been in charge during a rare season when there was no European football at Anfield.

HOULLIER 2000-2001   (Premiership, three points for a win)
TROPHIES WON   FA Cup, League Cup, UEFA Cup

RECORD									
	Pld	W	D	L	F	A	Pts	Pos	% Wins
LEAGUE	38	20	9	9	71	39	69	3rd	52.63
FA CUP	6	6	0	0	17	6	-	-	100.00
LGE CUP	6	5	0	1	20	4	-	-	83.33
EUROPE	13	8	4	1	19	9	-	-	61.54
OVERALL	63	39	13	11	127	58	-	-	61.90

Houllier's most successful season, as continued strengthening of the squad yielded a unique cup treble - while qualification for the Champions League was confirmed on the final day of the season. The only difference in league record to the previous season was 1 win replacing 1 draw - plus 20 extra goals - while FA Cup glory was achieved with 6 wins from 6.

HOULLIER TWO-SEASON TOTAL								
	Pld	W	D	L	F	A	Pts	% Wins
LEAGUE	76	39	19	18	122	69	136	51.32
FA CUP	8	7	0	1	19	7	-	87.50
LGE CUP	9	7	0	2	30	9	-	77.78
EUROPE	13	8	4	1	19	9	-	61.54
OVERALL	106	61	23	22	190	94	-	57.55

TWO-SEASON WONDER

Having taken over from Graeme Souness in January 1994, former Liverpool defender Roy Evans, who was also the final graduate of Bill Shankly's original bootroom, was able to lead the Reds back to the upper echleons of the table. The following statistics highlight his first two full seasons at the Anfield helm.

ROY EVANS

EVANS 1994-1995   **(Premiership, three points for a win)**
TROPHIES WON   **League Cup**

RECORD									
	Pld	W	D	L	F	A	Pts	Pos	% Wins
LEAGUE	42	21	11	10	65	37	74	4th	50.00
FA CUP	7	3	3	1	6	4	-	-	42.86
LGE CUP	8	8	0	0	16	4	-	-	100.00
OVERALL	57	32	14	11	87	45	-	-	56.14

As well as winning half of their league games, Liverpool won an impressive 8 successive games in clinching League Cup success and qualification for the UEFA Cup.

EVANS 1995-1996   **(Premiership, three points for a win)**
TROPHIES WON   **None**

RECORD									
	Pld	W	D	L	F	A	Pts	Pos	% Wins
LEAGUE	38	20	11	7	70	34	71	3rd	52.63
FA CUP	7	5	1	1	19	2	-	-	71.43
LGE CUP	4	3	0	1	7	1	-	-	75.00
EUROPE	4	1	2	1	2	2	-	-	25.00
OVERALL	53	29	14	10	98	39	-	-	54.72

An improvement in league form saw the Reds finish in the top 3, with more goals being scored despite there being four less games with the Premier League being reduced to 20 teams. Liverpool also reached the FA Cup final, although there was less success in the League Cup and in Europe.

TWO-SEASON TOTAL									
	Pld	W	D	L	F	A	Pts		% Wins
LEAGUE	80	41	22	17	135	71	145	-	51.25
FA CUP	14	8	4	2	25	6	-	-	57.14
LGE CUP	12	11	0	1	23	5	-	-	91.67
EUROPE	4	1	2	1	2	2	-	-	25.00
OVERALL	110	61	28	21	185	84	-	-	55.45

GRAEME SOUNESS

Another mid-season appointment following the shock resignation of Kenny Dalglish, former Reds midfield legend Graeme Souness arrived at Anfield having enjoyed huge success north of the border with Glasgow Rangers. His two full seasons in charge are documented here.

SOUNESS 1991-1992   (Division One, three points for a win)
TROPHIES WON   FA Cup

RECORD	Pld	W	D	L	F	A	Pts	Pos	% Wins
LEAGUE	42	16	16	10	47	40	64	6th	38.10
FA CUP	9	6	3	0	14	5	-	-	66.67
LGE CUP	5	2	2	1	11	8	-	-	40.00
EUROPE	8	4	0	4	16	8	-	-	50.00
OVERALL	64	28	21	15	88	61	-	-	43.75

A period of rebuilding saw Liverpool struggle for consistency, although they were still able to claim a top-six finish in the final season of Division One. There was an early exit in the League Cup and a run to the 4th round of the UEFA Cup, although these failings were redeemed by FA Cup success.

SOUNESS 1992-1993   (Premiership, three points for a win)
TROPHIES WON   None

RECORD	Pld	W	D	L	F	A	Pts	Pos	% Wins
LEAGUE	42	16	11	15	62	55	59	6th	38.10
FA CUP	2	0	1	1	2	4	-	-	00.00
LGE CUP	6	2	3	1	13	8	-	-	33.33
EUROPE	4	2	0	2	10	8	-	-	50.00
C. SHIELD	1	0	0	1	3	4	-	-	00.00
OVERALL	55	20	15	20	90	79	-	-	36.36

There was little league improvement - with five more defeats, although the Reds were more freescoring. Souness' win percentage was also the same, while overall his win percentage was the lowest of all 8 managers. The closest Liverpool came to silverware was a 4-3 defeat to Leeds United in the Charity Shield.

TWO-SEASON TOTAL	Pld	W	D	L	F	A	Pts	% Wins
LEAGUE	84	32	27	25	109	95	123	38.10
FA CUP	11	6	4	1	16	9	-	54.55
LGE CUP	11	4	5	2	24	16	-	36.36
EUROPE	12	6	0	6	26	16	-	50.00
C. SHIELD	1	0	0	1	3	4	-	00.00
OVERALL	119	48	36	35	178	140	-	40.34

TWO-SEASON WONDER

KENNY DALGLISH

The first player-manager in Liverpool's history, Dalglish also achieved another Reds first in his managerial career in his first season in charge, after taking over in the summer of 1985.

DALGLISH 1985-1986   **(Division One, three points for a win)**
TROPHIES WON   **League, FA Cup**

	Pld	W	D	L	F	A	Pts	Pos	% Wins
RECORD									
LEAGUE	42	26	10	6	89	37	88	1st	61.90
FA CUP	8	6	2	0	18	5	-	-	75.00
LGE CUP	7	5	1	1	19	6	-	-	71.43
S. SPORT	6	4	2	0	12	4	-	-	66.67
OVERALL	63	41	15	7	138	52	-	-	65.08

The first manager to achieve a league and cup double at Liverpool, Dalglish inherited a squad who had been pipped to the league title by Everton the previous season. This time the roles were reversed, Dalglish scoring the vital winner at Chelsea that secured the Championship, while Everton were also beaten in the FA Cup final. The only domestic blip in the first season of English clubs being banned from European competition was defeat to QPR in the semi-final of the League Cup. The Screen Sport Super Cup, arranged for clubs affected by the European ban, saw the Reds reach the final, to be played the following season.

DALGLISH 1986-1987   **(Division One, three points for a win)**
TROPHIES WON   **Charity Shield (shared), Screen Sport Super Cup**

	Pld	W	D	L	F	A	Pts	Pos	% Wins
RECORD									
LEAGUE	42	23	8	11	72	42	77	2nd	54.76
FA CUP	3	0	2	1	0	3	-	-	00.00
LGE CUP	9	6	2	1	25	6	-	-	66.67
S. SPORT	2	2	0	0	7	2	-	-	100.00
C. SHIELD	1	0	1	0	1	1	-	-	00.00
OVERALL	57	31	13	13	105	54	-	-	54.39

Less wins = a lower win percentage and ultimately failure as Liverpool lost the league title to Everton. There was an early exit too in the FA Cup, while League Cup success eluded the Reds when Arsenal claimed victory in the final. There was silverware of sorts to cheer, although a two-legged final victory over Everton in the Screen Sport Super Cup was of minor consolation - as was sharing the Charity Shield with the same opposition after a 1-1 draw.

	Pld	W	D	L	F	A	Pts	% Wins
TWO-SEASON TOTAL								
LEAGUE	84	49	18	17	161	79	165	58.33
FA CUP	11	6	4	1	18	8	-	54.55
LGE CUP	16	11	3	2	44	12	-	68.75
S. SPORT	8	6	2	0	19	6	-	75.00
C. SHIELD	1	0	1	0	1	1	-	00.00
OVERALL	120	72	28	20	243	106	-	60.00

Despite only being in charge for these two seaons, Joe Fagan's tenure following his promotion from the bootroom maintained Liverpool's run of success both at home and abroad.

FAGAN 1983-1984 **(Division One, three points for a win)**
TROPHIES WON **League, League Cup, European Cup**

						RECORD				
	Pld	W	D	L	F	A	Pts	Pos	% Wins
LEAGUE	42	22	14	6	73	32	80	1st	52.38
FA CUP	2	1	0	1	4	2	-	-	50.00
LGE CUP	13	7	6	0	25	8	-	-	53.85
EUROPE	9	8	1	0	16	3	-	-	88.89
C. SHIELD	1	0	0	1	0	2	-	-	00.00
OVERALL	67	38	21	8	118	47	-	-	56.72

Over half of their league games won and only 6 defeats were key in Liverpool claiming Championship success. An early exit from the FA Cup and Charity Shield disappointment aside, there was a clutch of further honours to come. Eight wins and only one draw were achieved as the Reds claimed a 4th European Cup, while although less impressive statistically, Liverpool also clinched success in the League Cup - again their 4th win in the competition.

FAGAN 1984-1985 **(Division One, three points for a win)**
TROPHIES WON **None**

						RECORD				
	Pld	W	D	L	F	A	Pts	Pos	% Wins
LEAGUE	42	22	11	9	68	35	77	2nd	52.38
FA CUP	7	4	2	1	19	5	-	-	57.14
LGE CUP	3	1	1	1	2	1	-	-	33.33
EUROPE	9	6	1	2	18	5	-	-	66.67
SUPER CUP	1	0	0	1	0	2	-	-	00.00
WORLD	1	0	0	1	0	1	-	-	00.00
C. SHIELD	1	0	0	1	0	1	-	-	00.00
OVERALL	64	33	15	16	107	50	-	-	51.56

Although the same win percentage was achieved, 3 extra defeats proved crucial as Liverpool finished as runners-up to Everton in the league. There was to be no fifth successive League Cup success, while the Reds fell in the FA Cup semi-final. Further afield Liverpool were runners-up in the European Cup, the World Club Cup and European Super Cup - as well as the Charity Shield in a rare season in the 1980s when the Anfield trophy room was bare.

						TWO-SEASON TOTAL			
	Pld	W	D	L	F	A	Pts	% Wins
LEAGUE	84	44	25	15	141	67	157	52.38
FA CUP	9	5	2	2	23	7	-	55.56
LGE CUP	16	8	7	1	27	9	-	50.00
EUROPE	19	14	2	3	34	10	-	73.68
WORLD	1	0	0	1	0	1	-	00.00
C. SHIELD	2	0	1	2	0	3	-	00.00
OVERALL	131	71	36	24	225	97	-	54.20

TWO-SEASON WONDER

BOB PAISLEY

In terms of trophies won, Bob Paisley's tenure yielded a total of 14 in only nine seasons. Taking over from Bill Shankly during the summer of 1974, the changeover proved seamless - despite the failure to land a major trophy in his first season.

PAISLEY 1974-1975 (Division One, two points for a win)
TROPHIES WON Charity Shield

RECORD									
	Pld	W	D	L	F	A	Pts	Pos	% Wins
LEAGUE	42	20	11	11	60	39	51	2nd	47.62
FA CUP	2	1	0	1	2	1	-	-	50.00
LGE CUP	4	2	1	1	6	2	-	-	50.00
EUROPE	4	2	2	0	13	1	-	-	50.00
C. SHIELD	1	1	0	0	1	1	-	-	100.00
OVERALL	53	26	14	13	82	44	-	-	49.06

A failure to break the 50% win barrier proved decisive as the Reds fell one short in the league, while there was disappointment in the domestic cup competitions. Despite being unbeaten, the Reds also failed to progress beyond round 2 in the European Cup Winners' Cup although Charity Shield success was achieved over Leeds United following a penalty shootout.

PAISLEY 1975-1976 (Division One, two points for a win)
TROPHIES WON League, UEFA Cup

RECORD									
	Pld	W	D	L	F	A	Pts	Pos	% Wins
LEAGUE	42	23	14	5	66	31	60	1st	54.76
FA CUP	2	1	0	1	2	1	-	-	50.00
LGE CUP	3	1	1	1	2	2	-	-	33.33
EUROPE	12	8	3	1	25	9	-	-	66.67
OVERALL	59	33	18	8	95	43	-	-	55.93

An improvement in wins and 6 less defeats were key in Liverpool clinching the league title - as were an improved goals record for and against. In addition, the UEFA Cup was brought back to Anfield, 8 wins from 12 games proving key although there was little cheer in the other cup competitions.

TWO-SEASON TOTAL								
	Pld	W	D	L	F	A	Pts	% Wins
LEAGUE	84	43	25	16	126	70	111	51.19
FA CUP	4	2	0	2	4	2	-	50.00
LGE CUP	7	3	2	2	8	4	-	42.86
EUROPE	16	10	5	1	38	10	-	62.50
C. SHIELD	1	1	0	0	1	1	-	100.00
OVERALL	112	59	32	21	177	87	-	52.68

BILL SHANKLY

Recognised as the man who breathed life into an ailing club, Bill Shankly arrived from Huddersfield Town in December 1959, with the club struggling in Division 2. Although it took a little time, Shankly would eventually lead the club to Division One - and glory awaited.

SHANKLY 1960-1961 (Division Two, two points for a win)
TROPHIES WON None

RECORD									
	Pld	W	D	L	F	A	Pts	Pos	% Wins
LEAGUE	42	21	10	11	87	58	52	3rd	50.00
FA CUP	2	1	0	1	3	4	-	-	50.00
LGE CUP	3	1	1	1	7	5	-	-	33.33
OVERALL	47	23	11	13	97	67	-	-	48.94

Shankly's first full season in charge laid the foundations for the following season. The Reds won half of their games but were one place from promotion. The cup competitions, meanwhile, could wait.

SHANKLY 1961-1962 (Division Two, two points for a win)
TROPHIES WON League

RECORD									
	Pld	W	D	L	F	A	Pts	Pos	% Wins
LEAGUE	42	27	8	7	99	43	62	1st	64.29
FA CUP	5	2	2	1	6	5	-	-	40.00
LGE CUP				Did not compete					
OVERALL	47	29	10	8	105	48	-	-	61.70

With Liverpool choosing not to compete in the League Cup and a run in the FA Cup again proving elusive, it was left to the league for the Reds to earn their success. A win percentage of nearly 65%, with 99 goals scored, was key in Shankly leading his side to Championship glory.

TWO-SEASON TOTAL								
	Pld	W	D	L	F	A	Pts	% Wins
LEAGUE	84	48	18	18	186	101	114	57.14
FA CUP	7	3	2	2	9	9	-	42.86
LGE CUP	3	1	1	1	7	5	-	33.33
OVERALL	94	52	21	21	202	115	-	55.32

MOST SUCCESSFUL LIVERPOOL MANAGER OVER THEIR FIRST 2 SEASONS IN CHARGE (ALL COMPETITIONS)			
RATING	MANAGER	% Wins	TROPHIES WON
1	DALGLISH	60.00	Division 1, FA Cup, Charity Shield, Screensport Super Cup
2	BENITEZ	59.02	FA Cup, European Cup, European Super Cup
3	HOULLIER	57.55	FA Cup, League Cup, UEFA Cup
4	EVANS	55.45	League Cup
5	SHANKLY	55.32	Division 2
6	FAGAN	54.20	Division 1, League Cup, European Cup
7	PAISLEY	52.68	Division 1, UEFA Cup, Charity Shield
8	SOUNESS	40.34	FA Cup

MOST SUCCESSFUL LIVERPOOL MANAGER OVER THEIR FIRST 2 SEASONS IN CHARGE (LEAGUE)			
RATING	MANAGER	% Wins	TROPHIES WON
1	DALGLISH	58.33	Division 1, FA Cup, Charity Shield, Screensport Super Cup
2	SHANKLY	57.14	Division 2
3	BENITEZ	55.26	FA Cup, European Cup, European Super Cup
4	FAGAN	52.38	Division 1, League Cup, European Cup
5	HOULLIER	51.32	FA Cup, League Cup, UEFA Cup
6	EVANS	51.25	League Cup
7	PAISLEY	51.19	Division 1, UEFA Cup, Charity Shield
8	SOUNESS	38.10	FA Cup

THE SQUAD 2006/07

Scott Carson (on loan at Charlton Athletic)

Position	Goalkeeper
Born	Whitehaven
Age (at start of 06/07)	20
Birth date	03/09/85
Height	6ft 3ins
Other clubs	Leeds United, Sheffield Wednesday
Liverpool debut	05/03/05 v Newcastle United - Premiership
Liverpool appearances	9
Liverpool goals	0
International caps	0
International goals	0

Jerzy Dudek

Position	Goalkeeper
Born	Rybnik, Poland
Age (at start of 06/07)	33
Birth date	23/03/73
Height	6ft 2ins
Other clubs	Sokol Tychy, Feyenoord
Liverpool debut	08/09/01 v Aston Villa - Premiership
Liverpool appearances	178 + 2 as substitute
Liverpool goals	0
International caps	55
International goals	0

Chris Kirkland (on loan at Wigan Athletic)

Position	Goalkeeper
Born	Leicester
Age (at start of 06/07)	25
Birth date	02/05/81
Height	6ft 3ins
Other clubs	Coventry City, West Bromwich Albion, Wigan Athletic
Liverpool debut	09/10/01 v Grimsby Town - League Cup
Liverpool appearances	45
Liverpool goals	0
International caps	0
International goals	0

David Martin

Position	Goalkeeper
Born	Romford
Age (at start of 06/07)	20
Birth date	22/01/86
Height	6ft 1ins
Other clubs	Milton Keynes Dons
Liverpool debut	-
Liverpool appearances	0
Liverpool goals	0
International caps	0
International goals	0

Jose Manuel Reina Paez

Position	Goalkeeper
Born	Madrid, Spain
Age (at start of 06/07)	23
Birth date	31/08/82
Height	6ft 2ins
Other clubs	Barcelona, Villarreal
Liverpool debut	13/07/05 v TNS - European Cup
Liverpool appearances	53
Liverpool goals	0
International caps	3
International goals	0

Daniel Agger

Position	Defence
Born	Hvidovre, Denmark
Age (at start of 06/07)	21
Birth date	12/12/84
Height	6ft 3ins
Other clubs	Rosenhoj, Brondby
Liverpool debut	01/02/06 v Birmingham City - Premiership
Liverpool appearances	4
Liverpool goals	0
International caps	4
International goals	1

Fabio Aurelio

Position	Defence
Born	Sao Carlos, Brazil
Age (at start of 06/07)	26
Birth date	24/09/79
Height	6ft 0ins
Other clubs	Sao Paulo, Valencia
Liverpool debut	-
Liverpool appearances	0
Liverpool goals	0
International caps	0
International goals	0

Jamie Carragher

Position	Defence
Born	Bootle, Liverpool
Age (at start of 06/07)	28
Birth date	28/01/78
Height	6ft 1ins
Other clubs	-
Liverpool debut	08/01/97 (as a sub) at Middlesbrough - League Cup
Liverpool appearances	401 + 16 as substitute
Liverpool goals	3
International caps	29
International goals	0

Steve Finnan

Position	Defence/Midfield
Born	Limerick, Republic of Ireland
Age (at start of 06/07)	30
Birth date	20/04/76
Height	6ft 0ins
Other clubs	Welling, Birmingham City, Notts County, Fulham
Liverpool debut	17/08/03 (as sub) v Chelsea - Premiership
Liverpool appearances	123 + 12 as substitute
Liverpool goals	1
International caps	38
International goals	1

Jack Hobbs

Position	Defence
Born	Portsmouth
Age (at start of 06/07)	18
Birth date	18/08/88
Height	6ft 3ins
Other clubs	Lincoln City
Liverpool debut	-
Liverpool appearances	0
Liverpool goals	0
International caps	0
International goals	0

Sami Hyypia

Position	Defence
Born	Porvoo, Finland
Age (at start of 06/07)	32
Birth date	07/10/73
Height	6ft 4ins
Other clubs	Pallo-Pelkot, Ku Mu, My Pa Anjalankoski, Willem II Tilburg
Liverpool debut	07/08/99 at Sheffield Wednesday - Premiership
Liverpool appearances	371 + 1 as substitute
Liverpool goals	26
International caps	75
International goals	4

Gabriel Paletta

Position	Defence
Born	Buenos Aires, Argentina
Age (at start of 06/07)	20
Birth date	15/02/86
Height	6ft 2ins
Other clubs	Club Atletico Banfield
Liverpool debut	-
Liverpool appearances	0
Liverpool goals	0
International caps	0
International goals	0

Xabi Alonso

Position	Midfield
Born	Tolosa, Spain
Age (at start of 06/07)	24
Birth date	25/11/81
Height	6ft 0ins
Other clubs	Eibar, Real Sociedad
Liverpool debut	29/08/04 at Bolton Wanderers - Premiership
Liverpool appearances	74 + 11 as substitute
Liverpool goals	8
International caps	29
International goals	1

Paul Anderson

Position	Midfield
Born	Leicester
Age (at start of 06/07)	18
Birth date	23/07/88
Height	5ft 9ins
Other clubs	Hull City
Liverpool debut	-
Liverpool appearances	0
Liverpool goals	0
International caps	0
International goals	0

Salif Diao

Position	Midfield
Born	Kedougou, Senegal
Age (at start of 06/07)	29
Birth date	10/02/77
Height	6ft 1ins
Other clubs	Monaco, Epinal, Sedan, Birmingham City, Portsmouth
Liverpool debut	28/08/02 (sub) at Blackburn Rovers - Premiership
Liverpool appearances	35 + 26 as substitute
Liverpool goals	3
International caps	39
International goals	4

Luis Javier Garcia Sanz

Position	Midfield
Born	Barcelona, Spain
Age (at start of 06/07)	28
Birth date	24/06/78
Height	5ft 10ins
Other clubs	Valladolid, Toledo, Tenerife, Atletico Madrid, Barcelona
Liverpool debut	29/08/04 at Bolton Wanderers - Premiership
Liverpool appearances	68 + 26 as substitute
Liverpool goals	24
International caps	13
International goals	3

Steven Gerrard

Position	Midfield
Born	Whiston, Merseyside
Age (at start of 06/07)	26
Birth date	30/05/80
Height	6ft 0ins
Other clubs	-
Liverpool debut	29/11/98 (sub) v Blackburn Rovers - Premiership
Liverpool appearances	306 + 30 as substitute
Liverpool goals	64
International caps	47
International goals	9

Mark Gonzalez

Position	Midfield/Forward
Born	Durban, South Africa
Age (at start of 06/07)	22
Birth date	10/07/84
Height	5ft 9ins
Other clubs	Universidad Catolica, Albacete, Real Sociedad
Liverpool debut	-
Liverpool appearances	0
Liverpool goals	0
International caps (Chile)	14
International goals	3

35

Harry Kewell

Position	Midfield/Forward
Born	Smithfield, Australia
Age (at start of 06/07)	27
Birth date	22/09/78
Height	5ft 11ins
Other clubs	Leeds United
Liverpool debut	17/08/03 v Chelsea - Premiership
Liverpool appearances	100 + 21 as substitute
Liverpool goals	15
International caps	23
International goals	7

Jan Kromkamp

Position	Defence/Midfield
Born	Makkinga, Holland
Age (at start of 06/07)	26
Birth date	17/08/80
Height	6ft 3ins
Other clubs	Go Ahead Eagles, AZ Alkmaar, Villarreal
Liverpool debut	07/01/06 (as sub) at Luton Town - FA Cup
Liverpool appearances	7 + 10 as substitute
Liverpool goals	0
International caps	11
International goals	0

Lee Peltier

Position	Defence/Midfield
Born	Aigburth, Liverpool
Age (at start of 06/07)	19
Birth date	11/12/86
Height	5ft 10ins
Other clubs	-
Liverpool debut	-
Liverpool appearances	0
Liverpool goals	0
International caps	0
International goals	0

Jermaine Pennant

Position	Midfield
Born	Nottingham
Age (at start of 06/07)	23
Birth date	15/01/83
Height	5ft 8ins
Other clubs	Notts County, Arsenal, Watford, Leeds United, Birmingham City
Liverpool debut	-
Liverpool appearances	0
Liverpool goals	0
International caps	0
International goals	0

Darren Potter (on loan at Wolves)

Position	Midfield
Born	Liverpool
Age (at start of 06/07)	21
Birth date	21/12/84
Height	6ft 1ins
Other clubs	Southampton
Liverpool debut	10/08/04 (sub) at Graz AK - European Cup
Liverpool appearances	10 + 7 as substitute
Liverpool goals	0
International caps	0
International goals	0

John Arne Riise

Position	Defence/Midfield
Born	Molde, Norway
Age (at start of 06/07)	25
Birth date	24/09/80
Height	6ft 1ins
Other clubs	Aalesunds F.K., Monaco
Liverpool debut	12/08/01 v Manchester United - FA Community Shield
Liverpool appearances	221 + 35 as substitute
Liverpool goals	26
International caps	54
International goals	5

Mohamed Sissoko

Position	Midfield
Born	Mont-Saint-Aignan, France
Age (at start of 06/07)	21
Birth date	22/01/85
Height	6ft 2ins
Other clubs	Auxerre, Valencia
Liverpool debut	26/07/05 (sub) at FBK Kaunas - European Cup
Liverpool appearances	37 + 8 substitute
Liverpool goals	0
International caps (Mali)	7
International goals	1

Stephen Warnock

Position	Defence/Midfield
Born	Ormskirk, Lancashire
Age (at start of 06/07)	24
Birth date	12/12/81
Height	5ft 9ins
Other clubs	Bradford City, Coventry City
Liverpool debut	10/08/04 (sub) at Graz AK - European Cup
Liverpool appearances	40 + 20 as substitute
Liverpool goals	1
International caps	0
International goals	0

Boudewijn Zenden

Position	Midfield
Born	Maastricht, Holland
Age (at start of 06/07)	30
Birth date	15/08/76
Height	5ft 10ins
Other clubs	PSV Eindhoven, Barcelona, Chelsea, Middlesbrough
Liverpool debut	13/07/05 (sub) v TNS - European Cup
Liverpool appearances	11 + 6 substitute
Liverpool goals	2
International caps	54
International goals	7

Craig Bellamy

Position	Attack
Born	Cardiff, Wales
Age (at start of 06/07)	27
Birth date	13/07/79
Height	5ft 9ins
Other clubs	Norwich City, Coventry City, Newcastle United, Celtic, Blackburn Rovers
Liverpool debut	-
Liverpool appearances	0
Liverpool goals	0
International caps	33
International goals	9

Djibril Cisse (on loan at Marseille)

Position	Attack
Born	Arles, France
Age (at start of 06/07)	25
Birth date	12/08/81
Height	6ft 1ins
Other clubs	Auxerre, Marseille
Liverpool debut	10/08/04 at Graz AK - European Cup
Liverpool appearances	43 + 36 as substitute
Liverpool goals	24
International caps	30
International goals	9

Peter Crouch

Position	Attack
Born	Macclesfield
Age (at start of 06/07)	25
Birth date	12/08/81
Height	6ft 7ins
Other clubs	Tottenham Hotspur, QPR, Portsmouth, Aston Villa, Norwich City, Southampton
Liverpool debut	26/07/05 at FBK Kaunas - European Cup
Liverpool appearances	42 + 7 substitute
Liverpool goals	13
International caps	11
International goals	6

Robbie Fowler

Position	Attack
Born	Toxteth, Liverpool
Age (at start of 06/07)	31
Birth date	09/04/75
Height	5ft 9ins
Other clubs	Liverpool, Leeds United, Manchester City
Liverpool debut (2nd)	01/02/06 v Birmingham City - Premiership
Liverpool appearances	299 + 47 as substitute
Liverpool goals	176
International caps	26
International goals	7

Anthony Le Tallec (on loan at Sochaux)

Position	Midfield/Attack
Born	Hennebont, France
Age (at start of 06/07)	21
Birth date	03/10/84
Height	6ft 1ins
Other clubs	Le Havre, St Etienne, Sunderland
Liverpool debut	13/09/03 (sub) at Blackburn Rovers - Premiership
Liverpool appearances	13 + 19 as substitute
Liverpool goals	1
International caps	0
International goals	0

Neil Mellor

Position	Attack
Born	Sheffield
Age (at start of 06/07)	23
Birth date	04/11/82
Height	6ft 0ins
Other clubs	West Ham United, Wigan Athletic
Liverpool debut	04/12/02 v Ipswich Town - League Cup
Liverpool appearances	15 + 7 as substitute
Liverpool goals	6
International caps	0
International goals	0

Florent Sinama-Pongolle

Position	Attack
Born	Saint-Pierre, Reunion Islands
Age (at start of 06/07)	21
Birth date	20/10/84
Height	5ft 7ins
Other clubs	Le Havre (and on loan), Blackburn Rovers
Liverpool debut	15/10/03 (sub) v Olimpija Ljubljana - Uefa Cup
Liverpool appearances	22 + 43 as substitute
Liverpool goals	9
International caps	0
International goals	0

Dirk Kuyt

Position	Attack
Born	Katwijk, Holland
Age (at start of 06/07)	26
Birth date	22/07/80
Height	6ft 0ins
Other clubs	FC Utrecht, Feyenoord
Liverpool debut	-
Liverpool appearances	0
Liverpool goals	0
International caps	22
International goals	4

SQUAD NUMBERS
2006/07

1 Jerzy Dudek
2 Jan Kromkamp
3 Steve Finnan
4 Sami Hyypia
5 Daniel Agger
6 John Arne Riise
7 Harry Kewell
8 Steven Gerrard
9 Robbie Fowler
10 Luis Garcia
11 Mark Gonzalez
12 Fabio Aurelio

14 Xabi Alonso
15 Peter Crouch
16 Jermaine Pennant
17 Craig Bellamy
18 Dirk Kuyt
22 Mohamed Sissoko
23 Jamie Carragher
24 Florent Sinama-Pongolle
25 Jose Reina
28 Stephen Warnock
29 Gabriel Paletta
32 Boudewijn Zenden

33 Neil Mellor
35 Danny Guthrie
38 David Mannix

Others
Paul Anderson
Salif Diao
Jack Hobbs
David Martin
Lee Peltier

RESERVES

RESERVES LEAGUE NORTH TABLE 2005/06

		Pld	W	D	L	F	A	Pts
1	Man Utd	28	19	2	7	68	32	59
2	Aston Villa	28	16	8	4	59	26	56
3	Man City	28	15	8	5	47	37	53
4	Middlesboro	28	15	7	6	50	27	52
5	Newcastle	28	12	8	8	45	40	44
6	**Liverpool**	**28**	**13**	**5**	**10**	**31**	**31**	**44**
7	Sunderland	28	11	7	10	40	41	40
8	Everton	28	10	8	10	31	35	38
9	Leeds United	28	9	11	8	27	31	38
10	Blackburn	28	8	7	13	38	46	31
11	Birmingham	28	7	9	12	32	36	30
12	Wolves	28	6	8	14	28	37	26
13	Bolton W	28	6	6	16	25	46	24
14	West Brom	28	6	6	16	26	55	24
15	Wigan Ath	28	5	4	19	24	51	19

RESERVES LEAGUE FIXTURES 2005/06

			Result*
16.08.05	Everton	H	2-3
22.08.05	Newcastle United	H	2-2
30.08.05	West Bromwich Alb	A	1-0
14.09.05	Wolverhampton W	H	1-0
19.09.05	Bolton Wanderers	A	3-2
27.09.05	Leeds United	H	0-1
18.10.05	Wigan Athletic	A	2-0
26.10.05	Blackburn Rovers	H	0-3
02.11.05	Manchester City	H	1-1
22.11.05	Birmingham City	A	0-2
29.11.05	Sunderland	H	1-0
05.12.05	Manchester United	A	2-0
09.01.06	Newcastle United	A	1-2
24.01.06	Wolverhampton W	A	1-0
02.02.06	Middlesbrough	A	1-4
09.02.06	Bolton Wanderers	H	0-0
16.02.06	Everton	A	1-0
22.02.06	Leeds United	A	0-0
20.03.06	Wigan Athletic	H	2-0
23.03.06	Aston Villa	H	1-1
28.03.06	Middlesbrough	H	0-2
03.04.06	Birmingham City	H	1-0
05.04.06	Sunderland	A	1-2
10.04.06	Blackburn Rovers	A	2-1
24.04.06	Aston Villa	A	0-3
27.04.06	West Bromwich Alb	H	4-0
30.04.06	Manchester United	H	1-0
02.05.06	Manchester City	A	0-2

* Liverpool score shown first

RESERVES APPEARANCES & GOALS 2005/06

	Appearances	Goals
Daniel Agger	4	0
Paul Anderson	18	2
Godwin Antwi	24	0
Charlie Barnett	1	0
Antonio Barragan	21	3
Paul Barratt	1	0
Ramon Calliste	27	7
Peter Crouch	1	0
Salif Diao	1	0
Jerzy Dudek	4	0
Ryan Flynn	6	0
Robbie Fowler	1	1
Robbie Foy	12	2
James Frayne	2	0
Luis Garcia	1	0
Danny Guthrie	25	3
Dietmar Hamann	1	1
Adam Hammill	16	1
Jack Hobbs	27	0
Besian Idrizaj	17	3
Josemi	1	0
Harry Kewell	1	0
Jan Kromkamp	2	0
Craig Lindfield	6	1
David Mannix	13	1
David Martin	15	0
Neil Mellor	2	1
Michael Nardiello	3	0
Danny O'Donnell	21	0
Lee Peltier	22	0
Conal Platt	1	0
Darren Potter	6	0
David Raven	12	1
Miki Roque	23	0
Florent Sinama-Pongolle	5	3
James Smith	19	0
Robbie Threlfall	2	0
Lee Tomlin	2	0
Djimi Traore	2	0
James Tunnicliffe	1	0
Stephen Warnock	1	0
Zak Whitbread	6	1
Ryan Wilkie	1	0
Paul Willis	9	0
Calum Woods	1	0

FA PREMIER RESERVE LEAGUE NORTHERN SECTION FIXTURES 2006-07

AUGUST

29 Manchester City (H)

SEPTEMBER

12 Everton (A)

OCTOBER

03 Newcastle United (H)
17 Middlesbrough (H)

NOVEMBER

01 Wigan Athletic (A) - 7.30pm KO
21 Sheffield United (A)

DECEMBER

07 Manchester United (H)
11 Blackburn Rovers (A)
20 Bolton Wanderers (A)

JANUARY

23 Everton (H

FEBRUARY

12 Newcastle United (A)
20 Bolton Wanderers (H)

MARCH

06 Middlesbrough (A)
13 Wigan Athletic (H)
20 Blackburn Rovers (H)

APRIL

03 Manchester City (A)
11 Sheffield United (H)
19 Manchester United (A)

All fixtures 7pm,
subject to change.

Paul Anderson (left) and Lee Peltier (right) - Liverpool reserve stars looking to break through in 2006/07

THE ACADEMY

Ten years after the club's only FA Youth Cup triumph, John Owens guided the Reds to a second success to complete a unique Cup double for the club in 2005/06. Craig Lindfield top-scored with seven goals during the competition which saw the Reds overcome Cardiff City (2-0), Ipswich Town (2-1), Burnley (3-0), Carlisle United (6-0) and Southampton (5-4 on penalties after the two-legged semi-final had finished 4-4), before the final against Manchester City.

In the first leg at Anfield, Robbie Threlfall, Ryan Flynn and Miki Roque were on target in a 3-0 victory before City hit back at Eastlands, coming through 2-0 although it was not enough as Liverpool held on for a 3-2 aggregate triumph. Incidentally five members of the squad - Threlfall, Lindfield, Flynn, David Roberts and Stephen Darby have since been promoted to the reserves.

FA PREMIER ACADEMY 2005/06 GROUP C

	P	W	D	L	F	A	Pts
1 Blackburn	28	17	3	8	51	36	54
2 Man Utd	28	16	4	8	56	30	52
3 Man City	28	14	7	7	50	37	49
4 Everton	28	14	7	7	33	24	49
5 Liverpool	**28**	**13**	**5**	**10**	**47**	**35**	**44**
6 Stoke City	28	10	8	10	42	37	38
7 Bolton	28	9	11	8	31	35	38
8 Crewe	28	9	8	11	38	42	35
9 West Brom	28	6	9	13	39	52	27
10 Wolves	28	6	8	14	25	39	26

UNDER-18s APPEARANCES & GOALS 2005/06

	Appearances	Goals
Paul Anderson	1	0
Godwin Antwi	1	0
Charlie Barnett	24	6
Paul Barratt	22	3
Stephen Behan	10	0
Michael Burns	14	0
Stephen Darby	25	1
Ryan Flynn	19	2
James Frayne	15	4
Adam Hammill	12	4
Jack Hobbs	2	0
Jordan Holmes	23	0
Besian Idrizaj	1	0
Paul Lancaster	10	0
Craig Lindfield	19	7
Joseph Mills	1	0
Josh Mimms	2	0
Michael Nardiello	21	3
Lee Peltier	2	0
Conal Platt	19	4
Jonathan Pringle	8	2
Raymond Putterill	3	1
David Roberts	16	0
Miki Roque	1	1
James Ryan	27	2
Francis Smith	20	1
Jay Spearing	9	1
Robbie Threlfall	19	1
Ryan Wignall	15	1
Calum Woods	21	1
Lee Woodward	2	0

UNDER-18s' LEAGUE FIXTURES 2005/06

			Result*
20.08.05	Cardiff City	A	2-1
27.08.05	Ipswich Town	H	2-3
03.09.05	Middlesbrough	A	6-2
10.09.05	Leeds United	H	3-1
17.09.05	Huddersfield Town	A	5-1
24.09.05	Stoke City	A	1-0
01.10.05	Everton	H	0-1
08.10.05	West Bromwich Albion	A	4-2
15.10.05	Bolton Wanderers	H	0-0
22.10.05	Crewe Alexandra	H	3-1
05.11.05	Blackburn Rovers	A	0-1
12.11.05	Manchester United	A	0-4
19.11.05	Manchester City	H	0-1
03.12.05	Wolverhampton W	A	2-1
09.12.05	Stoke City	H	2-0
07.01.06	West Bromwich Albion	H	5-3
21.01.06	Crewe Alexandra	A	1-2
04.02.06	Blackburn Rovers	H	0-1
11.02.06	Manchester United	H	1-0
15.02.06	Manchester City	H	1-2
25.02.06	Wolverhampton W	H	1-2
21.03.06	Derby County	H	0-1
30.03.06	Everton	A	2-0
01.04.06	Sheffield Wednesday	H	2-2
06.04.06	Nottingham Forest	H	2-2
08.04.06	Sheffield United	A	1-0
26.04.06	Sunderland	A	1-1
29.04.06	Bolton Wanderers	H	0-0

* Liverpool score shown first

FA PREMIER ACADEMY LEAGUE
FIXTURES 2006-07

AUGUST
19 Chelsea (H)
26 Crystal Palace (A)

SEPTEMBER
02 Leeds United (H)
09 Sunderland (A)
16 Barnsley (H)
23 Bolton Wanderers (A)
30 Wolverhampton W. (H)

OCTOBER
07 Everton (A)
14 Crewe Alexandra (H)
21 Manchester City (A)

NOVEMBER
04 Manchester United (H)
11 West Bromwich Albion (A)
18 Blackburn Rovers (A)

DECEMBER
02 Stoke City (H)
09 Crewe Alexandra (A)

JANUARY
06 Manchester City (H)
13 Manchester United (A)
20 West Bromwich Albion (H)

FEBRUARY
03 Blackburn Rovers (H)
10 Stoke City (A)
17 Bolton Wanderers (H)

MARCH
03 Everton (H)
10 Huddersfield Town (A)
17 Sheffield Wednesday (H)
24 Middlesbrough (H)

APRIL
14 Sheffield United (A)
21 Newcastle United (H)

All fixtures 11am,
subject to change.

FA WOMEN'S PREMIER LEAGUE
NORTHERN SECTION FIXTURES 2006-07

AUGUST
20 Nottingham Forest (H)
27 Lincoln City (A)

SEPTEMBER
03 Preston North End (A)
17 Stockport County (A)
24 Tranmere Rovers (H)

OCTOBER
01 Newcastle United (A)
04 Crewe Alexandra (H)
15 Wolverhampton W. (A)
22 Curzon Ashton (A)
29 Aston Villa (H)

NOVEMBER
08 Nottingham Forest (A)
12 Lincoln City (H)
19 Stockport County (H)
26 Manchester City (A)

DECEMBER
03 FA Cup 3rd round
10 Preston North End (H)
17 Tranmere Rovers (A)

JANUARY
07 FA Cup 4th round
14 Newcastle United (H)
21 Crewe Alexandra (A)
28 FA Cup 5th round

FEBRUARY
04 Wolverhampton W. (H)
11 FA Cup 6th round
18 Manchester City (H)
25 Curzon Ashton (H)

MARCH
04 Aston Villa (A)
11 FA Cup semi-final

Fixtures subject to change. Home fixtures played at Prescot Cables FC (Valerie Park), 2pm
kick-off subject to change. FA Cup final to be played on May 7, 2007.

The FA
125
CUP

46

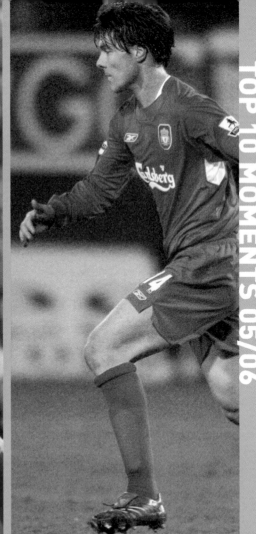

WINNERS
EFA SUPER CUP 2005

47

Clean sheet King

In a record-breaking season, Jose Reina and the Reds defence manage to overcome the previous best set by Kenny Dalglish's 1987/88 side by keeping an 11th successive clean sheet against Deportivo Saprissa in the Club World Championship.

9

Crouch at the double

Peter Crouch ends his Reds scoring drought, netting twice in his 19th game for the club against Wigan.

Seventh heaven

The 7-0 FA Cup quarter-final victory over Birmingham City at St Andrews - as well as banishing Rafa Benitez's record of never having beaten Blues - was also the Reds' record win in the competition.

European glory night

Another addition to the trophy cabinet as Liverpool overcome CSKA Moscow 3-1 after extra time in the European Super Cup in Monaco back in August.

God is back!

January 27, 2006 and the day most Liverpool fans thought would never happen. Robbie Fowler's return to his spiritual home is confirmed, coming on as a sub to make his second debut for the club the following Wednesday against Birmingham City at Anfield.

Kewell and the gang

Down to 10 men following Steven Gerrard's dismissal, the Reds deservedly clinched a derby double - Harry Kewell firing the crucial third late on at Anfield.

4

67 yards from glory

Never had a Liverpool player scored from his own half until Xabi Alonso in the 5-3 FA Cup third-round win at Luton Town.

3

Crouch ends 85 years of hurt

Peter Crouch is the Liverpool hero as his header sends Manchester United to a 1-0 defeat in the FA Cup fifth round at Anfield - 85 years after the Reds' last win over United in the competition.

2

Next stop Anfield South

Luis Garcia's stunning second goal proves crucial as Chelsea are defeated 2-1 in the FA Cup semi-final at Old Trafford.

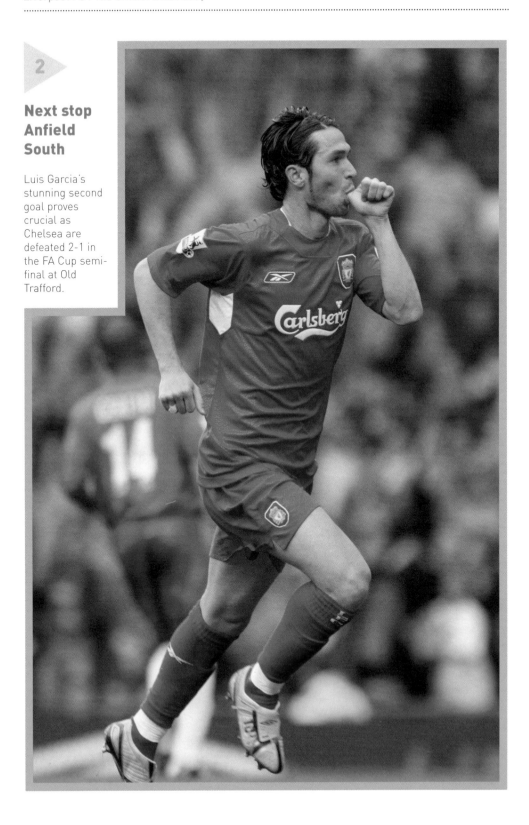

1

The FA Cup final

3-2 down to West Ham, 89 minutes gone and the game looks up. Up steps skipper Steven Gerrard with an unstoppable volley to send the FA Cup final into extra time, penalties and ultimate victory to round off another memorable season.

SUPER CUP
MONACO

PRESENTED BY

Carlsberg

Team line-ups

Liverpool (4-4-2):

Le Tallec Morientes

Riise Alonso Gerrard Potter

Warnock Finnan
Hyypia Carragher

Reina

Subs: Zenden (Warnock) 64, Cisse (Potter) 76
Subs not used: Carson, Josemi, Whitbread,
Hamann, Baros

TNS (4-4-1-1):

Wilde

Wood

Ward Ruscoe Jackson King

Holmes Baker Evans Naylor

Doherty

Subs: Beck (Wilde) 59, Lawless (Holmes) 72,
Leah (Ward) 82
Subs not used: Acton, Hogan, Lloyd Williams,
Toner

LIVERPOOL 3
TNS 0

UEFA Champions League
First Qualifying Round, 1st Leg,
Wednesday, July 13 2005.
Attendance: 44,760

Goals: Gerrard (8, 21, 89)
Booking: Baker (TNS)
Referee: Joeri van der Velde (Holland)

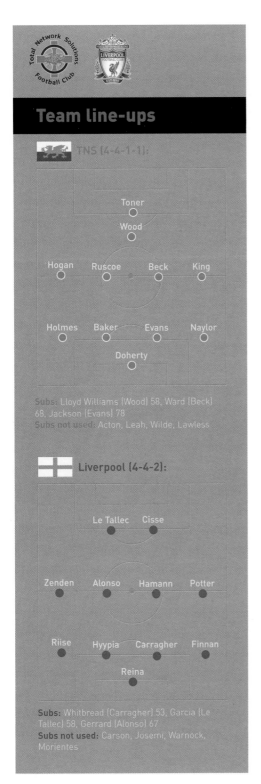

Team line-ups

TNS (4-4-1-1):

Toner

Wood

Hogan   Ruscoe   Beck   King

Holmes   Baker   Evans   Naylor

Doherty

Subs: Lloyd Williams (Wood) 58, Ward (Beck) 68, Jackson (Evans) 78
Subs not used: Acton, Leah, Wilde, Lawless

Liverpool (4-4-2):

Le Tallec   Cisse

Zenden   Alonso   Hamann   Potter

Riise   Hyypia   Carragher   Finnan

Reina

Subs: Whitbread (Carragher) 53, Garcia (Le Tallec) 58, Gerrard (Alonso) 67
Subs not used: Carson, Josemi, Warnock, Morientes

TNS   0
LIVERPOOL   3

UEFA Champions League
First Qualifying Round, 2nd Leg,
Tuesday, July 19 2005.
Attendance: 8,009

Goals: Cisse (26), Gerrard (85, 86)
Bookings: None
Referee: Carlo Bertolini (Switzerland)

Team line-ups

FBK Kaunas (4-4-2):

Tamosauskas   Poderis

Baguzis   Klimek   Rimkevicius   Barevicius

Manchkhava   Zelmikas
          Kancelskis   Pacevicius

Kurskis

Subs: Petrenko (Pacevicius) 44, Papeckys
(Barevicius) 71, Maciulis (Tamosauskas) 86
Subs not used: Beniusis, Kijanskas, Kilijonas,
Kunevicius, Maciulis, Petrenko

Liverpool (4-4-2):

Crouch   Cisse

Zenden   Alonso   Gerrard   Potter

Riise   Hyypia   Carragher   Josemi

Reina

Subs: Sissoko (Gerrard) 60, Garcia (Potter) 63,
Morientes (Crouch) 74
Subs not used: Dudek, Hamann, Warnock,
Medjani

FBK KAUNAS 1
LIVERPOOL 3

UEFA Champions League,
Second Qualifying Round, 1st Leg,
Tuesday, July 26, 2005.
Attendance: 8,300

Goals: Barevicius (21), Cisse (27), Carragher
(30), Gerrard (54, pen)
Bookings: Petrenko (FBK Kaunas), Zenden
(Liverpool)
Referee: Knud Erik Fisker (Denmark)

Team line-ups

Liverpool (4-4-2):

Crouch   Morientes

Zenden   Sissoko   Hamann   Garcia

Warnock   Hyypia   Whitbread   Finnan

Carson

Subs: Cisse (Morientes) 45, Potter (Crouch) 55, Gerrard (Hamann) 75
Subs not used: Reina, Riise, Alonso, Carragher

FBK Kaunas (4-4-2):

Pehlic   Poderis

Petrenko   Kvaratskhelia   Kunevicius   Rimkevicius

Manchkhava   Baguzis   Zelmikas   Kancelskis

Kilijonas

Subs: Klimek (Petrenko) 45, Barevicius (Pehlic) 66, Maciulis (Poderis) 87
Subs not used: Kurskis, Kijanskas, Papeckys, Beniusis

LIVERPOOL   2
FBK KAUNAS   0

**UEFA Champions League,
Second Qualifying Round, 2nd Leg,**
Tuesday, August 2, 2005.
Attendance: 43,717

Goals: Gerrard (77), Cisse (86)
Bookings: None
Referee: Gianluca Paparesta (Italy)

Team line-ups

CSKA Sofia (4-4-2):

Zadi V. Dimitrov

Yanev   Gargorov
      Hdiouad Tiago Silva

Gueye   Zabavnik
      Todorov   Matic

          Hmaruc

Subs: P. Dimitrov (Yanev) 35, Sakaliev (D Dimitrov) 59, Yordanov (Zadi) 80
Subs not used: Maksic, Ivaylo Ivanov, Matko, Yurukov

Liverpool (4-4-2):

Morientes   Cisse

Warnock Alonso Gerrard   Garcia

Riise   Finnan
     Hyypia Carragher

          Reina

Subs: Hamann (Alonso) 64, Sissoko (Gerrard) 70, Barragan (Morientes) 79
Subs not used: Carson, Baros, Whitbread

CSKA SOFIA   1
LIVERPOOL   3

UEFA Champions League
Third Qualifying Round, 1st Leg,
Wednesday 10 August 2005.
Attendance: 16,512

Goals: Cisse (25), Morientes (31, 58), Dimitrov (45)
Bookings: Hdiouad (CSKA Sofia), Garcia, Warnock (Liverpool)
Referee: Jan Wegereef (Holland)

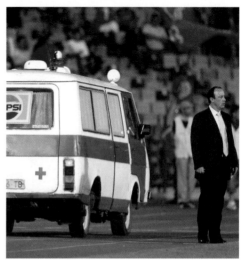

Team line-ups

Liverpool (4-4-2):

Morientes   Cisse

Riise   Sissoko   Hamann   Potter

Warnock   Hyypia   Josemi   Finnan

Carson

Subs: Garcia (Potter) 45, Zenden (Warnock) 64, Sinama-Pongolle (Cisse) 83
Subs not used: Reina, Alonso, Carragher, Barragan

CSKA Sofia (4-4-2):

V. Dimitrov   Zadi

Hdiouad   Todorov   Tiago Silva   Gargorov

Yurukov   Gueye   Iliev   Zabavnik

Maksic

Subs: Sakaliev (Yurukov) 72, P. Dimitrov (Zadi) 84
Subs not used: Kutchoukov, Ivankov, Zafirov, Ivanov, Matic

LIVERPOOL   0
CSKA SOFIA   1

UEFA Champions League
Third Qualifying Round, 2nd Leg,
Tuesday 23rd August 2005.
Attendance: 42,175

Goal: Iliev (16)
Bookings: None
Referee: Wolfgang Stark (Germany)

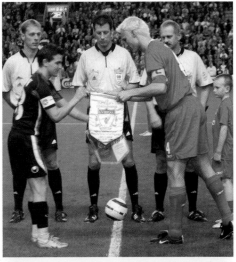

Team line-ups

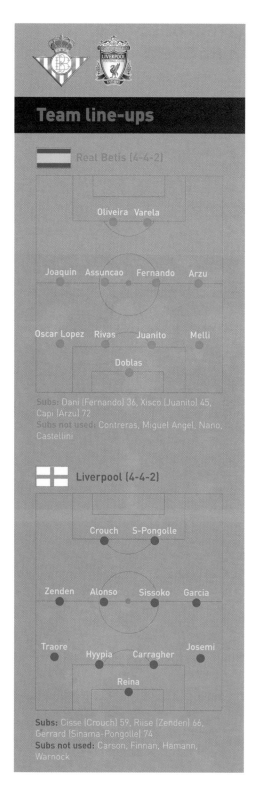

Real Betis (4-4-2)

Oliveira Varela

Joaquin Assuncao Fernando Arzu

Oscar Lopez Rivas Juanito Melli

Doblas

Subs: Dani (Fernando) 36, Xisco (Juanito) 45,
Capi (Arzu) 72
Subs not used: Contreras, Miguel Angel, Nano,
Castellini

Liverpool (4-4-2)

Crouch S-Pongolle

Zenden Alonso Sissoko Garcia

Traore Hyypia Carragher Josemi

Reina

Subs: Cisse (Crouch) 59, Riise (Zenden) 66,
Gerrard (Sinama-Pongolle) 74
Subs not used: Carson, Finnan, Hamann,
Warnock

REAL BETIS   1
LIVERPOOL   2

**UEFA Champions League,
Group G game 1,**
Tuesday, September 13, 2005.
Attendance: 45,000

Goals: Sinama-Pongolle (2), Garcia (14), Arzu
(51)
Bookings: Carragher, Reina (Liverpool)
Referee: Konrad Plautz (Austria)

Team line-ups

Liverpool (4-4-2):

Crouch   Morientes

Zenden   Gerrard
    Sissoko   Hamann

Riise   Finnan
   Hyypia   Carragher

Reina

Subs: Cisse (Morientes) 66, Kewell (Crouch) 83, Potter (Gerrard) 89
Subs not used: Dudek, Josemi, Traore, Warnock

Real Betis (4-4-2):

Fernando   Xisco

Arzu
Rivera   Joaquin
    Assuncao

Oscar Lopez   Melli
   Rivas   Juanito

Doblas

Subs: Capi (Assuncao) 69, Israel (Fernando) 78
Subs not used: Contreras, Canas, Castellini, Edu, Juanlu

LIVERPOOL   0
REAL BETIS   0

**UEFA Champions League,
Group G game 5,**
Wednesday, November 23, 2005.
Attendance: 42,077

Bookings: Hamann(Liverpool), Oscar Lopez (Real Betis)
Referee: Eric Poulat (France)

Team line-ups

Liverpool (4-4-2)

Crouch Cisse

Garcia Alonso Hamann Gerrard

Traore Hyypia Carragher Finnan

Reina

Subs: Sinama-Pongolle (Cisse) 78
Subs not used: Carson, Riise, Josemi,
Warnock, Zenden, Potter

Chelsea (4-5-1)

Drogba

Lampard

Robben Makelele Essien Duff

Gallas Terry Carvalho Ferreira

Cech

Subs: Wright-Phillips (Robben) 65, Crespo
(Duff) 75, Huth (Drogba) 90
Subs not used: Cudicini, J. Cole, Geremi,
Gudjohnsen

LIVERPOOL 0
CHELSEA 0

**UEFA Champions League,
Group G game 2,**
Wednesday, September 28, 2005.
Attendance: 42,743

Bookings: Alonso (Liverpool), Lampard,
Makelele, Robben, Terry (Chelsea)
Referee: Massimo de Santis (Italy)

Team line-ups

Chelsea (4-4-1-1):

Drogba
Gudjohnsen
Robben Lampard Essien Duff
Gallas Terry Carvalho Ferreira
Cech

Subs: Del Horno (Ferreira) 46, Wright-Phillips (Duff) 73, C. Cole (Robben) 73
Subs not used: Cudicini, C. Cole, Geremi, Diarra, Huth

Liverpool (4-4-1-1):

Crouch
Garcia
Riise Sissoko Hamann Gerrard
Traore Hyypia Carragher Finnan
Reina

Subs: Kewell (Riise) 61, Morientes (Crouch) 68, Sinama-Pongolle (Garcia) 81
Subs not used: Carson, Cisse, Josemi, Warnock

CHELSEA   0
LIVERPOOL   0

**UEFA Champions League,
Group G game 6,**
Tuesday, December 6, 2005.
Attendance: 41,598

Bookings: Lampard, Carvalho (Chelsea), Traore (Liverpool)
Referee: Herbert Fandel (Germany)

Team line-ups

Anderlecht (4-4-2)

Jestrovic Mpenza

Goor Vanderhaeghe Zetterberg Wilhelmsson

Borre Deman Tihinen Deschacht

Proto

Subs: L. Traore (Tihinen) 50, Baseggio (Vanderhaeghe) 61, Akin (Deschacht) 75
Subs not used: Zitka, Zewlakow, Pujol, Hasi

Liverpool (4-5-1)

Cisse

Alonso

Riise Hamann Sissoko Garcia

Traore Hyypia Carragher Josemi

Reina

Subs: Kewell (Cisse) 74, Zenden (Sissoko) 82, Warnock (Riise) 88
Subs not used: Carson, Finnan, Crouch, Morientes

ANDERLECHT 0
LIVERPOOL 1

**UEFA Champions League,
Group G game 3,**
Wednesday, October 19, 2005.
Attendance: 25,000

Goal: Cisse (20)
Bookings: Alonso, Reina (Liverpool)
Referee: Massimo Busacca (Switzerland)

Team line-ups

Liverpool (4-4-2)

Crouch Morientes

Garcia Alonso Sissoko Gerrard

Riise Hyypia Carragher Finnan

Reina

Subs: Zenden (Morientes) 52, Cisse (Crouch) 72, Kewell (Gerrard) 78
Subs not used: Dudek, Hamann, Josemi, Warnock

Anderlecht (4-4-1-1)

Mpenza

Wilhelmsson

Akin Vanderhaeghe Zetterberg Deman

Goor Juhasz Tihinen Zewlakow

Proto

Subs: Jestrovic (Akin) 70, Pujol (Vanderhaeghe) 70, Baseggio (Mpenza) 82
Subs not used: Zitka, Deschacht, Hasi, L. Traore

LIVERPOOL 3
ANDERLECHT 0

**UEFA Champions League,
Group G game 4,**
Tuesday, November 1, 2005.
Attendance: 42,607

Goals: Morientes (34), Garcia (61), Cisse (89)
Booking: Sissoko (Liverpool)
Sending off: Jestrovic (Anderlecht)
Referee: Kim Milton Nielsen (Denmark)

Team line-ups

Benfica (4-5-1)

Gomes

Robert   Fernandes   Beto   Sabrosa

Petit

Leo   Anderson   Luisao   Alcides

Moretto

Subs: Karagounis (Beto) 58, Nelson (Robert) 76, Rocha (Leo) 87
Subs not used: Quim, Mantorras, Kariaka, Augusto

Liverpool (4-4-2)

Fowler   Morientes

Kewell   Alonso   Sissoko   Garcia

Riise   Hyypia   Carragher   Finnan

Reina

Subs: Hamann (Sissoko) 35, Cisse (Fowler) 65, Gerrard (Morientes) 78
Subs not used: Dudek, Crouch, Traore, Warnock

BENFICA   1
LIVERPOOL   0

**UEFA Champions League,
Last 16, 1st Leg,**
Tuesday, February 21, 2006.
Attendance: 65,000

Goal: Luisao (84)
Bookings: Beto (Benfica), Garcia, Hamann (Liverpool)
Referee: Konrad Plautz (Austria)

Team line-ups

Liverpool (4-4-2):

Crouch
Morientes
Kewell   Garcia
Alonso Gerrard
Warnock   Finnan
Traore Carragher
Reina

Subs: Cisse (Kewell) 63, Hamann (Warnock) 70, Fowler (Morientes) 70
Subs not used: Dudek, Hyypia, Anderson, Barragan

Benfica (4-5-1):

Gomes
Robert Fernandes Geovanni Sabrosa
Beto
Leo   Alcides
Anderson Luisao
Moretto

Subs: Karagounis (Geovanni) 60, Rocha (Robert) 70, Miccoli (Gomes) 76
Subs not used: Quim, Kariaka, Marcel, Nelson

LIVERPOOL   0
BENFICA   2

**UEFA Champions League,
Last 16, 2nd Leg,**
Wednesday, March 8, 2006.
Attendance: 42,745

Goals: Sabrosa (36), Miccoli (89)
Bookings: Alonso, Crouch, Gerrard (Liverpool),
Fernandes, Gomes, Robert (Benfica)
Referee: Massimo de Santis (Italy)

Team line-ups

Liverpool (4-4-1-1):

Morientes

Garcia

Zenden Alonso Hamann Finnan

Riise Hyypia Carragher Josemi

Reina

Subs: Sinama-Pongolle (Finnan) 55, Sissoko (Alonso) 71, Cisse (Riise) 79
Subs not used: Carson, Warnock

CSKA Moscow (4-4-1-1):

Love

Carvalho

Rahimic Krasic
Aldonin Zhirkov

Ordia Ignashevich
V. Berezutsky A. Berezutsky

Akinfeev

Subs: Semberas (Zhirkov) 66, Dudu (Krasic) 85, Gusev (Ordia) 90
Subs not used: Mandrykin, Samodin

28' CARV

LIVERPOOL   3
CSKA MOSCOW 1
(after extra time)

European Super Cup Final, Monaco
Friday, August 26, 2005.
Attendance: 18,000

Goals: Cisse (82, 102), Garcia (109), Carvalho (28)
Bookings: Hyypia, Garcia, Sinama-Pongolle, Zenden (Liverpool), Dudu, Rahimic (CSKA Moscow)
Referee: Rene Temmink (Holland)

Team line-ups

Liverpool (4-4-2):

Crouch   Cisse

Riise   Alonso   Sissoko   Gerrard

Traore   Hyypia   Carragher   Josemi

Reina

Subs: Sinama-Pongolle (Gerrard) 64, Garcia (Hyypia) 72, Hamann (Alonso) 79
Subs not used: Dudek, Carson, Warnock, Finnan, Kewell, Morientes

Saprissa (4-4-2):

Badilla   Bennett

Gomez   Azofeifa   Centeno   Saborio

Cordero   Drummond   Gonzalez   Bolanos

Porras

Subs: Solis (Bennett) 46, Drummond (Gomez) 76, Aleman (Saborio) 83
Subs not used: Gonzalez, Navas, Parks, Brenes, Esquivel, Nunez, Phillips, Lopez, Fonseca

LIVERPOOL   3
SAPRISSA   0

FIFA Club World Championship Semi-Final, Yokohama,
Thursday, December 15, 2005.
Attendance: 43,902

Goals: Crouch (3, 58), Gerrard (32)
Booking: Azofeifa (Saprissa)
Referee: Carlos Chandia (Chile)

Team line-ups

 Liverpool (4-4-1-1):

Subs: Sinama-Pongolle (Sissoko) 79, Riise (Warnock) 79, Crouch (Morientes) 85
Subs not used: Dudek, Carson, Cisse, Hamann, Josemi, Traore

Sao Paulo (4-4-2):

Subs: Grafite (Aloisio) 75
Subs not used: Bosco, Flavio Kretzer, Christian, Alex, Denilson, Fabio Santos, Renan, Flavio Donizete, Thiago, Richarlyson, Souza

LIVERPOOL   0
SAO PAULO   1

FIFA Club World Championship Final, Yokohama,
Sunday, December 18, 2005.
Attendance: 66,821

Goal: Mineiro (27)
Bookings: Lugano, Rogerio Ceni (Sao Paulo)
Referee: Benito Armando Archundia (Mexico)

EUROPEAN/WORLD ROLL OF HONOUR

EUROPEAN CUP
WINNERS
1976-1977, 1977-1978, 1980-1981, 1983-1984, 2004-2005

RUNNERS-UP
1984-1985

UEFA CUP
WINNERS
1972-1973, 1975-1976, 2000-2001

EUROPEAN CUP WINNERS' CUP
RUNNERS-UP
1965-1966

WORLD CLUB CHAMPIONSHIP
RUNNERS-UP
1981, 1984, 2005

EUROPEAN SUPER CUP
WINNERS
1977, 2001, 2005

RUNNERS-UP
1978, 1985

EUROPEAN RESULTS

Despite ultimate disappointment for Liverpool in the defence of their Champions League crown in 2005-06, there was another addition to the European trophy cabinet. The European Super Cup success over CSKA Moscow took the club's tally to 11 major European trophies, outlining their credentials as the most successful British side in overseas competition. Five European Cups, three UEFA Cups and three European Super Cup successes have been secured, while 2006-07 will be the Reds' 34th season in European competition - the club having failed to qualify in only three seasons since their first venture overseas in 1964-65 (apart from when English clubs were forced to sit out European football).

Success in European competition has also brought about some eye-catching results, as well as some impressive scores. There have been three matches where the Reds have reached double figures, and the following pages will record each result. From Liverpool's European debut against Icelandic part-timers KR Reykjavik in the European Cup in August 1964, up to the Champions League last 16 defeat to Benfica in March 2006, each game is noted - including match details.

LIVERPOOL'S FULL LIST OF RESULTS IN EUROPE

Season	Round	Venue	Opponents	Opponent Country	Score	Scorers	Att
1964-65	EUROPEAN CUP						
17th Aug	1 Leg 1	(a)	Reykjavik	Ice	W 5-0	Wallace 2, Hunt 2, Chisnall	10,000
14th Sept	1 Leg 2	(h)	Reykjavik	"	W 6-1	Byrne, St John 2, Hunt, Graham, Stevenson	32,957
25th Nov	2 Leg 1	(h)	Anderlecht	Bel	W 3-0	St John, Hunt, Yeats	44,516
16th Dec	2 Leg 2	(a)	Anderlecht	"	W 1-0	Hunt	60,000
10th Feb	3 Leg 1	(a)	FC Cologne	W.Ger	D 0-0		40,000
17th Mar	3 Leg 2	(h)	FC Cologne	"	D 0-0		48,432
24th Mar	Replay	Rotterdam	FC Cologne	"	D 2-2	St John, Hunt	45,000
			(Liverpool won on toss of a coin)				
4th May	SF Leg 1	(h)	Inter Milan	Ita	W 3-1	Hunt, Callaghan, St John	54,082
12th May	SF Leg 1	(a)	Inter Milan	"	L 0-3		90,000
1965-66	EUROPEAN CUP WINNERS' CUP						
29th Sept	Pr Leg 1	(a)	Juventus	Ita	L 0-1		12,000
13th Oct	Pr Leg 2	(h)	Juventus	"	W 2-0	Lawler, Strong	51,055
1st Dec	1 Leg 1	(h)	Standard Liege	Bel	W 3-1	Lawler 2, Thompson	46,112
15th Dec	1 Leg 2	(a)	Standard Liege	"	W 2-1	Hunt, St John	35,000
1st Mar	2 Leg 1	(a)	Honved	Hun	D 0-0		20,000
8th Mar	2 Leg 2	(h)	Honved	"	W 2-0	Lawler, St John	54,631
14th Apr	SF Leg 1	(a)	Celtic	Sco	L 0-1		80,000
19th Apr	SF Leg 2	(h)	Celtic	"	W 2-0	Smith, Strong	54,208
5th May	Final	Glasgow	B. Dortmund	W.Ger	L 1-2 aet	Hunt	41,657
1966-67	EUROPEAN CUP						
28th Sept	Pr Leg 1	(h)	Petrolul Ploesti	Rom	W 2-0	St John, Callaghan	44,463
12th Oct	Pr Leg 2	(a)	Petrolul Ploesti	"	L 1-3	Hunt	20,000
19th Oct	Replay	Brussels	Petrolul Ploesti	"	W 2-0	St John, Thompson	15,000
7th Dec	1 Leg 1	(a)	Ajax Amsterdam	Hol	L 1-5	Lawler	65,000
14th Dec	1 Leg 2	(h)	Ajax Amsterdam	"	D 2-2	Hunt 2	53,846
1967-68	FAIRS CUP						
19th Sept	1 Leg 1	(a)	Malmo	Swe	W 2-0	Hateley 2	14,314
4th Oct	1 Leg 2	(h)	Malmo	"	W 2-1	Yeats, Hunt	39,795
7th Nov	2 Leg 1	(h)	TSV Munich 1860	W.Ger	W 8-0	St John, Hateley, Smith (pen) Hunt 2, Thompson, Callaghan 2	44,812
14th Nov	2 Leg 2	(a)	TSV Munich 1860	"	L 1-2	Callaghan	10,000
28th Nov	3 Leg 1	(a)	Ferencvaros	Hun	L 0-1		30,000
9th Jan	3 Leg 2	(h)	Ferencvaros	"	L 0-1		46,892
1968-69	FAIRS CUP						
18th Sept	1 Leg 1	(a)	Athletic Bilbao	Spa	L 1-2	Hunt	35,000
2nd Oct	1 Leg 2	(h)	Athletic Bilbao	"	W 2-1 aet	Lawler, Hughes	49,567
			(Liverpool lost on toss of coin)				
1969-70	FAIRS CUP						
16th Sept	1 Leg 1	(h)	Dundalk	Rep. Ire	W 10-0	Evans 2, Lawler, Smith 2, Graham 2, Lindsay, Thompson, Callaghan	32,562
30th Sept	1 Leg 2	(a)	Dundalk	"	W 4-0	Thompson 2, Graham, Callaghan	6,000
12th Nov	2 Leg 1	(a)	Vitoria Setubal	Por	L 0-1		16,000
26th Nov	2 Leg 2	(h)	Vitoria Setubal	"	W 3-2	Smith (pen), Evans, Hunt	41,633

Season	Round	Venue	Opponents	Opponent Country	Score	Scorers	Att
1970-71	FAIRS CUP						
15th Sept	1 Leg 1	(h)	Ferencvaros	Hun	W 1-0	Graham	37,531
29th Sept	1 Leg 2	(a)	Ferencvaros	"	D 1-1	Hughes	25,000
21st Oct	2 Leg 1	(h)	D. Bucharest	Rom	W 3-0	Lindsay, Lawler, Hughes	36,525
4th Nov	2 Leg 2	(a)	D. Bucharest	"	D 1-1	Boersma	45,000
9th Dec	3 Leg 1	(a)	Hibernian	Sco	W 1-0	Toshack	30,296
22nd Dec	3 Leg 2	(h)	Hibernian	"	W 2-0	Heighway, Boersma	37,815
10th Mar	4 Leg 1	(h)	Bayern Munich	W.Ger	W 3-0	Evans 3	45,616
24th Mar	4 Leg 2	(a)	Bayern Munich	"	D 1-1	Ross	23,000
14th Apr	SF Leg 1	(h)	Leeds United	Eng	L 0-1		52,577
28th Apr	SF Leg 2	(a)	Leeds United	"	D 0-0		40,462
1971-72	EUROPEAN CUP WINNERS' CUP						
15th Sept	1 Leg 1	(a)	Servette Geneva	Swi	L 1-2	Lawler	16,000
29th Sept	1 Leg 2	(h)	Servette Geneva	"	W 2-0	Hughes, Heighway	38,591
20th Oct	2 Leg 1	(h)	Bayern Munich	W.Ger	D 0-0		42,949
3rd Nov	2 Leg 2	(a)	Bayern Munich	"	L 1-3	Evans	40,000
1972-73	UEFA CUP						
12th Sept	1 Leg 1	(h)	E. Frankfurt	W.Ger	W 2-0	Keegan, Hughes	33,380
26th Sept	1 Leg 2	(a)	E. Frankfurt	"	D 0-0		20,000
24th Oct	2 Leg 1	(h)	AEK Athens	Gre	W 3-0	Boersma, Cormack, Smith (pen)	31,906
7th Nov	2 Leg 2	(a)	AEK Athens	"	W 3-1	Hughes 2, Boersma	25,000
29th Nov	3 Leg 1	(a)	Dynamo Berlin	E.Ger	D 0-0		19,000
13th Dec	3 Leg 2	(h)	Dynamo Berlin	"	W 3-1	Boersma, Heighway, Toshack	34,140
7th Mar	4 Leg 1	(h)	Dynamo Dresden	E.Ger	W 2-0	Hall, Boersma	33,270
21st Mar	4 Leg 2	(a)	Dynamo Dresden	"	W 1-0	Keegan	35,000
10th Apr	SF Leg 1	(h)	Tottenham H.	Eng	W 1-0	Lindsay	42,174
25th Apr	SF Leg 2	(a)	Tottenham H.	"	L 1-2	Heighway	46,919
10th May	F Leg 1	(h)	B. Moench'bach	W.Ger	W 3-0	Keegan 2, Lloyd	41,169
23rd May	F Leg 2	(a)	B. Moench'bach	"	L 0-2		35,000
1973-74	EUROPEAN CUP						
19th Sept	1 Leg 1	(a)	Jeunesse D'Esch	Lux	D 1-1	Hall	5,000
3rd Oct	1 Leg 2	(h)	Jeunesse D'Esch	"	W 2-0	Mond o.g., Toshack	28,714
24th Oct	2 Leg 1	(a)	R.S. Belgrade	Yug	L 1-2	Lawler	40,000
6th Nov	2 Leg 2	(h)	R.S. Belgrade"		L 1-2	Lawler	41,774
1974-75	EUROPEAN CUP WINNERS' CUP						
17th Sept	1 Leg 1	(h)	Stromsgodset	Nor	W 11-0	Lindsay (pen), Boersma 2, Thompson 2, Heighway, Cormack, Hughes, Smith Callaghan, Kennedy	24,743
1st Oct	1 Leg 2	(a)	Stromsgodset	"	W 1-0	Kennedy	17,000
23rd Oct	2 Leg 1	(h)	Ferencvaros	Hun	D 1-1	Keegan	35,027
5th Nov	2 Leg 2	(a)	Ferencvaros	"	D 0-0		30,000
1975-76	UEFA CUP						
17th Sept	1 Leg 1	(a)	Hibernian	Sco	L 0-1		19,219
30th Sept	1 Leg 2	(h)	Hibernian	"	W 3-1	Toshack 3	29,963
22nd Oct	2 Leg 1	(a)	Real Sociedad	Spa	W 3-1	Heighway, Callaghan, Thompson	20,000
4th Nov	2 Leg 2	(h)	Real Sociedad	"	W 6-0	Toshack, Kennedy 2, Fairclough Heighway, Neal	23,796

Season	Round	Venue	Opponents	Opponent Country	Score	Scorers	Att
1975-76	UEFA CUP (cont)						
26th Nov	3 Leg 1	(a)	Slask Wroclaw	Pol	W 2-1	Kennedy, Toshack	46,000
10th Dec	3 Leg 2	(h)	Slask Wroclaw	"	W 3-0	Case 3	17,886
3rd Mar	4 Leg 1	(a)	Dynamo Dresden	E.Ger	D 0-0		33,000
17th Mar	4 Leg 2	(h)	Dynamo Dresden	"	W 2-1	Case, Keegan	39,300
30th Mar	SF Leg 1	(a)	Barcelona	Spa	W 1-0	Toshack	70,000
14th Apr	SF Leg 2	(h)	Barcelona	"	D 1-1	Thompson	55,104
28th Apr	F Leg 1	(h)	FC Bruges	Bel	W 3-2	Kennedy, Case, Keegan (pen)	49,981
19th May	F Leg 2	(a)	FC Bruges	"	D 1-1	Keegan	33,000
1976-77	EUROPEAN CUP						
14th Sept	1 Leg 1	(h)	Crusaders	N.Ire	W 2-0	Neal (pen), Toshack	22,442
28th Sept	1 Leg 2	(a)	Crusaders	"	W 5-0	Keegan, Johnson 2, McDermott Heighway	10,500
20th Oct	2 Leg 1	(a)	Trabzonspor	Tur	L 0-1		25,000
3rd Nov	2 Leg 2	(h)	Trabzonspor	"	W 3-0	Heighway, Johnson, Keegan	42,275
2nd Mar	3 Leg 1	(a)	St Etienne	Fra	L 0-1		38,000
16th Mar	3 Leg 2	(h)	St Etienne	"	W 3-1	Keegan, Kennedy, Fairclough	55,043
6th Apr	SF Leg 1	(a)	FC Zurich	Swi	W 3-1	Neal 2 (1 pen), Heighway	30,500
20th Apr	SF Leg 2	(h)	FC Zurich	"	W 3-0	Case 2, Keegan	50,611
25th May	Final	Rome	B. Moench'bach	W.Ger	W 3-1	McDermott, Smith, Neal (pen)	57,000
1977-78	EUROPEAN CUP						
19th Oct	2 Leg 1	(h)	Dynamo Dresden	E.Ger	W 5-1	Hansen, Case 2, Neal (pen) Kennedy	39,835
2nd Nov	2 Leg 2	(a)	Dynamo Dresden	"	L 1-2	Heighway	33,000
1st Mar	3 Leg 1	(a)	Benfica	Por	W 2-1	Case, Hughes	70,000
15th Mar	3 Leg 2	(h)	Benfica	"	W 4-1	Callaghan, Dalglish, McDermott, Neal	48,364
29th Mar	SF Leg 1	(a)	B. Moench'bach	W.Ger	L 1-2	Johnson	66,000
12th Apr	SF Leg 2	(h)	B. Moench'bach	"	W 3-0	Kennedy, Dalglish, Case	51,500
10th May	Final	Wembley	FC Bruges	Bel	W 1-0	Dalglish	92,000
1977-78	EUROPEAN SUPER CUP						
22nd Nov	Leg 1	(a)	SV Hamburg	W.Ger	D 1-1	Fairclough	16,000
6th Dec	Leg 2	(h)	SV Hamburg	"	W 6-0	Thompson, Mc Dermott 3 Fairclough, Dalglish	34,931
1978-79	EUROPEAN CUP						
13th Sept	1 Leg 1	(a)	Nottingham Forest	Eng	L 0-2		38,316
27th Sept	1 Leg 2	(h)	Nottingham Forest	"	D 0-0		51,679
1978-79	EUROPEAN SUPER CUP						
4th Dec	1 Leg 1	(a)	Anderlecht	Bel	L 1-3	Case	35,000
19th Dec	1 Leg 2	(h)	Anderlecht	"	W 2-1	Hughes, Fairclough	23,598
1979-80	EUROPEAN CUP						
19th Sept	1 Leg 1	(h)	Dynamo Tblisi	Rus	W 2-1	Johnson, Case	35,270
3rd Oct	1 Leg 2	(a)	Dynamo Tblisi	"	L 0-3		80,000

Season	Round	Venue	Opponents	Opponent Country	Score	Scorers	Att
1980-81		**EUROPEAN CUP**					
17th Sept	1 Leg 1	(a)	Oulu Palloseura	Fin	D 1-1	McDermott	14,000
1st Oct	1 Leg 2	(h)	Oulu Palloseura	"	W 10-1	Souness 3 (1pen), McDermott 3, Lee, R.Kennedy, Fairclough 2	21,013
22nd Oct	2 Leg 1	(a)	Aberdeen	Sco	W 1-0	McDermott	24,000
5th Nov	2 Leg 2	(h)	Aberdeen	"	W 4-0	Miller o.g., Neal, Dalglish, Hansen	36,182
4th Mar	3 Leg 1	(h)	CSKA Sofia	Bul	W 5-1	Souness 3, Lee, McDermott	37,255
18th Mar	3 Leg 2	(a)	CSKA Sofia	"	W 1-0	Johnson	65,000
8th Apr	SF Leg 1	(h)	Bayern Munich	W.Ger	D 0-0		44,543
22nd Apr	SF Leg 2	(a)	Bayern Munich	"	D 1-1	R.Kennedy	77,600
27th May	Final	Paris	Real Madrid	Spa	W 1-0	A.Kennedy	48,360
1981-82		**EUROPEAN CUP**					
16th Sept	1 Leg 1	(a)	Oulu Palloseura	Fin	W 1-0	Dalglish	8,400
30th Sept	1 Leg 2	(h)	Oulu Palloseura	"	W 7-0	Dalglish, McDermott 2, R.Kennedy, Johnson, Rush, Lawrenson	20,789
21st Oct	2 Leg 1	(a)	AZ '67 Alkmaar	Hol	D 2-2	Johnson, Lee	15,000
4th Nov	2 Leg 2	(h)	AZ '67 Alkmaar	"	W 3-2	McDermott (pen), Rush, Hansen	29,703
3rd Mar	3 Leg 1	(h)	CSKA Sofia	Bul	W 1-0	Whelan	27,388
17th Mar	3 Leg 2	(a)	CSKA Sofia	"	L 0-2 aet		60,000
1982-83		**EUROPEAN CUP**					
14th Sept	1 Leg 1	(a)	Dundalk	Rep. Ire	W 4-1	Whelan 2, Rush, Hodgson	16,500
28th Sept	1 Leg 2	(h)	Dundalk	"	W 1-0	Whelan	12,021
19th Oct	2 Leg 1	(a)	JK Helsinki	Fin	L 0-1		5,722
2nd Nov	2 Leg 2	(h)	JK Helsinki	"	W 5-0	Dalglish, Johnson, Neal, A.Kennedy 2	16,434
2nd Mar	3 Leg 1	(a)	Widzew Lodz	Pol	L 0-2		45,531
16th Mar	3 Leg 2	(h)	Widzew Lodz	"	W 3-2	Neal (pen), Rush, Hodgson	44,494
1983-84		**EUROPEAN CUP**					
14th Sept	1 Leg 1	(a)	BK Odense	Den	W 1-0	Dalglish	30,000
28th Sept	1 Leg 2	(h)	BK Odense	"	W 5-0	Robinson 2, Dalglish 2, Clausen o.g.	14,985
19th Oct	2 Leg 1	(h)	Athletic Bilbao	Spa	D 0-0		33,063
2nd Nov	2 Leg 2	(a)	Athletic Bilbao	"	W 1-0	Rush	47,500
7th Mar	3 Leg 1	(h)	Benfica	Por	W 1-0	Rush	39,096
21st Mar	3 Leg 2	(a)	Benfica	"	W 4-1	Whelan 2, Johnston, Rush	70,000
11th Apr	SF Leg 1	(h)	D. Bucharest	Rom	W 1-0	Lee	36,941
25th Apr	SF Leg 2	(a)	D. Bucharest	"	W 2-1	Rush 2	60,000
30th May	Final	Rome	AS Roma	Ita	W 1-1 aet	Neal	69,693
			(Liverpool won 4-2 on penalties)				
1984-85		**EUROPEAN CUP**					
19th Sept	1 Leg 1	(a)	Lech Poznan	Pol	W 1-0	Wark	35,000
3rd Oct	1 Leg 2	(h)	Lech Poznan	"	W 4-0	Wark 3, Walsh	22,143
24th Oct	2 Leg 1	(h)	Benfica	Por	W 3-1	Rush 3	27,733
7th Nov	2 Leg 2	(a)	Benfica	"	L 0-1		50,000
6th Mar	3 Leg 1	(a)	Austria Vienna	Aut	D 1-1	Nicol	21,000
20th Mar	3 Leg 2	(h)	Austria Vienna	"	W 4-1	Walsh 2, Nicol, Obermayer o.g.	32,761

Season	Round	Venue	Opponents	Opponent Country	Score	Scorers	Att
1984-85	EUROPEAN CUP (cont)						
10th Apr	SF Leg 1 (h)		Panathinaikos	Gre	W 4-0	Wark, Rush 2, Beglin	39,488
24th Apr	SF Leg 2 (a)		Panathinaikos	"	W 1-0	Lawrenson	60,000
29th May	Final	Brussels	Juventus	Ita	L 0-1		60,000
1984-85	EUROPEAN SUPER CUP						
16th Jan		(a)	Juventus	Ita	L 0-2		60,000
1991-92	UEFA CUP						
18th Sept	1 Leg 1	(h)	Kuusysi Lahti	Fin	W 6-1	Saunders 4, Houghton 2	17,131
2nd Oct	1 Leg 2	(a)	Kuusysi Lahti	"	L 0-1		8,435
23rd Oct	2 Leg 1	(a)	Auxerre	Fra	L 0-2		16,500
6th Nov	2 Leg 2	(h)	Auxerre	"	W 3-0	Molby (pen), Marsh, Walters	23,094
27th Nov	3 Leg 1	(a)	Swarovski Tirol	Aut	W 2-0	Saunders 2	12,500
11th Dec	3 Leg 2	(h)	Swarovski Tirol	"	W 4-0	Saunders 3, Venison	16,007
4th Mar	4 Leg 1	(a)	Genoa	Ita	L 0-2		40,000
18th Mar	4 Leg 2	(h)	Genoa	"	L 1-2	Rush	38,840
1992-93	EUROPEAN CUP WINNERS' CUP						
16th Sept	1 Leg 1	(h)	Apollon Limassol	Cyp	W 6-1	Stewart 2, Rush 4	12,769
29th Sept	1 Leg 2	(a)	Apollon Limassol	"	W 2-1	Rush, Hutchison	8,000
22nd Oct	2 Leg 1	(a)	Spartak Moscow	Rus	L 2-4	Wright, McManaman	60,000
4th Nov	2 Leg 2	(h)	Spartak Moscow	"	L 0-2		37,993
1995-96	UEFA CUP						
12th Sept	1 Leg 1	(a)	S. Vladikavkaz	Rus	W 2-1	McManaman, Redknapp	43,000
26th Sept	1 Leg 2	(h)	S. Vladikavkaz	"	D 0-0		35,042
17th Oct	2 Leg 1	(a)	Brondby	Den	D 0-0		37,648
31st Oct	2 Leg 2	(h)	Brondby	"	L 0-1		35,878
1996-97	EUROPEAN CUP WINNERS' CUP						
12th Sept	1 Leg 1	(a)	MyPa 47	Fin	W 1-0	Bjornebye	5,500
26th Sept	1 Leg 2	(h)	MyPa 47	"	W 3-1	Berger, Collymore, Barnes	39,013
17th Oct	2 Leg 1	(a)	Sion	Swi	W 2-1	Fowler, Barnes	16,500
31st Oct	2 Leg 2	(h)	Sion	"	W 6-3	McManaman, Bjornebye Barnes, Fowler 2, Berger	38,514
6th Mar	3 Leg 1	(a)	Brann Bergen	Nor	D 1-1	Fowler	12,700
20th Mar	3 Leg 2	(h)	Brann Bergen	"	W 3-0	Fowler 2 (1 pen), Collymore	40,326
10th Apr	SF Leg 1 (a)		Paris St Germain	Fra	L 0-3		35,142
24th Apr	SF Leg 2 (h)		Paris St Germain	"	W 2-0	Fowler, Wright	38,984
1997-98	UEFA CUP						
16th Sept	1 Leg 1	(a)	Celtic	Sco	D 2-2	Owen, McManaman	48,526
30th Sept	1 Leg 2	(h)	Celtic	"	D 0-0		38,205
21st Oct	2 Leg 1	(a)	RC Strasbourg	Fra	L 0-3		18,813
4th Nov	2 Leg 2	(h)	RC Strasbourg	"	W 2-0	Fowler (pen), Riedle	32,426

Season	Round	Venue	Opponents	Opponent Country	Score	Scorers	Att
1998-99	UEFA CUP						
15th Sept	1 Leg 1	(a)	FC Kosice	Slovakia	W 3-0	Berger, Riedle, Owen	4,500
29th Sept	1 Leg 2	(h)	FC Kosice	"	W 5-0	Redknapp 2, Ince, Fowler 2	23,792
20th Oct	2 Leg 1	(h)	Valencia	Spa	D 0-0		36,004
3rd Nov	2 Leg 2	(a)	Valencia	"	D 2-2	McManaman, Berger	49,000
24th Nov	3 Leg 1	(a)	Celta Vigo	Spa	L 1-3	Owen	32,000
8th Dec	3 Leg 2	(h)	Celta Vigo	"	L 0-1		30,289
2000-01	UEFA CUP						
14th Sept	1 Leg 1	(a)	Rapid Bucharest	Rom	W 1-0	Barmby	12,000
28th Sept	1 Leg 2	(h)	Rapid Bucharest	"	D 0-0		37,954
26th Oct	2 Leg 1	(h)	Slovan Liberec	Cz Rep	W 1-0	Heskey	29,662
9th Nov	2 Leg 2	(a)	Slovan Liberec	"	W 3-2	Barmby, Heskey, Owen	6,808
23rd Nov	3 Leg 1	(a)	Olympiakos	Gre	D 2-2	Barmby, Gerrard	43,855
7th Dec	3 Leg 2	(h)	Olympiakos	"	W 2-0	Heskey, Barmby	35,484
15th Feb	4 Leg 1	(a)	AS Roma	Ita	W 2-0	Owen 2	59,718
22nd Feb	4 Leg 2	(h)	AS Roma	"	L 0-1		43,688
8th Mar	5 Leg 1	(a)	FC Porto	Por	D 0-0		21,150
15th Mar	5 Leg 2	(h)	FC Porto	"	W 2-0	Murphy, Owen	40,502
5th Apr	SF Leg 1	(a)	Barcelona	Spa	D 0-0		90,000
19th Apr	SF Leg 2	(h)	Barcelona	"	W 1-0	McAllister	44,203
16th May	Final	Dortmund	Alaves	Spa	W 5-4 aet	Babbel, Gerrard, McAllister (pen), Fowler, Geli o.g.	65,000
			(Liverpool won on golden goal)				
2001-02	EUROPEAN CUP						
8th Aug	Q. Leg 1	(a)	FC Haka	Fin	W 5-0	Heskey, Owen 3, Hyypia	33,217
21st Aug	Q. Leg 2	(h)	FC Haka	"	W 4-1	Fowler, Redknapp, Heskey, Wilson o.g.	31,602
			First Group Stage				
11th Sept	Group B	(h)	Boavista	Por	D 1-1	Owen	30,015
19th Sept	Group B	(a)	B. Dortmund	Ger	D 0-0		50,000
26th Sept	Group B	(h)	Dynamo Kiev	Ukr	W 1-0	Litmanen	33,513
16th Oct	Group B	(a)	Dynamo Kiev	"	W 2-1	Murphy, Gerrard	55,000
24th Oct	Group B	(a)	Boavista	Por	D 1-1	Murphy	6,000
30th Oct	Group B	(h)	B. Dortmund	Ger	W 2-0	Smicer, Wright	41,507
			Second Group Stage				
20th Nov	Group B	(h)	Barcelona	Spa	L 1-3	Owen	41,521
5th Dec	Group B	(a)	AS Roma	Ita	D 0-0		57,819
20th Feb	Group B	(h)	Galatasaray	Tur	D 0-0		41,605
26th Feb	Group B	(a)	Galatasaray	"	D 1-1	Heskey	22,100
13th Mar	Group B	(a)	Barcelona	Spa	D 0-0		75,362
19th Mar	Group B	(h)	AS Roma	Ita	W 2-0	Litmanen (pen), Heskey	41,794
3rd Apr	QF Leg 1	(h)	B. Leverkusen	Ger	W 1-0	Hyypia	42,454
9th Apr	QF Leg 2	(a)	B. Leverkusen	"	L 2-4	Xavier, Litmanen	22,500
2001-02	EUROPEAN SUPER CUP						
24th Aug		Monaco	Bayern Munich	Ger	W 3-2	Riise, Heskey, Owen	15,000

Season	Round	Venue	Opponents	Opponent Country	Score	Scorers	Att
2002-03	EUROPEAN CUP						
			First Group Stage				
17th Sept	Group B	(a)	Valencia	Spa	L 0-2		43,000
25th Sept	Group B	(h)	FC Basel	Swi	D 1-1	Baros	37,634
2nd Oct	Group B	(h)	Spartak Moscow	Rus	W 5-0	Heskey 2, Cheyrou, Hyypia, Diao	40,812
22nd Oct	Group B	(a)	Spartak Moscow	"	W 3-1	Owen 3	15,000
30th Oct	Group B	(h)	Valencia	Spa	L 0-1		41,831
12th Nov	Group B	(a)	FC Basel	Swi	D 3-3	Murphy, Smicer, Owen	35,000
2002-03	UEFA CUP						
28th Nov	3 Leg 1	(a)	Vitesse Arnhem	Hol	W 1-0	Owen	28,000
12th Dec	3 Leg 2	(h)	Vitesse Arnhem	"	W 1-0	Owen	23,576
20th Feb	4 Leg 1	(a)	Auxerre	Fra	W 1-0	Hyypia	20,452
27th Feb	4 Leg 2	(h)	Auxerre	"	W 2-0	Owen, Murphy	34,252
13th Mar	5 Leg 1	(a)	Celtic	Sco	D 1-1	Heskey	59,759
20th Mar	5 Leg 2	(h)	Celtic	"	L 0-2		44,238
2003-04	UEFA CUP						
24th Sept	1 Leg 1	(a)	Olimpija Ljubljana	Slovenia	D 1-1	Owen	10,000
15th Oct	1 Leg 2	(h)	Olimpija Ljubljana	"	W 3-0	LeTallec, Heskey, Kewell	42,880
6th Nov	2 Leg 1	(a)	Steaua Bucharest	Rom	D 1-1	Traore	25,000
27th Nov	2 Leg 2	(h)	Steaua Bucharest	"	W 1-0	Kewell	42,837
26th Feb	3 Leg 1	(h)	Levski Sofia	Bul	W 2-0	Gerrard, Kewell	39,149
3rd Mar	3 Leg 2	(a)	Levski Sofia	"	W 4-2	Gerrard, Owen, Hamann, Hyypia	40,281
11th Mar	4 Leg 1	(h)	O. Marseille	Fra	D 1-1	Baros	41,270
25th Mar	4 Leg 2	(a)	O. Marseille	"	L 1-2	Heskey	50,000
2004-05	EUROPEAN CUP						
10th Aug	Q. Leg 1	(a)	AK Graz	Aut	W 2-0	Gerrard 2	15,000
24th Aug	Q. Leg 2	(h)	AK Graz	"	L 0-1		42,950
			Group Stage				
15th Sept	Group A	(h)	AS Monaco	Fra	W 2-0	Cisse, Baros	33,517
28th Sept	Group A	(a)	Olympiakos	Gre	L 0-1		33,000
19th Oct	Group A	(h)	D. La Coruna	Spa	D 0-0		40,236
3rd Nov	Group A	(a)	D. La Coruna	"	W 1-0	Andrade o.g.	32,000
23rd Nov	Group A	(a)	AS Monaco	Fra	L 0-1		15,000
8th Dec	Group A	(h)	Olympiakos	Gre	W 3-1	Sinama-Pongolle, Mellor, Gerrard	42,045
22nd Feb	L. 16 L1	(h)	B. Leverkusen	Ger	W 3-1	Garcia, Riise, Hamann	40,942
9th Mar	L. 16 L2	(a)	B. Leverkusen	"	W 3-1	Garcia 2, Baros	23,000
5th Apr	QF Leg 1	(h)	Juventus	Ita	W 2-1	Hyypia, Garcia	41,216
13th Apr	QF Leg 1	(a)	Juventus	"	D 0-0		55,464
27th Apr	SF Leg 1	(a)	Chelsea	Eng	D 0-0		40,497
3rd May	SF Leg 1	(h)	Chelsea	"	W 1-0	Garcia	42,529
25th May	Final	Istanbul	AC Milan	Ita	W 3-3 aet	Gerrard, Smicer, Alonso	65,000

(Liverpool won 3-2 on penalties)

Season	Round	Venue	Opponents	Opponent Country	Score	Scorers	Att
2005-06	EUROPEAN CUP						
13th July	Q.1 Leg 1	(h)	TNS	Wal	W 3-0	Gerrard 3	44,760
19th July	Q.1 Leg 2	(a)	TNS	"	W 3-0	Cisse, Gerrard 2	8,009
26th July	Q.2 Leg 1	(a)	FBK Kaunas	Lith	W 3-1	Cisse, Carragher, Gerrard (pen)	8,300
2nd Aug	Q.2 Leg 2	(h)	FBK Kaunas	"	W 2-0	Gerrard, Cisse	43,717
10th Aug	Q.3 Leg 1	(a)	CSKA Sofia	Bul	W 3-1	Cisse, Morientes 2	16,512
23rd Aug	Q.3 Leg 2	(h)	CSKA Sofia	"	L 0-1		42,175
			Group Stage				
13th Sept	Group G	(a)	Real Betis	Spa	W 2-1	Sinama-Pongolle, Garcia	45,000
28th Sept	Group G	(h)	Chelsea	Eng	D 0-0		42,743
19th Oct	Group G	(a)	Anderlecht	Bel	W 1-0	Cisse	25,000
1st Nov	Group G	(h)	Anderlecht	Bel	W 3-0	Morientes, Garcia, Cisse	42,607
23rd Nov	Group G	(h)	Real Betis	Spa	D 0-0		42,077
6th Dec	Group G	(a)	Chelsea	Eng	D 0-0		41,598
21st Feb	L. 16 L1	(a)	Benfica	Por	L 0-1		65,000
8th Mar	L. 16 L2	(h)	Benfica	Por	L 0-2		42,745
2005-06	EUROPEAN SUPER CUP						
26th Aug		Monaco	CSKA Moscow	Rus	W 3-1 aet	Cisse 2, Garcia	18,000

Stand-in skipper Jamie Carragher shows off the European Super Cup following Liverpool's 3-1 extra-time victory over CSKA Moscow in August, 2005

When it all began...Bill Shankly shows off the UEFA Cup, Liverpool's first European trophy, following the 3-2 aggregate victory over Borussia Moenchengladbach (top)

European Cup winners - 1977 captain Emlyn Hughes (left picture), and 1981 matchwinner Alan Kennedy (left in right picture), with skipper Phil Thompson (right)

LIVERPOOL'S EUROPEAN OPPONENTS

With Serbia and Montenegro becoming independent states in 2006, the number of countries the Reds have yet to visit in European competition has gone up to 20. These are:

Albania, Andorra, Armenia, Azerbaijan, Belarus, Bosnia-Herzegovina, Croatia, Estonia, FYR Macedonia, Faroe Islands, Georgia, Israel, Kazakhstan, Latvia, Liechtenstein, Malta, Moldova, Montenegro, San Marino and Serbia.

In terms of most frequent opposition, it seems apt - in light of the current Spanish influence at Anfield - that with Liverpool being drawn to play Primera Liga side Real Betis last season, the Reds have now played a record 9 clubs from the country in European competition. The former West German sides (7) and French clubs (6) are the others most commonly visited, while Bayern Munich and Juventus remain the most common opposition, having been faced four times each in competition. 'Big' clubs (in terms of competing in Europe on a regular basis) Liverpool have yet to face in European competition include: Manchester United, Arsenal, Lyon, PSV Eindhoven, Feyenoord, Lazio, Rosenborg, Sporting Lisbon, Rangers and Fenerbahce.

The countries, and the clubs who Liverpool have faced (up to and including the 2005-06 season) are listed below and opposite:

AUSTRIA (3)
AK Graz, Austria Vienna, Swarovski Tirol.
BELGIUM (3)
FC Bruges, Anderlecht, Standard Liege.
BULGARIA (2)
CSKA Sofia, Levski Sofia.
CYPRUS (1)
Apollon Limassol.
CZECH REPUBLIC (1)
Slovan Liberec.
DENMARK (2)
Brondby, Odense.
ENGLAND (4)
Chelsea, Leeds United, Nottingham Forest, Tottenham Hotspur.
EAST GERMANY (2)
Dynamo Dresden, Dynamo Berlin.
FINLAND (5)
FC Haka , HJK Helsinki, Kuusysi Lahti, MyPa 47, Oulu Palloseura.
FRANCE (6)
Auxerre, Olimpique Marseille, Monaco, Paris St Germain, RC Strasbourg, St Etienne.
GERMANY (2)
Borussia Dortmund, Bayer Leverkusen.
GREECE (3)
AEK Athens, Olympiakos, Panathinaikos.
HOLLAND (3)
Ajax Amsterdam, AZ '67 Alkmaar, Vitesse Arnhem.
HUNGARY (2)
Ferencvaros, Honved.

LIVERPOOL'S EUROPEAN OPPONENTS

ICELAND (1)
Reykjavik.
ITALY (5)
Juventus, AS Roma, Genoa, Inter Milan, AC Milan.
LITHUANIA (1)
FBK Kaunas.
LUXEMBOURG (1)
Jeunesse D'Esch.
NORTHERN IRELAND (1)
Crusaders.
NORWAY (2)
Brann Bergen, Stromsgodset.
POLAND (3)
Lech Poznan, Slask Wroclaw, Widzew Lodz.
PORTUGAL (4)
Benfica, Boavista, FC Porto, Vitoria Setubal.
REPUBLIC OF IRELAND (1)
Dundalk.
ROMANIA (4)
Dinamo Bucharest, Petrolul Ploesti, Rapid Bucharest, Steaua Bucharest.
RUSSIA (4)
Dynamo Tblisi, Spartak Moscow, Spartak Vladikavkaz, CSKA Moscow.
SCOTLAND (3)
Celtic, Hibernian, Aberdeen.
SLOVAKIA (1)
FC Kosice.
SLOVENIA (1)
Olimpija Ljubljana.
SPAIN (9)
Alaves, Atletico Bilbao, Barcelona, Celta Vigo, Deportivo La Coruna, Real Betis, Real Madrid, Real Sociedad, Valencia.
SWEDEN (1)
Malmo.
SWITZERLAND (4)
Servette Geneva, FC Sion, FC Zurich, FC Basel.
TURKEY (2)
Trabzonspor, Galatasaray.
WALES (1)
Total Network Solutions.
WEST GERMANY (7)
Bayern Munich, Borussia Moenchengladbach, Borussia Dortmund, FC Cologne, Eintracht Frankfurt, Hamburg, 1860 Munich.
UKRAINE (1)
Dynamo Kiev.
YUGOSLAVIA (1)
Red Star Belgrade.

Liverpool in action for the first time in European competition against FBK Kaunas, CSKA Moscow and Real Betis in 2005/06

ALL THOSE WHO HAVE A RED HEART CAN REJOICE, FOR THEY HAVE SEEN 'GOD.'

Mt. 4:23

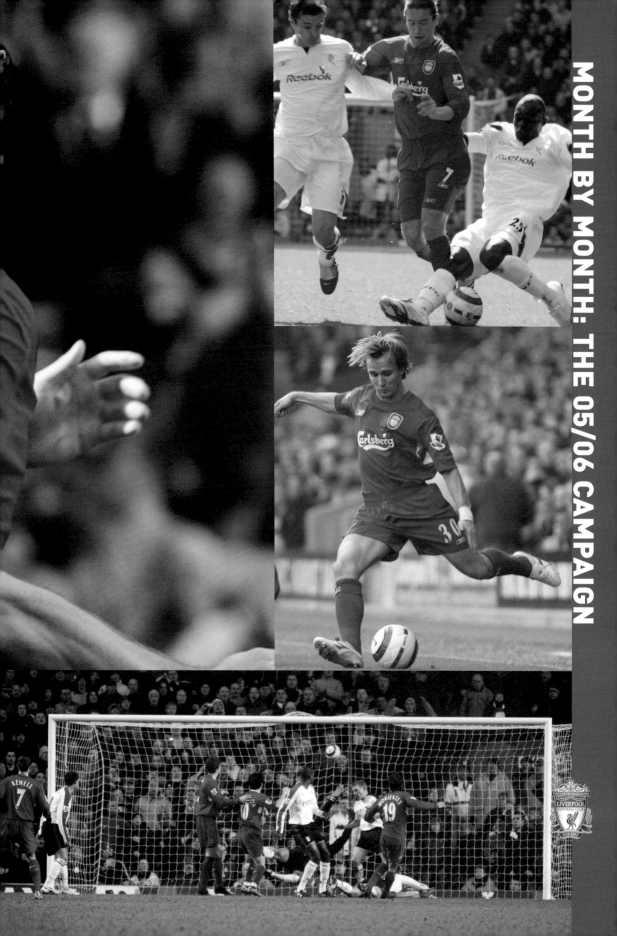

IT'S A MARATHON NOT A SPRINT . . .

From July 13th at Anfield against Welsh champions TNS through to the following May at the Millennium Stadium in Cardiff (exactly 10 months or 305 days later), Liverpool endured the longest season in their history - although one of their most memorable. The succession of records broken has been documented elsewhere, as has the continued success of the club under Rafa Benitez. So allow us now to recap what went on...

July
Steven Gerrard makes a U-turn in his decision to leave Liverpool for Chelsea, agreeing a new four-year contract extension while Jamie Carragher agrees to extend his stay. Among the Reds' moves in the transfer market, they beat Everton and Chelsea to the signature of Mohamed Sissoko, while Wrexham are defeated 4-3 in Liverpool's only pre-season friendly before the Champions League qualifiers begin.
Liverpool are successful in their three qualifying games this month, with Jamie Carragher scoring only his third goal for the Reds - his first for six years - at FBK Kaunas.

Incoming: Jose Reina (Villarreal), Boudewijn Zenden (Middlesbrough), Antonio Barragan (Sevilla), Peter Crouch (Southampton), Mohamed Sissoko (Valencia).
Outgoing: Mauricio Pellegrino (Alaves), Igor Biscan (Panathinaikos), Stephane Henchoz (Wigan Athletic), Gregory Vignal (Portsmouth), Jon Ostemobor (Rotherham United), Richie Partridge (Sheffield Wednesday).
Injuries: Harry Kewell (hernia).
Quote of the month: "It has been such a long time, it has been embarrassing really. I probably deserve the man-of-the-match ball after that. Me scoring? It's like someone scoring a hat-trick!"
Jamie Carragher

August
Rafa welcomes Jose Mourinho's comments questioning Steven Gerrard's decision to stay at Liverpool. "I like it when Jose talks about us because it means we are doing well. He must be worried about us." Milan Baros finally leaves following a summer of speculation linking the Czech striker with Schalke 04, Monaco and Everton, among others. However, Michael Owen will not be returning to Anfield, the England striker moving to Newcastle for £17m while target Luis Figo joins Inter Milan.
Djibril Cisse insists he will score 20 goals this season, while Xabi Alonso admits his relief at avoiding Everton in the Champions League third-qualifying round. Didi Hamann expects a title challenge this term, due to the "spirit of Istanbul", a view mirrored by Sven-Goran Eriksson while the Reds fail to land Chile winger Mark Gonzalez, due to work permit problems.
Sami Hyypia and Stephen Warnock extend their contracts to 2008. Steven Gerrard is voted the Most Valuable Player in last season's Champions League, accepting his award at a ceremony prior to the Champions League group draw.

Incoming: Jack Hobbs (Lincoln City), Godwin Antwi (Real Zaragoza), Miquel Roque (Lleida), Besian Idrizaj (Linzer ASK), Ramon Castille (unattached).
Outgoing: Antonio Nunez (Celta Vigo), Milan Baros (Aston Villa), Anthony Le Tallec (Sunderland, loan), Chris Kirkland (West Brom, loan), Carl Medjani (Metz, loan).
Injuries: Peter Crouch (hamstring), Jerzy Dudek (elbow), Djimi Traore (thigh).
Quote of the month: "These are good times for Liverpool and I'd like to repay the faith the supporters have shown in me by winning more trophies."
Sami Hyypia

September

Josemi vows to regain his place in the Reds XI while Momo Sissoko believes he can be a better player than Patrick Vieira. Patrik Berger claims Liverpool made a mistake in selling Milan Baros. Rafa backs Peter Crouch to shine for England following his return from injury, while also warning that his Liverpool side are the team to beat after their Champions League success in May. In addition, Florent Sinama-Pongolle could be the answer to the Reds' right-sided problem according to the boss.

Djibril Cisse is keen to repay the fans' "love" for him after coming off the bench to rescue a point from the spot in the 2-2 draw at Birmingham. Rafa also dismisses suggestions the Reds are out of the title race: "After all, you can lose or gain six points in eight days over Christmas. Why do you need to think about it in September? Of course I want to see us reduce the gap, but there's still a long way to go." Ahead of their Champions League Group G encounter at Anfield, Chelsea mysteriously hold their pre-match press conference near Liverpool John Lennon Airport, rather than at the stadium while they also refuse to train on the pitch. Jose Mourinho looks forward to the game, claiming that in the Champions League semi-final, second leg at Anfield the previous April: "Liverpool beat us without scoring a goal and I will say that for as long as I live."

Injuries: Fernando Morientes (hamstring), Momo Sissoko (thigh).

Quote of the month: "Carra is one of the best defenders in the world. The only problem is I don't understand a lot of what Carra is saying. I'm trying to learn to speak good English as soon as possible so we're still going to improve."

Jose Reina

October

Rafa claims that Chelsea have emerged as Liverpool's biggest rivals while Xabi Alonso admits the team need new blood.

Steven Gerrard backs Peter Crouch to be a big success at Anfield, while Stephen Warnock receives a late call-up to the England squad for the games against Austria and Poland, having been omitted following his call for games last month against Wales and Northern Ireland.

Stockport defender James Tunnicliffe, 16, is offered a week's trial by Liverpool while Liverpool and Juventus youth teams play a friendly in aid of victims of the Heysel tragedy at Arezzo's Comunale Stadium near Florence.

Former players from Liverpool and Everton will reunite to replay the 1986 FA Cup final on May Bank Holiday Monday, with proceeds to go to Marina Dalglish's Cancer Charity, while Steven Gerrard is named on the shortlist for FIFA's World Player of the Year and European Footballer of the Year awards, Jamie Carragher and Luis Garcia also being nominated for the latter.

Rafa backs Fernando Morientes to find his goalscoring form, while former player Christian Ziege retires through injury.

Steven Gerrard returns from injury to net his 50th goal for Liverpool in the 2-1 Carling Cup defeat at Crystal Palace, later apologising to the fans on behalf of the team for their exit from the competition.

Injuries: Steven Gerrard (calf), Antonio Barragan (knee).

Quote of the month: "I've been pleased with my performances when I have played but I would say there is definitely a lot more to come from me. The fans haven't seen the best of me in a Liverpool shirt yet. I can give much more than I've done so far."

Bolo Zenden

IT'S A MARATHON NOT A SPRINT . . .

November
Milan Baros fails to fire as Liverpool record their first Premiership away win of the season, 2-0 at Aston Villa with sub Peter Crouch helping to turn the game.

Liverpool are revealed as the No 1 club in the world by the International Federation of Football History and Statistics (IFFHS). The rankings took into account the past 12 months' performances, assigning weighted points for wins in various competitions. Manchester United are fifth, while Chelsea were 12th.

Steven Gerrard reveals he would like to stay involved with the club after he hangs up his boots. Luis Garcia scores a hat-trick on his first start for Spain, in a 5-1 hammering of Slovakia in the first leg of their World Cup play-off.

Hull City winger Paul Anderson reveals his determination to be a success at Liverpool as it is confirmed he will join the Reds in January, with John Welsh joining the Tigers as part of the deal. The 17-year-old impressed during a trial in September.

Peter Crouch sees a penalty saved as his goalless run is extended against Portsmouth, while Rafael Benitez believes that Steven Gerrard deserves to win the European Footballer of the Year award - he finishes third behind Frank Lampard and Ballon d'Or winner Ronaldinho. The 2-0 win at Sunderland is the club's fifth Premiership victory in a row without conceding a goal.

Outgoing: Zak Whitbread (Millwall, loan).
Injuries: Xabi Alonso (knee and ankle), Luis Garcia (hip), Bolo Zenden (knee).
Quote of the month: "I can see why people don't like him. He is not very pleasing on the eye and he is not silky. What you have to admire about Crouch is no matter how the game goes, or how his form is, he will not hide. Having said that, I will dislike him intensely on Saturday and we want to stop him, even if it takes a pair of ladders!"

Stuart Pearce

December
Peter Crouch breaks his goalscoring duck with a deflected effort against Wigan (going on to hit a second) in a 3-0 victory - in his 19th game for the Reds. Neil Mellor makes his comeback in the reserves nearly a year after suffering a serious knee injury against Watford in the Carling Cup.

Rafael Benitez rubbishes rumours linking him with the top job at Real Madrid, while the Reds boss is named the Barclays manager of the month for November.

Bolo Zenden is ruled out for the rest of the season after learning he needs surgery to repair damage to the cruciate ligament in his right knee, while the 2-0 defeat of Middlesbrough extends the Reds' Premiership winning run to seven - their best run for three years. Jose Reina's clean sheet also equalled the club record of 10 set by Kenny Dalglish's side in 1987/88 - although Reina has the goalkeeper's record, as the 1987/88 run was shared by Bruce Grobbelaar and Mike Hooper. The following game against Deportivo Saprissa in the Club World Championship in Japan saw the Reds beat the record - although they went down 1-0 to Sao Paulo in the final, having three goals disallowed in the process.

Steven Gerrard is named the seventh best player in the world as Ronaldinho adds the FIFA World Player of the Year award to his European gong. Liverpool win the Merseyside derby 3-1 at Goodison Park, their ninth successive Premiership win which has yielded 20 goals - while James Beattie's goal ended the Reds' run of clean sheets. The New Year's Eve win over West Brom makes it a perfect 10.

Injuries: Darren Potter (back), Dietmar Hamann (leg), Fernando Morientes (knee).
Quote of the month: "I cannot speak highly enough of the supporters. They were willing me to score and this is a goal not just for me and the team but for them as well."

Peter Crouch

January

An astonishing FA Cup third-round tie at Championship side Luton Town ends with Liverpool winning 5-3 - having been 3-1 down. Zak Whitbread's loan spell at Millwall is extended until the end of the season, while Liverpool legend Ian Rush helps to train Northwich Victoria in the build-up to their FA Cup tie at Sunderland - but the non-leaguers go down 3-0.

Deportivo Saprissa winger Christian Bolanos fails to earn a contract with the Reds after completing a brief trial spell, while it's praise all round for Harry Kewell as the Australian nets the winner in the 1-0 victory over Tottenham Hotspur.

Steven Gerrard and Luis Garcia are named in UEFA's team of the year for 2005 though Jamie Carragher is just pipped to a place in central defence, while Rafael Benitez misses out on the top coach award - to Jose Mourinho.

Neil Mellor is hopeful of impressing Rafa while on loan at Wigan, while John Arne Riise agrees a new contract, keeping him at Anfield until at least 2009.

Rafa claims he would like to stay in charge of "the same club" for 20 years - like Sir Alex Ferguson. He adds: "If I could do that at Liverpool it would mean we will have won many trophies."

Jamie Carragher is given the freedom of Sefton, in recognition of his local charity work, although there is a setback when the Reds fail in their attempts to secure a work permit for Mark Gonzalez - the Chilean winger will now return to La Liga, spending the rest of the season on loan to Real Sociedad. And...God returns.

Incoming: Jan Kromkamp (Villarreal), Daniel Agger (Brondby), Paul Anderson (Hull City), David Martin (MK Dons), Robbie Fowler (Manchester City).

Outgoing: Josemi (Villarreal), John Welsh (Hull City), Neil Mellor (Wigan Athletic, loan), Darren Potter (Southampton, loan), David Raven (Tranmere Rovers, loan), Mark Gonzalez (Real Sociedad, loan), Florent Sinama-Pongolle (Blackburn Rovers, loan).

Injuries: David Mannix (broken leg), Luis Garcia (knee), Sami Hyypia (illness), Jan Kromkamp (ankle).

Quote of the month: "I'm so happy it's frightening. Just to travel back to Anfield was great and to actually get into the office and put pen-to-paper was something that I have wanted to happen for a long time. Obviously since I have left deep down I've always wanted to come back and it has been a long time but I'm glad to say I'm back now!"

Robbie Fowler

February

Sami Hyypia earns the Reds a first win in five against Wigan, while it is confirmed that Argentine defender Gabriel Paletta will join the Reds at the end of the season from Banfield. Jamie Carragher passes the 400 appearance mark, and it is confirmed that Adidas will become the official sportswear supplier to the club in July.

Liverpool move up to eighth in the list of the world's richest clubs and youngsters Adam Hammill and Calum Woods are moved up from the Academy to train at Melwood.

The FA Cup fifth-round victory over Manchester United is the Reds' first over their rivals in the competition for 85 years. Jamie Carragher's performance in the tie also sees him voted the player of the round. Momo Sissoko damages the retina in his right eye during the Champions League clash against Benfica - although fears his career could be over are dismissed.

Injuries: Steven Gerrard (knee), Peter Crouch (heel), Xabi Alonso (leg), Momo Sissoko (eye), Steve Finnan (neck).

Quote of the month: "I really think I have improved in every aspect of my game and I have to give the manager credit for that. I am working with one of the most respected managers in Europe and he is very much a training ground boss. He is always there, watching, teaching and talking. I have not been used to that at previous clubs."

Peter Crouch

IT'S A MARATHON NOT A SPRINT . . .

March

Ahead of England's friendly with Uruguay at Anfield, coach Sven-Goran Eriksson says: "You can smell the history of this stadium. Liverpool have won the Champions League five times. It is one of those great, great clubs." In the game Peter Crouch scores his first international goal in a 2-1 win. Robbie Fowler finally hits his first goal for the club - in his second spell - in the 5-1 rout of Fulham, having seen two goals disallowed in previous games.

Momo Sissoko, who suffered a detached retina against Benfica, reveals that a doctor in Portugal claimed he could lose the vision in his right eye. The Reds midfielder is back in training only two weeks after the incident - and plays the full 90 minutes in a 7-0 demolition of Birmingham City that sees the Reds book a FA Cup semi-final against Chelsea. Liverpool's U18s also reach the FA Youth Cup final for the first time in 10 years.

An eventful Anfield derby sees 10-man Liverpool defeat Everton - who themselves were reduced to 10 in the second half - with Phil Neville's own goal, Luis Garcia and Harry Kewell the Reds' scorers in a 3-1 win. Steven Gerrard and Andy Van der Meyde were the men given their marching orders while there were also nine bookings. Another side issue in the match was in Gerrard and James Beattie becoming the first Premiership players to be allowed to alter their squad numbers mid-campaign by the Premier League, both being allowed to wear '08' on their backs rather than '8' to advertise Liverpool's City of Culture year.

Outgoing: Scott Carson (Sheffield Wednesday, loan).
Major injuries: Sami Hyypia (hamstring), Djimi Traore (knee), Chris Kirkland (finger), Neil Mellor (knee).
Quote of the month: "It's too physical. Sometimes the penalty area is like a boxing ring. Some of the strikers are built like boxers and play like them without the gloves on."

Jose Reina

April

Steven Gerrard is voted player of the round for the FA Cup quarter-finals, while Robbie Fowler's goal in the 2-0 defeat of West Bromwich Albion sees the striker rise to fifth in the all-time Liverpool scorers list - above Kenny Dalglish.

Reserve boss and scout Paco Herrera will return to Spain to be with his family in the summer. Despite going down 2-0 in the second leg, a 3-0 first-leg win secures Liverpool their first FA Youth Cup success in 10 years, at the expense of Manchester City. It is the first of three weekend successes for the club. Things get better and better when the Reds see off Chelsea 2-1 to reach their 13th FA Cup final - while Steven Gerrard is named the PFA Player of the Year.

The 1-0 win at Blackburn Rovers on Easter Sunday gives Jose Reina his 30th clean sheet of the season. The statistic also means that Reina has a better goals against record than Ray Clemence for his first 50 games for the Reds (29 goals in 50 games compared to Clemence's 32 in 50) while Liverpool have now kept 33 clean sheets this season - the club record is 34.

Liverpool win the FA Cup final dress rehearsal, 2-1 at Upton Park - although Luis Garcia, as well as the Hammers' Hayden Mullins, will miss the showpiece in Cardiff following their red cards due to a clash in the second half.

The 3-1 victory over Aston Villa means it has been the Reds' best season at Anfield for 15 years, winning 15, drawing 3 and losing only 1 of their 19 games - conceding only 8 goals in the process and keeping 14 clean sheets.

Injuries: Daniel Agger (shin), Steven Gerrard (hamstring), Harry Kewell (thigh).
Quote of the month: "It's Stevie G who teases me about my clothes. Sometimes I go to the showers, and when I come back he's wearing my clothes. I have funny underwear, like zebra print, so he puts on my underpants and walks around the dressing room."

Djibril Cisse

May

Liverpool beat Everton 1-0 in a replay of the 1986 FA Cup final. Played to raise money for the Marina Dalglish Appeal, nearly 33,000 turned up at Anfield to see John Durnin win it with a last-minute strike. Luis Garcia is voted player of the round following his match-winning semi-final display against Chelsea, some consolation at least in light of missing the final due to suspension. Mark Gonzalez, proving a hit at Real Sociedad, is hopeful there will be no problems in him moving to Liverpool in the summer. Former Liverpool defender Richard Money becomes the new manager of Walsall, while Robbie Fowler reveals his delight having been offered a new contract - going on to score his fifth goal in only 10 league and cup starts in the 3-1 final-day victory at Portsmouth. The three points also means that it is Liverpool's best-ever Premiership points total (82), and their 11th win in a row, their best sequence for over 15 years. If the Premiership had started in October, then the Reds would be champions.

There are no surprises as far as Liverpool's England contingent are concerned, as Steven Gerrard, Jamie Carragher and Peter Crouch are named in Sven-Goran Eriksson's World Cup squad (Scott Carson is later added as a replacement for the injured Robert Green). There's another award for the Liverpool skipper, being named Premiership Player of the Month for April while Jose Reina scoops the 'Golden Gloves' award for the most clean sheets.

In what is dubbed as one of the greatest-ever FA Cup finals, Liverpool hold off the spirited challenge of underdogs West Ham to clinch their seventh success in the competition. The 3-1 penalty shootout success - with Jose Reina saving three of the Hammers' four penalties - after the match finishes 3-3 (Liverpool were never ahead) creates further landmarks in a season full of records. The inspired two-goal display from skipper Steven Gerrard means that the midfielder has now scored in every major cup final for the Reds, while it is the Reds' ninth shootout success in 10 ties.

Quote of the month: "Getting measured for suits and being constantly asked for tickets is all part and parcel of being in the FA Cup final. I've had people on from school who I haven't spoken to for 10 years and they're not just asking for one ticket - they're after four or five! Sorting everyone out with tickets is an impossible job so I've just changed my mobile phone number! As for the suits I'm not really bothered what the suits look like - so long as they're not cream!"

Steven Gerrard

Liverpool line up before the 1986 FA Cup final replay against Everton at Anfield in May, played in aid of the Marina Dalglish Appeal. The Reds won 1-0 thanks to a late John Durnin goal

JULY

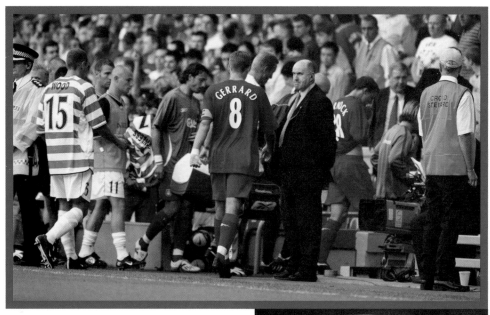

THE GAMES

13	TNS	H	3-0	(Gerrard 3)
19	TNS	A	3-0	(Cisse, Gerrard 2)
26	FBK Kaunas	A	3-1	(Cisse, Carragher, Gerrard pen)

RAFA SAYS . . .

'I saw Vieira when he was 18 and he was no better than Sissoko. He will be more dynamic than Vieira and a better player.'

AUGUST

THE GAMES

2	FBK Kaunas	H	2-0	(Gerrard, Cisse)
10	CSKA Sofia	A	3-1	(Cisse, Morientes 2)
13	Middlesboro	A	0-0	
20	Sunderland	H	1-0	(Alonso)
23	CSKA Sofia	H	0-1	
26	CSKA Moscow	N	3-1 aet	(Cisse 2, Garcia)

WHERE THEY STOOD

7	Arsenal
8	Aston Villa
9	West Ham United
10	**Liverpool**
11	Blackburn Rovers
12	Middlesbrough
13	Birmingham City

RAFA SAYS . . .

'We will win more games because we have a better squad and a better team. We will be closer this time.'

SEPTEMBER

THE GAMES

10	Tottenham	A	0-0	
13	**Real Betis**	**A**	**2-1**	(S-Pongolle, Garcia)
18	Man Utd	H	0-0	
24	Birmingham	A	2-2	(Garcia, Cisse pen)
28	**Chelsea**	**H**	**0-0**	

WHERE THEY STOOD

10	Newcastle United
11	Middlesbrough
12	Blackburn Rovers
13	**Liverpool**
14	Birmingham City
15	Aston Villa
16	Portsmouth

RAFA SAYS . . .

'Crouch is going to be good for us and crucial to our away form. I've bought a quality player.'

OCTOBER

THE GAMES

2	Chelsea	H	1-4	(Gerrard)
15	Blackburn	H	1-0	(Cisse)
19	**Anderlecht**	**A**	**1-0**	(Cisse)
22	Fulham	A	0-2	
25	Crystal Pal.	A	1-2	(Gerrard)
29	West Ham	H	2-0	(Alonso, Zenden)

WHERE THEY STOOD

10	Newcastle United
11	Middlesbrough
12	Blackburn Rovers
13	**Liverpool**
14	Portsmouth
15	Fulham
16	Aston Villa

RAFA SAYS . . .

'When Harry Kewell is back it'll be like signing a new player because he has a lot of quality.'

NOVEMBER

THE GAMES

1	**Anderlecht**	H	**3-0**	(Morientes, Garcia, Cisse)
5	Aston Villa	A	2-0	(Gerrard pen, Alonso)
19	Portsmouth	H	3-0	(Zenden, Cisse, Morientes)
23	**Real Betis**	H	**0-0**	
26	Man City	A	1-0	(Riise)
30	Sunderland	A	2-0	(Garcia, Gerrard)

WHERE THEY STOOD

1	Chelsea
2	Manchester United
3	Arsenal
4	**Liverpool**
5	Wigan Athletic
6	Tottenham Hotspur
7	Bolton Wanderers

RAFA SAYS . . .

'The League is physical, the Champions League is more tactical. In Europe you need brain and muscle.'

DECEMBER

THE GAMES

3	Wigan	H	3-0	(Crouch 2, Garcia)
6	**Chelsea**	**A**	**0-0**	
10	Middlesboro	H	2-0	(Morientes 2)
15	Saprissa	N	3-0	(Crouch 2, Gerrard)
18	Sao Paulo	N	0-1	
26	Newcastle	H	2-0	(Gerrard, Crouch)
28	Everton	A	3-1	(Crouch, Gerrard, Cisse)
31	West Brom	H	1-0	(Crouch)

WHERE THEY STOOD

1	Chelsea
2	Manchester United
3	**Liverpool**
4	Tottenham Hotspur
5	Wigan Athletic
6	Arsenal
7	Bolton Wanderers

RAFA SAYS . . .

'Jamie Carragher is like a sponge. I know SpongeBob from when my children watch television! '

JANUARY

THE GAMES

2	Bolton	A	2-2	(Gerrard pen, Garcia)
7	Luton	A	5-3	(Gerrard, S-Pongolle 2, Alonso 2)
14	Tottenham	H	1-0	(Kewell)
22	Man Utd	A	0-1	
29	Portsmouth	A	2-1	(Gerrard pen, Riise)

WHERE THEY STOOD

1	Chelsea
2	Manchester United
3	**Liverpool**
4	Tottenham Hotspur
5	Wigan Athletic
6	Arsenal
7	Bolton Wanderers

RAFA SAYS . . .

'Robbie Fowler will act as an example to every player here in how much he loves Liverpool. '

FEBRUARY

THE GAMES

1	Birmingham	H	1-1	(Gerrard)
5	Chelsea	A	0-2	
8	Charlton	A	0-2	
11	Wigan	A	1-0	(Hyypia)
14	Arsenal	H	1-0	(Garcia)
18	Man Utd	H	1-0	(Crouch)
21	**Benfica**	**A**	**0-1**	
26	Man City	H	1-0	(Kewell)

WHERE THEY STOOD

1	Chelsea
2	Manchester United
3	**Liverpool**
4	Tottenham Hotspur
5	Blackburn Rovers
6	Bolton Wanderers
7	Arsenal

RAFA SAYS . . .

'After 85 years to beat Manchester United is fantastic. Our supporters were fantastic and the team responded to them.'

MARCH

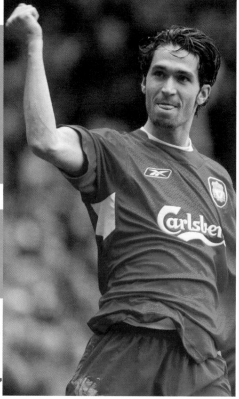

THE GAMES

4	Charlton	H	0-0	
8	**Benfica**	**H**	**0-2**	
12	Arsenal	A	1-2	(Garcia)
15	Fulham	H	5-1	(Fowler, Brown o.g., Morientes, Crouch, Warnock)
19	Newcastle	A	3-1	(Crouch, Gerrard, Cisse pen)
21	Birmingham	A	7-0	(Hyypia, Crouch 2, Morientes, Riise, Tebily o.g., Cisse)
25	Everton	H	3-1	(Neville o.g., Garcia, Kewell)

WHERE THEY STOOD

1	Chelsea
2	Manchester United
3	**Liverpool**
4	Tottenham Hotspur
5	Blackburn Rovers
6	Arsenal
7	Bolton Wanderers

RAFA SAYS . . .

'We have won one cup this season, and we hope the FA Cup can be the second.'

APRIL

THE GAMES

1	West Brom	A	2-0	(Fowler, Cisse)
9	Bolton	H	1-0	(Fowler)
16	Blackburn	A	1-0	(Fowler)
22	Chelsea	N	2-1	(Riise, Garcia)
26	West Ham	A	2-1	(Cisse 2)
29	Aston Villa	H	3-1	(Morientes, Gerrard 2)

WHERE THEY STOOD

1	Chelsea
2	Manchester United
3	**Liverpool**
4	Tottenham Hotspur
5	Arsenal
6	Blackburn Rovers
7	Newcastle United

RAFA SAYS . . .

'If a player is offside he must be offside. We could talk about the rule for hours. We need to make it easier for referees.'

MAY

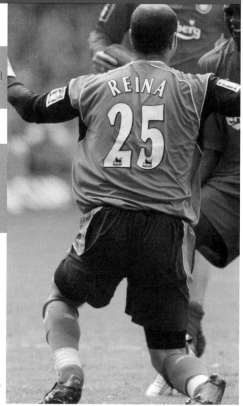

THE GAMES

| 7 | Portsmouth | A | 3-1 | (Fowler, Crouch, Cisse) |
| 13 | West Ham | N | 3-3*aet | (Cisse, Gerrard 2) |

*Liverpool win 3-1 on penalties

WHERE THEY FINISHED

1	Chelsea
2	Manchester United
3	**Liverpool**
4	Arsenal
5	Tottenham Hotspur
6	Blackburn Rovers
7	Newcastle United

RAFA SAYS . . .

'I must give credit to my players. A lot of them had cramp but they kept going, never gave up and have done a fantastic job.'

CURRENT APPEARANCES & GOALS FOR LIVERPOOL

UP TO AND INCLUDING 31ST JULY 2006

	LGE GMS	LGE GLS	FA GMS	FA GLS	L. CUP GMS	L. CUP GLS (inc Spr Cup)	EURO GMS	EURO GLS (inc C. Shield & C. World)	OTHER GMS	OTHER GLS	LFC GMS	LFC GLS
DUDEK	125	0	8	0	9	0	37	0	1	0	180	0
KROMKAMP	13	0	4	0	0	0	0	0	0	0	17	0
FINNAN	88	1	9	0	5	0	32	0	1	0	135	1
HYYPIA	252	18	24	1	16	1	76	6	4	0	372	26
AGGER	4	0	0	0	0	0	0	0	0	0	4	0
RIISE	172	20	12	3	11	1	57	2	4	0	256	26
KEWELL	81	11	9	0	4	1	26	3	1	0	121	15
GERRARD	232	37	19	5	16	5	66	16	3	1	336	64
CISSE	49	13	6	2	0	0	23	9	1	0	79	24
GARCIA	60	15	3	1	4	0	25	8	2	0	94	24
FOWLER	250	125	24	12	32	27	40	12	0	0	346	176
LE TALLEC	17	0	4	0	2	0	9	1	0	0	32	1
ALONSO	59	5	5	2	0	0	19	1	2	0	85	8
CROUCH	32	8	6	3	1	0	8	0	2	2	49	13
CARSON	4	0	1	0	1	0	3	0	0	0	9	0
SISSOKO	26	0	6	0	0	0	11	0	2	0	45	0
CARRAGHER	290	2	24	0	22	0	78	1	3	0	417	3
S-P'GOLLE	38	4	5	2	8	1	12	2	2	0	65	9
REINA	33	0	5	0	0	0	13	0	2	0	53	0
WARNOCK	39	1	3	0	5	0	12	0	1	0	60	1
ZENDEN	7	2	0	0	0	0	10	0	0	0	17	2
MELLOR	12	2	2	0	6	3	2	1	0	0	22	6
POTTER	2	0	1	0	5	0	9	0	0	0	17	0
DIAO	37	1	2	0	8	1	14	1	0	0	61	3
KIRKLAND	25	0	3	0	6	0	11	0	0	0	45	0

MAN OF THE SEASON

It will come as little surprise that Liverpool's Player of the Year, as voted for by readers of the LFC Magazine, was none other than Steven Gerrard. The Reds skipper, who also proved himself a class above in the Premiership by scooping the PFA Player of the Year award, held off the challenge of the likes of Jamie Carragher, Steve Finnan, Sami Hyypia and Young Player of the Year Momo Sissoko.

His season was best summed up in the FA Cup final, delivering when the club needed him most in 90 minutes, and stepped up to score a penalty in the shootout despite the fact he could hardly walk due to cramp, displaying courage, class and leadership in equal measure.

Legend:
- ● Game played
- ■ Substitute
- ▲ Unused sub
- ● Goal scored
- ● Substituted player
- ◆ Substituted sub

2005/06

Players (columns):

1 Jerzy Dudek · 2 Jan Kromkamp · 3 Steve Finnan · 4 Sami Hyypia · 5 Daniel Agger · 6 John Arne Riise · 7 Harry Kewell · 8 Steven Gerrard · 9 Djibril Cisse · 10 Luis Garcia · 11 Robbie Fowler · 14 Xabi Alonso · 15 Peter Crouch · 16 Dietmar Hamann · 19 Fernando Morientes · 20 Scott Carson · 21 Djimi Traore · 22 Mohamed Sissoko · 23 Jamie Carragher · 24 Florent Sinama-Pongolle · 25 Jose Reina · 26 Paul Anderson

DATE	OPPONENTS		RES	ATT
July				
13	TNS (CL Q1 1st)	H	3-0	44,760
19	TNS (CL Q1 2nd)	A	3-0	8,009
26	FBK Kaunas (CL Q2 1st)	A	3-1	8,300
August				
2	FBK Kaunas (CL Q2 2nd)	H	2-0	43,717
10	CSKA Sofia (CL Q3 1st)	A	3-1	16,512
13	Middlesbrough	A	0-0	31,908
20	Sunderland	H	1-0	44,913
23	CSKA Sofia (CL Q3 2nd)	H	0-1	42,175
26	CSKA Moscow (Super Cup)	N	3-1*	18,000
September				
10	Tottenham	A	0-0	36,148
13	Real Betis (CL group 1)	A	2-1	45,000
18	Man Utd	H	0-0	44,917
24	Birmingham	A	2-2	27,733
28	Chelsea (CL group 2)	H	0-0	42,743
October				
2	Chelsea	H	1-4	44,235
15	Blackburn	H	1-0	44,679
19	Anderlecht (CL group 3)	A	1-0	25,000
22	Fulham	A	0-2	22,480
25	C Palace (Carling Cup 3rd)	A	1-2	19,673
29	West Ham	H	2-0	44,537
November				
1	Anderlecht (CL group 4)	H	3-0	42,607
5	Aston Villa	A	2-0	42,551
19	Portsmouth	H	3-0	44,394
23	Real Betis (CL group 5)	H	0-0	42,077
26	Man City	A	1-0	47,105
30	Sunderland	A	2-0	32,679
December				
3	Wigan	H	3-0	44,098
6	Chelsea (CL group 6)	A	0-0	41,598
10	Middlesbrough	H	2-0	43,510
15	Deportivo Saprissa (CWC s-f)	N	3-0	43,902
18	Sao Paulo (CWC final)	N	0-1	66,821
26	Newcastle	H	2-0	44,197
28	Everton	A	3-1	40,158
31	West Brom	H	1-0	44,192
January				
2	Bolton	A	2-2	27,604
7	Luton (FA Cup 3rd)	A	5-3	10,170
14	Tottenham	H	1-0	44,983
22	Man Utd	A	0-1	67,874
29	Portsmouth (FA Cup 4th)	A	2-1	17,247
February				
1	Birmingham	H	1-1	43,851
5	Chelsea	A	0-2	42,316
8	Charlton	A	0-2	27,111
11	Wigan	A	1-0	25,023
14	Arsenal	H	1-0	44,065
18	Man Utd (FA Cup 5th)	H	1-0	44,039
21	Benfica (CL last 16 1st)	A	0-1	65,000
26	Man City	H	1-0	44,121
March				
4	Charlton	H	0-0	43,892
8	Benfica (CL last 16 2nd)	H	0-2	42,745
12	Arsenal	A	1-2	38,221
15	Fulham	H	5-1^	42,293
19	Newcastle	A	3-1	52,302
21	Birmingham (FA Cup QF)	A	7-0^	27,378
25	Everton	H	3-1^	44,923
April				
1	West Brom	A	2-0	27,576
9	Bolton	H	1-0	44,194
16	Blackburn	A	1-0	29,142
22	Chelsea (FA Cup SF)	N	2-1	64,575
26	West Ham	A	2-1	34,852
29	Aston Villa	H	3-1	44,479
May				
7	Portsmouth	A	3-1	20,240
13	West Ham (FA Cup final)	N	3-3**	71,140

^ Own goals v Fulham (Brown); v Birmingham (Tebily); v Everton (Neville);
*aet; ** aet (Liverpool win 3-1 on pens)

Stephen Warnock · Boudewijn Zenden · David Raven · Besian Idrizaj · Neil Mellor · Darren Potter · Daniel Guthrie · Antonio Barragan · Zak Whitbread · David Mannix · Robbie Foy · Anthony Le Tallec · Carl Medjani · Milan Baros · Josemi

28 29 30 31 32 33 34 35 36 37 38 42

FINAL TABLE

BARCLAYS PREMIERSHIP TABLE 2005/06

Team	Pd	HOME					AWAY					Pts	GD
		W	D	L	F	A	W	D	L	F	A		
1. Chelsea	38	18	1	0	47	9	11	3	5	25	13	91	+50
2. Manchester Utd	38	13	5	1	37	8	12	3	4	35	26	83	+38
3. Liverpool	38	15	3	1	32	8	10	4	5	25	17	82	+32
4. Arsenal	38	14	3	2	48	13	6	4	9	20	18	67	+37
5. Tottenham Hotspur	38	12	5	2	31	16	6	6	7	22	22	65	+15
6. Blackburn Rovers	38	13	3	3	31	17	6	3	10	20	25	63	+9
7. Newcastle United	38	11	5	3	28	15	6	2	11	19	27	58	+5
8. Bolton Wanderers	38	11	5	3	29	13	4	6	9	20	28	56	+8
9. West Ham United	38	9	3	7	30	25	7	4	8	22	30	55	-3
10. Wigan Athletic	38	7	3	9	24	26	8	3	8	21	26	51	-7
11. Everton	38	8	4	7	22	22	6	4	9	12	27	50	-15
12. Fulham	38	13	2	4	31	21	1	4	14	17	37	48	-10
13. Charlton Athletic	38	8	4	7	22	21	5	4	10	19	34	47	-14
14. Middlesbrough	38	7	5	7	28	30	5	4	10	20	28	45	-10
15. Manchester City	38	9	2	8	26	20	4	2	13	17	28	43	-5
16. Aston Villa	38	6	6	7	20	20	4	6	9	22	35	42	-13
17. Portsmouth	38	5	7	7	17	24	5	1	13	20	38	38	-25
18. Birmingham City	38	6	5	8	19	20	2	5	12	9	30	34	-22
19. West Brom	38	6	2	11	21	24	1	7	11	10	34	30	-27
20. Sunderland	38	1	4	14	12	37	2	2	15	14	32	15	-43

MINUTES ON PITCH 2005-2006

	LEAGUE	FA CUP	LEAGUE CUP	CHAMPS LEAGUE	SUPER CUP	CLUB WORLD	TOTAL
DUDEK	457	0	0	0	0	0	457
KROMKAMP	603	162	0	0	0	0	765
FINNAN	3021	490	0	990	55	90	4646
HYYPIA	3163	570	90	1080	120	162	5185
BAROS	38	0	0	0	0	0	38
AGGER	360	0	0	0	0	0	360
RIISE	2354	570	0	805	79	101	3909
KEWELL	2010	373	65	201	0	90	2739
GERRARD	2817	541	90	723	0	154	4325
CISSE	1727	334	0	627	41	90	2819
GARCIA	1670	200	25	815	120	108	2938
FOWLER	773	0	0	85	0	0	858
LE TALLEC	0	0	0	148	0	0	148
ALONSO	2571	427	0	761	71	169	3999
CROUCH	2140	381	90	601	0	95	3307
HAMANN	1215	139	90	626	120	11	2201
JOSEMI	262	0	0	270	120	90	742
MORIENTES	1823	248	62	608	120	85	2946
CARSON	0	90	90	180	0	0	360
TRAORE	889	34	14	360	0	90	1387
SISSOKO	1954	537	0	635	49	169	3344
CARRAGHER	3240	570	0	953	120	180	5063
SINAMA-PONGOLLE	292	33	28	90	65	37	545
REINA	2962	480	0	990	120	180	4732
WARNOCK	1314	91	76	378	0	79	1938
ZENDEN	451	0	0	540	120	0	1111
RAVEN	0	0	90	0	0	0	90
POTTER	0	0	90	310	0	0	400
BARRAGAN	0	0	0	11	0	0	11
WHITBREAD	0	0	90	127	0	0	217
WELSH	0	0	0	0	0	0	0

Up to and including 13th May 2006

PLAYER GOALS 2005-2006 SEASON

ALL COMPETITIONS UP TO AND INCLUDING: 13TH MAY 2006				
	1ST HALF	2ND HALF	EXTRA-TIME	TOTAL
GERRARD	11	12	0	23
CISSE	8	10	1	19
CROUCH	9	4	0	13
GARCIA	2	8	1	11
MORIENTES	3	6	0	9
ALONSO	2	3	0	5
FOWLER	4	1	0	5
RIISE	2	2	0	4
KEWELL	1	2	0	3
SINAMA-PONGOLLE	1	2	0	3
OWN GOALS	2	1	0	3
HYYPIA	2	0	0	2
ZENDEN	1	1	0	2
CARRAGHER	1	0	0	1
WARNOCK	0	1	0	1
TOTAL	49	53	2	104

Steven Gerrard's second wonder goal in the FA Cup final was voted the LFC goal of the season

MOST POINTS WON BY TEAMS IN PREMIER LEAGUE HISTORY

(up to end of 2005-2006 season)

		POINTS	HIGHEST POS	SEASONS IN PREMIERSHIP
1	MANCHESTER UNITED	1143	1st (8 times)	14
2	ARSENAL	1013	1st (3 times)	14
3	LIVERPOOL	931	2nd (2001-2002)	14
4	CHELSEA	930	1st (2 times)	14
5	NEWCASTLE UNITED	786	2nd (2 times)	13
6	ASTON VILLA	767	2nd (1992-1993)	14
7	TOTTENHAM HOTSPUR	728	5th (2005-2006)	14
8	BLACKBURN ROVERS	695	1st (1994-1995)	13
9	LEEDS UNITED	692	3rd (1999-2000)	12
10	EVERTON	677	4th (2004-2005)	14
11	SOUTHAMPTON	587	8th (2002-2003)	13
12	WEST HAM UNITED	555	5th (1998-1999)	11
13	MIDDLESBROUGH	513	7th (2004-2005)	11
14	MANCHESTER CITY	410	8th (2004-2005)	9
15	COVENTRY CITY	409	11th (2 times)	9
16	SHEFFIELD WEDNESDAY	392	7th (3 times)	8
17	WIMBLEDON (MK DONS)	391	6th (1993-1994)	8
18	LEICESTER CITY	342	8th (1999-2000)	8
19	CHARLTON ATHLETIC	327	7th (2003-2004)	7
20	BOLTON WANDERERS	320	6th (2004-2005)	7
21	DERBY COUNTY	263	8th (1998-1999)	6
22	NOTTINGHAM FOREST	239	3rd (1994-1995)	5
23	FULHAM	236	9th (2003-2004)	5
24	SUNDERLAND	229	7th (2 times)	6
25	IPSWICH TOWN	224	5th (2000-2001)	5
26	QUEENS PARK RANGERS	216	5th (1992-1993)	4
27	NORWICH CITY	201	3rd (1992-1993)	4
28	BIRMINGHAM CITY	177	10th (2003-2004)	4
29	CRYSTAL PALACE	160	18th (2004-2005)	4
30	PORTSMOUTH	122	13th (2003-2004)	3
31	SHEFFIELD UNITED	94	14th (1992-1993)	2
32	WEST BROMWICH ALB.	90	17th (2004-2005)	3
33	OLDHAM ATHLETIC	89	19th (1992-1993)	2
34	BRADFORD CITY	62	17th (1999-2000)	2
35	WIGAN ATHLETIC	51	10th (2005-2006)	1
36	BARNSLEY	35	19th (1997-1998)	1
37	WOLVERHAMPTON W.	33	20th (2003-2004)	1
38	SWINDON TOWN	30	22nd (1994-1995)	1
39	WATFORD	24	20th (1999-2000)	1

THE LEAGUE FINISHES

DIVISION ONE/PREMIERSHIP - 91 SEASONS

	Number of times
First	18
Second	11
Third	6
Fourth	7
Fifth	9
Sixth	2
Seventh	4
Eighth	4
Ninth	4
Tenth	2
Eleventh	5
Twelfth	4
Thirteenth	2
Fourteenth	1
Fifteenth	1
Sixteenth	4
Seventeenth	3
Eighteenth	2
Nineteenth	1
Twentieth	0
Twenty-first	0
Twenty-second	1

DIVISION TWO - 11 SEASONS

	Number of times
First	4
Third	4
Fourth	2
Eleventh	1

**Rob Jones, Steve McManaman and Ian Rush celebrate a Reds goal - the trio were amongst
Liverpool's star men in the early days of the Premier League era**

**Robbie Fowler celebrates one of his three goals for Liverpool against Arsenal in August 1994 -
the quickest hat-trick in Premier League history**

**John Arne Riise in action against Wigan (above left) - the Reds boast a 100% Premiership
record against the Latics, while Peter Crouch (right) scores against West Brom, a side who the
Reds have scored over 3 goals a game in Premiership games**

PREMIER LEAGUE: CLUB BY CLUB

LIVERPOOL'S PREMIER LEAGUE RECORD - CLUB BY CLUB
(At end of 2005-06 season. Only teams in Premier League in 2005-06 included)

	PLAYED	WON	DREW	LOST	FOR	AGAINST
ARSENAL	164	67	40	57	232	206
ASTON VILLA	162	76	35	51	286	240
BIRMINGHAM CITY	94	46	20	28	157	132
BLACKBURN ROVERS	116	48	35	33	207	161
BOLTON WANDERERS	106	43	29	34	164	132
CHARLTON ATHLETIC	54	28	7	19	88	68
CHELSEA	126	57	26	43	200	181
EVERTON	174	65	54	55	238	209
FULHAM	38	21	11	6	74	40
MANCHESTER CITY	140	71	32	37	257	188
MANCHESTER UNITED	146	49	43	54	192	202
MIDDLESBROUGH	128	54	37	37	221	164
NEWCASTLE UNITED	142	66	37	39	242	181
PORTSMOUTH	52	21	13	18	93	82
SUNDERLAND	140	60	31	49	234	210
TOTTENHAM HOTSPUR	126	58	33	35	199	143
WEST BROMWICH ALBION	114	53	33	28	176	127
WEST HAM UNITED	98	50	28	20	158	90
WIGAN ATHLETIC	2	2	0	0	4	0

LIVERPOOL GOALS v PREMIER LEAGUE OPPONENTS

	GAMES PLAYED	GOALS IN FIXTURE	AVE. PER GAME	LIVERPOOL GOALS	AVE. PER GAME
ARSENAL	28	62	2.21	37	1.32
ASTON VILLA	28	73	2.61	45	1.61
BARNSLEY	2	6	3.00	3	1.50
BIRMINGHAM CITY	8	23	2.88	12	1.50
BLACKBURN ROVERS	24	67	2.79	38	1.58
BOLTON WANDERERS	14	40	2.86	25	1.79
BRADFORD CITY	4	8	2.00	6	1.50
CHARLTON ATHLETIC	14	36	2.57	22	1.57
CHELSEA	28	72	2.57	32	1.14
COVENTRY CITY	18	44	2.44	27	1.50
CRYSTAL PALACE	8	26	3.25	20	2.50
DERBY COUNTY	12	30	2.50	22	1.83
EVERTON	28	63	2.25	35	1.25
FULHAM	10	30	3.00	20	2.00
IPSWICH TOWN	10	27	2.70	20	2.00
LEEDS UNITED	24	71	2.96	48	2.00
LEICESTER CITY	16	33	2.06	19	1.19
MANCHESTER CITY	18	50	2.78	32	1.78
MANCHESTER UNITED	28	72	2.57	31	1.11
MIDDLESBROUGH	22	50	2.27	32	1.45
NEWCASTLE UNITED	26	81	3.12	49	1.88
NORWICH CITY	8	24	3.00	17	2.13
NOTTINGHAM FOREST	10	29	2.90	18	1.80
OLDHAM ATHLETIC	4	12	3.00	8	2.00
PORTSMOUTH	6	16	2.67	12	2.00
QUEENS PARK RANGERS	8	20	2.50	13	1.62
SHEFFIELD UNITED	4	7	1.75	3	0.75
SHEFFIELD WEDNESDAY	16	43	2.69	27	1.69
SOUTHAMPTON	26	78	3.00	45	1.73
SUNDERLAND	12	19	1.58	13	1.08
SWINDON TOWN	2	9	4.50	7	3.50
TOTTENHAM HOTSPUR	28	78	2.79	46	1.64
WATFORD	2	6	3.00	3	1.50
WEST BROMWICH ALBION	6	19	3.17	19	3.17
WEST HAM UNITED	22	50	2.27	34	1.55
WIGAN ATHLETIC	2	4	2.00	4	2.00
WIMBLEDON	16	39	2.44	22	1.37
WOLVERHAMPTON WANDERERS	2	3	1.50	2	1.00

(Up to and including end of 2005-06 season)

PREMIER LEAGUE NUMBERS GAME

SQUAD NUMBERS

Number Players (with Premiership appearances in brackets)

1	Grobbelaar (29),	James (171),	Westerveld (75),	Dudek (90)
2	R.Jones (125),	Henchoz (135)	Kromkamp (13)	
3	Burrows (4),	Dicks (24),	Scales (3),	Kvarme (45),	Ziege (16),
	Xavier (14),	Finnan (88)		
4	Nicol (35),	McAteer (100),	Song (34),	Hyypia (179)
5	M.Wright (104),	Staunton (44),	Baros (68),	Agger (4)
6	Hutchison (11),	Babb (128),	Babbel (42),	Riise (69)
7	Clough (39),	McManaman (101),	Smicer (91),	Kewell (81)
8	Stewart (8),	Collymore (61),	Leonhardsen (37),	Heskey (150),	Gerrard (62)
9	Rush (98),	Fowler (128),	Anelka (20),	Diouf (55),	Cisse (49)
10	Barnes (135),	Owen (178),	Garcia (60)	
11	Walters (35),	Redknapp (103),	Smicer (30),	Fowler (14)
12	Whelan (23),	Scales (62),	Harkness (38),	Hyypia (73),	Dudek (35),
	P.Jones (2),	Pellegrino (12)		
13	James (14),	Riedle (60),	Murphy (130),	Le Tallec (4)
14	Molby (25),	Ruddock (19),	Heggem (54),	Alonso (59)
15	Redknapp (99),	Berger (148),	Diao (11),	Crouch (32)
16	Thomas (99),	Dundee (3),	Hamann (191)	
17	McManaman (108),	Ince (65),	Gerrard (129),	Josemi (21)
18	Rosenthal (3),	Owen (38),	Ferri (2),	Meijer (24),	Riise (103),
	Nunez (18)			
19	Piechnik (1),	Kennedy (16),	Friedel (14),	Arphexad (2),	Morientes (41)
20	Bjornebye (128),	Barmby (32),	Le Tallec (13),	Carson (4)
21	Marsh (2),	Matteo (127),	McAllister (55),	Diao (26),	Traore (48)
22	Harkness (43),	Camara (33),	Kirkland (25),	Sissoko (26)
23	Fowler (108),	Carragher (290)		
24	L.Jones (3),	Murphy (40),	Diomede (2),	Sinama-Pongolle (38)
25	Ruddock (96),	Thompson (48),	Biscan (72),	Reina (33)
27	Vignal (11)			
28	Gerrard (41),	Cheyrou (31),	Warnock (39)	
29	Friedel (11),	S.Wright (14),	Luzi (1)	
30	Traore (40),	Zenden (7)		
31	Raven (1)			
32	Newby (1),	Welsh (4)		
33	Mellor (12)			
34	Potter (2)			
36	Otsemobor (4)			
37	Litmanen (26)			

MOST APPEARANCES/GOALS IN PREMIER LEAGUE

Top 10 total appearances in Premier League		Top 10 goalscorers in Premier League	
Jamie Carragher	290	Robbie Fowler	125
Sami Hyypia	252	Michael Owen	118
Robbie Fowler	250	Ian Rush	45
Steve McManaman	240	Steve McManaman	41
Steven Gerrard	232	Emile Heskey	39
Jamie Redknapp	231	Steven Gerrard	37
Michael Owen	216	Jamie Redknapp	29
David James	214	Patrik Berger	28
Dietmar Hamann	191	Stan Collymore	26
John Arne Riise	172	Danny Murphy	25

PREMIER LEAGUE RED CARDS

Date	Player	Opponents	Venue	Minute of Dismissal	Result
19th Dec 1992	Jamie Redknapp	Coventry City	(a)	69	Lost 5-1
1st May 1993	David James	Norwich City	(a)	61	Lost 1-0
5th May 1993	Don Hutchison	Oldham Athletic	(a)	76	Lost 3-2
1st Sept 1993	Rob Jones	Coventry City	(a)	70	Lost 1-0
4th Feb 1995	Phil Babb	Nottingham Forest	(a)	52	Drew 1-1
16th Apr 1997	Robbie Fowler	Everton	(a)	82	Drew 1-1
1st Nov 1997	Robbie Fowler	Bolton Wanderers	(a)	76	Drew 1-1
10th Apr 1998	Michael Owen	Manchester United	(a)	41	Drew 1-1
31st Oct 1998	Jason McAteer	Leicester City	(a)	85	Lost 1-0
6th Feb 1999	Dominic Matteo	Middlesbrough	(h)	64	Won 3-1
13th Feb 1999	Jamie Carragher	Charlton Athletic	(a)	68	Lost 1-0
18th Sept 1999	David Thompson	Leicester City	(a)	90	Drew 2-2
27th Sept 1999	Sander Westerveld	Everton	(h)	75	Lost 1-0
27th Sept 1999	Steven Gerrard	Everton	(h)	90	Lost 1-0
2nd Oct 1999	Steve Staunton	Aston Villa	(a)	31	Drew 0-0
21st Aug 2000	Gary McAllister	Arsenal	(a)	39	Lost 2-0
21st Aug 2000	Dietmar Hamann	Arsenal	(a)	78	Lost 2-0
31st Mar 2001	Danny Murphy	Manchester United	(h)	69	Won 2-0
13th Apr 2001	Steven Gerrard	Leeds United	(h)	71	Lost 2-1
16th Apr 2001	Igor Biscan	Everton	(a)	77	Won 3-2
8th Sept 2001	Steven Gerrard	Aston Villa	(h)	74	Lost 3-1
27th Oct 2001	Stephen Wright	Charlton Athletic	(a)	88	Won 2-0
25th Nov 2001	Dietmar Hamann	Sunderland	(h)	44	Won 1-0
1st Jan 2003	Salif Diao	Newcastle United	(a)	65	Lost 1-0
5th Apr 2003	Sami Hyypia	Manchester United	(a)	4	Lost 4-0
11th May 2003	Steven Gerrard	Chelsea	(a)	90	Lost 2-1
7th Jan 2004	El-Hadji Diouf	Chelsea	(a)	86	Won 1-0
16th Oct 2004	Josemi	Fulham	(a)	77	Won 4-2
20th Mar 2005	Milan Baros	Everton	(h)	77	Won 2-1
30th Nov 2005	Mohamed Sissoko	Sunderland	(a)	65	Won 2-0
5th Feb 2006	Jose Reina	Chelsea	(a)	82	Lost 2-0
12th Mar 2006	Xabi Alonso	Arsenal	(a)	81	Lost 2-1
25th Mar 2006	Steven Gerrard	Everton	(h)	18	Won 3-1
26th Apr 2006	Luis Garcia	West Ham United	(a)	82	Won 2-1

Midfielders Momo Sissoko and Steven Gerrard - amongst the Liverpool 'bad boys' in 2005-06

Michael Owen (top) and Jamie Carragher - amongst the goals in Liverpool's record Premiership victory, a 7-1 win over Southampton at Anfield in January 1999

PREMIER LEAGUE FACTS & FIGURES

PREMIER LEAGUE RECORD

Season	P	W	D	L	F	A	Pts	Pos
1992-1993	42	16	11	15	62	55	59	6
1993-1994	42	17	9	16	59	55	60	8
1994-1995	42	21	11	10	65	37	74	4
1995-1996	38	20	11	7	70	34	71	3
1996-1997	38	19	11	8	62	37	68	4
1997-1998	38	18	11	9	68	42	65	3
1998-1999	38	15	9	14	68	49	54	7
1999-2000	38	19	10	9	51	30	67	4
2000-2001	38	20	9	9	71	39	69	3
2001-2002	38	24	8	6	67	30	80	2
2002-2003	38	18	10	10	61	41	64	5
2003-2004	38	16	12	10	55	37	60	4
2004-2005	38	17	7	14	52	41	58	5
2005-2006	38	25	7	6	57	25	82	3

BIGGEST PREMIER LEAGUE WINS (TOP FIVE)

Date	Opponents	Venue	Score	Scorers	Attendance
16th Jan 1999	Southampton	Home	Won 7-1	Fowler 3, Matteo, Carragher, Owen, Thompson	44,011
26th Apr 2003	West Brom	Away	Won 6-0	Owen 4, Baros 2	27,128
9th Feb 2002	Ipswich Town	Away	Won 6-0	Abel Xavier, Heskey 2, Hyypia, Owen 2	25,608
28th Oct 1995	Manchester City	Home	Won 6-0	Rush 2, Redknapp, Fowler 2, Ruddock	39,267
20th Aug 1994	Crystal Palace	Away	Won 6-1	Fowler, McManaman 2, Molby (pen), Rush 2	18,084

BIGGEST PREMIER LEAGUE DEFEATS (TOP SIX)

Date	Opponents	Venue	Score	Scorer	Attendance
19th Dec 1992	Coventry City	Away	Lost 5-1	Redknapp	19,779
5th Apr 2003	Manchester United	Away	Lost 4-0		67,639
2nd Oct 2005	Chelsea	Home	Lost 4-1	Gerrard	44,235
16th Dec 2001	Chelsea	Away	Lost 4-0		41,174
25th Apr 1998	Chelsea	Away	Lost 4-1	Riedle	34,639
3rd Apr 1992	Blackburn Rovers	Away	Lost 4-1	Rush	15,032

AVERAGE ATTENDANCES

Season	High	Low	Average
1992-1993	44,619	29,574	37,009
1993-1994	44,601	24,561	38,503
1994-1995	40,014	27,183	34,175
1995-1996	40,820	34,063	39,552
1996-1997	40,892	36,126	39,776
1997-1998	44,532	34,705	40,628
1998-1999	44,852	36,019	43,321
1999-2000	44,929	40,483	44,074
2000-2001	44,806	38,474	43,698
2001-2002	44,371	37,153	43,389
2002-2003	44,250	41,462	43,243
2003-2004	44,374	34,663	42,677
2004-2005	44,224	35,064	42,587
2005-2006	44,983	42,293	44,236

SEVEN-UP

In celebration of Liverpool's seventh FA Cup triumph, the following pages look at each successful FA Cup campaign in a little more detail, including additional notes and the odd pictorial reminder! Liverpool's FA Cup traditions could hardly have been described as impressive before Bill Shankly's men embarked on their campaign in the competition with a tricky-looking tie at West Bromwich Albion in January 1965. With only two runners-up additions to the club's honours list being the sum total of their exertions in the competition, it became one of Shanks' main ambitions upon taking the helm at Anfield. The 2-1 success would begin the journey to Wembley that finally ended Liverpool's Cup hoodoo, when a Gerry Byrne-inspired Reds side deservedly saw off Leeds United 2-1 after extra time. The following day an estimated 250,000 packed the city centre, inspiring Shankly to declare the following:

"There has never been a reception like this in the whole history of the game. This has been fantastic - there is no other word for it. I have been in football all my life and had my ups and downs and played in Cup finals both losing and winning. This, without doubt, is the happiest moment of my life. I am not happy just for myself but for my players and club. No manager had a greater bunch of players."

1964-1965			
Round 3	West Bromwich Albion (a)	Won 2-1	Hunt, St. John
Round 4	Stockport County (h)	Drew 1-1	Milne
Replay	Stockport County (a)	Won 2-0	Hunt (2)
Round 5	Bolton Wanderers (a)	Won 1-0	Callaghan
Round 6	Leicester City (a)	Drew 0-0	
Replay	Leicester City (h)	Won 1-0	Hunt
Semi-final	Chelsea (Villa Park)	Won 2-0	Thompson, Stevenson (pen)
Final	Leeds United (Wembley)	Won 2-1 (aet)	Hunt, St. John

Final teams:
Liverpool: Lawrence, Lawler, Byrne, Strong, Yeats (captain), Stevenson, Callaghan, Hunt, St John, Smith, Thompson.
Leeds: Sprake, Reaney, Bell, Bremner, Charlton, Hunter, Giles, Storrie, Peacock, Collins (captain), Johanneson.
Referee: W. Clements.
Appearances:
Byrne 8, Callaghan 8, Hunt 8, Lawler 8, Lawrence 8, St John 8, Smith 8, Stevenson 8, Thompson 8, Yeats 8, Milne 6, Arrowsmith 1, Strong 1.
Goals:
Hunt 5, St John 2, Callaghan 1, Milne 1, Stevenson 1.

In the fourth round Liverpool struggled to overcome Stockport County, who finished the season in 92nd place in the Football League.
Liverpool went five successive games in the competition without conceding a goal for the first time.
All the goals in the final came in extra time - Hunt 93 minutes, Bremner (Leeds) 95, St. John 113.
Gerry Byrne broke his collar bone in the early minutes but insisted on playing on. In fact, he supplied the pass that led to Hunt's goal.
Geoff Strong made his FA Cup debut for the Reds in the final.
Gordon Milne missed the final through injury just as his father Jim had done in 1938 when his victorious Preston side included Bill Shankly.
It was Liverpool's first FA Cup success in their 63rd season of taking part in the world's oldest Cup competition.

1973-74

Round 3	Doncaster Rovers (h)	Drew 2-2	Keegan (2)
Replay	Doncaster Rovers (a)	Won 2-0	Heighway, Cormack
Round 4	Carlisle United (h)	Drew 0-0	
Replay	Carlisle United (a)	Won 2-0	Boersma, Toshack
Round 5	Ipswich Town (h)	Won 2-0	Hall, Keegan
Round 6	Bristol City (a)	Won 1-0	Toshack
Semi-final	Leicester City (Old Trafford)	Drew 0-0	
Replay	Leicester City (Villa Park)	Won 3-1	Hall, Keegan, Toshack
Final	Newcastle United (Wembley)	Won 3-0	Keegan (2), Heighway

Final teams:
Liverpool: Clemence, Smith, Lindsay, Thompson, Cormack, Hughes (captain), Keegan, Hall, Heighway, Toshack, Callaghan. Sub: Lawler.
Newcastle: McFaul, Clark, Kennedy, McDermott, Howard, Moncur (captain), Smith (Gibb), Cassidy, Macdonald, Tudor, Hibbitt.
Referee: G. Kew

Appearances (total with sub apps in brackets):
Callaghan 9, Clemence 9, Hughes 9, Keegan 9, Lindsay 9, Thompson 9, Cormack 8, Hall 8 (1), Smith 7, Heighway 6, Toshack 6, Boersma 5 (1), Lloyd 3, Waddle 2, Rylands 1, Storton 1.

Goals:
Keegan 6, Toshack 3, Hall 2, Heighway 2, Boersma 1, Cormack 1.

Liverpool set a club record, which still stands today, of six consecutive clean sheets in the FA Cup.
In the third round, Dave Rylands made his only appearance for Liverpool.
Doncaster hit the woodwork in the last minute of that third-round tie at Anfield. Had they scored the Third Division side would have caused a major shock.
Kevin Keegan's goals in the final came after 57 and 88 minutes with Steve Heighway scoring the second on 74.
Future Liverpool heroes Alan Kennedy and Terry McDermott played against the Reds in the final.
The final turned out to be Bill Shankly's last game in charge of the club.

Skipper Emlyn Hughes and the Liverpool players parade the FA Cup at Wembley following the comprehensive 3-0 victory over Newcastle United in 1974

SEVEN-UP

1985-86			
Round 3	Norwich City (h)	Won 5-0	MacDonald, Walsh, McMahon, Whelan, Wark
Round 4	Chelsea (a)	Won 2-1	Rush, Lawrenson
Round 5	York City (a)	Drew 1-1	Molby (pen)
Replay	York City (h)	Won 3-1 (aet)	Wark, Molby, Dalglish
Round 6	Watford (h)	Drew 0-0	
Replay	Watford (a)	Won 2-1 (aet)	Molby (pen), Rush
Semi-final	Southampton (White Hart Lane)	Won 2-0 (aet)	Rush (2)
Final	Everton (Wembley)	Won 3-1	Rush (2), Johnston

Final teams:

Liverpool: Grobbelaar, Lawrenson, Beglin, Nicol, Whelan, Hansen (captain), Dalglish, Johnston, Rush, Molby, MacDonald. Sub: McMahon.

Everton: Mimms, Stevens (Heath), Van den Hauwe, Ratcliffe (captain), Mountfield, Reid, Steven, Lineker, Sharp, Bracewell, Sheedy.

Referee: A. Robinson

Appearances (total with sub apps in brackets):

Grobbelaar 8, Hansen 8, Johnston 8 (2), Molby 8, Rush 8, Beglin 7, Lawrenson 7, Whelan 7, Dalglish 6, Gillespie 5, McMahon 4, Nicol 4, Wark 4 (2), Lee 3, MacDonald 2, Walsh 2, Seagraves 1.

Goals:

Rush 6, Molby 3, Wark 2, Dalglish 1, Johnston 1, Lawrenson 1, MacDonald 1, McMahon 1, Walsh 1, Whelan 1.

Liverpool were four minutes away from going out of the Cup in the quarter-final. Jan Molby's 86th-minute penalty took the game into extra time at Watford after John Barnes had given the home team the lead.

In the semi-final, Southampton's Mark Wright (later to captain the Reds to success in the competition) broke his leg.

Liverpool and Everton met in the first all-Merseyside FA Cup final.

For the first time since 1970 the team trailing at half-time came back to win the Cup.

Gary Lineker gave Everton a 28th-minute lead. Ian Rush scored on 57 and 84 with Craig Johnston finding the net after 63.

For the first time in Cup final history a team (Liverpool) did not include a player in the starting XI qualified to play for England.

Kenny Dalglish became the first player-manager to lead his team to FA Cup final success.

Ian Rush strokes home the equaliser in the 1986 all-Merseyside FA Cup final against Everton, with Craig Johnston (left) following in

1988-89

Round 3	Carlisle United (a)	Won 3-0	McMahon (2), Barnes
Round 4	Millwall (a)	Won 2-0	Aldridge, Rush
Round 5	Hull City (a)	Won 3-2	Aldridge (2), Barnes
Round 6	Brentford (h)	Won 4-0	Beardsley (2), McMahon, Barnes
Semi-final	Nottingham Forest (Old Trafford)	Won 3-1	Aldridge (2), Laws (o.g.)
Final	Everton (Wembley)	Won 3-2 (aet)	Rush (2), Aldridge

Final teams:

Liverpool: Grobbelaar, Ablett, Staunton (Venison), Nicol, Whelan (captain), Hansen, Beardsley, Aldridge (Rush), Houghton, Barnes, McMahon.

Everton: Southall, McDonald, Van den Hauwe, Ratcliffe (captain), Watson, Bracewell (McCall), Nevin, Steven, Cottee, Sharp, Sheedy (Wilson).

Referee: J.Worrall

Appearances (total with sub apps in brackets):

Ablett 6, Aldridge 6, Barnes 6, McMahon 6, Nicol 6, Beardsley 5, Grobbelaar 5, Houghton 5, Whelan 5, Burrows 3, Molby 3, Staunton 3, Gillespie 2, Hansen 2, Rush 2 (1), Watson 2 (1), Hooper 1, Venison 1 (1).

Goals:

Aldridge 6, Barnes 3, McMahon 3, Rush 3, Beardsley 2, own goals 1.

Liverpool reached the final for the first time ever without the aid of a replay.

Stuart McCall became the first substitute to score twice in an FA Cup final - beating Ian Rush by two minutes.

The final goal times were: Aldridge 4, Rush 94, 104 (Liverpool); McCall 89, 102 (Everton).

Steve McMahon played against a former club in the final, as did Kevin Sheedy.

Barry Venison's only appearance of the Cup run came in the final as a substitute.

It's that man Rush again, as Ian slays Everton once again in the 1989 FA Cup final with another brace in the 3-2 extra-time success

SEVEN-UP

1991-92			
Round 3	Crewe Alexandra (a)	Won 4-0	Barnes (3), McManaman
Round 4	Bristol Rovers (a)	Drew 1-1	Saunders
Replay	Bristol Rovers (h)	Won 2-1	McManaman, Saunders
Round 5	Ipswich Town (a)	Drew 0-0	
Replay	Ipswich Town (h)	Won 3-2 (aet)	Houghton, Molby, McManaman
Round 6	Aston Villa (h)	Won 1-0	Thomas
Semi-final	Portsmouth (Highbury)	Drew 1-1 (aet)	Whelan
Replay	Portsmouth (Villa Park)	0-0 (aet)	
		(Liverpool won 3-1 on penalties)	
Final	Sunderland (Wembley)	Won 2-0	Thomas, Rush

Final teams:

Liverpool: Grobbelaar, Jones, Burrows, Nicol, Molby, Wright (captain), Saunders, Houghton, I. Rush, McManaman, Thomas. Subs: Marsh, Walters.

Sunderland: Norman, Owers, Ball, Bennett, Rogan, D. Rush (Hardyman) , Bracewell (captain), Davenport, Armstrong (Hawke), Byrne, Atkinson.

Referee: P.Don

Appearances (total with sub apps in brackets):

Grobbelaar 9, R. Jones 9, Wright 9, Houghton 8, McManaman 8, Nicol 8, Saunders 8, Burrows 6, Marsh 6 (2), Molby 6 (1), Rush 5 (1), Thomas 5, Barnes 4, Rosenthal 3 (2), Venison 3 (2), Walters 3 (1), Whelan 3, Kozma 2 (2), Redknapp 2, Tanner 2, Harkness 1.

Goals:

Barnes 3, McManaman 3, Saunders 2, Thomas 2, Houghton 1, Molby 1, Rush 1, Whelan 1.

Aston Villa provided Liverpool with their only top-flight opponents of the Cup run.

The semi-final was the first ever to be decided on penalties. John Barnes, Ian Rush and Dean Saunders scored Liverpool's spot-kicks.

Ian Rush scored his fifth FA Cup final goal - a competition record.

The trophy which Mark Wright collected at the end of the final was being presented for the first time and was the fourth used in the history of the competition.

Ronnie Moran led Liverpool out, though Graeme Souness had recovered sufficiently from illness to attend the game. Sunderland's Malcolm Crosby was also in temporary charge of his side.

Sunderland's Paul Bracewell lost to Liverpool in the final for the third time (the first two with Everton).

Ian Rush completes the scoring in 1992 against Sunderland - a record fifth in the final

2000-01

Round 3	Rotherham United (h)	Won 3-0	Heskey (2), Hamann
Round 4	Leeds United (a)	Won 2-0	Barmby, Heskey
Round 5	Manchester City (h)	Won 4-2	Litmanen (pen), Heskey, Smicer (pen), Babbel
Round 6	Tranmere Rovers (a)	Won 4-2	Murphy, Owen, Gerrard, Fowler (pen)
Semi-final	Wycombe Wanderers (Villa Park)	Won 2-1	Heskey, Fowler
Final	Arsenal (Cardiff)	Won 2-1	Owen (2)

Final teams:

Liverpool: Westerveld, Babbel, Henchoz, Hyypia (capt.), Carragher, Murphy (Berger), Hamann (McAllister), Gerrard, Smicer (Fowler), Heskey, Owen. Unused subs: Arphexad, Vignal.

Arsenal: Seaman, Dixon (Bergkamp), Keown, Adams (capt.), Cole, Ljungberg (Kanu), Grimandi, Vieira, Pires, Henry, Wiltord (Parlour). Unused subs: Manninger, Lauren.

Referee: S. Dunn

Appearances (total with sub apps in brackets):

Carragher 6, Hyypia 6, Westerveld 6, Babbel 5, Barmby 5 (3), Fowler 5 (2), Hamann 5, Henchoz 5, Heskey 5 (2), McAllister 5 (1), Murphy 5 (1), Owen 5 (1), Smicer 5 (1), Biscan 4 (1), Gerrard 4 (2), Ziege 3 (1), Litmanen 2 (1), Berger 1 (1), Vignal 1 (1), Wright 1.

Goals:

Heskey 5, Owen 3, Fowler 2, Babbel 1, Barmby 1, Gerrard 1, Hamann 1, Litmanen 1, Murphy 1, Smicer 1.

Liverpool won the first FA Cup final to be played outside England.

Liverpool defeated Arsenal for the first time in three FA Cup final attempts after losing in 1950 and 1971.

Liverpool, wearing gold shirts and navy blue shorts, won the FA Cup in a change strip for the first time.

The final was the first time both sides had been managed by foreigners - Gerard Houllier and Arsene Wenger.

Patrik Berger made his only appearance of the 2000-01 FA Cup campaign in the final itself and made the pass for the winning goal.

Freddie Ljungberg gave Arsenal a 72nd-minute lead before Michael Owen pounced on 83 and 88 minutes to win the Cup.

It was the first time since 1991 a team had come from behind to win the Cup.

Liverpool became only the second team (after Arsenal) to win the League Cup and FA Cup in the same season.

Michael Owen volleys a dramatic equaliser in 2001 in Cardiff

SEVEN-UP

2005-06			
Round 3	Luton Town (a)	Won 5-3	Gerrard, Sinama-Pongolle (2), Alonso (2)
Round 4	Portsmouth (a)	Won 2-1	Gerrard (pen), Riise
Round 5	Manchester United (h)	Won 1-0	Crouch
Round 6	Birmingham City (a)	Won 7-0	Hyypia, Crouch (2), Morientes, Riise, Tebily (o.g.), Cisse
Semi-final	Chelsea (Old Trafford)	Won 2-1	Riise, Garcia
Final	West Ham United (Cardiff)	3-3 (aet)	Cisse, Gerrard (2)

(Liverpool won 3-1 on penalties)

Final teams:

Liverpool: Reina, Finnan, Carragher, Hyypia, Riise, Gerrard (capt.), Alonso (Kromkamp), Sissoko, Kewell (Morientes), Cisse, Crouch (Hamann). Unused subs: Dudek, Traore.

West Ham: Hislop, Scaloni, Ferdinand, Gabbidon, Konchesky, Benayoun, Fletcher (Dailly), Reo-Coker (capt.), Etherington (Sheringham), Ashton (Zamora), Harewood. Unused subs: Walker, Collins.

Referee: A. Wiley

Appearances (total with sub apps in brackets):

Carragher 6, Cisse 6 (3), Crouch 6 (1), Finnan 6 (1), Gerrard 6, Hyypia 6, Kewell 6 (2), Riise 6, Sissoko 6, Alonso 5, Morientes 5 (3), Reina 5, Kromkamp 4 (3), Garcia 3 (1), Hamann 2 (1), Traore 2 (1), Warnock 2 (1), Carson 1, Sinama-Pongolle 1 (1).

Goals:

Gerrard 4, Crouch 3, Riise 3, Alonso 2, Cisse 2, Sinama-Pongolle 2, Garcia 1, Hyypia 1, Morientes 1, own goal 1.

In the third round Liverpool scored five goals in an away FA Cup tie for the first time since 1947.

Liverpool defeated Manchester United in the FA Cup for the first time since 1921 and the first time at Anfield since February 1898.

At Birmingham in round six records tumbled. Liverpool recorded their biggest-ever away win in the competition and their second biggest ever on their travels in all competitions. It was also the biggest away win by any team at that stage of the FA Cup since 1890.

Rafa Benitez became the fifth overseas manager to lead his team to FA Cup final success.

Benitez also became the first manager in Liverpool history to win a major trophy in each of his first two seasons in charge.

Liverpool became the first team since 1966 to win the final after being two goals down.

The Reds became the second team to win the trophy on penalties after Arsenal the year before.

Liverpool equalled a club record of 20 FA Cup goals in a season.

Manager Rafa Benitez delivers his team talk before extra time in the 2006 final (opposite left), while the boss and skipper Steven Gerrard parade the trophy (above)

THE FA CUP RECORD

Date	Round	Venue	Opponents	Opponent Division	Score	Scorers	Att
1892-93							
15th Oct	1st Qual	(a)	Nantwich	Non Lge	W 4-0	Miller 3, Wyllie	700
29th Oct	2nd Qual	(h)	Newtown	Non Lge	W 9-0	Wyllie 3, McVean 2, McCartney H.McQueen, Cameron, Townsend o.g.	4,000
19th Nov	3rd Qual	(a)	Northwich Victoria	Non Lge	L 1-2	Wyllie	1,000
1893-94							
27th Jan	1	(h)	Grimsby Town	2	W 3-0	Bradshaw (2), McQue	8,000
10th Feb	2	(h)	Preston North End	1	W 3-2	Henderson (2), McVean	18,000
24th Feb	3	(a)	Bolton Wanderers	1	L 0-3		20,000
1894-95							
2nd Feb	1	(a)	Barnsley St Peters	Non Lge	*D 2-1	Mc Vean, Ross	4,000
11th Feb	1 Rep.	(h)	Barnsley St Peters	Non Lge	W 4-0	Bradshaw, Drummond, McVean, H.McQueen	4,000
16th Feb	2	(h)	Nottingham Forest	1	L 0-2		5,000
1895-96							
1st Feb	1	(h)	Millwall	Non Lge	W 4-1	Ross, Becton, Allan, Bradshaw	10,000
15th Feb	2	(a)	Wolverhampton W.	1	L 0-2		15,000
1896-97							
30th Jan	1	(h)	Burton Swifts	2	W 4-3	Hannah, Allan, Cleghorn, Ross	4,000
13th Feb	2	(a)	West Bromwich Alb.	1	W 2-1	McVean, Neill	16,000
27th Feb	3	(h)	Nottingham Forest	1	D 1-1	Becton	15,000
3rd Mar	3 Rep.	(a)	Nottingham Forest	1	W 1-0	Allan	10,000
20th Mar	S.F.	Bramall La.	Aston Villa	1	L 0-3		30,000
1897-98							
29th Jan	1	(h)	Hucknall St John's	Non Lge	W 2-0	Becton, McQue	8,000
12th Feb	2	(a)	Newton Heath	2	D 0-0		12,000
16th Feb	2 Rep	(h)	Newton Heath	2	W 2-1	Wilkie, Cunliffe	6,000
25th Feb	3	(a)	Derby County	1	D 1-1	Bradshaw	20,000
2nd Mar	3 Rep	(h)	Derby County	1	L 1-5	Becton (pen)	15,000
1898-99							
28th Jan	1	(h)	Blackburn Rovers	1	W 2-0	Cox, Allan	14,000
11th Feb	2	(h)	Newcastle United	1	W 3-1	Morgan, Raisbeck, Higgins o.g.	7,000
25th Feb	3	(a)	West Bromwich Alb.	1	W 2-0	Morgan, Robertson	17,124
18th Mar	S.F.	Nottingham	Sheffield United	1	D 2-2	Allan, Morgan	35,000
23rd Mar	S.F. Rep	Bolton	Sheffield United	1	D 4-4	Walker, Allan, Boyle o.g., Cox	20,000
30th Mar	S.F.Rep (2)	Derby	Sheffield United	1	L 0-1		20,000
1899-1900							
27th Jan	1	(a)	Stoke City.	1	D 0-0		8,000
1st Feb	1 Rep	(h)	Stoke City	1	W 1-0	Hunter	10,000
17th Feb	2	(h)	West Bromwich Alb.	1	D 1-1	Cox	15,000
21st Feb	2 Rep	(a)	West Bromwich Alb.	1	L 1-2	Robertson	13,000
1900-01							
5th Jan	Qual	(a)	West Ham United	Non Lge	W 1-0	Raybould	6,000
9th Feb	1	(a)	Notts County	1	L 0-2		15,000

* (Match counted as a draw after Barnsley protest)

Date	Round	Venue	Opponents	Opponent Division	Score	Scorers	Att
1901-02							
25th Jan	1	(h)	Everton	1	D 2-2	T.Robertson (pen), Hunter	25,000
30th Jan	1 Rep	(a)	Everton	1	W 2-0	Raisbeck, Hunter	20,000
8th Feb	2	(a)	Southampton	Non Lge	L 1-4	Fleming	20,000
1902-03							
7th Feb	1	(a)	Manchester United	2	L 1-2	Raybould	15,000
1903-04							
6th Feb	1	(a)	Blackburn Rovers	1	L 1-3	Raybould	10,000
1904-05							
4th Feb	1	(h)	Everton	1	D 1-1	Parkinson	28,000
8th Feb	1 Rep	(a)	Everton	1	L 1-2	Goddard	40,000
1905-06							
13th Jan	1	(h)	Leicester Fosse	2	W 2-1	Raybould, Goddard	12,000
3rd Feb	2	(h)	Barnsley	2	W 1-0	West	10,000
24th Feb	3	(h)	Brentford	Non Lge	W 2-0	Hewitt, Goddard	20,000
10th Mar	4	(h)	Southampton	Non Lge	W 3-0	Raybould 3	20,000
31st Mar	S.F.	Villa Park	Everton	1	L 0-2		37,000
1906-07							
12th Jan	1	(h)	Birmingham City	1	W 2-1	Raybould 2	20,000
2nd Feb	2	(a)	Oldham Athletic	Non Lge	W 1-0	McPherson	21,500
23rd Feb	3	(h)	Bradford City	2	W 1-0	Cox	18,000
9th Mar	4	(a)	Sheffield Wed.	1	L 0-1		30,000
1907-08							
11th Jan	1	(h)	Derby County	2	W 4-2	Cox, Gorman, Bradley, Parkinson	15,000
1st Feb	2	(h)	Brighton	Non Lge	D 1-1	Cox	36,000
5th Feb	2 Rep	(a)	Brighton	Non Lge	W 3-0	Bradley 2, Cox	10,000
22nd Feb	3	(a)	Newcastle United	1	L 1-3	Saul	45,987
1908-09							
16th Jan	1	(h)	Lincoln City	Non Lge	W 5-1	Orr 3, Hewitt, Parkinson	8,000
6th Feb	2	(h)	Norwich City	Non Lge	L 2-3	Cox, Robinson	25,000
1909-10							
15th Jan	1	(a)	Bristol City	1	L 0-2		10,000
1910-11							
14th Jan	1	(h)	Gainsborough Trin.	2	W 3-2	Bowyer 2, Goddard	15,000
4th Feb	2	(a)	Everton	1	L 1-2	Parkinson	50,000
1911-12							
13th Jan	1	(h)	Leyton	Non Lge	W 1-0	Parkinson	33,000
3rd Feb	2	(a)	Fulham	2	L 0-3		30,000

Date	Round	Venue	Opponents	Opponent Division	Score	Scorers	Att
1912-13							
15th Jan	1	(h)	Bristol City	2	W 3-0	Goddard (pen), Peake, Lacey	15,000
1st Feb	2	(a)	Arsenal	1	W 4-1	Metcalf 3, Lacey	8,653
22nd Feb	3	(h)	Newcastle United	1	D 1-1	Lacey	37,903
26th Feb	3 Rep	(a)	Newcastle United	1	L 0-1		45,000
1913-14							
10th Jan	1	(h)	Barnsley	2	D 1-1	Lacey	33,000
15th Jan	1 Rep	(a)	Barnsley	2	W 1-0	Lacey	23,999
31st Jan	2	(h)	Gillingham	Non Lge	W 2-0	Lacey, Ferguson	42,045
21st Feb	3	(a)	West Ham United	Non Lge	D 1-1	Miller	15,000
25th Feb	3 Rep	(h)	West Ham United	Non Lge	W 5-1	Lacey 2, Miller 2, Metcalf	43,729
7th Mar	4	(h)	QPR	Non Lge	W 2-1	Sheldon, Miller	43,000
28th Mar	S.F.	Tottenham	Aston Villa	1	W 2-0	Nicholl 2	27,474
25th Apr	Final	Crystal Pal.	Burnley	1	L 0-1		72,778
1914-15							
9th Jan	1	(h)	Stockport County	2	W 3-0	Pagnam 2, Metcalf	10,000
30th Jan	2	(a)	Sheffield United	1	L 0-1		25,000
1919-20							
10th Jan	1	(a)	South Shields	2	D 1-1	Lewis	10,000
14th Jan	1 Rep	(h)	South Shields	2	W 2-0	Lewis, Sheldon	40,000
31st Jan	2	(a)	Luton Town	Non Lge	W 2-0	Lacey 2	12,640
23rd Feb	3	(h)	Birmingham City	2	W 2-0	Sheldon, T.Miller	50,000
6th Mar	4	(a)	Huddersfield Town	2	L 1-2	T.Miller	44,248
1920-21							
8th Jan	1	(h)	Manchester United	1	D 1-1	Chambers	36,000
12th Jan	1 Rep	(a)	Manchester United	1	W 2-1	Lacey, Chambers	29,189
29th Jan	2	(a)	Newcastle United	1	L 0-1		61,400
1921-22							
7th Jan	1	(a)	Sunderland	1	D 1-1	Forshaw	30,000
11th Jan	1 Rep	(h)	Sunderland	1	W 5-0	Forshaw 2, Chambers 2, W.Wadsworth	46,000
28th Jan	2	(h)	West Bromwich Alb.	1	L 0-1		50,000
1922-23							
13th Jan	1	(h)	Arsenal	1	D 0-0		37,000
17th Jan	1 Rep	(a)	Arsenal	1	W 4-1	Chambers 2, Johnson, McKinlay (pen)	40,000
3rd Feb	2	(a)	Wolverhampton W.	2	W 2-0	Johnson, Forshaw	40,079
24th Feb	3	(h)	Sheffield United	1	L 1-2	Chambers	51,859
1923-24							
12th Jan	1	(h)	Bradford City	2	W 2-1	Chambers 2	25,000
2nd Feb	2	(a)	Bolton Wanderers	1	W 4-1	Walsh 3, Chambers	51,596
23rd Feb	3	(a)	Southampton	2	D 0-0		18,671
27th Feb	3 Rep	(h)	Southampton	2	W 2-0	Chambers, Forshaw	49,000
8th Mar	4	(a)	Newcastle United	1	L 0-1		56,595

Date	Round	Venue	Opponents	Opponent Division	Score	Scorers	Att
1924-25							
10th Jan	1	(h)	Leeds United	1	W 3-0	Shone 2, Hopkin	39,000
31st Jan	2	(a)	Bristol City	3 Sth	W 1-0	Rawlings	29,362
21st Feb	3	(h)	Birmingham City	1	W 2-1	Rawlings, Shone	44,000
7th Mar	4	(a)	Southampton	2	L 0-1		21,501
1925-26							
9th Jan	3	(a)	Southampton	2	D 0-0		18,031
13th Jan	3 Rep	(h)	Southampton	2	W 1-0	Forshaw	42,000
30th Jan	4	(a)	Fulham	2	L 1-3	Forshaw	36,381
1926-27							
8th Jan	3	(a)	Bournemouth	3 Sth	D 1-1	Hodgson	13,243
12th Jan	3 Rep	(h)	Bournemouth	3 Sth	W 4-1	Hopkin, Chambers 3	36,800
29th Jan	4	(h)	Southport	3 Nth	W 3-1	Hodgson, Chambers, Edmed	51,600
19th Feb	5	(a)	Arsenal	1	L 0-2		43,000
1927-28							
14th Jan	3	(h)	Darlington	3 Nth	W 1-0	Chambers	28,500
28th Jan	4	(a)	Cardiff City	1	L 1-2	Edmed (pen)	20,000
1928-29							
12th Jan	3	(a)	Bristol City	2	W 2-0	Salisbury, Hodgson	28,500
26th Jan	4	(h)	Bolton Wanderers	1	D 0-0		55,055
30th Jan	4 Rep	(a)	Bolton Wanderers	1	L 2-5 aet	Lindsay, Hodgson	41,808
1929-30							
11th Jan	3	(h)	Cardiff City	2	L 1-2	McPherson	50,141
1930-31							
10th Jan	3	(h)	Birmingham City	1	L 0-2		40,500
1931-32							
9th Jan	3	(a)	Everton	1	W 2-1	Gunson, Hodgson	57,090
23rd Jan	4	(a)	Chesterfield	2	W 4-2	Barton 4	28,393
13th Feb	5	(h)	Grimsby Town	1	W 1-0	Gunson	49,479
27th Feb	6	(h)	Chelsea	1	L 0-2		57,804
1932-33							
14th Jan	3	(a)	West Bromwich Alb.	1	L 0-2		29,170
1933-34							
13th Jan	3	(h)	Fulham	2	D 1-1	Hodgson	45,619
17th Jan	3 Rep	(a)	Fulham	2	W 3-2 aet	Hanson, Bradshaw, S.Roberts	28,319
27th Jan	4	(h)	Tranmere Rovers (match played at Anfield)	3 Nth	W 3-1	English 2, Nieuwenhuys	61,036
17th Feb	5	(h)	Bolton Wanderers	2	L 0-3		54,912
1934-35							
12th Jan	3	(a)	Yeovil & Petters	Non Lge	W 6-2	Nieuwenhuys, Wright, Hodgson 2, Roberts 2	13,000
26th Jan	4	(a)	Blackburn Rovers	1	L 0-1		49,546

Date	Round	Venue	Opponents	Opponent Division	Score	Scorers	Att
1935-36							
11th Jan	3	(h)	Swansea Town	2	W 1-0	Wright	33,494
25th Jan	4	(h)	Arsenal	1	L 0-2		53,720
1936-37							
16th Jan	3	(a)	Norwich City	2	L 0-3		26,800
1937-38							
8th Jan	3	(a)	Crystal Palace	3 Sth	D 0-0		33,000
12th Jan	3 Rep	(h)	Crystal Palace	3 Sth	W 3-1 aet	Shafto, Collins o.g., Fagan (pen)	35,919
22nd Jan	4	(a)	Sheffield United	2	D 1-1	Hanson	50,264
26th Jan	4 Rep	(h)	Sheffield United	2	W 1-0	Johnson o.g.	48,297
12th Feb	5	(h)	Huddersfield Town	1	L 0-1		57,682
1938-39							
7th Jan	3	(h)	Luton Town	2	W 3-0	Balmer 2, Paterson	40,431
21st Jan	4	(h)	Stockport County	3 Nth	W 5-1	Nieuwenhuys 2, Eastham, Balmer 2	39,407
11th Feb	5	(a)	Wolverhampton W.	1	L 1-4	Fagan (pen)	61,315
1945-46							
5th Jan	3 Leg 1	(a)	Chester	3 Nth	W 2-0	Liddell, Fagan	12,000
9th Jan	3 Leg 2	(h)	Chester	3 Nth	W 2-1	Fagan 2	11,207
26th Jan	4 Leg 1	(a)	Bolton Wanderers	1	L 0-5		39,692
30th Jan	4 Leg 2	(h)	Bolton Wanderers	1	W 2-0	Balmer, Nieuwenhuys	35,247
1946-47							
11th Jan	3	(a)	Walsall	3 Sth	W 5-2	Foulkes o.g., Done, Liddell, Balmer 2	18,379
25th Jan	4	(h)	Grimsby Town	1	W 2-0	Stubbins, Done	42,265
8th Feb	5	(h)	Derby County	1	W 1-0	Balmer	44,493
1st Mar	6	(h)	Birmingham City	2	W 4-1	Stubbins 3, Balmer	51,911
29th Mar	S.F.	Ewood Pk	Burnley	2	D 0-0 aet		52,570
12th Apr	S.F. Rep	Maine Rd	Burnley	2	L 0-1		72,000
1947-48							
10th Jan	3	(h)	Nottingham Forest	2	W 4-1	Priday, Stubbins 2, Liddell	48,569
24th Jan	4	(a)	Manchester United	1	L 0-3		74,721
			(match played at Goodison Park due to bomb damage)				
1948-49							
8th Jan	3	(a)	Nottingham Forest	2	D 2-2 aet	Fagan, Done	35,000
15th Jan	3 Rep	(h)	Nottingham Forest	2	W 4-0	Payne, Balmer 2, Stubbins	52,218
29th Jan	4	(h)	Notts County	3 Sth	W 1-0	Liddell	61,003
12th Feb	5	(a)	Wolverhampton W.	1	L 1-3	Done	54,983
1949-50							
7th Jan	3	(a)	Blackburn Rovers	2	D 0-0		52,468
11th Jan	3 Rep	(h)	Blackburn Rovers	2	W 2-1	Payne, Fagan	52,221
28th Jan	4	(h)	Exeter City	3 Sth	W 3-1	Baron, Fagan, Payne	45,209
11th Feb	5	(a)	Stockport County	3 Nth	W 2-1	Fagan, Stubbins	27,833
4th Mar	6	(h)	Blackpool	1	W 2-1	Fagan, Liddell	53,973
25th Mar	S.F.	Maine Rd	Everton	1	W 2-0	Paisley, Liddell	72,000
29th Apr	Final	Wembley	Arsenal	1	L 0-2		98,249

Date	Round	Venue	Opponents	Opponent Division	Score	Scorers	Att
1950-51							
6th Jan	3	(a)	Norwich City	3 Sth	L 1-3	Balmer	34,641
1951-52							
12th Jan	3	(h)	Workington Town	3 Nth	W 1-0	Payne	52,581
2nd Feb	4	(h)	Wolverhampton W.	1	W 2-1	Paisley, Done	61,905
23rd Feb	5	(a)	Burnley	1	L 0-2		52,070
1952-53							
10th Jan	3	(a)	Gateshead	3 Nth	L 0-1		15,193
1953-54							
9th Jan	3	(a)	Bolton Wanderers	1	L 0-1		45,341
1954-55							
8th Jan	3	(a)	Lincoln City	2	D 1-1	Evans	15,399
12th Jan	3 Rep	(h)	Lincoln City	2	W 1-0 aet	Evans	32,179
29th Jan	4	(a)	Everton	1	W 4-0	Liddell, A'Court, Evans 2	72,000
19th Feb	5	(h)	Huddersfield Town	1	L 0-2		57,115
1955-56							
7th Jan	3	(h)	Accrington Stanley	3 Nth	W 2-0	Liddell 2	48,385
28th Jan	4	(h)	Scunthorpe United	3 Nth	D 3-3	Liddell 2, Payne	53,393
6th Feb	4 Rep	(a)	Scunthorpe United	3 Nth	W 2-1 aet	Liddell, Arnell	19,500
18th Feb	5	(a)	Manchester City	1	D 0-0		70,640
22nd Feb	5 Rep	(h)	Manchester City	1	L 1-2	Arnell	57,528
1956-57							
5th Jan	3	(a)	Southend United	3 Sth	L 1-2	Wheeler	18,253
1957-58							
4th Jan	3	(h)	Southend United	3 Sth	D 1-1	Smith o.g.	43,454
8th Jan	3 Rep	(a)	Southend United	3 Sth	W 3-2	Molyneux, White, Rowley	20,000
25th Jan	4	(h)	Northampton Town	3 Sth	W 3-1	Liddell, Collins o.g., Bimpson	56,939
15th Feb	5	(a)	Scunthorpe United	3 Nth	W 1-0	Murdoch	23,000
1st Mar	6	(a)	Blackburn Rovers	2	L 1-2	Murdoch	51,000
1958-59							
15th Jan	3	(a)	Worcester City	Non Lge	L 1-2	Twentyman (pen)	15,011
1959-60							
9th Jan	3	(h)	Leyton Orient	2	W 2-1	Hunt 2	40,343
30th Jan	4	(h)	Manchester United	1	L 1-3	Wheeler	56,736
1960-61							
7th Jan	3	(h)	Coventry City	3	W 3-2	Hunt, Lewis, Harrower	50,909
28th Jan	4	(h)	Sunderland	2	L 0-2		46,185
1st Feb	4 Rep	(h)	Burnley	1	W 2-1 aet	St John, Moran (pen)	57,906
16th Mar	5	(a)	Arsenal	1	W 2-1	Melia, Moran (pen)	55,245
30th Mar	6	(h)	West Ham United	1	W 1-0	Hunt	49,036
27th Apr	S.F.	H'borough	Leicester City	1	L 0-1		65,000

Ian St John wheels away in delight following his winner in the 1965 FA Cup final (top page), while the squad remain positive on their open-top bus tour following the 1971 final (above)

Date	Round	Venue	Opponents	Opponent Division	Score	Scorers	Att
1961-62							
6th Jan	3	(h)	Chelsea	1	W 4-3	St John 2, Hunt, A'Court	48,455
27th Jan	4	(a)	Oldham Athletic	4	W 2-1	St John 2	42,000
17th Feb	5	(h)	Preston North End	2	D 0-0		54,967
20th Feb	5 Rep	(a)	Preston North End	2	D 0-0 aet		37,831
26th Feb	5 Rep (2)	Old Trafford	Preston North End	2	L 0-1		43,944
1962-63							
9th Jan	3	(a)	Wrexham	3	W 3-0	Hunt, Lewis, Melia	29,992
26th Jan	4	(a)	Burnley	1	D 1-1	Lewis	49,885
21st Feb	4 Rep	(h)	Burnley	1	W 2-1 aet	St John, Moran (pen)	57,906
16th Mar	5	(a)	Arsenal	1	W 2-1	Melia, Moran (pen)	55,245
30th Mar	6	(h)	West Ham United	1	W 1-0	Hunt	49,036
27th Apr	S.F.	Hillsborough	Leicester City	1	L 0-1		65,000
1963-64							
4th Jan	3	(h)	Derby County	2	W 5-0	Arrowsmith 4, Hunt	46,460
25th Jan	4	(h)	Port Vale	3	D 0-0		52,327
27th Jan	4 Rep	(a)	Port Vale	3	W 2-1 aet	Hunt, Thompson	42,179
15th Feb	5	(a)	Arsenal	1	W 1-0	St John	61,295
29th Feb	6	(h)	Swansea Town	2	L 1-2	Thompson	52,608
1964-65							
9th Jan	3	(a)	West Bromwich Alb.	1	W 2-1	Hunt, St John	28,360
30th Jan	4	(h)	Stockport County	4	D 1-1	Milne	51,587
3rd Feb	4 Rep	(a)	Stockport County	4	W 2-0	Hunt 2	24,080
20th Feb	5	(a)	Bolton Wanderers	2	W 1-0	Callaghan	52,207
6th Mar	6	(a)	Leicester City	1	D 0-0		39,356
10th Mar	6 Rep	(h)	Leicester City	1	W 1-0	Hunt	53,324
27th Mar	S.F.	Villa Park	Chelsea	1	W 2-0	Thompson, Stevenson (pen)	67,686
1st May	Final	Wembley	Leeds United	1	W 2-1aet	Hunt, St John	100,000
1965-66							
22nd Jan	3	(h)	Chelsea	1	L 1-2	Hunt	54,097
1966-67							
28th Jan	3	(a)	Watford	3	D 0-0		33,000
1st Feb	3 Rep	(h)	Watford	3	W 3-1	St John, Hunt, Lawler	54,451
18th Feb	4	(h)	Aston Villa	1	W 1-0	St John	52,447
11th Mar	5	(a)	Everton	1	L 0-1		64,851
			(a further 40,149 watched on closed-circuit TV at Anfield)				
1967-68							
27th Jan	3	(a)	Bournemouth	3	D 0-0		24,388
30th Jan	3 Rep	(h)	Bournemouth	3	W 4-1	Hateley, Thompson, Hunt Lawler	54,075
17th Feb	4	(a)	Walsall	3	D 0-0		21,066
19th Feb	4 Rep	(h)	Walsall	3	W 5-2	Hateley 4, Strong	39,113
9th Mar	5	(a)	Tottenham Hotspur	1	D 1-1	Hateley	54,005
12th Mar	5 Rep	(h)	Tottenham Hotspur	1	W 2-1	Hunt, Smith (pen)	53,658
30th Mar	6	(a)	West Bromwich Alb.	1	D 0-0		53,062
8th Apr	6 Rep	(h)	West Bromwich Alb.	1	D 1-1aet	Hateley	54,273
18th Apr	6 Rep (2)	Maine Rd	West Bromwich Alb.	1	L 1-2	Hateley	56,000

Date	Round	Venue	Opponents	Opponent Division	Score	Scorers	Att
1968-69							
4th Jan	3	(h)	Doncaster Rovers	4	W 2-0	Hunt, Callaghan	48,330
25th Jan	4	(h)	Burnley	1	W 2-1	Smith (pen), Hughes	53,677
1st Mar	5	(a)	Leicester City	1	D 0-0		42,002
3rd Mar	5 Rep	(h)	Leicester City	1	L 0-1		54,666
1969-70							
7th Jan	3	(a)	Coventry City	1	D 1-1	Graham	33,688
12th Jan	3 Rep	(h)	Coventry City	1	W 3-0	Ross, Thompson, Graham	51,261
24th Jan	4	(h)	Wrexham	4	W 3-1	Graham 2, St John	54,096
7th Feb	5	(h)	Leicester City	2	D 0-0		53,785
11th Feb	5 Rep	(a)	Leicester City	2	W 2-0	Evans 2	42,100
21st Feb	6	(a)	Watford	2	L 0-1		34,047
1970-71							
2nd Jan	3	(h)	Aldershot	4	W 1-0	McLaughlin	45,500
23rd Jan	4	(h)	Swansea Town	3	W 3-0	Toshack, St John, Lawler	47,229
13th Feb	5	(h)	Southampton	1	W 1-0	Lawler	50,226
6th Mar	6	(h)	Tottenham Hotspur	1	D 0-0		54,731
16th Mar	6 Rep	(a)	Tottenham Hotspur	1	W 1-0	Heighway	56,283
27th Mar	S.F.	Old Trafford	Everton	1	W 2-1	Evans, Hall	62,144
8th May	Final	Wembley	Arsenal	1	L 1-2 aet	Heighway	100,000
1971-72							
15th Jan	3	(a)	Oxford United	2	W 3-0	Keegan 2, Lindsay	18,000
5th Feb	4	(h)	Leeds United	1	D 0-0		56,300
9th Feb	4 Rep	(a)	Leeds United	1	L 0-2		45,821
1972-73							
13th Jan	3	(a)	Burnley	2	D 0-0		35,730
16th Jan	3 Rep	(h)	Burnley	2	W 3-0	Toshack 2, Cormack	56,124
3rd Feb	4	(h)	Manchester City	1	D 0-0		56,296
7th Feb	4 Rep	(a)	Manchester City	1	L 0-2		49,572
1973-74							
5th Jan	3	(h)	Doncaster Rovers	4	D 2-2	Keegan 2	31,483
8th Jan	3 Rep	(a)	Doncaster Rovers	4	W 2-0	Heighway, Cormack	22,499
26th Jan	4	(h)	Carlisle United	2	D 0-0		47,211
29th Jan	4 Rep	(a)	Carlisle United	2	W 2-0	Boersma, Toshack	21,262
16th Feb	5	(h)	Ipswich Town	1	W 2-0	Hall, Keegan	45,340
9th Mar	6	(a)	Bristol City	2	W 1-0	Toshack	37,671
30th Mar	S.F.	Old Trafford	Leicester City	1	D 0-0		60,000
3rd Apr	S.F. Rep	Villa Park	Leicester City	1	W 3-1	Hall, Keegan, Toshack	55,619
4th May	Final	Wembley	Newcastle United	1	W 3-0	Keegan 2, Heighway	100,000
1974-75							
4th Jan	3	(h)	Stoke City	1	W 2-0	Heighway, Keegan	48,723
25th Jan	4	(a)	Ipswich Town	1	L 0-1		34,708
1975-76							
3rd Jan	3	(a)	West Ham United	1	W 2-0	Keegan, Toshack	32,363
24th Jan	4	(a)	Derby County	1	L 0-1		38,200

Date	Round	Venue	Opponents	Opponent Division	Score	Scorers	Att
1976-77							
8th Jan	3	(h)	Crystal Palace	3	D 0-0		44,730
11th Jan	3 Rep	(a)	Crystal Palace	3	W 3-2	Keegan, Heighway 2	42,644
29th Jan	4	(h)	Carlisle United	2	W 3-0	Keegan, Toshack, Heighway	45,358
26th Feb	5	(h)	Oldham Athletic	2	W 3-1	Keegan, Case, Neal (pen)	52,455
19th Mar	6	(h)	Middlesbrough	1	W 2-0	Fairclough, Keegan	55,881
23rd Apr	S.F.	Maine Rd	Everton	1	D 2-2	McDermott, Case	52,637
27th Apr	S.F. Rep	Maine Rd	Everton	1	W 3-0	Neal (pen), Case, Kennedy	52,579
21st May	Final	Wembley	Manchester United	1	L 1-2	Case	100,000
1977-78							
7th Jan	3	(a)	Chelsea	1	L 2-4	Johnson, Dalglish	45,449
1978-79							
10th Jan	3	(a)	Southend United	3	D 0-0		31,033
17th Jan	3 Rep	(h)	Southend United	3	W 3-0	Case, Dalglish, R.Kennedy	37,797
30th Jan	4	(h)	Blackburn Rovers	2	W 1-0	Dalglish	43,432
28th Feb	5	(h)	Burnley	2	W 3-0	Johnson 2, Souness	47,161
10th Mar	6	(a)	Ipswich Town	1	W 1-0	Dalglish	31,322
31st Mar	S.F.	Maine Rd	Manchester United	1	D 2-2	Dalglish, Hansen	52,584
4th Apr	S.F. Rep	Goodison	Manchester United	1	L 0-1		53,069
1979-80							
5th Jan	3	(h)	Grimsby Town	3	W 5-0	Souness, Johnson 3, Case	49,706
26th Jan	4	(a)	Nottingham Forest	1	W 2-0	Dalglish, McDermott (pen)	33,277
16th Feb	5	(h)	Bury	3	W 2-0	Fairclough 2	43,769
8th Mar	6	(a)	Tottenham Hotspur	1	W 1-0	Mc Dermott	48,033
12th Apr	S.F.	Hillsborough	Arsenal	1	D 0-0		50,174
16th Apr	S.F. Rep	Villa Park	Arsenal	1	D 1-1 aet	Fairclough	40,679
28th Apr	S.F.Rep (2)	Villa Park	Arsenal	1	D 1-1 aet	Dalglish	42,975
1st May	S.F.Rep (3)	Highfield Rd	Arsenal	1	L 0-1		35,335
1980-81							
3rd Jan	3	(h)	Altrincham	Non Lge	W 4-1	McDermott, Dalglish 2, R.Kennedy	37,170
24th Jan	4	(a)	Everton	1	L 1-2	Case	53,804
1981-82							
2nd Jan	3	(a)	Swansea City	1	W 4-0	Hansen, Rush 2, Lawrenson	24,179
23rd Jan	4	(a)	Sunderland	1	W 3-0	Dalglish 2, Rush	28,582
13th Feb	5	(a)	Chelsea	2	L 0-2		41,422
1982-83							
8th Jan	3	(a)	Blackburn Rovers	2	W 2-1	Hodgson, Rush	21,967
29th Jan	4	(h)	Stoke City	1	W 2-0	Dalglish, Rush	36,666
20th Feb	5	(h)	Brighton	1	L 1-2	Johnston	44,868
1983-84							
6th Jan	3	(h)	Newcastle United	2	W 4-0	Robinson, Rush 2, Johnston	33,566
29th Jan	4	(a)	Brighton	2	L 0-2		19,057

Date	Round	Venue	Opponents	Opponent Division	Score	Scorers	Att
1984-85							
5th Jan	3	(h)	Aston Villa	1	W 3-0	Rush 2, Wark	36,877
27th Jan	4	(h)	Tottenham Hotspur	1	W 1-0	Rush	27,905
16th Feb	5	(a)	York City	3	D 1-1	Rush	13,485
20th Feb	5 Rep	(h)	York City	3	W 7-0	Whelan 2, Wark 3, Neal, Walsh	43,010
10th Mar	6	(a)	Barnsley	2	W 4-0	Rush 3, Whelan	19,838
13th Apr	S.F.	Goodison	Manchester United	1	D 2-2 aet	Whelan, Walsh	51,690
17th Apr	S.F. Rep	Maine Rd	Manchester United	1	L 1-2	McGrath o.g.	45,775
1985-86							
4th Jan	3	(h)	Norwich City	2	W 5-0	MacDonald, Walsh, McMahon Whelan, Wark	29,082
26th Jan	4	(a)	Chelsea	1	W 2-1	Rush, Lawrenson	33,625
15th Feb	5	(a)	York City	3	D 1-1	Molby (pen)	12,443
18th Feb	5 Rep	(h)	York City	3	W 3-1 aet	Wark, Molby, Dalglish	29,362
11th Mar	6	(h)	Watford	1	D 0-0		36,775
17th Mar	6 Rep	(a)	Watford	1	W 2-1 aet	Molby (pen), Rush	28,097
5th Apr	S.F.	Tottenham	Southampton	1	W 2-0 aet	Rush 2	44,605
10th May	Final	Wembley	Everton	1	W 3-1	Rush 2, Johnston	98,000
1986-87							
11th Jan	3	(a)	Luton Town	1	D 0-0		11,085
26th Jan	3 Rep	(h)	Luton Town	1	D 0-0 aet		34,822
28th Jan	3 Rep (2)	(a)	Luton Town	1	L 0-3		14,687
1987-88							
9th Jan	3	(a)	Stoke City	2	D 0-0		31,979
12th Jan	3 Rep	(h)	Stoke City	2	W 1-0	Beardsley	39,147
31st Jan	4	(a)	Aston Villa	2	W 2-0	Barnes, Beardsley	46,324
21st Feb	5	(a)	Everton	1	W 1-0	Houghton	48,270
13th Mar	6	(a)	Manchester City	2	W 4-0	Houghton, Beardsley (pen) Johnston, Barnes	44,077
9th Apr	S.F.	Hillsborough	Nottingham Forest	1	W 2-1	Aldridge 2 (1 pen)	51,627
14th May	Final	Wembley	Wimbledon	1	L 0-1		98,203
1988-89							
7th Jan	3	(a)	Carlisle United	4	W 3-0	Barnes, McMahon 2	18,556
29th Jan	4	(a)	Millwall	1	W 2-0	Aldridge, Rush	23,615
18th Feb	5	(a)	Hull City	2	W 3-2	Barnes, Aldridge 2	20,058
18th Mar	6	(h)	Brentford	3	W 4-0	McMahon, Barnes, Beardsley 2	42,376
7th May	S.F.	Old Trafford	Nottingham Forest	1	W 3-1	Aldridge, Laws o.g.	38,000
20th May	Final	Wembley	Everton	1	W 3-2aet	Aldridge, Rush 2	82,800
1989-90							
6th Jan	3	(a)	Swansea City	3	D 0-0		16,098
9th Jan	3 Rep	(h)	Swansea City	3	W 8-0	Barnes 2, Whelan, Rush 3, Beardsley, Nicol	29,194
28th Jan	4	(a)	Norwich City	1	D 0-0		23,152
31st Jan	4 Rep	(h)	Norwich City	1	W 3-1	Nicol, Barnes, Beardsley (pen)	29,339
17th Feb	5	(h)	Southampton	1	W 3-0	Rush, Beardsley, Nicol	35,961
11th Mar	6	(a)	QPR	1	D 2-2	Barnes, Rush	21,057
14th Mar	6 Rep	(h)	QPR	1	W 1-0	Beardsley	38,090
8th Apr	S.F.	Villa Park	Crystal Palace	1	L 3-4 aet	Rush, McMahon, Barnes (pen)	38,389

Date	Round	Venue	Opponents	Opponent Division	Score	Scorers	Att
1990-91							
5th Jan	3	(a)	Blackburn Rovers	2	D 1-1	Atkins o.g.	18,524
8th Jan	3 Rep	(h)	Blackburn Rovers	2	W 3-0	Houghton, Rush, Staunton	34,175
26th Jan	4	(h)	Brighton	2	D 2-2	Rush 2	32,670
30th Jan	4 Rep	(a)	Brighton	2	W 3-2 aet	McMahon 2, Rush	14,392
17th Feb	5	(h)	Everton	1	D 0-0		38,323
20th Feb	5 Rep	(a)	Everton	1	D 4-4 aet	Beardsley 2, Rush, Barnes	37,766
27th Feb	5 Rep (2)	(a)	Everton	1	L 0-1		40,201
1991-92							
6th Jan	3	(a)	Crewe Alexandra	4	W 4-0	McManaman, Barnes 3 (1 pen)	7,400
5th Feb	4	(a)	Bristol Rovers	2	D 1-1	Saunders	9,464
11th Feb	4 Rep	(h)	Bristol Rovers	2	W 2-1	McManaman, Saunders	30,142
16th Feb	5	(a)	Ipswich Town	2	D 0-0		26,140
26th Feb	5 Rep	(h)	Ipswich Town	2	W 3-2 aet	Houghton, Molby, McManaman	27,335
8th Mar	6	(h)	Aston Villa	1	W 1-0	Thomas	29,109
5th Apr	S.F.	Highbury	Portsmouth	2	D 1-1 aet	Whelan	41,869
13th Apr	S.F. Rep	Villa Park	Portsmouth	2	W 0-0 aet		40,077
			(Liverpool won 3-1 on penalties)				
9th May	Final	Wembley	Sunderland	2	W 2-0	Thomas, Rush	79,544
1992-93							
3rd Jan	3	(a)	Bolton Wanderers	2	D 2-2	Winstanley o.g., Rush	21,502
13th Jan	3 Rep	(h)	Bolton Wanderers	2	L 0-2		34,790
1993-94							
19th Jan	3	(a)	Bristol City	1	D 1-1	Rush	21,718
25th Jan	3 Rep	(h)	Bristol City	1	L 0-1		36,720
1994-95							
7th Jan	3	(a)	Birmingham City	2	D 0-0		25,326
18th Jan	3 Rep	(h)	Birmingham City	2	W 1-1aet	Redknapp	36,275
			(Liverpool won 2-0 on penalties)				
28th Jan	4	(a)	Burnley	1	D 0-0		20,551
7th Feb	4 Rep	(h)	Burnley	1	W 1-0	Barnes	32,109
19th Feb	5	(h)	Wimbledon	Prem	D 1-1	Fowler	25,124
28th Feb	5 Rep	(a)	Wimbledon	Prem	W 2-0	Barnes, Rush	12,553
11th Mar	6	(h)	Tottenham Hotspur	Prem	L 1-2	Fowler	39,592
1995-96							
6th Jan	3	(h)	Rochdale	3	W 7-0	Fowler, Collymore 3, Valentine o.g., Rush, McAteer	28,126
18th Feb	4	(a)	Shrewsbury Town	2	W 4-0	Collymore, Walton o.g., Fowler McAteer	7,752
28th Feb	5	(h)	Charlton Athletic	1	W 2-1	Fowler, Collymore	36,818
10th Mar	6	(a)	Leeds United	Prem	D 0-0		34,632
20th Mar	6 Rep	(h)	Leeds United	Prem	W 3-0	McManaman 2, Fowler	30,812
31st Mar	S.F	Old Trafford	Aston Villa	Prem	W 3-0	Fowler 2, McAteer	39,072
11th May	Final	Wembley	Manchester United	Prem	L 0-1		79,007
1996-97							
4th Jan	3	(h)	Burnley	2	W 1-0	Collymore	33,252
26th Jan	4	(a)	Chelsea	Prem	L 2-4	Fowler, Collymore	27,950

Date	Round	Venue	Opponents	Opponent Division	Score	Scorers	Att
1997-98							
3rd Jan	3	(h)	Coventry City	Prem	L 1-3	Redknapp	33,888
1998-99							
3rd Jan	3	(a)	Port Vale	1	W 3-0	Owen (pen), Ince, Fowler	16,557
24th Jan	4	(a)	Manchester United	Prem	L 1-2	Owen	54,591
1999-2000							
12th Dec	3	(a)	Huddersfield Town.	1	W 2-0	Camara, Matteo	23,678
10th Jan	4	(h)	Blackburn Rovers	1	L 0-1		32,839
2000-01							
6th Jan	3	(h)	Rotherham United	2	W 3-0	Heskey 2, Hamann	30,689
27th Jan	4	(a)	Leeds United	Prem	W 2-0	Barmby, Heskey	37,108
18th Feb	5	(h)	Manchester City	Prem	W 4-2	Litmanen (pen), Heskey, Smicer (pen), Babbel	36,231
11th Mar	6	(a)	Tranmere Rovers	1	W 4-2	Murphy, Owen, Gerrard Fowler (pen)	16,334
8th Apr	S.F.	Villa Park	Wycombe W.	2	W 2-1	Heskey, Fowler	40,037
12th May	Final	Cardiff	Arsenal	Prem	W 2-1	Owen 2	74,200
2001-02							
5th Jan	3	(h)	Birmingham City	1	W 3-0	Owen 2 ,Anelka	40,875
27th Jan	4	(a)	Arsenal	Prem	L 0-1		38,092
2002-03							
5th Jan	3	(a)	Manchester City	Prem	W 1-0	Murphy (pen)	28,586
26th Jan	4	(a)	Crystal Palace	1	D 0-0		26,054
5th Feb	4 Rep	(h)	Crystal Palace	1	L 0-2		35,109
2003-04							
4th Jan	3	(a)	Yeovil Town	3	W 2-0	Heskey, Murphy (pen)	9,348
24th Jan	4	(h)	Newcastle United	Prem	W 2-1	Cheyrou 2	41,365
15th Feb	5	(h)	Portsmouth	Prem	D 1-1	Owen	34,669
22nd Feb	5 Rep	(a)	Portsmouth	Prem	L 0-1		19,529
2004-05							
18th Jan	3	(a)	Burnley	Champ	L 0-1		19,033
2005-06							
7th Jan	3	(a)	Luton Town	Champ	W 5-3	Gerrard, Sinama-Pongolle 2, Alonso 2	10,170
29th Jan	4	(a)	Portsmouth	Prem	W 2-1	Gerrard (pen), Riise	17,247
18th Feb	5	(h)	Manchester United	Prem	W 1-0	Crouch	44,039
21st Mar	6	(a)	Birmingham City	Prem	W 7-0	Hyypia, Crouch 2, Morientes, Riise, Tebily o.g., Cisse	27,378
22nd Apr	S.F.	Old Trafford	Chelsea	Prem	W 2-1	Riise, Garcia	64,575
13th May	Final	Cardiff	West Ham United	Prem	W 3-3 aet	Cisse, Gerrard 2	74,000

(Liverpool won 3-1 on penalties)

Ronnie Whelan celebrates his late equaliser in the 1992 FA Cup semi-final at Highbury (top page) - while Steven Gerrard enjoys the success of the 2001 final in Cardiff (above)

THE LEAGUE CUP

Date	Round	Venue	Opponents	Opponent Division	Score	Scorers	Att
1960-61							
19th Oct	2	(h)	Luton Town	2	D 1-1	Leishman	10,502
24th Oct	2 Rep	(a)	Luton Town	2	W 5-2	Lewis 2, Hickson, Hunt 2	6,125
16th Nov	3	(h)	Southampton	2	L 1-2	Hunt	14,036
1967-68							
13th Sept	2	(h)	Bolton Wanderers	2	D 1-1	Thompson	45,957
27th Sept	2 Rep	(a)	Bolton Wanderers	2	L 2-3	Smith (pen), Callaghan	31,500
1968-69							
4th Sept	2	(h)	Sheffield United	2	W 4-0	Hunt, Lawler, Callaghan, Thompson	32,358
25th Sept	3	(h)	Swansea Town	4	W 2-0	Lawler, Hunt	31,051
15th Oct	4	(a)	Arsenal	1	L 1-2	Lawler	39,299
1969-70							
3rd Sept	2	(a)	Watford	2	W 2-1	Slater o.g., St John	21,149
24th Sept	3	(a)	Manchester City	1	L 2-3	A.Evans, Graham	28,019
1970-71							
8th Sept	2	(a)	Mansfield Town	3	D 0-0		12,532
22nd Sept	2 Rep	(h)	Mansfield Town	3	W 3-2 aet	Hughes, Smith (pen), A.Evans	31,087
6th Oct	3	(a)	Swindon Town	2	L 0-2		23,992
1971-72							
7th Sept	2	(h)	Hull City	2	W 3-0	Lawler, Heighway, Hall (pen)	31,612
5th Oct	3	(h)	Southampton	1	W 1-0	Heighway	28,964
27th Oct	4	(a)	West Ham United	1	L 1-2	Graham	40,878
1972-73							
5th Sept	2	(a)	Carlisle United	2	D 1-1	Keegan	16,257
19th Sept	2 Rep	(h)	Carlisle United	2	W 5-1	Keegan, Boersma 2, Lawler, Heighway	22,128
3rd Oct	3	(a)	West Bromwich Alb.	1	D 1-1	Heighway	17,756
10th Oct	3 Rep	(h)	West Bromwich Alb.	1	W 2-1 aet	Hughes, Keegan	26,461
31st Oct	4	(h)	Leeds United	1	D 2-2	Keegan, Toshack	44,609
22nd Nov	4 Rep	(a)	Leeds United	1	W 1-0	Keegan	34,856
4th Dec	5	(h)	Tottenham Hotspur	1	D 1-1	Hughes	48,677
6th Dec	5 Rep	(a)	Tottenham Hotspur	1	L 1-3	Callaghan	34,565
1973-74							
8th Oct	2	(a)	West Ham United	1	D 2-2	Cormack, Heighway	25,823
29th Oct	2 Rep	(h)	West Ham United	1	W 1-0	Toshack	26,002
21st Nov	3	(a)	Sunderland	2	W 2-0	Keegan, Toshack	36,208
27th Nov	4	(a)	Hull City	2	D 0-0		19,748
4th Dec	4 Rep	(h)	Hull City	2	W 3-1	Callaghan 3	17,120
19th Dec	5	(a)	Wolverhampton W.	1	L 0-1		15,242
1974-75							
10th Sept	2	(h)	Brentford	4	W 2-1	Kennedy, Boersma	21,413
8th Oct	3	(a)	Bristol City	2	D 0-0		25,573
16th Oct	3 Rep	(h)	Bristol City	2	W 4-0	Heighway 2, Kennedy 2	23,694
12th Nov	4	(h)	Middlesbrough	1	L 0-1		24,906

Date	Round	Venue	Opponents	Opponent Division	Score	Scorers	Att
1975-76							
10th Sept	2	(a)	York City	2	W 1-0	Lindsay (pen)	9,421
7th Oct	3	(h)	Burnley	1	D 1-1	Case	24,607
14th Oct	3 Rep	(a)	Burnley	1	L 0-1		20,022
1976-77							
31st Aug	2	(h)	West Bromwich Alb.	1	D 1-1	Callaghan	23,378
6th Sept	2 Rep	(a)	West Bromwich Alb.	1	L 0-1		22,662
1977-78							
30th Aug	2	(h)	Chelsea	1	W 2-0	Dalglish, Case	33,170
26th Oct	3	(h)	Derby County	1	W 2-0	Fairclough 2	30,400
29th Nov	4	(h)	Coventry City	1	D 2-2	Fairclough, Neal (pen)	33,817
20th Dec	4 Rep	(a)	Coventry City	1	W 2-0	Case, Dalglish	36,105
17th Jan	5	(a)	Wrexham	3	W 3-1	Dalglish 3	25,641
7th Feb	S.F.Leg 1	(h)	Arsenal	1	W 2-1	Dalglish, Kennedy	44,764
14th Feb	S.F.Leg 2	(a)	Arsenal	1	D 0-0		49,561
18th Mar	Final	Wembley	Nottingham Forest	1	D 0-0 aet		100,000
22nd Mar	Final Rep.	Old Trafford	Nottingham Forest	1	L 0-1		54,375
1978-79							
28th Aug	2	(a)	Sheffield United	2	L 0-1		35,753
1979-80							
29th Aug	2 Leg 1	(a)	Tranmere Rovers	4	D 0-0		16,759
4th Sept	2 Leg 2	(h)	Tranmere Rovers	4	W 4-0	Thompson, Dalglish 2, Fairclough	24,785
25th Sept	3	(h)	Chesterfield	3	W 3-1	Fairclough, Dalglish, McDermott	20,960
30th Oct	4	(h)	Exeter City	3	W 2-0	Fairclough 2	21,019
5th Dec	5	(a)	Norwich City	1	W 3-1	Johnson 2, Dalglish	23,000
22nd Jan	S.F.Leg 1	(a)	Nottingham Forest	1	L 0-1		32,234
12th Feb	S.F.Leg 2	(h)	Nottingham Forest	1	D 1-1	Fairclough	50,880
1980-81							
27th Aug	2 Leg 1	(a)	Bradford City	4	L 0-1		16,232
2nd Sept	2 Leg 2	(h)	Bradford City	4	W 4-0	Dalglish 2, R.Kennedy, Johnson	21,017
23rd Sept	3	(h)	Swindon Town	3	W 5-0	Lee 2, Dalglish, Cockerill o.g., Fairclough	16,566
28th Oct	4	(h)	Portsmouth	3	W 4-1	Dalglish, Johnson 2, Souness	32,021
5th Dec	5	(h)	Birmingham City	1	W 3-1	Dalglish, McDermott, Johnson	30,236
14th Jan	S.F.Leg 1	(a)	Manchester City	1	W 1-0	R.Kennedy	48,045
10th Feb	S.F.Leg 2	(h)	Manchester City	1	D 1-1	Dalglish	46,711
14th Mar	Final	Wembley	West Ham United	2	D 1-1aet	A.Kennedy	100,000
1st Apr	Final Rep	Villa Park	West Ham United	2	W 2-1	Dalglish, Hansen	36,693
1981-82							
7th Oct	2 Leg 1	(h)	Exeter City	3	W 5-0	Rush 2, McDermott, Dalglish, Whelan	11,478
28th Oct	2 Leg 2	(a)	Exeter City	3	W 6-0	Rush 2, Dalglish, Neal, Sheedy, Marker o.g.	11,740
10th Nov	3	(h)	Middlesbrough	1	W 4-1	Sheedy, Rush, Johnson 2	16,145
1st Dec	4	(a)	Arsenal	1	D 0-0		37,917
8th Dec	4 Rep	(h)	Arsenal	1	W 3-0 aet	Johnston, McDermott (pen), Dalglish	21,375
12th Jan	5	(h)	Barnsley	2	D 0-0		33,707
19th Jan	5 Rep	(a)	Barnsley	2	W 3-1	Souness, Johnson, Dalglish	29,639

Date	Round	Venue	Opponents	Opponent Division	Score	Scorers	Att

1981-82 (cont)

Date	Round	Venue	Opponents	Opponent Division	Score	Scorers	Att
2nd Feb	S.F.Leg 1	(a)	Ipswich Town	1	W 2-0	McDermott, Rush	26,690
9th Feb	S.F.Leg 2	(h)	Ipswich Town	1	D 2-2	Rush, Dalglish	34,933
13th Mar	Final	Wembley	Tottenham Hotspur	1	W 3-1 aet	Whelan 2, Rush	100,000

1982-83

Date	Round	Venue	Opponents	Opponent Division	Score	Scorers	Att
5th Oct	2 Leg 1	(a)	Ipswich Town	1	W 2-1	Rush 2	19,328
26th Oct	2 Leg 2	(h)	Ipswich Town	1	W 2-0	Whelan, Lawrenson	17,698
11th Nov	3	(h)	Rotherham United	2	W 1-0	Johnston	20,412
30th Nov	4	(h)	Norwich City	1	W 2-0	Lawrenson, Fairclough	13,235
18th Jan	5	(h)	West Ham United	1	W 2-1	Hodgson, Souness	23,953
8th Feb	S.F.Leg 1	(h)	Burnley	2	W 3-0	Souness, Neal (pen), Hodgson	33,520
15th Feb	S.F.Leg 2	(a)	Burnley	2	L 0-1		20,000
26th Mar	Final	Wembley	Manchester United	1	W 2-1 aet	Kennedy, Whelan	100,000

1983-84

Date	Round	Venue	Opponents	Opponent Division	Score	Scorers	Att
5th Oct	2 Leg 1	(a)	Brentford	3	W 4-1	Rush 2, Robinson, Souness	17,859
25th Oct	2 Leg 2	(h)	Brentford	3	W 4-0	Souness (pen), Hodgson, Dalglish, Robinson	9,902
8th Nov	3	(a)	Fulham	2	D 1-1	Rush	20,142
22nd Nov	3 Rep	(h)	Fulham	2	D 1-1 aet	Dalglish	15,783
29th Nov	3 Rep (2)	(a)	Fulham	2	W 1-0 aet	Souness	20,905
20th Dec	4	(a)	Birmingham City	1	D 1-1	Souness	17,405
22nd Dec	4 Rep	(h)	Birmingham City	1	W 3-0	Nicol, Rush 2 (1 pen)	11,638
17th Jan	5	(a)	Sheffield Wed.	2	D 2-2	Nicol, Neal (pen)	49,357
25th Jan	5 Rep	(h)	Sheffield Wed.	2	W 3-0	Rush 2, Robinson	40,485
7th Feb	S.F.Leg 1	(h)	Walsall	3	D 2-2	Whelan 2	31,073
14th Feb	S.F.Leg 2	(a)	Walsall	3	W 2-0	Rush, Whelan	19,591
25th Mar	Final	Wembley	Everton	1	D 0-0 aet		100,000
28th Mar	Final Rep	Maine Rd	Everton	1	W 1-0	Souness	52,089

1984-85

Date	Round	Venue	Opponents	Opponent Division	Score	Scorers	Att
24th Sept	2 Leg 1	(a)	Stockport County	4	D 0-0		11,169
9th Oct	2 Leg 2	(h)	Stockport County	4	W 2-0 aet	Robinson, Whelan	13,422
31st Oct	3	(a)	Tottenham Hotspur	1	L 0-1		38,690

1985-86

Date	Round	Venue	Opponents	Opponent Division	Score	Scorers	Att
24th Sept	2 Leg 1	(h)	Oldham Athletic	2	W 3-0	McMahon 2, Rush	16,150
9th Oct	2 Leg 2	(a)	Oldham Athletic	2	W 5-2	Whelan 2, Wark, Rush, MacDonald	7,719
29th Oct	3	(h)	Brighton	2	W 4-0	Walsh 3, Dalglish	15,291
26th Nov	4	(h)	Manchester United	1	W 2-1	Molby 2 (1 pen)	41,291
21st Jan	5	(h)	Ipswich Town	1	W 3-0	Walsh, Whelan, Rush	19,762
12th Feb	S.F.Leg 1	(a)	QPR	1	L 0-1		15,051
5th Mar	S.F.Leg 2	(h)	QPR	1	D 2-2	McMahon, Johnston	23,863

1986-87

Date	Round	Venue	Opponents	Opponent Division	Score	Scorers	Att
23rd Sept	2 Leg 1	(h)	Fulham	3	W 10-0	Rush 2, Wark 2, Whelan, McMahon 4, Nicol	13,498
7th Oct	2 Leg 2	(a)	Fulham	3	W 3-2	McMahon, Parker o.g., Molby (pen)	7,864
29th Oct	3	(h)	Leicester City	1	W 4-1	McMahon 3, Dalglish	20,248
19th Nov	4	(a)	Coventry City	1	D 0-0		26,385
26th Nov	4 Rep	(h)	Coventry City	1	W 3-1	Molby 3 (3 pens)	19,179
21st Jan	5	(a)	Everton	1	W 1-0	Rush	53,325
11th Feb	S.F.Leg 1	(a)	Southampton	1	D 0-0		22,818

Date	Round	Venue	Opponents	Opponent Division	Score	Scorers	Att
1986-87 (cont)							
11th Feb	S.F.Leg 1	(a)	Southampton	1	D 0-0		22,818
25th Feb	S.F.Leg 2	(h)	Southampton	1	W 3-0	Whelan, Dalglish, Molby	38,481
5th Apr	Final	Wembley	Arsenal	1	L 1-2	Rush	96,000
1987-88							
23rd Sept	2 Leg 1	(a)	Blackburn Rovers	2	D 1-1	Nicol	13,924
6th Oct	2 Leg 2	(h)	Blackburn Rovers	2	W 1-0	Aldridge	28,994
28th Oct	3	(h)	Everton	1	L 0-1		44,071
1988-89							
28th Sept	2 Leg 1	(h)	Walsall	2	W 1-0	Gillespie	18,084
12th Oct	2 Leg 2	(a)	Walsall	2	W 3-1	Barnes, Rush, Molby (pen)	12,015
2nd Nov	3	(h)	Arsenal	1	D 1-1	Barnes	31,951
9th Nov	3 Rep	(a)	Arsenal	1	D 0-0		54,029
23rd Nov	3 Rep (2)	Villa Park	Arsenal	1	W 2-1	McMahon, Aldridge	21,708
30th Nov	4	(a)	West Ham United	1	L 1-4	Aldridge (pen)	26,971
1989-90							
19th Sept	2 Leg 1	(h)	Wigan Athletic	3	W 5-2	Hysen, Rush 2, Beardsley, Barnes	19,231
4th Oct	2 Leg 2	(a)	Wigan Athletic (match played at Anfield)	3	W 3-0	Staunton 3	17,954
25th Oct	3	(a)	Arsenal	1	L 0-1		40,814
1990-91							
25th Sept	2 Leg 1	(h)	Crewe Alexandra	3	W 5-1	McMahon, Gillespie, Houghton, Rush 2	17,228
9th Oct	2 Leg 2	(a)	Crewe Alexandra	3	W 4-1	Rush 3, Staunton	7,200
31st Oct	3	(a)	Manchester United	1	L 1-3	Houghton	42,033
1991-92							
25th Sept	2 Leg 1	(h)	Stoke City	3	D 2-2	Rush 2	18,389
9th Oct	2 Leg 2	(a)	Stoke City	3	W 3-2	McManaman, Saunders, Walters	22,335
29th Oct	3	(h)	Port Vale	2	D 2-2	McManaman, Rush	21,553
20th Nov	3 Rep	(a)	Port Vale	2	W 4-1	McManaman, Walters, Houghton, Saunders	18,725
3rd Dec	4	(a)	Peterborough Utd	3	L 0-1		14,114
1992-93							
22nd Sept	2 Leg 1	(h)	Chesterfield	3	D 4-4	Rosenthal, Hutchison, Walters Wright	12,533
6th Oct	2 Leg 2	(a)	Chesterfield	3	W 4-1	Hutchison, Redknapp, Walters Rush	10,632
28th Oct	3	(a)	Sheffield United	Prem	D 0-0		17,856
11th Nov	3 Rep	(h)	Sheffield United	Prem	W 3-0	McManaman 2, Marsh (pen)	17,654
1st Dec	4	(h)	Crystal Palace	Prem	D 1-1	Marsh (pen)	18,525
16th Dec	4 Rep	(a)	Crystal Palace	Prem	L 1-2 aet	Marsh (pen)	19,622

Date	Round	Venue	Opponents	Opponent Division	Score	Scorers	Att
1993-94							
22nd Sept	2 Leg 1	(a)	Fulham	2	W 3-1	Rush, Clough, Fowler	13,599
5th Oct	2 Leg 2	(h)	Fulham	2	W 5-0	Fowler 5	12,541
27th Oct	3	(h)	Ipswich Town	Prem	W 3-2	Rush 3	19,058
1st Dec	4	(h)	Wimbledon	Prem	D 1-1	Molby (pen)	19,290
14th Dec	4 Rep	(a)	Wimbledon	Prem	L 2-2 aet	Ruddock, Segers o.g.	11,343
			(Liverpool lost 3-4 on penalties)				
1994-95							
21st Sept	2 Leg 1	(h)	Burnley	1	W 2-0	Scales, Fowler	23,359
5th Oct	2 Leg 2	(a)	Burnley	1	W 4-1	Redknapp 2, Fowler, Clough	19,032
25th Oct	3	(h)	Stoke City	1	W 2-1	Rush 2	32,060
30th Nov	4	(a)	Blackburn Rovers	Prem	W 3-1	Rush 3	30,115
11th Jan	5	(h)	Arsenal	Prem	W 1-0	Rush	36,004
15th Feb	S.F.Leg 1	(h)	Crystal Palace	Prem	W 1-0	Fowler	25,480
8th Mar	S.F.Leg 2	(a)	Crystal Palace	Prem	W 1-0	Fowler	18,224
2nd Apr	Final	Wembley	Bolton Wanderers	1	W 2-1	McManaman 2	75,595
1995-96							
20th Sept	2 Leg 1	(h)	Sunderland	1	W 2-0	McManaman, Thomas	25,579
4th Oct	2 Leg 2	(a)	Sunderland	1	W 1-0	Fowler	20,560
25th Oct	3	(h)	Manchester City	Prem	W 4-0	Scales, Fowler, Rush, Harkness	29,394
29th Nov	4	(h)	Newcastle United	Prem	L 0-1		40,077
1996-97							
23rd Oct	3	(a)	Charlton Athletic	1	D 1-1	Fowler	15,000
13th Nov	3 Rep	(h)	Charlton Athletic	1	W 4-1	Wright, Redknapp, Fowler 2	20,714
27th Nov	4	(h)	Arsenal	Prem	W 4-2	McManaman, Fowler 2 (1 pen) Berger	32,814
8th Jan	5	(a)	Middlesbrough	Prem	L 1-2	McManaman	28,670
1997-98							
15th Oct	3	(a)	West Bromwich Alb.	1	W 2-0	Berger, Fowler	21,986
18th Nov	4	(h)	Grimsby Town	2	W 3-0	Owen 3	28,515
7th Jan	5	(a)	Newcastle United	Prem	W 2-0 aet	Owen, Fowler	33,207
27th Jan	S.F.Leg 1	(h)	Middlesbrough	1	W 2-1	Redknapp, Fowler	33,438
18th Feb	S.F.Leg 2	(a)	Middlesbrough	1	L 0-2		29,828
1998-99							
27th Oct	3	(h)	Fulham	2	W 3-1	Morgan o.g., Fowler (pen), Ince	22,296
10th Nov	4	(h)	Tottenham Hotspur	Prem	L 1-3	Owen	20,772
1999-2000							
14th Sept	2 Leg 1	(a)	Hull City	3	W 5-1	Murphy 2, Meijer 2, Staunton	10,034
21st Sept	2 Leg 2	(h)	Hull City	3	W 4-2	Murphy, Maxwell, Riedle 2	24,318
13th Oct	3	(a)	Southampton	Prem	L 1-2	Owen	13,822
2000-01							
1st Nov	3	(h)	Chelsea	Prem	W 2-1 aet	Murphy, Fowler	29,370
29th Nov	4	(a)	Stoke City	2	W 8-0	Ziege, Smicer, Babbel, Fowler 3 (1 pen), Hyypia, Murphy	27,109
13th Dec	5	(h)	Fulham	1	W 3-0 aet	Owen, Smicer, Barmby	20,144
10th Jan	S.F.Leg 1	(a)	Crystal Palace	1	L 1-2	Smicer	25,933
24th Jan	S.F.Leg 2	(h)	Crystal Palace	1	W 5-0	Smicer, Murphy 2, Biscan Fowler	41,854
25th Feb	Final	Cardiff	Birmingham City	1	W 1-1 aet	Fowler	73,500
			(Liverpool won 5-4 on penalties)				

Date	Round	Venue	Opponents	Opponent Division	Score	Scorers	Att
2001-02							
9th Oct	3	(h)	Grimsby Town	1	L 1-2 aet	McAllister (pen)	32,672
2002-03							
6th Nov	3	(h)	Southampton	Prem	W 3-1	Berger, Diouf, Baros	35,870
4th Dec	4	(h)	Ipswich Town	1	W 1-1	Diouf (pen)	26,305
			(Liverpool won 5-4 on penalties)				
18th Dec	5	(a)	Aston Villa	Prem	W 4-3	Murphy 2, Baros, Gerrard	38,530
8th Jan	S.F.Leg 1	(a)	Sheffield United	1	L 1-2	Mellor	30,095
21st Jan	S.F.Leg 2	(h)	Sheffield United	1	W 2-0 aet	Diouf, Owen	43,837
2nd Mar	Final	Cardiff	Manchester United	Prem	W 2-0	Gerrard, Owen	74,500
2003-04							
29th Oct	3	(a)	Blackburn Rovers	Prem	W 4-3	Murphy (pen), Heskey 2, Kewell	16,918
3rd Dec	4	(h)	Bolton Wanderers	Prem	L 2-3	Murphy, Smicer	33,185
2004-05							
26th Oct	3	(a)	Millwall	Champ	W 3-0	Diao, Baros 2	17,655
10th Nov	4	(h)	Middlesbrough	Prem	W 2-0	Mellor 2	28,176
1st Dec	5	(a)	Tottenham Hotspur	Prem	W 1-1 aet	Sinama-Pongolle (pen)	36,100
			(Liverpool won 4-3 on penalties)				
11th Jan	S.F.Leg 1	(h)	Watford	Champ	W 1-0	Gerrard	35,739
25th Jan	S.F.Leg 2	(a)	Watford	Champ	W 1-0	Gerrard	19,797
27th Feb	Final	Cardiff	Chelsea	Prem	L 2-3 aet	Riise, Nunez	71,622
2005-06							
25th Oct	3	(a)	Crystal Palace	Champ	L 1-2	Gerrard	19,673

Manager Bob Paisley leads his Liverpool side out before the 1982 League Cup final against Tottenham Hotspur - a 3-1 extra-time success at Wembley

CLUB WORLD CHAMPIONSHIP

Date	Round	Venue	Opponents	Opponent Country	Score	Scorers	Att
1981							
13th Dec	Final	Tokyo	Flamengo	Bra	L 0-3		62,000
1984							
9th Dec	Final	Tokyo	Independiente	Arg	L 0-1		62,000
2005							
15th Dec	S.F.	Yokohama	Saprissa	CRi	W 3-0	Crouch 2, Gerrard	43,902
18th Dec	Final	Yokohama	Sao Paulo	Bra	L 0-1		66,821

THE CHARITY SHIELD (FA COMMUNITY SHIELD)

Date	Round	Venue	Opponents	Opponent Division	Score	Scorers	Att
1922							
10th May		Old Trafford	Huddersfield Town	1	L 0-1		20,000
1964							
15th Aug		Anfield	West Ham United	1	D 2-2	Wallace, Byrne	38,858
1965							
14th Aug		Old Trafford	Manchester United	1	D 2-2	Stevenson, Yeats	48,502
1966							
13th Aug		Goodison P	Everton	1	W 1-0	Hunt	63,329
1971							
7th Aug		Filbert St	Leicester City	1	L 0-1		25,014
1974							
10th Aug		Wembley	Leeds United (Liverpool won 6-5 on penalties)	1	W 1-1	Boersma	67,000
1976							
14th Aug		Wembley	Southampton	2	W 1-0	Toshack	76,500
1977							
13th Aug		Wembley	Manchester United	1	D 0-0		82,000
1979							
11th Aug		Wembley	Arsenal	1	W 3-1	McDermott 2, Dalglish	92,000
1980							
9th Aug		Wembley	West Ham United	2	W 1-0	McDermott	90,000
1982							
21st Aug		Wembley	Tottenham Hotspur	1	W 1-0	Rush	82,500
1983							
20th Aug		Wembley	Manchester United	1	L 0-2		92,000
1984							
18th Aug		Wembley	Everton	1	L 0-1		100,000
1986							
16th Aug		Wembley	Everton	1	D 1-1	Rush	88,231
1988							
20th Aug		Wembley	Wimbledon	1	W 2-1	Aldridge 2	54,887
1989							
12th Aug		Wembley	Arsenal	1	W 1-0	Beardsley	63,149
1990							
18th Aug		Wembley	Manchester United	1	D 1-1	Barnes	66,558
1992							
12th Aug		Wembley	Leeds United	Prem	L 3-4	Rush, Saunders, Strachan o.g.	61,291
2001							
12th Aug		Cardiff	Manchester United	Prem	W 2-1	McAllister (pen), Owen	70,227
2002							
11th Aug		Cardiff	Arsenal	Prem	L 0-1		67,337

Liverpool skipper Sami Hyypia shows off the FA Community Shield following a 2-1 victory over Manchester United in 2001

SCREEN SPORT SUPER CUP

Date	Round	Venue	Opponents	Opponent Division	Score	Scorers	Att
1985-86							
			Group stage				
17th Sept	Group	(h)	Southampton	1	W 2-1	Molby, Dalglish	16,189
22nd Oct	Group	(a)	Southampton	1	D 1-1	Walsh	10,503
3rd Dec	Group	(h)	Tottenham Hotspur	1	W 2-0	MacDonald, Walsh	14,855
14th Jan	Group	(a)	Tottenham Hotspur	1	W 3-0	Rush 2, Lawrenson	10,078
5th Feb	SF Leg 1	(a)	Norwich City	1	D 1-1	Dalglish	15,330
6th May	SF Leg 2	(h)	Norwich City	1	W 3-1	MacDonald, Molby (pen), Johnston	26,696
1986-87							
16th Sept	F Leg 1	(h)	Everton	1	W 3-1	Rush 2, McMahon	20,660
30th Sept	F Leg 2	(a)	Everton	1	W 4-1	Rush 3, Nicol	26,068

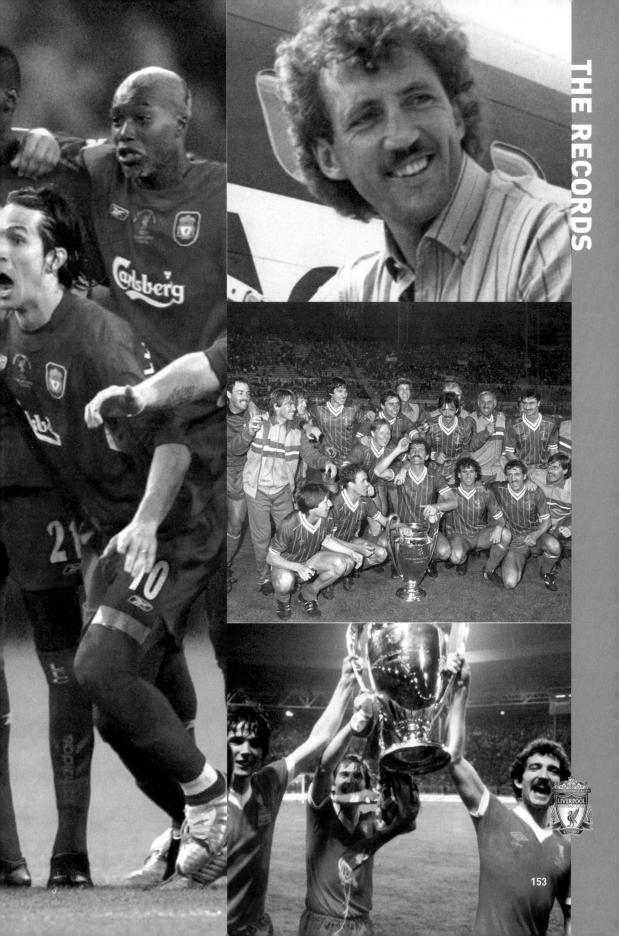

153

RECORD BREAKERS

In another season of success, Liverpool's run of results, particularly from November onwards, ensured there would be a revision of club records. Jose Reina's magnificent first season resulted in a clean sheet record while the run of successive wins at the end of the campaign also created a new mark. The following tables highlight these new records and how they compare with previous campaigns.

MOST SUCCESSIVE CLEAN SHEETS (IN ALL COMPETITIONS)

GAMES	PERIOD COVERED
11	29th October 2005-15th December 2005
10	19th December 1987 - 6th February 1988
8	14th January 1920 - 21st February 1920
8	16th February 1974 - 30th March 1974
7	31st December 1898 - 4th February 1899
7	1st March 1966 - 9th April 1966
7	12th February 1972 - 25th March 1972
7	13th February 1979 - 10th March 1979

MOST SUCCESSIVE WINS (IN ALL COMPETITIONS)

GAMES	PERIOD COVERED
12*	5th March 2006-13th May 2006
11	18th February 1989-11th April 1989
10	2nd December 1893-10th February 1894
10	7th September 1904-19th November 1904
10	20th March 1982-1st May 1982
10	1st January 1983-12th February 1983
10	31st March 1986-10th May 1986
9	25th August 1990-9th October 1990

* 3-3 result in FA Cup final noted as a victory courtesy of the penalty shootout win.

HIGHEST NUMBER OF GOALSCORERS IN AN AWAY FA CUP TIE

DATE	ROUND	TEAM	GOALS	SCORELINE
21/3/2006	6	BIRMINGHAM CITY	7	7-0
12/1/1935	3	YEOVIL & PETTERS	6	6-2
11/1/1947	3	WALSALL	5	5-2
7/1/2006	3	LUTON TOWN	5	5-3

MOST MINUTES WITHOUT CONCEDING A GOAL IN EUROPEAN COMPETITION

LENGTH OF TIME	PERIOD COVERED	RUN ENDED
573 minutes	13th September 2005-21st February 2006	Benfica
561 minutes	16th March 1983-21st March 1984	Benfica
454 minutes	14th September 1964-24th March 1965	Cologne
426 minutes	21st October 1997-3rd November 1998	Valencia
423 minutes	12th November 2002-13th March 2003	Celtic
407 minutes	22nd February 2001-16th May 2001	Alaves

EUROPEAN SUPER CUP (MOST WINS)

WINS	TEAM	YEARS
4	AC Milan	1989, 1990, 1994, 2003
3	Ajax Amsterdam	1972, 1973, 1995
3	Liverpool	1977, 2001, 2005
2	Anderlecht	1976, 1978
2	Barcelona	1992, 1997
2	Juventus	1984, 1996
2	Valencia	1980, 2004

In safe hands - Jose Reina with the European Super Cup in 2005, making it a Liverpool hat-trick

PENALTY KINGS

Liverpool's penalty shootout success in May's FA Cup final not only ensured a seventh victory in the competition, but it also established the Reds as undisputed penalty kings. An unprecedented nine shootouts have been won by the Reds from 10 attempts - including their last two European Cup final wins. These 10 matches are listed below, including penalty takers and penalty outcomes.

PENALTY SHOOTOUT 1

10th August 1974   FA CHARITY SHIELD (Wembley)
Attendance   67,000
                          LIVERPOOL 1-1 LEEDS UNITED
Scorers   Liverpool: Boersma; Leeds United: Cherry
                          LIVERPOOL WON 6-5 ON PENALTIES
                          (LEEDS TOOK THE FIRST KICK):

LEEDS UNITED:	LORIMER (SCORED),	LIVERPOOL:	LINDSAY (SCORED),
	GILES (SCORED),		HUGHES (SCORED),
	GRAY (SCORED),		HALL (SCORED),
	HUNTER (SCORED),		SMITH (SCORED),
	CHERRY (SCORED),		CORMACK (SCORED),
	HARVEY (MISSED).		CALLAGHAN (SCORED).

GOALKEEPER: HARVEY   GOALKEEPER: CLEMENCE

In what proved to be the first penalty shootout to decide the showpiece to the new season, the match was also notable for the sendings off of Kevin Keegan and Leeds United's Billy Bremner early in the second half. It was also the first year that the fixture was played at a neutral venue, while the recently retired Bill Shankly was given the privilege of leading Liverpool out.
The shootout was won courtesy of Ian Callaghan, after Leeds United goalkeeper David Harvey had blasted the sixth penalty over the bar.

PENALTY SHOOTOUT 2

30th May 1984   EUROPEAN CUP FINAL (Rome)
Attendance   69,693
                          LIVERPOOL 1-1 AS ROMA (aet)
Scorers   Liverpool: Neal; AS Roma: Pruzzo
                          LIVERPOOL WON 4-2 ON PENALTIES
                          (LIVERPOOL, TOOK THE FIRST KICK):

LIVERPOOL:	NICOL (MISSED),	AS ROMA:	DI BARTOLOMEI (SCORED),
	NEAL (SCORED),		CONTI (MISSED),
	SOUNESS (SCORED),		RIGHETTI (SCORED),
	RUSH (SCORED),		GRAZIANI (MISSED),
	A. KENNEDY (SCORED).		

GOALKEEPER: GROBBELAAR   TANCREDI

Liverpool's fourth European Cup triumph was secured despite Steve Nicol missing the target with the Reds' first penalty against the Italians, playing in their home stadium. Conti's second penalty went over the bar, and then Graziani did likewise, arguably pre-occupied by Grobbelaar's spaghetti legs impression. Alan Kennedy, who scored the winner in the 1981 final, stroked home to win it.

PENALTY SHOOTOUT 3

13th April 1992
Attendance

FA CUP SEMI-FINAL REPLAY (Villa Park)
40,077
LIVERPOOL 0-0 PORTSMOUTH
LIVERPOOL WON 3-1 ON PENALTIES
(PORTSMOUTH TOOK THE FIRST KICK)

PORTSMOUTH: KUHL (MISSED),
SYMONS (SCORED),
NEILL (SAVED),
BERESFORD (MISSED).

LIVERPOOL: BARNES (SCORED),
RUSH (SCORED),
SAUNDERS (SCORED),

GOALKEEPER: KNIGHT

GOALKEEPER: GROBBELAAR

The first FA Cup semi-final to be decided on a shootout saw the Reds hold their nerve after Second Division Portsmouth had battled through two games, the first at Highbury seeing a late Ronnie Whelan goal earn Liverpool a replay. Only Kit Symons scored for Pompey in the shootout, with John Beresford's miss ensuring Graeme Souness' side a place in the 1992 final.

Alan Kennedy converts the crucial fifth penalty which secured the 1984 European Cup

PENALTY SHOOTOUT 4

14th December 1993
Attendance

Scorers

LEAGUE CUP FOURTH-ROUND REPLAY
11,343
WIMBLEDON 2-2 LIVERPOOL (aet)
Wimbledon: Holdsworth, Earle;
Liverpool: Ruddock, Segers (o.g.)
LIVERPOOL LOST 4-3 ON PENALTIES
(LIVERPOOL TOOK THE FIRST KICK)

LIVERPOOL: RUDDOCK (SCORED),
REDKNAPP (SAVED),
BARNES (SCORED),
WALTERS (SAVED),
FOWLER (SCORED),

WIMBLEDON: FASHANU (SCORED),
HOLDSWORTH (SCORED),
JONES (SAVED),
McALLISTER (SCORED),
ARDLEY (SCORED).

GOALKEEPER: GROBBELAAR

GOALKEEPER: SEGERS

In blizzard conditions at Selhurst Park, Liverpool went down to their first and only competitive defeat in a shootout. Hans Segers made up for his last-minute own goal by saving three pens - one from John Barnes in extra time, and then from Jamie Redknapp and Mark Walters in the shootout.

PENALTY KINGS

PENALTY SHOOTOUT 5

18th January 1995   FA CUP THIRD-ROUND REPLAY
Attendance   36,275
                           LIVERPOOL 1-1 BIRMINGHAM CITY (aet)
Scorers   Liverpool: Redknapp, Birmingham City: Otto
                           LIVERPOOL WON 2-0 ON PENALTIES

(BIRMINGHAM CITY TOOK THE FIRST KICK):

BIRMINGHAM: WARD (MISSED),   LIVERPOOL: RUDDOCK (SAVED),
              McGAVIN (SAVED),   REDKNAPP (SCORED),
              DAISH (MISSED),   BJORNEBYE (SCORED),
              COOPER (MISSED).

GOALKEEPER: BENNETT   JAMES

Following a goalless draw at St Andrews, Liverpool were again held by the Second Division leaders and after extra time failed to yield a result, it was left to penalties to decide the outcome. Despite Neil Ruddock missing Liverpool's first kick, Blues missed all of theirs to hand the Reds victory.

PENALTY SHOOTOUT 6

25th February 2001   LEAGUE CUP FINAL (CARDIFF)
Attendance   73,500
                           LIVERPOOL 1-1 BIRMINGHAM CITY (aet)
Scorers   Liverpool: Fowler; Birmingham City: Purse (pen)
                           LIVERPOOL WON 5-4 ON PENALTIES

(LIVERPOOL TOOK THE FIRST KICK):

LIVERPOOL: McALLISTER (SCORED),   BIRMINGHAM: GRAINGER (SAVED),
              BARMBY (SCORED),   PURSE (SCORED),
              ZIEGE (SCORED),   MARCELO (SCORED),
              HAMANN (SAVED),   LAZARIDIS (SCORED),
              FOWLER (SCORED),   HUGHES (SCORED),
              CARRAGHER (SCORED),   A. JOHNSON (SAVED).

GOALKEEPER: WESTERVELD   BENNETT

Liverpool clinched the League Cup for a record sixth time, and in so doing became the first English club to win a domestic final on penalties. In normal time Darren Purse's last-minute penalty levelled Robbie Fowler's first-half volley, but Liverpool again proved too astute for Birmingham in the shootout. Andrew Johnson's kick was saved by Sander Westerveld, which also meant that the Reds became the first winners of a major football final at the Millennium Stadium in Cardiff.

PENALTY SHOOTOUT 7

4th December 2002
Attendance

Scorers

LEAGUE CUP FOURTH ROUND
26,305
LIVERPOOL 1-1 IPSWICH TOWN (aet)
Liverpool: Diouf (pen); Ipswich Town: Miller
LIVERPOOL WON 5-4 ON PENALTIES
(IPSWICH TOWN TOOK THE FIRST KICK):

IPSWICH:	HOLLAND (SCORED),	LIVERPOOL:	GERRARD (SCORED),
	CLAPHAM (MISSED),		BAROS (SCORED),
	MAGILTON (SCORED),		RIISE (SCORED),
	MILLER (SCORED),		CARRAGHER (SCORED),
	ARMSTRONG (SCORED),		DIOUF (SCORED).
GOALKEEPER:	MARSHALL		DUDEK

With replays abolished in the League Cup, Liverpool hit back from a goal down against Championship side Ipswich Town. Penalties again proved to the Reds' liking, with Jamie Clapham's miss from the visitors' second penalty proving crucial.

PENALTY SHOOTOUT 8

1st December 2004
Attendance

Scorers

LEAGUE CUP FIFTH ROUND
36,100
TOTTENHAM HOTSPUR 1-1 LIVERPOOL (aet)
Tottenham Hotspur: Defoe; Liverpool: Sinama-Pongolle (pen)
LIVERPOOL WON 4-3 ON PENALTIES
(TOTTENHAM TOOK THE FIRST KICK):

TOTTENHAM:	DEFOE (SCORED),	LIVERPOOL:	HENCHOZ (SCORED),
	CARRICK (SCORED),		PARTRIDGE (SCORED),
	KANOUTE (SAVED),		POTTER (SAVED),
	BROWN (MISSED),		WELSH (SCORED),
	ZIEGLER (SCORED),		S-PONGOLLE (SCORED).
GOALKEEPER:	ROBINSON		DUDEK

A weakened Liverpool side booked their passage into the semi-final courtesy of Florent Sinama-Pongolle's decisive spot-kick, the striker having earned penalties with a late extra-time penalty equaliser after Freddie Kanoute (who also saw his penalty saved in the shootout) had handled.

Florent Sinama-Pongolle converts to send Liverpool through to the 2005 League Cup semi-final

PENALTY KINGS

PENALTY SHOOTOUT 9

25th May 2005	EUROPEAN CUP FINAL (ISTANBUL)
Attedance	65,000
	AC MILAN 3-3 LIVERPOOL (aet)
Scorers	AC Milan: Maldini, Crespo 2;
	Liverpool: Gerrard, Smicer, Alonso
	LIVERPOOL WON 3-2 ON PENALTIES
	(AC MILAN TOOK THE FIRST KICK):

AC MILAN: SERGINHO (MISSED),   LIVERPOOL: HAMANN (SCORED),
                    PIRLO (SAVED),   CISSE (SCORED),
                    TOMASSON (SCORED),   RIISE (SAVED),
                    KAKA (SCORED),   SMICER (SCORED),
                    SHEVCHENKO (SAVED).

GOALKEEPER: DIDA   DUDEK

With Liverpool 3-0 down at half-time, penalties would have been beyond their wildest dreams. But three goals in a six-minute spell in the second half, together with some inspired performances all around the pitch earned the penalty kings their moment of destiny. Despite John Arne Riise missing their third kick (Dietmar Hamann also scored despite suffering from a broken foot), an inspired goalkeeping display by Jerzy Dudek, who saved two penalties while Serginho also missed the target with AC Milan's first, earned the club a fifth European Cup.

**Jerzy Dudek saves Andriy Shevchenko's fifth penalty to secure Liverpool's European Cup
triumph in Istanbul in 2005**

PENALTY SHOOTOUT 10

13th May 2006	FA CUP FINAL (CARDIFF)
Attendance	71,140
	LIVERPOOL 3-3 WEST HAM UNITED (aet)
Scorers	Liverpool: Cisse, Gerrard 2;
	West Ham United: Carragher (o.g.), Ashton, Konchesky
	LIVERPOOL WON 3-1 ON PENALTIES
	(LIVERPOOL TOOK THE FIRST KICK):

LIVERPOOL:		WEST HAM:	
	HAMANN (SCORED),		ZAMORA (SAVED),
	HYYPIA (SAVED),		SHERINGHAM (SCORED),
	GERRARD (SCORED),		KONCHESKY (SAVED),
	RIISE (SCORED),		FERDINAND (SAVED).
GOALKEEPER:	REINA		HISLOP

A year after the drama in Istanbul, Liverpool were again involved in another similarly dramatic final. The Reds were never ahead in the match, and after being 2-0 down in the first half, they hit back to 2-2 in the second half. Paul Konchesky's attempted cross seemed to have ended the Reds' hopes before skipper Steven Gerrard again proved inspirational, volleying home spectacularly in the last minute. Battle-weary Liverpool survived extra time, thanks to Jose Reina's late save from Nigel Reo-Coker's header and once in the shootout, Liverpool again held their nerve. Dietmar Hamann, in taking and scoring their first kick, became the only player to have taken penalties in three different major finals, while Reina was the hero, saving three spot-kicks.

Jose Reina is mobbed by Liverpool team-mates as his save from Anton Ferdinand confirms a seventh FA Cup success for the Reds in 2006

THE MARATHON MEN

CORRECT AT END OF MAY 2006 - Games played includes substitute appearances

OVERALL APPEARANCES (500+ GAMES)

1	Ian Callaghan	857
2	Ray Clemence	665
=	Emlyn Hughes	665
4	Ian Rush	660
5	Phil Neal	650
6	Tommy Smith	638
7	Bruce Grobbelaar	628
8	Alan Hansen	620
9	Chris Lawler	549
10	Billy Liddell	534
11	Kenny Dalglish	515

Ian Callaghan - Most Reds appearances

LEAGUE APPEARANCES (400+ GAMES)

1	Ian Callaghan	640
2	Billy Liddell	492
3	Emlyn Hughes	474
4	Ray Clemence	470
5	Ian Rush	469
6	Tommy Smith	467
7	Phil Neal	455
8	Bruce Grobbelaar	440
9	Alan Hansen	434
10	Elisha Scott	430
11	Chris Lawler	406
12	Roger Hunt	404

Ray Clemence   **Alan Hansen**

EUROPE APPEARANCES (40+ GAMES)

1	Ian Callaghan	89
2	Tommy Smith	85
3	Ray Clemence	80
4	Emlyn Hughes	79
5	Jamie Carragher	78
6	Sami Hyypia	76
7	Phil Neal	74
8	Steve Heighway	67
9	Steven Gerrard	66
=	Chris Lawler	66
11	Dietmar Hamann	61
12	John Arne Riise	57
13	Kenny Dalglish	51
14	Ray Kennedy	50
=	Michael Owen	50
=	Phil Thompson	50
17	Alan Hansen	46
=	Danny Murphy	46
19	Emile Heskey	45
20	Peter Thompson	43

Jamie Carragher - European veteran

FA CUP APPEARANCES (45+ GAMES)

1	Ian Callaghan	79
2	Bruce Grobbelaar	62
=	Emlyn Hughes	62
4	Ian Rush	61
5	Alan Hansen	58
6	Ray Clemence	54
7	Tommy Smith	52
8	John Barnes	51
9	Steve Nicol	50
=	Ron Yeats	50
11	Ian St John	49
12	Chris Lawler	47

LEAGUE CUP APPEARANCES (40+ GAMES)

1	Ian Rush	78
2	Bruce Grobbelaar	70
3	Alan Hansen	68
4	Phil Neal	66
5	Kenny Dalglish	59
6	Ray Clemence	55
7	Mark Lawrenson	50
=	Ronnie Whelan	50
9	Emlyn Hughes	46
10	Alan Kennedy	45
=	Graeme Souness	45
12	Phil Thompson	43
13	Ian Callaghan	42
=	Steve Nicol	42

Bruce Grobbelaar - The goalkeeper is joint second on the list of most FA Cup appearances for Liverpool

Ian Rush, Liverpool's League Cup appearance record holder

THE RECORD GOALSCORERS

CORRECT AT END OF MAY 2006 – Games played includes substitute appearances

OVERALL (100+ GOALS)

		TIME WITH CLUB	GAMES	GOALS
1	Ian Rush	1980-87 & 1988-96	660	346
2	Roger Hunt	1959-1970	492	286
3	Gordon Hodgson	1925-1936	379	241
4	Billy Liddell	1945-1961	534	228
5	Robbie Fowler	1993-2001 & 2006-	346	176
6	Kenny Dalglish	1977-1990	515	172
7	Michael Owen	1997-2004	297	158
8	Harry Chambers	1919-1928	339	151
9	Jack Parkinson	1899-1914	222	130
10	Sam Raybould	1899-1907	224	127
11	Dick Forshaw	1919-1927	288	124
12	Ian St John	1961-1971	425	118
13	Jack Balmer	1935-1952	310	110
14	John Barnes	1987-1997	407	108
15	Kevin Keegan	1971-1977	323	100

LEAGUE (100+ GOALS)

1	Roger Hunt	1959-1970	404	245
2	Gordon Hodgson	1925-1936	360	233
3	Ian Rush	1980-87 & 1988-96	469	229
4	Billy Liddell	1945-1961	492	215
5	Harry Chambers	1919-1928	310	135
6	Jack Parkinson	1899-1914	203	125
=	Robbie Fowler	1993-2001 & 2006-	250	125
8	Sam Raybould	1899-1907	211	119
9	Michael Owen	1997-2004	216	118
=	Kenny Dalglish	1979-1990	355	118
11	Dick Forshaw	1919-1927	266	117

EUROPE (11+ GOALS)

1	Michael Owen	1997-2004	50	22
2	Ian Rush	1980-87 & 1988-96	38	20
3	Roger Hunt	1959-1970	31	17
4	Steven Gerrard	1998-	66	16
5	Terry McDermott	1974-1982	34	15
6	Jimmy Case	1974-1981	35	13
=	Emile Heskey	2000-2004	45	13
8	Robbie Fowler	1993-2001 & 2006-	40	12
=	Kevin Keegan	1971-1977	40	12
=	Ray Kennedy	1974-1982	50	12
11	Kenny Dalglish	1979-1990	51	11
=	Steve Heighway	1970-1981	67	11
=	Chris Lawler	1962-1975	66	11
=	Phil Neal	1974-1985	74	11

FA CUP (10+ GOALS)			
		TIME WITH CLUB	GAMES	GOALS

		TIME WITH CLUB	GAMES	GOALS
1	Ian Rush	1980-87 & 1988-96	61	39
2	Roger Hunt	1959-1970	44	18
3	Harry Chambers	1919-1928	28	16
=	John Barnes	1987-1997	51	16
5	Kevin Keegan	1971-1977	28	14
6	Kenny Dalglish	1979-1990	37	13
=	Billy Liddell	1945-1961	42	13
8	Jack Balmer	1935-1952	21	12
=	Robbie Fowler	1993-2001 & 2006-	24	12
=	Ian St John	1961-1971	49	12
11	Peter Beardsley	1987-1991	25	11
=	Billy Lacey	1911-1924	28	11
13	Willie Fagan	1937-1952	24	10

LEAGUE CUP (10+ GOALS)				
1	Ian Rush	1980-87 & 1988-96	78	48
2	Robbie Fowler	1993-2001 & 2006-	32	27
=	Kenny Dalglish	1979-1990	59	27
4	Ronnie Whelan	1980-1994	50	14
5	Steve McMahon	1985-1991	27	13
6	Danny Murphy	1997-2004	16	11
7	David Fairclough	1975-1983	20	10
=	Steve McManaman	1990-1999	33	10

Robbie Fowler - Up to fifth in the all-time goals scored for Liverpool chart

ROBBIE RETURNS

Friday 27th January proved another significant date in Liverpool FC's history. We are often told to expect the unexpected, although even by the Reds' recent standards the return of one of the greatest goalscorers ever to grace the Anfield turf was something of a surprise. But after nearly five years away, the return of Robbie Fowler in a Liverpool shirt against Birmingham City was as welcome as when another striking great returned to his favourites, when Ian Rush returned from Italy back in 1988.

As well as the rejoicing of fans in the return of 'God', Rafa Benitez was impressed upon meeting the player, saying:

"We have signed a player with so much passion for this football club and I think he will act as an example to every player here in how much he loves Liverpool. I'm not sure I've ever seen a player quite so happy to be joining a club before."

The transfer window purchase proved an astute piece of business. With Fowler regaining match sharpness and fitness, he ended the Premiership campaign with five goals in nine league starts - including the winning goal against Bolton Wanderers and Blackburn Rovers, earning himself another year's contract and the opportunity to continue his love affair with the Anfield faithful. Further recollections come from the great man himself, and the legend whose goals record he surpassed to reach fifth in the all-time list of goalscorers for Liverpool FC, Kenny Dalglish:

ROBBIE FOWLER (On his dream return)
"I'm so happy it's frightening. Just to travel back to Anfield was great and to actually get into the office and put pen-to-paper was something that I have wanted to happen for a long time. Obviously since I have left deep down I've always wanted to come back and it has been a long time but I'm glad to say I'm back now!"

ROBBIE FOWLER (On going above Kenny Dalglish in the all-time LFC scorers list)
"It's fantastic for me. Kenny Dalglish is a proper Liverpool legend and to get anywhere near him is an achievement. To go one past him makes me very happy."

KENNY DALGLISH (On Robbie Fowler overtaking him in the all-time scoring list)
"I won't be ringing him. He's now scored more goals than me so I'm not talking to him. In fact, I wish he hadn't come back, who's bright idea was that?"

ROBBIE FOWLER (On being offered a new contract)
"You can imagine how happy I was when the manager offered me another year. I can't put my feelings into words, this is something I have wanted for a long time. I feel as though I've done alright and the manager has been pleased with me as well. I'm looking forward to next season now. I was buzzing when I got a six-month deal so you can imagine how happy I am to have been given another year. I am absolutely over the moon."

RAFA BENITEZ (On Robbie Fowler)
"We are very lucky to have a player like Fowler who has shown that he plays for passion and not money. The fans love him and it was great for him to score."

ROBBIE FOWLER'S DOMESTIC GOALS FOR LIVERPOOL

	LEAGUE		FA CUP		LEAGUE CUP		TOTAL	
	GAMES	GOALS	GAMES	GOALS	GAMES	GOALS	GAMES	GOALS
ASTON VILLA	13	12	1	2	-	-	14	14
ARSENAL	13	9	1	0	2	2	16	11
FULHAM	1	1	-	-	4	7	5	8
CHARLTON ATHLETIC	7	4	1	1	2	3	10	8
SOUTHAMPTON	12	8	-	-	-	-	12	8
LEEDS UNITED	13	7	3	1	-	-	16	8
TOTTENHAM HOTSPUR	11	6	1	1	1	0	13	7
CHELSEA	14	5	1	1	1	1	16	7
NEWCASTLE UNITED	15	6	-	-	2	1	17	7
BOLTON WANDERERS	5	6	-	-	1	0	6	6
DERBY COUNTY	7	6	-	-	-	-	7	6
NOTTINGHAM FOREST	7	6	-	-	-	-	7	6
MIDDLESBROUGH	9	5	-	-	3	1	12	6
MANCHESTER UNITED	12	6	2	0	-	-	14	6
EVERTON	15	6	-	-	-	-	15	6
LEICESTER CITY	9	5	-	-	-	-	9	5
WEST HAM UNITED	11	5	-	-	-	-	11	5
CRYSTAL PALACE	3	1	-	-	3	3	6	4
MANCHESTER CITY	6	3	1	0	1	1	8	4
STOKE CITY	-	-	-	-	2	3	2	3
BLACKBURN ROVERS	10	3	-	-	1	0	11	3
WIMBLEDON	10	2	2	1	2	0	14	3
OLDHAM ATHLETIC	2	2	-	-	-	-	2	2
WEST BROMWICH ALBION	1	1	-	-	1	1	2	2
NORWICH CITY	3	2	-	-	-	-	3	2
BURNLEY	-	-	2	0	2	2	4	2
IPSWICH TOWN	5	2	-	-	1	0	6	2
SUNDERLAND	5	1	-	-	2	1	7	2
SHEFFIELD WEDNESDAY	10	2	-	-	-	-	10	2
PORTSMOUTH	1	1	-	-	-	-	1	1
PORT VALE	-	-	1	1	-	-	1	1
ROCHDALE	-	-	1	1	-	-	1	1
SHREWSBURY TOWN	-	-	1	1	-	-	1	1
TRANMERE ROVERS	-	-	1	1	-	-	1	1
WYCOMBE WANDERERS	-	-	1	1	-	-	1	1
BIRMINGHAM CITY	1	0	2	0	1	1	4	1
QUEENS PARK RANGERS	5	1	-	-	-	-	5	1
COVENTRY CITY	9	1	1	0	-	-	10	1
BRISTOL CITY	-	-	1	0	-	-	1	0
SWINDON TOWN	1	0	-	-	-	-	1	0
WATFORD	1	0	-	-	-	-	1	0
WIGAN ATHLETIC	1	0	-	-	-	-	1	0
SHEFFIELD UNITED	2	0	-	-	-	-	2	0
TOTAL	**250**	**125**	**24**	**12**	**32**	**27**	**306**	**164**

ROBBIE FOWLER'S EUROPEAN GOALS FOR LIVERPOOL

	TOTAL			TOTAL	
	GAMES	GOALS		GAMES	GOALS
BRANN BERGEN	2	3	MY PA '47	1	0
FC SION	2	3	BENFICA	2	0
FC KOSICE	2	2	BRONDBY	2	0
CD ALAVES	1	1	CELTA VIGO	2	0
FC HAKA	2	1	FC PORTO	2	0
PARIS ST GERMAIN	2	1	RAPID BUCHAREST	2	0
RC STRASBOURG	2	1	ROMA	2	0
BAYERN MUNICH	1	0	SLOVAN LIBEREC	2	0
BOAVISTA	1	0	SPARTAK VLADIKAVKAZ	2	0
BORUSSIA DORTMUND	1	0	VALENCIA	2	0
CELTIC	1	0	BARCELONA	3	0
DYNAMO KIEV	1	0			
TOTAL	**40**	**12**			

THE OLDEST/YOUNGEST

Oldest player

	Final game	Age
Ted Doig	April 11 1908	41 years & 165 days

Oldest player (post-War)

Kenny Dalglish	May 1 1990	39 years & 58 days
Billy Liddell	August 31 1960	38 years & 234 days
Gary McAllister	May 11 2002	37 years & 137 days
Paul Jones	January 17 2004	36 years & 274 days
Bruce Grobbelaar	February 19 1994	36 years & 136 days
Phil Taylor	December 25 1953	36 years & 98 days
Jack Balmer	February 16 1952	36 years & 10 days
Ian Callaghan	February 4 1978	35 years 300 days
Berry Nieuwenhuys	February 1 1947	35 years 88 days
Bob Paisley	March 13 1954	35 years 49 days

Youngest player (post-War)

	Debut	Age
Max Thompson	May 8 1974	17 years & 128 days
Michael Owen	May 6 1997	17 years & 144 days
Johnny Morrissey	September 23 1957	17 years & 158 days
Reginald Blore	October 17 1959	17 years & 213 days
Phil Charnock	September 16 1992	17 years & 215 days

Youngest player to score on debut

Michael Owen	May 6 1997	17 years & 144 days

Kenny Dalglish and Gary McAllister - Two of Liverpool's 'golden oldies'

MOST GOALS FOR LIVERPOOL IN A LEAGUE SEASON

Name	Season	Division	Games	Goals	Goal average
Roger Hunt	1961-62	2	41	41	1
Gordon Hodgson	1930-31	1	40	36	1.11
Ian Rush	1983-84	1	41	32	1.28
Sam Raybould	1902-03	1	33	31	1.06
Roger Hunt	1963-64	1	41	31	1.32
Jack Parkinson	1909-10	1	31	30	1.03
Gordon Hodgson	1928-29	1	38	30	1.27
Billy Liddell	1954-55	2	40	30	1.33
Ian Rush	1986-87	1	42	30	1.4
Roger Hunt	1965-66	1	37	29	1.28
John Evans	1954-55	2	38	29	1.31
Robbie Fowler	1995-96	Prem	38	28	1.36
Dick Forshaw	1925-26	1	32	27	1.19
Gordon Hodgson	1934-35	1	34	27	1.26
Billy Liddell	1955-56	2	39	27	1.44
Gordon Hodgson	1931-32	1	39	26	1.5
John Aldridge	1987-88	1	36	26	1.38
George Allan	1895-96	2	20	25	0.8
Roger Hunt	1964-65	1	40	25	1.6
Roger Hunt	1967-68	1	40	25	1.6
Robbie Fowler	1994-95	Prem	42	25	1.68

MOST GOALS FOR LIVERPOOL IN A SEASON
- ALL COMPETITIONS

Name	Season	Games	Goals	Goal average
Ian Rush	1983-84	65	47	1.38
Roger Hunt	1961-62	46	42	1.1
Roger Hunt	1964-65	58	37	1.57
Gordon Hodgson	1930-31	41	36	1.14
Robbie Fowler	1995-96	53	36	1.47
Ian Rush	1986-87	57	35	1.63
John Evans	1954-55	42	33	1.27
Roger Hunt	1963-64	46	33	1.39
Ian Rush	1985-86	56	33	1.7
Sam Raybould	1902-03	34	32	1.06
Gordon Hodgson	1928-29	41	32	1.28
Billy Liddell	1955-56	44	32	1.38
Roger Hunt	1965-66	46	32	1.44
Billy Liddell	1954-55	44	31	1.42
Robbie Fowler	1996-97	44	31	1.42
John Aldridge	1988-89	47	31	1.52
Ian Rush	1982-83	51	31	1.65
Robbie Fowler	1994-95	57	31	1.84
Kenny Dalglish	1977-78	62	31	2

BIGGEST-EVER VICTORIES

Date	Opponents	Venue	Competition	Score
17th Sept 1974	Stromsgodset	Home	European Cup Winners' Cup	Won 11-0
16th Sept 1969	Dundalk	Home	Inter Cities' Fairs Cup	Won 10-0
23rd Sept 1986	Fulham	Home	League Cup	Won 10-0
18th Feb 1896	Rotherham Utd	Home	League	Won 10-1
1st Oct 1980	Oulu Palloseura	Home	European Cup	Won 10-1
29th Oct 1892	Newtown	Home	FA Cup	Won 9-0
12th Sept 1989	Crystal Palace	Home	League	Won 9-0
26th Dec 1928	Burnley	Home	League	Won 8-0
7th Nov 1967	TSV Munich 1860	Home	Inter Cities' Fairs Cup	Won 8-0
9th Jan 1990	Swansea City	Home	FA Cup	Won 8-0
29th Nov 2000	Stoke City	Away	League Cup	Won 8-0
6th Dec 1902	Grimsby Town	Home	League	Won 9-2
8th Apr 1905	Port Vale	Home	League	Won 8-1
29th Feb 1896	Burton Swifts	Away	League	Won 7-0
28th Mar 1896	Crewe A	Away	League	Won 7-0
4th Jan 1902	Stoke City	Home	League	Won 7-0
2nd Sept 1978	Tottenham H	Home	League	Won 7-0
21st Mar 2006	Birmingham City	Away	FA Cup	Won 7-0

BIGGEST-EVER DEFEATS

Date	Opponents	Venue	Competition	Score
11th Dec 1954	Birmingham C	Away	League	Lost 9-1
10th Nov 1934	Huddersfield T	Away	League	Lost 8-0
1st Jan 1934	Newcastle Utd	Away	League	Lost 9-2
7th May 1932	Bolton W	Away	League	Lost 8-1
1st Sept 1934	Arsenal	Away	League	Lost 8-1
7th Dec 1912	Sunderland	Away	League	Lost 7-0
1st Sept 1930	West Ham United	Away	League	Lost 7-0
19th Apr 1930	Sunderland	Home	League	Lost 6-0
28th Nov 1931	Arsenal	Away	League	Lost 6-0
11th Sept 1935	Manchester City	Away	League	Lost 6-0
26th Sept 1953	Charlton Athletic	Away	League	Lost 6-0

THE INDIVIDUAL HONOURS

FOOTBALL WRITERS FOOTBALLER OF THE YEAR

Honours won (that season)

1974	Ian Callaghan	FA Cup
1976	Kevin Keegan	First Division, UEFA Cup
1977	Emlyn Hughes	First Division, European Cup, Charity Shield
1979	Kenny Dalglish	First Division
1980	Terry McDermott	First Division, Charity Shield
1983	Kenny Dalglish	First Division, League Cup, Charity Shield
1984	Ian Rush	First Division, League Cup, European Cup
1988	John Barnes	First Division
1989	Steve Nicol	FA Cup, Charity Shield
1990	John Barnes	First Division, Charity Shield

PFA PLAYER OF THE YEAR

1980	Terry McDermott	First Division, Charity Shield
1983	Kenny Dalglish	First Division, League Cup, Charity Shield
1984	Ian Rush	First Division, League Cup, European Cup
1988	John Barnes	First Division
2006	Steven Gerrard	FA Cup, European Super Cup

PFA YOUNG PLAYER OF THE YEAR

1983	Ian Rush	First Division, League Cup, Charity Shield
1995	Robbie Fowler	League Cup
1996	Robbie Fowler	
1998	Michael Owen	
2001	Steven Gerrard	FA Cup, League Cup, UEFA Cup

EUROPEAN FOOTBALLER OF THE YEAR

2001	Michael Owen	FA Cup, League Cup, UEFA Cup

MANAGER OF THE YEAR

1973	Bill Shankly	First Division, UEFA Cup
1976	Bob Paisley	First Division, UEFA Cup
1977	Bob Paisley	First Division, European Cup, European Super Cup, Charity Shield
1979	Bob Paisley	First Division
1980	Bob Paisley	First Division, Charity Shield
1982	Bob Paisley	First Division, League Cup
1983	Bob Paisley	First Division, League Cup, Charity Shield
1984	Joe Fagan	First Division, League Cup, European Cup
1986	Kenny Dalglish	First Division, FA Cup
1988	Kenny Dalglish	First Division
1990	Kenny Dalglish	First Division, Charity Shield

PLAYER WITH MOST MEDALS

20	Phil Neal (8 League, 1 FA Cup runner-up, 4 League Cup, 1 runner-up, 5 European, 1 runner-up)

NATIONALITIES

With Liverpool being given the green light to complete the signing of Mark Gonzalez during the summer of 2006, there is set to be a further addition to the list of nationalites to have represented the Reds. Indeed, the South African-born Chile international is not the only first - full-back Fabio Aurelio will become the first Brazilian to play for the club, while Argentine defender Gabriel Paletta will also be added to the list.

Below is a comprehensive list of those players to have represented Liverpool in a first-team game:

COUNTRIES REPRESENTED	PLAYERS
Argentina	Mauricio Pellegrino
Australia	Harry Kewell
Cameroon	Rigobert Song
Croatia	Igor Biscan
Czech Republic	Patrik Berger, Vladimir Smicer, Milan Baros
Denmark	Jan Molby, Jorgen Nielsen, Torben Piechnik, Daniel Agger
Finland	Sami Hyypia, Jari Litmanen
France	Jean-Michel Ferri, Pegguy Arphexad, Bernard Diomede, Gregory Vignal, Nicolas Anelka, Bruno Cheyrou, Patrice Luzi, Anthony Le Tallec, Florent Sinama-Pongolle, Djibril Cisse
Germany	Karlheinz Riedle, Dietmar Hamann, Markus Babbel, Christian Ziege, Sean Dundee
Guinea	Titi Camara
Holland	Erik Meijer, Sander Westerveld, Bolo Zenden, Jan Kromkamp
Hungary	Istvan Kozma
Israel	Avi Cohen, Ronny Rosenthal
Mali	Djimi Traore, Mohammed Sissoko
Norway	Stig Inge Bjornebye, Oyvind Leonhardsen, Bjorn Tore Kvarme, Vegard Heggem, Frode Kippe, John Arne Riise
Poland	Jerzy Dudek
Portugal	Abel Xavier
Senegal	El-Hadji Diouf, Salif Diao
South Africa	Lance Carr, Hugh Gerhadi, Gordon Hodgson, Dirk Kemp, Berry Nieuwenhuys, Robert Priday, Arthur Riley, Doug Rudham, Charlie Thompson, Harman Van Den Berg
Spain	Josemi, Luis Garcia, Xabi Alonso, Antonio Nunez, Fernando Morientes, Jose Reina, Antonio Barragan
Sweden	Glenn Hysen
Switzerland	Stephane Henchoz
USA	Brad Friedel, Zak Whitbread
Zimbabwe	Bruce Grobbelaar

* Note Craig Johnston (born in South Africa) represented England at 'B' and U21 level and has not been included – likewise John Barnes (born in Jamaica) played for England.

Top 5 capped Liverpool players

England
60	Michael Owen
59	Emlyn Hughes
56	Ray Clemence
50	Phil Neal
48	John Barnes

Scotland
55	Kenny Dalglish
37	Graeme Souness
28	Billy Liddell
27	Steve Nicol
26	Alan Hansen

Wales
67	Ian Rush
26	John Toshack
18	Joey Jones
16	Maurice Parry
10	Ernest Peake

Northern Ireland (3 players only)
27	Elisha Scott
12	Billy Lacey
3	David McMullen

Republic of Ireland
51	Ronnie Whelan
38	Steve Staunton
34	Ray Houghton
33	Steve Heighway
25	Phil Babb

**Michael Owen: Most capped Liverpool player
to represent England at international level**

**Emlyn Hughes
and Kenny
Dalglish, on
opposite sides
for England
and Scotland**

WORLD CUP REDS

With last summer's World Cup in Germany boasting no less than nine Liverpool-registered players in action in the finals, the tournament provided the club with their biggest-ever tally of players on the world stage. The following list looks at the players who have previously played in the finals, beginning in 1950 with Lawrence Hughes.

1950 - BRAZIL Lawrence Hughes (England)

| | STATISTICS | | | |
	Played	Starts	Sub	Goals
Hughes	3	3	0	0

Despite beating Chile 2-0 in their first group game, subsequent 1-0 defeats to USA and group winners Spain saw England bow out early - the defeat to the Americans seen as one of the most embarrassing the country has ever experienced.
26-year-old Hughes, a centre-back, played in all 3 games having not played for England before the finals in Brazil.

1958 - SWEDEN Alan A'Court (England), Tommy Younger (Scotland)

| | STATISTICS | | | |
	P	Starts	Sub	Goals
A'Court	3	3	0	0
Younger	2	2	0	0

A'Court played in three of England's four games at outside left. The 23-year-old had scored in his only previous England appearance before the finals - although he failed to score in Sweden.
A'Court came in after Tom Finney was injured following the 2-2 draw with USSR in England's first game. Subsequent matches were against Brazil (0-0), Austria (2-2) and USSR again, this time going down 1-0.
Liverpool goalkeeper Younger captained Scotland in their first two games against Yugoslavia (1-1) and Paraguay (2-3), winning the last of his 24 international caps against the South Americans, although he was subsequently left out of the final group game, a 2-1 defeat to France.

1962 - CHILE Roger Hunt (England)

With one cap and one goal to his name, Hunt was included in the squad to travel to Chile. However, the 23-year-old failed to make an appearance, with England having played Hungary (1-2), Argentina (3-1), Bulgaria (0-0) and Brazil (1-3).

1966 - ENGLAND Roger Hunt, Gerald Byrne, Ian Callaghan (England)

| | STATISTICS | | | |
	P	St	Sb	Gls
Byrne	0	0	0	0
Callaghan	1	1	0	0
Hunt	6	6	0	3

1966 - ENGLAND (continued)

An integral member of the 1966 World Cup-winning side, Hunt played in all six games as England took the trophy, scoring three goals to add to his 12 goals in 13 appearances before then.
Of the other Liverpool trio, Callaghan replaced Terry Paine in the 2-0 victory over France in England's final group game - a match that saw Hunt score both goals (Hunt's other goal came in the previous group game - a 2-0 defeat of Mexico).
Gerald Byrne meanwhile never saw any action, the left-back being understudy to the ever-present Everton man Ray Wilson.
Incidentally, the selection process meant other Liverpool players were in contention for the squad up to eight days before the finals began. FIFA required that each national side provide a list of 40 players before the end of May 1966, and the final squad of 22 by July 3 - with these 22 not needing to have been whittled down from the original 40.
Manager Alf Ramsey named his provisional list of 40 in early April, to give as much notice as possible to the affected clubs.
The 40 included Chris Lawler, Gordon Milne, Tommy Smith and Peter Thompson.
A month later Ramsey announced a list of 28 who, of the 40, included Milne and Thompson. The duo were cut on June 18 - although asked to remain in training at Melwood in the event of an emergency.

Liverpool striker Roger Hunt in action during the 1966 World Cup final

1970 - MEXICO   Emlyn Hughes (England)

The 22-year-old failed to add to his six England caps in Mexico, who along with Manchester United duo Alex Stepney and Nobby Stiles, were the only players not to make an appearance.

1974 - WEST GERMANY   Peter Cormack (Scotland)

The 27-year-old was squad No 15 in West Germany - but never made an appearance as the Scots bowed out at the first-round stage despite not losing a game.

WORLD CUP REDS

1978 - ARGENTINA   Kenny Dalglish, Graeme Souness (Scotland)

STATISTICS

	P	St	Sb	Gls
Dalglish	3	3	0	1
Souness	1	1	0	0

Kenny Dalglish played the whole game against Peru in Argentina, a 3-1 defeat. He was taken off in the second half of the 1-1 draw v Iran, but scored the first goal in the 3-2 victory over Holland - when Graeme Souness made his first appearance. But it was not enough...

1982 - SPAIN   Terry McDermott, Phil Neal, Phil Thompson (England); Graeme Souness, Alan Hansen, Kenny Dalglish (Scotland)

STATISTICS

	P	St	Sb	Gls
Neal	2	1	1	0
McDermott	0	0	0	0
Thompson	5	5	0	0
Dalglish	2	1	1	1
Hansen	3	3	0	0
Souness	3	3	0	1

Phil Thompson, having been overlooked to captain England in Spain (with Mick Mills taking the captaincy), played every minute of the finals, mainly partnering Terry Butcher at the heart of the defence. Phil Neal made two appearances (a brief sub appearance against France and a start against Kuwait), while there was disappointment for Terry McDermott, who failed to add to his 25 England caps. Incidentally, excepting Kevin Keegan and the three goalkeepers, manager Ron Greenwood assigned squad numbers according to the alphabetical order of their surnames. Thus McDermott was No 10, Neal No 14 and Thompson No 18.

Scotland included all three Liverpool players in their side for their opening victory, a 5-2 defeat of New Zealand, with Kenny Dalglish netting the first while future player John Wark netted a brace. Three days later Brazil proved too strong in a 4-1 victory despite Scotland taking the lead, although Dalglish could only make the bench - coming on in the second half. Dalglish was left out for the final group game, a 2-2 draw with USSR which saw skipper Souness level three minutes from time.

Kenny Dalglish on target against Holland in the 1978 World Cup

1986 - MEXICO   Steve Nicol (Scotland)

	P	St	Sb	Gls
	STATISTICS			
Nicol	3	3	0	0

Liverpool's only representative at the 1986 World Cup, Nicol played all three group games, being subbed in the latter two, a 2-1 defeat to eventual runners-up West Germany and the 0-0 draw against Uruguay. Incidentally Graeme Souness, then of Sampdoria, skippered the side in the first two games but missed the final group game.

1990 - ITALY   Peter Beardsley, John Barnes, Steve McMahon (England); Gary Gillespie (Scotland); Steve Staunton, Ronnie Whelan, Ray Houghton (Eire); Glenn Hysen (Sweden)

	P	St	Sb	Gls
	STATISTICS			
Barnes	5	5	0	0
Beardsley	5	3	2	0
McMahon	4	3	1	0
Gillespie	1	0	1	0
Houghton	5	5	0	0
Staunton	5	5	0	0
Whelan	1	0	1	0
Hysen	2	2	0	0

Italia '90 proved a mixed tournament for Liverpool's English trio. Beardsley started three games and was a sub for two, failing to find the target. John Barnes started the first five games but was substituted in the last two, missing the semi-final against West Germany due to injury and being absent for the third-place play-off against the hosts. McMahon started three games but his only sub appearance, in the first game against the Republic of Ireland, saw him give the ball away before former Reds reserve Kevin Sheedy rifled home the equaliser in a 1-1 draw. He was also booked soon after.

Ray Houghton and Steve Staunton started against England, Egypt and Holland in the group games, while Ronnie Whelan came on as a sub in that vital third match against the Dutch. In the second round against Romania, the 0-0 draw saw Staunton substituted in extra time while Houghton played the 120 minutes. The penalty shootout saw Houghton on target as the Republic claimed a last-eight berth although Italy proved a step too far.

Gary Gillespie was a member of the Scotland squad, but made only one appearance as a first-half sub for the injured Murdo McLeod in the final group game, a 1-0 defeat to Brazil. In the same group, Glenn Hysen played and captained Sweden in their last two group games in a dire campaign for the Swedes, who lost each game. He played in 2-1 defeats to Scotland and Costa Rica.

1994 - USA   Ronnie Whelan (Eire); Stig Inge Bjornebye (Norway)

	P	St	Sb	Gls
	STATISTICS			
Whelan	1	0	1	0
Bjornebye	3	3	0	0

Ronnie Whelan was included in the Republic of Ireland squad four years later, but was again a peripheral figure. Former Red Ray Houghton scored the winner as they stunned Italy in the opening game, with Steve Staunton, Phil Babb, Jason McAteer and John Aldridge also in the squad. Whelan came on as a sub in the 0-0 draw with Norway that booked a second-round berth against Holland, with Stig Inge Bjornebye in the Norway side (he was an ever-present).

WORLD CUP REDS

1998 - FRANCE   Paul Ince, Steve McManaman, Michael Owen (England); Stig Inge
Bjornebye, Oyvind Leonhardsen (Norway); Brad Friedel (USA)

STATISTICS			
	P	St	Sb	Gls
Ince	4	4	0	0
McManaman	1	0	1	0
Owen	4	2	2	2
Bjornebye	4	4	0	0
Leonhardsen	3	3	0	0
Friedel	1	1	0	0

Michael Owen rose to prominence in France, after only one full season in the Reds first team.
Having only been on the bench for the first two games - against Tunisia and Romania, where he
found the target - the 18-year-old played in England's other two matches, including the memorable
second-round exit to Argentina, where he netted a fine solo goal as well as a penalty in the losing
shootout.
Just 17 minutes as a sub in the 2-0 defeat of Colombia was Steve McManaman's World Cup while
Paul Ince started each game, going off injured against Romania although he missed a penalty in
the shootout defeat to the South American side.
Of the other World Cup participants, Norway's Stig Inge Bjornebye was an ever-present as his
county bowed out in the second round to Italy while Oyvind Leonhardsen missed only one game
(both played in their final group game, a 2-1 victory over Brazil which earned them a place in the
last 16). Brad Friedel played once for the USA in their final group game against Yugoslavia (0-1) as
they bowed out in the first round.

2002 - JAPAN/S. KOREA   Michael Owen, Emile Heskey (England); Dietmar Hamann (Germany);
Jerzy Dudek (Poland); Abel Xavier (Portugal).

STATISTICS			
	P	St	Sb	Gls
Owen	5	5	0	2
Heskey	5	5	0	1
Hamann	6	6	0	0
Diouf	5	5	0	0
Dudek	2	2	0	0
Xavier	1	0	1	0

Both Steven Gerrard and his replacement, Danny Murphy, were forced to miss the finals due to
injury, leaving forwards Heskey and Owen to fly the red flag. Both started all five games, with the
former scoring against Denmark and Owen netting twice, against Denmark - where he also went
off injured - and against Brazil in the 2-1 quarter-final defeat.
The main success story was Dietmar Hamann, who missed only one game and became the first
Liverpool player since Roger Hunt in 1966 to play in a World Cup final, Germany going down to a
2-0 defeat to favourites Brazil.
Forward El-Hadji Diouf had been signed from Lens before the tournament and despite not scoring,
he helped inspire Senegal to the quarter-finals.
There was disappointment for both Jerzy Dudek and Abel Xavier, who both had disappointing
tournaments as their respective countries fell at the first hurdle, while Salif Diao (Senegal) had not
signed a contract with the Reds until after the finals.

Michael Owen celebrates his goal in the 3-0 victory over Denmark at the 2002 World Cup

2006 - GERMANY   Steven Gerrard, Jamie Carragher, Peter Crouch, Scott Carson
(England); Jose Reina, Xabi Alonso, Luis Garcia (Spain); Harry Kewell
(Australia); Jan Kromkamp (Holland)

STATISTICS

	P	St	Sb	Gls
Carragher	4	2	2	0
Crouch	4	2	2	1
Gerrard	5	4	1	2
Carson	0	0	0	0
Alonso	3	3	0	1
Garcia	3	2	1	0
Reina	0	0	0	0
Kewell	3	2	1	1
Kromkamp	0	0	0	0

Liverpool's biggest-ever England contingent in a World Cup, with Steven Gerrard involved in every
game including the quarter-final exit. Gerrard and Crouch scored the goals in the 2-0 group win
over Trinidad & Tobago, with Gerrard also on target in the 2-2 group draw with Sweden.
Unfortunately Gerrard and Carragher failed to score in the vital shootout defeat to Portugal, while
Scott Carson was third-choice goalkeeper.
Xabi Alonso and Luis Garcia were integral to Spain's hopes, both players being rested for their third
group game against Saudi Arabia when they had already qualified. Alonso scored his first
international goal in the 4-0 demolition of Ukraine, although they were helpless as eventual
runners-up France (for whom Djibril Cisse missed out through injury) won their second-round
clash 3-1. Jose Reina was in the squad as a back-up keeper.
In Australia's first World Cup since 1974, Harry Kewell scored the vital equaliser against Croatia in
their final group game, a 2-2 draw although injury ruled him out of the second-round game with
eventual winners Italy (0-1). Incidentally Jan Kromkamp was an unused Holland squad member.

ARSENAL

FINAL STANDINGS 05-06

		W	D	L	PTS
3	Liverpool	25	7	6	82
4	**Arsenal**	**20**	**7**	**11**	**67**
5	Tottenham	18	11	9	65

ALL-TIME RECORD

(League matches only)

	PL	W	D	L
Home:	82	47	14	21
Away:	82	20	26	36
Overall:	164	67	40	57

LAST 2 MEETINGS

12/03/2006

Arsenal	2-1	Liverpool
Henry 21, 83		Garcia 76

14/02/2006

Liverpool	1-0	Arsenal
Garcia 87		

CLUB DETAILS

Nickname: The Gunners
Ground: Emirates Stadium, capacity 60,000
Manager: Arsene Wenger (app. 30/09/96)
Assistant: Pat Rice
Year formed: 1886

USEFUL INFORMATION

Website: www.arsenal.com
Address: Emirates Stadium, Avenell Road, Highbury, London N5 1BU
Switchboard: 0207 704 4000

TRAVEL INFORMATION

By Train: The nearest underground stations are Arsenal and Holloway Road (Piccadilly line); Finsbury Park (Piccadilly) and Highbury & Islington (Victoria) are also within walking distance.

By Bus: Main bus stops are located on Holloway Road, Nag's Head, Seven Sisters Road, Blackstock Road and Highbury Corner. Regular services will take you to within 10 minutes walk of the ground.

ASTON VILLA

FINAL STANDINGS 05-06

		W	D	L	PTS
15	Man City	13	4	21	43
16	**Aston Villa**	**10**	**12**	**16**	**42**
17	Portsmouth	10	8	20	38

ALL-TIME RECORD

(League matches only)

	PL	W	D	L
Home:	81	51	16	14
Away:	81	25	19	37
Overall:	162	76	35	51

LAST 2 MEETINGS

29/04/2006

Liverpool	3-1	Aston Villa
Morientes 4, Gerrard 61, 66		Barry 58

05/11/2005

Aston Villa	0-2	Liverpool
		Gerrard 85 (p), Alonso 89

CLUB DETAILS

Nickname: The Villans
Ground: Villa Park, capacity 42,584
Manager: Martin O'Neill (app. 05/08/06)
Assistant: John Robertson
Year formed: 1874

USEFUL INFORMATION

Website: www.avfc.co.uk
Address: Villa Park, Trinity Road, Birmingham B6 6HE
Switchboard: 0121 327 2299

TRAVEL INFORMATION

By Train: Trains run from Birmingham New Street to either Aston or Witton station (10-15 minute journey). Witton is nearer, only a few minutes walk from the ground.

By Bus: The number 7 runs from Birmingham City Centre directly to the ground, while numbers 11a and 11c also serve Villa Park.

BLACKBURN ROVERS

FINAL STANDINGS 05-06

		W	D	L	PTS
5	Tottenham	18	11	9	65
6	**Blackburn**	**19**	**6**	**13**	**63**
7	Newcastle	17	7	14	58

ALL-TIME RECORD

(League matches only)

	PL	W	D	L
Home:	58	34	15	9
Away:	58	14	20	24
Overall:	116	48	35	33

LAST 2 MEETINGS

16/04/2006

Blackburn Rovers 0-1	Liverpool
	Fowler 29

15/10/2005

Liverpool	1-0	Blackburn Rovers
Cisse 75		

CLUB DETAILS

Nickname:	Rovers
Ground:	Ewood Park, capacity 31,367
Manager:	Mark Hughes (app. 15/09/04)
Assistant:	Mark Bowen
Year formed:	1875

USEFUL INFORMATION

Website:	www.rovers.co.uk
Address:	Ewood Park, Blackburn, Lancashire BB2 4JF
Switchboard:	08701 123232

TRAVEL INFORMATION

By Train: Blackburn Station is 1 1/2 miles away, while Mill Hill is 1 mile from the stadium.

By Bus: The central bus station is next to the railway station. Services 1, 3 and 225 all go from Stand N to Ewood Park. From Stand M a Darwen-bound bus passes near the ground, which is under 2 miles away.

BOLTON WANDERERS

FINAL STANDINGS 05-06

		W	D	L	PTS
7	Newcastle	17	7	14	58
8	**Bolton**	**15**	**11**	**12**	**56**
9	West Ham	16	7	15	55

ALL-TIME RECORD

(League matches only)

	PL	W	D	L
Home:	53	27	16	10
Away:	53	16	13	24
Overall:	106	43	29	34

LAST 2 MEETINGS

09/04/2006

Liverpool	1-0	Bolton Wanderers
Fowler 45		

02/01/2005

Bolton Wanderers 2-2	Liverpool
Jaidi 10, Diouf 71	Gerrard (p) 67, Garcia 82

CLUB DETAILS

Nickname:	The Trotters
Ground:	Reebok Stadium, capacity 28,000
Manager:	Sam Allardyce (app. 19/10/99)
Assistant:	Sammy Lee
Year formed:	1874

USEFUL INFORMATION

Website:	www.bwfc.co.uk
Address:	Reebok Stadium, Burnden Way, Lostock, Bolton BL6 6JW
Switchboard:	01204 673673

TRAVEL INFORMATION

By Train: Horwich Parkway Station serves the stadium, with regular trains from Bolton Station.

By Bus: The club run buses from Bolton town centre, while the number 539 bus runs directly to the ground.

CHARLTON ATHLETIC

FINAL STANDINGS 05-06

		W	D	L	PTS
12	Fulham	14	6	18	48
13	**Charlton**	**13**	**8**	**17**	**47**
14	Middlesboro	12	9	17	45

ALL-TIME RECORD

(League matches only)

	PL	W	D	L
Home:	27	16	5	6
Away:	27	12	2	13
Overall:	54	28	7	19

LAST 2 MEETINGS

04/03/2006

Liverpool	0-0	Charlton Athletic

08/02/2006

Charlton Athletic	2-0	Liverpool

D. Bent (p) 42,
Young 45

CLUB DETAILS

Nickname: Addicks
Ground: The Valley, capacity 27,100
Head Coach: Iain Dowie (app. 30/05/06)
Assistant: Les Reed
Year formed: 1905

USEFUL INFORMATION

Website: www.cafc.co.uk
Address: The Valley, Floyd Road, Charlton, London SE7 8BL
Switchboard: 0208 333 4000

TRAVEL INFORMATION

By Train: Frequent London services depart from Charing Cross, Waterloo East and London Bridge to Charlton Station. North Greenwich (Jubilee line) is a short bus ride from the ground. From Kent, some services come through Dartford to Charlton.
By Bus: Numerous routes serve the ground including the 53, 54, 161, 177, 180, 422, 472 and the 486.

CHELSEA

FINAL STANDINGS 05-06

		W	D	L	PTS
1	**Chelsea**	**29**	**4**	**5**	**91**
2	Man Utd	25	8	5	83
3	Liverpool	25	7	6	82

ALL-TIME RECORD

(League matches only)

	PL	W	D	L
Home:	63	42	13	8
Away:	63	15	13	35
Overall:	126	57	26	43

LAST 2 MEETINGS (LEAGUE)

05/02/2006

Chelsea	2-0	Liverpool

Gallas 35, Crespo 68

02/10/2005

Liverpool	1-4	Chelsea

Gerrard 36 — Lampard (p) 27, Duff 43, Cole 63, Geremi 82

CLUB DETAILS

Nickname: The Blues
Ground: Stamford Bridge, capacity 42,360
Manager: Jose Mourinho (app. 02/06/04)
Assistants: Steve Clarke/Baltemar Brito
Year formed: 1905

USEFUL INFORMATION

Website: www.chelseafc.com
Address: Stamford Bridge, Fulham Road, London SW6 1HS
Switchboard: 0870 300 1212

TRAVEL INFORMATION

By Train: Fulham Broadway (tube) is on the District Line, around 5 minutes walk. The nearest overground station is West Brompton, which is served by trains from Clapham Junction.
By Bus: Numbers 14, 414 and 211 go along Fulham Road. The 11, 14, 28, 211, 295, 391, 414 and 424 all stop near the stadium.

EVERTON

FINAL STANDINGS 05-06

		W	D	L	PTS
10	Wigan	15	6	17	51
11	**Everton**	**14**	**8**	**16**	**50**
12	Fulham	14	6	18	48

ALL-TIME RECORD

(League matches only)

	PL	W	D	L
Home:	87	37	27	23
Away:	87	28	27	32
Overall:	174	65	54	55

LAST 2 MEETINGS

25/03/2006

Liverpool	3-1	Everton
Neville (og) 45, Garcia 47, Kewell 84		Cahill 61

28/12/2005

Everton	1-3	Liverpool
Beattie 42		Crouch 11, Gerrard 18, Cisse 47

CLUB DETAILS

Nickname:	The Toffees
Ground:	Goodison Park, capacity 40,260
Manager:	David Moyes (app. 15/03/02)
Assistant:	Alan Irvine
Year formed:	1878

USEFUL INFORMATION

Website:	www.evertonfc.com
Address:	Goodison Park, Goodison Road, Liverpool L4 4EL
Switchboard:	0151 330 2200

TRAVEL INFORMATION

By Train: From Liverpool Central, take any train heading for Ormskirk or Kirkby and get off at Kirkdale - from there it is a 10-minute walk.

By Bus: From Queen's Square Bus Station in Liverpool city centre, numbers 1, 2, 19, 20, 311, 345 and 350 go past the stadium.

FULHAM

FINAL STANDINGS 05-06

		W	D	L	PTS
11	Everton	14	8	16	50
12	**Fulham**	**14**	**6**	**18**	**48**
13	Charlton	13	8	17	47

ALL-TIME RECORD

(League matches only)

	PL	W	D	L
Home:	19	14	5	0
Away:	19	7	6	6
Overall:	38	21	11	6

LAST 2 MEETINGS

15/03/2006

Liverpool	5-1	Fulham
Fowler 16, Brown (og) 34, Morientes 71, Crouch 89, Warnock 90		John 25

22/10/2005

Fulham	2-0	Liverpool
John 30, Boa Morte 90		

CLUB DETAILS

Nickname:	Cottagers
Ground:	Craven Cottage, capacity 22,000
Manager:	Chris Coleman (app. 17/04/03)
Assistant:	Steve Kean
Year formed:	1879

USEFUL INFORMATION

Website:	www.fulhamfc.com
Address:	Craven Cottage, Stevenage Road, Fulham, London SW6 6HH
Switchboard:	0870 442 1222

TRAVEL INFORMATION

By Train: Alight at Putney Bridge (District line). Turn left out of station and right down Ranleigh Gardens. At the end of the road (before the Eight Bells pub) turn left into Willow Bank and right through the underpass into Bishops Park. Walk along river to ground (note park is closed after evening games).

By Bus: The numbers 74 and 220 both run along Fulham Palace Road.

MANCHESTER CITY

FINAL STANDINGS 05-06

		W	D	L	PTS
14	Middlesboro	12	9	17	45
15	**Man City**	**13**	**4**	**21**	**43**
16	Aston Villa	10	12	16	42

ALL-TIME RECORD

(League matches only)

	PL	W	D	L
Home:	70	43	14	13
Away:	70	28	18	24
Overall:	140	71	32	37

LAST 2 MEETINGS

26/02/2006

Liverpool	1-0	Manchester City
Kewell 40		

26/11/2005

Manchester City	0-1	Liverpool
		Riise 61

CLUB DETAILS

Nickname: Blues/The Citizens
Ground: City of Manchester Stadium, capacity 48,000
Manager: Stuart Pearce (app. 11/03/05)
First-team coach: Derek Fazackerley
Year formed: 1887

USEFUL INFORMATION

Website: www.mcfc.co.uk
Address: City of Manchester Stadium, Sportcity, Rowsley Street, Manchester M11 3FF
Switchboard: 0870 062 1894

TRAVEL INFORMATION

By Train: The nearest station is Ashburys (a 10-minute walk), which is a five-minute train ride from Manchester Piccadilly (which itself is a 20-25 minute walk).
By Bus: Numbers 216 and 217 are the main services from the city centre, but 185, 186, 230, 231, 232, 233, 234, 235, 236, 237, X36 and X37 also run here.

MANCHESTER UNITED

FINAL STANDINGS 05-06

		W	D	L	PTS
1	Chelsea	29	4	5	91
2	**Man Utd**	**25**	**8**	**5**	**83**
3	Liverpool	25	7	6	82

ALL-TIME RECORD

(League matches only)

	PL	W	D	L
Home:	73	35	18	20
Away:	73	14	25	34
Overall:	146	49	43	54

LAST 2 MEETINGS

22/01/2006

Manchester Utd	1-0	Liverpool
Ferdinand 90		

18/09/2005

Liverpool	0-0	Manchester Utd

CLUB DETAILS

Nickname: Red Devils
Ground: Old Trafford, capacity 74,800
Manager: Sir Alex Ferguson (app. 06/11/86)
Assistant: Carlos Queiroz
Year formed: 1878

USEFUL INFORMATION

Website: www.manutd.com
Address: Old Trafford, Manchester M16 0RA
Switchboard: 0870 442 1994

TRAVEL INFORMATION

By Train: Special services run from Manchester Piccadilly to the clubs own railway station. There is also a Metrolink service, with the station located next to Lancashire County Cricket Club on Warwick Road, which leads up to Sir Matt Busby Way.
By Bus: Numbers 114, 230, 252 and 253 all run from the city centre to the ground.

MIDDLESBROUGH

FINAL STANDINGS 05-06

		W	D	L	PTS
13	Charlton	13	8	17	47
14	**Middlesbro**	**12**	**9**	**17**	**45**
15	Man City	13	4	21	43

ALL-TIME RECORD

(League matches only)

	PL	W	D	L
Home:	64	34	17	13
Away:	64	20	20	24
Overall:	128	54	37	37

LAST 2 MEETINGS (LEAGUE)

10/12/2005

Liverpool	2-0	Middlesbrough
Morientes 72, 77		

13/08/2005

Middlesbrough	0-0	Liverpool

CLUB DETAILS

Nickname:	Boro
Ground:	Riverside Stadium, capacity 35,100
Manager:	Gareth Southgate (app. 07/06/06)
Assistant:	Steve Round
Year formed:	1876

USEFUL INFORMATION

Website:	www.mfc.co.uk
Address:	Riverside Stadium, Middlesbrough, Cleveland TS3 6RS
Switchboard:	0870 421 1986

TRAVEL INFORMATION

By Train: Middlesbrough Station is about 15 minutes walk from the stadium, served by trains from Darlington. Take the back exit from the station, turn right then after a couple of minutes right again into Wynward Way for the ground.

By Bus: Numbers 36, 37 and 38 go from the town centre close to the ground.

NEWCASTLE UNITED

FINAL STANDINGS 05-06

		W	D	L	PTS
6	Blackburn	19	6	13	63
7	**Newcastle**	**17**	**7**	**14**	**58**
8	Bolton	15	11	12	56

ALL-TIME RECORD

(League matches only)

	PL	W	D	L
Home:	71	46	14	11
Away:	71	20	23	28
Overall:	142	66	37	39

LAST 2 MEETINGS

19/03/2006

Newcastle	1-3	Liverpool
Ameobi 41		Crouch 10, Gerrard 35, Cisse (p) 52

26/12/2005

Liverpool	2-0	Newcastle
Gerrard 14, Crouch 43		

CLUB DETAILS

Nickname:	Magpies
Ground:	St James' Park, capacity 52,387
Manager:	Glenn Roeder (app. 16/05/06)
Assistant:	Kevin Bond
Year formed:	1881

USEFUL INFORMATION

Website:	www.nufc.co.uk
Address:	St James' Park, Newcastle- upon-Tyne NE1 4ST
Switchboard:	0191 201 8400

TRAVEL INFORMATION

By Train: St James' Park is a 10-minute walk from Newcastle Central Station. The stadium is also served by its own Metro station (St James' Metro).

By Bus: Any bus from the town centre heading towards Gallowgate. Numbers 36, 36B, 71, 87 and 88 run from Berwick Street, opposite the station.

PORTSMOUTH

FINAL STANDINGS 05-06

		W	D	L	PTS
16	Aston Villa	10	12	16	42
17	**Portsmouth**	**10**	**8**	**20**	**38**
18	Birmingham	8	10	20	34

ALL-TIME RECORD

(League matches only)

	PL	W	D	L
Home:	26	13	9	4
Away:	26	8	4	14
Overall:	52	21	13	18

LAST 2 MEETINGS (LEAGUE)

07/05/2006

Portsmouth	1-3	Liverpool
Koroman 85		Fowler 52, Crouch 84, Cisse 89

19/11/2005

Liverpool	3-0	Portsmouth
Zenden 23, Cisse 39, Morientes 80		

CLUB DETAILS

Nickname: Pompey
Ground: Fratton Park, capacity 20,200
Manager: Harry Redknapp (app. 07/12/05)
Assistant: Tony Adams
Year formed: 1898

USEFUL INFORMATION

Website: www.pompeyfc.co.uk
Address: Fratton Park,
Frogmore Road,
Portsmouth,
Hants PO4 8RA
Switchboard: 0239 273 1204

TRAVEL INFORMATION

By Train: Fratton Station is a 10-minute walk from the ground - on arrival by train you pass the ground on your left. Portsmouth Station is at least a 25-minute walk.
By Bus: 3, 13, 14, 16a, 24, 27 and 57 all run to Fratton Station

READING

FINAL C'SHIP STANDINGS 05-06

		W	D	L	PTS
1	**Reading**	**31**	**13**	**2**	**106**
2	Sheff Utd	26	12	8	90
3	Watford	22	15	9	81

ALL-TIME RECORD

(League matches only)

	PL	W	D	L
Home:	0	0	0	0
Away:	0	0	0	0
Overall:	0	0	0	0

LAST 2 MEETINGS (LEAGUE)

NONE

CLUB DETAILS

Nickname: The Royals
Ground: Madejski Stadium, capacity 24,225
Manager: Steve Coppell (app. 09/10/03)
Assistant: Kevin Dillon
Year formed: 1871

USEFUL INFORMATION

Website: www.readingfc.co.uk
Address: Madejski Stadium, Junction 11, M4, Reading, Berkshire RG2 0FL
Switchboard: 0118 968 1100

TRAVEL INFORMATION

By Train: Reading Central is 3 miles away - but could take over an hour on foot. From the station a bus service is available - outside the main entrance turn right and they should be about 200 yards down the road on the opposite side.
By Bus: The shuttle bus services (Number 79) are provided between the stadium and the station, running from 1pm on a Saturday (for 3pm kick-offs).

SHEFFIELD UNITED

FINAL C'SHIP STANDINGS 05-06

		W	D	L	PTS
1	Reading	31	13	2	106
2	Sheff Utd	26	12	8	90
3	Watford	22	15	9	81

ALL-TIME RECORD

(League matches only)

	PL	W	D	L
Home:	58	37	12	9
Away:	58	17	14	27
Overall:	116	54	26	36

LAST 2 MEETINGS

02/04/1994

Liverpool	1-2	Sheffield United
Rush 4		Flo 46, 72

26/12/1993

Sheffield United	0-0	Liverpool

CLUB DETAILS

Nickname: The Blades
Ground: Bramall Lane, capacity 30,936
Manager: Neil Warnock (app. 02/12/1999)
Assistant: Stuart McCall
Year formed: 1889

USEFUL INFORMATION

Website: www.sufc.co.uk
Address: Bramall Lane, Sheffield, South Yorkshire. S2 4SU
Switchboard: 0870 787 1960

TRAVEL INFORMATION

By Train: From Sheffield mainline station, it is a 10-15 minute walk. Turn left at the island in front of the station and continue down this street to the ground.
By Bus: From the Sheffield Interchange, services 47 and 48 will take you to Shoreham Street near the ground.

TOTTENHAM HOTSPUR

FINAL STANDINGS 05-06

		W	D	L	PTS
4	Arsenal	20	7	11	67
5	Tottenham	18	11	9	65
6	Blackburn	19	6	13	63

ALL-TIME RECORD

(League matches only)

	PL	W	D	L
Home:	63	40	18	5
Away:	63	18	15	30
Overall:	126	58	33	35

LAST 2 MEETINGS

14/01/2006

Liverpool	1-0	Tottenham H.
Kewell 59		

10/09/2005

Tottenham H.	0-0	Liverpool

CLUB DETAILS

Nickname: Spurs
Ground: White Hart Lane, capacity 36,240
Manager: Martin Jol (app. 05/11/04)
Assistant: Chris Hughton
Year formed: 1882

USEFUL INFORMATION

Website: www.spurs.co.uk
Address: 748 High Road, Tottenham, London N17 0AP
Switchboard: 0208 365 5000

TRAVEL INFORMATION

By Train: The nearest tube station is Seven Sisters (Victoria line), which is around a 25-minute walk. The nearest station is White Hart Lane, approx 5 minutes walk, on the Liverpool Street-Enfield Town line.
By Bus: Numbers 149, 259 and 279 all go along Tottenham High Road.

WATFORD

FINAL C'SHIP STANDINGS 05-06

		W	D	L	PTS
2	Sheffield Utd	26	12	8	90
3	**Watford**	**22**	**15**	**9**	**81**
4	Preston	20	20	6	80

ALL-TIME RECORD

(League matches only)

	PL	W	D	L
Home:	7	6	0	1
Away:	7	4	1	2
Overall:	14	10	1	3

LAST 2 MEETINGS (LEAGUE)

15/01/2000

Watford	2-3	Liverpool
Johnson 44,		Berger 10, Thompson 41,
Helguson 46		Smicer 71

14/08/1999

Liverpool	0-1	Watford
		Mooney 14

CLUB DETAILS

Nickname: The Hornets
Ground: Vicarage Road, capacity 22,000
Manager: Adrian Boothroyd (app. 29/03/05)
Assistant: Keith Burkinshaw
Year formed: 1881

USEFUL INFORMATION

Website: www.watfordfc.co.uk
Address: Vicarage Road Stadium, Watford, Hertforshire WD18 0ER
Switchboard: 01923 496000

TRAVEL INFORMATION

By Train: Watford High Street is a 10-minute walk away from the ground, while Watford Junction is about a 20-minute walk. There is also Watford tube station on the Metropolitan line, about 1 mile away.
By Bus: The No 7, 10 and 11 run from Market Street in the town centre to Vicarage Road.

WEST HAM UNITED

FINAL STANDINGS 05-06

		W	D	L	PTS
8	Bolton	15	11	12	56
9	**West Ham**	**16**	**7**	**15**	**55**
10	Wigan	15	6	17	51

ALL-TIME RECORD

(League matches only)

	PL	W	D	L
Home:	49	33	13	3
Away:	49	17	15	17
Overall:	98	50	28	20

LAST 2 MEETINGS (LEAGUE)

26/04/2006

West Ham	1-2	Liverpool
Reo-Coker 46		Cisse 19, 54

29/10/2005

Liverpool	2-0	West Ham
Alonso 18, Zenden 82		

CLUB DETAILS

Nickname: The Hammers
Ground: Upton Park, capacity 35,647
Manager: Alan Pardew (app. 20/10/03)
Assistant: Peter Grant
Year formed: 1895

USEFUL INFORMATION

Website: www.whufc.com
Address: Boleyn Ground, Green Street, Upton Park, London E13 9AZ
Switchboard: 0208 548 2748

TRAVEL INFORMATION

By Train: Upton Park is the closest tube station, around 45 minutes from Central London on the District (and also Hammersmith & City) line. When you exit the station turn right, the stadium is then a two-minute walk. East Ham and Plaistow Stations, which are further away, may also be worth using to avoid congestion after the match.
By Bus: Routes 5, 15, 58, 104, 115, 147, 330 and 376 all serve The Boleyn Ground.

WIGAN ATHLETIC

FINAL STANDINGS 05-06

		W	D	L	PTS
9	West Ham	16	7	15	55
10	**Wigan**	**15**	**6**	**17**	**51**
11	Everton	14	8	16	50

ALL-TIME RECORD

(League matches only)

	PL	W	D	L
Home:	1	1	0	0
Away:	1	1	0	0
Overall:	2	2	0	0

LAST 2 MEETINGS

11/02/2006

Wigan	0-1	Liverpool
		Hyypia 30

03/12/2006

Liverpool	3-0	Wigan
Crouch 19, 42, Garcia 70		

CLUB DETAILS

Nickname: The Latics
Ground: JJB Stadium, capacity 25,023
Manager: Paul Jewell (app. 12/06/01)
Assistant: Chris Hutchings
Year formed: 1932

USEFUL INFORMATION

Website: www.wiganlatics.co.uk
Address: JJB Stadium, Robin Park, Newtown, Wigan WN5 0UZ
Switchboard: 01942 774000

TRAVEL INFORMATION

By Train: Wigan Wallgate and Wigan North Western are a 20-minute walk from the stadium. From either station head under the railway bridge and keep to the right - following the road (A49) for 10 minutes. The complex should soon be visible.
By Bus: No particular route, as the venue is within easy distance of the station.

Watford's Vicarage Road - Liverpool make a Premiership return to Hertfordshire in January

LIVERPOOL FC 3 - ARSENAL

MATCH TIME 42 MINUTES

READ ME   ON/OFF

Choose match coverage type :

AUDIO COMMENTARY WITH WEBCAMS
▶ PLAY

AUDIO COMMENTARY WITH STILLS
▶ PLAY

AUDIO COMMENTARY ONLY
▶ PLAY

PRE-MATCH PRESS CONFERENCE
▶ PLAY

POST-MATCH PRESS CONFERENCE
▶ PLAY

WHATS NEW
LIVE MATCH COVERAGE
ALL MATCH ARCHIVE
CH 1 : PREMIERSHIP
CH 2 : EUROPE
CH 3 : OFF THE PITCH
CH 4 : FEATURES
CH 5 : RETRO
CH 6 : RESERVES & YOUTH
CH 7 : THE FANS
MY FAVOURITES

SEARCH | HELP

PLAYLIST

Chris's Selection

Title	Length	
	Clear All	X
Aston Villa	5m 13s	X
Rafa Press C	6m 13s	X
Leeds After	5m 13s	X
Goals	5m 13s	X
Example Clip	5m 13s	X
Total	7m 30 sec	

▶ PLAY CLIPS

SAVE PLAYLIST

LIVERPOOL FC   OPPOSITION   SUBS

MINUTE BY MINUTE   OTHER SCORES   OTHER INFO

BARCLAYS PREMIERSHIP - LATEST SCORES

Birmingham 2 - 1 Newcastle : Owen 89

Liverpool 3 - 0 Arsenal : Riise 87

Birmingham 1 - 0 Newcastle : Forseli 75

Liverpool 2 - 0 Arsenal : Kewell 60

Man City 5 - 2 Fulham : Pearce 54

Man City 4 - 2 Fulham : HT

Wigan 3 - 1 Portsmouth : HT

TICKETS

Address	Ticket Office,
	PO Box 204,
	Liverpool
	L69 4PQ

Telephone Numbers	24-Hour Ticket Information Line	0870 444 4949
	Credit Card Booking Line	0870 220 2151
	FA/League Cup Line	0870 220 0056
	European Line	0870 220 0034
	Away Ticket Line	0870 787 2000
	PTS Booking Line	0870 220 0408
	Customer Services	0870 220 2345
	Late Availability Line	0870 428 8687

Ticket Office Hours	Monday-Friday 8.15am-5.30pm
	Matchdays 9.15am to kick-off, then 15 minutes after end of game
	Non Match Saturdays/Sundays 9.15am-1.00pm

Prices	CAT B	CAT A
Kop	£30	£32
Over 65	£22.50	£24
Disabled and Visually Impaired	£24	£25.50
Main Stand	£32	£34
Over 65	£24	£25.50
Centenary	£32	£34
Over 65	£24	£25.50
Paddock	£32	£34
Over 65	£24	£25.50
Disabled and Visually Impaired	£24	£25.50
Anfield Road	£32	£34
Over 65	£24	£25.50
Combined 1 Adult/1 Child (16 or under)	£48	£51
Disabled and Visually Impaired	£24	£25.50

(Free for Disabled and Visually Impaired Assistants)

Category A matches

Arsenal, Aston Villa, Blackburn Rovers, Chelsea, Everton, Manchester City, Manchester United, Newcastle United and Tottenham Hotspur.

Family tickets

For adult/child combined tickets a ratio of two adults to one child, or two children to one adult is allowed. In the event that the number of children exceeds the ratio of 2:1 the additional tickets will be charged at the adult rate.

Buying tickets

General sales begin 18 days before a home fixture and are available through the credit card hotline (Monday-Friday 8.30am-5.30pm - a maximum of four tickets, minimum booking fee of 50p per ticket applies), postal application and for Fan Card holders, online (subject to a booking fee of £2.50 per ticket). A small number are often made available online on the date of general sale.

TICKETS

By post
State the match and number of tickets you require, with the correct remittance and a stamped addressed envelope, to LFC Ticket Office, PO Box 204, Liverpool L69 4PQ. You can pay by cheque, postal order, credit or debit card. Cheques must be made payable to Liverpool FC. If you want to pay by credit or debit card, include card number and expiry date, plus debit card issue number where applicable. If applications exceed the number of tickets, they will be allocated through a ballot.

By phone
You can apply for a maximum of four tickets, by calling the credit card hotline, quoting your credit or debit card number and expiry date. A minimum booking fee of 50p per ticket will be charged. Tickets booked more than three days before the match will be sent out by post, those booked after this must be collected from the credit card collections window at the ticket office, and you must produce the card used to book the tickets.

In person
Any remaining tickets will go on sale at the ticket office 11 days in advance. A maximum of four tickets may be purcased in one transaction (subject to change). However, tickets usually sell out through phone and postal bookings.

Away matches (Premiership)
Tickets go on sale first based on a priority system (i.e. to supporters who have attended the most away fixtures in the Premiership during season 2005/06 - and subsequently 2006/07). The number of matches attended will be determined from the information held on the ticket office database.

Cup matches
Ticket information concerning European and domestic Cup match allocations are made as soon as possible after each draw has taken place. Supporters are advised that they should quote their Fan Card number for all ticket purcahses, and to retain their ticket stubs for potential use for any additional fixtures allocated on a voucher system or in the ven of a home match being abandoned.

THE LFC FAN CARD

About the Fan Card
Fan Cards are used to record attendance and help prevent ticket fraud. If you do not have a Fan Card, you can purchase from the ticket office (for a one-off fee of £3.50 for a multi-season card). Season-ticket holders, Priority Ticket Scheme, Official Liverpool Supporters' Club and e-Season Ticket members all receive Fancard details automatically.

Buying Tickets
When purchasing tickets you must provide your Fan Card customer number either by handing your Fan Card to the ticket office, quoting it via the telephone booking line or by post, or using it to log in online. Further information may be requested for security reasons. Purchases made online will require your Fan Card customer number and password.
Only one ticket per match will be recorded on your Fan Card. If applying for tickets as a group it will be necessary for you to disclose each Fan Card customer number and the customer name.

What Happens If I Lose My Fan Card?
Please let the ticket office know immediately in writing. Your Fan Card will then be deactivated and a new Fan Card will be issued for a fee of £10. The data held on your lost or stolen Fan Card will be transferred onto your new Fan Card.

Should you change address, please inform the ticket office in writing, quoting your old address and enclosing a copy of a utility bill (gas, electric, water or telephone) to the ticket office.

GETTING TO ANFIELD

How to get there - by car
Follow the M62 until you reach the end of the motorway. Then follow the A5058 towards Liverpool for 3 miles, then turn left at the traffic lights into Utting Avenue (there is a McDonalds on the corner of this junction). Proceed for one mile and then turn right at The Arkles pub for the ground. It is recommended that you arrive at least two hours before kick-off in order to secure your parking spec. Otherwise, you can park in the streets around Goodison Park and walk across Stanley Park to Anfield, or you can park in a secure parking area at Goodison.

How to get there - by train
Kirkdale Station is the closest to Anfield (about a mile away), although Sandhills Station the stop before has the benefit of a bus service to the ground (Soccerbus). Both stations can be reached by first getting a train from Liverpool Lime Street (which is over 3 miles from the ground) to Liverpool Central (Merseyrail Northern Line), and then changing there for trains to Sandhills (2 stops away) or Kirkdale (3 stops). Note: only trains to Ormskirk or Kirkby go to Kirkdale station. A taxi from Liverpool Lime Street should cost between £5 and £7.

How to get there - Soccerbus
There are frequent shuttle buses from Sandhills Station, to Anfield for all Liverpool home Premiership and Cup matches. Soccerbus will run for two hours before each match (last bus from Sandhills Station is approximately 15 minutes before kick-off) and for 50 minutes after the final whistle (subject to availability). You can pay as you board the bus. Soccerbus is FREE for those who hold a valid TRIO, SOLO or SAVEAWAY ticket or Merseytravel Free Travel Pass.

How to get there - by bus
Take a 26 (or 27) from Paradise Street Bus Station or a 17B, 17C, 17D, or 217 from Queen Square bus station directly to the ground. The 68 and 168 which operate between Bootle and Aigburth and the 14 (from Queen Square) and 19 stop a short walk away.

How to get there - by air
Liverpool John Lennon Airport is around 10 miles from the ground, and taxis should be easily obtainable. Alternatively, you can catch the 80A bus to Garston Station and change at Sandhills for the Soccerbus service.

How to get there - on foot
From Kirkdale Station, turn right and then cross the railway bridge, where you will see the Melrose Abbey pub. Walk past up Westminster Road for around 1/3 of a mile before you arrive at the Elm Tree pub. Follow the road around the right-hand bend and then turn left into Bradwell Street. At the end of the road you will come to County Road (A59). Cross over at the traffic lights and then go down the road to the left of the Aldi superstore. At the end of this road you will reach Walton Lane (A580). You should be able to see Goodison Park on your left and Stanley Park in front of you. Cross Walton Lane and either enter Stanley Park, following the footpath through the park (keeping to the right) which will exit into Anfield Road. As an alternative to going through Stanley Park, bear right down Walton Lane and then turn left down the road at the end of Stanley Park to the ground.

To check bus and train times (8am-8pm, 7 days a week):

Traveline Merseyside   0870 608 2 608
Soccerbus   0151 330 1066

MUSEUM & STADIUM TOUR

The Museum tells the story of England's most successful football club from the early days right until the present. With the permanent addition of the Champions League trophy, which is surrounded by the sights and sounds of that glorious night in Istanbul, the Museum & Stadium Tour continues to bring in unprecedented numbers. This was followed last May by the greatest FA Cup final ever played, and the Museum can now boast the trophy, as well as the FA Youth Cup to the displays!

The Stadium Tour takes you behind the scenes at Anfield, visiting the dressing rooms, down the tunnel to the sound of the crowd, a chance to touch the famous 'This Is Anfield' sign and sit on the team bench.

Address:	Museum & Tour Centre, Anfield Road, Liverpool, L4 0TH
Telephone:	0151 260 6677 (bookings)
Opening times:	Daily 10.00-17.00 - last admission 16.00 or 1 hour before kick-off on matchdays. NO STADIUM TOURS ON MATCHDAYS (tours on day before a match will be MINI TOURS, at special reduced prices.
Prices	
Museum and Tour:	£10 adults, children & OAPs £6, family £25.00
Museum:	£5 adults, children & OAPs £3, family £13.00 (Contact club for family tickets)
Recommend:	Booking in advance for stadium tours - please arrive 15 minutes prior to tour. There is no need to pre-book a museum-only visit.
Facilities:	Disabled access, Gift shop, Parking, Toilets
Security Information:	We regret that we cannot accept suitcases and other large and bulky items into either the Museum or Stadium. There is no place to store such items in the ground.

Some of the sights on show at the club museum

WEBSITE

Launched in April 2001, liverpoolfc.tv has proved the most visited football club website in the world for the past five years and is currently one of the top 10 most popular sports sites in the world, with over 43 million page impressions a month. These are some of the reasons why:

News: All the latest official Reds news.

Match: Fixtures, results, match reports and expert analysis.

Shop: Order official LFC merchandise from the online store.

Interactive: Messageboards, games, fans gallery and downloads.

Mobile: Everything to get Anfield on your mobile!

Tickets: How to apply, availability and date of sales.

Team: Profiles of the first team, youth and reserves squads.

History: 1892 to the present, honours, trophies and legends. Everything you need to know about England's most successful football club.

Club: Includes all LFC-related initiatives and bodies.

Premium Content:

In order to enjoy 100% official audio and video coverage of Liverpool FC's 2006/07 campaign, you can sign up for an e-Season Ticket – the access-all-areas online pass.

For as little as 11p a day, e-Season Ticket brings the following unrivalled benefits and coverage at the click of a mouse:

* Live audio match coverage of all first-team matches.
* Highlights of all reserve-team matches.
* Extended highlights of all Liverpool's Premiership matches.
* Exclusive online messageboard with extended opening hours.
* Download every Premiership LFC goal scored since 2000.
* An exclusive weekly video interview with the manager.
* Watch press conferences in full.
* Brilliant retro clips of some of the club's greatest moments.
* Exclusive video interviews with first-team players.
* The complete '100 Days That Shook The Kop' video series.
* Exclusive video interviews with the Academy youngsters.
* The complete '100 Players Who Shook The Kop' video series.
* 500 tickets for each Premiership home game available to buy through a ballot, only for e-Season Ticket Holders.

Available to fans worldwide, you can pay by direct debit (UK only), credit card or cheque on a choice of monthly and annual payment plans. For more details or a FREE PREVIEW, visit:

http://www.liverpoolfc.tv/preview/

Website homepage (above, left) and the e-Season Ticket console (above, right)

CLUB STORES

Selling everything from the new replica kits to the latest toys and games, both club stores within Liverpool provide Reds fans with a wealth of souvenirs. With the new Adidas range having been unveiled, there remains a wealth of choice for the 2006/07 season.

Addresses and contact details are as follows:

Williamson Square Official Club Store
11 Williamson Square, Liverpool, L1 1EQ
United Kingdom
Tel +44 (0)151 330 3077
Opening times: Mon-Sat 9.00am - 5.30pm
Sundays 11.00am - 5.00pm

Anfield Official Club Store
Kop grandstand +44 (0)151 263 1760
Fax +44 (0)151 264 9088
Opening times Mon - Fri 9.00am - 5.00pm
Saturdays 9.00am - 5.00pm
Sundays 10.00am - 4.00pm
Match Saturdays 9.00am - 45 mins after game
Match Sundays 10.00am - 45 mins after game
Match Evenings 9.00am - 45 mins after game

Online Store
www.liverpoolfc.tv

Liverpool FC Order hotline: 0870 600 0532 **International calls:** +44 138 685 2035
Lines open 8am-9pm Mon-Sun

Goalkeeper Jose Reina in unfamiliar territory, sporting the new Liverpool away strip

MATCHDAY PROGRAMME AND OFFICIAL MAGAZINE

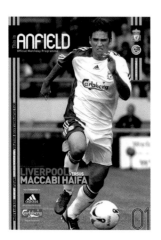

Official Matchday Programme

Liverpool's award-winning official matchday programme is written and produced in Liverpool by Sport Media on behalf of the club. The traditionally sized programme includes regular features like the nostalgia-based Kop'n'Goal Years, an L4 interview with one of Rafa's squad, a message from the manager himself plus captain's notes while new features include a regular cartoon strip depicting moments from Liverpool history.

How to subscribe

Phone: 0845 143 0001 (Monday-Friday 9am-5pm)
Website: www.liverpoolfc.tv/match/magazine
(Also available in braille and other formats - contact community department on 0151 264 2316 for details)

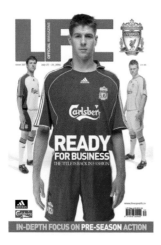

LFC Magazine

Liverpool are the only club boasting an official weekly magazine in the Premiership. The Sport Media-produced glossy LFC Magazine, priced £1.95, provides up-to-date news and views on all aspects of the club, from exclusive player interviews, match previews and reports to features on former players and famous Reds and stats. Popular back page feature asks fans to Spot The Kop Idol from a Liverpool crowd scene while regular columnists are Chief Executive Rick Parry, plus legendary duo Kenny Dalglish and Alan Hansen.

How to subscribe

Phone: 0845 143 0001 (Monday-Friday 9am-5pm)
Website: www.liverpoolfc.tv/match/magazine

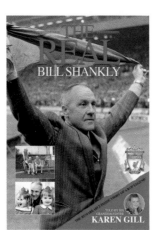

The Real Bill Shankly

Marking the 25th anniversary of the death of the man who made Liverpool FC one of the bastions of world football, this new release by Sport Media highlights the many sides to the legendary Scottish manager. Compiled by Karen Gill, the great man's granddaughter, *The Real Bill Shankly* will provide a fascinating insight into the mind of this unique character through recollections from the fans who idolised him, the players who responded to his inspirational team talks and the
family who loved him.

How to order

Phone: 0845 143 0001 (Monday-Friday 9am-5pm)

OFFICIAL LIVERPOOL SUPPORTERS CLUB

The membership package has kept the elements we know members love, including 10% off in official club stores and the OLSC magazine, and as ever we have built on this.

Both PTS and Adult members will receive the exclusive OLSC DVD "7" looking at the relationship between Liverpool FC and the number 7, including the 0-7 FA Cup victory over Birmingham in 2006, 7 minutes in Istanbul and 7 managers from Shankly to Benitez plus much more!

As well as the DVD there is a fantastic shirt shaped photo frame, an exclusive football pen and an OLSC coaster not to mention the competitions and discounts available to members.

Junior members receive an OLSC slide puzzle, a brilliant red and white beach ball as well as a logo bug and rosette stickers to show the world they support the best team.

Contact 08707 020207 or write to Membership Dept, Liverpool FC, Anfield Road, L'pool L4 0TQ.

Adult and Junior Members will receive a £2 discount if you choose to pay by Direct Debit.

PTS Scheme (PRICE: £50 including P&P)

- Free Fan Card if required
- 1 in 2 chance to buy tickets for FAPL home games
- SMS and e-mail alerts on first day of sales
- Quarterly Member Magazines inc exclusive comps
- OLSC Members DVD
- LFC photo frame
- Exclusive football pen
- OLSC coaster
- 10% off merchandise in official club stores
- Monthly Mega Draw
- 2 for 1 museum offer
- Free entry to reserve matches
- Exclusive LFC magazine offers

Adult Scheme (PRICE: £29.95 including P&P)

- Free Fan Card if required
- Quarterly Member Magazines inc exclusive comps
- OLSC Members DVD
- LFC photo frame
- Exclusive football pen
- OLSC coaster
- 10% off merchandise in official club stores
- Monthly Mega Draw
- 2 for 1 museum offer
- Free entry to reserve matches
- Exclusive LFC magazine offers

Junior Scheme (PRICE: £19.95 including P&P)

- Free Fan Card if required
- Quarterly Member Magazines inc exclusive comps
- Beach ball
- Slide puzzle
- Logo bug
- Rosette stickers
- Football pen
- Chance to be a mascot
- Chance to attend the Christmas Party at Anfield
- 10% off merchandise in official club stores
- Monthly Mega Draw
- 2 for 1 museum offer
- Free entry to Reserve Matches
- Exclusive LFC Magazine Offers

ASSOCIATION OF INTERNATIONAL BRANCHES

There are almost 200 Association of International Branches, and several new ones are being formed each season. Benefits of affiliating include passes to watch the first team train at the pre-season Fans Day at Anfield, an exclusive Q&A session with a Reds legend, as well as meeting like-minded supporters in your area. However, please note that new branches have restricted access to tickets.

If there isn't an AIB near you, why not form one. You'll need 25 supporters and will have to pay a small fee and sign up to AIB regulations. For further details or information on your nearest branch, please call: +44-(0)-151-261-1444 or fax 0151 261 1695.

LIVERPOOL DISABLED SUPPORTERS ASSOCIATION

The Liverpool Disabled Supporters Association (LDSA) was formed in January 2004 with help from LFC Disability Liaison Officer Jodi Unsworth and a small group of LFC disabled supporters. The aims and objectives of this association are to act in partnership with Liverpool Football Club to promote inclusiveness for the disabled fans of the club, the disabled fans of visiting clubs as well as those individuals who support disabled people and those with impairments.

This association recognises that all fans should have an equal opportunity to participate in an enjoyable matchday experience and that people with disabilities and/or impairments must have their interests recognised and promoted by LFC with equal status to that of all other fans of the club. The LDSA committee is made up of 10 members, who are all LFC supporters. The group meets once a month with Jodi Unsworth to discuss disability issues at LFC.

If you would like anymore information about the LDSA then please send an email to LDSA@liverpoolfc.tv or write to LDSA, Liverpool Football Club, 69 Anfield Road, Liverpool, L4 0TH.

REDUC@TE

Since opening, thousands of children have now enjoyed the opportunity to learn in the exciting and inspirational environment of Liverpool Football Club. Staffed by a Centre Manager and students from the three Universities in Liverpool, Reduc@te aims to help children improve their skills in the key areas of literacy, numeracy and ICT. Resources are made available in Reduc@te on a daily basis and use football, sport and contemporary issues to help motivate young people to learn. Great emphasis is placed on rewarding achievement and building up the self-esteem of the children to give them more confidence when learning. Staff use the unique environment to make the educational experience as special as possible and groups are offered learning opportunities in the club shop, the LFC Museum, the Academy and around Anfield.

All of the curriculum materials are designed to be fun and enjoyable and study support groups attend after normal school hours on weekdays Monday to Thursday. Fridays are set aside for Special Needs schools or schools who wish to make a full day visit to the centre. Reduc@te is well equipped with ICT hardware and is always willing to embark on new and exciting projects. Recently primary schools have visited Reduc@te for French or Spanish lessons during the school day and a number of secondary schools attend Reduc@te for 'business days' where they focus on the off-field activities of the club for their GCSE and A-Level courses.

Further details on Reduc@te may be obtained from the Centre Manager, Keith White:
Tel: 0151 263 1313 **Email:**   krwhite.lfc.study@talk21.com or Reducate@liverpoolfc.tv

LFC IN THE COMMUNITY

Led by Community Coaching co-ordinator Bill Bygroves, who is also Liverpool FC's club chaplain, this thriving department work very closely with the local community and are involved in a host of activities both locally and world wide. Bill works alongside former professional footballer Owen Brown in leading a very dedicated and enthusiastic team working with the community. There are community coaches including Head Coach Eddie Sullivan, Disability Liaison Officer Jodi Unsworth and Admin Co-ordinator Tracy Boden, and six full-time coaching community staff. The community department works closely with youngsters and visits schools throughout the Merseyside region.

We pioneered the successful SweeperZone project. The club were chosen as the first Premiership club to kick this project off with the aim of kicking litter off the streets, encouraging local kids to help with this initiative on a matchday, and as a reward earning a free ticket for the match.
One of the club's most successful initiatives has also been the 'Jamie Carragher Young Person of the Year' awards night. With categories recognising Schools, Youth and Community and Special Achievements to name but three, the night recognises good in the community and is a reward for those who have shown courage, bravery, overcome an illness or have contributed significantly in the local area. Current projects set up by Disability Liaison Officer Jodi Unsworth include a North West Wheelchair Football Premiership League, a visually impaired football team, a deaf football team, and a mini football league within special schools across Merseyside.

LFC in the Community have been instrumental in the Kick Racism Out Of Football campaign

PUBLIC RELATIONS

Fronted by former playing star Brian Hall, Liverpool's PR Department provides a vital role in promoting the good name of Liverpool Football Club. The department handles a variety of different queries and requests, a recent example being when a fan undertook a fund-raising bicycle ride around every Premiership club. Brian ensured a warm welcome at Anfield.
Brian's team also ensure that the club's image is used positively to aim social messages at youngsters i.e. anti-smoking, anti-drugs and anti-street crime. Brian seeks and gets the support of our stars to reinforce these important themes.
Videos and DVDs playing on this format will aim to reach every school in Liverpool. The PR team strive to ensure the club's image is nothing less than top class. Fans write in asking for many things and while the club cannot satisfy all demands, Brian's team do all they can to provide a vital link with supporters and the community, even when it comes to organising the players' fan mail.
PR will also deal with information relating to school projects. A recent one related to the possible abuse of child labour in places like India regarding the production of kit and footballs. Brian, after talking to our supportive kit sponsors Adidas, was able to reassure the schoolchildren who posed the query that our standards ensure this is not the case.
We also look after requests from special-needs groups as well as those from charitable organisations. Again, the club cannot satisfy all requests, but there is total focus to maintain our proud reputation all over the world.

INSIDE ANFIELD

Hospitality

Heathcotes at Anfield is based at Liverpool Football Club, which has one of the regions most remarkable venues. The club is synonymous with achievement and success – great teams built on the perfect blend of skill, flair and determination, and this is highlighted in the service we offer.

Our experience in accommodating large numbers of hospitality guests – typically 2,500 people on match days – offers valuable reassurance that all events will run smoothly. And because of our considerable resources, we'll do our best to help if you are working to a tight deadline.

You'd be correct in thinking that any culinary experience that bears the name of Paul Heathcote has to be special. Under the direction of award-winning head chef Christian Grall you can enjoy a range of inspired menu options covering everything from conference luncheons to fine dining.

To find out details regarding conferencing, events and weddings and private events, further details can be obtained from the following contacts:

Telephone: 0151 263 7744
Email: events@liverpoolfc.tv
Website: www.liverpoolfc.tv/club/banqueting.htm

Some of the facilities on offer in the Trophy Room Suite at Anfield

LIVERPOOL IN THE MEDIA

LOCAL MEDIA

Liverpool Echo
Local evening daily, Monday-Saturday.
Saturday edition contains the 'Football Echo'.
Price: 42p

Liverpool Daily Post
Local morning daily, Monday-Saturday.
Price: 45p

LOCAL RADIO

BBC Radio Merseyside
Provides full coverage of all Liverpool first-team games, with Gary Gillespie the main summariser. Post-match fans' debate is a regular feature, while football is covered throughout the week, with Fridays usually previewing the weekend action.
Frequency: 95.8FM/1485AM

Radio City/Magic
Ian St John is a prominent figure of a Saturday during the football season, while full commentary on all Liverpool matches is provided with guest summarisers including John Aldridge, who also plays a popular agony uncle to fans on the station's post-match debate.
Frequency: 96.7FM/1548AM

Century FM
Coverage of all first-team games is available, with a daily football phone-in Monday-Saturday (known as the 'Legends' phone-in), including Alan Kennedy.
Frequency: 105.4FM

OTHER UNOFFICIAL PUBLICATIONS

The KOP magazine
Important grass roots tabloid-style publication providing an alternative take on all things Red, established since 1994. On sale locally in newsagents or outside the ground on matchdays. Subscribe by calling 0845 143 0001.

Price: £1.50

The Liverpool Way
Alternative view of Liverpool FC since 1999, copies are available around Anfield on matchdays. Usually priced £2, issue 53, featuring a Jamie Carragher exclusive, costs £3.50.

Through The Wind And Rain
Long-running publication, available on matchdays with issue 72 (Spring 2006) priced £2.

Red All Over The Land
Having celebated its 10th anniversary, RAOTL is on sale at most home and away games. Including postage, the Summer 2006 issue could be ordered for £2.50.

2007	Jan	Feb	March	April	May	June
Monday						
Tuesday					1	
Wednesday					2	
Thursday		1	1		3	
Friday		2	2		4	1
Saturday		3	3		5	2
Sunday		4	4	1	6	3
Monday	1	5	5	2	7	4
Tuesday	2	6	6	3	8	5
Wednesday	3	7	7	4	9	6
Thursday	4	8	8	5	10	7
Friday	5	9	9	6	11	8
Saturday	6	10	10	7	12	9
Sunday	7	11	11	8	13	10
Monday	8	12	12	9	14	11
Tuesday	9	13	13	10	15	12
Wednesday	10	14	14	11	16	13
Thursday	11	15	15	12	17	14
Friday	12	16	16	13	18	15
Saturday	13	17	17	14	18	16
Sunday	14	18	18	15	20	17
Monday	15	18	18	16	21	18
Tuesday	16	20	20	17	22	18
Wednesday	17	21	21	18	23	20
Thursday	18	22	22	18	24	21
Friday	18	23	23	20	25	22
Saturday	20	24	24	21	26	23
Sunday	21	25	25	22	27	24
Monday	22	26	26	23	28	25
Tuesday	23	27	27	24	29	26
Wednesday	24	28	28	25	30	27
Thursday	25		29	26	31	28
Friday	26		30	27		29
Saturday	27		31	28		30
Sunday	28			29		
Monday	29			30		
Tuesday	30					
Wednesday	31					

Make: AVR Programming

Elliot Williams

SEBASTOPOL, CA

Make: AVR Programming

by Elliot Williams

Printed in the United States of America.

Published by Maker Media, Inc., 1160 Battery Street East, Suite 125, San Francisco, CA 94111.

Maker Media books may be purchased for educational, business, or sales promotional use. Online editions are also available for most titles (*http://my.safaribooksonline.com*). For more information, contact O'Reilly Media's corporate/institutional sales department: 800-998-9938 or *corporate@oreilly.com*.

Editor: Patrick Di Justo	**Indexer:** Judy McConville
Production Editor: Kara Ebrahim	**Cover Designer:** Shawn Wallace
Copyeditor: Kim Cofer	**Interior Designer:** Monica Kamsvaag
Proofreader: Amanda Kersey	**Illustrator:** Rebecca Demarest

February 2014:   First Edition

Revision History for the First Edition:

2014-01-24:   First release

2014-02-14:   Second release

2015-03-03:   Third release

See *http://oreilly.com/catalog/errata.csp?isbn=9781449355784* for release details.

ISBN: 978-1-449-35578-4

[LSI]

Table of Contents

Preface . . . . **xi**

Part I. The Basics

1. Introduction **3**
What Is a Microcontroller? The Big Picture 3
   A Computer on a Chip… 3
   …But a Very Small Computer 4
   What Can Microcontrollers Do? 5
Hardware: The Big Picture 5
   The Core: Processor, Memory, and I/O 8
   Peripherals: Making Your Life Easier 9

2. Programming AVRs **13**
Programming the AVR 13
   Toolchain 14
The Software Toolchain 16
   Linux Setup 18
   Windows Setup 18
   Mac Setup 20
   Arduino Setup 20
   Make and Makefiles 20
AVR and the Arduino 21
   Arduino Pros 21
   Arduino Cons 22

The Arduino: Hardware or Software? Both! 24
The Arduino Is an AVR 25
The Arduino Is an AVR Programmer 27
Other Hardware Programmers 30
Flash Programmers I Have Known and Loved 30
Getting Started: Blinking LEDs 31
Hookup 32
ISP Headers 35
AVRDUDE 37
Configuring Your Makefile 40
Flash 42
Troubleshooting 42

3. **Digital Output** **45**
blinkLED Redux 46
The Structure of AVR C Code 47
Hardware Registers 48
blinkLED Summary 51
POV Toy 51
Building the Circuit 52
Pretty Patterns: The POV Toy Code 56
Experiment! 58

4. **Bit Twiddling** **61**
Working Through the Code: Cylon Eyes 62
Bit Twiddling and Cylon Eyes 63
Bit Shifting 64
Advanced Bit Twiddling: Above and Beyond Cylon Eyes 66
Setting Bits with OR 70
Toggling Bits with XOR 71
Clearing a Bit with AND and NOT 72
Showing Off 74
Summary 78

5. **Serial I/O** **79**
Serial Communication 79
Implementing Serial Communication on the AVR: Loopback Project 83
Setup: Configuring the AVR 83
Setup: Your Computer 85
Setup: USB-Serial Adapter 85
Putting It All Together: Test Out Your Loopback 88
Troubleshooting Serial Connections 89
Configuring USART: The Nitty-Gritty Details 90
AVR Square-Wave Organ 97
Making Music with Your Micro 98

The Organ Library 100
The Code 101
Extra Goodies 104
Summary 105

6. Digital Input **107**
Pushbuttons, Switches, Etc. 107
    Configuring Input: DDRs, PORTs, and PINs 110
    Interpreting Button Presses 111
Changing State 114
Debouncing 115
    Debounce Example 117
AVR Music Box 119
    The Code 119
Boss Button 121
    Desktop-side Scripting 122
    Extensions 126

7. Analog-to-Digital Conversion I **127**
ADC Hardware Overview 128
Light Meter 131
    The Circuit 131
    The Code 137
    ADC Initialization 139
    Extensions 141
Slowscope 142
    The AVR Code 143
    The Desktop Code 145
    Synergies 147
AVR Night Light and the Multiplexer 147
    Multiplexing 147
    Setting the Mux Bits 148
    The Circuit 150
    The Code 150
Summary 152

Part II. Intermediate AVR

8. Hardware Interrupts **155**
External Interrupts 101: Real-time Button Pressing Examples 157
    External Interrupt 0 Example 158
    Pin-Change Interrupt Example 163
Capacitive Sensor 166
    The Sensor 167

The Code 170
Global, Volatile Variables 172
Debugging the Circuit 175

9. **Introduction to the Timer/Counter Hardware 177**
Timer/Counters: Why and How? 177
Test Your Reaction Time 180
Using Timer 0 for a Better 8-Bit Organ 184
AM Radio 188
The Circuit 190
CPU Speed 191
AM Radio: The Code 192
Summary 198

10. **Pulse-Width Modulation 201**
Bright and Dim LEDs: PWM 202
Brute-Force PWM Demo 204
Timers PWM Demo 206
Initializing Timers for PWM Mode 208
PWM on Any Pin 210
PWM on Any Pin Demo 211
Closing: Alternatives to PWM and a Timer Checklist 213

11. **Driving Servo Motors 217**
Servos 218
The Secret Life of Servos 219
The Circuit 220
The Code 221
Servo Sundial 225
The Build 226
Ready the Lasers! 229
The Code 231
Servo Sundial Calibration 238

12. **Analog-to-Digital Conversion II 245**
Voltage Meter 246
The Circuit 247
The Code 250
The Footstep Detector 254
The Circuit 255
The Theory 260
Exponentially Weighted Moving Averages 261
The Code 264
Summary 268

Part III. Advanced AVR Topics

13. Advanced PWM Tricks 271
Direct-Digital Synthesis 272
Making a Sine Wave 276
Next Steps: Mixing and Volume 279
Mixing 279
Dynamic Volume Control 282
Polling USART 285
ADSR Envelope 285
Auxiliary Files 286

14. Switches 289
Controlling Big Loads: Switches 290
Bipolar-Junction Transistors 292
MOSFETs 293
Power MOSFETs 295
Relays 296
Triacs and SSRs 297
Switches: Summary 298
DC Motors 299

15. Advanced Motors 307
Going in Reverse: H-Bridges 308
Code: Taking Your H-Bridge Out for a Spin 311
Experts-Only H-Bridge 314
PWM and the H-Bridge 315
Drive Modes: Sign-Magnitude 316
Drive Modes: Locked Anti-phase 316
Drive Modes: Comparison 317
Stepper Motors 320
Kinds of Stepper Motors 321
Full Stepping and Half Stepping 322
Identification of Stepper Motor Wires 325
Too Many Wires! 325
Dual H-Bridge Chips: The SN754410 327
The Code 329
Acceleration Control 333
Microstepping 336

16. SPI 339
How SPI Works 340
Bit Trading Example 342
Shift Registers 342

EEPROM External Memory 345
   External Memory 346
SPI Demo Hookup 349
SPI Demo Code 350
   SPI EEPROM Library Header 352
   SPI EEPROM Library C Code 354
   initSPI 356
   SPI_tradeByte 357
   Convenience Functions 358
Summary 359

17. I2C **361**
How I2C Works 363
I2C Demo Hookup 367
I2C Demo Library 368
I2C Thermometer Demo 372
SPI and I2C Data Logger 374
   Pointers in EEPROM 378
   The UART Serial Menu 379
   The Logger's Event Loop 380

18. Using Flash Program Memory **381**
Using Flash Program Memory 381
   Memory Addresses 383
   The Address-Of Operator: & 384
Pointers 387
   Pointers in Brief 387
   Pointers as Arguments to Functions 390
   Summary 394
   Optional: Dereferencing Pointers 395
Talking Voltmeter 396
   PROGMEM Data Structures and the Header File 397
   Sound Playback and Voltage Reading: The .c File 402
Generating the Audio Data 406
   Differential Pulse-Code Modulation 406
   Encoding Two-bit DPCM 407
   Encoding DPCM: wave2DPCM.py 410

19. EEPROM **415**
Using EEPROM 416
   Storing in Memory 416
   Reading from Memory 421
   Saving and Loading EEPROM 424
   Organizing Data in EEPROM 425
Project: Vigenère Cipher Encoder/Decoder 428

20. Conclusion, Parting Words, and Encouragement
.... **439**
Learning AVR: The Missing Chapters 439
   The Watchdog Timer 439
   Power Savings 440
   Crystals and Alternate Clock Sources 440
   Bootloaders 440
   Analog Comparator 441
Debugging 441
Put This Book Down and Build! 442

Index **443**

Preface

Microcontroller projects are ubiquitous in the hobbyist/hacker/Maker world, and with good reason. Microcontrollers stand directly in the middle ground between the hardware world of buttons, motors, and lights and the software world of algorithms, connectivity, and infinite possibility. Microcontrollers are part computer and part electrical component. They can also be the metaphorical glue between the real world and the virtual world.

Why This Book?

Are you sending a balloon with a small payload to near space? Need a small bit of computing power to read your temperature sensors and accelerometer and log the data to an SD card without using too much power? A microcontroller is just what you need. Would you like to build your own small robot or a cute interactive toy for your niece? There's a microcontroller application there, too. I'm sure that you've seen a million interesting projects online, wondered, "How'd they do that?" and gotten the answer: a microcontroller. Without their capable microcontroller brains, the homegrown 3D printing scene would be nowhere. Microcontrollers are at the center of an emerging culture of people building the previously impossible.

The goal of this book is to get you building projects with microcontrollers and writing your own firmware (or using libraries from other people) in C. I've chosen the Atmel AVR series microcontrollers to focus on because they have a fantastic free and open toolchain, easily available programming hardware, and many of you probably have one or two already on hand in the form of Arduinos. A large part of the collaborative hacker community uses these chips, so it's as good a starting point as any. The ATmega168 chip family that we'll be using is right now the sweet spot in price-per-functionality, but it is not hard to port your code to smaller and cheaper if you want to or move over to other AVR chips if you need to.

I picked the C language because it's pretty much the standard for programming microcontrollers. It's just at the right point, for my taste, in terms of being abstract enough to read but low-level enough that turning an individual bit on or off doesn't require subclassing or overriding anything. Your C code will compile down to something that is nearly as efficient as the best-written assembler, but it's a heck of a lot easier to maintain. There's also a *ton* of code examples out there on the Web for you to look at and learn from. (That said, if you really want a good feel for how the hardware works, teach yourself AVR assembler when you're done with this book.)

On the other hand, this book is really a book about programming and using microcontrollers in general. Though the particular naming conventions and some of the implementation details are different across different brands of microcontrollers, the basic principles will be the same. More on this in just a minute.

Software Type or Hardware Type?

In a class on programming microcontrollers that I taught at my local hackerspace, I discovered that the students would identify largely as either hardware types or software types. Some people coded JavaScript for web applications all day, while others worked in electrical and machine shops. One guy had never seen a for loop, and another didn't know that the red wire is the positive side of a battery pack. Everyone had something to learn, but it was almost never the same thing for everyone.

In building your microcontroller projects, you're going to need to think both like a software type and a hardware type, even if only one of these initially comes naturally to you. At times you're going to need to debug code algorithms, and at other times you're going to need to figure out exactly what's going on electrically when that button is pushed or that motor is energized. This need to put on two different hats, sometimes even at the same time, characterizes microcontroller and embedded applications.

Throughout this book, there'll be some concepts that are too obvious to you, but which may be entirely perplexing to others. I'll be swapping my software-type and hardware-type hats accordingly. In the end, you'll become familiar enough with both worlds that you'll be able to navigate the middle ground. You'll know you've reached embedded-design nirvana when you begin coding *with* the hardware. Then you'll have become a microcontroller type!

Manifesto!

And so we come to my sincerest goal in writing this book instead of simply another blinky-LEDs-on-an-Arduino manual—to turn you into a true microcontroller type. Although the Arduino environment is good for getting people hooked on microcontrollers, it's a cheap high. Arduino/Wiring goes to great lengths to abstract away from the microcontroller's hardware. Here, I want to teach you *about the hardware*—because it's useful—so getting further away from it won't help. (My friend Ash once described working with the Arduino environment as being "like knitting in boxing gloves.")

I don't think that the built-in hardware timer modules are something to be abstracted away from. I believe the timers should be understood thoroughly enough to be abused to create a small AM radio transmitter that can play the Mario theme song within a room using nothing more than a wire or your finger as an antenna (in Chapter 9). And I believe that this code should fit in under 500 bytes of program memory.

More seriously, many of the hardware peripherals inside the AVR are common to most microcontrollers, from the "prehistoric" 8051 or the tiniest PIC or ATtiny chips, through the MSP430s and the ATmegas, to the mighty XMega and ARM chips. These hardware peripherals have been developed and honed over 40 years of microcontroller design development, and they're not going away any time soon because they have been designed to be *helpful* to getting your project realized. The microcontroller hardware has been designed by very clever engineers to solve your problems. My goal in writing this book is to show you how common problems are solved. You need to learn the hardware, and apply the hardware, to love the hardware.

Although every microcontroller design implements things a little bit differently, once you've seen it here, it will make sense there. Every microcontroller that I've ever come across is programmable in C. Almost all of what you learn working through this book is *transferable* to other chips and other architectures, because what you're learning here is the way things work rather than an abstraction wrapped around the way things work, designed to protect you from the way things work. Some of what you learn (for instance bitwise binary manipulations in Chapter 4) might seem boring, but in the end it will give you simple and direct access to the common hardware bits that are put there to help you, and the techniques will work with any brand of microcontroller that you choose to use.

In short, almost none of the time you spend learning about how to create projects on the AVR in C will be wasted. Yeah, it's a bit harder than just reusing someone's shields and code. Yeah, you might need to stop sometimes and leaf through a C programming book or an electronics text (or just look it up on the Net). But when you find out that you need more processing power, or a different set of peripherals, you can just buy yourself a $8 chip in place of the $4 one you were using and bring most of your code, and more importantly your knowledge, along with you.

This book is meant to be the red pill, and I sincerely hope that you find it worth your time once you've seen how deep the rabbit hole goes.

You Will Need...

Before we get too much into detail about the AVR chips and what they can do for you, let me provide you with a shopping list. Order this stuff now so that you can be ready to start programming chips in a few days when the delivery truck shows up.

The Basic Kit

Here is a basic kit of parts that you'll need throughout the rest of your AVR life. A lot of this gear is multipurpose, and you'll have some of these parts on hand if you're playing around with electronics. The following is the basic kit that you'll use for programming AVRs throughout the book:

- A solderless breadboard or two or three. I like the 800-contact type because of the extra working space, but a few smaller breadboards can be nice for building subcircuits on. You can never have too much workspace.

- A number of wire jumpers to plug in to the breadboard. I really like the prebuilt ones with rubber grips and pins on the end. You can often find these sold in combination with breadboards for cheap at online auction websites.

- You should probably have a small resistor assortment on hand. You'll need a bunch in the 200–500 ohm range for LEDs, a few around 1k ohm, and at least five in the 10k ohm range.

- An ISP programmer (see "Flash Programmers I Have Known and Loved" on page 30 for recommendations) or Arduino (see "AVR and the Arduino" on page 21).

- An ATmega168, 168A, 168P, or 168PA. Make sure you get one in the DIP package if you want to plug it into the breadboard. The parts I'm using at the moment are called ATMEGA 168A-PU, where the "PU" denotes a DIP part. See "The AVR Family of Microcontrollers" on page 11 for more on chip selection.

- A USB-to-serial adapter. I'm a big fan of the FTDI USB-Serial cable. Get the 3.3 V-compatible one for maximum flexibility. It works painlessly with all operating systems, and at all speeds. A variety of online geekery stores have slightly cheaper options as well.

- At least 10 LEDs (any color) and 10 appropriately sized resistors: 200–500 ohms. You can never have enough LEDs.

- A source of 5 V DC power (optional). Many of the ISP programmers provide power to the breadboard. If yours doesn't, cutting up a 5 V wall-wart power supply or using a 4xAA battery pack will work. Rechargeable batteries are even better.

For the Basic Projects

- A small 8 ohm (normal) speaker and roughly 10–100 uF capacitor. I got my speaker from an old keyboard toy.
- Two or more pushbuttons. Normally open. Cheap tactile switches are great.
- At least 5x 2N7000 MOSFETs.
- Two light-dependent resistors (LDRs), but you might as well buy an assorted pack.
- Two potentiometers. 10k ohms is ideal. Anything above 1k ohms will work.

For the Intermediate Projects

- A piezo disk, preferably with wires attached.
- A servo. Any old hobby servo will do. I get my cheap ones from Tower Hobbies.
- A laser pointer that you're willing to take apart.
- An I2C device to talk to—my example uses the very common LM75 temperature sensor.
- An SPI device to talk to. Here, I'm using a 25LC256 32K SPI EEPROM chip.

For the Motors and H-Bridge Chapters

- A small DC motor (3–12 V is good). I got mine from a racecar toy.
- MOSFETs for building an H-Bridge. I use two IRF9530s and two IRF530s.
- SN754410 or L293D motor driver chip instead of or in addition to the MOSFETs.
- A stepper motor and a power supply to drive it.
- Random switch-like devices: relays, SSRs, Darlington transistors (TIP120, etc.).
- Random DC-powered devices like LED lamps or pumps or fans or solenoids or kids' toys or...
- A 5 V relay.

Deluxe and Frills

- A standalone voltmeter.
- An amplified speaker—computer speakers are ideal.
- A soldering iron and some solder.
- A prototype board for soldering up your circuits permanently.

- Extras of everything in the first list so that you can create permanent versions of each chapter's project that you like. Nothing beats having a bunch of souvenirs around to show off what you've learned and to go back to and modify later on.

Conventions Used in This Book

The following typographical conventions are used in this book:

Italic
> Indicates new terms, URLs, email addresses, filenames, and file extensions.

`Constant width`
> Used for program listings, as well as within paragraphs to refer to program elements such as variable or function names, databases, data types, environment variables, statements, and keywords.

`Constant width bold`
> Shows commands or other text that should be typed literally by the user.

`Constant width italic`
> Shows text that should be replaced with user-supplied values or by values determined by context.

 This icon signifies a tip, suggestion, or general note.

 This icon indicates a warning or caution.

Using Code Examples

Supplemental material (code examples, exercises, etc.) is available for download at *https://github.com/hexagon5un/AVR-Programming*.

This book is here to help you get your job done. In general, you may use the code in this book in your programs and documentation. You do not need to contact us for permission unless you're reproducing a significant portion of the code. For example, writing a program that uses several chunks of code from this book does not require permission. Selling or distributing a CD-ROM of examples from MAKE books does require permission. Answering a question by citing this book and quoting example code does not require permission. Incorporating a significant amount of example code from this book into your product's documentation does require permission.

We appreciate, but do not require, attribution. An attribution usually includes the title, author, publisher, and ISBN. For example: "*Make: AVR Programming* by Elliot Williams (MAKE). Copyright 2014 Elliot Williams, 978-1-4493-5578-4."

If you feel your use of code examples falls outside fair use or the permission given here, feel free to contact us at *bookpermissions@makermedia.com*.

Safari® Books Online

 *Safari Books Online* is an on-demand digital library that delivers expert content in both book and video form from the world's leading authors in technology and business.

Technology professionals, software developers, web designers, and business and creative professionals use Safari Books Online as their primary resource for research, problem solving, learning, and certification training.

Safari Books Online offers a range of product mixes and pricing programs for organizations, government agencies, and individuals. Subscribers have access to thousands of books, training videos, and prepublication manuscripts in one fully searchable database from publishers like Maker Media, O'Reilly Media, Prentice Hall Professional, Addison-Wesley Professional, Microsoft Press, Sams, Que, Peachpit Press, Focal Press, Cisco Press, John Wiley & Sons, Syngress, Morgan Kaufmann, IBM Redbooks, Packt, Adobe Press, FT Press, Apress, Manning, New Riders, McGraw-Hill, Jones & Bartlett, Course Technology, and dozens more. For more information about Safari Books Online, please visit us online.

How to Contact Us

Please address comments and questions concerning this book to the publisher:

Maker Media, Inc.
1160 Battery Street East, Suite 125
San Francisco, CA 94111

MAKE unites, inspires, informs, and entertains a growing community of resourceful people who undertake amazing projects in their backyards, basements, and garages. MAKE celebrates your right to tweak, hack, and bend any technology to your will. The MAKE audience continues to be a growing culture and community that believes in bettering ourselves, our environment, our educational system—our entire world. This is much more than an audience, it's a worldwide movement that Make is leading—we call it the Maker Movement.

For more information about MAKE, visit us online:

MAKE magazine: *http://makezine.com/magazine/*
Maker Faire: *http://makerfaire.com*
Makezine.com: *http://makezine.com*
Maker Shed: *http://makershed.com/*

We have a web page for this book, where we list errata, examples, and any additional information. You can access this page at:

http://oreil.ly/avr-programming

To comment or ask technical questions about this book, send email to:

bookquestions@oreilly.com

Acknowledgments

I would like to thank the members of HacDC, and especially those who were subjected to my first couple of classes teaching microcontroller programming. I've learned as much from you all as you have from me. And you're all the inspiration for this book in the first place!

Special thanks go out to Gareth Branwyn and Alberto Gaitan for pushing me into writing this crazy thing. You are truly overlords and enablers. Respect!

To anyone who has contributed to the greater hive-mind that is the global hacker/Maker community: if you've put anything microcontroller-related out there, you've probably contributed to this book in a six-degrees-of-separation sort of way. I hope you enjoy it.

This book couldn't have been made without the help of the tremendous folks at O'Reilly and Maker Media. Patrick DiJusto edited the text with a fine-tooth comb and provided much helpful feedback. Brian Jepson, Shawn Wallace, and Dale Dougherty provided high-level direction. Kara Ebrahim helped pull it all together. Also, much thanks to Eric Weddington for his technical review. Writing a book is a team effort, and I thank you all.

Finally, my wife Christina has my endless gratitude for letting me see this long project through. Hab dich lieb, Schatz.

## PART I

The Basics

This first section of the book covers the material you'll need to know for most AVR projects. These chapters build directly on one another, and you're probably going to want to work through them in order. Chapter 1 starts out with an overview of the chip and what it can do for you, then we move on to doing it.

The first task is to learn how to write and compile code for the AVR, and then get that code written into the chip's flash program memory. By the end of Chapter 2, you'll have an LED blinking back at you from your breadboard. Chapter 3 introduces the topic of digital output in general, and we'll build a POV illusion gadget that you can program yourself. Chapter 4 is an introduction to bit-level manipulations using bitwise logic functions. Though not a particularly sexy chapter, it's fundamentally important.

Chapter 5 connects your AVR to the outside world: in particular, your desktop computer. Bridging the computer world and the real world is where microcontrollers excel, and the serial port is the easiest way to do so. To show off a little, we'll make an organ that you can play from your desktop's keyboard.

Chapter 6 introduces you to the world of button pressing. We'll make a standalone AVR music box where you control the tempo and length of the notes that are preprogrammed into the chip and leverage the serial connection from the previous chapter to make a dedicated web page–launching button.

Chapter 7 brings the outside world of analog voltages into your AVR, by introducing the built-in analog-to-digital converter (ADC) hardware. Knowing how to use the ADC opens up the world of sensors. We'll build a light meter, expand on this to build a knob-controllable night light, and finally combine the ADC with serial output and your desktop to implement a simple and slow, but still incredibly useful, oscilloscope.

Introduction | 1

The first question to ponder is what, exactly, is a microcontroller? Clearly it's a chunk of silicon, but what's inside of it?

What Is a Microcontroller? The Big Picture

Rhetorical questions aside, it's well worth getting the big-picture overview before we dive headfirst into flipping bits, flashing program memory, and beyond.

A Computer on a Chip...

Microcontrollers are often defined as being complete computers on a single chip, and this is certainly true.

At their core, microcontrollers have a processor that is similar to the CPU on your computer. The processor reads instructions from a memory space (in flash memory rather than on a hard drive), sends math off to an arithmetic logic unit (instead of a math coprocessor), and stores variables in RAM while your program is running.

Many of the chips have dedicated serial hardware that enables them to communicate to the outside world. For instance, you'll be able to send and receive data from your desktop computer in Chapter 5. OK, it's not gigabit Ethernet, but your microcontroller won't have to live in isolation.

Like any computer, you have the option of programming the microcontroller using a variety of languages. Here we use C, and if you're a software type, the code examples you see in this book will be an easy read. It'll contain things like for loops and assigning variables. If you're used to the design-code-compile-run-debug cycle, or you've got your favorite IDE, you'll feel at home with the software side of things.

So on one hand, microcontrollers are just tiny little computers on a chip.

...But a Very Small Computer

On the other hand, the AVR microcontrollers are *tiny little* computers on a chip, and their small scale makes development for microcontrollers substantially different from development for "normal" computers.

One thing to notice is that the chips in the AVR product line, from ATtiny15 to ATmega328, include the flash program memory space in kilobytes in the chip's name. Yeah, you read that right: we're talking about 1 KB to 32 KB of room for your code. Because of this limited program memory space, the scope of your program running on a single chip is necessarily smaller than, for example, that Java enterprise banking system you work on in your day job.

Microcontrollers have limited RAM as well. The ATmega168 chips that we'll be focusing on here have a nice, round 1 KB. Although it's entirely possible to interface with external RAM to get around this limitation, most of the time, the limited working memory is just something you'll have to live with. On the other hand, 1,024 bytes isn't that limiting most of the time. (How many things do *you* need 1,024 of?) The typical microcontroller application takes an input data stream, processes it relatively quickly, and shuttles it along as soon as possible with comparatively little buffering.

And while we're talking specs, the CPU core clocks of the AVR microprocessors run from 1 to 20 megahertz (when used with an external crystal), rather than the handful of gigahertz you're probably used to. Even with the AVR's RISC design, which gets close to one instruction per cycle, the raw processing speed of a microcontroller doesn't hold a candle to a modern PC. (On the other hand, you'll be surprised how much you can do with *a few million* operations per second.)

Finally, the AVR family of microcontrollers have 8-bit CPUs without a floating-point math coprocessor inside. This means that most of the math and computation you do will involve 8-bit or 16-bit numbers. You *can* use 32-bit integers, but higher precision comes with a slight speed penalty. There is a floating-point math library for the AVRs, but it eats up a large chunk of program memory, so you'll often end up redesigning your software to use integers cleverly. (On the other hand, when you have memory sitting unused, go for it if it helps make your life easier.)

Because the computer that's inside the microcontrollers is truly *micro*, some more of the niceties that you're probably used to on your PC aren't present. For instance, you'll find no built-in video, sound, keyboard, mouse, or hard drives. There's no operating system, which means that there's no built-in provision for multitasking. In Part II, I'll show you how the built-in hardware interrupt, clock, and timer peripherals help you get around this limitation.

On the other hand, microcontrollers have a range of hardware peripherals built in that make many of the common jobs much easier. For instance, the built-in hardware serial interface means you don't have to write serial drivers, but merely put your byte in the right place and wait for it to get transmitted. Built-in pulse-width modulation hardware allows you to just write a byte in memory and then the AVR will toggle a voltage output accordingly with fractional microsecond precision.

What Can Microcontrollers Do?

Consumer examples of microcontrollers include the brains behind your microwave oven that detect your fingers pressing on the digit buttons, turn that input into a series of programmed on-times, and display it all on a screen for you to read. The microcontroller in your universal remote control translates your key presses into a precise series of pulses for an infrared LED that tells the microcontroller inside your television to change the channel or increase the volume.

On the other end of the cost spectrum, microcontrollers also run braking and ac-celeration code in streetcars in Norway and provide part of the brains for satellites.

Hacker projects that use microcontrollers basically span everything that's cool these days, from the RepRap motor-control and planning electronics, to quadcop-ter inertial management units, to high-altitude balloon data-loggers; Twittering toilets and small-scale robotics; controls for MAME cabinets and disk-drive emu-lators for C64s. If you're reading this book, you've probably got a couple applica-tions in mind already; and if you don't, it'll only take one look at Hack-a-day or the Make blog to get your creative juices flowing.

(If you want to know *why* you'd ever want to get your toilet to tweet each time you flush, I'm afraid I can't help you. I'm just hear to show you *how*.)

Hardware: The Big Picture

So a microcontroller is a self-contained, but very limited computer—halfway be-tween a *computer* and a *component*. I've been talking a lot about the computer side. What about the AVR chips as components? Where can you hook stuff up? And how exactly do they do all that they do? Figure 1-1 lays out all of the chip's pins along with the mnemonics that describe their main functions.

If you're coming at this from no background, you're probably wondering how a microcontroller does all this marvellous stuff. The short answer is by reading vol-tages applied to its various pins or by setting up output voltages to these very same pins. Blinking an LED is an obvious example—when the output voltage is high, the LED lights up, and when the voltage is low, it doesn't. More complicated examples include the serial ports that communicate numbers by encoding them in binary, with high voltage standing in for a 1 and low voltage standing in for a 0, and changing the voltage on the pins over time to convey arbitrary messages.

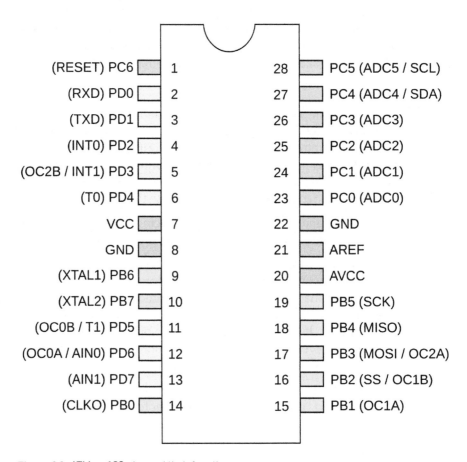

ATMega168 pins and their functions

Each pin on the AVR has a name, and you'll see later on how you can refer to them all in code. So if I hook an LED up to pin number 14, I can then write a high voltage or low voltage out to that pin by referring to it as PB0. Most of the pins on the AVR also have secondary functions, and these are listed as mnemonics in parentheses. For instance, RXD and TXD are the receive and transmit functions for the serial port functionality and live on pins PD0 and PD1, respectively. By the end of this book, you'll know what all of the terms in parentheses mean and will have played around with almost all of their special functionalities.

Internally, and somewhat according to function, the pins are arranged into banks of eight pins. I've color-coded the pins according to their banks. (I wish they were all located in consecutive blocks, but there's nothing you can do about that without building your own circuit board.) Because each bank, for instance, "bank B," has a maximum of eight pins in it, you can refer to them by an eight-bit binary number to turn on or off their voltage source. You'll see a lot more of this in Chapter 3 and onward.

Rounding out the miles-high overview here, you can access all of these pins and their various functions from within your code by reading from and writing to special *I/O registers* in the chip, which your code will be able to access as if they were any other variable. For instance, a register PINB contains the input pin state of all of the pins in Bank B. You'll read it in with code like:

```
thePins = PINB;
```

and then you can do whatever you'd like with the variable thePins that has captured the current pin states. Similarly, a register "variable" PORTB can be assigned to as if it were a normal variable:

```
PORTB = 42;
```

with the side effect that certain pins in bank B will get set to the logic high voltage level, and others will get set to 0 V. And changing the voltage level on these pins turns on and off motors or LEDs, plays sounds on speakers, or encodes and transmits numerical data.

All of the above is actually worth a couple of chapters, so don't worry if it's not crystal clear yet. The point is that code you write has physical side effects on the chip: directly controlling or reading the voltage levels on the pins. And with that, it turns out, you can do anything. The rest is just the details.

Datasheets

Newcomers to AVR microcontrollers are often surprised when they eventually figure out how *useful* the datasheets are. They answer just about every question you've got about how the chips work. For instance, I adapted Figure 1-1 from page 2 of the datasheet.

But the datasheets are imposing—the ATmega 48/88/168 series is 450 pages long! And the datasheets don't seem helpful at first—the datasheet tells you everything about how the chip works, but almost nothing about how you should work with the chip. Some sections of the datasheets are nearly impenetrable unless you already know the basics of what's going on inside the chip already.

The trick is to approach the datasheet like a reference book rather than a novel. If you're learning a new foreign language, you don't start by opening up a dictionary to page one and reading onward. A dictionary is most useful when you already have a basic idea of how the language works, but you've just forgotten how to say "lemur" in Portuguese.

And so it is here. I'll refer to the datasheets throughout this book as you learn to use new functions. One of the important skills you'll learn working through this book is how to read the datasheets.

So take a moment right now to go fetch the full datasheet for the chip we're going to be using, the ATmega168 (*http://bit.ly/KGy3cx*). Read the first page and then stop for now. If your PDF reader supports indexing, enable the index sidepane and maybe give it a look-through. But don't dive in head first just yet—we'll be dipping into the datasheets frequently throughout this book, and you'll get a feel for them as we work along.

So without further ado, here is a whirlwind tour of the hardware that's built into an AVR microcontroller and what it's good for.

The Core: Processor, Memory, and I/O

CPU

The central processing unit (CPU) of the AVR is basically very similar to that in your laptop or desktop computer. It is a bit of electronic circuitry that has a bunch of predefined logical and mathematical operations built in, and knows where to find a list of these operations to follow (your program) and where to get the data it needs to execute them.

Memory

AVR microcontrollers have no fewer than three different memory types, each with different uses.

1. *Flash*. Your compiled program code gets stored in nonvolatile flash memory. It doesn't disappear when the chip loses power. In fact, it's guaranteed to only lose 1 bit per million after 100 years at room temperature. We'll discuss uploading your code to flash memory in Chapter 2.

2. *RAM*. Naturally, there is some memory for storing temporary variables while doing calculations and so forth.

3. *EEPROM*. EEPROM is slow to write to, and there's not much of it, but like flash program memory, it stays around when the power goes out. We'll talk about using EEPROM in Chapter 19.

Clocks

All computers need a sense of time. In the AVR chips, there are multiple clocks that are all derived from the same common timebase but often divided down through their own individual prescalers. We'll use the internal RC oscillator as the master clock source. It runs at around 8 MHz. The *CPU clock* is then divided down from the master clock, and runs at 1 MHz by default, but sometimes when we need the extra speed, we'll bump it up to the full 8 MHz.

Following the CPU clock come all the other peripheral clocks, most of which have their own prescalers relative to the CPU. There are clocks for the I/O subsystem, the analog-to-digital converter, RAM, and Flash and EEPROM. When you're using any of the peripheral subsystems, remember the clock prescalers —you'll often have to set their values. These multiple clocks derived from the same source keep everything running on schedule together.

Outputs

Almost all of the pins on the AVR chips can be configured so that they're usable as digital outputs, meaning that the pin can be commanded in software to output either the supply voltage level or the ground voltage level. (Call these voltage levels VCC and GND, or ground.) Any way you slice it, digital output is the heart and soul of microcontroller programming. It's how you "speak" to the outside world. We'll go into digital output in great depth in Chapter 3.

"Analog" Outputs

*If you've used the Arduino platform, you might think of some of the outputs as "analog" outputs, but there aren't really any truly analog outputs on the AVR series micros. What the Arduino code is doing behind the scenes is switching the pin state very rapidly between the high and low voltages so that the average voltage is somewhere in the middle. This is called pulse-width modulation, and we'll cover it in detail in **Chapter 10**.*

Inputs

Just as almost all the pins can be set up as outputs, they can also be configured as digital inputs, where they detect if the voltage applied to the pin externally is high or low. Specifically, if the voltage on the pin is greater than half of the supply voltage, the chip sets a bit in an internal variable to one. If the voltage is lower than the threshold, that same bit reads as zero.

Hook up a button to the supply voltage through a resistor on one side, and connect this junction to one of the AVR's pins that's configured for input. Connect the other side of the button to ground. When the button isn't pressed, the AVR will read the VCC voltage, but when you do press the button the AVR's input pin will be grounded. Thus, by reading in the voltage on the pin, the AVR is able to detect whether or not you've pressed the button.

Physical states are turned into voltage levels, which are in turn converted to logic values inside the chip.

You'll see a lot more about digital inputs and pushbuttons in Chapter 6.

So far, I've described a tiny computer that can run programs that read and write values out to pins in the form of digital logic voltages. That's essentially all there is to it—with this framework you can implement nearly anything. And a broad range of very useful microcontroller applications can be built with just this ability.

The rest of the microcontroller's hardware is dedicated to making your life as a programmer easier and to making many common tasks more reliable.

Peripherals: Making Your Life Easier

Serial communications

One of my favorite uses of microcontrollers is as the connector between a real computer and interesting hardware. Say you want to strap accelerometers to your body, dance around like it's 1999, and pass this data off to your laptop, which renders a 3D figure of you in real time. The job of the microcontroller here is simple: talk to the accelerometers, do a little math and light up some LEDs perhaps, and send all of the data to your laptop. But what language do the accelerometers speak? How about your desktop?

The AVR has three serial communications peripherals built in. Plain-vanilla USART serial described in Chapter 5 is useful for communicating with your desktop computer, radio modems, and GPS units. SPI (Chapter 16) is good for ultra-fast communication over very short distances with peripherals like memories, ADCs, and DACs. I2C (Chapter 17) is like a small network, allowing you to connect up to 127 different sensors to the same couple of wires. Devices that move around a moderate amount of data tend to use I2C. That's a good choice for the network of accelerometers.

Because each of these serial hardware peripherals is separate inside the AVR, you can use each of these at the same time. Your AVR can communicate with virtually anything.

Analog to digital converter

A number of the useful sensors that you'd like to connect to your projects don't speak the microcontroller's native digital language; rather, they speak in terms of continuous analog voltages. To read in these values and manipulate them like you'll manipulate any other digital data, you'll need to run them through an analog to digital converter (ADC). In Chapter 7, you'll make good use of the ADCs in building a light sensor and variable-threshold night light. In Chapter 12 I'll go over some more advanced ADC applications, including building a vibration sensor that can detect footsteps indoors, and introduce you to oversampling and exponential smoothing—two techniques that can get you more precision or remove noise from your ADC readings.

Interrupts

You'd like your program to be able to react to the outside world: you press a button, you'd like something to happen. Heck, that's half of the fun of writing code for a microcontroller. Or maybe you'd like your program to do something every so often, as the examples using timers/counters make clear. Hardware-level interrupts are just the ticket.

An *interrupt service routine* is a software function that you can write that automatically executes whenever an interrupt condition is met. They're called interrupt routines because the processor stops whatever it was doing in the main flow of your program and runs the appropriate function. After it's done with the interrupt routine, the processor picks up your program's normal operation where it left off.

There are many ways to trigger interrupts in the AVR microcontroller. These interrupt conditions include a press on the reset button, a changing input value, an internal clock tick, a counter value being reached, data coming in on the serial port, an analog-to-digital conversion finishing, or many others. The point here is that there are loads of interrupt conditions and they each can trigger their own function calls.

Interrupts and interrupt service routines are fundamental to advanced AVR programming, and along with timers form most of the content of Part II.

Timers/counters

The AVR microprocessors have built-in hardware counters. The counters are basically what they sound like—they keep a running count of how many times a pin or internal source has changed its voltage level.

The simplest counter application is hooking up the internal counter to a button. Now whenever your program wants, you can tell how many times that button's been pushed by just reading the counter's register. (You can write to the counter as well, so you can reset it to zero at the beginning of any day, for instance.)

Counters really come into their own when paired up with clocks, and this is why they're often referred to as timer/counters. With a clock and a timer, you can measure either how long some event takes, or figure out the event's frequency. You'll even be able to output to certain AVR pins (OCRxn in the pinout diagram) and fire off special subroutines periodically. The timer/counter peripherals are tremendously configurable and turn out to provide more functionality than you would have thought. Which is great, because there are three of them.

You'll see a lot more applications of the timer/counters throughout Part II.

The AVR Family of Microcontrollers

Although we've settled on the AVR ATmega168 for the purposes of this book, you might want to tailor the chip to your specific project later on. There are many, many AVR microcontroller chips to choose from, each with different capabilities at different price points. Finding the one that's right for your project can be intimidating. You can spend hours choosing the chip that has the peripherals you need and enough memory to fit your code, and then locating the least expensive part.

If you're just working on a prototype and you want to get something working as fast as you can, you probably shouldn't worry about spending an extra 50 cents per chip. You're better served by having a few chip types on hand, and just picking the best fit from what you've got. Here's my current working set:

Small: ATtiny45

The x5 series chips are small and cheap, great for when you only need five I/O pins. They also have a high-speed peripheral clock that can run up to 66 MHz, which makes them uniquely great for PWM applications, and for use in conjunction with the V-USB firmware USB library to build your own USB peripheral devices.

The only differences between the 25, 45, and 85 are the amount of program memory (2 kB, 4 kB, and 8 kB) and the price, so there's a trade-off. For me, 4 kB of memory is the sweet spot.

ATtiny45s cost around $1 singly or $0.65 in bulk as of this writing.

Medium: ATtiny 44

An attractive step up from the 45 when you don't need the high-speed PWM of the Tiny45. For just a few cents more, you get 11 I/O pins and a 16-bit timer. Even though they're relatively new on the market, these chips are becoming my go-to for small projects as well.

ATtiny44s cost around $1.15 singly or $0.75 in bulk as of this writing.

Large: ATmega xx8 Family

Now we're talking—the Mega xx8 chips are deluxe! If you're going to focus on one chip series, this is the one. At this level, you get 20 I/O pins, hardware USART, three timers, and a whopping 16 kB of program memory. There's a reason the wildly popular Arduino platform is based on Mega 168s and 328s.

And because the Mega 48, 88, 168, and 328 all have the same features outside of program memory, it's often possible to just swap out a chip and save a few dollars on a project. The Mega48s give you the same functionality for half the price of the mega168s that we're using when you don't need the extra memory.

ATmega168s cost around $2.25 singly or $1.50 in bulk as of this writing.

Now, there are lots of other options besides the chip family and member. Searching for "mega168" at an electronics house yields over 50 results: ATmega168PA-10PU, ATmega168-AU, and so on.

The letters after the part number (168P or 168PA or 168A) represent different versions of the chips. The "V" variants are guaranteed to run at lower voltages, but are only guaranteed to run at reduced speed. The "P" and "V" series are an older design. The "A" and "PA" variants represent newer designs that use less power (P) or run full-range across speed and voltages (A) or both.

The extensions represent the package size and will often be described in words. PU (PDIP) is the largest, and is the through-hole standard part. AU (TQFP) is 1.0 mm spacing surface-mount and is entirely doable if you're comfortable with SMT. The MU packages are very difficult to solder by hand.

The number in the extension is a speed grade, and chips that end in 10, for instance, are only guaranteed to run up to 10 MHz. When there is no numeric extension (as with the modern chips), the chip runs at full rated speed, which is usually 20 MHz at 5 V.

So which variant, in which package? P, A, or PA are safe bets, and I'm basically indifferent among them. The P variants seem to be cheapest at the moment. For packages, pick PU (PDIP) if you've got little or no experience soldering, and AU (TQFP) if you enjoy surface-mount work.

Programming AVRs | 2

Hello World!

In this chapter, you'll get set up with everything you need for coding, compiling, and flashing your programs into the bare silicon of the AVR chips that are sitting on your desk right now. To do so, you're going to need some hardware (a flash programmer) and some software (a code editor, C compiler, and the program that'll communicate with the hardware flash programmer). Finally, you'll need to hook up some wires from the programmer to the AVR chip and get set up with a power supply.

In this process, there are a *lot* of different approaches that will get you to the top of the same mountain. Ultimately, the different approaches are all basically the same at some abstract level, but we'll step through some details of a few of the most popular options to make things clearer.

On the hardware side, most of the flash programmers work about the same, and the differences there won't amount to much more than a few tweaks to a file that you'll use over and over again. Flash programmers, after all, are just USB devices that send bytes of your code across to the AVR chip. On the software side, different development packages will have different looks and feels, but in the end it all comes down to editing code, compiling it, and then sending it off to the hardware programmer.

Programming the AVR

The words "program," "programmer," and "programming" are overloaded in the microcontroller world. We (as programmers) write programs, compile them, and then use a flash programmer to program the AVRs, which then runs our program. Pshwew! Let's step through the actual procedure and see what's actually going on.

What You Need

For this chapter, you'll just need the basic kit as described in "The Basic Kit" on page xiv. For convenience, I've summarized that here:

- A solderless breadboard.

- Wire jumpers to plug in to the breadboard.

- An ISP programmer.

- An ATmega168, 168A, 168P, or 168PA.

- An LED (any color) and an appropriately sized resistor: 200–500 ohms.

- A source of 5 V DC power (if not supplied by your ISP); a 4xAA battery pack is nice anyway.

- One 100 nF (0.1 µF) capacitor to smooth out the AVR's power supply.

Toolchain

It's a long and winding road from the code you type into your editor to a chip on your desk that turns a light on and off. Getting from typed letters on a computer screen to a working piece of electronic machinery requires a chain of tools called, predictably, a toolchain!

Toolchain overview

1. Write your source code in an *editor*.

2. Turn your source code into machine code with a *compiler* (and associated software tools).

3. Using *uploader software* on your big computer and a *hardware flash programmer*, send the machine code to your target AVR chip, which stores the instructions in its nonvolatile flash memory.

4. As soon as the flash programmer is done, the AVR chip resets and starts running your code.

Figure 2-1 sketches out the main steps in AVR firmware development along with which tools you'll use for each step.

The first step in your toolchain is going to be a text editor, or whatever you're most comfortable writing code in. For the Linux folks out there, *gedit* is quite nice. On Windows platforms, you'll probably find the editor that comes with WinAVR, *Programmer's Notepad*, will work pretty well, but I prefer the freeware *Notepad++*. Many Mac coders swear by *TextMate*. If you've already got a favorite code editor, by all means feel free to use it. Nice features to look for include syntax highlighting, automatic formatting and indenting, parenthesis matching, and maybe even code folding. (Put your copy of Microsoft Word away—that's not what we're looking for here.)

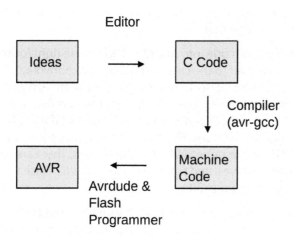

Editor

Ideas ⟶ C Code

Compiler
(avr-gcc)

AVR ⟵ Machine
Code

Avrdude &
Flash
Programmer

Figure 2-1. *AVR programming toolchain*

Aside on Windows Editors

Both *Programmer's Notepad* and *Notepad++* let you compile and flash code directly from the editor with a single button push, which is handy because the Windows command line isn't very familiar to most folks.

In *Programmer's Notepad*, there are options for calling your makefile in the Tools pull-down menu, and you'll see the results of your compilation and uploading in the "Output" panel at the bottom of the screen.

In *Notepad++*, use the Run pull-down menu, and type in `cmd /K cd /d $(CURRENT_DIRECTORY) &&` `make flash` to open up a command window in the current directory, compile your code, and flash it to the AVR. The `/K` leaves the window open after it's done, so you can read any errors in compiling or uploading that may have occurred. You can also run it with `/C` if you don't want to see the output.

With both of these editors, you can also bind these actions to a key combination so that compiling and uploading your code is as easy as it would be in an IDE. Pretty slick.

Anyway, once you can write and edit code, you need to compile it for the AVR, turning your human-readable C code into machine code for the AVR. The compiler we're using, avr-gcc, is the AVR-specific version of the popular open source compiler GCC. (In fact, I would argue that the support from Atmel for avr-gcc and an open source toolchain is the main reason for the chip's amazing success in the hacker community.)

In addition to the compiler, you'll need a few more software tools from the avr-gcc suite to go from source code to machine code that's ready for uploading. A script called a *makefile* is commonly used to automate all of the repetitive, intermediate bits of the process. See "Make and Makefiles" on page 20 if you want to learn a little more about what's going on with the makefiles, but don't sweat it if it's too much info—you can do everything you need to by simply editing a few lines, and I'll walk you through that.

Once you've compiled your C code into machine code in the right format, it's time to send the machine code over to the chip and write it into nonvolatile flash memory. The *flash programmer* is a piece of hardware that sits in between your computer and the target AVR microcontroller. The AVR microcontrollers, when put into programming mode, listen over their serial peripheral interface (SPI) bus for incoming data to flash into program memory. The flash programmer's job is to relay the compiled machine code to the target AVR over the SPI bus. There are tons of flash programmers available, and I've listed some of my favorites in "Flash Programmers I Have Known and Loved" on page 30.

A lot of you will have an Arduino sitting around. If so, it turns out to be fantastically easy to turn that Arduino (temporarily) into an AVR programmer. I'll walk you through the steps to do so, and how to wire it up, in "AVR and the Arduino" on page 21. So if you don't have a dedicated hardware SPI programmer just yet, I'll get you up and running with an Arduino.

Now, stepping back to your main computer, you'll need to run software that feeds the compiled machine code to the flash programmer. Far and away the most popular software uploader is AVRDUDE, which is available for all platforms and supports a wide variety of programmers. How wide? So wide that almost any way that you can think of communicating in SPI with the target AVR will work with AVRDUDE, from a few wires hooked up to your parallel port to dedicated USB programmers with their own AVR microcontroller brains.

The Software Toolchain

The main feature of the style of software development that we'll use in this book is cross-platform compatibility. That is, if you're used to the whole workflow of writing code and compiling it on a Mac, you'll have the same tools available for you on Windows or Linux, and you can be sure that you'll always know what you're doing wherever you go. After all, the target of all our work here is a little 8-bit microcontroller that doesn't know anything about what operating system you use.

To Recap:

1. *Plan*. This stage just requires your brain, some paper and a pencil, and maybe the AVR datasheet so you can figure out which parts the onboard hardware can help you with. Think through what you need the chip to do, and break it up into functions for each logical step.

2. *Code*. Write your program using whatever text/code editor makes you happy. Here you're just translating the ideas behind the functions into valid C code.

3. *Compile*. Turn your C code into AVR machine code with avr-gcc and its associated tools, most likely run from a makefile. Type **make** and read through the compiler errors, then go back and fix them.

4. *Flash*. Hook up a flash programmer to your target AVR and then run AVRDUDE to send the machine code through the programmer to the AVR chip, which saves it in flash memory. (Or just type **make flash** and watch it go.) Did flashing work?

5. *Test*. Once you've uploaded your code to the AVR, does it do what you want it to? Test it under many differing conditions before you're sure. You'll find all sorts of interesting real-world situations where your sensors aren't reporting data as you thought they would. Now's a good time to find that out, so you can recode around it.

6. *Debug*. There are many tricks for figuring out what's going wrong with your code—from lighting up status LEDs, to transferring variable data information over the serial line to your desktop computer, to stepping through the code with a debugger.

Programming the AVR—What's Really Going On?

AVR microcontrollers are able to write into their own flash program memory space. All of the ATmega series microcontrollers are set up so that when you reset them, they start listening for data on the SPI lines, and with the right instructions can program themselves.

A flash programmer works by grounding the RESET line, which halts the CPU and signals the AVR to start listening on the SPI bus. The programmer then transmits programming instructions over the SPI bus. After each instruction or section of code, the AVR writes the received data to flash memory. Some of the tiny AVR chips flash the data to program memory after every few bytes, which can be slow. Larger and newer chips store the incoming data in a temporary page memory and then write it all at once, which is much, much faster.

After the programming is complete, you can read the data back out of the AVR's flash program memory to verify again that its correct. The -v flag for AVRDUDE does this for you.

For a deep read on programming the AVR chips, for instance, if you want to implement your own flash programmer or write your own bootloader once you're done working through this book, see Atmel's "Application Note AVR910" (*http://www.atmel.com/Images/doc0943.pdf*).

Linux Setup

Setting up the toolchain for programming AVRs on Linux is tremendously simple. If you're using a Debian-based distribution (like Ubuntu or Mint or, heck, Debian) you can simply type (all on one line):

```
sudo apt-get install avrdude avrdude-doc binutils-avr avr-libc gcc-avr
gdb-avr
```

Red Hat and Fedora users type:

```
sudo yum install avrdude avr-gcc avr-binutils avr-libc avr-gdb
```

All other Linux users will find that it's easy enough to find source packages for all of the above. See *http://www.nongnu.org/avr-libc/user-manual/install_tools.html* or *http://avr-eclipse.sourceforge.net/wiki/index.php/The_AVR_GCC_Toolchain* for details.

Windows Setup

Windows users have three options for the software toolchain, and each has its quirks. The first is to download Atmel's official Atmel Studio. The downside is that it's absolutely huge and requires its own learning curve just to get familiar with the IDE. On the other hand, it's the de facto standard for programming Atmel's line of chips, and there's plenty of documentation out there to help you learn to use it.

If you use Atmel Studio you'll need to set a couple of "symbols" in the project properties to make up for macro variables otherwise defined in the project's makefile. In particular, you need to define the AVR's processor speed and baud rate (for serial communications) in two symbols F_CPU and BAUD. This will make sense once you're used to the Studio environment. Similarly, if you use someone else's software, you'll need to add a symbol for every macro variable defined in their project's makefile.

*Support for non-Atmel hardware programmers has also been variable, and the utility that's included in Studio isn't nearly as flexible as the open-source AVRDUDE program that I recommend. (For instance, if you'd like to program an Arduino using the Arduino bootloader, you'll need AVRDUDE.) To use AVRDUDE with Studio, you can create an "External Tool" command that calls AVRDUDE with the correct options for your programmer and chip. See **http://waihung.net/programming-arduino-using-atmel-studio-6/** for an example setup.*

Another option for the software toolchain in Windows is to download WinAVR. The project was frozen in 2010, but it's still available and works well, for the most part. You can download WinAVR from SourceForge (*http://sourceforge.net/projects/winavr/files/WinAVR/20100110/*). The good news is that WinAVR comes with everything you'd need to get going, including a decent code editor and AVRDUDE.

※ *The gotcha with WinAVR is that it's old and this causes trouble when you're pro-*
gramming a chip that didn't exist when WinAVR was last updated. The solution is
to copy a recent configuration file for AVRDUDE (avrdude.conf) into your installa-
tion. I've included one in the software bundle for the book, so all you need to do is copy the
file into C:\WinAVR-20100110\bin and you should be set.

During the installation, WinAVR will offer to change your PATH variable so that all
of the binary files (importantly *make*, *avrdude*, and *avr-gcc*) are available without
typing the full pathnames in. Be sure that you allow this.

The third option is the one that I'd recommend most these days. Even though it's
a little bit of hassle, it's the most powerful and flexible.

In addition to the full-blown IDE, Atmel also makes the AVR cross-compiler available
separately here: AVR Toolchain for Windows (*http://www.atmel.com/tools/ATME
LAVRTOOLCHAINFORWINDOWS.aspx*). It's compact, up-to-date, and pretty much
bulletproof. The caveat here is that you'll need to flesh out the rest of the toolchain
yourself, notably AVRDUDE and the make program that tells the compiler how to
put all the pieces together. But to make your life easy, I've included them in the
book's software bundle in a folder called *avrdude_utilities*.

※ *If you download Atmel's compiler and the additional tools, you'll need to put the*
folders somewhere and then make sure that your OS knows where to find the
programs. Easiest is to move both folders into your Program Files directory and
then hand-edit your PATH environment variable to point to them. To set an environment
variable, open the Control Panel, search for "Environment", and choose "Edit environment
variables for your account". Edit the PATH variable, and taking care to not modify any existing
values, append a ; to the end of the path, followed by the full path to the bin and avrdude-
utilities directories (separated by a ;), which should be something like C:\Program Files\avr-8-
gnu-toolchain\bin ` and `C:\Program Files\avrdude-utilities.

If you go either of the two non-IDE ways, you'll need an external editor ("Aside on
Windows Editors" on page 15), and you might be interested in the following shortcut. Assuming you've downloaded the project code from the website, open up
your code editor and save something like the following to a file called something
like *blinkLED.bat* (you'll need to change *C:\Users\elliot* to wherever you've extracted the sample code directory).

```
cd C:\Users\elliot\AVR-Programming-master\Chapter02_Programming-AVRs\blinkLED
make flash
cmd
```

When you double-click on this batch file, it will open up a command window, change to the appropriate directory, compile and flash the code to your target AVR, and then leave the command window open so that you can look out for errors in the process or issue other make commands quickly and easily. You can edit it to point to whatever code you're working on and then compiling and flashing AVR code is just a click away.

Mac Setup

AVR CrossPack (*http://www.obdev.at/products/crosspack/index.html*) is the way to go for Mac. It includes all the compile tools, AVRDUDE, and more. It's kept up to date and should just work.

Arduino Setup

As a fourth option, the Arduino IDE is available for all three OS platforms. Heck, most of you will have it installed already. If you've got Arduino up and running, there are some modifications you can make to turn your Arduino IDE into a working generic AVR C-language environment. See "AVR and the Arduino" on page 21 and, in particular, "Writing C in the Arduino IDE" on page 25 for details.

If you'd like to use your Arduino as a hardware flash programmer, but don't plan to use the Arduino IDE, you can do that too. In addition to the Arduino install, install the software toolchain for your OS.

Make and Makefiles

The C programming language lets you split up one big program or task into a bunch of individual functions, and lets you keep collections of functions together in their own files for easier maintenance and portability. That way, if you want to frequently reuse some serial-port input/output functions, for instance, all you have to do is include the serial library code files (by name) in your main code, and then tell the compiler where to find these files. Separating your code into functionally different files is good software design, but it means that you need to remember all of the dependencies among the different files in your codebase and type out potentially many filenames each time you compile.

Keeping track of all of these dependencies manually can quickly become unreasonable, and it was only a few years after C was invented that the *make* utility was designed to help. Instead of compiling your files together manually, a file called a *makefile* contains a bunch of dependency rules and instructions for processing them, and then you just run the make command and everything compiles. (That's the idea, anyway.)

So, for instance, you can explicitly compile all of your source files together like this:

```
gcc main.c another_file.c serialLibrary.c -o main
```

which makes an executable file, *main*, from all of the listed *.c* files. Or, you can write a makefile that maps out these dependencies:

```
main: main.c another_file.c serialLibrary.c
```

and then simply type **make main** or even simpler, **make**. The make program knows that names on the left side of the ":" are targets, and on the right, their dependencies. If you need to run special commands to make the targets from their dependencies, these commands are listed on the next line, indented with a tab.

Dependencies can, in turn, have other dependencies, and make will keep digging deeper until it can resolve them. Things get complicated with makefiles when you add in variables and wildcards that match any filenames. You can start to write generic rules that compile any *.c* files together, for example, and then you only have to change the variable definitions when you move a makefile from project to project.

I'm including a preconfigured makefile for each project in this book's code repository. You may be able to use them as is, but we also might have different AVR programmers and different serial ports, so you'll eventually want to at least modify some of the definitions. We'll step through configuring the makefile to fit your setup in "Configuring Your Makefile" on page 40.

Now that you've got the software set up, all you need is to connect up a flash programmer to the chip and test it out. Here, you'll have two choices. If you don't have a dedicated AVR flash programmer yet, but you have an Arduino lying around, the next chapter is for you. If you'd like to buy a dedicated AVR flash programmer, I have some advice in "Other Hardware Programmers" on page 30. Otherwise, if you've already got a flash programmer, you may proceed straight to "Getting Started: Blinking LEDs" on page 31 and get started.

AVR and the Arduino

A bunch of you are going to be used to the Arduino programming environment. That's great! In this book, I'll be teaching you all of the powerful nitty-gritty that Arduino hides from you in the name of easy accessibility. But that doesn't mean that there's any reason to let your Arduino gather dust—in fact, the Arduino platform can be a great generic AVR playground, once you know how to (ab)use it.

Arduino Pros

One very real advantage of the Arduino hardware setup is that the chip comes pre-flashed with a *bootloader*, which is code that enables the chip to communicate with your computer over the serial line in order to flash program itself. This means that you can do away with the requirement for an external bit of hardware to flash the chip—there's a tiny bit of bootloader code already running in your Arduino that'll flash the chip for you!

The second highlight of the Arduino package is that it comes with a built-in USB-to-serial converter, so you don't have to buy a separate one just yet. I personally get a lot of mileage out of my USB-Serial cable, and you will too if you want to play around with freestanding microcontrollers, GPS units, old terminals, hacked WiFi routers, and other devices. If you're going to get serious about embedded electronics hacking, you're going to want a standalone USB-Serial adapter eventually, but it's sweet that the Arduino lets you get away without buying one for the time being.

And finally, although it's not such a big deal, the Arduino is powered by your computer's USB power supply. This is handy if you're developing code on your laptop in a park or on a plane. You don't need to find a wall plug for your power adapter or remember to bring batteries along with you—all you need for flashing, communications, and power is a USB cable.

Arduino Cons

As good as the Arduino hardware is as a generic AVR development platform, it's not perfect. For use with this book and our examples, there are a number of disadvantages to using an Arduino instead of just plugging an AVR chip into a breadboard.

Probably the first among these disadvantages is the lack of the breadboard itself. Shields are great for finished products, but when I'm building up a hardware section for the first time, it's nice to test it out on something more flexible like a breadboard. I find that the more complicated my external circuitry gets, the less suitable working on the Arduino becomes. The Arduino is great for plugging a few LEDs or a couple of sensors into. But when things get interesting, I end up having to jumper the Arduino into the breadboard with 10 or more wires like some demented spider, and then my dog knocks something loose, and it takes a long while to debug the problem, and that's when I wish I'd just stuck a chip into the breadboard in the first place. (True story.)

Another downside to using an Arduino as an AVR development platform is that a few ports and pins are already irreversibly wired up and unavailable for use. For instance, when we make an eight-LED POV toy in Chapter 3, you'll discover that two of the pins that I'd like to use for LEDs are already hard-wired up to the crystal oscillator. It's a design trade-off—because it's clocked with a 16 MHz crystal oscillator, the Arduino is able to run twice as fast as an AVR using only its internal timebase.

But because the Arduino ties up two of the pins in PORTB, you'll only be able to make a six-LED cylon without having to do some elaborate coding as a workaround. If you want to display a byte's worth of data on PORTB, you'll be missing the most significant two bits.

Arduino boards aren't cheap either; just compare an Arduino Uno with the AVR ATmega328p chip that powers it. You can buy 8 or 10 AVRs (or 20 ATtiny 45s) for the price of one Arduino. This is because the Arduino has extra hardware—power regulation, USB-to-serial, and other circuitry onboard—which makes them over-qualified for many trivial applications. This also makes an Arduino too expensive to commit to a one-off quickie project, and that's a real shame because nothing in the world is better than giving your young niece a goofy microcontroller-based toy that you made for around $5 in parts. (That said, if you can prototype the toy faster because everything's wired up for you on the Arduino, go for it. A goal of this book is that you'll be able to move fluently between the "Real AVR" world and Arduino.)

More trivially, it's a minor pain to be always going back and forth between the pin names in the datasheet ("PB5" and similar) and the Arduino's pin names ("Digital 13" and so on). Figure 2-2, which is similar to the sweet ASCII art in *arduino-1.0.4/ hardware/arduino/variants/standard/pins_arduino.h*, should help.

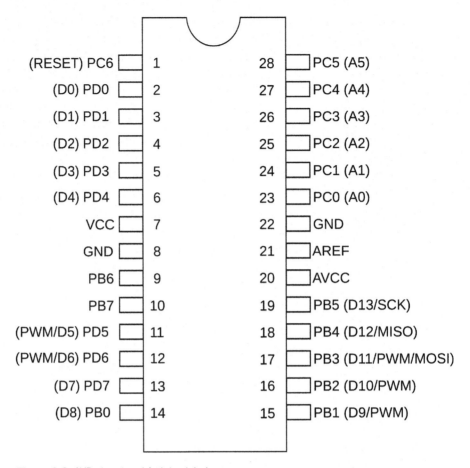

Figure 2-2. *AVR pinout and Arduino labels*

So if you're working along with code from this book, and you need an LED connected to pin PB0, for instance, you'll want to hook up the same LED to your Arduino's Digital 8 pin. (And see how the Arduino doesn't use pins PB6 and PB7?)

But don't let these gripes overshadow the main point—an Arduino can also be turned into a fine C-language AVR-programming platform. And besides, if you've got one sitting on your desk, you might as well use it.

The Arduino: Hardware or Software? Both!

In the next two sections, I'll show you how to use the Arduino—both the software IDE *and* the physical hardware—as an AVR learning platform. The first section covers programming the AVR chip that's inside the Arduino (as you normally would) but using standard C instead of the strange Arduino dialect. This way, if you've already got an Arduino in hand, but AVR chips and a breadboard in the mail, you can get started working through this book by programming the Arduino board directly.

The second section treats the case where you've already got your AVR chip on a breadboard, and you want to use your Arduino as a hardware flash programmer to transfer the code to the target AVR. Following some simple steps, you can (temporarily and reversibly) use the Arduino as a hardware programmer to flash your code into the bare AVR. And then you can decide to continue using the Arduino IDE to compile and send your code, or you can use any other code editor and the standard AVR development toolchain. The choice is yours.

Choices, Choices!

From my perspective as an experienced coder and microcontroller user, I like to use my own favorite development tools rather than the Arduino IDE. It's also a lot easier and faster to prototype circuits with a bare AVR on a breadboard than using the Arduino hardware.

However, using the Arduino as a hardware programmer is tremendously comfortable, even if you're used to more advanced tools. With just six wires between the Arduino and your breadboard, you've got a source of power and a flash programmer that's just as good as any other.

If you're willing to learn a bit more about the non-Arduino toolchain—programming in standard C, using makefiles, and all that—you'll be learning some transferrable skills that will work on other hardware platforms and microprocessor architectures. And then if you eventually swap out the Arduino-as-programmer for dedicated hardware, you won't even notice.

The Arduino Is an AVR

If you're shy about leaving the comfortable Arduino IDE, you don't have to. With a few tweaks, the Arduino compiler can be fooled into compiling standard C code, which you can then flash directly to the AVR that lives inside the Arduino hardware. So if you're coming from the Arduino world and you'd like to get started with this book right away—you can!

The reason that this all works is that the Arduino environment is really just a thin GUI layer that ties together the standard AVR toolchain—GCC as a compiler and AVRDUDE to talk to the flash programmer. In short, you can start off with the full Arduino IDE and slowly migrate over to doing everything manually, or vice versa.

Writing C in the Arduino IDE

If you're used to the Arduino IDE and don't want to try out another code editor, for instance, the following steps will enable you to compile and flash valid C code with minimal changes to your old workflow. Follow these steps whether you're programming for the Arduino's onboard AVR chip or for an external AVR target on a breadboard—anytime you want to write straight AVR C code within the Arduino environment.

To get running in C with the Arduino IDE, there are two things that you'll have to do only once, *before* you even start the IDE:

- Copy over whatever libraries you need to go with your code. In writing the code for this book, I ended up using a few bits of common code in almost every project. It makes more sense to put all of these common files in one place. To use this "library" of common code, create a directory in your libraries folder (*~/sketchbook/libraries* on Linux and *Documents/Arduino/libraries* on Windows) and copy your common code here. Now you'll be able to use it within any other program by simply by importing the library. So copy the *AVR-Programming-Library* folder out of the code directory and into your sketches library right now.

- If you're going to be coding for an ATmega 328P, either in an Arduino (the Uno, for instance) or as a standalone chip, fix up your *portpins.h* file. See "portpins.h and the Arduino IDE" on page 26. If you're going to use an ATmega168 or other chips, you don't have to follow this step, but it won't hurt.

Now that your Arduino IDE is set up, it's time to get coding. In this example, I'll assume that you'd like to copy some code out of one of the book's projects, but the same basic steps apply for when you're writing it yourself:

1. Start the Arduino IDE.

2. Import the header files into the project using the Sketch → Import Library pulldown, where you should find the *AVR-Programming-Library* folder at the bottom of the list. Notice that the Arduino IDE adds include lines for each header file in your directory.

3. Save this (mostly blank) sketch with a descriptive name. This will create a directory for you to put your code in.

4. Outside of Arduino, copy the C code file that you'd like to use into the sketches directory. If you press Open and reopen the sketch, you should see this newly added code in a new tab.

5. Alternatively, you can write new C code in the sketch by opening up a new tab (Ctrl-Shift-N, or from the arrow menu in the top-right corner) and then entering the code directly.

6. To make sure that all works, click on the Verify button. If it does, then you're ready to flash the code.

Flashing the Arduino as target

This is super simple from within the Arduino IDE, because programming the Arduino is what it's meant to do. The only difference here is that you're writing your code in real, portable C rather than Arduinoese:

portpins.h and the Arduino IDE

The code compiler that the Arduino IDE uses is the same GCC as you'd use if you were compiling manually. As such, it doesn't care if you pass it code written in C for the AVR, or in C++, using the Arduino libraries. Along the way, though, I found a gotcha.

For whatever reason, the *portpins.h* include file that comes with Arduino 1.0.4 and previous is old (2006!) and doesn't conform to modern usage. The end result is that standard pin-name macros like PB1 don't end up getting defined for the mega328 chip, while the old-style PORTB1 macros are.

If you want to compile for an ATmega 328P chip (as is found on the Arduino Uno, for instance), you'll want to replace the *portpins.h* file with a more recent version. On my system, I found the file in *arduino-1.0.4/ hardware/tools/avr/lib/avr/include/avr/portpins.h*. Replace this file with the version that I've included with the book's code library, and you should be able to just write C.

If you see errors like PB1 undeclared (first use in this function), that's the *portpins.h* bug.

1. Verify that your board type is selected in Tools → Board.
2. Make sure you've included your library using Sketch → Import Libraries, and that the #include lines appear in the first sketch tab.
3. Click Upload (or type Ctrl-U) to flash your code into the AVR inside the Arduino hardware. Easy.

The Arduino Is an AVR Programmer

Or at least it can be. In this section, you're not going to be writing your code into the Arduino as a target, but rather using it as the middleman. You've got an AVR chip that you've stuck into a breadboard, and you're going to use the Arduino as the hardware programmer, thanks to example code that converts the Arduino into an Arduino In-System Programmer (ISP). You can do this either from within the Arduino software IDE, or you can use an editor and the avr-gcc toolchain independently.

Wiring your Arduino as a flash programmer

The first step toward using your Arduino as a flash programmer is hooking it up to your breadboard. The essential six connections are power, ground, RESET/PC6, SCK/ PB5, MISO/PB4, and MOSI/PB3. (You'll find these pin names in Figure 2-5 on page 2 of the AVR datasheet, or you can also just refer to Figure 2-3.)

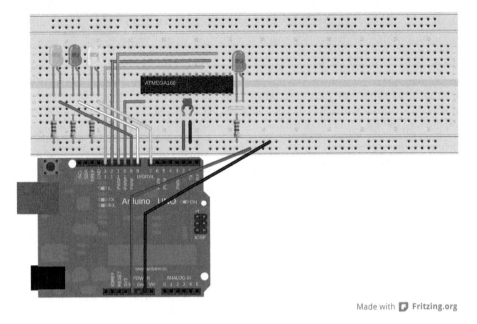

Made with **Fritzing.org**

Figure 2-3. *Arduino as flash programmer*

The single red LED hooked up to pin PB0 on the target AVR is the LED in question if you're uploading this chapter's blinkLED code.

The three (optional, colored) LEDs hooked up to the Arduino are status lights. Green will pulse while the ArduinoISP is waiting for input, yellow will light when it's transferring code to the AVR, and red will light if there's an error. You can leave these out, but they make everything look so professional, no?

Resistor values for the LEDs aren't too critical, but something over 200 ohms is a good idea for normal LEDs, which commonly have around a 1.7 V threshold voltage, and are rated for around 20 milliamps: (5 V – 1.7 V) / 220 ohms = 15 milliamps.

Flashing AVR chips using the Arduino as a programmer

Now that the hardware is wired up, let's use it to program the AVR chip! Following these instructions will turn your Arduino into a flash programmer. (When you want your Arduino back as an Arduino, you can just reprogram it as usual.)

1. Verify that your Arduino board type is set up correctly (Tools → Board → Uno in my case).

2. Flash the example code "ArduinoISP" into the Arduino hardware the usual Arduino way.

3. If you don't have a sketch ready to upload yet, go back to "Writing C in the Arduino IDE" on page 25 and set up *blinkLED.c*.

4. Select Tools → Programmer → Arduino as ISP to program *through* the Arduino hardware instead of programming the Arduino itself.

5. Select Tools → Board → Arduino Pro Mini (8 MHz) w/ ATmega168, because we're targeting an ATmega168 running at 8 MHz. (Nobody will know it's not inside an Arduino Pro.)

6. *Shift*-click on the Upload button (Shift-Ctrl-U) to flash your code into the AVR target. If you're too accustomed to just clicking the Upload button and forget to press Shift here, you'll get an error like avrdude: `stk500_disable(): protocol error, expect=0x14, resp=0x10`.

7. If you want to see what's going on in the background, click File → Preferences → Show verbose output.

8. Otherwise, sit back and watch your AVR target get programmed. Does it blink? Sweet!

Using Arduino as hardware programmer without the Arduino IDE

Because it's possible to use your Arduino as a flash programmer from within the Arduino IDE, you're probably wondering if it's possible to flash arbitrary AVR chips without using the Arduino IDE as well. Of course it is!

First, make sure that your Arduino is wired up as in Figure 2-3 and that you've uploaded the ArduinoISP sketch to the Arduino. Once you've done that, you won't need to touch the Arduino IDE again if you don't want to.

Open up the *blinkLED* directory from the software that accompanies this book. Because you're using makefiles to configure and compile your code, you're going to need to edit *Makefile* by hand so that it knows how to use the Arduino programmer. In short, you want to use programmer type "avrisp" at 19,200 baud on the correct serial port.

For Linux, try:

```
PROGRAMMER_TYPE = avrisp
PROGRAMMER_ARGS = -b 19200 -P /dev/ttyACM0
```

For Windows, try:

```
PROGRAMMER_TYPE = avrisp
PROGRAMMER_ARGS = -b 19200 -P com5
```

For Macintosh using the Uno or Mega 2560, try:

```
PROGRAMMER_TYPE = avrisp
PROGRAMMER_ARGS = -b 19200 -P /dev/tty.usbmodemXXXXXXX
```

For Macintosh using any other Arduino, try:

```
PROGRAMMER_TYPE = avrisp
PROGRAMMER_ARGS = -b 19200 -P /dev/tty.usbserialXXXXXXX
```

You can figure out which port name the Arduino connects to from within the Arduino environment, under Tools → Serial Port. On Windows systems it will be a COM port, and on Linux or OSX systems it will be /dev/tty-something.

Once your makefile is configured for the Arduino-as-programmer, you're all set to flash the code over to your chip. If you've got a terminal window open, and you're in the *blinkLED* directory, typing make flash should do it.

Other Hardware Programmers

If you don't have an Arduino handy, or if you'd like the convenience of a dedicated hardware flash programmer, you've got a lot of good choices. If you've got the software already set up, a flash programmer is your missing link. (If you already got your firmware flashed by following the previous Arduino instructions, you can skip this section, or read on for curiosity's sake.)

Flash Programmers I Have Known and Loved

You have a large number of choices for hardware flash programmers. A programmer can be as simple as a handful of wires, but most of them actually use an AVR or other microcontroller to interface between your computer and the AVR that you'd like to program. Here is a shortened list of some of the good choices you have available:

Parallel port
> The first programmer I ever used was not really any programmer at all, but instead just a cable with five wires soldered to a parallel port D-sub connector. This works because AVRDUDE knows how to toggle the lines of a parallel port to program your AVR chips directly. Unfortunately this programming method requires a parallel port on your computer, which is a luxury that fewer and fewer of us have. On the other hand, if you'd like to go this route, search the Web for a DAPA (Direct AVR Parallel Access) cable. Many of the schematics will include "safety" resistors—feel free to ignore them unless you're hooking up your AVR to voltages higher than 15 V. If you've got an unused parallel printer cable lying around, you've got your first programmer.

Atmel AVRISP mkII
> Atmel's current official USB in-system programmer, the AVRISP mkII is a very nice programmer that's capable of programming the whole AVR line, including the newest XMega devices. It's a bit more expensive than other programmers, but it's rock solid and is quite a bargain all in all.

USBTiny and USBasp
> These two USB-based AVR programmers have super simple hardware designs with open source firmware. You can make one yourself, although you will ironically have to find a way to flash the firmware into the AVR in the programmer (an Arduino ISP is perfect for this). You can also find these designs for sale all

over—I've got a USBasp-based programmer that I bought for $5 online, and it's just fine. Both of these designs have a jumper that allows you to power your breadboard off of your computer's USB port, which is handy for most applications in this book.

LadyAda's USBTinyISP

This is an improved version of the USBTiny, with input and output buffering. I've used one of these for a few years. They come in kits, don't cost too much money, and have very good build instructions and support. Like the USBTiny project that it's based on, LadyAda's programmer can power your project off the USB bus. If you'd like an easy kit to solder together that builds a useful tool, this is a good way to go.

A family portrait of some of my programmers can be found in Figure 2-4, from center-top and going clockwise:

1. An Arduino and six wires makes a totally workable flash programmer.
2. USBTinyISP
3. USBasp, from BaiTe in China
4. USBTiny, tiny version from ehajo.de
5. A homemade programming spider, which plugs into a breadboard around the AVR chip and connects up the programming, power, and reset pins the right way every time. If you're at all handy with a soldering iron and perfboard, you should make one of these.

Getting Started: Blinking LEDs

OK, let's get down to business and compile, flash, and test our first AVR microcontroller project. This is *not* the coolest, most interesting project in this book. The point is to verify that all parts of the programming toolchain are working for you before we start to get a little fancy. In order to minimize the possible ways to mess up, we'll build up the simplest possible project that puts the software toolchain together with the flash programmer, an AVR chip, and the most minimal possible feedback—a single LED.

To download the code for this project—and for the rest of the book—visit *https://github.com/hexagon5un/AVR-Programming* and click the "Download ZIP" button. The blinking LED example is in this chapter's folder.

Please double-check that you've installed an appropriate software toolchain for your OS, or modified the Arduino environment to work with C language code. If you're using an Arduino as a hardware programmer, make sure that you've flashed ArduinoISP. Fasten your seatbelts—here we go!

Figure 2-4. *Some programmer options*

Hookup

The overview of wiring for this chapter is that we're going to be hooking up the programmer (including its power-supply pins) to the AVR chip. Each of these pins has a specific function, and they're labelled in Figure 2-5. The whole point is to make sure that the programmer's MOSI pin is connected to the AVR's MOSI pin (PB3) and so on. We'll also wire up an LED for display purposes, and optionally wire up another as a power-on indicator.

If you're using an Arduino as your programmer, your wiring will end up looking like Figure 2-3, but you can also assemble the circuit piecewise as we're doing here. First hook up the power and verify that it's working, and then move on to the MOSI, MISO, SCK, and RESET wires. The principle is exactly the same.

For the first step, let's set up the power rails of your breadboard to double-check that we've got the pinout from the programmer's connector right. You're going to need some red wire for 5 V and some black wire for GND. If you're using an Arduino as programmer, the 5 V and GND connections are nicely labelled on the board. Use red and black wires to hook them up to the breadboard's power rails.

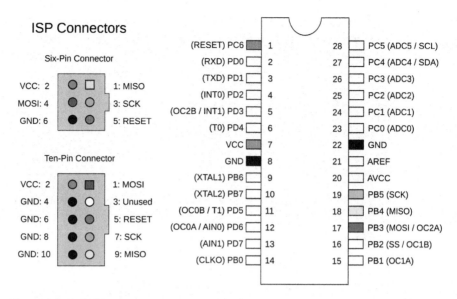

ISP Connectors

Figure 2-5. *AVR ISP programming pins*

If you're using a programmer that ends in a standard 6-pin or 10-pin two-row IDC connector, getting the pinout correct can be a little bit tricky. For orientation, set the connector on the table so that you're looking down into the holes, and notice the location of the plastic tab. The cable should also have a red stripe on the same side that has the VCC pin, which is a very helpful mnemonic. Hook up the power pins so that they look like Figure 2-6.

If you're going to use a power-on LED, now's the time to plug it into the board to verify that you've got power. Wire it up as in Figure 2-7. Note polarity matters with LED, and you'll need to make sure that the positive side is connected to VCC and the negative to ground. You can recognize the negative side of an LED by its shorter pin (think of it as the "minus" side having something *subtracted* from its length), or by the slight flat spot on the flange of round LEDs, or by the larger structure inside the LED itself. Connect the resistor up to the negative pin.

Plug your USB programmer into your computer. If the LED glows, the power supply is ready to go. If not, and you're using a programmer like the USBTiny, you may have to install a jumper across two pins to enable the power-supply passthrough. (See the instructions that came with your programmer for how to make the programmer supply power to the AVR.) If this still isn't working, double-check your 6-pin connector again. Or maybe your programmer doesn't supply power over the VCC and GND pins (the Atmel ones don't). In that case, it's up to you to find a 5V power supply and plug it into the power rails. A four-AA battery pack works great if you've got one.

After you've gotten the power-on LED light working, you know for sure that you're getting power on the breadboard's supply rails. On to the next step!

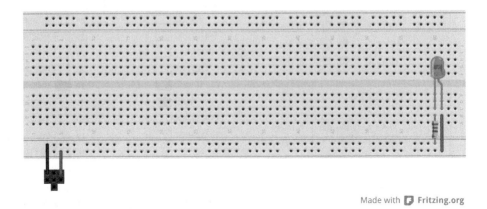

Made with **Fritzing.org**

Figure 2-6. AVR programmer layout—no chip yet

Now plug the AVR somewhere in the middle of the board. Locate pins 7 and 8, which are power and ground for the chip, and plug a 100 nF (0.1 µF) capacitor across the two power pins. Using a red wire, connect pin 7 to the VCC rail. Wire up pin 8 with a black wire to the GND rail. Now you've completed the setup in Figure 2-7.

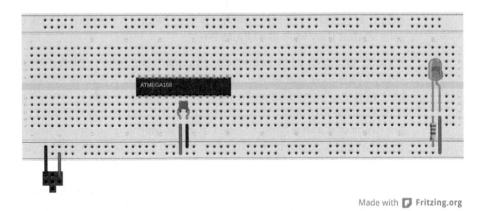

Made with **Fritzing.org**

Figure 2-7. AVR programmer layout—power

Now hook up the rest of the programmer's pins. Look carefully at Figure 2-5 if it's not clear which pins are which. Double-check that MOSI on the connector is wired to MOSI on the AVR, etc. Finally, connect up the demo output LED and its resistor as shown in Figure 2-8. When you're done with this, we're ready to test it out.

Full Power Connections

The astute datasheet readers out there will notice that there are more pins on the AVR devoted to powering the chip than we're connecting here. On the right side of the chip, pins 20 and 22 are labelled AVCC and GND respectively. AVCC provides power to the analog to digital converter (ADC), which you'll first learn how to use in Chapter 7.

The extra GND line exists to provide a low resistance return line to the digital pins on the right side of the chip. Inside the integrated circuit package, there's a tiny wire connecting the two GND pins, but it's thin enough that it actually has measurable resistance. (I get around 2 Ohms with my multimeter.) In most circumstances, this won't matter.

We're skipping the not-entirely-essential power lines here in the name of simplicity — too many wires on the breadboard when you're starting out provides more points of failure. On the other hand, if you're designing a PCB that's going to use an AVR along with other integrated circuits, it's certainly good practice to connect up both of the GND pins.

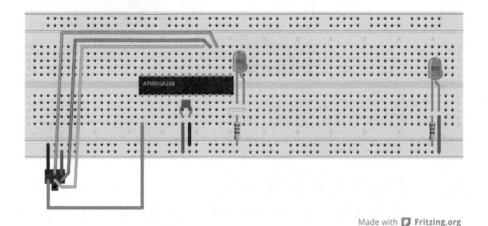

Made with **Fritzing.org**

Figure 2-8. *BlinkLED full setup*

ISP Headers

The Atmel-standard 6-pin and 10-pin headers are nice for manufactured boards because they're compact, but they're not at all breadboard-friendly, and that's why we end up with all these wires all over. Sparkfun (and probably others) sell adapters that convert the 5 × 2 and 3 × 2 layouts into a 6 × 1 inline layout that plugs nicely into the breadboard and labels the signal lines as well. If you're ever placing an order with them, these little tools are well worth a dollar.

Alternatively, you can take some perfboard and wire up a similar breakout yourself. You'll need a bunch of breakaway header pins, a bit of wire, and some patience. Make sure you test and label the outputs when you're done.

For the long run, I'd recommend making yourself a programming adapter of some kind. The idea is to hardwire up a connector that either plugs into a breadboard or sits on top of the chip that you can use to replace the multiple wires that connect the programmer to the chip. Figure 2-9 demonstrates a variety of ways to simplify connections between your AVR and programmer.

Figure 2-9. *Programming adapters for ISP 6-pin headers*

From the top, going clockwise:

1. A USBTiny programmer with the standard 6-pin ISP header.

2. A zero insertion force (ZIF) socket that I wired up to connect to the 6-pin ISP header and the ATmegax8 series chips. For fun, I also added a power-on LED and an external power connection so that it can work with non-self-powered flash programmers. You can find ZIF sockets cheap at online auction sites. The underlying perfboard came from Radio Shack.

3. Next is a (deluxe!) custom board that I had made as a precursor to a board I used in teaching an AVR class. This one breaks out all the ports into banks, has a 6-pin SPI header, an external power connector, on-board capacitors and power lights, and a 6-pin inline header that's compatible with the FTDI USB-Serial cable pinouts.

4. On the bottom is an experimental 6-pin ISP adaptor that just barely squeezes on top of an AVR chip, holding itself in place by bending the pins a little bit. I got the idea from *http://elm-chan.org/works/avrx/report_e.html*, but I added on a serial interface as well. It's hard to maintain contact with all the pins at once, and I only use this connector in emergencies.

5. Last, on the far left, is the homemade programming spider that I use almost all the time. It plugs into a breadboard just around the AVR and connects up everything you need to flash the chip. It's the bee's knees, and if you're handy with a soldering iron or looking for an excuse to learn, making a connector like this is well worth your time.

AVRDUDE

After you've gotten the circuit breadboarded and the AVR connected up to the programmer, you're ready to start talking to the AVR to test the connection. And, believe it or not, the easiest way to do this is to type a little bit.

Open up a command-line window. If you're in Linux or Mac OS, open up Terminal. For Windows, open up a Run dialog from the Start menu, type in **cmd**, and hit Enter. You can then type **avrdude** to double-check your installation. You should see a helpful listing of all the command-line flags and arguments that you can use. You can read up on the most useful ones in "AVRDUDE Options" on page 37.

If you don't get AVRDUDE running from the command line, you're going to need to make sure that it's installed and that your OS knows the correct path to find it. If you're on Windows, the easiest way is probably to uninstall WinAVR and reinstall, allowing it to set up the PATH variable for you this time. Linux and Mac people should not have this issue.

 Drivers and Windows

If you're running Windows, you may not automatically have the correct drivers for your programmer installed. This is notably the case with Windows Vista and Windows 7 and the USBTiny and USBasp type programmers. If you get a warning message like "usbtiny device not found," it's very likely that your drivers aren't set up right.

You should probably follow whatever instructions your programmer comes with. For me, I had to download a newer libusb from LadyAda's website, install it, and then do a manual install of the USBTiny drivers through the Device Manager. This step is no fun, but you only have to do it once.

Now let's try to talk to the programmer directly. Type something like **avrdude -p m168p -c usbtiny** to interrogate the chip (only substitute your programmer in place of the "usbtiny") and optionally add a serial port and baud rate. If all is hooked up well, it will respond with something about the chip's signature and fuses and say OK. Success looks something like this:

```
avrdude: AVR device initialized and ready to accept instructions
Reading | ################################################## | 100% 0.01s
```

AVRDUDE Options

Whoa! That's a lot of choices. Let's look at a few of the ones that we'll use:

-c <programmer>
Here you specify the type of flash programmer that you're using. Many serial programmers, including the ArduinoISP, use the generic av risp type (not the arduino type, which programs the Arduino itself). There are also configurations for both usbasp and usbtiny programmers. If you'd like to see the full list, type **avrdude -c ?**.

-p <partno>
Here you specify the type of AVR chip that you're programming for. In our case "m168" is an ATmega168 chip or "m168p" if you've got that version.

-P <port>
If you're not using a native USB programmer (for instance, if you're using an ArduinoISP), you'll need to know which serial port the programmer is connected to. See "Common AVRDUDE Configurations" on page 40 for details. On Windows, it's usually something like COM3; on Linux and Mac OS, it's in the /dev/tty* lineup.

-b <baud>
This sets the baud rate if you're using a serial programmer. You'll have to know what speed your programmer wants, or use trial and error.

-n
Write-nothing mode. This one lets you test out commands without worrying that you'll accidently mess up the chip.

-t
Terminal mode. This mode lets you talk to the AVR chip directly. After the programmer has connected, type **sig** to read the AVR's device signature, which makes a quick test of basic communication between the programmer and chip. Type **help** to see all the options.

-C <config-file>
This lets you use a nonstandard configuration file. If the version of AVRDUDE that you've got doesn't support a particular chip or programmer, you can often fix it by getting a more recent configuration file. I've included mine in the book's software bundle.

-U
This the command that reads or writes to memory. You'll almost always be calling this from a makefile, but if you'd like to dump the memory of an AVR chip to a file, or flash in a *.hex* file that someone has already compiled for you, this is how you'd do it.

```
avrdude: Device signature = 0x1e9406
avrdude: safemode: Fuses OK
avrdude done.   Thank you.
```

AVRDUDE errors

On the other hand, you might get an error. There are basically four possible errors you'll get, depending on whether you've messed up the wiring, specified the wrong chip or programmer type, or don't have adequate permissions to use the interface. Let's break them down into cases.

You get an an error that reads:

```
avrdude: initialization failed, rc=-1
        Double check connections and try again, or use -F to override
        this check.
```

The dreaded rc=-1 error message means that your wiring is messed up. Despite what it suggests, using -F won't help you—99.9% of the time when you see this error, your problem is that the six wires connecting your programmer to the AVR chip aren't hooked up right. This error can occur when you don't have power to the chip, when any of the RESET, MISO, MOSI, or SCK lines aren't connected properly, or even if you've got something else plugged into any of these pins that's interfering with your setup. Double-check everything until the problem is fixed; maybe even unplug and replug your USB programmer.

You get an an error that reads:

```
avrdude: Device signature = 0x1e9406
avrdude: Expected signature for ATmega168P is 1E 94 0B
        Double check chip, or use -F to override this check.
```

This probably means that you've got the AVR chip type wrong. In the previous example, I used a mega168 but told it I had a mega168P. In this case, you just need to change the chip type that you're passing as an argument to AVRDUDE. If AVR-DUDE doesn't have a configuration for the chip you're using, you should try using a newer (or custom) configuration file with the -C flag (see "AVRDUDE Options" on page 37).

The other source of the Expected signature error is that there's something wrong with the communication channel. If the programmer sees a signature like 0xffffff or 0x000000 or the signature changes from one trial to the next, you've most likely got something wired up to your ISP lines that's blocking the communications, or you've got a loose wire. Fix these problems and try again.

You get an an error that reads:

```
avrdude: stk500_recv(): programmer is not responding
avrdude done.  Thank you.
```

or:

```
avrdude: error: could not find USB device with vid=0x16c0 pid=0x5dc
vendor='www.fischl.de' product='USBasp'
```

or:

```
avrdude: Error: Could not find USBtiny device (0x1781/0xc9f)
```

This means AVRDUDE is having trouble finding your programmer. In the case of a serial programmer like when you're using the Arduino, double-check the serial port and baud-rate flags that you're passing to AVRDUDE. If you're using a USB programmer, make sure that it's recognized by the system. On Linux you can type lsusb and look for the programmer in the list. On Windows, check for it in the Device Manager.

Finally, if you're on Linux and you receive a permissions error, you can fix it by typing **sudo avrdude** instead of **avrdude**. When you get tired of the extra typing, you can give yourself permission to write to USB serial ports. In Ubuntu-like distributions, this means adding yourself to the dialout group. For all flavors of Linux you could alternatively write a *udev* script for the specific programmer. You'll find specific directions online if you search "avrdude udev" and your programmer type.

Common AVRDUDE Configurations

AVRDUDE supports more than 70 programmers and 100 chip types, and runs on three different operating systems, so the number of possible configurations is ridiculous. Here are some examples of the types of configurations that you'll encounter to get you started:

Windows, Linux, or Mac OS with USBTiny, ATmega168P

```
avrdude -p m168p -c usbtiny
```

(Because USBTiny and USBasp programmers don't need any additional options, the command is the same across all three operating systems.)

For the following, you need to type the commands all on one line:

Windows with ArduinoISP, ATmega168p

```
avrdude -p m168p -c avrisp -P com5
-b 19200
```

Linux with ArduinoISP, ATmega168p

```
avrdude -p m168p -c avrisp -P
/dev/ttyACM0 -b 19200
```

Mac OS with ArduinoISP, ATmega168p

```
avrdude -p m168p -c avrisp -P
/dev/tty.usbserial-A5307bQf -b 19200
```

ArduinoISP needs the -P flag for the serial port. To find out which serial port you need, open up the Arduino IDE and look under Tools → Serial Ports with the Arduino plugged in. (The Arduino plugs into USB, but it's got an onboard serial emulator that makes it show up as a serial port device.)

Windows with parallel port programming cable, ATmega88

```
avrdude -p m88 -c dapa -P lpt1
```

Linux with parallel port programming cable, ATmega168p

```
avrdude -p m88 -c dapa -P /dev/parport0
```

I hope these examples get you squared away, or at least put you on the right path. If not, an Internet search will probably yield results. In most all situations, just a couple of tweaks to the same basic command options will work.

Configuring Your Makefile

Playing around with AVRDUDE by itself is good for debugging and making sure everything works, but you'd hate to have to remember all this, much less type this all out every time. And that's where the makefile comes in.

As mentioned in "Make and Makefiles" on page 20, most of the makefile is generic info for the compiler about how to compile and link program files for the AVR, and you'll never need to modify these generic bits. On the other hand, the top few lines include some definitions that are specific to the project at hand and to your compilation and flash programming setup. We're going to need to edit some of these by hand. Copy the *blinkLED* folder from the book's source code library and open up *Makefile* with your programming editor. Let's step through the bits you'll need to change:

MCU

> This is the type of AVR chip you're using. In our case, we're using an ATmega168, so it reads atmega168. For a complete list of supported chips, type **avr-gcc --target-help** and about halfway down you'll find a list of "Known MCU names."

F_CPU

> This definition tells the compiler what clock speed your chip is running at. If you don't have an external clock source, like a crystal, this is either 1000000 or 8000000 for the ATmega chips—one megahertz or eight megahertz. Getting this right will matter for the timing of serial communication, and anything else where timing is key.

BAUD

> This is the baud rate that you're going to use for computer-to-AVR serial communications, and 9,600 baud is a good conservative default.

LIBDIR

> The code for this book reuses a common base for many projects. Instead of copying these files into each project's folder, the common files are stored in a directory that I've called *AVR-Programming-Library*. By default, it's located two directories above each project. If you move things around, you'll need to change this variable to point at the new location of the *AVR-Programming-Library*. Later on, if your code doesn't rely on this library, you can leave the variable blank or change it to fit.

PROGRAMMER_TYPE

> The two "programmer" options are for AVRDUDE, along with information about what chip we're programming from MCU. Here, you enter the type of flash programmer that you're using, and the makefile passes it to AVRDUDE using the -c option. If you're using a USBTiny or USBasp, for instance, you enter that here. If you're using the Arduino as a flash programmer, enter **avrisp**.

PROGRAMMER_ARGS

> The other "programmer" option is for any of the other necessary AVRDUDE options. If you're using a USBTiny or USBasp, you won't have to enter anything here; just leave the line blank. If you are using a serial-based programmer, you'll need to specify the serial port and baud rate using the -P and -b options, respectively.

> See "Common AVRDUDE Configurations" on page 40 for hints, or scroll down to the very bottom of the makefile to see some examples for common programmers and configurations. And remember, this is just passing these options on to AVRDUDE, so whatever it took to get AVRDUDE working on the command line (except for processor and programmer type), you'll need to add in here.

Flash

OK, by now you're dying to see some blinking lights. I can't blame you. If you've already got a command-line window open, change directory to the blinkLED project and type make flash. If all of the preparations up to now went well, congratulations! Your sweet reward is a slowly blinking LED on the breadboard!

You want more? Open up the *blinkLED.c* file in your editor, and read through. Try changing the delay times to change the blink rate of the LED—for instance, make it blink on for just a very short time between long periods of being off. Each time you edit the code, save it and then type make flash again. Or if you're using an editor that lets you compile and flash from within it, it's even simpler.

Take the time now to get used to the "edit-compile-flash" cycle, while the toolchain is unfamiliar but the code is simple. Once the code and/or the circuits start to get complicated, you'll be glad to have faith in the toolchain.

Troubleshooting

We did most of the troubleshooting for this project as we went along. Is the power working? It should be, as long as the power LED is lit. Does the AVR receive this power? A quick way to double-check is to put an LED with a series resistor across the AVR power pins, where you've got a capacitor.

The next things to check are the connections, because it's easy to get these wrong. But because we tested them using AVRDUDE, we know that the programmer is able to communicate with the AVR chip, so all should be well.

So with the hardware all debugged, that only leaves the software, and in this case, it's about as simple as can be. What's more, I've double-checked it about a billion times, so it should compile just fine. (Barring the *pindefs.h* problem if you're using an Arduino IDE for compiling, in which case see "portpins.h and the Arduino IDE" on page 26.)

Because everything's working just fine, a good exercise at this point is to break the code and see what happens. C compilers are great when it comes to complaining *that* something's wrong, but not as helpful as you'd like when it comes to pinpointing the *cause* of the error. For instance, pick a line of code that ends with a ";" and delete the semicolon. Save the bad code and type make to see what happens. All sorts of errors, no? But none of them tell you "you deleted a semicolon." Learning to deal with the error messages is an important part of coding.

If you deleted a semicolon as suggested, you'll probably see an error like:

```
blinkLED.c: In function 'main':
blinkLED.c:22:5: error: called object '_delay_ms(1.0e+3)' is not a function
```

The compiler is telling you that something went wrong around line 22 in the code, specifically something that starts at line 22, column 5. It doesn't know there's a missing semicolon, but it gets you in the right neighborhood. This is where you have to do a little detective work. (The meaning of the error is that lines that look like something() without a semicolon at the end are supposed to be function definitions, but in this case it's not. The compiler can't know that you meant *use* a function rather than define one if you don't add that semicolon on the end.)

It could be worse. Sometimes there will be a string of many errors all in a row. Don't give up! It's not necessarily the case that you made many errors, but maybe the first one caused a bunch of follow-on problems to arise. If the compiler gives you multiple errors, it's often a good idea to start fixing the first one (by line number) and then see if that resolves the rest.

Anyway, fix up that semicolon and reflash your valid code with a make flash. Notice what a successful flashing looks like. Heck, if you're feeling nerdy, scroll back up to see the exact string of commands the makefile ran on your behalf and revisit "Make and Makefiles" on page 20. If you just want to get on with more programming, and everything worked, we're done here.

Digital Output 3

POV Toy

If you got the project from Chapter 2 running, you've gotten yourself a little bit familiar with the AVR toolchain. You've hooked up a simple circuit on the breadboard, and you've seen the first sweet blinkies of success! Now you're ready to take the next step: even more blinkies blinking even faster, and looking at what's going on under the hood.

The project for this chapter is a persistence-of-vision (POV) pattern generator. By turning eight LEDs on and off really quickly, the POV toy exploits your eye's slow response to light in order to draw patterns that seem to float in midair when you scan your eyes across the LEDs. For an example of how this looks, see Figure 3-1. POV toys are fun, and you'll have something neat to show for your efforts at the end of the chapter. You could spend an entire rainy Saturday making up neat patterns to display on the POV toy. (Don't ask me how I know!)

What You Need

In this chapter, in addition to the programming setup from Chapter 2, you will need:

- Eight LEDs and current-limiting resistors.

- One 2N7000 MOSFET. This is not strictly essential, but highly recommended. The MOSFET acts as a switch to allow you to share some of the AVR pins between duty as LED outputs and flash-programming inputs. (See "MOSFET trickery" on page 54 for details.)

- (Optionally) a soldering iron to solder the resistors permanently to the LEDs.

- (Optionally) a 4xAA battery pack so that you can swing the POV toy around.

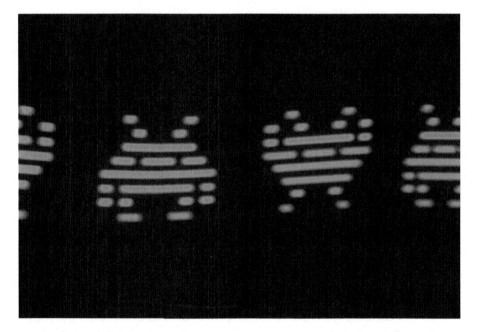

Figure 3-1. *POV invasion*

Digital output is both the simplest and most common way that your microcontroller programs are going to control other devices in the outside world. By setting the voltage on an AVR pin, you can light an LED or activate a circuit that turns a motor on or off. So as we're going through these exercises, if you'd like to think of each LED as standing in for a motor you'd like to turn on, or a switch you'd like to flip somewhere, I won't stop you from daydreaming.

Along the way, you'll learn how to configure the AVR's pins to output a digital logic voltage, a bit about how the AVR represents numbers as eight-bit binary bytes, and some of the basics of writing code in C. That's a lot to cover, so lets get to it!

blinkLED Redux

Before we take on anything truly new, let's have a look at the code that's hopefully still blinking away inside the chip on your desktop, because we'll be expanding on that program in this chapter. See Example 3-1 to refresh your memory.

Example 3-1. **blinkLED.c listing**

```
                                        /* Blinker Demo */

// ------- Preamble -------- //
#include <avr/io.h>                      /* Defines pins, ports, etc */
#include <util/delay.h>                  /* Functions to waste time */
```

```
int main(void) {

  // -------- Inits --------- //
  DDRB = 0b00000001;              /* Data Direction Register B:
                                     writing a one to the bit
                                     enables output. */


  // ------ Event loop ------ //
  while (1) {

    PORTB = 0b00000001;           /* Turn on first LED bit/pin in PORTB */
    _delay_ms(1000);                                      /* wait */

    PORTB = 0b00000000;           /* Turn off all B pins, including LED */
    _delay_ms(1000);                                      /* wait */

  }                                          /* End event loop */
  return (0);                       /* This line is never reached */
}
```

The Structure of AVR C Code

Looking over the *blinkLED.c* code, notice that the code falls into the following rough sections:

```
[preamble & includes]
[possibly some function definitions]
int main(void){
    [chip initializations]
    while(1) { [event loop]
        [do this stuff forever]
    }
    return(0);
}
```

The preamble is where you include information from other files, define global variables, and define functions. If you're going to be using a library of functions from some other source, or even just reusing your own code, this is where you'll do it.

After the preamble comes the main() function. The name "main" is special—regardless of how many other functions are defined, your C program *must* have exactly one main() function. main is where the AVR starts executing your code when the power first goes on. It's the entry point.

Inside the main function you'll find a while(1) loop, often referred to as the "main loop" or "event loop." while() loops are loops that continue running over and over as long as the condition inside the parentheses is true. And in C, 0 always resolves as false, and 1 always resolves as true. So everything that's within this loop will run over and over again forever. As long as you're giving the AVR microcontroller power, it's going to keep going round and round the main event loop, turning your one LED on and off until it burns out.

Why the return(0)?

I just said that the event loop is an infinite while() loop, and thus never finishes. So why is there a return(0) following it?

For programs that run on your desktop computer, it's important for the operating system to know whether they ran correctly or not. For that reason, GCC, our compiler, wants every main() to end with a return code. Return codes are totally superfluous for AVR code, which runs freestanding without any supporting operating system; nevertheless, the compiler raises a warning if you don't end main with return(). And I'd rather that you take compiler warnings seriously, because the warnings often help you debug bigger issues.

There *is* another way around the whole issue, and that's to prototype the main function like so before you define it: void main(void) __attribute__((noreturn));, but almost nobody does this, even though it would be strictly correct. Instead, almost everyone gives the compiler the return(0); it expects, just to keep it quiet. Or they ignore the compiler warnings entirely—but there's a special level in Hades allocated for those folks.

Hardware Registers

Now we get down to actually doing something in the code. The lines that are mostly in all caps (DDRB = 0b00000001;) need some explaining. Let's tackle the left side first. DDRB and PORTB are definitions that point to the AVR's internal hardware registers.

As mentioned in Chapter 1, almost all of the pins on the AVR chips are configurable as either input or output pins. That is, they can be internally hooked up as either voltage-sensing components or as transistor switches that will connect the pin through to the VCC or GND voltage levels. The way we're going to configure the pins as either input or output is deceptively simple in code—assigning a variable a certain value—but what goes on inside the dark wiring heart of the chip is interesting.

When you save a value in a "normal" variable, for instance with code that looks something like a = 7, the compiler picks a free slot from the chip's available RAM, calls that slot "a", and stores the value 7 there. Later on, when you add one to your variable a = a + 1; the compiler looks up "a" to see in which slot in memory it stored the value, pulls the value out of the memory slot, adds one to it, and puts it back in its slot. (For much more detail about the AVR's use of memory, see Chapter 19.)

Each slot in the AVR's memory is a byte, and each byte has eight bits. For a "normal" RAM location, these bits are used to encode (in binary) the number you'd like to store. Inside the chip, each bit in RAM is hooked up to a network of transistors that keep whatever electrical state was last imposed on them. The ATmega168, for instance, has 8,192 of these single-bit memory networks, or 1,024 bytes of RAM.

When you want to configure a microcontroller pin, it looks the same in code as saving a value into a variable. And that's because the same thing is going on inside the chip. The chip's hardware registers are just like the RAM storage slots that you use for variables, only they each have side effects. So when you write DDRB = 0b00000001;, you're not just storing the number one in a memory location; you're also flipping the transistor switches that are directly wired to each of the eight memory cells.

Inside the AVR chip, the data-direction register (DDR) memory locations are physically wired up to the transistor switches that determine whether a given pin is in input or output mode. When you write the numeric value one to that register, it's remembered. But it doesn't end there—the register's output is additionally connected to two switches. When a one is stored in that register bit, the output switch is closed, the input switch is open, and the pin is configured as output. When a zero is stored in that bit in your code, the output switch is open, the input switch is closed, and the pin is configured as input.

Because hardware registers are special memory locations, the compiler can't treat them exactly the same as variables. When you create a normal variable, the compiler can pick any convenient place in memory for it. Because the hardware registers are physically connected to the input/output circuitry, the location can't change. These register locations are spelled out in the *io.h* header file so that we don't have to remember their numerical value, but rather mnemonic names like DDRB, for "data-direction register B." Anyway, the upshot is that, once you've included the *io.h* file in your code, you can treat the hardware registers like normal variables and write code like DDRB = 0b00000001;, DDRB = 23;, or DDRB = DDRB + 7;.

Hardware registers: the bottom line

Whether or not you care about what's going on deep under the hood inside the chip, you need to take away two things from all this: hardware registers can be accessed just like "normal" variables from your code, but inside the chip they have extra connections that let them influence the way the rest of the chip behaves.

Consequently, when you need to tell the chip to put out a high voltage level on a given pin, it ends up being a matter of figuring out which number corresponds to the bits that correspond to the pins you'd like activated, and then writing that number into memory. Try to think of each register as being a row of eight switches, and writing a number into that register is the equivalent of flipping some of the switches. In particular, if you know how your number is represented in binary, each of the bits that has a 1 in it is a switch turned on, and each 0 is a switch turned off.

The three most important hardware registers

Each bank of pins (B, C, and D on the Mega series AVRs) has three hardware register memory locations associated with it. Let x stand for each bank's letter: so DDRx will be DDRB, DDRC, or DDRD depending on which bank of pins you mean:

DDRx *data-direction registers (port x)*

These registers control whether each pin is configured for input or output—the data direction. After a reset or power-up, the default state is all zeros, corresponding to the pins being configured for input. To enable a pin as output, you write a one to its slot in the DDR.

PORTx *port x data registers*

When the DDRx bits are set to one (output) for a given pin, the PORT register controls whether that pin is set to logic high or low (i.e., the VCC voltage or ground). Switching between these voltage levels could, for instance, turn on and off attached LEDs.

With the DDR configured for input, setting the PORT bits on a pin will control whether it has an internal pull-up resistor attached or whether it's in a "hi-Z" (high-impedance) state, effectively electrically disconnected from the circuit, but still able to sense voltage. We'll talk more about this in Chapter 6.

PINx *port x input pins address*

The PIN register addresses are where you read the digital voltage values for each pin that's configured as input. Each PINx memory location is hooked up to a comparator circuit that detects whether the external voltage on that pin is high or low. You can't write to them, so they're not really memory, but you can read from the PINx registers like a normal variable in your code to see which pins have high and low voltages on them.

All of these hardware registers are readable, so you can always query the input/output direction or state of any pin at any time. The PINx addresses aren't writable, because they just reflect the voltage values (high or low) on the corresponding pins.

Configuring output: DDRs, PORTs

Let's quickly step through what you need to do in order to light up some LEDs. When an AVR chip first gets power, it starts off in a default state with all its pins in input mode, with the pins essentially electrically disconnected from the circuit. To output a voltage on a given pin, you'll need to:

1. Configure the relevant pin for output mode by writing to the data-direction register (DDR).

2. Assign a high or low value to the individual pin by writing to the PORT hardware register.

Get Your DDRs, PINs, and PORTs Straight!

A common beginner mistake, and one I even make from time to time, is trying to write to the PORT register and expecting a voltage out when the DDR hasn't been set to output yet. So when you're debugging your code, and can't figure out why the LEDs aren't lighting up, the first thing you should do is make sure that you've enabled the pins in question for output.

*The other related gotcha is forgetting which register you're writing to—writing to the DDR or the PIN registers when you want to be writing to the PORT register, for instance. Try to think of the PIN registers as "**P**ort **IN**put," and the PORT registers as "**P**ort **O**utput **R**egister **T**hing."*

When things aren't working as expected, double-check the logic of your DDRs, PINs, and PORTs!

blinkLED Summary

Look back at the *blinkLED.c* code, and make sure you know what's going on. The first two lines include files that are part of the AVR standard C library. *avr/io.h* is the file that defines all the PORTs and DDRs. *util/delay.h* provides us with the _de lay_ms() function that we use to delay between blinks. You'll end up including a few more of these AVR library files as we move through the book.

int main(void) starts the main function—when the microcontroller starts up, it'll start here. Unlike big-computer programs, the microcontroller main() function usually never returns. We'll initialize our variables, configure the chip, and then enter a neverending event loop.

Our initialization here consists of writing a 1 in one bit of the DDRB register, which is enough to set up that pin as output. And then, in the event loop, we go back and forth between turning on and off the first LED by writing a 1 to the bit in the PORT register that's connected to our LED, with a delay to make it visible. That's the one-two combo for setting up digital output.

POV Toy

That should be *more* than enough detail about how to blink a single LED on and off slowly! Now let's take some time to solidify all that information and make something cool with it. Specifically, a programmable POV toy.

With all this newfound bit-twiddling power, it's time to show off a little. POV toys are pretty neat, and take our LED-blinking skills up to the next level. POV stands for persistence of vision, the phenomenon in which an afterimage persists on the retina for approximately 1/25 of a second. The point with a POV toy is that you turn LEDs on and off so quickly that the eye can't react to them. If you swing the device around, the afterimage patterns that they make seem to float in the air. They're pretty cool, and the only thing cooler is one that's loaded up with patterns you made yourself.

POV Toys: How Do They Work?

The human eye doesn't react instantly. Rather, if a light blinks on and off quickly enough, it's perceived as being constantly on. This is, of course, how movies work—they flash images at you 24 to 32 times per second, and your brain interprets them as being a fluid stream.

Persistence-of-vision toys exploit this slow response to make animations "magically" float in midair. If you swing a single LED quickly, persistence of vision would make it look like a streak. By turning the LED on and off rapidly, you can make a dashed line or a series of dots instead of a solid streak. Now by doing the same with multiple LEDs, you can make a low-resolution image just like with old dot-matrix printers.

It's also fun (and sometimes frustrating) to take photos of your POV toy in action. Getting the timing of the camera shutter just right takes a bit of practice.

If you think that persistence of vision is just for toys, it might surprise you to know that almost all LEDs are driven in pulses these days, either for a dimming effect (known as pulse-width modulation, or PWM, and the subject of Chapter 10) or for energy efficiency. To see for yourself, scan your eyes across any LED tail lights on a car, or stoplight at an intersection (do this while you're standing on the sidewalk, or while you're not behind the wheel of a car, please). See the blinking? Wouldn't the world be a cooler place if they embedded patterns in them?

Building the Circuit

In building the blinkLED circuit from the previous chapter, you've already hooked up an LED and resistor to PB0 on the AVR. For the POV toy, you're going to need to do that seven more times. At some point, it becomes convenient to solder the LED and the resistor together directly, because they're always used together anyway. If you'd like to take a 10-minute soldering break, make yourself some *blinkenlights*.

Blinkenlights

You're going to want to test voltages all of the time to make sure that everything is working as you expect, and for digital circuits the easiest way is to light (or not!) an LED. But LEDs can burn out if you run too much current through them, so we almost always add on a current-limiting resistor. So warm up your soldering iron, and take a few minutes to make yourself some tools—LEDs with integrated resistors used for diagnostic purposes: blinkenlights. (Look up "blinkenlights" on Wikipedia if this doesn't ring a bell.)

To make a blinkenlight, all you'll need to do is clip the negative/cathode side of the LED short and solder on an appropriate resistor. If you're only going to be using 5 V, a 220 ohm resistor will work fine. But for maximum utility, use something like a 1,000 ohm resistor, and you'll be able to light the LED off sources up to 15 V without fear of burning out your LED. Figure 3-2 shows you the three simple steps.

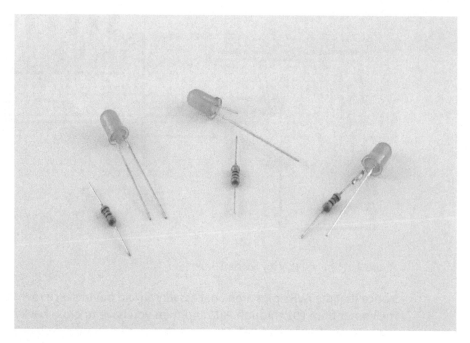

Figure 3-2. *Constructing blinkenlights*

If you're going to be working through this book with a breadboard, you'll need 8 LEDs for the POV toy project alone, so go ahead and make 10 or 12. Everywhere in our circuit diagrams that you see an LED and a resistor, you can substitute a blinkenlight. Having the resistors prewired can save you a bunch of extra connections on your breadboard.

When you're done with this book and you start up a new project, attach a blinkenlight to the power lines of your breadboard to use as a power indicator. Then you'll never have to worry about whether the breadboard is "on" or not. Scatter them liberally around your breadboard wherever you want to test a logic value (and the current draw of 20 mA isn't too excessive). Making 10 or 12 may seem like a lot at once, but trust me; you'll find a use for them all someday. If you've got LEDs of different colors, make a few of each. Go nuts!

Simplest POV Toy

The simplest version of the POV circuit is just eight LEDs, each with its own current-limiting resistor, all hooked up to the pins PB0 through PB7 on the AVR. This way, you can write a one to selected bits of the eight-bit byte in PORTB, and the corresponding LEDs will light up. Hook up the circuit shown in Figure 3-3.

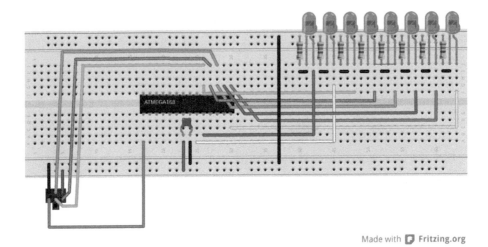

Figure 3-3. *Simplest POV toy hookup*

Notice that the AVR's pins aren't necessarily all laid out in a nice row. PD0 is around the corner from PD1 through PD5, and then you have to cross back over the chip again to get to PD6 and PD7. Pay attention to this strange ordering, or else the resulting images won't look right! If you need a refresher, look at the pinout diagram in Figure 2-5.

For instant gratification, temporarily unplug the black wire that connects the bottom ground rail to the top ground rail that has the LEDs plugged into it. Now flash your code into the AVR and reconnect the black wire between the ground rails again. You should see the LEDs spring to life! Success. Sort of.

Now try to flash the code into the chip again. It will very probably fail, and the chances of success depend on the interior electrical details of your flash programming setup and your choice of current-limiting resistors for the LEDs. What's going on? Well, you see those three AVR pins that are shared between the LEDs and the programmer? The LEDs are interfering with your programmer-to-AVR communication. When the programmer tries to write a logic-high voltage to the AVR or vice versa, the LEDs can draw enough current to pull the voltage down and turn ones into zeros.

When you'd like to reflash the chip, pull out the ground wire on the LEDs again. Now they're not connected into the circuit, and communication between AVR and programmer is normal. And then when you want to see the LED output, plug the black wire back in.

MOSFET trickery
After you've done the disconnect-program-reconnect-blink dance enough times, you'll start to get bored of it. You could connect a two-way switch in place of the black wire, flipping it one way to enable the LEDs and the other way to enable the

programmer. A nice twist on this idea is to use an electrical switch to automatically connect and disconnect the LEDs for you. In our case, the electrical switch that we'll use is a 2N7000 MOSFET.

(If you got "lucky," and you're able to program the AVR's flash with the LEDs still connected, you might be tempted to skip the MOSFET. You can do that at your own risk—just remember later on when you have random trouble flashing the AVR that I told you so. You can always test out if this is the case by temporarily pulling the ground wire that supplies the LEDs.)

What Is a MOSFET?

A MOSFET is a transistor. We'll be using it in full-on and full-off modes, so for now you can think of it as an electrically controlled switch. All MOSFETs have three pins, and we'll almost always connect one (the source pin) to ground and another (the drain) to the part of the circuit that we'd like to turn on and off. This switching action is accomplished by putting a voltage on the remaining pin, the gate.

Inside the MOSFET is a channel that connects the source to the drain. The gate lies physically between them and is a metal plate that's insulated from the drain-source channel. Voltages applied to the gate actually attract or repel electrons in the channel, making it more or less conductive. At the extremes, it's like an open circuit (disconnected) when there is no voltage on the gate, and very conductive with five volts on the gate.

*We'll cover FETs in much more detail in **Chapter 14**.*

Back to our wiring-up problem. We'd like our MOSFET switch to automatically disconnect the LED's ground rail when we're programming the AVR, and reconnect the ground rail so that the chip can blink LEDs when we're done programming. The clever bit in this next circuit uses the fact that the AVR uses its RESET pin to enter programming mode. And we have the good luck that the RESET pin (PC6, blue wire from the programmer) is held at 5 V by the AVR when the chip is running, and pulled low to 0 V by the programmer to signal the AVR to enter programming mode.

We can thus connect the MOSFET to the AVR's RESET pin and use the RESET action to connect and disconnect the LED's ground rail. When the AVR is running normally, the RESET pin is pulled up to 5 V and the gate on the MOSFET is pulled up along with it. This closes the MOSFET switch, which connects the ground rail from the LEDs to the circuit ground and the LED's blink. When the programmer pulls the RESET line low, it simultaneously sets the AVR into programming mode and also draws the gate of the MOSFET to ground, opening the MOSFET switch and disconnecting the LEDs. See Figure 3-4 for a breadboard wiring diagram.

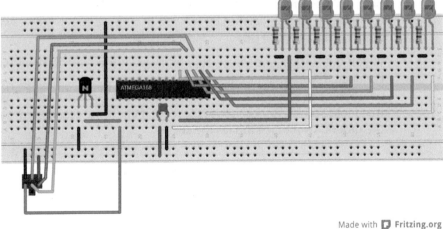

Made with **□ Fritzing.org**

Figure 3-4. *POV toy hookup on a breadboard*

When hooking up this circuit, notice that the MOSFET has a front side with a flat face and part labelling. If you're looking at it front-on, the far left pin is the source that gets connected to ground. The far right pin on a 2N7000 is the drain, which gets connected to the LED's ground rail. The center pin is the gate pin, which controls the switching action and gets connected to the AVR's RESET pin, PC6.

If you don't have a suitable MOSFET lying around, you can make do with a manual switch if you have one, or just keep plugging and unplugging the ground wire. We're going to be using 2N7000s for a number of tasks throughout the book, though, so it's a good time to order some. And if you are using any other MOSFET, be sure to check the datasheet to make sure that you know which pins are gate, drain, and source. Believe it or not, they're not all the same.

Pretty Patterns: The POV Toy Code

OK, that was a lot of detailed wiring-up. If you're feeling brave, you can now play around with a full byte's worth of LEDs and modify the *blinkLED.c* code to display whatever blinking patterns you'd like. What would happen, for instance, if you replaced PORTB = 0b00000001; with PORTB = 0b01010101;? Or alternate between PORTB = 0b10101010; and PORTB = 0b01010101; with a small delay in-between? You could start to make animations.

Flash the *povToy.c* code into the chip and see what happens. If it's not convenient to shake the breadboard around, try turning off the lights in the room and running your eyes across the tabletop with the device on it. The trick is to *not* focus on the blinking lights, but rather to let them trace their pattern across the back of your eyes. Try jumping your eyes between a point a foot or two to the left of the POV toy and a point a foot or two off to the right.

Once you get tired of my preprogrammed pattern, it's time to work through the code in Example 3-2 so that you can create your own!

Example 3-2. *povToy.c listing*

```c
// POV toy demo framework //

// ------- Preamble -------- //
#include <avr/io.h>
#include <util/delay.h>

// -------- Functions --------- //
void POVDisplay(uint8_t oneByte) {
  PORTB = oneByte;
  _delay_ms(2);
}

int main(void) {
  // -------- Inits --------- //
  DDRB = 0xff;                    /* Set up all of LED pins for output */
  // ------ Event loop ------ //
  while (1) {                                          /* mainloop */
    POVDisplay(0b00001110);
    POVDisplay(0b00011000);
    POVDisplay(0b10111101);
    POVDisplay(0b01110110);
    POVDisplay(0b00111100);
    POVDisplay(0b00111100);
    POVDisplay(0b00111100);
    POVDisplay(0b01110110);
    POVDisplay(0b10111101);
    POVDisplay(0b00011000);
    POVDisplay(0b00001110);

    PORTB = 0;
    _delay_ms(10);
  }                                              /* end mainloop */
  return (0);
}
```

At the base of the POV toy routine is a really simple function, POVDisplay(), but if it's the first function declaration in C you've ever seen, it's worth a short explanation.

Let's look at what the POVDisplay function does. It takes in a single byte and then turns around and writes it straight back out to the PORTB. This is just like what goes on in blinkLED. Every bit that's set to a one in the number we pass to POVDisplay has a corresponding illuminated LED. Here, we also delay for a few milliseconds to display the pattern for just a tiny bit.

Now look down at the `main()` functions. The first step to using the AVR's digital outputs is to configure the data-direction register (DDRB) so that any subsequent values written to the PORTB register will appear as either high or low voltage values on the corresponding pins.

Functions in C

When your code gets to the point that it's doing many, many different things, it can really help both the readability and the logical flow to encapsulate whatever parts of it you can into functions. *In C, a function takes variables as arguments (or inputs) and returns either nothing or a single value as a result. Each time you call the function from any other place in the code, the code inside the function is run.*

Variables that are defined within the function stay in the function (this is called their scope) *and aren't accessible outside the function's context, so you don't have to worry about one i overwriting another. Variables that are defined outside the function can be changed by code within the function.*

C insists on knowing the type of each of these arguments and return values. In this example, POVDisplay() is a function that takes in an unsigned integer (uint8_t) variable as its input, uses the input to set the LEDs, and then waits. It doesn't return any values, hence the void *in it's definition.*

If you're new to C, you'll see a lot more function definitions throughout the rest of the book, and you'll pick it up as we go along.

The event loop is where the action happens. The POVDisplay() function is called repeatedly with a binary value. I could have written this part of the code using the decimal representation of these numbers, but if you squint your eyes just right and tilt your head, you can almost see the pattern that's displayed in the ones and zeros. (How readable would it be if I wrote POVDisplay(189);? Quick, which LEDs are on and which are off?)

After displaying the desired pattern, all of the LEDs are turned off with PORTB=0; and a relatively long delay time separates one run of the pattern from the next. Then the infinite while() loop starts up again at the top.

Experiment!

Now I'd like you to start messing around with the code. Increase the delay inside the POVDisplay() function so that it's long enough that you can see the individual steps. Compare them to the binary values getting written to the PORTB register. See how numbers being written around in your code is making electrical things happen in the real world. Experience the zen of hardware registers.

How short can you make the delay before you can no longer swing your arm (or move your eyes) fast enough to see the pattern anymore? If you need to decrease the delay down below one millisecond, there is a _delay_us() function that delays in increments of microseconds, or thousandths of a millisecond.

Finally, and here's the part where I lost a Saturday afternoon, try coding up some of your own patterns using this simple function. I found that it helps to draw out the patterns horizontally across eight rows of graph paper first, and then read the binary numbers out down the vertical columns.

In the *povToy* directory, I've included some more examples and even an example POV font so that you can easily spell words. The code for running all of these is a little advanced for the first serious chapter of this book but was written with easy extensibility in mind, so feel free to flash them in or modify them and see what happens.

The easiest way to program in another bit of code from within the same directory is to edit the makefile and change the target from MAIN = povToy.c to something like MAIN = 1up.c or whatever. Alternatively, if you're running make from the command line, you can just type make MAIN=1up.c flash and it will compile the new code and flash it into your microcontroller without having to touch the makefile.

If you've made some patterns that you're really proud of, you'll want to show them off to other people. You may want to make this whole setup a little bit more portable, and the easiest way to do that is to unplug the flash programmer and supply power using batteries.

Once you've exhausted all of the eight-LED POV possibilities, pick up again with the next chapter where you'll learn a much more flexible method of controlling the AVR's output from code.

Battery Power!

To make the POV toy swingable, it's nice to unplug it from the wall or your USB tether. The easiest way to do this is by battery-powering your circuit, and you've got a couple of ways to do this.

My favorite power supply for AVR projects is a set of four AA-cell rechargeable batteries. Rechargeables have two advantages: they're cheaper in the long run, and they have a lower voltage than normal batteries. While four fresh standard AA cells start off at 6 V (4 × 1.5 V), most single-cell rechargeables run around 1.2 V, making four of them together just right at 4.8 V—meaning you won't have to modify most of your 5 V circuits.

On the other hand, the AVR chips run reliably as low as 3 V, so you *can* get by with two or three regular AA batteries or even three rechargeables. (My version of the circuit keeps on blinking until around 2 V, but is a little dim on two rechargeables.) If you've designed your LED circuit with 5 V in mind, you'll find that the LEDs run a little bit dim on three or four volts. Oh well. You're probably swinging your POV toy around in a dark room anyway.

Bit Twiddling 4.

Cylon Eyes and More

In this chapter we'll make a cylon-eye-type LED back-and-forth scanner. Everyone needs one. Scanning lights were the only thing, besides maybe menace, that gave the cylons their personality. Would KITT have been half as useful to David Hasselhoff without his scrolling red lights? I think not. And now you can build your very own.

But I won't lie to you. We're building cylon eyes in order to learn a fundamental concept in microcontroller-specific programming: how to flip individual bits on and off inside a hardware register. And while that may not sound sexy, you'll be using the ideas from this chapter in every AVR or microcontroller project you ever make from here on out. Flipping bits is just that important in embedded devices.

If you don't believe me yet, think back on how we turned on LED3. We wrote something like:

```
PORTB = 0b00001000;
```

And that worked, as long as we knew for sure that we wanted all of the other LEDs turned off. But what if you need to turn on or off a particular LED without disturbing any of the others? Bitwise logical operations—"bit twiddling"—lets us modify any one bit out of the register byte without having to think explicitly about the others. Because we'll be setting bits in registers to configure nearly every aspect of the AVR hardware, we'll get a lot of mileage out of this investment.

Because this chapter is mostly theory, let's get the project up and running so you have something pretty to look at. Assuming that you still have all the LEDs hooked up as in Chapter 3, all you have to do is enter the *cylonEyes* directory, open up *cylonEyes.c* in your editor, and run make to compile the firmware and upload it to the chip.

What You Need

In this chapter, in addition to the basic kit, you will need:

- The eight LEDs and their resistors that you hooked up in Chapter 3.

- That's it. Well, it wouldn't hurt to have your thinking cap on, because we're going to be using a bunch of bitwise binary logic.

If you have trouble uploading the program to the chip, please double-check the ISP connectors according to Figure 3-4 and make sure you've got the MOSFET set up right. If in doubt about the MOSFET part of the circuit, go back to the wire between the top ground rail to the bottom ground rail to double-check that's the problem.

Working Through the Code: Cylon Eyes

You got it running? Great! Now let's look at the code in Example 4-1 and see what makes it tick. Essentially, it's the same as with the one-LED blinker code, only instead of switching on and off only one of the bits in the PORTB register, we can toggle eight of them.

Example 4-1. *cylonEyes.c listing*

```
                                              /* Cylon Eyes */

// ------- Preamble -------- //
#include <avr/io.h>                  /* Defines pins, ports, etc */
#include <util/delay.h>              /* Functions to waste time */

#define DELAYTIME 85                      /* milliseconds */
#define LED_PORT        PORTB
#define LED_PIN         PINB
#define LED_DDR         DDRB

int main(void) {

  // -------- Inits --------- //
  uint8_t i = 0;
  LED_DDR = 0xff;              /* Data Direction Register B:
                                  all set up for output */

  // ------ Event loop ------ //
  while (1) {

    while (i < 7) {
      LED_PORT = (1 << i);          /* illuminate only i'th pin */
      _delay_ms(DELAYTIME);                       /* wait */
```

```
    i = i + 1;                              /* move to the next LED */
  }

  while (i > 0) {
    LED_PORT = (1 << i);                    /* illuminate only i'th pin */
    _delay_ms(DELAYTIME);                               /* wait */
    i = i - 1;                             /* move to the previous LED */
  }

}                                          /* End event loop */
return (0);
}
```

You should recognize the general form of the code from *blinkLED.c*. In fact, the only big differences are that we have loops inside our event loop, and we have the cryptic PORTB = (1 << i); statement—our first introduction to bit twiddling! Before we get on to the main course, though, I'll introduce our first #define statement ("C Asides: #defines" on page 63). Feel free to skim through if you're already comfortable with C.

Bit Twiddling and Cylon Eyes

Looking back briefly at how we implemented *blinkLED.c* and even *povToy.c*, you'll see that the code turns on and off the bit that controls our LED quite directly: PORTB = 0b0000001;. We could make a cylon eyes animate in the same way. To make the traditional back-and-forth scanner, we hook up eight LEDs to the same port, and light them up one at a time, moving from right to left and left to right. Our naive code might look something like this:

```
DDRB  = 0b11111111;        // enable all pins for output

while(1){
        PORTB = 0b00000001;        // set the 0th pin in PORT B high
        _delay_ms(100);
        PORTB = 0b00000010;        // set the 1st pin in PORT B high
        _delay_ms(100);
        PORTB = 0b00000100;        // set the 2nd pin in PORT B high
        (etc.)
        ...
}
```

As you can see, that's going to involve a lot of typing, and in the end the code is going to be difficult to maintain, tweak, and extend. So we're going to need a better way. Enter bit twiddling! The C programming language allows the user to access bits individually, and the AVR *libc* (the microcontroller-specific library routines) helps even more, but it's going to take a little getting used to.

C Asides: #defines

#define statements improve code readability and portability by defining human-friendly synonyms for constants or code fragments. For instance, in a setup with only one LED like our *blinkLED.c*, I'll usually define LED as a synonym for a particular pin on the AVR (PB0) partly to remind myself how to hook up the circuit, but also partly to make it easy to change later.

For instance, if you were reproducing the *blinkLED.c* code, but you'd like to physically wire the LED to pin PB5, you could go through the code and change every occurrence of PB0 to PB5. If instead, as here, you define the LED pin at the top of the code, something like #define LED PB0 and then consistently only use LED in the main body, you'll only have to change PB0 to PB5 in the one place where it's defined, right up at the top of your code or in a suitably named include file. Defining your hardware layout makes it easier to modify later, and makes your code easier to read. (What was hooked up to PB0 again?)

This is handled by the preprocessor, which goes through your code and does a search-and-replace for all your #defines before handing the result off to the compiler. Because #define statements are simple substitutions made by the preprocessor, they're not variables, take up no memory in the AVR, and can't be changed from within your code.

To keep from forgetting their special nature, the names of #defines are usually written in ALL_CAPS_SEPARATED_WITH_UNDERSCORES. This makes #defines stand out in your code, and reminds you that they're not normal variables.

In addition to user-defined #defines, if you look in the *avr/io.h* file that we include in all our example codes, you'll find that there's a #define for every hardware register that's listed in the datasheet. (Include files are also handled by the preprocessor, before the code is compiled.) These definitions point in turn to the correct memory locations of the AVR's hardware registers.

This is a more general pattern in AVR C: a lot of the low-level details of the layout and configuration of the chip (like what locations in memory are hardware registers) are provided for you in #define statements, and the names are a vaguely helpful mnemonic for something that's written in the datasheet.

For now, think of #defines as handy shortcuts for keeping track of values that you might later like to change or would like to make more clear. Using #defines for pin-layouts also makes your code flexible across different hardware setups, and helps remind you later which pin your accelerometer was hooked up to. Good use of #defines is good practice.

Bit Shifting

Wouldn't it be nice, instead of having to write out 0b00001000, if we could just say "give me a number with a 1 in bit number three"? (If you thought that one was in bit number four, see "Bits, Numbering, and Significance" on page 64.) That way we could code our cylon eyes by incrementing or decrementing a variable and then putting a *1* in the corresponding bit's place.

It turns out that the technique known as bit shifting will do exactly that for us. You're going to be surprised at how often we use bit shifting in microprocessor-style C code.

Bit shifts have the effect of rolling all of the bit positions to the left or right, depending on your command. Bits that fall off either end just disappear, and any new

Bits, Numbering, and Significance

A byte is made up of eight bits, and the AVR chip organizes its pins for purposes of input and output in banks of eight. Coincidence? Not at all! It makes our lives easier.

But something that unsettles newcomers to C is its zero-indexing convention. That is, when you count in C you don't start counting with 1, but with 0. Counting eight elements looks like this: 0,1,2,3,4,5,6,7.

That's why, when we hook up eight LEDs to our AVR chip, you're going to have to think of the first one as "LED Number Zero" in your head. And the AVR chip designers are in on the zero-indexed conspiracy as well. Our first LED will be hooked up to pin PB0. The eighth LED, which I want you to call "LED7," connects to PB7. If you think of it any other way, you'll get confused.

Zero-indexing is natural if you think of everything in terms of a base location and an offset, which is why it's done in C. If the hardware register for Port B is at a given location in memory (byte number five in the mega168, as it turns out), then the location of the first pin is at byte five plus zero bits. The second pin (PB1) is located at byte five plus one bit, etc.

If you can just remember to think of the first LED as "LED Number Zero" or "The LED at PORTB + 0" then you're on your way. You'll also see how this fits naturally with the way we're going to access single bits through bit shifting later on.

We'll be representing numbers in binary in most-significant-bit-first order. Now this isn't strange: when you say "three hundred and twenty one", you're also working in most-significant-bit-first order, right? But it can sometimes be confusing for people to see the first bit, bit 0, all the way on the far right of the number, rather than right up front. Just remember that it represents a number, and we usually write numbers with the most-important digits up front. 321 is $3 \times 10^2 + 2 \times 10^1 + 1 \times 10^0$, just like 0b11001 is $1 \times 2^4 + 1 \times 2^3 + 1 \times 2^0$.

So when you look at a port of eight pins in the datasheet, or when you write to the hardware register, you'll want to remember which end is which. And when you're naming your eight LEDs as they're laid out in a row, to avoid confusion you're going to want to call them LED7, LED6, LED5, …, LED0, with LED7 on the left side and LED0 on the right (see below).

bits added are all zeros. The C language instruction for shifting all the bits in a number to the left or right is << or >>, respectively. Now let's see how they're used.

| LED 7 | LED 6 | LED 5 | LED 4 | LED 3 | LED 2 | LED 1 | LED 0 |

Bit shift examples:

```
  0b00001110 >> 3
= 0b00000001  (Three new zeros were added to the left,
                  and the bits on the right just rolled off the edge.)

  0b00001110 << 2
= 0b00111000  (Two new bits, both zeros, are rolled in from the right.)
```

What this means to you as a programmer is that if you want a single 1 bit in position number three, say, you can start off with the number that has a 1 bit in position zero, and roll it to the left three spaces.

The bit-shift roll:

```
1         =  0b00000001
(1 << 0) =  0b00000001
(1 << 1) =  0b00000010
...
(1 << 3) =  0b00001000
...
(1 << 7) =  0b10000000
```

Take a minute to make sure you've got the logic of the bit-shift roll down. It's a standard idiom in microcontroller coding, and you'll be using it in nearly every program you write. Any time you want to set the nth bit to a 1, you'll shift the value 1 over to the left n times.

Now you're starting to see how the cylon eyes work: start off with the number 1, roll the bit one position, and then write that to an output hardware register, rinse, and repeat. Shift bits left until you end up at LED7, then switch to shifting bits right until you hit LED0.

So before we leave this section, let's recap the meat of the cylon eyes code. Make sure that it makes sense to you, because we'll be using the bit-shift roll extensively from here on out:

```
while(i < 7){
    LED_PORT = (1 << i);      /* illuminate only i'th pin */
    _delay_ms(DELAYTIME);     /* wait */
    i = i + 1;                /* increase shift amount */
}
while(i > 0){
    LED_PORT = (1 << i);      /* illuminate only i'th pin */
    _delay_ms(DELAYTIME);     /* wait */
    i = i - 1;                /* decrease shift amount */
}
```

There are two while loops, driving the variable i up to seven and back down to zero. Inside each loop there is a delay, which is fairly self-explanatory. All the action that matters is in the LED_PORT = (1 << i); command. We want a binary number with a 1 in the ith place, which will turn on only the ith LED in our series. We implement it by starting with a 1 in the zeroth position and rolling it over i times to the left.

Advanced Bit Twiddling: Above and Beyond Cylon Eyes

So that's all there is to making cylon eyes: just shifting a bit to the left or right as appropriate, and waiting. But what if we wanted to make an even more interesting pattern? Multiple lights on at once? Or random toggling? Or maybe we just need to control one bit out of a byte, without changing any of the others.

The serious limitation in the preceding code is that each time through the while() loop, we're writing a whole byte to the LED port. This works in cylon eyes because we know that we'd only like one LED on at a time. But what about the case where we've already got a few LEDs lit up, and we'd like to add another? Say just LED1? If we wrote LED_PORT = (1<<1);, we'd turn on LED1 all right, but in the process, we'll have turned off all the rest.

In this section, we're going to learn some essential bit-twiddling techniques that will allow us to manipulate single bits easily without clobbering the rest of the contents of the register. Think of each byte in the AVR's hardware registers as being a row of eight little switches; in this section, we're going to use bitwise logic functions to set or toggle each switch individually without modifying the rest.

Even if you've programmed C since you were seven years old, it's quite possible that you haven't spent much time on bit-level manipulations. If you've ever learned a little bit about logic, digital or otherwise, the bitwise operators will seem familiar to you, but the context may be brand new. For some of you, this is all going to be brand new. Hold on to your hats.

Bitwise logical operators take full bytes as their input. They do logical operations on those bytes one bit at a time, hence the name. This makes the bitwise operators an absolutely perfect match for manipulating the individual bits inside a register byte.

To give you a bit of the flavor, the bitwise operator NOT takes each bit in the byte and toggles, or flips, it. A 1 becomes a 0, and a 0 becomes a 1: 10001110 turns into 01110001. The operation happens all at once inside the AVR chip, but you can think of it as reading bit 0 and then writing the logical opposite to bit 0 of the result byte. This same operation repeats seven more times, *bitwise*, for each bit in the byte.

There are four bitwise logical operators in total, so let's work through each with an example. I find it helpful to think of the two input bytes stacked on top of each other so that the bits being compared are aligned vertically. Work through the following sidebar and make sure that you see how the logical operation is being applied, bitwise down the columns, to get the final result.

Bitwise logic definitions are all well and good, and you may have seen all this already. It's how bitwise logic is *used* in microcontroller coding that's interesting, especially when combined with the side effects of setting, clearing, and testing bits in hardware registers. In short, we care about twiddling bits inside bytes a lot more in AVR programming than in most other computer programming, because bitwise logic allows us to configure the AVR's internal hardware, and read from and write to individual pins.

The _BV() Macro

Bit shifting is so common in AVR programming that there's even a macro defined that gets included with *io.h*: it's called _BV() and stands for "bit value."

Before 2006, this macro used to be called BV(), and it used to be used quite commonly. Sometime around 2007, it got renamed to _BV(), where the underscore indicates that it's intended for internal use within the avr-libc libraries, because it isn't part of official Standard C.

The _BV() macro is just our bit-shift roll in disguise. In fact, it's even defined as:

```
`#define _BV(bit) (1 << (bit))`
```

So should you use _BV(2) or (1 << 2)? Well, they end up being exactly the same thing once the preprocessor has done its text replacing, so it's just a matter of style. You'll definitely see code written both ways, so I want you to be able to read both.

There are a couple of arguments for the use of _BV(). If you saw (1 << 2) and were new to microcontroller programming, you might have to think for a while about what the purpose of the "1" was—is it a numerical value to be treated like a number, or is it just the simplest way of representing a 1 in a single bit? So the first argument for _BV() is that it *does* read a little more clearly in code. On the other hand, the bit-shift roll is so common in microcontroller C and assembly code that the _BV() doesn't really gain much in readability after you've been at it a few months.

Secondly, many old AVR programmers are used to having the macro around, and they wrote a bunch of code with BV() in it, and it's trivial to find-replace all their code to read _BV()—people also use _BV() because they're used to it.

The arguments against _BV() basically boil down to it not being Standard C. If you want to compile your code on some other platform to test it out, for instance, it probably won't have the _BV() macro already defined.

So what if you like the clarity of BV() as a macro, but also want to keep your code maximally portable? Define BV() yourself! It's easy and hardly costs anything. If you define it yourself in your code, you won't have to worry about your code being portable, because it'll be right there. In the sidebar "Bit Twiddling for the Impatient" on page 76, I've listed an example with a bunch of bit-shifting macros that I routinely include in my own code.

In the interest of teaching you standard microcontroller-style C I'll use (1 << 3) in the code most of the time. If you can read code written this way, you can read anything; this idiom is used across microcontroller families and compilers. But in your own code, feel free to use the built-in _BV() macro, or better still, define your own.

Bitwise Logical Operators

OR (|)

For each bit position, a bitwise OR returns 1 if either bit in the comparison is 1. OR returns a 1 if this bit is 1 *or* that bit is 1. OR returns 0 only when *both* bits are 0:

```
  1010
| 1100
= 1110
```

AND (&)

Bitwise AND compares two bits and returns 1 only if *both* of the bits are 1. If either of the bits are 0, AND returns 0:

```
  1010
& 1100
= 1000
```

XOR (^)

XOR (or "exclusive or") returns 1 if *only one* of the two bits compared is a 1. If both bits are 1 or if both bits are 0, XOR returns 0:

```
  1010
^ 1100
= 0110
```

NOT (~)

NOT takes all the bits and flips their logical sense —each 1 becomes a 0 and each 0 becomes a 1. It's also the only logical operator that takes only one input:

```
~ 1100
= 0011
```

 Stupid Bitwise Tricks

As a quick demo of the utility of bitwise logical operators, you can convert the Cylon Eyes demo into Inverse-Video Cylon Eyes with the NOT operator. Just replace each:

LED_PORT = (1 << i);

with:

LED_PORT = ~(1 << i);

Every LED that was previously on will be off, and vice versa.

For a different display that uses tools you'll learn in the remainder of this section, change the first LED_PORT line into LED_PORT |= (1 << i); and the second into LED_PORT &= ~(1 << i); See what you get!

So let's get down to the business at hand: manipulating individual bits within a byte. For concreteness, take the eight LEDs and suppose that we already have a few LEDs lit: LEDs zero, one, six, and seven. If we looked at the value currently stored in PORTB, it would read 0b11000011. Now say we want to turn on and off LED2 without changing the states of any of the other LEDs. Or maybe we want to turn on or off LEDs two and four at the same time. How can we do this?

Setting Bits with OR

For our first trick, let's learn how to set an individual bit in a register, leaving all the other bits as they were. Thinking back on the bitwise logical operators, let's revisit the way the OR operator works. In particular, let's think about ORing some bit with either a fixed 0 or a fixed 1.

Consider ORing a bit with zero. If you OR a 1 with a 0, the result is 1. If you OR a 0 with a 0, the result is 0. That is, ORing a bit with 0 doesn't change the initial logical bit at all. But ORing with a 1 always yields a 1. This behavior lays the groundwork for using OR to turn bits on using bitmasks:

```
OR with 0:
 0 | 0 -> 0
 1 | 0 -> 1

OR with 1:
 0 | 1 -> 1
 1 | 1 -> 1
```

A *bitmask* is just a normal old byte, but we're thinking of it as being made up of ones and zeros in particular places that we specify rather than representing a numerical value. We use a bitmask, along with a bitwise logical operator, to change some bits in a target byte.

I like to think of bitmasks almost like stencils used for spray painting. You cut away parts of the stencil where you want to change (paint) the underlying surface, and you leave the stencil intact where you don't want paint to go.

In particular, if we want to turn on some bits in PORTB while leaving the others untouched, we'll create a bitmask with ones in the bit locations we'd like turned on. This works because a one ORed with anything will return a one. So we read in PORTB and OR it with the bitmask. The result should be the unaltered contents of PORTB everywhere that we had a zero, and ones everywhere our bitmask had a one. If we write this back out to PORTB, we're set—PORTB has all its old bits intact, except those where there was a 1 in the bitmask have been turned on. I've worked this all through in detail in Example 4-2.

Example 4-2. Using OR to set bits
If LED2 is initially off:

```
  PORTB  : 0b11000011  // the current LED state
(1 << 2) = 0b00000100  // the LED we want to turn on
    |    = 0b11000111  // hooray!
```

LED2 is turned on, and none of the others are changed.

If LED2 is initially on:

```
       PORTB  : 0b11000111  // the current LED state
  (1 << 2) = 0b00000100  // the LED we want to turn on
       |   = 0b11000111  // hooray!
```

LED2 is still on, and none of the others are changed.

We can also set multiple bits at once. All we have to do is create a bitmask with the two bits (say LED2 and LED4) that we'd like to turn on. Since:

```
0b00010100       // the desired bitmask
 = (0b00000100 | 0b00010000)
 = ( (1 << 2)  | (1 << 4) )
```

then:

```
       PORTB          = 0b11000011  // the current LED state
  ((1 << 2) | (1 << 4)) = 0b00010100  // bits two and four
       |            = 0b11010111  // turned both on!
```

We've just seen how to get a copy of the byte currently in PORTB, and how to turn on LED2 and LED4 using OR and a bitmask. That gives us a new byte, which we just write out to PORTB, and we're done:

```
PORTB = PORTB | (1 << 2);
```

This type of operation is so common that there's a shorthand for it in C:

```
PORTB |= (1 << 2);
```

Either way you write it, the code ends up the same after compilation, so pick a style that makes you happy. Both of them have the effect of turning on LED2 and leaving the other bits as they were.

Toggling Bits with XOR

Now imagine that you want to flip a bit or two. You don't really care if it's on or off right now, you just want it in the *other* state, whatever that is. Imagine that you want to blink LED2 while leaving the rest of the LEDs unchanged. To do this, you'd toggle the bit that corresponds to LED2, delay a while, and then toggle it again, etc. To toggle a bit, you'll use a bitmask and the XOR operator.

Let's look at XOR again. If you XOR any bit with a fixed 0, you get a 1 if that bit is a 1 and a 0 if that bit is 0. (Remember, this is the "exclusive" or and is only true if one or the other is true, but not both.) So XORing with a zero gives you the input back again.

If you XOR with a 1, what happens? Starting with a 0 and XORing 1 returns a 1, and starting with a 1 and XORing 1 yields 0. XORing with a 1 seems a good way to toggle bits!

```
XOR with 0:
 0 ^ 0 -> 0
```

```
   1 ^ 0 -> 1

XOR with 1:
   0 ^ 1 -> 1
   1 ^ 1 -> 0
```

As we did with OR for setting bits, we'll make a bitmask with a 1 where we want to toggle a bit and zeros everywhere else. To toggle a bit in a register, we XOR the current register value with the bitmask, and write it back into the register. Boom. For more detail, see Example 4-3.

Example 4-3. Using XOR to toggle a bit

If LED2 is initially off:

```
  PORTB    : 0b11000011  // the current LED state
(1 << 2) = 0b00000100  // bitmask LED2
    ^      = 0b11000111  // LED2 bit flipped on
```

After the XOR, LED2 is turned on, and none of the others are changed.

And if LED2 is initially on:

```
  PORTB    : 0b11000111  // the current LED state
(1 << 2) = 0b00000100  // bitmask LED2
    ^      = 0b11000011  // LED2 bit flipped off
```

After the XOR, LED2 is turned off, and none of the others are changed.

So to toggle a bit, we create a bitmask for the bit we'd like to toggle, XOR it with the contents of our register, and write the result back out to the register. In one line:

```
PORTB = PORTB ^ (1 << 2);
```

or:

```
PORTB ^= (1 << 2);
```

for short. You can, of course, toggle more than one bit at once with something like:

```
PORTB ^= ((1 << 2) | (1 << 4));
```

Clearing a Bit with AND and NOT

Clearing a bit (setting it to zero) is just inconvenient, but you'll have to do it so often that you'll eventually find it second nature. So far, we've used OR to set bits and XOR to toggle them. You may not be entirely surprised that we're going to use AND to clear bits. Let's run through the usual analysis.

If we AND any bit with 0, the result is guaranteed to be 0. There's no way they can both be 1 if one of them was a 0 to start with. This is how we'll turn bits off:

```
AND with 0:
  0 & 0 -> 0
  1 & 0 -> 0

AND with 1:
  0 & 1 -> 0
  1 & 1 -> 1
```

This suggests using a bitmask with AND to turn bits off. The bitmask we'll have to use should have a 1 where we want to keep the old data and a 0 where we want to clear a bit. That is, to turn off LED2, we'll use an AND bitmask that looks like 0b11111011.

But wait a minute! That bitmask is the exact opposite of the bitmasks we've used before—it has ones where the others had zeros and vice versa. There's a million stupid ways to create such a mask, but the easy way is to first create the mask with a 1 where we want it, and then use NOT to flip all the bits.

So to make a bitmask to turn off LED2, we'll first shift a 1 over into the right spot and then NOT the whole mask:

```
 (1 << 2) -> 0b00000100
~(1 << 2) -> 0b11111011
```

Now we AND that with the original value and we're home free. I work through all of the steps for you in Example 4-4.

Example 4-4. *Using AND and NOT to clear a bit*
If LED2 is initially off:

```
     PORTB  =  0b11000011
~(1 << 2)  =  0b11111011
        &  =  0b11000011
```

LED2 stays off, and none of the others are changed.

And if LED2 is initially on:

```
     PORTB  =  0b11000111
~(1 << 2)  =  0b11111011
        &  =  0b11000011
```

LED2 is turned off, and none of the others are changed.

Reassigning to PORTB and writing these as one-liners, we get:

```
PORTB = PORTB & ~(1 << 2);
```

or:

```
PORTB &= ~(1 <<2);
```

And as with the other examples, you can of course turn off multiple bits in one statement:

```
PORTB &= ~((1 << 2) | (1 << 4));
```

being careful with the NOT outside the parentheses, because you want to have two zeros in your bitmask.

Showing Off

Now that we've got all this bit-level manipulation under our belts, let's make some demo code to show off a little bit. Being able to set, clear, and toggle individual bits allows a little more flexibility than cylon eyes code had, and it should give you enough basis to start experimenting. Let's work through Example 4-5.

Example 4-5. *showingOffBits.c listing*

```
                /* Showing off some patterns to practice our bit-twiddling */

// ------- Preamble -------- //
#include <avr/io.h>
#include <util/delay.h>

#define DELAYTIME 85                            /* milliseconds */
#define LED_PORT        PORTB
#define LED_DDR         DDRB

int main(void) {

  uint8_t i;
  uint8_t repetitions;
  uint8_t whichLED;
  uint16_t randomNumber = 0x1234;

  // -------- Inits --------- //
  LED_DDR = 0xff;                    /* all LEDs configured for output */
  // ------ Event loop ------ //
  while (1) {
                                                /* Go Left */
    for (i = 0; i < 8; i++) {
      LED_PORT |= (1 << i);             /* turn on the i'th pin */
      _delay_ms(DELAYTIME);                          /* wait */
    }
    for (i = 0; i < 8; i++) {
      LED_PORT &= ~(1 << i);           /* turn off the i'th pin */
      _delay_ms(DELAYTIME);                          /* wait */
    }
    _delay_ms(5 * DELAYTIME);                      /* pause */

                                                /* Go Right */
    for (i = 7; i < 255; i--) {
      LED_PORT |= (1 << i);             /* turn on the i'th pin */
      _delay_ms(DELAYTIME);                          /* wait */
```

```
  }
  for (i = 7; i < 255; i--) {
    LED_PORT &= ~(1 << i);                /* turn off the i'th pin */
    _delay_ms(DELAYTIME);                             /* wait */
  }
  _delay_ms(5 * DELAYTIME);                          /* pause */


                              /* Toggle "random" bits for a while */
  for (repetitions = 0; repetitions < 75; repetitions++) {
                                   /* "random" number generator */
    randomNumber = 2053 * randomNumber + 13849;
                               /* low three bits from high byte */
    whichLED = (randomNumber >> 8) & 0b00000111;
    LED_PORT ^= (1 << whichLED);             /* toggle our LED */
    _delay_ms(DELAYTIME);
  }
  LED_PORT = 0;                               /* all LEDs off */
  _delay_ms(5 * DELAYTIME);                         /* pause */


  }                                      /* End event loop */
  return (0);              /* This line is never reached */
}
```

Reading down from the top, I include the standard *avr/io.h* file, which includes all the DDR and PORT macros and AVR part definitions, and then the delay utilities. Next, a delay time and the pinouts are defined in case you want to play around with them later on.

Down in the main() routine, there's not much to do for initialization. A few variables that we'll be needing are defined, and then the DDRB is configured for output on all of the pins. (0xff is 255 in hexadecimal, and is equivalent to 0b11111111.)

The event loop (while(1){...) is divided into three different "animations": one that turns on all the LEDs starting from LED0, and then turns them all off starting from LED0; one that does the same thing in reverse; and one that "randomly" toggles individual LEDs on and off.

The "go left" routine is a lot like cylon eyes, except that it doesn't turn off any LEDs until they're all on, and it uses a for() loop. Turning on each LED one at a time, without turning them back off, ends up with all eight LEDs on. The next for() loop in the "go left" section turns off the LEDs one at a time, from right to left. This makes it look like a block of LEDs, eight wide, passes through our viewing range.

 **For Loops**

You'll be seeing a lot more for() loops in this book, but this one's the first one. So make sure you know what's going on inside the loop's parentheses.

First, a loop variable is initialized (i=0). Then a test is done on that variable (i<8). If the test is true, the rest of the code in curly brackets is run. If not, the loop is over and the code moves on. Finally, each time it's done with a loop, the third argument in the for() parentheses is run. In our case, we're adding one (i++) to the variable.

The "go right" code is a little bit more interesting, and here's a potential trap when coding for microcontrollers. Conceptually, it's easiest to think of starting with i=7 and subtracting one until it's reached zero. The problem with this is how we test for the end condition. We want to run the for loop when i=0 and turn off LED0.

If you set up the loop like this:

```
for (i=7; i>0; i--){}
```

it will stop as soon as i is zero, so it will never set or unset LED0. You might try to fix this by comparing with a greater-than-or-equal-to:

```
for (i=7; i>=0; i--){}
```

then you end up with a surprising infinite loop! The reason for this gotcha is that i is defined as an *unsigned* integer, which counts from 0 to 255—it's only defined for positive numbers. When you subtract one from zero, it rolls back around to the maximum value, which is 255 in the 8-bit case. This means the condition i>=0; is *always* true.

Because we want the for loop to run when i is 0, and then stop afterwards when i equals 255, we can test for i < 255, which is exactly what the code, as written, does.

Finally, have a brief look at the "random toggling" section of the code. The "random number" isn't really random at all, but it looks pretty close, so it is good enough. You can see how I used bit-masking to take a 16-bit random number and turn it into a number in the range zero to seven, to match up with our LED numbers. You'll end up seeing these tricks again, so I'll at least introduce them here.

First, we convert the 16-bit randomNumber variable into an 8-bit number by bit shifting the randomNumber over eight times: whichLED = (randomNumber >> 8);. This keeps the most significant eight bits, which are the most "random" using this quick-and-dirty algorithm.

Bit Twiddling for the Impatient

In summary, here's a recap of the three important bit-twiddling operations. Let's say you're trying to write bit i in byte BYTE:

Set a bit
```
BYTE |= (1 << i);
```

Clear a bit
```
BYTE &= ~(1 << i);
```

Toggle a bit
```
BYTE ^= (1 << i);
```

Of course, you can substitute more complicated bit shifts in for the parentheses. For instance, if you want to set bits i and j, use BYTE |= ((1<<i)|(1<<j));.

It's "hardcore" to do the bit shifting and negation stuff by hand, and this book's code is also written in that style because I think it's good for you, like doing situps or drinking wheatgrass juice. In the end, you *will* have to read other people's code, and they *will* do bitwise operations this way. You can't escape it, so you might as well get used to it—it's part of the language idiom.

But on days when you're not feeling hardcore, you can also define some macros to do the same thing, and this can make your code more easily readable. If you'd like to take this path, these will do the trick:

```
#define BV(bit)              (1 << (bit))
#define setBit(byte, bit)    (byte |= BV(bit))
#define clearBit(byte, bit)  (byte &= ~BV(bit))
#define toggleBit(byte, bit) (byte ^= BV(bit))
```

The main limitation of the macros is that they can only change one bit at a time, while the standard method can accept any kind of bitmask, but this rarely makes any practical difference except to how it reads in your code. In the rare cases that you need to flip four bits or more really quickly or really frequently, you'll get it done faster the hardcore way. Anyway, in my opinion, it's good to have options.

Next, we need to limit the random number to the range zero through seven. And what's the largest number you can count to with three bits? Seven. So the trick is to keep only the lowest three bits, zeroing out the upper five. And the quickest and easiest way to do this is using AND and a bitmask: whichLED = whichLED & 0b00000111;. Now our variable whichLED will be in the range of the number of LEDs we actually have.

Finally, if whichLED contains a number like zero or three or seven, all that's left for us to do is use XOR and a bit-shift roll to toggle the randomly selected bit. Voila! A random blinker, powered by bit twiddling.

Summary

You learned a lot about bit twiddling in this chapter, so let's recap. In the last chapter you saw how to set up the data-direction registers to enable any given pin for output, and then how writing a logical one or zero to the same bit number in another register set the output voltage on that pin to 5 V or 0 V, respectively.

And because digital output is all about controlling individual bits, you dove head-first into more advanced bit twiddling. First, using the bit-shift roll, you saw how to get a one bit in any given position. Then you saw how to use the various bitwise logical operations (OR, XOR, AND, and NOT) to set, toggle, or clear bits in a byte individually or in groups. Here, I also introduced the idea of a bitmask that's used with the logical operations to tweak specific bits individually or together:

Set a bit
```
BYTE |= (1 << i);
```

Clear a bit
```
BYTE &= ~(1 << i);
```

Toggle a bit
```
BYTE ^= (1 << i);
```

And that's a lot of bit twiddling for one chapter, but the groundwork we've laid here will serve you throughout the rest of the book and for the rest of your life with microcontrollers.

Serial I/O | 5

Square-Wave Organ

This chapter gives you a lot of bang for the buck. Before it's all over, you're going to have learned how to communicate between the AVR and your desktop or laptop computer and constructed a cheesy computer-controlled musical instrument.

Along the way, you're going to learn a little about serial communications protocols, and how you can generate quick-and-dirty audio with the AVRs. Serial communication is the simplest possible way to interface your microcontroller with your desktop or laptop computer, your first step toward bridging the world of the physical and the virtual.

What You Need

In addition to the basic kit, you will need:

- A speaker with a DC-blocking capacitor around 10 uF.

- A USB-Serial adapter.

- (Optionally) an amplifier if you want to play it loud.

Serial Communication

How do computers or integrated circuit components actually talk to each other? The (too-short) answer is that it's almost exactly like what we were doing in Chapter 3. One side sends a signal by outputting high and low voltage pulses on a wire that connects it to the other device. The other side, in input mode, listens to the voltages on the wire.

The rules for encoding data into voltage pulses and decoding the voltage pulses back into data is called a *serial protocol*. We'll get into a lot more of the nitty-gritty of other serial protocols in Chapter 16 and Chapter 17. For now, we'll limit ourselves to the most common serial mode—universal asynchronous receive and transmit (UART) serial.

To understand what's going on with UART serial, start by thinking of two people who want to talk to each other by sending voltage signals over a few wires. Let's say Alice wants to send the number 10 to her friend Bob over a wire. For concreteness, let's say that the wire's got a pull-up resistor on it so that it's constantly at five volts. On Alice's side of the wire, there's a switch connected to ground, and on Bob's side, there's also an LED so that he can see what the voltage on the wire is by whether or not the LED lights up.

Alice is going to send the number 10 to Bob by pressing her button, grounding the wire, and turning off Bob's LED on the other side. Now, she could send the number by just blinking the LED off 10 times, but that system's going to break down when she wants to send the number 253, or worse, 64,123. So instead she writes out 10 in binary, 0b00001010, and sends a corresponding pattern of flashes.

Bob and Alice have to agree on a bunch of things beforehand for this to work—the serial protocol. First they need to decide on an encoding: they agree beforehand that a button press (a zero-volt signal on the wire) indicates a zero, and no-press (five volts) indicates a one, and that they'll send the numbers least-significant-bit first.

Next, they need to agree how often Alice presses or doesn't press the button. Let's say they choose to signal once per second. This is the *baud rate*—how often the voltage is allowed to change on the line, and conversely how often the receiver needs to read in a new voltage.

How does Bob tell when the transmission begins and ends? They've agreed to wrap the eight bits with two extra bits: a *start bit*, which will always be a zero so that you can tell when the transmission starts, and a *stop bit*, which is a one.

Bob is sitting at his end, staring at the LED, when he sees the LED blink. It blinks off for a second—the start bit! Now once every second after the start bit, he notes down whether the LED is on or off. After the first blink, he sees off, on, off, on, off, off, off, off, and then the LED stays on for a while. He writes down his eight bits, 01010000. He then flips the bit-ordering around, and sees that Alice has sent the number 10!

The oscilloscope trace in Figure 5-1 is a real example of an AVR transmitting the digit 10 to my computer. Instead of one bit per second I used 9,600 bits per second (baud), so each bit takes about 104 microseconds. But you can make out the pattern: 1111100101000011111. Remember that the first low bit is the start bit, then count out eight bits, check that the ninth is high, flip the order, and read it out in binary.

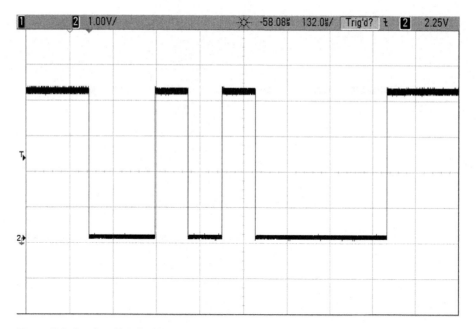

Figure 5-1. *Sending 10 in Serial*

Now if Bob wants to reply, the simplest solution is just to repeat the same physical setup and protocol, but in reverse—that is, give Bob a button and Alice an LED. That way, Bob and Alice can signal each other at any time, sending numbers back and forth. It takes two signal wires to make this work, but the advantages of dedicated lines are simplicity and data throughput.

Figure 5-2 is the trace when two bytes in a row are sent: 9 and then 10. Notice in the center that the stop bit that lies between the two digits is slightly longer—the AVR was doing work and not sending data for an extra few microseconds. This doesn't bother the receiving computer, which starts timing again only when it receives the next start bit.

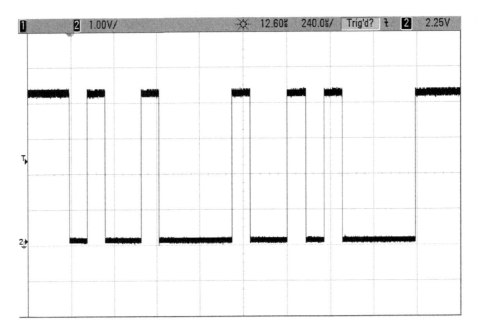

Figure 5-2. *Sending 9 and 10 in Serial*

See Figure 5-3 for the logic interpretation of the signals, and try to read out the bits from the scope trace if you're so inclined.

Start	0	1	2	3	4	5	6	7	Stop	Start	0	1	2	3	4	5	6	7	Stop
0	1	0	0	1	0	0	0	0	1	0	0	1	0	1	0	0	0	0	1

Figure 5-3. *Sending 9 and 10*

Encoding and decoding this data seems like a lot of work, and getting the timing exactly right to send and receive data at baud rates in the tens of thousands of bits per second is no picnic either. That's why all of the AVR Mega microcontrollers have at least one dedicated hardware peripheral, called a *Universal Synchronous and Asyncronous Receiver and Transmitter* (USART) device built in. In the rest of this chapter, we'll look into how to configure and use the USART hardware, as well as how to set up your desktop computer to talk to the AVR.

 **UART and USART**

In the introduction, I said we'd be using UART (universal asynchronous receive and transmit) serial, but the AVR's peripheral is called a USART. What's the difference? Why the extra "S"?

*The AVR's serial hardware is capable of running both in a synchronous mode—using a clock that helps with data timing—and in asynchronous mode without a clock, hence "USART" (universal synchronous and asynchronous receiver and transmitter). But until **Chapter 16**, we'll be exclusively concerned with asynchronous serial communications, so you can feel free to ignore the "S" in the AVR's USART for now.*

Implementing Serial Communication on the AVR: Loopback Project

The first thing you're going to want to do is make sure that your serial link between computer and microcontroller is up and running, and get used to using it. Time to get your chips talking to your desktop computer.

Our setup here is going to involve three different stages:

1. Configuring the AVR
2. Installing serial terminal software on your computer
3. Connecting them together

Setup: Configuring the AVR

Because the AVR microprocessors have dedicated USART circuitry inside, all we have to do to communicate is configure the interface, and then dump our bytes into the special hardware registers designated for sending and receiving. The hardware peripheral will take care of the rest. That's fantastically handy.

First, just to make sure everything is working, we'll flash in a quick demo program. If you've got the LEDs still plugged in from the last few chapters, that's great! If not, you'll miss on out seeing the ASCII numeric representation of each character's value as you type it out. Before we dive into the nitty-gritty of configuring the USART hardware, let's see how we can use it by working through Example 5-1.

Example 5-1. serialLoopback.c listing

```
/*
A simple test of serial-port functionality.
Takes in a character at a time and sends it right back out,
 displaying the ASCII value on the LEDs.
*/
```

```
// ------- Preamble -------- //
#include <avr/io.h>
#include <util/delay.h>
#include "pinDefines.h"
#include "USART.h"

int main(void) {
  char serialCharacter;

  // --------- Inits --------- //
  LED_DDR = 0xff;                          /* set up LEDs for output */
  initUSART();
  printString("Hello World!\r\n");              /* to test */

  // ------ Event loop ------ //
  while (1) {

    serialCharacter = receiveByte();
    transmitByte(serialCharacter);
    LED_PORT = serialCharacter;
                       /* display ascii/numeric value of character */

  }                                        /* End event loop */
  return (0);
}
```

Skip straight down to the event loop, and you can see that there's only three things our program is doing. It receives a byte from the serial line using the function receiveByte(). Then it transmits that same byte back out using transmitByte(). Finally, the LED displays the byte that it just sent across in ASCII.

In the initialization section, you shouldn't be surprised to find that we're initializing the LEDs for output just as we did in the previous chapter. What's new are the functions initUSART() and printString(). They must be defined somewhere, but where? Scrolling up to the preamble, you'll see that I've included a new file, USART.h. If you open that file up, you'll find their prototypes, and we'll go into detail about the configuration routine in "Configuring USART: The Nitty-Gritty Details" on page 90 and including modules in "Modules in C" on page 96. For now, we'll focus on making sure everything is up and running.

Functions as Verbs

It's a style question, but I find that if I name all of my functions with verbs that describe what they do, and all the variables as descriptive nouns, C code can start to read like a sentence.

Sure, you may have to type a little more the first time, but consider yourself coming back to look at this code six months from now. Will you be able to browse through the code and find the section that you'd like to modify? You will, if your functions and variables have descriptive names.

That's the overview. If you haven't already, now's a good time to flash the `serial` Loopback project code into your AVR.

Setup: Your Computer

On your computer, it's just a matter of installing the right software. In particular, you need to connect to a *terminal* application that'll let you type to the AVR and read what it types back. If you've got a favorite terminal application, by all means feel free to use it. Otherwise, I've got a few suggestions.

Setup: USB-Serial Adapter

So your AVR is flashed with the `serialLoopback` code, and your computer's got brand-new serial terminal software loaded and running. Time to hook them up together.

If you've got one of the ubiquitous FTDI cables, it's got a pinout, as summarized in Table 5-1.

Table 5-1. FTDI cable pinout

Color	Signal
Black	GND
Brown	CTS#
Red	VCC
Orange	TXD
Yellow	RXD
Green	RTS#

If you don't have an FTDI cable, the lines you're looking for are going to be labeled something like RX, TX, GND, and optionally VCC. You can choose between powering the project from an external source of 5V, which is the right way to do it, or powering the whole circuit from the USB cable, which is convenient but will probably be drawing more current through the FTDI cable than its specifications allow.

Terminal Emulator Software

Linux

gtkterm is nice and easy to configure and should work on most Linuxes. Another option is *screen*, which is available on both Mac OS and Linux, but which you may not realize is a serial terminal in disguise. Invoking *screen* with **screen [portName] 9600** should get you talking to your AVR directly. Ctrl-A followed by Ctrl-? will get you help. Ctrl-A then Ctrl-K will kill your current session. Linux users can find out which USB serial port is connected by typing **ls /dev/ tty***.

Mac OS

CoolTerm and ZTerm are nice serial terminal applications for Macs. If they don't detect your serial port automatically, you can find it by opening up a regular terminal and typing **ls /dev/ *usbserial***. You're looking for something like /dev/cu.usbserial-XXXX.

Windows

There are a bazillion terminal programs for Windows systems. In the olden days, Hyperterminal was the default and came under Accessories. In recent times, I've used Bray's Terminal, which is minimalistic and gets the job done. If you're not sure which port the USB serial is connected to, check in Device Manager under Ports → USB Serial Port.

Cross-platform, Python

If you've already got Python and the serial library installed, you can run the included serial terminal emulator. Typing **python -m seri al.tools.miniterm --cr [portName] 9600** should get you talking. Note that you type Ctrl-] to quit and Ctrl-T then Ctrl-H for help. (And make a shortcut for this if you know how.)

Cross-platform, Arduino

If you've got the Arduino IDE set up on your computer, you'll find its serial terminal program under Tools → Serial Monitor. This "terminal" program works well enough to listen to the AVR, but it requires you to hit Enter after every character you type in order to send it. For text, you can send a line at a time this way, but for anything interactive, it's inconvenient. In short, I can't recommend the Arduino Serial Moni tor as a general-purpose terminal program, even though it works fine if you only need to receive data from the AVR.

Double-check that you've hooked up the computer/FTDI cable's RX pin to the AVR's TX pin, and vice versa. On the breadboard, with an FTDI cable represented by the rainbow-colored, six-pin header strip, it'll look like Figure 5-4.

Hooking Up Serial Pins

Connecting your serial adapter to the AVR is as simple as connecting three wires, and the first one's simple: it's GND. The other two are "tricky." You need to connect the RX of one device to the TX of the other, and the TX of one to the RX of the other.

"Crossing" the wires this way makes sense electronically, but note that the naming convention is totally different from the way that the SPI pins that we used in the programmer were named! There, MOSI on the programmer connects to MOSI on the AVR, SCK to SCK, etc. Almost all of the modern serial protocols are specified this way: pins with the same names are connected together.

The newer convention makes labelling the cable that runs between them particularly easy as well. The wire that connects MOSI to MOSI should be labelled "MOSI." But what do you label the wire that connects RX to TX? Or the one that connects TX to RX? Usually, the answer is something like "TXA - RXB" and "RXA - TXB," but besides being a mouthful, you then have to remember which device is "A" and which is "B." It's a mess.

Engineers learned their lesson after the crappy naming convention of old-school serial ports, but that doesn't help us here, in USART-land. So just remember: when using (old-school) USART serial, you connect RX to TX, and vice versa. Schematically, your setup should look like Figure 5-5.

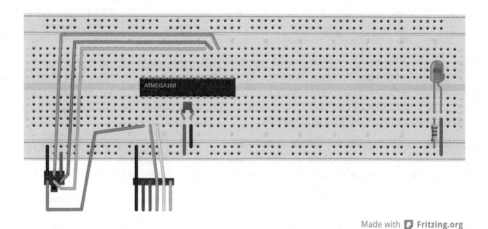

Made with **F** Fritzing.org

Figure 5-4. *Serial I/O breadboard hookup*

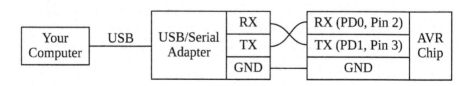

Figure 5-5. *RX-TX hookup*

Again, notice that we've hooked up the RX and TX wires, and connected the ground from the FTDI cable to the ground that's shared between our AVR chip and the programmer. (And if you've still got the LEDs hooked up from last chapter, that's a bonus.)

Putting It All Together: Test Out Your Loopback

So if you've flashed the serialLoopback code to your chip, hooked up the RX/TX pins (and GND) to the USB-Serial converter, and plugged it into your computer, it's time to test this baby out.

Open up the terminal program, make sure it's configured for the right port (the USB converter) and with the right baud rate (9600). If it's got an option for "local echo," set it to no—we're going to be echoing back from the AVR chip. If you've got local echo on, you'll see everything you type twice, "lliikkee tthhiiss".

Now type something. The LED's should display the binary values that correspond to the letter you typed in ASCII. Success! And if you unplug and replug power to the AVR (or momentarily ground the RESET pin), you should be greeted with a friendly "Hello World!" If you're at this point, you've got it all working.

ASCII

When sending 8-bit bytes across the serial line, it's natural to think of them as numbers. But if you want to send letters, we'll have to work out a mapping from the numbers into letters. Enter the American Standard Code for Information Interchange (ASCII).

Have a look at an ASCII table on the Web, or type **man ascii** in Linux or OS X. Otherwise, you'll be well-oriented just by knowing that 'A' is at 0x41, 'B' is at 0x42, 'a' is at 0x61, and '0' is at 0x30. What comes in between should be self-explanatory.

C and ASCII work very well together. You can transition seamlessly between letters and numbers, and because the characters are defined in corresponding alphabetical and numerical order, there's all sorts of tricks you can play with ASCII. 'A' + 2 = 'C' for instance, and '0' + 3 = '3'. This means that if you have the variable a=3; and you'd like to send single digits represented as their ASCII characters, then you can send '0' + a. The printByte() function from my USART library exploits this fact to send a byte as its text representation:

```
void printByte(uint8_t number){
    /* Hundreds */
    transmitByte('0'+ (number/100));
    /* Tens */
    transmitByte('0'+ ((number/10) % 10));
    /* Ones */
    transmitByte('0'+ (number % 10));
}
```

With all this in mind, load up the *serialLoopback.c* demo, type some letters on your keyboard, and watch the blinking (ASCII binary numeric) lights. You're watching the ghost in the machine!

---

printBinaryByte in Lieu of LEDs

If you don't have the LEDs connected but would still like to see how individual characters look as binary ASCII bits, you can replace the line:

```
transmitByte(serialCharacter);
```

in serialLoopback.c with:

```
printBinaryByte(serialCharacter);
printString("\r\n");
```

and then, instead of a simple echo, you'll get the ASCII value of the character you just typed sent back to you. A character-to-ASCII converter!

Troubleshooting Serial Connections

Something's not working? Let's step through it:

1. You've installed terminal software, right?

2. When you plug in the USB-Serial cable, does your computer recognize it? On Linux, type **lsusb** and look for "FT232 USB-Serial" (get a Mac version at *https://github.com/jlhonora/lsusb.*) On Windows, check Device Manager→Ports.

3. On Windows, did you install the correct driver? If not, try unplugging and re-plugging the FTDI cable. If the driver is not installed, it should walk you through it.

4. Do you have the right port name? In Linux and Mac, it'll be something like */dev/ttyUSB0* or */dev/XXX.usbserial-XXXXXXXX*. In Windows, click on the FTDI device in the Device Manager and select the Hardware tab. It should show you which port it's connected to.

5. Do you have permissions? On Linux and Mac, if you're getting hassled, try running your terminal with sudo. (sudo is a command that lets you temporarily run one command at a time as super user—the user with maximum permissions. When something won't run because of permissions issues, you can side-step it quickly by using sudo.) In the long term, you may need to add yourself to a group with read/write permissions to the USB-Serial adapter. Search "serial port permissions" plus your operating system name if you don't already know how to do this.

6. Do you have the TX and RX lines mixed up? It's a quick experiment to switch them and see if that fixes things.

7. Finally, you can remove the AVR from the picture and make sure that your computer isn't to blame by using a hardware loopback. Take a wire and connect

it between the TX and RX lines of your USB-Serial adapter. Now open up your terminal program and type something. The signal should go out the TX, back into the RX, and be typed back out on your screen. If this works, it's possible that the wires connecting to your AVR aren't appropriately crossed, or you've set the baud rates wrong somewhere. Double-check.

8. Once you've got it all working, take a picture of the circuit. You can refer back to this later when you're hooking things up again.

If you have the serialLoopback program up and running, then all is well with your computer, the AVR chip, and the connection between them. Now you are ready to start using the serial port for something. If you want to move straight on down to the AVR Organ project in "AVR Square-Wave Organ" on page 97, feel free. If you'd like a little more detail on just exactly how the USART library that we're including works, keep on reading.

Configuring USART: The Nitty-Gritty Details

In this section, I'm going to go into a bit of detail on how the initUSART() code does its work. You'll see similar examples of hardware configuration and initialization routines in almost every chapter of this book. It can be a little bit intimidating on the first pass, but after working through it a couple of times, either in this chapter or any of the later chapters in this book, you'll get it.

The essential outline of the hardware configuration is that there are a handful of registers for each of the AVR's built-in peripherals. Each bit in a register byte is a switch that enables or disables some functions of the peripheral. Setting up the hardware to do its job, then, is just a matter of figuring out which switches you need to set and bit twiddling them into the right states.

To dig in, let's look at the USART.h and USART.c files. The .h file is pretty standard— it defines a default BAUD rate if you haven't already specified one, and then introduces the functions with descriptive comments. Any macro defines you may need in USART.c are also found here.

So on to the source file, USART.c where the functions are actually defined. I've partially excerpted the file in Example 5-2.

To read along with the USART.c file, you'll want to get the datasheet for the mega168 chip, and open up to the chapter labeled "USART0." Feel free to read the overview section of the datasheet, and then jump on down to the section on "USART Initialization."

Example 5-2. USART.c partial listing

```
/*
  Quick and dirty functions that make serial communications work.
```

```
*/

#include <avr/io.h>
#include "USART.h"
#include <util/setbaud.h>

void initUSART(void) {                                /* requires BAUD */
  UBRR0H = UBRRH_VALUE;                             /* defined in setbaud.h */
  UBRR0L = UBRRL_VALUE;
#if USE_2X
  UCSR0A |= (1 << U2X0);
#else
  UCSR0A &= ~(1 << U2X0);
#endif
                                    /* Enable USART transmitter/receiver */
  UCSR0B = (1 << TXEN0) | (1 << RXEN0);
  UCSR0C = (1 << UCSZ01) | (1 << UCSZ00);   /* 8 data bits, 1 stop bit */

}

void transmitByte(uint8_t data) {
                                    /* Wait for empty transmit buffer */
  loop_until_bit_is_set(UCSR0A, UDRE0);
  UDR0 = data;                                          /* send data */
}

uint8_t receiveByte(void) {
  loop_until_bit_is_set(UCSR0A, RXC0);       /* Wait for incoming data */
  return UDR0;                                /* return register value */
}


// Example of a useful printing command
void printString(const char myString[]) {
  uint8_t i = 0;
  while (myString[i]) {
    transmitByte(myString[i]);
    i++;
  }
}
```

Because this is your first time configuring an AVR hardware peripheral, I'll take you through the configuration steps in some detail. Have a look at the general structure of the initUSART() function. What's going on? Well, we're writing some numbers into registers UBRR0H and UBRR0L at the top of the code. At the bottom, we're setting a couple of bits in the UCSR0B and UCSR0C registers using a bit-shift roll. In particular, for instance, I'll claim that UCSR0B = (1 << TXEN0) | (1 << RXEN0) sets the "transmit enable" bit and the "receive enable" bit for USART0. But how do I know what any of these uppercase macro definitions stand for? Where are they defined?

The meanings of all these cryptic uppercase macro definitions are found in the AVR datasheet, and they're all #defined in the header file *avr/io.h* that we include at the top of our code. Similarly to how the DDRB register definition that we used in Chapter 3 pointed to the register that switched pin-modes between input and output, UCSR0B points to a configuration register for the serial hardware that contains eight bits that act as switches to control up to eight different hardware functions.

To figure out the specifics of what these serial hardware configuration registers do, we'll consult the datasheet for the AVR. In particular, find the "Register Description" section of the "USART0" chapter, and scroll down until you find UCSR0B. (OK, I'll excerpt a diagram from the register description in Figure 5-6, but you should really get used to looking through the datasheet.)

UCSR0B -- USART Control and Status Register 0B

RXCIE0	TXCIE0	UDRIE0	RXEN0	TXEN0	UCSZ02	RXB80	TXB80
7	6	5	4	3	2	1	0

Figure 5-6. *The UCSR0B register: bits and their names*

In a typical configuration register like UCSR0B, each bit is essentially a switch, and each switch has its own function. These functions are laid out in the datasheet, along with a "mnemonic" name associated with it, and these are the same names that get assigned to these pin numbers in the AVR-specific *avr/io.h* file that we included at the top of our code.

What this means is that you don't have to remember if the bit to enable transmission is bit two or bit three in the control register, but you can instead refer to it as TXEN0 and the preprocessor substitutes a three for you because a define statement in *io.h* maps this to bit three. Unfortunately, you *do* have to remember which of the many control registers you need to be accessing, and sometimes the mnemonics aren't really all that clear, but it's better than nothing. If your code reads UCSR0B |= (1<<4), you'd have absolutely no idea what was going on, whereas if it reads UCSR0B |= (1 << RXEN0), you at least stand a chance of figuring out that the line enables the serial receiver hardware bit.

 *avr/io.h*

Actually, the avr/io.h file in turn includes a different subfile depending on which chip you are writing for so that you don't have to change much of your code when you change chips. For instance, using an ATmega168P, the file that actually gets included is called iom168p.h. Looking through this file, you can see all the special register definitions for each register byte and its bits.

Scrolling down to the USART section, we find that:

```
#define UCSR0B _SFR_MEM8(0xC1)
#define TXB80   0
#define RXB80   1
#define UCSZ02  2
#define TXEN0   3
#define RXEN0   4
#define UDRIE0  5
#define TXCIE0  6
#define RXCIE0  7
```

But bear in mind that the macro definition doesn't do everything for you—all it does is substitute a four everywhere it finds RXEN0, for instance. The real meaning of that bit number is only realized when you flip that bit in the right register, UCSR0B. Which is to say, when you have to configure some AVR peripheral by hand, there's no substitute for the "Register Description" sections of the AVR datasheet.

 The "Register Description" Section

When I'm approaching an AVR peripheral configuration problem, I almost always start off by rereading the "Features" and "Overview" sections, and then jump straight across to the "Register Description." After the first two sections, I have a good idea of what the hardware is supposed to do. The "Register Description" section then describes how to do it.

The first hunk of code in initUSART() makes use of some macro definitions from the *util/setbaud.h* include file to set up the USART configuration registers. UBRR0L and UBRR0H contain, respectively, the low byte and high byte of a 16-bit number that determines what baud rate the AVR will use for serial communications. To sample the serial line at just the right times, the AVR divides the system CPU clock, which usually runs between 1 MHz to 20 MHz, down to a baud-rate clock running between 9,600 Hz and 115,200 Hz. The divisor for this clock is stored in UBRR0.

Because there's such a wide range of possible system clocks and desired baud rates, the AVR also has a double-speed mode to handle the higher speeds. A USE_2X macro is defined in *setbaud.h* that figures out whether we should use the regular or double-speed modes. The #if, #else, and #endif commands are like #define statements; they're intended for the preprocessor. This is the only time I'll use preprocessor #if statements, so don't sweat this if you don't want to.

Next, the code enables the USART hardware by writing the enable bits for both transmit and receive. When we do this, the AVR takes over the normal operation of these ports for the USART, setting the data direction registers and pull-up resistors and everything else appropriately for serial communication. Finally, we set a few extra configuration bits that set the USART for 8-bit bytes and one stop bit.

Feel free to skim through the "Register Description" section in the datasheet to see what all the special register configuration bits can do. We'll only use a very small subset of the options here, because we're doing the default—speaking "normal" hardware serial to the computer. In particular, if you'd like to change the number of bits per frame, or include a parity bit or extra stop bits, you'll see which bits you need to set here in the register description.

Once the USART is configured, using it is a piece of cake. Look at the functions transmitByte() and receiveByte(). They both check bits in the UCSR0A (USART Control and Status Register 0 A) register to make sure that the hardware is ready, then read or write their target byte to a special hardware register, UDR0 (USART Data Register), that you use for reading and writing data to and from the USART hardware.

To transmit, you simply wait until the UDRE0 (USART Data Register Empty) bit in the status register is set and then load your byte to transmit into UDR0. The USART hardware logic then shuttles that data along to another memory where it writes it out bit by bit over the serial line as described in the Bob and Alice example.

Similarly, there is a receive-complete bit (RXC0) in the status register UCSR0A that lets you know when a byte has been received. When that bit is set, you can read out the data that just came in. Indeed, if you didn't want to loop around until data came in over the USART—say you wanted the AVR to process other events in the meantime—instead of using a loop_until_bit_is_set(UCSR0A, RXC0); construct, you could simply test if the RXC0 bit is set from within your main event loop and act on the new data when it comes in. You'll see examples of this style of code later on.

The Registers: Using USART

Sending

Wait until the USART data register is clear, indicated by the UDRE0 bit in UCSR0A being set, then write your data to UDR0.

Receiving

When data comes in, the RXC0 bit in UCSR0A will be set, and you can read the incoming data out of UDR0.

The function `printString()` just loops through all the characters in a string until the end, transmitting them one at a time. How does it know when it's come to the end? C strings end in the NULL character, a character with the special value of zero, which you can test easily enough for in an `if()` or `while()` statement.

Two more functions, `printByte()` and `printBinaryByte()`, are mostly for your convenience and to help make pretty output for your computer. `printByte()` takes the numeric value of an 8-bit byte and turns it into the three ASCII digits it represents and sends them out. So if a=56, `printByte(a)` sends "0" and then "5" and then "6" across the serial line:

```
void printByte(uint8_t byte){
  /* Converts a byte to a string of decimal text, sends it */
  transmitByte('0'+ (byte/100));        /* Hundreds */
  transmitByte('0'+ ((byte/10) % 10)); /* Tens     */
  transmitByte('0'+ (byte % 10));       /* Ones     */
  }
```

`printBinaryByte()` does a similar thing, but in binary; `printBinaryByte(56)` prints out "00111000" to your terminal:

```
void printBinaryByte(uint8_t byte){
  /* Prints out a byte as a series of 1's and 0's */
  uint8_t bit;
  for (bit=7; bit < 255; bit--){
    if ( bit_is_set(byte, bit) )
      transmitByte('1');
    else
      transmitByte('0');
  }
}
```

Because we're used to reading binary in most-significant-bit order, the `for()` loop in `printBinaryByte()` runs the variable bit from seven to zero. The `if()` statement tests each bit and sends a 1 or 0 character accordingly.

If you look into the full version of the *USART.h* and *USART.c* files, you'll find a few more useful functions that we'll employ at various points in the rest of the book. But feel free to hold off on that for later. It's time to start *using* this stuff.

Modules in C

All of this USART code, wrapped up in the *USART.h* and *USART.c* files, is written in a way so that it's maximally easy to import it into your own code. When your projects get complex enough, you're going to want to do this, too. So let's take a minute to look at the ways people bundle up their code into reusable modules in C.

Generally speaking, the *.c* file is where your code goes, and the *.h*, or *header* file is reserved for #defines that the user is likely to want to change and for descriptions of the functions that are included in the *.c* file. This makes the header file the first place to look when looking at someone else's code—the header file should provide an overview.

Additionally, in strict C, every function should be *prototyped* before it is defined or used, and the traditional way to make sure this happens is to put function prototypes in the header files. A function prototype is very similar to a function definition, just without the code. The important part is that you must declare what type of variables each function takes as arguments, and what value it will return. But while you're at it, you might as well write some nice explanations of what everything does. This makes the header files very valuable.

To use functions from a given module, say *module.c*, into your code, you've got to first include all the function prototypes by including the *module.h* file at the top of your main file. (See how I do that with #include "USART.h" at the top of the code in this chapter?) Next, you've got to tell the compiler where to find the *module.c* file in which the actual code for the functions are stored. Much of the project-specific detail, like locations of module files and so on, is incorporated into the project's makefile.

Makefiles automate a bunch of the repetitive and otherwise boring parts of software compilation by defining which parts of the project depend on which other parts. So when you're adding a new module to your code, you'll need to tell the makefile where it can find the *module.c* file, so that it can compile it along with your main program's *.c* file.

If you are only using a given module for this one project, it makes sense to keep its header and code files in the same folder as your main code. If, on the other hand, you are reusing the same code across multiple projects, you may want to store the module in some other "library" directory and include it from there.

In my makefiles, I provide options for both of these possibilities. If you'd like to include *.c* files that are in the same directory as the rest of your project, you can add the filenames to the LOCAL_SOURCE variable. If you'd like to include library functions that you've stored somewhere else, you can pass the directory name to EXTRA_SOURCE_DIR and the filenames to EXTRA_SOURCE_FILES. Other makefiles will have similar definitions.

So, in short, if you want to include a module module into your main code, you need to:

1. Copy the *module.h* and *module.c* files into your project directory or include the directory where you've stored the files in your makefile.

2. #include module.h at the top of your code before you use any of the functions.

3. Add the *.c* file to your makefile as extra source to be compiled.

Now you know what makes it all work. Again, because the USART code is all bundled up in the .h and .c files, all you need to do to use serial in your code is include the .h file in your preamble and add the .c file into your makefile. Then you can have your AVR talk freely to your computer, and tremendous power becomes yours.

Other Uses for USART

Besides communicating with your computer, here are some other uses of the USART:

- Debugging. The ability to send out info about the AVR's state over the serial line can be priceless. The functions printByte(), print Word(), and printBinaryByte() make it painless.

- Using LCD and VFD displays that take serial input.

- Making your own GPS datalogger is fairly easy, because GPS modules usually send out their location data using a USART-style serial protocol.

- Integrating card-readers, both magnetic-stripe and RFID, into your designs, because they often send their data to you in USART serial.

- Sending data via radio protocols, because most use USART encoded in various ways.

- Building other examples in this book: we'll set up a low-speed "oscilloscope" using the ADC in Chapter 7.

AVR Square-Wave Organ

It's time to make some noise, and put our serial-port to good use. I love sound projects, and thought an AVR organ would be a nice demonstration. But then, if you're going to play an organ, you certainly need a keyboard. Rather than build one out of ebony, ivory, and 88 keyswitches, we'll hijack your computer's keyboard and use the serial port to connect the computer with the AVR. Let's get started.

Hearing is frankly amazing. In case you don't share my sense of wonder, think about this: periodic pressure waves in the air around you press on a thin skin membrane that wiggles some tiny bones that are configured like a lever, amplifying the movements and pressing on a fluid-filled sac that contains hairs that are connected to nerves that sense vibrations. When the longer hairs are vibrated by the fluid, you hear bass tones. When the shorter ones are vibrated, you hear treble.

Right. So the hearing part is already sorted out by Mother Nature. All that's left for us to do is make the corresponding periodic pressure waves in the air. And for that, we'll use a paper cone that we've strapped an electromagnet onto, and use electricity to wiggle the electromagnet and cone back and forth in the field of a permanent magnet. And we'll call this device a speaker. Now all we have to do is send time-varying voltages to the speaker coil, and we'll hear tones. Glorious!

Making Music with Your Micro

Microcontrollers are *not* meant to drive speakers. Speakers have a very low resistance to direct current (DC), around 8 ohms. For instance, if we run our AVR at 5 volts and we connect it directly to an 8-ohm speaker, a current of 625 milliamps (5 volts divided by 8 ohms) will be drawn, which is significantly more than the 20 to 50 milliamps that an AVR pin is good for. The solution is to add a *blocking capacitor* to the circuit, as shown in Figure 5-7.

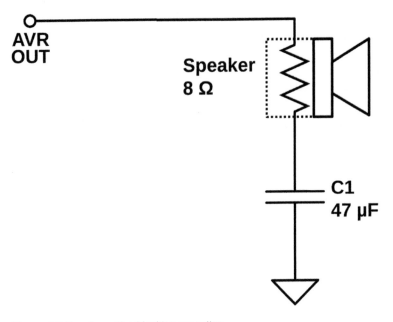

AVR OUT

Speaker 8 Ω

C1 47 µF

Figure 5-7. *Speaker with a blocking capacitor*

When a capacitor is subject to a DC voltage, it lets a little current through until it is "charged up" to that voltage, then it blocks further current. This means that capacitors pass current only for *changes* in voltage. This is perfect for our speaker! The changing signal that makes up the audio is passed through, while the speaker doesn't overload the AVR's output current when the voltage is held high.

But do note that if you're using an electrolytic capacitor (one that comes in a metal tube-shaped can), they often have a positive and negative sides to them. We're not running enough current through the capacitor to damage it anyway, but you might as well hook it up with the stripe (negative terminal) to ground. On the breadboard, it will look like Figure 5-8.

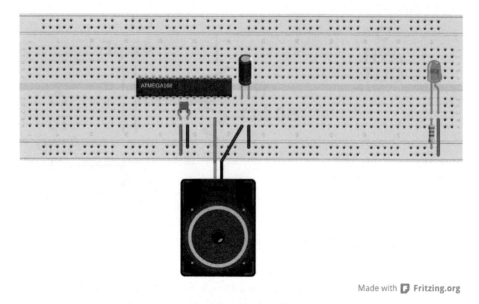

Made with 🐟 Fritzing.org

Figure 5-8. *Speaker with a blocking capacitor on the breadboard*

Just how large a capacitor to use depends on your desired bass response, the particulars of the speaker, and how willing you are to overdrive the AVR's outputs. In my experience, anything between 10 and 100 microfarads works well, and I tend to use 47 microfarads. Experiment with whatever values you can get your hands on; it's unlikely that you can break anything.

Amplification

It's equally unlikely that the AVR will be driving your speaker to deafening levels, so to truly annoy your neighbors, you may need to redirect the audio signal to whatever amplification you've got handy: amplified computer speakers, your stereo, a mixing board, etc. But first, you'll have to attenuate the signal. The 5 V signal that the AVR puts out is not enough to drive your speaker very loudly, but it's too loud for direct input into an amplifier.

Most amplified devices expect a "line level" signal; that is, something from one to two volts peak to peak. Assuming the AVR is running on 5 V, you'll want to cut the signal at least in half before sending it on. The easiest way to do this is to place a voltage-divider in the circuit before the capacitor to limit the output. Any potentiometer with a resistance in the 10 kΩ to 100 kΩ range makes a good voltage divider, and a volume-adjust knob to boot. See Figure 5-9 for the circuit diagram.

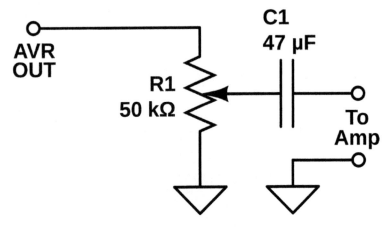

Figure 5-9. *Audio with pot, blocking capacitor*

This circuit will work very nicely with self-powered "computer monitor" type speakers. In fact, you'll probably want to use something small and cheap rather than your hi-fi equipment. I have an old powered computer speaker; I've chopped the plug off and replaced it with three alligator clips (for stereo). This comes in handy quite often, and I'm not really worried about destroying it. Given the very harsh square waves we'll be producing, I would caution against plugging this straight into your stereo's line in unless you really know what you're doing.

Once you've hooked up the speakers, powered or otherwise, you're ready to go. Flash in the *serialOrgan.c* code, and then fire up your terminal program, and play some notes on the home row of the keyboard.

The Organ Library

I went module crazy in this program. Most of the code for making the actual sound is stored in the *organ.h* and *organ.c* libraries so that you can use them again in your own code if you'd like. Let's look them over quickly.

As usual, have a first look at *organ.h*. Two functions are defined there: play Note(uint16_t wavelength, uint16_t duration) and rest(uint16_t dura tion). If you look at any of the player programs, they all include the file *scale16.h* as well, which provides #defines for a scale in terms of the wavelengths that the playNote function requires. So let's look at playNote() in Example 5-3 and see what's going on.

Example 5-3. *playNote function listing*

```
void playNote(uint16_t wavelength, uint16_t duration){
  uint16_t elapsed;

  uint16_t i;
  for(elapsed = 0; elapsed < duration; elapsed += wavelength){
```

```
/* For loop with variable delay selects the pitch */
for (i = 0; i < wavelength; i++){
  _delay_us(1);
}
SPEAKER_PORT ^= (1 << SPEAKER);
  }
}
```

playNote() takes a wavelength (essentially the inverse of a frequency or pitch) and a duration, and plays a note of the corresponding pitch and length. It does this by toggling the SPEAKER bit between zero and one at a given frequency, and because the speaker pin is configured for output, this sends 5 V and then 0 V to the speaker cone, making it move back and forth and creating a tone.

The innermost for loop is doing nothing but waiting for a precise amount of time. By waiting one microsecond per trip through the i loop, the loop creates a delay of approximately wavelength microseconds. Thus, larger values of wavelength correspond to slower back-and-forths of the speaker cone, and thus to lower frequencies. If we choose these times just right, we'll have musical pitches.

The outermost for loop (looping over elapsed) has one little bit of cleverness that's worth noting. Musically we want to be able to specify a note that lasts for a given duration, hence the duration argument. But at the same time, the pitch of the note we play is varied by changing how long our innermost loop takes per step—wavelength microseconds. How do we write the outer loop so that it knows exactly how many times to loop around the inner loop while the inner loop takes a variable amount of time?

Although we often increment the counting variable in a for() loop by one each time through, we don't have to. For each trip through the inner loop, wavelength microseconds have elapsed. The outer loop keeps track of the total elapsed time by adding wavelength microseconds to the elapsed variable each time it moves through the loop. So instead of adding only one to elapsed per loop through, the increment to elapsed is made to depend on the length of time that the inner loop took: wavelength microseconds. Now it's easy to exit the loop as soon as elapsed time is no longer less than the duration.

The Code

If you've been too distracted by all of this coding mumbo-jumbo, please flash in the *serialOrgan.c* code, open up a serial terminal, and press some keys. If you've hooked up the speaker, you should be able to play some simple songs using your computer's keyboard. Enjoy this for a while, and then let's get down to figuring out what makes it all tick in Example 5-4.

Example 5-4. **serialOrgan.c** *listing*

```
/*

serialOrgan.c

Reads a character in serial from the keyboard, plays a note.

See organ.h for pin defines and other macros
See organ.c (and include it in the Makefile) for playNote() and rest()

*/

// ------- Preamble -------- //
#include <avr/io.h>
#include <util/delay.h>
#include "organ.h"
#include "scale16.h"
#include "pinDefines.h"
#include "USART.h"

#define NOTE_DURATION     0xF000          /* determines long note length */

int main(void) {

  // -------- Inits --------- //
  SPEAKER_DDR |= (1 << SPEAKER);                   /* speaker for output */
  initUSART();
  printString("----- Serial Organ ------\r\n");

  char fromCompy;                          /* used to store serial input */
  uint16_t currentNoteLength = NOTE_DURATION / 2;
  const uint8_t keys[] = { 'a', 'w', 's', 'e', 'd', 'f', 't',
    'g', 'y', 'h', 'j', 'i', 'k', 'o',
    'l', 'p', ';', '\''
  };
  const uint16_t notes[] = { G4, Gx4, A4, Ax4, B4, C5, Cx5,
    D5, Dx5, E5, F5, Fx5, G5, Gx5,
    A5, Ax5, B5, C6
  };
  uint8_t isNote;
  uint8_t i;

  // ------ Event loop ------ //
  while (1) {

                                                        /* Get Key */
    fromCompy = receiveByte();       /* waits here until there is input */
    transmitByte('N');     /* alert computer we're ready for next note */

                                                        /* Play Notes */
    isNote = 0;
    for (i = 0; i < sizeof(keys); i++) {
```

```
      if (fromCompy == keys[i]) {        /* found match in lookup table */
        playNote(notes[i], currentNoteLength);
        isNote = 1;                      /* record that we've found a note */
        break;                            /* drop out of for() loop */
      }
    }


                        /* Handle non-note keys: tempo changes and rests */
    if (!isNote) {
      if (fromCompy == '[') {             /* code for short note */
        currentNoteLength = NOTE_DURATION / 2;
      }
      else if (fromCompy == ']') {        /* code for long note */
        currentNoteLength = NOTE_DURATION;
      }
      else {                              /* unrecognized, just rest */
        rest(currentNoteLength);
      }
    }


  }                                       /* End event loop */
  return (0);
}
```

First and foremost, look at the laundry list of include files. We want to use the playNote() function from the *organ.c* and *organ.h* files, so I've included that here. I'll also use the predefined scale data from the *scale16.h* file. ("16" because the scale makes use of 16-bit numbers for greater pitch accuracy.) And finally, I include the *USART.h* file that includes the utility serial functions that we've already seen.

And speaking of the USART library, look down to the main() function. Notice that before entering the event loop, in the initializations section, I call the initU SART() function and print out something friendly to the serial port. As you saw earlier, initUSART() selects the baud rate and configures the USART hardware appropriately. The print command gives us something to look for in the serial terminal window to verify that all's well with the serial connection. And before we leave the initialization section, notice that we've set up the speaker pin for output by setting the correct bit in the DDR.

Finally, inside the event loop, the program starts off by waiting for a serial byte from your computer. Once it gets a byte, it acknowledges it back to your computer, which will let you play around with scripting the serial organ later, and then the routine plays an appropriate note depending on which key you've sent. The way the code maps these keys to notes is a tiny bit advanced, so feel free to skip the following sidebar if you'd like.

Converting Keypresses to Notes

The organ code needs to take input from your serial terminal program and map those keys to notes in a way that's intuitive for you. To code this lookup in a flexible and maintainable manner, I use two constant arrays, one with the list of keypresses and the other with a list of the pitches. This is actually a pretty common case for dealing with user input, so I thought I'd mention it here.

The "trick" to the lookup is the for(i=0; i < sizeof(keys); i++){} loop. The code looks through all of the possible keys that correspond to notes. If it matches one of them, it plays the i'th note immediately and drops out of the for() loop. Slick, no?

There's one nuance in the for loop that I'd like to point out. Notice that i is only incremented as long as i < sizeof(keys). Because the code indexes the keys[] array with i, this seems natural. But we should double-check that i never gets bigger than the size of the array. Because each key[] entry is a byte and the array is 18 bytes long, the sizeof(keys) command will return 18, and the maximum value i will ever take on is 17. That is, we only want to run the for() loop as long as i < sizeof(keys).

The error that new C programmers make here is to write something like i <= sizeof(keys), because we have 18 bytes and we'd like to loop over all of them, right? Right, but wrong! Because C indexes its arrays starting at position 0, the last element is keys[17] and not keys[18]. That is, the less-than-or-equal-to construction ends up indexing one past the end of the array, which is no good.

If you're still new at C, you'll probably want to double-check the variables you use to index arrays each time you see one. Just remember that the maximum index for an array is one less than its length because we started counting at zero rather than one.

If the program hasn't received a valid note command, it checks to see if you've changed the note length, and sets the appropriate value if you have. If none of these have happened, it defaults to resting (not playing a note) for the duration.

And that's it. You can now play your AVR from your laptop's keyboard, and that's pretty cool. But this is just the beginning of a long and fruitful friendship; your computer and your AVR are a match made in hacker heaven.

Extra Goodies

I've also included two more files that might be interesting in the software bundle for the serialOrgan project. Both of them are written in Python, rather than being written in C. Python is an interpreted language, and includes modules that let you do basically anything, easily. I'll use it throughout the book for projects that require computer/AVR interaction, or for doing any sort of computations that are too demanding for the AVR.

Creating the *scale16.h* header file that contains the note pitch data is an example of something that you'll really want to do with a simple routine on your big computer, rather than reimplementing on the fly in the AVR. I've included the *generateScale.py* file that created the header file in the software distribution for this project.

I've also included a simple script (*autoPlay.py*) that demonstrates one way to interface your desktop computer with the AVR. The code relies on Python and the `pyserial` library. This script sends a character to the organ to play a note, and then waits for the AVR's response before sending the next note—you'll recall the AVR acknowledges when it's ready to continue.

Though it's a little bit difficult to get the timing right, and even to remember which keys are which while playing the AVR organ live, it's a lot easier to type in strings of characters and let a Python routine shuttle them out to the AVR for you. And for pure frivolity, I have the demonstration program fetch text from a web page that contains "song" data, and play it across on the organ.

Neither of these programs are necessary to your understanding of the AVR serial peripheral, so I'm going to leave digging into the code up to you—they're just here to whet your appetite. If you've already got Python installed on your computer, feel free to run them both. If you don't have Python or `pyserial` installed yet and you just can't wait, flip ahead to "Installing Python and the Serial Library" on page 123 and install them both. If you'd like to get on to more and better AVR programming, don't sweat it; I'll catch you up on the whole Python thing later.

Summary

After digging deep into a complex application like this, you may have forgotten the reason we came here—to learn something about the AVR's serial peripheral.

Using the USART:

1. Choose a baud rate, here by defining BAUD, and write the appropriate values to the baud rate registers UBRRL and UBRRH. (The *setbaud.h* library will help you with this.)

2. Enable the serial receive and transmit register bits.

3. If you're transmitting, wait until the hardware is ready (`loop_un til_bit_is_set(UCSR0A, UDRE0)`) and then load your byte data into UDR0. The AVR's hardware handles everything else automatically.

4. If you're waiting for data, check the data-received bit (`bit_is_set(UCSR0A, RXC0)`) and then read the data out of UDR0. Reading UDR0 automatically clears the data-received bit, and the AVR gets ready for the next received byte.

Additionally, I've wrapped up these simple statements into a few functions that I find convenient. I use `initUSART()`, `transmitByte()`, and `receiveByte()` in my code all the time. If you feel adventurous, you can look through the *USART.c* file and see how I've implemented other useful serial functions, like printing out a byte as its binary or hexadecimal equivalent, and printing whole strings at a time.

Connecting your big desktop computer to the little computer that lives inside the AVR provides you with many creative possibilities. Your computer can fetch and parse websites, check up on stock prices, and do incredible amounts of math. The AVR can move motors, blink LEDs, sense light levels, respond to pushbuttons in real time, and generally interface with the world of DIY electronics. Putting these two together is a recipe for winning, and the serial port is your link.

Digital Input

AVR Music Box and a Boss Button

If you want to build a standalone AVR device, there's no substitute for the tried-and-true pushbutton. Look around the room you're now in. How many electronic devices with pushbuttons are you surrounded by? (Feel free to stop counting after five or ten.) Pushbuttons are cheap, ubiquitous, and the natural choice for quick and mostly painless human/AVR interaction.

In this chapter, we'll take the humble pushbutton as a stand-in for all types of digital input, but there are also a few quirks in using pushbuttons that you will need to know about. Most importantly, they often *bounce* very rapidly between the on and off states when pressed or released. Additionally, you're often interested in running some action *when* the button is first pressed rather than continuously *while* it's pressed.

What You Need

In this chapter, in addition to the basic kit, you will need:

- A pushbutton or two.

- A speaker and blocking capacitor, around 10µF.

- A USB-Serial adapter.

Pushbuttons, Switches, Etc.

As soon as you start having plans for more interesting AVR devices, you're going to want some degree of user interaction. And what's simpler than the humble pushbutton? Still, there are a couple of things you're going to need to know before you can start using switches and buttons as inputs to the AVR.

The AVR inputs are good at sensing voltages. In particular, they're very good at sensing whether an applied voltage on a particular pin is higher or lower than half of the supply voltage. Your first task, then, is to figure out how to apply logic high and low voltages to an AVR pin by way of a pushbutton.

The naïve circuit shown in Figure 6-1 connects one end of the pushbutton to ground and the other end to the AVR. That way, whenever you press the button the AVR end is connected to ground, too, so it's pretty much guaranteed to be at 0 V.

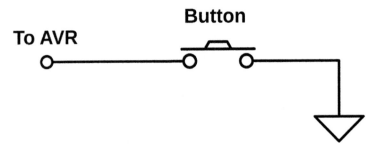

Figure 6-1. *Naive button circuit*

But when you let go of the button (or open the switch), what is the voltage at the AVR end of the switch? Short answer: nobody knows. A wire that's just dangling in the air, on the unconnected side of a switch, can act as an antenna. The voltage on that wire will wiggle around between high and low logic states at whatever frequency the strongest local radio stations (or even "noisy" electrical appliances) broadcast. The only thing you *do* know about this voltage is that it's unreliable.

Instead of some random value, you want the side of the button that you connect to the AVR to have a nice, defined high voltage level when the button isn't pressed. But you can't hook the AVR-side of the button directly to VCC, because if you did, you'd be shorting out the power supply when you pressed the button—hooking VCC up directly to GND is a recipe for disaster. Enter the *pull-up* resistor, shown in Figure 6-2.

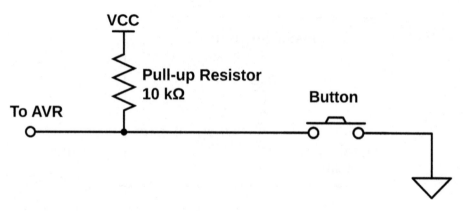

Figure 6-2. *Pull-up resistor button circuit*

A pull-up resistor is a resistor of a relatively high value that "pulls up" the nonground side of the button to the high voltage level in the absence of a button press. Think of pull-up (or pull-down) resistors as setting a default electrical value for the button when it's not pressed.

Relatively large-valued resistors (10k ohms–100k ohms) are used for pull-ups so that when the switch is pressed, it creates a lower-resistance path to ground, and only a small amount of current will flow through the circuit. If the pull-up's resistance is large enough, the voltage seen by the AVR will be very close to 0 V.

Now here's the cool bit. The AVR chips provide you a built-in pull-up resistor for each pin, and you have the option to activate it for any pin that is in input mode. That way the AVR side reads a well-defined high voltage level (pulled up by the internal resistor) until you press the button, when the lower-resistance connection to ground through the button dominates, and the pin reads 0 V. The final circuit with the AVR's internal pull-up resistor enabled is shown in Figure 6-3.

So in the end, it looks like we're back to the naïve circuit from Figure 6-1, with the exception that this one will actually work as intended, thanks to the AVR's optional internal pull-up resistor. Add the button to your breadboard as in Figure 6-4 (pushbutton to pin PD2), and let's get to configuration. (Leave the LEDs and everything else you've got on the board in place.)

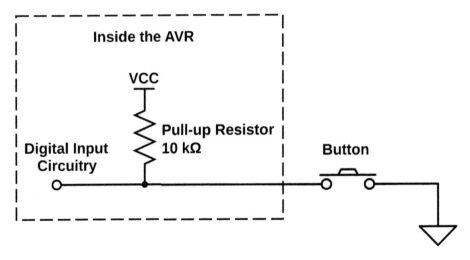

Figure 6-3. *AVR circuit with internal pull-up resistor enabled*

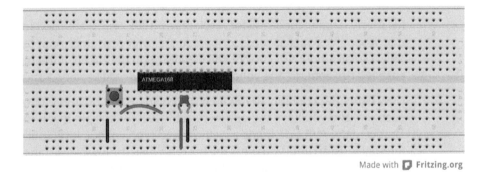

Made with 🟥 Fritzing.org

Figure 6-4. *AVR with pushbutton*

Configuring Input: DDRs, PORTs, and PINs

Just as you can configure the AVR's pins for output, you can also set the data direction registers to enable the pins as inputs. Only this time it's a lot easier—input is the default mode for the chip. If you haven't touched the DDR yet, you're already in input mode. Otherwise, you can select input mode for a pin at any time by clearing the bits that correspond to your pins in the right DDR.

Suppose you want to read the state of pin PD2, the pin that you've connected to your pushbutton. When the chip powers up, every pin is already in input mode, so all that remains is to enable the pull-up resistor. And to enable the pull-up, unsurprisingly, you need to set a bit in a hardware special register.

But the surprise is *which* hardware register you need to set a bit in: the output pin hardware register. That is, if you'd like to enable the pull-up on PD2, you need to set PORTD's corresponding bit high:

```
DDRD &= ~(1 << PD2); // makes double-sure we're in input mode
PORTD |= (1 << PD2); // enables pull-up resistor
```

The way I remember this is that writing a bit to the PORTD register when it's configured for output would pull the pin high, so doing the same when it's configured for input also pulls it high, but only weakly—that is, through the pull-up resistor.

You might be wondering why the Atmel engineers would reuse the same hardware register for both setting the output value in output mode *and* for enabling or disabling the pull-up resistor in input mode. Well, me too. My only guess is that it costs them more space in the IC's internal circuitry to set up another dedicated eight bits of memory for (yet another) register. Because you're never going to have a given pin both in output and input mode, they can use the PORT registers to do double duty. The point is, though, that you're going to have to remember this double role of the PORT registers in input mode.

Great. So you're configured. Now how do you access the bits? Very similarly to how you wrote to them: reading out a byte from a hardware register and doing some bit twiddling. Only this time you're twiddling the input hardware register address: PIND. (Think "**Pin IN**put **D**.")

Let's say that you haven't attached anything to any of the other pins in bank D except for your pushbutton on PD2. Further, you've just reset the chip, so all of the pins are in input mode. One more thing: let's write a 1 to all the bits in PORTD, enabling all of the pull-ups:

```
DDRD  = 0x00;   // all pins in input mode, just to be sure
PORTD = 0xff;   // all pins pull-ups enabled
```

If you look at the eight bits in PIND, you'll see:

```
PIND:  11111111
```

Why? Because nothing is grounded, and the pull-ups guarantee that everything is in logic-high state. Now let's say you push your button, grounding pin PD2. What happens? All the other bits in PIND stay the same, but because the button has *much* lower resistance than the internal pull-up resistor, the ground voltage wins out, the voltage on PD2 drops near zero, and PIND reads:

```
PIND:  11111011
```

Now you've got something you can work with!

Interpreting Button Presses

So you've configured the pin with your button for input, you've set the pull-up resistor, and you're ready to go! How do you read the value of a single bit in the register without reading all the others? If your instincts tell you that it's something to do with bitwise logical operators, you are on your way to microcontroller mastery.

Testing bit states is done with the AND operator. You know that an AND will only return 1 if *both* bits are 1. If you perform an AND operation in which you compare an unknown bit value against a known 1, you'll get the state of the mystery bits as the result. So you'll bit-shift a 1 into the bit location you're interested in, then AND the two bytes together. The result will either be all zeros if the target bit was zero, or it will be a byte with a 1 in the target location if it was 1.

Testing bits with AND
Say we're interested in testing if bit two is set. The first step is to create a bitmask with a 1 in bit two:

```
(1 << 2) : 00000100
```

Then we AND that byte with whatever is in the input register, PIND:

```
PIND     : xxxxxxxx
(1 << 2) : 00000100
&        : 00000x00
```

If the value we were interested in knowing is a zero, the result is eight zeros. If the result isn't zero, then we know the pin in the input register must have been set. Voilà!

So we can test this:

```
if (PIND & (1<<2)){
    doStuff();
}
```

using the C language convention that *only* a value of zero returns false, and anything else is true.

GCC convenience macros
Because all of this shifting and ANDing can get tiresome, you won't be surprised that there are some convenience macros defined to help you out. Now I've almost never seen other people's code using these macros, so you're going to have to remain used to reading the bitmask-and-AND method. These macros are probably not defined by any compiler other than GCC, for all I know.

On the other hand, these macros are in avr-libc for your use, and I do find they lead to nicely readable code. I'll use them in my code sometimes, but then also use the standard C bitmask method sometimes too just to keep you on your toes.

Helpful input macros (included with *avr/io.h*):

```
#define _BV(bit)  (1 << (bit))
```

```
#define bit_is_set(sfr, bit)                (_SFR_BYTE(sfr) & _BV(bit))
#define bit_is_clear(sfr, bit)              (!(_SFR_BYTE(sfr) & _BV(bit)))

#define loop_until_bit_is_set(sfr, bit)     do { } while (bit_is_clear(sfr, bit))
#define loop_until_bit_is_clear(sfr, bit)   do { } while (bit_is_set(sfr, bit))
```

simpleButton demo code

As a quick example of reading button input, flash the *simplePushbutton.c* test program into your chip now and then have a look at the code listed in Example 6-1.

Example 6-1. simpleButton.c listing

```
/*
   Demo of the simplest on/off button code
   Button connected to PD2
   LEDs connected to PB0..PB7
*/

// ------- Preamble -------- //
#include <avr/io.h>
#include <util/delay.h>

int main(void) {
  // -------- Inits --------- //
  PORTD |= (1 << PD2);  /* initialize pullup resistor on our input pin */
  DDRB = 0xff;                          /* set up all LEDs for output */

  // ------- Event loop ------ //
  while (1) {
    if (bit_is_clear(PIND, PD2)) {            /* look for button press */
                      /* equivalent to if ((PIND & (1 << PD2)) == 0 ){ */
      PORTB = 0b00111100;                               /* pressed */
    }
    else {                                    /* not pressed */
      PORTB = 0b11000011;
    }
  }                                       /* End event loop */
  return (0);
}
```

It's not all that complicated, so I'm not going to explain it in excruciating detail, but there are two points worth mentioning. First, notice that the code enables the pull-up resistor for the button pin (PD2) by writing to PORTD. In Cylon Eyes, we used PORTB for controlling output state. In input mode, PORTD controls the pull-up resistor.

The second detail is that our logic is reversed. Because a high voltage on the AVR's pin results in a logical 1 inside the AVR, and the switch voltage is high when the button is *not* pressed, PIND has a 1 in bit PD2 when the button is *not* pressed. Contrariwise, when the button *is* pressed, the bit will read 0. So if you're testing for a press in an if() statement, you'll want to use bit_is_clear(PIND, PD2) or equivalently (PIND & (1<< PD2)) == 0 as the test.

Careful with Those Parentheses

Note that I used (PIND & (1 << PD2)) == 0 and not PIND & (1 << PD2) == 0 in the preceding test. This is because the == is evaluated before the & otherwise. If you forget the parentheses, (1 << PD2) == 0 returns zero, and PIND & 0 is also going to be zero, no matter whether the button is pressed or not. The parentheses make it evaluate the & before the ==.

Of course, you can avoid all this thinking and use bit_is_clear() instead, which I find much more readable anyway. (And note that the macro is defined with the outer parentheses for you.)

Changing State

Depending on what your device does, you may be interested in whether the button is currently pressed, or whether the button just got pressed. That is, you may want to know what state the button is in (pressed or not), or you may alternatively want to know that the button has changed state (just got pressed or just released).

Because the English language is a little imprecise on these matters, but the AVR is brutally literal, you'll need to think like a computer here. When you say "do something if the button is pressed," you'll have to think about whether you mean "while the button is pressed" or "when the button enters the pressed state."

The difference? Imagine that you want to turn on or off an LED with a button press. If you write naïve code:

```
while(1) {
    if (buttonIsPressed){
        toggleLED();
    }
}
```

the LED is going to be toggling around 100,000 times per second while you're holding the button down, and whichever state it ends up in when you let go of the button is pretty much random. This is probably not what you want.

Instead, if you save the current state of the button in a variable, you'll be able to see when the button changes state easily. The code shown in Example 6-2 toggles the LED every time you press a button.

Example 6-2. *toggleButton.c listing*

```
/*
    Demonstrates using state to detect button presses
*/

// ------- Preamble -------- //
#include <avr/io.h>
#include "pinDefines.h"

int main(void) {
  // -------- Inits --------- //
  uint8_t buttonWasPressed;                              /* state */
  BUTTON_PORT |= (1 << BUTTON);     /* enable the pullup on the button */
  LED_DDR = (1 << LED0);               /* set up LED for output */

  // ------- Event loop ------ //
  while (1) {
    if (bit_is_clear(BUTTON_PIN, BUTTON)) {   /* button is pressed now */
      if (buttonWasPressed == 0) {      /* but wasn't last time through */
        LED_PORT ^= (1 << LED0);                       /* do whatever */
        buttonWasPressed = 1;                     /* update the state */
      }
    }
    else {                           /* button is not pressed now */
      buttonWasPressed = 0;                     /* update the state */
    }
  }                                          /* End event loop */
  return (0);                      /* This line is never reached */
}
```

In this code, the state of the button after the last pass through the event loop is stored in the variable buttonWasPressed. If the button is pressed right now, but it wasn't pressed the last time we looked, then we know that there's been a change of state—the button has just been pressed. In this code, we toggle an LED, but you can imagine doing something fancy.

Debouncing

If you play around with the *toggleButton.c* code for long enough, it will glitch. That is, you'll press the button, and instead of turning the LED on, it will turn on and then off again so quickly that you might not even see it. But the end effect will be that you thought you were turning the LED on, and it didn't go on.

Or sometimes it'll happen that you've just turned the LED on with a press, and then when you release the button, it turns back off again. Is there a bug in the code? Nope. You're just suffering from button *bounce*.

When you press a switch closed, two surfaces are brought into contact with each other. Often they don't fit together quite perfectly, and electrical contact will get made and unmade a few times before you've smooshed the two plates together firmly enough that a good reliable connection is made. The same is true when you release a button, but in reverse. You let go, the plates start to separate, but one gets a little sideways and just taps the other before they're far enough apart that they never touch.

This physical open-close-open-close nature of switches makes the voltage on the circuit bounce between high and low logic voltages over a timescale from a few microseconds to a few milliseconds. The really annoying thing about button bounce is that most of the time it doesn't happen. You can test your button 10 times and declare it working, only to have it bounce on the thirteenth press.

Figure 6-5 displays two oscilloscope traces from the pushbutton on my breadboard. Because the button is normally held high by the AVR's internal pull-up resistor, the first frame represents a button press while the second is a button release. I've cherry-picked two of the worst examples just for you.

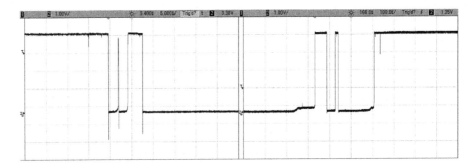

Figure 6-5. *Pushbutton bounce example*

So that's what's going on with our toggling code! When we release the button, for instance, it can momentarily go high and then low again before finally taking the correct high voltage value. If the AVR is checking the button state frequently enough, it can see this high-low transition that occurs during the release bounce and interpret it as a button press, even though no human could ever release and then repress a button that quickly.

The easiest solution is to have the AVR wait a few milliseconds and then check to see if the button is still pressed or not before making any decisions. Because the buttons bounce only for a "short" time, waiting for a little bit longer and then double-checking will ensure that we're not mistaking bounce for a true change.

The trick with debouncing-by-waiting is getting the timing right. The characteristic time that a switch bounces varies from switch to switch, but all that I've ever seen settle down within a couple milliseconds. We can therefore very conservatively wait around 5 ms and test the button again. Bearing in mind that human response time is on the order of tens of milliseconds, this won't result in a noticeable delay to the user, either. Of course, I recommend varying the wait time and trying it out in your particular setup.

 (More than) All You Ever Wanted to Know About Debouncing...

You can find a nice writeup of debouncing at **http://www.ganssle.com/debouncing.htm**, *and a compilation of software debouncing routines on* **http://hackaday.com/2010/11/09/ debounce-code-one-post-to-rule-them-all/**. *Both are good reads.*

Debounce Example

So let's add a debouncing routine to our `toggleLED` code. The result is shown in Example 6-3.

Example 6-3. **debouncer.c listing**

```
// ------- Preamble -------- //
#include <avr/io.h>
#include "pinDefines.h"

#include <util/delay.h>
#define DEBOUNCE_TIME  1000                          /* microseconds */

uint8_t debounce(void) {
  if (bit_is_clear(BUTTON_PIN, BUTTON)) {     /* button is pressed now */
    _delay_us(DEBOUNCE_TIME);
    if (bit_is_clear(BUTTON_PIN, BUTTON)) {          /* still pressed */
      return (1);
    }
  }
  return (0);
}

int main(void) {
  // -------- Inits --------- //
  uint8_t buttonWasPressed;                              /* state */
  BUTTON_PORT |= (1 << BUTTON);    /* enable the pullup on the button */
  LED_DDR = (1 << LED0);                 /* set up LED for output */

  // ------- Event loop ------ //
  while (1) {
    if (debounce()) {                     /* debounced button press */
      if (buttonWasPressed == 0) {   /* but wasn't last time through */
        LED_PORT ^= (1 << LED0);              /* do whatever */
        buttonWasPressed = 1;               /* update the state */
      }
```

```
  }
  else {                             /* button is not pressed now */
    buttonWasPressed = 0;                   /* update the state */
  }

}                                        /* End event loop */
  return (0);                    /* This line is never reached */
}
```

The *debouncer.c* code here is almost exactly the same as that in the bouncy *toggleButton.c* earlier. The debounce() function is new, I added a definition for the debounce delay, and I changed the line:

```
    if (bit_is_clear(BUTTON_PIN, BUTTON)){
```

to:

```
    if (debounce()){
```

but that's it. All of the rest of the logic of the code (in particular, keeping track of the button state) is just the same, so you don't have to rethink that through.

To Debounce, or Not to Debounce?

As much as I love debouncing routines (and I love them a lot!) there's a time and a place for everything.

To debounce

Fundamentally, you need to debounce whenever you're counting button press events. This goes equally for on/off toggling, scrolling through elements of a menu, or switching among modes.

You'll also want to debounce if you're timing an event. How long was the button pressed? Well, that will depend on when you define the button press as beginning. If you accidentally time one of the early spikes, you might erroneously conclude that the user pressed and released the button within microseconds, when it was just a bounce.

Not to debounce

If you don't care about counting button presses or events, there's no need to spend the code on debouncing. For instance, if you'd like a circuit to light up when you press a button, a simple logic test will suffice. If your LED blinks a couple times during the first few microseconds, but it's faster than a human's flicker-fusion rate, nobody will notice.

Similarly, if you've got a built-in delay, the bounce may not matter as much. If your code is doing a lot, and only makes it through the main event loop once in a few milliseconds, then you don't really have to worry about debouncing—the delay you would have written into your debounce code is already built in to your (slow) main event loop.

Hardware debouncing

There's also a third option, and this is the way buttons were debounced in the old days before microcontrollers reduced the issue to just a few extra lines of code. Putting a capacitor across the two contacts of a switch forces the voltage to rise slowly, and can ensure that it will not jump up and down along the way. In industry, almost everyone debounces in code, saving a few cents per capacitor.

The debounce() function handles debouncing in the simplest way possible—checking if the button is pressed twice with a delay in between. The function returns a one only if the button was pressed both times. If the button wasn't pressed for either of the two checks, debounce() returns a zero, and the if(debounce()) statement is false. This, for a long-enough value of the defined DEBOUNCE_TIME, guarantees debounce-free toggling.

Try it out and see. I've defined the debounce timeout in microseconds (millionths of a second), which will enable you to experiment. You can set the delay short enough that your button still bounces, and then you can adjust it so it doesn't. I encourage you to play around with it. For instance, my button still bounces sometimes at 200 microseconds, but doesn't seem to at 700 microseconds. Even 1,000 microseconds, or one millisecond, is very, very fast on human timescales. Your mileage will vary. Play around.

Just to reiterate, debouncing can be as simple as waiting a fixed time and retesting the button. It's a good thing to know about debouncing, and to understand that it's no big deal. If you didn't know, and you were trying to debug an infrequent glitch like switch bounce in your system, you'd be pulling your hair out.

AVR Music Box

Here is a simple musical application of everything that you've learned so far. We've all seen music boxes, right? The ones with the small crank on the outside that turns a drum that plucks little tines to play a song? When you turn the crank faster or slower, you can influence the tempo of the song, but the notes are "hardcoded" in to the pins on the turning drum.

You can easily do the same with the AVR: you already know how to play notes so all that's left is using the pushbutton to allow you to control the tempo. If you've got the speaker and blocking capacitor and the pushbutton set up, there's nothing more for you to do other than flash in this simple code.

The Code

This code is basically just a small tweak on the serial organ in Chapter 5. It calls the same playNote() that we used in the organ routine repeatedly, each time with a different note. The notes themselves are stored in an array called song[]. Each time you press the button (that is, the button state changes to pressed), a variable is incremented that points to the next note in the song. While the button is held down, the same note continues to play. This gives you total control over both the tempo and duration of each note.

Flash it in, play around, and see if you can figure out what the tune is! Once you do, feel free to extend the song[] array to play anything you want. The code for the example is found in Example 6-4.

Example 6-4. avrMusicBox.c listing

```
// Music Box Input Demo

// ------- Preamble -------- //
#include <avr/io.h>
#include <util/delay.h>
#include "organ.h"
#include "scale16.h"
#include "pinDefines.h"

#define SONG_LENGTH  (sizeof(song) / sizeof(uint16_t))

int main(void) {
  const uint16_t song[] = {
    E6, E6, E6, C6, E6, G6, G5,
    C6, G5, E5, A5, B5, Ax5, A5,
    G5, E6, G6, A6, F6, G6, E6, C6, D6, B5,
    C6, G5, E5, A5, B5, Ax5, A5,
    G5, E6, G6, A6, F6, G6, E6, C6, D6, B5,
                                                /* etc */
  };
  /* starting at end b/c routine starts by incrementing and then playing
     this makes the song start at the beginning after reboot */
  uint8_t whichNote = SONG_LENGTH - 1;
  uint8_t wasButtonPressed = 0;

  // -------- Inits --------- //
  SPEAKER_DDR |= (1 << SPEAKER);                /* speaker for output */
  BUTTON_PORT |= (1 << BUTTON);                  /* pullup on button */

  // ------ Event loop ------ //
  while (1) {
    if (bit_is_clear(BUTTON_PIN, BUTTON)) {
      if (!wasButtonPressed) {                 /* if it's a new press ... */
        whichNote++;                           /* advance to next note */
                                        /* but don't run over the end */
        if (whichNote == SONG_LENGTH) {
          whichNote = 0;
        }
        wasButtonPressed = 1;
      }
      playNote(song[whichNote], 1600);
    }
    else {
      wasButtonPressed = 0;
    }
  }                                             /* End event loop */
  return (0);
}
```

The bulk of the main() routine looks just like the toggleButton code, and that's no surprise. First, the button is tested for input. If it's pressed, but it wasn't pressed last time, we advance to the next note. If that takes us past the last note in the song, we loop back to the beginning. Outside of the first-press logic, the code updates the button-press state and plays our note. If the button is not pressed this time through the loop, wasButtonPressed is naturally set to zero.

If you're new to C, the way the code moves through the song[] array is worth looking at. The number of notes in the song is computed by the #define macro SONG_LENGTH. Why can't we just use the sizeof() command directly? Because the note values happen to all be 16-bit numbers, and sizeof() returns the number of bytes. So for a 10-note song, sizeof() will return 20. But because I know that I've got an array of uint16_t numbers, I can get the number of entries either by dividing by two or dividing by sizeof(uint16_t), which I think makes it clearer why we're doing the division in the first place.

Also notice that we test for running over the end of the song with:

```
if (whichNote == SONG_LENGTH) { ...
```

Remember that arrays start at zero in C. Because of this, if you've got a 10-element array, the first element is number 0 and the last is 9. On the one hand, this is hard to remember and is the cause of many off-by-one errors. On the other hand, it makes it super easy to test for whether you've gone too far with just a simple test of equality, as we do here.

Finally, the last strange bit about this code is that we start off with the note indexing variable whichNote set to SONG_LENGTH -1. What gives? If you followed the discussion about zero-indexing, you'll recognize that whichNote is set to the last valid note in the song. I ended up having to do this because of the button-press logic, which updates the song position first, then plays the note afterward. (I suppose I could have changed the logic to update the note when the button is released, but I wanted it to be a mirror of the toggleButton code.) Anyway, because I wanted the song to start with the first note on reboot, but it advances a note with every press, the solution is to start on the last note so that when you press the button the first time it will wrap around back to the beginning.

And that's it. The simple button-pressing routine we developed here turns into a music box with very little extra effort. I hope you enjoy the quick demo. Now what can you do with a pushbutton and some quick programming logic?

Boss Button

While we're on the topic of pushbuttons and the AVR, I can't resist but throw in a project that uses the AVR as a frontend for code that runs on your desktop. Why? Because I think it's awesome to have a pushbutton that opens a web page. So let's make a quick-and-dirty Boss Button.

Pushbutton Checklist

1. Set DDR for input. It's the default pin state, but if you're not sure, it doesn't hurt to set it explicitly with something like DDRD &= ~(1 << PD2).

2. Set the internal pull-up if you don't have a physical pull-up resistor in the circuit: PORTD |= (1 << PD2).

3. Read the button voltage in your code. If you'd like to test that the button is pressed, you can do so two ways: with something like if(! (PIND & (1 << PD2))) or using the macro

bit_is_clear(PIND, PD2), which I find more readable, and less error-prone.

4. Think about whether you want something to happen while the button is pressed, or when it becomes pressed. Store the previous state and test for changes if you're interested in the latter.

5. If you're trying to detect a single button-press event, consider debouncing. The simplest way to debounce is to simply wait a few milliseconds and test if the button is still pressed.

What's a Boss Button? You know, when you're surfing the Web, or generally goofing off and your boss comes by? You're going to need to hide the evidence on your computer screen quickly. But how are you going to do this without mousing all around and generally looking klutzy and suspicious? The answer is the Boss Button. One click on your trusty (and totally work-related) AVR microcontroller project that just happens to be sitting on your desk, and your browser is loaded with all sorts of businessy looking stuff.

OK, so that's the pitch. But once you're done with this project, you can simply add a few more buttons and modify the desktop code to launch whatever web pages you'd like with each press. You'll have your own dedicated physical favorite-website-launcher machine.

To open the browser window to a website, we'll need to do some scripting on the computer side. And for that, we'll use Python. So if you don't have Python and pyserial installed on your computer yet, now's the time. After you've got that set up and understood, the rest is child's play.

If you're more focused on simply learning the AVR chip than playing around with desktop computer programming, at least take the few minutes to install Python and the serial module (see "Installing Python and the Serial Library" on page 123) because we'll be using them throughout the rest of the book. But don't fret—you won't have to learn Python on top of C unless you'd like to.

Desktop-side Scripting

I do most of my computer-side scripting in Python, mostly because it's very easy to extend your work from one domain to another. Most of the stuff that's almost impossible to implement on a microcontroller is trivial in Python (and vice versa).

For instance, if you'd like to write a website hit counter that moves a physical arm, it couldn't be easier—fetching and parsing a web page is easy with Python. Now all that remains is turning the data into a byte or two, and taking care of the physical interfacing with the AVR, which is where it excels.

Installing Python and the Serial Library

First off, if you don't have Python installed already, let's do that. And even if you do, we'll need to make sure you've got the `serial` library (confusingly contained in a package called `pyserial`) installed.

On Linux and Mac OS X
On any modern distribution, you'll very likely have Python installed, which means that you can simply open up a terminal window and type **`easy_install pyserial`** to get the serial port libraries. If your system can't find `easy_install` and you're on a Debian system, try **`sudo apt-get install python-setuptools`**. If all that fails, a web search for how to install `setuptools` on your system should set you straight.

On Windows
The easiest way to go is with ActiveState's Python distribution. Click on downloads and save the Python 2.7 installer for your system. If in doubt, get the 32-bit version. Run the installer and install in the default directories (Python27). Now you'll need to get `pyserial` (the serial port library). Run `cmd.exe` to get a terminal window and type in **`pypm install pyserial`** and you should be all set.

To verify that all's well, open IDLE, the included GUI editor and shell, and type **`import serial`**. If there's no error, you're all set.

And if you're new to Python development, The Python Tutorial (*http://docs.python.org/2/tutorial/*) is the traditional place to start. But because we've got some demo code coming right up, I'd start there for now.

In this project, we'll be working through two fairly straightforward bits of code. The first is in Python (but you don't have to worry too much about the details unless you'd like to), and the other is AVR C. Let's start off with the Python file listed in Example 6-5.

Example 6-5. bossButton.py listing
```
## Simple demo
## Sits forever listening to serial port
## When you press button, opens website of your choosing.
## Extend this to many buttons and you'll have a physical
##   web-launcher.

BOSS_SITE = "http://www.cartalk.com/content/boss-redirect"
## or perhaps more topical...
XKCD = "http://xkcd.com/353/"

SERIAL_PORT = "/dev/ttyUSB0"
BAUD_RATE = 9600

import serial
```

```python
import webbrowser

sp = serial.Serial(SERIAL_PORT, BAUD_RATE, timeout = 5)
sp.flush()

while(1):                         # Sit and wait forever
    response = sp.read(1)         # get one byte
    if response == "O":
        print "Got OK Byte.  Waiting for button press."
    elif response == "X":
        print "Got Boss Byte!  Alarm!"
        webbrowser.open(BOSS_SITE)
    else:
        print "Got nothing.  Still waiting."
```

The first few lines are simple defines. If you'd like your button to open up a different web page, this is where you modify things. If you're not using Linux, you'll definitely need to change the SERIAL_PORT line to point to your USB-Serial port. In Windows, it's going to be something like COM4 or similar. Leave the baud rate as is for now.

One thing that's marvelous about Python for this type of quick, yet awesome, hack is that most everything is built-in. (Yes, yes, we had to install the serial library, and that was kind of a pain. But from here on, it's smooth sailing.) For instance, opening a page in a browser requires you to import the webbrowser library and then call webbrowser.open(), and then you're done. So all you need to do is wait until you get the signal from your microcontroller over the serial port.

And using the serial port in Python is almost just as easy. First, import the serial library. Then, create a serial port object with the location of your USB-Serial adapter, the baud rate, and an optional timeout. When you later ask for a byte over the serial line, this timeout value tells you how long, in seconds, your program will wait until it gives up and returns nothing. I set it to a relatively low five seconds, but you can set it to whatever you'd like. Longer values will just mean fewer messages indicating that the program is still waiting.

The sp.flush() command clears out the serial input and output buffers. Your big computer collects all of the values that it's seen in a serial buffer and waits for some program to read from it. You don't want the serial buffer clogged up with other data before you start your program, so you flush it. This step may or may not be necessary on your system, but it won't hurt.

Then you enter an infinite loop, where you continually read a byte from the serial port and then print messages or open a browser window, depending on the value received from the AVR. You can see how to generalize this to multiple buttons here —for each button, simply send out a different character over the serial line and assign it a different action. Simplicity itself.

Try resetting your AVR by either unplugging its power or temporarily grounding the RESET line, and verify that your Python-side program says that it's received the OK byte. Now press the Boss Button and smile with glee as it opens up a browser. The power!!!

What's fun about the AVR code in *bossButton.c* is that it's even more trimmed-down than our "simple" loopback routine. Aside from the usual configurations and including the USART files, Example 6-6 lists the AVR-side code.

*Example 6-6. **bossButton.c** listing*

```
/*
bossButton.c

As long as we've got a button wired up to the AVR,
might as well have some fun.

Upload this code to your AVR, run bossButton.py.
Press button.

*/

// ------- Preamble -------- //
#include <avr/io.h>
#include <util/delay.h>
#include "pinDefines.h"
#include "USART.h"

static inline void blinkLED(void) {
  LED_PORT = (1 << LED0);
  _delay_ms(1000);
  LED_PORT &= ~(1 << LED0);
}


int main(void) {

  // -------- Inits --------- //
  BUTTON_PORT |= (1 << BUTTON);          /* input mode, turn on pullup */

  LED_DDR = (1 << LED0);
  blinkLED();

  initUSART();
  transmitByte('O');

  // ------ Event loop ------ //
  while (1) {

    if (bit_is_clear(BUTTON_PIN, BUTTON)) {
      transmitByte('X');
      blinkLED();
```

```
    }

  }                                       /* End event loop */
  return (0);
}
```

Yup. All the AVR does is sit in the event loop, looking for the button press. When it sees a button press, it sends your secret code character "X" and blinks an LED. The Python code on your big computer takes care of the rest. You don't have to worry about debouncing and sending multiple "X"s per button press either, because you're delaying for one second per button press, so the AVR is basically unburdened.

Extensions

Although the Boss Button application is probably a little bit trivial, it demonstrates some of the real power of connecting your AVR to your computer. If you can serve web pages, you can have them display real-time status from anything you can hook your AVR up to. Any of the further projects we undertake in this book can be trivially webified. Need a remote light sensor? Send the data out from our project in Chapter 7 to a web server. Or tweet it. Or whatever. Your imagination is the limit.

If you'd like to get even fancier, and have the AVR take some of the load, see the example in the pyserial Python module documentation of a serial-to-TCP/IP bridge. Now you can connect to your AVR remotely by accessing the relevant network port. Using this, you can serve web pages directly from your AVR. (That's overkill in my opinion—it's better to send the data to your desktop, and have the desktop generate the web page. But you may have your reasons.)

Analog-to-Digital Conversion I | 7

Light Sensors and Slowscope

If there's one thing I like about microcontrollers, it's connecting the real world with the code world. And a lot of the real world is *analog*: voltages, currents, light levels, forces, etc., all take on continuously variable values. Deep inside the AVR, on the other hand, everything is binary: on or off. Going from the analog world to the digital is the job of the *analog-to-digital converter* (ADC) hardware. Using the built-in ADC, we'll see how to use the AVR to take (voltage) readings from analog sensors and turn them into numbers that we can use inside our code.

Imagine that you're building a robot or an interactive art piece. You might be interested in measuring temperature, distance to the nearest object, force and acceleration, sound pressure level, brightness, magnetic force, or other physical characteristics. The first step is to convert all of these physical quantities into a voltage using a specifically designed sensor of some sort. Then, you might have to modify this voltage input so that it's in a range that's usable by the AVR. Finally, the voltage is connected up to an AVR pin, and the internal ADC hardware converts the continuous voltage value into a number that you can use in your code like any other.

In this chapter, we'll use the ADC and a serial connection to make a slow "oscilloscope." We'll interface with a light sensor, making a simple LED-display light meter. Finally, we'll add in a potentiometer to create an adjustable-threshold night-light that turns a bunch of LEDs on when it gets dark enough. How dark? You get to decide by turning a knob!

Analog sensors and electronics are by themselves huge topics, so I won't be able to cover everything, but I'll try to point out further interesting opportunities in passing. In this chapter, I'll focus on simply using the AVR's ADC hardware—taking continuous readings through clever use of interrupt service routines, and using the multiplexer so that you can read analog voltages from more than one source.

Topics like input voltage scaling and oversampling and noise smoothing will have to wait for Chapter 12.

Sensors

With the exception of a battery-charge monitor or something similar, you're almost never interested in measuring a voltage directly. But because measuring voltages is so darn easy, you'll find that many, many analog sensors convert whichever physical quantities they're designed to measure (light, noise, or temperature) into a voltage. And once you've got a properly scaled voltage, you're all set to read the value in through the ADC.

Designing sensors to put out carefully calibrated voltages in response to the physical world is both a science and an art in itself. When you don't need absolute accuracy, though, there are a lot of interesting physical effects that end up in a voltage signal. For you as the microcontroller designer, browsing around through the world of different sensing possibilities can be inspirational.

One good source of cheap-and-easy ideas for sensors is Forrest Mims' *Electronic Sensor Circuits & Projects* from the "Engineer's Mini Notebook" series (Master Publishing, Inc., 2004).

ADC Hardware Overview

The onboard ADC peripheral is an incredibly complex system. Have a look at the block diagram in the datasheet to see for yourself. You might be tempted to just treat it all as a black-box, and I'm sure a lot of people do. But a quick look behind the curtain will help make sense of all the configuration options and the few tricky bits that it pays to be aware of. Figure 7-1 lays out all the major components of the ADC peripheral.

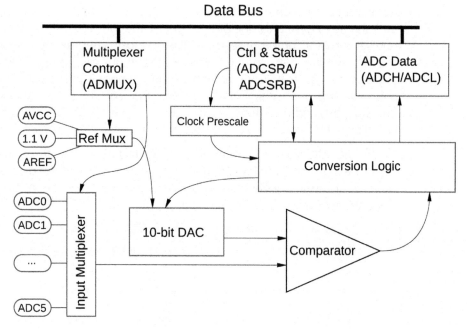

Figure 7-1. *ADC hardware*

At the heart of the ADC is actually a DAC—a digital-to-analog converter—and a comparator. The DAC generates a voltage that corresponds to a digital value that it takes as input. The comparator is a digital device that outputs a binary high or low value if the input signal coming from one of the ADC pins is higher or lower than the output of the DAC. Like playing a game of "20 Questions," the conversion logic sets a voltage level on the DAC and then reads the value off the comparator to figure out if the input voltage is higher or lower than this DAC voltage. The ADC repeats this until it has located the input voltage between two of the 10-bit voltage levels that it can produce with the DAC.

The ADC has a number of options for the reference voltage it applies to the internal DAC, which enable you to tailor the voltage range over which the 10 bits are spread so that you get maximum resolution in end use. The ADC also has a number of triggering options. You can start an ADC conversion from your code, or any of the internal timer compare or overflow conditions, the external INT0 pin, or even the ADC itself—resulting in the so-called free-running mode where it's continually sampling.

The ADC module can't run at the full CPU clock speed, though, so it needs its own clock source. The good news is that it's equipped with a clock prescaler (like the timers are) that can subdivide the CPU clock down to a usable speed. The bad news is that because you can change the CPU clock speed, it's also your responsibility to figure out an appropriate prescaler for the ADC clock.

Because of all this complexity, the ADC module is a large chunk of silicon. It would be a shame to have only one ADC on board, though, and only be able to sample one sensor. As a compromise, the AVR (and most other microprocessors) shares the ADC module out over a number of pins. In our case, pins PC0 to PC5 are all available for use as ADC inputs (plus a couple more if you're using the surface-mount version of the chips), with the catch that you can only take readings from one at a time, and you must switch between them. A multiway switch like this is called a *multiplexer*, or "mux" for short.

Finally, the ADC has to communicate with the rest of the chip through a bunch of hardware registers, both for configuration and for returning the digitized voltage value. So in summary, the ADC hardware is a beast. Heck, the ADC even draws power from its own separate power supply pin, AVCC!

How the ADC Works: Successive Approximation

The AVR is a fundamentally digital chip, so how can it figure out the analog voltage on the input pin? Well, it can't figure it out exactly, but it can figure out a range in which the analog value lies by asking a bunch of clever yes/no questions. The method the AVR's ADC uses is called *successive approximation*.

Successive approximation works by taking a reference voltage (on the AREF pin) and dividing it in half using an internal 10-bit digital-to-analog converter. Then the input voltage is compared with this DAC voltage. If the input is higher, the ADC writes down a 1 and then sets the internal DAC at half the difference between AREF and AREF/2. If the input is lower, the ADC writes down a 0 and sets the DAC halfway between GND and AREF/2.

The ADC repeats these tests 10 times for a 10-bit result, changing the DAC level each time to cut the possible voltage range in half. If the most significant bit is a 1, then you know that input voltage is greater than AREF/2. If the most significant bits are (1,0), then you know that the voltage is greater than 1/2 AREF, but less than 3/4 AREF, etc. For each bit, the possible voltage range that the input can be in is cut in half, so that by the end of 10 bits, the ADC knows which of 1,024 bins the voltage is in, and the resulting 10-bit binary number points exactly at it.

As the AVR goes through this process of successive approximation, it needs to have a constant version of the input voltage. To do this, there's a *sample and hold* circuit just on the frontend of the ADC that connects a capacitor to your voltage source and lets it charge up to the input voltage level. Then it disconnects the capacitor and the (now nearly constant) voltage on the capacitor is used in the successive approximation procedure. So even if the external voltage is changing rapidly, the ADC will have a snapshot of that voltage taken at the time that sampling started.

What does this mean for you, as chip-user and programmer? Using the ADC is going to boil down to first configuring an ADC clock speed (more on this later), and then instructing the ADC to start taking a sample by setting the "start conversion" bit in an ADC register. When the ADC is done, it writes this same bit back to zero. Between starting the ADC conversion and its finish, your code can either sit around and test for this flag, or set up an interrupt service routine to trigger when the ADC is done. Because the ADC is reasonably fast, I'll often just use the (simpler) blocking-wait method. On the other hand, when you're trying to squeeze out maximum speed from the CPU and ADC, the ISR method is the way to go. You'll see examples of both here.

We'll start with a minimum configuration and work our way up example by example to something more complex. To make full use of the ADC you can or must set:

- The ADC clock prescaler (default: disabled, which means no conversions)
- The voltage reference that defines the full scale (default: an externally supplied voltage)
- The analog channel to sample from (default: external pin PC0)
- An ADC trigger source (default: free-running if specified)
- Interrupts to call when an ADC conversion is complete (default: none)
- Other miscellaneous options including an 8-bit mode, turning off the digital input circuitry to save power, and more

Light Meter

Creating a simple light meter is a classic first ADC project. The sensor is cheap and simple to make, and there are a many different directions to extend the basic program just in software. Here, we'll use the LEDs to display the amount of light hitting the sensor. If you calibrated this sensor, you could use it as an exposure meter for a camera. If you shine a light on the circuit from across the room with a laser bounced off a bunch of mirrors, you could make a beam-break detector suitable for securing your diamonds.

The Circuit

The sensor portion of this project is basically a *voltage divider*. A voltage divider is really just two resistors (or similar) in series between one voltage level and ground. Because the bottom end of the lower resistor is at ground, and the top end of the upper resistor at, say VCC, the middle point where they join together must be at some voltage in the middle. If the two resistances are equal, the voltage in the middle will be 1/2 VCC. If the top resistance is less than the bottom, the output voltage will be higher than 1/2, and vice versa.

To make our light sensor, we're using an LDR for the top resistor and hooking up the middle-point output voltage to our ADC. So when the LDR is less resistive, we'll read more voltage. The LDR gets less resistive when more light shines on it, so we'll see a direct relationship between the light level and the voltage sent to the AVR— a simple light meter!

Cadmium-Sulfide Light Sensor

One of my favorite electronic components is the cadmium-sulfide, light-dependent resistor (LDR), also known simply as "photocells" or "photoresistors." They're cheap, relatively sturdy, and do just exactly what they are supposed to—provide a resistance that decreases as more and more light falls on them. Coupled with a fixed-value resistor, you get a voltage divider whose output depends on its illumination: a light-to-voltage converter.

LDRs are used everywhere: old-school camera light meters, streetlamp on/off circuits, automatic headlight sensors, beam-break detectors, and even sensors in telescopes. On the other hand, LDRs can be a little touchy to work with unless you know a few things:

- *LDRs vary a lot from one to the next in terms of their maximum resistance in the dark, so don't expect any two to have exactly the same resistance in the same conditions. If you've got an ohmmeter, measure a few in the dark to see what I mean.*
- *Lesser-known fact: LDRs also exhibit a temperature-dependent resistance.*
- *You can burn an LDR out if you run too much current through it. And because the resistance drops as the light hitting it gets brighter, the fixed resistor can't be too small: keep it above 200 ohms at 5 V.*
- *If your sensor saturates in bright light, try decreasing the fixed resistor in the voltage divider. If you need more dark sensitivity, increase the fixed resistor.*
- *LDRs are slow relative to microcontrollers, but faster than the human eye: they take between tens and hundreds of milliseconds to react to changes in light. My example LDR circuit is fast enough to detect the flicker in incandescent light bulbs that results from alternating current.*
- *LDRs are most sensitive to light in the red-green wavelength range, so they pair up beautifully with red LEDs or lasers. Some even see into the infrared. They're a little weaker in the blue-purple range. Their response curve is actually a lot like the human eye's.*

So connect one end of the LDR to VCC and the other to the fixed resistor to ground, as shown in Figure 7-2. The joint between the LDR and fixed resistor is our voltage output—connect this to pin PC0 on the AVR.

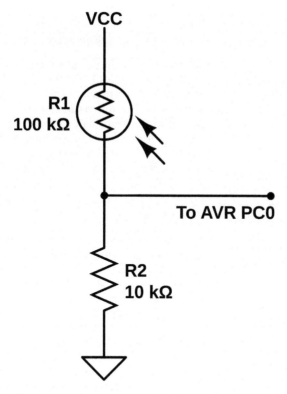

Figure 7-2. *LDR voltage divider*

A good rule of thumb for getting the maximum variability out of your LDR-based voltage divider is to use a fixed resistor that's approximately the square root of the LDR's resistance at the brightest light level, multiplied by the resistance at the lowest light level:

$$R = \sqrt{LDR_{bright} \times LDR_{dark}}$$

For instance, if the LDR measures 16k ohm in the light and 100k ohm when it's dark, you'll want roughly a 40k ohm resistor. For a sample of LDRs on my bench and indoor lighting conditions, the ideal resistor ended up in the 10k ohm to 100k ohm range, so measure and experiment in this range. (The value is also going to depend on how brightly lit your room is.) If you've got a 100k ohm potentiometer lying around, you can use that in place of the fixed resistor and you'll have control over the sensitivity.

Voltage Dividers

You'll start seeing voltage dividers everywhere once you know what to look for. Almost any time you have two passive components hooked together in series between two different voltage levels, and you're reading out the value from the middle—you've got a voltage divider.

The basic voltage divider is just two resistors hooked end-to-end between the VCC and GND rails. We're interested in the voltage in-between the two resistors, and this voltage is determined by the values of the two resistors. If both have the same resistance, the voltage taken from the midpoint is half of the input voltage. In general, you can get any voltage you'd like between GND and V_{in} by using the formula $V_{out} = V_{in} \times R_2 / (R_1 + R_2)$.

By analogy to water pressure in a piping system, where water pressure is like voltage, higher resistance corresponds to skinnier tubes. Smaller diameter piping restricts the flow of water, like higher resistance impedes the flow of electrons. If you pinch on a hose (increase the resistance), you'll see more pressure upstream of the pinch and less downstream. In the same way, if you use a large resistor for R_2, more of the original V_{in} voltage (pressure) is present at the midpoint. If you decrease the resistance in R_2, the current flows through it relatively unimpeded, and the voltage/pressure at the junction is much lower.

To remember whether it's R_1 or R_2 in the numerator, think about which resistor the voltage is measured across. One end of the pair of resistors is at 5 V, and the other end is at GND, 0 V. The total 5 V voltage difference from top to bottom must be split up between the two resistors. Because it takes more voltage to push a given current through a larger resistance, more of the voltage is dropped across the larger of the two resistors. If more voltage is dropped before we sample it, our V_{out} will be lower than half. If the larger resistor is on the bottom, most of the voltage drop occurs after we measure the voltage, so V_{out} will be greater than half.

Besides resistor-resistor voltage dividers, the resistor-capacitor lowpass filter we will use in Chapter 10 is another example of a voltage divider. Look at it again. We're taking our output signal from between a resistor and capacitor that are connected in series to GND. Capacitors have a resistance to passing current that's similar to resistors, except that it's frequency-dependent. Capacitors block direct current (DC) entirely, but let higher and higher frequency alternating current (AC) through with less and less resistance. (This resistance to AC is called *reactance*, but you can think of reactance as a frequency-dependent resistance.) So if you look at the filter this way, you'll see that the capacitor at the bottom of the circuit is more and more resistive as the frequency lowers, passing through more of the voltage at lower frequencies, and making a low-pass filter.

This circuit's great on a breadboard, because it's just two parts and a wire, or you can "sensorize" it by soldering the LDR and fixed resistor together and adding some wires. You can also increase the directionality of your sensor by wrapping the LDR in a bit of black electrical tape to make a snoot so that it is only sensitive to light falling on it from one direction. If you're making a beam-break detector, this'll also help protect the sensor from ambient light in the room, and make it more reliable. Figure 7-3 demonstrates the basic ideas.

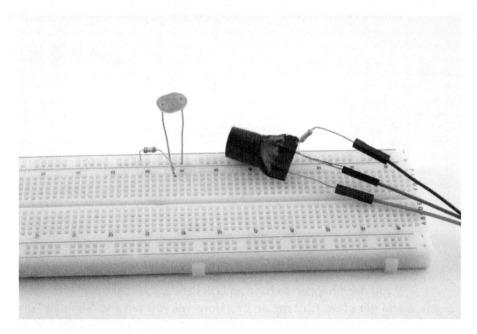

Figure 7-3. *LDR sensors*

ADC power pins

Aside from the sensor, there's one tweak we'll have to the AVR setup—powering up the ADC. There are two "special" pins connected to the ADC that are important for powering the hardware and for stabilizing the reference voltage. Good analog circuit design practice dictates that we use a separate source of 5 V for the chip (which has all sorts of quick switching and power spikes) and for the ADC, which needs a stable value to be accurate.

Ideally, you'd run a second wire directly from your 5 V source to the AVCC pin, rather than sharing the line that supplies the AVR with power. You should probably use this second, analog-only, 5 V rail to provide power to the light sensor as well. If you're measuring very small voltage differences or high-frequency signals, this all becomes much more important, and you may need to use even more tricks to stabilize the AVCC.

Here, we're not looking for millivolt accuracy, and we're only sampling a few times per second. Feel free to get power to AVCC and the sensor however you'd like—just make sure you get 5 V to AVCC somehow. Without power, the ADC won't run. I've made this mistake a bunch of times, and end up scratching my head about what's wrong in my ADC init code for far longer than is productive.

If you've hooked up the AVCC and the LDR with a resistor, you should have something that looks like Figure 7-4. Of course, you'll still have the programmer connections as well. You should also have the eight LEDs still hooked up to the B pins.

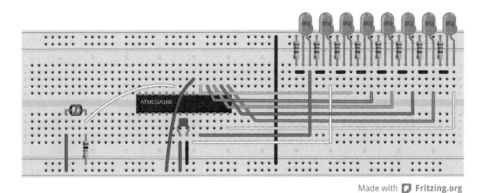

Made with ⬛ Fritzing.org

Figure 7-4. *LDR voltage divider on the breadboard*

LDR alternative: potentiometer

If you don't happen to have an LDR handy, you really owe it to yourself to go out and get a few. Trust me on this. However, you can also "simulate" one so that you can experiment with the code and the setup here. The LDR and it's resistor are simply making a variable voltage divider, so anything else along those lines will work as well. The obvious candidate is a potentiometer (pot). Any value of pot will do, as long as it's greater than 1k ohm resistance.

Potentiometers are three-terminal devices. Essentially there's a resistive track connecting the two outermost pins—that's the rated (maximum) resistance. The middle pin is connected to a *wiper* that scans across the surface of the resistor as you turn the knob. The result is that when you turn the potentiometer knob one way, the resistance between the wiper and one outside pin increases while the resistance between the wiper and the other decreases.

Imagine that you've got a 10k ohm linear potentiometer with the knob turned exactly to the middle. The resistance from the wiper to either side will read 5k ohms, and if you put a voltage across the two outside pins, you'd find exactly half of that voltage on the wiper. Turn the knob one way, and the 10k ohms is split up, perhaps, 7k and 3k. If you apply 5 V across the outside pins, and the 3k resistance is on the GND side, the voltage at the wiper will be $5 V \times 3 / (3 + 7) = 1.5 V$.

To make a long story short, a potentiometer tied to the voltage rails makes a nice adjustable voltage for experimenting around with ADCs, and also a tremendously useful input device if you need a user to select from more than a couple of choices —just mark them out on a dial and read the ADC values in. Even if you do have an LDR lying around to play with, it's probably worth your while to experiment some with potentiometers. An example circuit is shown in Figure 7-5.

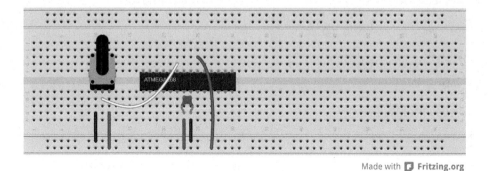

Made with ⚡ Fritzing.org

Figure 7-5. *Potentiometer voltage divider on the breadboard*

The Code

Because this is our first project with the ADC, we'll necessarily have to talk a little bit of hardware initialization. First, let's work through the event loop, as listed in Example 7-1, and then we'll come back and clean up the details.

Example 7-1. **lightSensor.c** *Listing*

```c
// Quick Demo of light sensor

// ------- Preamble -------- //
#include <avr/io.h>
#include <util/delay.h>
#include "pinDefines.h"

// -------- Functions --------- //
static inline void initADC0(void) {
  ADMUX |= (1 << REFS0);                      /* reference voltage on AVCC */
  ADCSRA |= (1 << ADPS1) | (1 << ADPS0);     /* ADC clock prescaler /8 */
  ADCSRA |= (1 << ADEN);                       /* enable ADC */
}

int main(void) {

  // -------- Inits --------- //
  uint8_t ledValue;
  uint16_t adcValue;
  uint8_t i;
```

```
initADC0();
LED_DDR = 0xff;

// ------ Event loop ------ //
while (1) {

    ADCSRA |= (1 << ADSC);                      /* start ADC conversion */
    loop_until_bit_is_clear(ADCSRA, ADSC);          /* wait until done */
    adcValue = ADC;                                     /* read ADC in */
                    /* Have 10 bits, want 3 (eight LEDs after all) */
    ledValue = (adcValue >> 7);
                                /* Light up all LEDs up to ledValue */
    LED_PORT = 0;
    for (i = 0; i <= ledValue; i++) {
      LED_PORT |= (1 << i);
    }
    _delay_ms(50);
}                                                   /* End event loop */
    return (0);                        /* This line is never reached */
}
```

The event loop starts off by directly triggering the start of a read from the ADC. Here, we first set the "ADC start conversion" (ADSC) bit in the "ADC Status Register A" to tell the ADC to sample voltage and convert it into binary for us. Because an ADC conversion doesn't take place instantaneously, we'll need to wait around for the result to become ready to use. In this example, I'm using a blocking-wait for the ADC; the loop_until_bit_is_clear() just spins the CPU's wheels until the ADC signals that it's done by resetting the ADSC bit.

If you're reading up on the ADC in the datasheet, this mode of triggering is called "single-conversion mode" because our code initiates the conversion, and when it's done, the ADC waits for further instructions. This is in contrast to "free-running mode," in which the ADC retriggers itself as soon as it's completed a conversion, or other triggering modes where you can assign the INT0 pin or even timer events to start an ADC conversion.

After a conversion is complete, the virtual register ADC contains a number from zero to 1,023 that represents the voltage (scaled by AREF) on the selected pin. I say "virtual" because the 10-bit ADC result is too large to fit in a normal 8-bit register, so it's spread out over two registers: ADCL contains the least significant eight bits and ADCH contains the most significant two bits, and is padded with zeros. The compiler, GCC, lets us access these two registers as if they were a single 16-bit number.

Finally, as eye-candy, the code displays the voltage/light level on our eight LEDs. Here's a trick I end up using a lot when displaying data on a small number of LEDs. We have eight LEDs, or three-bits worth of them. We can use yet another bit shift to reduce our current eight-bit value down to three. (Or you can think if it as dividing a number between 0 and 255 by 32 so that it's always between zero and eight.) Then to create a bargraph-like display, the code lights up each i'th LED in a for loop up to the one that represents the scaled ADC value.

Besides the visualization on the LEDs, you can display the values on your computer. The Python routine *serialScope.py* provides rather nice feedback when debugging something like this, and it's fun to watch the graph change as you wave your hand over the light sensor. When you're done playing around with that, let's look into the initialization.

ADC Initialization

Now let's look in-depth at the ADC initialization in the initADC0() function. There are three principle registers that configure the ADC: ADMUX controls the multiplexer and voltage source; ADCSRA (status register A) controls the prescaler, enables the ADC, and starts conversions; and ADCSRB controls the triggering. And because we'll be running in the so-called single conversion mode, we don't need to worry about trigger sources. So have a look at the datasheet for the ADMUX and ADCSRA registers and follow along.

First, we set up the voltage reference for the chip. Because we're using a light sensor that's set up to output voltage in the same 0–5 V range as the chip is operating, we'll set the reference voltage to AVCC. Because the AVR is internally connecting the AREF and AVCC pins together, we can add a decoupling capacitor between AREF and ground to further stabilize the analog reference voltage. It's not necessary here, but it's quick and easy if you'd like.

Next, we set up the ADC clock prescaler. Because we're running the chip at 1 MHz off of the internal oscillator, and the ADC wants to run between 50 kHz and 200 kHz, we'll pick a prescaler of 1/8, resulting in a 125 kHz sampling frequency. If you're feeling brave, you can change this to 250 kHz, but the results aren't guaranteed to work.

Providing the ADC with its own prescaled clock source is a pain if you're running the AVR's CPU clock at other frequencies, but at the end of the day, it's just math. The ADC prescaler gives you the choice of dividing the CPU clock by 2, 4, 8, 16, 32, 64, or 128. Your goal is to pick one of these divisors that sets the ADC clock between 50 kHz and 200 kHz. Rather than go through this calculation every time, Table 7-1 provides a cheat sheet.

Table 7-1. ADC prescaler options

CPU clock	Prescale	ADC frequency	ADCSRA bits set
1 MHz	4	250 kHz	ADPS1
	8	125 kHz	ADPS1 and ADPS0
	16	62.5 kHz	ADPS2
	32	31.25 kHz	ADPS2 and ADPS0
8 MHz	16	250 kHz	ADPS2
	32	125 kHz	ADPS2 and ADPS0
	64	62.5 kHz	ADPS2 and ADPS1
	128	31.25 kHz	ADPS2 and ADPS1 and ADPS0
12 MHz	64	187.5 kHz	ADPS2 and ADPS1
	128	93.75 kHz	ADPS2 and ADPS1 and ADPS0
16 MHz	64	250 kHz	ADPS2 and ADPS1
	128	125 kHz	ADPS2 and ADPS1 and ADPS0

Note that I've included a couple of ADC clock frequencies that are just outside of the official 50–200 kHz range. Although I can't figure why you'd want to run the ADC clock any slower than you have to, they seem to work. Maybe you save a little power?

On the fast end of things, the datasheet notes that running the ADC clock at speeds higher than 200 kHz is possible, with reduced resolution. I've included the clock settings for 250 kHz because I've found that it's worked for me. You're on your own here: Atmel only guarantees the ADC to run at 10-bits resolution up to 200 kHz, but I've never had trouble or noticed the lack of accuracy at 250 kHz.

Wrapping up the ADC initialization section, we'll enable the ADC circuitry. This final step, enabling the ADC, is one of those small gotchas—do not forget to enable the ADC by setting the ADEN bit when you're using the ADC!

So to recap the initialization: we've set the voltage reference. We've set the ADC clock prescaler. And finally, we've enabled the ADC. This is the simplest initialization routine that will work. What's missing? We didn't configure the multiplexer—but the default state is to sample from pin PC0, so we don't need to. And we didn't set up any triggering modes because we're going to trigger the ADC conversions ourselves from code. So we're set.

ADC Gotchas

So you're not getting output from the ADC or it's not changing? Here's a quick troubleshooting checklist:

1. *Did you hook up AVCC? The ADC needs power, and it needs to be within 0.3 V of the AVR's VCC.*
2. *Did you set a voltage reference with the REFSx bits in ADMUX? By default the AVR is looking for an external voltage reference on the AREF pin. If you'd like to use the AVCC as AREF, you have to set REFS0 in ADMUX.*
3. *Did you set the ADC prescaler? The ADC needs a clock source.*
4. *Did you set the ADEN bit to enable the ADC?*
5. *Do you have the correct channel selected in the multiplexer? Remember that they're referenced by binary value rather than bit value.*
6. *Finally, if you're reading the ADC values out independently, make sure that you read the low byte, ADCL, before you read the high byte, ADCH. For whatever reason, the ADCH bytes aren't updated until ADCL is read in 10-bit mode. (I just avoid this snafu by reading ADC, and letting the compiler take care of the ordering for me.)*

And if none of this is working, are you sure that your sensor is working? Try outputting the ADC data over the serial port and connecting the ADC pin to AREF and GND, respectively, to make sure that the problem lies in your code and not in a broken sensor. Or if you can, hook the sensor up to a voltmeter or oscilloscope. Is it behaving as you expect?

Extensions

OK, so now you've got a simple light meter. What can you *do* with it? First off, you could make a beam-break sensor. Aim a laser pointer or light of any kind at the light sensor and then walk through it. In your code, you can test if the value is greater or less than some threshold, and then light up LEDs or sound an alarm or something. Since you're sending the data across to your computer, you could even tweet when someone breaks the beam.

Or you can send data (slowly!) from one AVR to another using light. Just remember that the LDR has about a 10–20 ms reaction time, which means bitrates like 50–100 baud. (You can get a lot faster with a photodiode, but that's a different electrical setup.)

Or combine the AVR with some additional memory, and you can make a light-level logger. Put it out in your garden and record how many hours of what intensity sunlight your plants receive. Measure their growth along with it, and you've got the makings of some real plant science.

Vactrols

A fantastic application for LDRs (totally unrelated to the one in this chapter, but I can't resist) is providing microcontroller-controlled resistance for all sorts of circuits. Imagine that you had a circuit that relies on turning a potentiometer to create a variable resistance. (A perfect example is a guitar effect pedal, the kind that makes an electric guitar go waka-waka-wow-wow.) Wouldn't it be nice if you could have your microcontroller turn the knob for you?

The trick is to tape an LDR face-to-face with an LED using black electrical tape so that the only light hitting the LDR comes from the LED. Now you've effectively got an LED-controlled resistor. The idea here is old—going back to the early 1900s—but a popular implementation of the circuit was trademarked in the 1960s as the "Vactrol" and the name stuck. In the analog-circuits days, Vactrols were used to turn varying currents into varying resistances, by brightening or dimming a light and thus lowering or raising the resistance of the LDR.

Now let's digitize the Vactrol. In Chapter 10 you will see how you could pulse an LED quickly, using the duty cycle to make it appear to dim and brighten in a nearly continuous fashion. Taking advantage of the LDR's relatively slow response time, you can PWM the LED, and thus digitally control the LDR's resistance. Now you've got an 8-bit PWM-controlled resistor with a very wide range of resistances. Solder this into your guitar effects box, and your AVR chip can take care of the knob-twiddling for you.

The only limit to the PWM-Vactrol is that the LDR can't handle much power, so if you're substituting out a pot that moves significant current, you might want to consider hooking the LDR up to the base of a (power) transistor to supply the current. How to hook this up is application dependent, so if you're going to do this, you'll need to learn a thing or two about driving loads with transistors. I'll cover this a little bit in Chapter 15, but otherwise I recommend a good book on introductory electronics. *Practical Electronics for Inventors* by Paul Scherz (McGraw-Hill) is a good one. *The Art of Electronics* by Horowitz and Hall (Cambridge University Press) is a little tougher read, but is an absolute classic.

Slowscope

In the light sensor example, we triggered an ADC conversion and then displayed the light reading on eight LEDs. You could also kind of visualize the light levels by watching the LEDs light up and turn off. But if you wanted to look at simple voltages with more resolution, or see some trace of them over time, you'll want an oscilloscope. Old-school analog oscilloscopes would trace out a changing voltage over time by sweeping a light beam across a phosphorescent screen at a fixed speed, while the voltage applied to an input would deflect the beam up or down so that the end result was a display of the changing voltage levels over time. They're tremendously useful if, like me, you like to visualize signals to "see" what's going on.

When you're debugging an ADC circuit, for instance, an oscilloscope can be particularly useful. But what if you don't have one handy? Well, in this section you'll set up the AVR's ADC in free-running mode and transmit the digitized values back to your desktop computer. From there, you can either store it or plot it. To get a quick-and-dirty impression of what's going on with the ADC voltage, you can simply plot the values out on the screen, making a sort of serial-port-speed limited, zero-to-five-volt oscilloscope—the "slowscope." (Rhymes with "o-scope.")

Because you're already set up for measuring light levels as voltage using the LDR voltage divider, let's use that for the demo. Plus, it's nice to see what happens on your desktop computer's screen as you wave your hands around over the light sensor.

For the circuit, all that's left is to connect your USB-Serial converter to the AVR as you did in Chapter 5. In fact, all you'll need is to connect the TX line from the AVR to the RX line on your USB-Serial converter.

The AVR Code

The AVR code in Example 7-2 is a quick exercise in configuring the ADC to work in free-running mode where it's continually taking samples. Because there's always a fresh ADC value ready to be read out, you can simply write it out to the serial port whenever you feel like it—in this case after a fixed time delay that determines the sweep speed of your scope.

Example 7-2. *slowScope.c listing*

```c
// Slow-scope.  A free-running AVR / ADC "oscilloscope"

// ------- Preamble -------- //
#include <avr/io.h>
#include <util/delay.h>
#include "pinDefines.h"
#include "USART.h"

#define SAMPLE_DELAY  20 /* ms, controls the scroll-speed of the scope */

// -------- Functions --------- //
static inline void initFreerunningADC(void) {
  ADMUX |= (1 << REFS0);                    /* reference voltage on AVCC */
  ADCSRA |= (1 << ADPS1) | (1 << ADPS0);    /* ADC clock prescaler /8 */

  ADMUX |= (1 << ADLAR);      /* left-adjust result, return only 8 bits */

  ADCSRA |= (1 << ADEN);                              /* enable ADC */
  ADCSRA |= (1 << ADATE);                     /* auto-trigger enable */
  ADCSRA |= (1 << ADSC);                      /* start first conversion */
}

int main(void) {
  // -------- Inits --------- //
  initUSART();
  initFreerunningADC();
  // ------- Event loop ------ //
  while (1) {
    transmitByte(ADCH);        /* transmit the high byte, left-adjusted */
    _delay_ms(SAMPLE_DELAY);
  }                                          /* End event loop */
```

```
    return (0);                /* This line is never reached */
}
```

To get a feel for how little code is needed once you get all of AVR's hardware peripherals configured, have a look down at the main() function's event loop. All it does is delay for a few milliseconds so that your screen doesn't get overrun, and then sends across the current ADC value. All of the interesting details, and there are at least two of them, are buried in the ADC initialization function. What's different from the last example? Glad you asked!

The line:

```
    ADMUX |= (1 << ADLAR);     /* left-adjust result, return only 8 bits */
```

left-adjusts the ADC value. Because the ADC has a 10-bit resolution, there are two ways you can pack it into the two 8-bit ADC registers, ADCH and ADCL. If you'd like to use the entire 10-bit value, it's convenient to leave the left-adjust bit in its default state. These two options are illustrated in Figure 7-6. When the ADLAR bit is zero, the top byte, ADCH, only contains the top two bits of the ADC result. This way, if you read both bytes into a 16-bit result, you get the right number.

Right Adjusted: ADLAR = 0

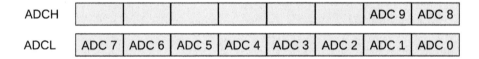

Left Adjusted: ADLAR = 1

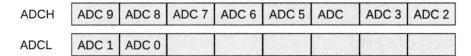

Figure 7-6. ADC result bit alignment

The alternative, which we use here, is to essentially throw away the least significant two bits by left-adjusting the top byte into ADCH and leaving the least significant two bits in ADCL. The AVR shifts the 10-bit byte over by six bits for you, so that the ADCH register contains a good 8-bit value. It's an easy shortcut that saves you the bit-shifting when you only need 8-bit precision.

The other bit of interest in the ADC initialization routine concerns setting up and enabling free-running mode. All three lines of:

```
ADCSRA |= (1 << ADEN);                    /* enable ADC */
ADCSRA |= (1 << ADATE);              /* auto-trigger enable */
ADCSRA |= (1 << ADSC);             /* start first conversion */
```

are needed to make free-running mode work. The first sets the ADC auto-trigger enable bit, which turns on free-running mode. This sets up the ADC to start another sample as soon as the current sample is finished. You still have to start up the initial conversion, so I set the ADSC bit as I did in normal, one-shot mode to start up the first conversion. Then, because ADATE is set, the next conversion follows along automatically.

If you read the datasheet section on the ADC auto-trigger source, you'll find that you can actually trigger conversions automatically a whole bunch of ways—when external pins changing logic state or from the AVRs internal timer/counter modules. But the default is to use the signal from the ADC's own conversion-complete bit to trigger the next conversion, and that's what we're doing here. This means that as soon as the ADC finishes one reading, it will start up the next without any user intervention: "free-running."

But you have to remember to kick it off initially at least that one time, hence the ADSC.

The Desktop Code

The AVR is sending data across the serial line to your desktop computer. All that's left to do is plot it. I find this short bit of Python code in Example 7-3 so useful that I had to throw it in here. There's all sorts of cosmetic and performance improvements you could make, but there's a lot to be said for just printing the numbers out on the screen.

Example 7-3. serialScope.py listing

```python
import serial

def readValue(serialPort):
    return(ord(serialPort.read(1)))

def plotValue(value):
    """ Displays the value on a scaled scrolling bargraph"""
    leadingSpaces = " " * (value*(SCREEN_WIDTH-3) / 255)
    print "%s%3i" % (leadingSpaces, value)

def cheapoScope(serialPort):
    while(1):
        newValue = readValue(serialPort)
        plotValue(newValue)


if __name__ == "__main__":
```

```python
PORT = '/dev/ttyUSB0'
BAUDRATE =  9600
TIMEOUT = None
SCREEN_WIDTH = 80

## Take command-line arguments to override defaults above
import sys
if len(sys.argv) == 3:
    port = sys.argv[1]
    baudrate = int(sys.argv[2])
else:                           # nothing passed, use defaults
    print ("Optional arguments port, baudrate set to defaults.")
    port, baudrate = (PORT, BAUDRATE)

serialPort = serial.Serial(port, baudrate, timeout=TIMEOUT)
serialPort.flush()
cheapoScope(serialPort)
```

The code makes heavy use of the Python pyserial library. If you don't already have this installed, go do so now! See "Installing Python and the Serial Library" on page 123 for installation instructions.

The three functions that make the scope work include readValue() that gets a single byte from the serial stream and converts it into an ordinal number. This way when the AVR sends 123, the code interprets it as the number 123 rather than {, which is ASCII character number 123.

Next plotValue() takes the value and prints an appropriate number of leading spaces, and then the number, padding to three digits with empty space. Finally, cheapoScope() just wraps an infinite loop around these two other functions. A new value is read in, then plotted. This goes on forever or until you close the window or press Ctrl-C to stop it.

If you call *serialScope.py* from the command line, it allows you to override the default serial port and baud rate configurations. On the other hand, once you know how your serial port is configured, you might as well hardcode it in here by editing the PORT and BAUDRATE definitions.

While looking through the defaults, if you'd like the program to quit after a few seconds with no incoming data, you can reset TIMEOUT to a number (in seconds). If you have a particularly wide or skinny terminal window, you can also change SCREEN_WIDTH.

The only little trick here is that before running the scope, the code flushes the serial port input buffer. Depending on your operating system, it may be collecting a bunch of past values from the serial port for you. This is normally a good idea, but here we'd like to start off with a clean slate so that we instantly read in the new

values from the AVR. Hence, we flush out the serial buffer before calling cheapo
Scope() and looping forever.

Synergies

This sort of simple desktop computer scripting can greatly expand on the capabilities and debugging friendliness of the AVR environment. You saw in Chapter 5 how you can expand the AVR's capabilities dramatically by taking in information from your desktop computer. Here, we're doing the opposite.

If you're adept with Python, I encourage you to make a fancier scope display if you'd like. The Python code could also easily be expanded out to a general-purpose data logger application if you'd like. Just open a file on your hard disk and start writing the values to it. Import the datetime module and timestamp them. Heck, import the csv module and you can import the data straight into a spreadsheet or statistics package. Even with such simple tools, if you combine them right, the world is your oyster.

Debugging the ADC is sometimes tricky. You won't always know a priori what types of values to expect. Writing code to detect a shadow is much easier when you know just exactly how dark the shadow is, or how light it is in the room the rest of the time. Seeing how your signal data looks in real time helps your intuition a lot.

I hope you get as much use out of these simple "oscilloscope" routines as I do. Or at least that you have a good time waving your hand over the light sensor for a little bit. I'm pretty sure I can tell which direction I'm moving my hand—the thumb and pinkie fingers cast different shadows. Who knew? I wonder if I can teach the AVR to detect that?

AVR Night Light and the Multiplexer

We just saw how to use single ADC conversions, and then ADC conversions in free-running mode. What's next? Learning how to use more than one of the ADC channels "at once"! We'll stick with our light sensor on ADC0 / PC0 and add in a potentiometer on ADC3 / PC3. Switching between the two rapidly and comparing their voltage values in software will give us an easily adjustable night light that turns on at precisely the level of darkness that we desire.

OK, I'll admit it's not that cool a project, but it gives us a good excuse to learn about the ADC multiplexer and play around with reading values from potentiometers, both of which are fundamental uses of the ADC hardware.

Multiplexing

Because the internal ADC is a fairly complex bit of circuitry, it's not too surprising that there's only one of them per microcontroller. But what to do if you'd like to monitor several analog sensors or voltages? The approach that the AVR, and most other microcontrollers, take is to *multiplex* the ADC out to multiple pins; the single input to the ADC on the inside of the chip is connected through a six-way switch to external pins, enabling you to sample analog voltages on *any one* of the six PCn pins at a time.

If you'd like to sample from two or three different analog sources, you'll need to switch between the pins, sampling each one at a time and then moving on to the next. And as always with the AVR's hardware peripherals, this is done by telling an internal hardware register which channel you'd like to sample from.

This sounds obvious, but you also have to take care to be sure that you switch channels in the multiplexer before the start of an ADC sampling cycle. This is only really a problem in "free-running" mode, in which the ADC samples continually. In free-running mode, when you change the multiplexer, the AVR doesn't restart the sampling automatically. This means that the first sample after you've changed the multiplexer will still be from the old analog source—you need to wait at least one complete ADC cycle before getting a value from the new channel. In my experience, it's a lot easier to trigger each sample yourself (through mainloop or interrupt), because it's easier to verify that you've set up the multiplexer correctly without any complex bookkeeping.

Setting the Mux Bits

The multiplexer is a tiny bit tricky to program, so I hope you haven't forgotten all you learned about bit twiddling from Chapter 4. The problem is the following: the low four bits control which ADC pin is used for input, but the upper three control the voltage reference and switch between 8-bit mode and 10-bit mode as we saw in the slowScope code. When you change the multiplexer channel in ADMUX, you want to change the bottom four bits without modifying the upper four. To see what I mean, look at Figure 7-7.

Bit 7	Bit 6	Bit 5	Bit 4	Bit 3	Bit 2	Bit 1	Bit 0
REFS1	REFS0	ADLAR	-	MUX3	MUX2	MUX1	MUX0

Figure 7-7. ADMUX register bits

To sample from ADC3, you set both the MUX0 and MUX1 bits and make sure that MUX2 and MUX3 are zeroed, because three in binary is 0011, right? But it's lousy to have to think about setting each bit individually. Wouldn't it be nicer to just write a three to the register? Sure, but then you'd end up clobbering the high bits. What if you just AND a three into the register? It doesn't clear out the other low bits, if any were set. For instance, if you were sampling on channel five before with MUX2 and MUX1 set, you'd need to make sure that the MUX2 bit was cleared to get back to channel three.

The easiest solution is to first clear out the bottom four bits, and then OR in your desired channel number. This takes two conceptual steps. To change to ADC3 for instance, you first clear all the low bits and then write the number three back in:

```
ADMUX = ADMUX & 0b11110000;    // clear all 4 mux bits
ADMUX = ADMUX | PC3;           // set the bits we want
```

Notice that the top four bits aren't changed by either of these instructions. You'll often see this written with the clear and set steps combined into one line like this:

```
ADMUX = (0b11110000 & ADMUX) | PC3;
/* or, the ADC macro synonyms */
ADMUX = (0b11110000 & ADMUX) | ADC3;
/* or, in hex for the lazy typer */
ADMUX = (0xf0 & ADMUX) | ADC3;
/* or with numbers instead of macros */
ADMUX = (0xf0 & ADMUX) | 3;
```

This bitmask-style code is easily extensible when you need to loop over all the ADC pins, sampling from each one. If you'd like to read which channel is being sampled, you can logically invert the bitmask, keeping the low four bits of the ADMUX register. For instance, here's an example code snippet that reads from each of the ADCs in a row and stores its value in an array:

```
uint16_t adcValues[6];
uint8_t channel;

for (channel = 0; channel < 6; channel++) {
  ADMUX = (0xf0 & ADMUX) | channel;        // set channel
  ADCSRA |= (1 << ADSC);                    // start next conversion
  loop_until_bit_is_clear(ADCSRA, ADSC);   // wait for conversion
  adcValues[channel] = ADC;                 // store the value in array
}
```

With code like this, running with the ADC clocked at 125 kHz, you can get over 1,500 cycles of all six channels in a second. You'll see in Chapter 8 how to use interrupts to avoid the blocking loop_until_bit_is_clear() step and use the extra CPU time for processing.

Another application of bit-masking and the MUX register is in reading out which channel has just been read from:

```
channelNumber = (0x0f & ADMUX);
```

To figure out which channel was just read from, you can create a bitmask for the lowest four bits and then AND that with the ADMUX register. That way, your channelNumber variable will only contain the value of the ADC sampling channel, and none of the upper bits.

The Circuit

If you've got the LEDs still attached, and you haven't yet disconnected the light sensor circuit from up above, you're most of the way there. All that remains is to hook up a potentiometer to PC3. As before, if you connect one side of the potentiometer to ground and the other to VCC, the center pin will take on all the intermediate values as you turn it back and forth. On a breadboard, it would look like Figure 7-8.

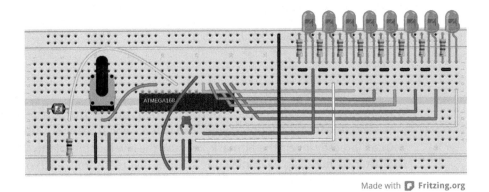

Made with **🄵** Fritzing.org

Figure 7-8. AVR night light circuit

You should also have at least a few of the LEDs still hooked up to this circuit so that you can see when the light is on or off. If you'd like to power something more significant than a couple of LEDs, you'll need to use a transistor or relay as a switch, but this way you could actually turn on a quite useful light automatically when a room gets dark. See Chapter 14 for more details on switching large loads with the AVR. Until then, you can think of the LEDs as a stand-in.

The Code

The code for this project is super simple. Basically, I just wanted an excuse to show you my favorite channel-changing, ADC-sampling routine. Have a look at Example 7-4.

Example 7-4. nightLight.c listing
```
// Quick and dirty adjustable-threshold night-light.

// ------- Preamble -------- //
#include <avr/io.h>
#include <util/delay.h>
#include "pinDefines.h"

uint16_t readADC(uint8_t channel) {
  ADMUX = (0xf0 & ADMUX) | channel;
  ADCSRA |= (1 << ADSC);
```

```
    loop_until_bit_is_clear(ADCSRA, ADSC);
    return (ADC);
}

int main(void) {
    // -------- Inits --------- //
    uint16_t lightThreshold;
    uint16_t sensorValue;
    // Set up ADC
    ADMUX  |= (1 << REFS0);                      /* reference voltage on AVCC */
    ADCSRA |= (1 << ADPS1) | (1 << ADPS0);   /* ADC clock prescaler  /8 */
    ADCSRA |= (1 << ADEN);                              /* enable ADC */

    LED_DDR = 0xff;
    // ------ Event loop ------ //
    while (1) {

        lightThreshold = readADC(POT);
        sensorValue = readADC(LIGHT_SENSOR);

        if (sensorValue < lightThreshold) {
            LED_PORT = 0xff;
        }
        else {
            LED_PORT = 0x00;
        }
    }                                                /* End event loop */
    return (0);                              /* This line is never reached */
}
```

In this example, I initialize the ADC inside the main() routine. By now, you're not surprised by any of these lines, I hope. I also turn on all the LEDs for output. (With eight yellow LEDs on my desktop right now, this night light would actually work pretty well!)

The event loop simply consists of reading the ADC value on the potentiometer and then the light sensor. If the value from the light sensor is lower, it turns the LEDs on, otherwise it turns them off. That's it! Too simple.

The reason for this night-light demo, however, is the function readADC( ). I probably reuse this function, or something similar enough, for tens of simple ADC applications. Taking a channel number as an input, it applies the bitmask to change the ADC channel, starts a conversion, waits for a result, and then returns it. Simple, effective, and it makes simple ADC sampling from multiple channels relatively painless.

Summary

You now know enough about using the ADC to do some pretty complicated sampling. Free-running mode is great when you're only interested in one channel and you'd like to always have a contemporaneous value available. Single-shot mode is great when you don't need to sample that often, or if you're switching channels a lot as we just did here. You know how to use all 10-bits of the ADCs sample or how to set the ADLAR bit to left-adjust down to an easy-to-read 8-bit value in ADCH. That's going to cover you for most simple sensor sampling situations.

We're not quite done with the ADC yet, though. In Chapter 12, I'll demonstrate some more advanced signal-processing methods (oversampling and smoothing) that are useful for getting more resolution from the sensor for stable signals and for getting smoother outputs from noisy signals. We'll also experiment around a little with signal conditioning—namely creating a frontend voltage divider to expand the voltage range over which you can read with the ADC, and adding in a DC-blocking capacitor and biasing circuit for use with input voltages that otherwise would go negative, like microphones and piezo sensors.

## PART II

Intermediate AVR

This section makes you a more efficient programmer of the chip and expands the universe of what you'll think an AVR can do. You'll start doing cool things with the internal hardware peripherals and some more sophisticated tricks in firmware using what you already know. This section provides the big payoff—the tools to do things with a bare AVR chip that you just can't do without knowing a little about how the hardware works.

Mastery of microcontrollers starts with good use of the interrupt system. Chapter 8 shows you how to allow events in the outside world to directly and instantaneously call portions of your code. You'll use this speed to build a noncontact capacitive touch sensor out of aluminum foil and tape that will detect your finger as far as a few centimeters away.

Chapter 9 introduces you to the three internal timers that the ATmega microcontroller comes with. Offloading timing from your code to the timer/counter hardware lets you do things with a precision and speed that you couldn't before, or even just do two things at once. Timers are shockingly versatile, and you'll use them to make a reaction timer, an improved square-wave organ, and even a tiny AM radio transmitter. What do these have in common? Time.

In Chapter 10, you finally get to output something other than ones and zeros from the AVR. (Sort of). Pulse-width modulation (PWM) is the most convenient way to dim LEDs and slow down motors. Between the timer and interrupt hardware, the AVR provides you with a few options for producing PWM, and we'll go through three.

Servo motors are the perfect match for microcontrollers. For so little circuitry, you get so much movement. In Chapter 11, you'll use the 16-bit timer to directly control a servo motor with almost no CPU overhead. The project for this chapter is a "sundial" in reverse—instead of the sun creating a moving shadow, you'll track a laser across the ceiling to show the time. As a bonus, you also get to make a real-time clock out of the AVR.

Rounding out the intermediate section, in Chapter 12 I'll show you two of my favorite mathematical techniques that help you get more out of the ADC: oversampling and exponential smoothing. These techniques let you build a 12-bit accurate voltmeter and a super-sensitive footstep detector built from a $2 piezo element.

Hardware Interrupts

Real-time Response, and a Capacitive Sensor

This chapter introduces perhaps the most useful of the AVR's hardware peripherals —the interrupt system. Up to now, our programs have been very much linear, going from one command to the next command to the next command. However, you often have to deal with input from the real world that arrives asynchronously, almost at random—you want the AVR to respond when you press the button, not when it's ready to have you press the button.

In this chapter, we'll take our first steps into interrupt programming. The first two examples will demonstrate how interrupts can run code for you any time an input pin changes state. And while it's pretty cool to have the interrupt hardware directly run a bit of your code when a button is pressed, it's a bit trivial. So we'll expand on that and build a capacitive touch sensor. (In fact, if you build a large sensor and tweak the code, it'll even detect your hand a centimeter or so away from the touch place.)

What You Need

In this chapter, in addition to the basic kit, you will need:

- An LED or a few. You may still have these hooked up.

- A pushbutton. You may still have this hooked up, too.

- A capacitive touch sensor: we'll make ours out of two pieces of aluminum foil, some tape, a piece of paper, two alligator clips, and a 100k ohm resistor.

- A USB-Serial adapter.

Elegant and skillful use of the interrupt system separates good programmers from good microcontroller programmers. When you're writing code that runs on a multitasking operating system, you don't have to worry nearly as much about what happens when, or how long it takes. The OS takes care of the nitty-gritty details like making sure that the video card is constantly fed with video data and that the mouse and keyboard are being constantly listened to. (*You* don't have to worry about it, because your OS is doing all this for you with its own system of hardware interrupts.)

Here in the land of microcontrollers, we don't often have the luxury of running an OS. Instead, if we'd like to have two things going on seemingly at once, we either cycle between them very quickly or set up a system where one can preemptively interrupt the other. The first strategy, called "polling" in the comp sci jargon, can suffice for a lot of applications. The event loop in a polling-style program is essentially a list of things that we'd like to check up on. (Is a button pressed? If it is, light an LED.) The AVR then runs through that list repeatedly as fast as it can. If we keep our event loop short enough that any given part comes around frequently enough, it's hard to tell that we're polling—when a button is pressed, the LED seems to light up instantly even if we caught the program in another part of the event loop.

Polling code frequently looks something like this:

```c
int main(void){
    // Event Loop
    while(1){

        if (checkLightSensor()){
            set_bit(LED_PORT, LED);
        }

        switchesState = checkSwitches();
        if (switchesState == DANGER_VALUE){
            turnOffKillerLaser();
        }

        doWhateverElse();
    }
}
```

One problem with polling in event loops is that there's no concept of priority. Even though we care more about the limit switches that control our laser than the light sensors, each separate check happens at the same frequency, once per trip through the event loop. That may work fine as long as the event loop is short enough. But if the doWhateverElse() routine takes a while, maybe because it uses a lot of CPU power, too much time can elapse between checks of the switches, and our death-laser-on-a-motor might end up cutting something that it shouldn't.

Handling multiple jobs at once is where interrupts excel. Interrupts do just what they sound like—they interrupt the normal flow of the program. When an interrupt is triggered, all of the variables that you're using are stashed in memory and then a special function, called an interrupt service routine (ISRs), is run. After the ISR is done, your program picks up again where it left off. Switching from one context to another like this takes an AVR chip four cycles (half a microsecond at 8 MHz) both going and returning, but otherwise the ISR happens just about instantly when the interrupt is flagged.

What are interrupts good for? There are *internally triggered interrupts* that respond to the internal AVR hardware peripherals. For instance, there are interrupts that can run ISR code when the analog-to-digital converter or USART has got new data or when the timer/counter peripheral has reached a certain value. Instead of waiting in a blocking loop until the peripheral is ready, we can write our ISR to handle that peripheral directly, and it will execute only when required. We'll be using internally triggered interrupts throughout the rest of the book, and when I introduce a new peripheral subsystem, I'll show you how it can trigger ISRs for you.

There are also *externally triggered interrupts* that can react to to a voltage change on any of the AVRs pins, and these external interrupts will be the focus of this chapter. Without interrupts, you have to check each button in the system to see if it's pressed, which wastes some processor cycles and can result in serious delay if parts of the event loop take a long time. By using interrupts for each AVR pin, you can dispatch code that executes within a microsecond of the button press.

From a coder's perspective, using interrupts judiciously can vastly streamline your work. For instance, when we wanted to test if a button had just been pressed, we had to store the old button state in a variable and check each time around the event loop to see if the current state is different from the old state. Then we had to replace the old state with the current one. By using interrupts, we can configure the interrupt routines to only fire when a pin changes state. (We still have to test whether it changed into a pressed or released state, but it's a lot simpler.)

I find that interrupts often match the way I'm thinking about a coding problem. I want the AVR to be doing one or two main things, but be ready to drop them and execute a third task for a while if it needs to react to a change coming in from the outside world. Interrupts make it much easier for my code to mirror the way I think about the problem.

Interrupts are a deep and rich topic, and we'll just be scratching the surface. That said, we've got a lot of surface area to scratch. In this chapter, we'll walk through a few exercises with external interrupts, we'll use internal interrupts paired with the timer/counter modules to create a system clocks, and then we'll combine both types to implement a capacitive touch sensor.

External Interrupts 101: Real-time Button Pressing Examples

The first use case for external hardware interrupts is to handle a button press asynchronously. That is, you write your event loop so that when an interrupt comes in from outside, the CPU drops whatever it was doing and executes your interrupt routine before getting back to the event loop.

There are two flavors of external interrupts: the fancy interrupts, INT0 and INT1, and the pin-change interrupts. We've wired our button up to pin PD2, which is the dedicated pin for the INT0 interrupt, but which also works with the pin-change interrupt mechanism like all the other I/O pins on the AVR chips.

The INT0 interrupt mechanism has more versatile triggering possibilities, allowing you trigger the interrupt on a rising voltage, a falling voltage, any change, or continuously for a low-voltage level, which is useful for interaction with other processors or peripherals. Due to their hardware complexity, there are only two of these type interrupts: INT0 and INT1, on pins PD2 and PD3.

The PCINT system, on the other hand, allows you to treat every I/O pin on the AVR as an interrupt source if you so desire, but only detects changes (not their direction) and thus requires a little more processing to interpret. The pin-change interrupts are grouped together in banks, so it's more accurate to say that there's a pin-change interrupt for the "B" pins, one for the "C" pins, and one for the "D" pins. We use pin-mask registers to select which of the pins from within the bank we want to trigger the interrupt. I'll discuss this more in the following code example.

External Interrupt 0 Example

First off, let's consider the INT0 and INT1 external interrupts. These are the two highest-priority interrupts in the chip, so in general, you'll want to reserve them for some signal that you really care about. (If you get a bunch of interrupts at the same time, the INT0 routine will run before any of the others.)

As an example, I built a logging accelerometer with GPS, which was mainly an exercise in coordinating among three devices—the GPS over the USART, the accelerometer using I2C serial, and external flash memory using SPI serial. (I'll cover the two advanced serial protocols in Chapter 16 and Chapter 17.)

The accelerometer (an LIS302D) updated at 100 Hz, so every 10 milliseconds, the AVR had to request new data from it or else it would miss the current value. Fortunately, the accelerometer provided a falling-voltage signal when it had new data ready. The simplest solution was to connect the data-ready signal from the accelerometer directly to pin PD2 on the AVR, and trigger an interrupt for a falling voltage. When the accelerometer had new data, it grounded the wire, the AVR detected the falling edge, triggered the interrupt, read the new data in, and saved it to memory. Easy peasy.

Many external peripherals will signal data-ready or otherwise demand your attention by either raising or lowering a voltage signal on a dedicated line, and that's exactly the situation that INT0 and INT1 are designed to handle. For the moment, we're simulating this all with a button press, so let's look at some code.

The first demo interrupt program does two things. In the main event loop, the AVR blinks an LED, LED0, with a delay—a pretty boring main task. In the ISR, which is triggered by the INT0 state change interrupt, we turn on another LED depending on whether the button is pressed or not. Again, that's pretty lame, but this is our first example with interrupts. Let's see how it's done in Example 8-1.

Example 8-1. *helloInterrupt.c listing*

```c
/*

Demo of using interrupts for doing what they do best --
two things at once.

Flashes LED0 at a fixed rate, interrupting whenever button is pressed.

 */

// ------- Preamble -------- //
#include <avr/io.h>
#include <util/delay.h>
#include <avr/interrupt.h>
#include "pinDefines.h"

ISR(INT0_vect) {              /* Run every time there is a change on button */
  if (bit_is_clear(BUTTON_PIN, BUTTON)) {
    LED_PORT |= (1 << LED1);
  }
  else {
    LED_PORT &= ~(1 << LED1);
  }
}

void initInterrupt0(void) {
  EIMSK |= (1 << INT0);                        /* enable INT0 */
  EICRA |= (1 << ISC00);           /* trigger when button changes */
  sei();                      /* set (global) interrupt enable bit */
}

int main(void) {
  // -------- Inits --------- //
  LED_DDR = 0xff;                          /* all LEDs active */
  BUTTON_PORT |= (1 << BUTTON);                 /* pullup */
  initInterrupt0();

  // ------- Event loop ------ //
  while (1) {

    _delay_ms(200);
    LED_PORT ^= (1 << LED0);

  }                                   /* End event loop */
```

```
    return (0);                     /* This line is never reached */
}
```

As usual, let's first skip down to the event loop and see what the main() routine does. At first glance, it looks like all it does is blink LED0 on and off again. There's nothing in the event loop concerning the button or LED1 at all!

Before we leave the event loop, think about how you'd program something similar without interrupts. If you took the easy way and tested the button once per trip around the event loop, just before or after the _delay_ms() statement, you'd notice a delay between the time when you press the button and the time that LED1 lights up, right? For extra credit, try to code up this functionality as a polled event-loop type program—just comment out the initInterrupt0() function and test bit_is_set() to toggle LED1 from within the event loop. You'll find that the button pressing action will start to feel horribly sluggish if it takes significant time to cycle through the event loop.

Let's see what's going on with the interrupts and LED1. First, there's the ISR() call itself. If you've been following along, you'll guess (correctly) that ISR being written in all-caps denotes a macro. (In this case, it's a fairly complicated macro that defines a function, defined in the *interrupt.h* header file that we included at the top of the program.)

ISRs are special routines that run when their interrupt flag is set, and their interrupt vector is called. For the nitty-gritty on interrupts, see "Interrupts: Under the Hood" on page 160. Otherwise, feel free to think of the ISR as being a function that gets called whenever its interrupt flag is set.

The ISR() Is a Special Function

ISRs are different from normal functions in two important ways, however. ISR() "functions" don't have a return value, and they take only their interrupt vector as an argument. This means you can't pass arguments to the ISR directly and have to use variables with global scope to get data in and out of the ISR. For now, just remember that an ISR is a special type of macro/function hybrid that has neither arguments nor return values.

In this example, we're setting the ISR for the INT0 interrupt, and so we use the special (macro) name INT0_vect. The interrupt macro names are defined in the normal *io.h* header file that's specific for the chip. In our case, that'd be *iomx8.h*, which covers the entire series of Mega chips in the "x8" series like the ATmega48, ATmega88P, etc.

Interrupts: Under the Hood

The interrupt system is a little bit involved at the hardware level, but it's not magic, and knowing how it works may someday help you track down interrupt-related bugs.

Like everything else in the AVR, it's all done with bits in registers. For each type of possible interrupt, there is a flag bit inside the AVR that can be set. When you press the button, the INT0 interrupt flag is set. There is also a global interrupt-enable bit that determines whether or not *any* interrupts are checked.

When this global flag is set, the AVR continually checks all of the interrupt flags to see if any of them are set. If one or more of the individual interrupt flags is set, the global interrupt-enable flag is first cleared, preventing any further interrupts, and then the system runs the ISR corresponding to the first individual flag it finds. When the first ISR is done, the system sets the global interrupt-enable flag again, and control either goes to the next ISR with a set flag or back to your main program where it left off. The ordering of the individual interrupt flags thus provides a priority scheme for executing the ISRs. (For the complete list, see Table 8-1, which is derived from a table from the datasheet.)

How does the interrupt mechanism know which section of code to run? At the very beginning of the machine-language version of your code lies the interrupt vector space. Each entry in this space can contain a command to jump to the memory location where the corresponding ISR code will be stored. When the CPU gets a USART_RX interrupt, for instance, signaling that some data has come in over the USART, the USART_RX interrupt flag is set. Because this flag is the 18th flag in the interrupt table, the 18th entry in the interrupt vector table is read out. The 18th slot of this table contains a command that tells the AVR to execute code at the location where the ISR routine's function starts.

In short, when an interrupt flag is thrown, the CPU drops what it's doing, disables further interrupts by turning off the global interrupt bit, looks up the corresponding memory address in the interrupt vector table, and then starts running whatever code it finds at that memory address—which is set to be the beginning of your ISR. Each ISR then ends with the RETI ("return from interrupt") command, which tells the CPU to turn the global interrupt flag back on, to recheck the interrupt flags register, and if none are set, to return to your code where it left off. If, while it was handling your first interrupt request, another interrupt flag has been set, the CPU handles the new interrupt before getting back to your main() routine.

What does all this mean for you as a programmer? Because the individual interrupt flags are prioritized, they'll reliably be run in the same order. Think about this when designing your hardware layout, and physically connect the most important signals to the most important interrupt pins. Additionally, the individual interrupt flags can be set even when the global interrupt flag isn't. Later on, when the global interrupt-enable flag is set, they'll all get processed in the normal priority order. Because interrupts are handled one after the other, if your interrupt routines take a long time to run, or the interrupt flags keep getting set very frequently, execution may take a while before it can get back to your main routine. And finally, because the individual interrupt flags are just like any other flag in a hardware register, you can trigger them from within your own code if you ever need to simulate a button press or whatever.

Table 8-1. Interrupt vector

Name in datasheet	Vector name for ISRs	Interrupt definition
RESET		External Pin Reset, Power-on Reset, Brown-out Reset, and Watchdog System Reset
INT0	INT0_vect	External Interrupt Request 0
INT1	INT1_vect	External Interrupt Request 1

Name in datasheet	Vector name for ISRs	Interrupt definition
PCINT0	PCINT0_vect	Pin Change Interrupt Request 0
PCINT1	PCINT1_vect	Pin Change Interrupt Request 1
PCINT2	PCINT2_vect	Pin Change Interrupt Request 2
WDT	WDT_vect	Watchdog Time-out Interrupt
TIMER2 COMPA	TIMER2_COMPA_vect	Timer/Counter2 Compare Match A
TIMER2 COMPB	TIMER2_COMPB_vect	Timer/Counter2 Compare Match B
TIMER2 OVF	TIMER2_OVF_vect	Timer/Counter2 Overflow
TIMER1 CAPT	TIMER1_CAPT_vect	Timer/Counter1 Capture Event
TIMER1 COMPA	TIMER1_COMPA_vect	Timer/Counter1 Compare Match A
TIMER1 COMPB	TIMER1_COMPB_vect	Timer/Coutner1 Compare Match B
TIMER1 OVF	TIMER1_OVF_vect	Timer/Counter1 Overflow
TIMER0 COMPA	TIMER0_COMPA_vect	Timer/Counter0 Compare Match A
TIMER0 COMPB	TIMER0_COMPB_vect	Timer/Counter0 Compare Match B
TIMER0 OVF	TIMER0_OVF_vect	Timer/Counter0 Overflow
SPI, STC	SPI_STC_vect	SPI Serial Transfer Complete
USART, RX	USART_RX_vect	USART Rx Complete
USART, UDRE	USART_UDRE_vect	USART, Data Register Empty
USART, TX	USART_TX_vect	USART, Tx Complete
ADC	ADC_vect	ADC Conversion Complete
EE READY	EE_READY_vect	EEPROM Ready
ANALOG COMP	ANALOG_COMP_vect	Analog Comparator
TWI	TWI_vect	2-wire Serial Interface
SPM READY	SPM_READY_vect	Store Program Memory Ready

In our code, we've got an event loop that blinks an LED, and we've got an ISR() that handles our button presses; it is called when the INT0 interrupt is triggered. How do we configure the triggering?

With all interrupts, at least two flags need to be set: one to enable our particular interrupt and one to enable interrupts in general. This two-tiered system is terribly handy when you want to enable or disable all interrupts at once or singly, but it means that you have to remember to set at least two flags during initialization.

To follow along with the initInterrupt0() function, it may help to look at the datasheet chapter titled "External Interrupts," and look in the "Register Description" section. Our initialization routine starts off by setting the INT0 bit in the Enable Interrupt Mask so that our specific interrupt will fire, then sets the bit that makes the interrupt trigger on any change in logical state. Why trigger on both changes?

Because we're using the ISR to turn the LED on and off, we need to trigger on both the rising and falling voltage edges. Finally, the initialization routine ends with a command that sets the global interrupt-enable bit, turning on all interrupts that we've configured so far: `sei();`.

Sometimes you'll find that you need to turn on or off all interrupts at once. The AVR designers have anticipated this and added a global interrupt bit and two commands to control it. `sei()` turns all interrupts on, and `cli()` turns them all off. For some timing-sensitive sections of code, especially if you have long-running interrupt service routines, you may want to disable interrupts before you call critical functions and reenable interrupts after you return.

Both `sei()` and `cli()` compile into machine-language instructions of the same name, so we're stuck with those names even though I don't find them particularly descriptive. In case you're wondering, "sei" is "Set Enable Interrupt" bit and "cli" is "CLear enable Interrupt" bit. (Hooray for inconsistent mnemonics!)

Also note that interrupts are automatically turned off when entering an ISR and turned back on again when finishing. This prevents a situation where an interrupt gets called from inside another interrupt, which itself had been called from inside another interrupt, and so on. Of course, if you'd like to have interruptable ISRs, you can specify that either manually by calling `sei()` in the ISR itself or by using a special `ISR_NOBLOCK` argument to the `ISR()` definition. Use this only if you know what you're doing!

And don't forget that interrupts are disabled by default, and that you need to explicitly enable them with an `sei()` somewhere in your code if you expect them to run. (Have I hammered that home enough? You'll still forget to do it sometimes.)

I can't count the number of times that I've written a brand-new ISR, compiled, flashed, and run the code only to find that my interrupt isn't working because I forgot to enable interrupts globally. Always remember that enabling interrupts is a two-step process; enable your specific interrupt vector, then enable the overall interrupt system with `sei()`.

Pin-Change Interrupt Example

As mentioned previously, the `INT0` and `INT1` interrupts are special. If you'd like to use any of the other pins to generate an interrupt, you'll have to use a pin-change interrupt. Initialization of pin-change interrupts is a tiny bit different, but the main difference is that there are only three pin-change interrupt flags, and each one stands for up to eight physical pins on the AVR. In order to select which of the eight pins in each bank you'd like to trigger the interrupt, you'll also need to set up a *pin mask*:

```
ISR(PCINT2_vect){
  ....
}
```

```
void initPinChangeInterrupt18(void){
  PCICR |= (1 << PCIE2);        /* set pin-change interrupt for D pins */
  PCMSK2 |= (1 << PCINT18);     /* set mask to look for PCINT18 / PD2 */
  // PCMSK2 |= (1 << PD2);      /* this will also work for the pin mask */
  sei();                        /* set (global) interrupt enable bit */
}
```

First, you'll notice that we're using a different interrupt vector. There's not much more to say about that—see Table 8-1 for the possible interrupts that can trigger ISRs. Inside the interrupt, we'll still test to see whether the button is pressed or not, just as before.

Setting up a pin-change interrupt is only a tiny bit more conceptually involved than using INT0. Remember that the pin-change interrupt system can respond to a change on any of the AVR's pins (except the power supply pins, naturally). To accommodate that many pins, they're broken up into interrupt bytes by bank.

 Which Pin-Change Interrupt?

For some reason, the AVR designers decided to label the pin-change interrupts by number instead of the letter-number pairs that they labeled the pins with. Don't let this confuse you! All of the pins PB0 through PB7 can potentially trigger the PCINT0 interrupt, PC0 through PC6 trigger PCINT1, and PD0 through PD7 trigger PCINT2. Because we attached the button to pin PD2, we'll need to enable PCINT2. (I would have called it PCINTD, but they didn't ask me—see **Table 8-2** *for the full list.)*

Table 8-2. Pin-change interrupts

Name in datasheet	Vector name for ISRs	Which pins are covered
PCINT0	PCINT0_vect	PB0 .. PB7
PCINT1	PCINT1_vect	PC0 .. PC6
PCINT2	PCINT2_vect	PD0 .. PD7

Because the pin-change interrupt can in principle trigger if *any* of the pins in the relevant bank change state, we'll need to tell the AVR which pins we'd like for it to watch specifically. This is done through the pin mask, which is just a normal 8-bit byte where the corresponding bit is set for each pin we'd like to be able to trigger the interrupt. See Figure 8-1, which is similar to the pinout diagram in the AVR datasheet, for the correspondence between physical pins and their pin-change interrupt numbering.

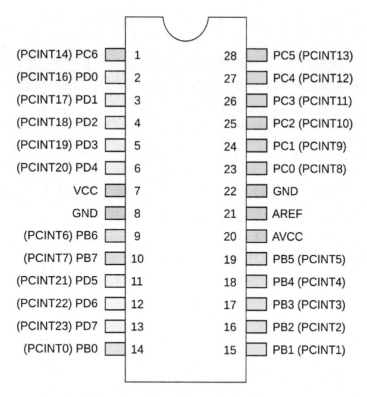

Figure 8-1. *AVR pinouts—PCINT names*

So if we want to trigger on PD2 and PD4, we can set the pin mask one of two ways. We can either use the pins' PCINTxx aliases, or the normal PD2 type pin references. For instance:

```
PCMSK2 |= ( (1 << PCINT18) | (1 << PCINT20) );
```

and:

```
PCMSK2 |= ( (1 << PD2) | (1 << PD4) );
```

both do the same thing: configure the pin-change interrupt to trigger if either PD2 or PD4 changes state.

If you have an interrupt that is triggered by multiple pins, you'll need to test which pin actually changed state in the ISR itself. For instance, continuing the preceding two-button example:

```
if (bit_is_clear(PIND, PD2)){
  // Do one thing...
}
if (bit_is_clear(PIND, PD4)){
  // Do another
}
```

Now you'll be able to respond nearly instantly to input on any or all of the AVR's pins.

Pin-Change Interrupts Made Easy

Using pin-change interrupts allows your code to respond instantaneously to a voltage change on any or all(!) AVR pins. Just remember the three-tiered system for configuring pin-change interrupts and you'll be all set:

1. Enable your specific interrupt in the control register: PCICR |= (1 << PCIEx)

2. Set which pins you'd like to react to in the appropriate pin-mask register: PCMSKx |= (1 << PCINTyy) or PCMSK0 |= (1 << PB2)

3. Enable interrupts globally with sei() when you're ready.

Now write the code that you'd like to run using the ISR(PCINTx_vect) macro:

1. If you're triggering off of multiple pins in the same bank, you will want to test which pin just caused the interrupt in your ISR with something like bit_is_clear(BUTTON_IN, BUTTON).

2. Even if you're triggering on only one pin in the bank, remember that pin-change interrupts trigger on any pin change. If you care whether the change is a press or release, you will need to test for that.

Capacitive Sensor

Capacitive sensors are pretty cool. I mean, who doesn't like a button that can be pressed through a piece of paper or even just by waving your hand near a metal plate? Regular pushbuttons are old-tech, reliable, and despite their debouncing requirements, quite easy to use. When you want something that's just a bit fancier, a little temperamental, and just a tad futuristic, you'll want a capacitive touch sensor. Touching metal plates is what they do in the "future."

The basic principle behind capacitive touch sensors is the same: timing how long it takes for a capacitor to charge or discharge. When nobody is nearby, the sensor plate itself will have some roughly fixed capacitance of its own, and it will take a given amount of time to charge and discharge at a given voltage. When you come along, your body capacitance couples with the circuit. The resulting capacitor—made up of you and the sensor—has more capacitance than the sensor's capacitor alone, and so takes longer to charge and discharge. Measuring the change in charge time, allowing for environmental variation and more, lets you determine when the "button" is pressed.

Timing the capacitor's discharge time directly involves detecting the difference between times that are on the order of two or more microseconds different from each other, and that's a little bit unreliable and hard to do with great sensitivity. Instead if you fire off a pin-change interrupt service routine that recharges the capacitor and adds one to a count variable, and then time how many of these cycles you get in 50 milliseconds, you'll get a number that ranges between 2,000 with your hand on the sensor plate, 8,000 with a thumb, 10,000 with a finger, 12,000 with your hand 1 cm above the plate, and 15,000 counts when you're nowhere near the sensor.

Capacitive Sensor Timing Methods

All capacitive sensor applications work by measuring the time it takes to charge or discharge a baseline capacitor, and then comparing that with the extra time it takes to charge or discharge the same capacitor when the capacitance changes due to the proximity of a human. The approaches differ in how the timing of an individual charge/discharge cycle is done, and how these times are averaged together.

The most intuitive method is to directly time the capacitor discharging with nobody touching it, then with someone touching it, and compute the difference in time. If a human body adds around 20–30 pF of extra capacitance, and the capacitor is drained through a 100k ohm resistor as we do here, the time difference is one or two microseconds. With the AVR's processor running at eight instructions per microsecond at best, we just don't have much resolution with times that are that short.

Instead, we indirectly time how long it takes the capacitor to discharge by discharging it to a fixed level (where the digital pin reads a logic change), fully charging it back up, and then repeating. Because we're always charging and discharging the capacitor, we can then count how many cycles take place in a fixed amount of time. This has the added advantage of averaging a bunch of cycles together—as many fit in our fixed time frame—so that if one cycle is a little too short due to some random fluctuation, and another cycle is too long, they cancel out.

In the end, the direct and indirect methods are very similar, and either is workable. I encourage you to make a direct-timing capacitive sensor if you'd like to experiment.

As demonstration code, a capacitive sensor lets me show you how interrupts let you do two things "at once." We'll use the plain-vanilla _delay_ms() function to implement the waiting time. Now normally, your code doesn't do anything while a delay is running. But here we'll be charging up the capacitor and keeping track of how many cycles we've seen in an interrupt that's fired automatically every time the capacitor is discharged. So every time the ISR is called, the chip stops delaying, recharges the capacitor, increments a counter, and then goes back to the delay function where it left off. Cool, no? But first, we'll need to build ourselves a sensor.

The Sensor

A capacitive sensor is basically just a capacitor. But unlike normal capacitors where the goal is to minimize the size and prevent it from interacting with electric fields in the environment, here you'll be building your own capacitor as large as you'd like and trying to integrate your hand into the electric field.

Consequently, you can make a fairly low-tech capacitor. In fact, a very nice sensor for this project can be made by taking two pieces of aluminum foil with a sheet of paper between them. For starters, cut one piece of foil approximately 10 × 10 cm

(3–4 inches on a side) to act as a ground plane. Clip an alligator clip to this foil. Put a sheet of paper on top of this, then a second smaller piece of aluminum foil. This piece of foil should be around half the size of the first in both dimensions—you want the ground plate to overlap the sensor plate at least where you're going to be touching it. Attach the second alligator clip to the sensor foil. In my installation, I taped both foils to the piece of paper, using both the tape and paper to strengthen the foil. The two foils should be totally insulated from each other by the paper, and make sure that the alligator clips aren't touching each other either. You can see how my completed sensor looks in Figure 8-2.

Figure 8-2. *Aluminum foil capacitive sensor*

Figure 8-3 shows you the resulting circuit diagram.

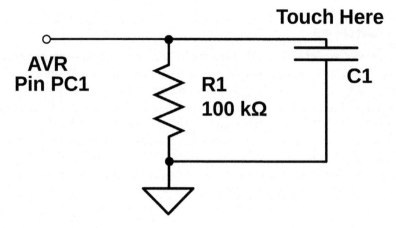

Figure 8-3. *Capacitive sensor circuit*

As you can see, the circuit is very simple. Connect a 100k ohm resistor from the AVR's PC1 to ground. Now connect the ground-plate alligator clip to ground, and the sensor-plate alligator clip to the resistor and the AVR's PC1. (See how the circuit diagram ends up looking just about like the two pieces of aluminum foil on your desk? This is no coincidence!) If you've already got an LED or two plugged in to PORTB, you're done! The result on your breadboard should look something like Figure 8-4.

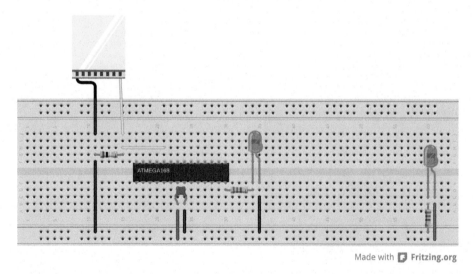

Made with 🔲 Fritzing.org

Figure 8-4. *Capacitive sensor breadboard*

The AVR will now charge up the capacitor and then switch to input mode. The large resistor will slowly discharge the capacitor back down to 0 V. And then you measure (indirectly) the time it takes for the capacitor to discharge and see if you're touching the plate or not.

Once you've gotten it working the "right" way, feel free to experiment around with other capacitor geometries. Any conductive surface held insulated over a ground plane should work, in principle. By reading the number of counts per sensing period over the serial port, you'll be able to figure out a suitable sensing time and threshold value for almost any capacitor. For instance, I dunked my alligator clip in a cup of tea that was sitting on top of grounded aluminum foil, and it could sense when I put my hand on the mug. You could also try taping the aluminum foil and paper sensor underneath a thin-seated chair to detect when a person sits down. You have a lot of room to experiment here.

The Code

OK, so down to business. To recap, we'll be repeatedly charging up the sense capacitor and letting it discharge through the resistor, counting up the number of cycles. A delay function keeps track of the time. Once the delay is over, the number of charge-discharge cycles can be used to detect a nearby hand. Example 8-2 implements these ideas in code.

Example 8-2. capSense.c listing

```
/*
    Capacitive touch sensor demo
*/

#include <avr/io.h>
#include <util/delay.h>
#include <avr/interrupt.h>
#include <avr/power.h>
#include "pinDefines.h"
#include "USART.h"

#define SENSE_TIME    50
#define THRESHOLD     12000

// ------- Global Variables ---------- //
volatile uint16_t chargeCycleCount;

// ------- Functions -------- //

void initPinChangeInterrupt(void) {
  PCICR |= (1 << PCIE1);     /* enable Pin-change interrupts 1 (bank C) */
  PCMSK1 |= (1 << PC1);    /* enable specific interrupt for our pin PC1 */
}

ISR(PCINT1_vect) {
  chargeCycleCount++;                            /* count this change */
```

```
   CAP_SENSOR_DDR |= (1 << CAP_SENSOR);                   /* output mode */
   _delay_us(1);                                        /* charging delay */

   CAP_SENSOR_DDR &= ~(1 << CAP_SENSOR);                 /* set as input */
   PCIFR |= (1 << PCIF1);              /* clear the pin-change interrupt */
}

int main(void) {
   // -------- Inits --------- //
   clock_prescale_set(clock_div_1);                       /* full speed */
   initUSART();
   printString("==[ Cap Sensor ]==\r\n\r\n");

   LED_DDR = 0xff;
   MCUCR |= (1 << PUD);                             /* disable all pullups */
   CAP_SENSOR_PORT |= (1 << CAP_SENSOR);     /* we can leave output high */

   initPinChangeInterrupt();

   // ------ Event loop ------ //
   while (1) {

     chargeCycleCount = 0;                               /* reset counter */
     CAP_SENSOR_DDR |= (1 << CAP_SENSOR);      /* start with cap charged */
     sei();                             /* start up interrupts, counting */
     _delay_ms(SENSE_TIME);
     cli();                                                    /* done */
     if (chargeCycleCount < THRESHOLD) {
       LED_PORT = 0xff;
     }
     else {
       LED_PORT = 0;
     }
     printWord(chargeCycleCount);                      /* for fine tuning */
     printString("\r\n");

   }                                                    /* End event loop */
   return (0);                          /* This line is never reached */
}
```

The pin-change interrupt initialization is the minimal setup—we set the pin-change interrupt for the bank of pins that we'd like to trigger and then the pin-mask for the particular pin we're interested in. The only thing this initialization doesn't do is enable the global interrupt vector. We'll do that from within main().

The interrupt service routine does three things. First it increments our cycle variable. Then it changes the DDR to output and delays a tiny bit to charge up the capacitor. (The delay may or may not be necessary depending on your setup. Try it without.) Then, the DDR is set back to input for the pin, and the pin-change interrupt flag is cleared by writing `PCIF1` into the pin-change interrupt flag register, `PCIFR`.

Resetting the pin-change interrupt flag is described in the datasheet, in the pin-change interrupts "Register Description" section if you'd like to read more. Why did we do this? Because, during the pin-change ISR, we change the voltage on the pin by charging up the capacitor, which sets the interrupt flag. If we didn't reset the flag, program execution would jump right back to the pin-change ISR as soon as the ISR is done.

Moving down to the `main()` routine, we set the chip to run at maximum speed and call the initialization routines. (I go into more depth on setting the CPU speed in "CPU Speed" on page 191, so sit tight until then. I've been trying to explain everything in place, but this code just works so much better with the AVR in high-speed mode that I had to do it.)

Because the ISR will be swapping between charging the capacitor and passively reading its voltage, we can leave the `PORT` register high for charging, but we don't want it to enable the internal pull-up resistor when we're sensing the voltage. It turns out that we can disable *all* of the internal pull-up resistors with a single bit: setting `MCUCR |= (1 << PUD);`, the pull-up disable bit in the MCU control register.

The event loop then resets the charge cycle counter, initially charges up the capacitor, and then enables interrupts. As soon as the voltage on the capacitor drops back down, the ISR will be called, which will add one to the counter and then charge the capacitor back up. This cycle loops around until the delay is up and the code again disables interrupts. Now we can test how many cycles happened during the delay time and decide whether a press happened or not.

Global, Volatile Variables

There's one more important detail in the capacitive sensor code that I brushed over in the preceding treatment, and that's the use of global variables with our interrupt service routine. Have a look back at where the variable `chargeCycleCount` is defined, way up at the top of the file. Being defined outside of any function like this makes the variable *global*, meaning that any of the other functions defined in this file can access it without explicitly passing it as an argument to that function. This makes the variable `chargeCycleCount` available to both our `main()` routine *and* the ISR.

Remember back in "The ISR() Is a Special Function" on page 160 where I said that ISRs were not entirely equivalent to functions? Here's where the difference really matters. We need to increment a variable in the ISR and then use it to make a decision in the `main()` function. How can we do that without passing arguments and return values between the ISR and `main()`? The answer is to define a global variable that's defined outside of both functions, and so its value isn't contained within the scope of either. The ISR can add to `chargeCycleCount` and `main()` can read it.

But `chargeCycleCount` also must be marked `volatile` because the compiler needs to be warned that it can change without notice in any given context. In fact, this distinction is so important that not declaring the variable as `volatile` will break the code. I'll explain why in a bit, but it's a little arcane.

If your eyes glaze over while reading the next section, just remember to *always* define your global variables using the special `volatile` keyword for the AVR, otherwise the compiler will optimize them away and your ISR won't work.

The volatile keyword

`volatile` warns the compiler that the declared variable can change at any time without warning, and that the compiler shouldn't optimize it away no matter how static it seems.

For a glimpse into the mind of the optimizing compiler, imagine you write code with a segment like this:

```
int main(void){
    char a;
    a = 'H';
    while(1){
        transmitByte(a);
    }
}
```

The compiler is going to notice that nothing in your `main()` function changes the value of the variable a, and the optimizer will get rid of it entirely. The optimizer will instead compile the equivalent of this code for you:

```
int main(void){
    while(1){
        transmitByte('H');
    }
}
```

which does the same thing, but is much shorter and doesn't involve allocating scarce memory for a variable that never varies. A win, right?

The optimizer is pretty good about finding shortcuts through our code, and if we write code that uses a variable that doesn't change, the optimizer is going to replace it with a constant. This is where we run afoul of interrupts. Because the ISRs are never explicitly called from within the `main()` function, the optimizer doesn't know that the ISR is changing a variable relevant for `main()`, and it replaces it with a constant value.

In the capacitive sensor code, it looks like the variable `chargeCycleCount` is set to zero and then it's never changed with the `main()` routine. An optimizing compiler will notice this and replace chargeCycleCount with 0 everywhere within main(). If the cycle count is always 0, the code thinks that the sensor is always being pressed, even when it's not, and the sensor routine won't work.

To tell the compiler that we expect our global variables to change without warning, we mark it volatile. Now the compiler won't make assumptions that it knows what the variable's value is.

What about the AVR's special memory registers like PINB that change all the time due to external input? If you dig deep enough into the include files (into *sfr_defs.h* to be precise), you'll find that the macros that define the hardware register variables, PORTB and PINB and so on, are *already* defined as volatile so that the compiler can't just ignore them, even if nothing in code changes them explicitly.

Forgetting to mark global shared variables as volatile is probably pitfall #1 in advanced AVR programming. If your ISR seems not to be working, and you're sure you've run sei(), double-check your volatiles.

Aside: volatile in for loops

Another place you'll want to define a variable as volatile is when you're using a loop to do nothing but delay. Because it's doing nothing, the compiler will optimize it away. The compiler *loves* to help your code run faster!

So when you write something like:

```
uint8_t i;
/* I'd really like to delay here */
for (i = 0; i < 200; i++){
   ;
}
```

hoping to slow the program down for something like 200 CPU cycles, the compiler notices the empty for loop and optimizes it to:

```
uint8_t i;
/* Compiler: I found a shortcut! */
```

Instead, if you declare the variable i to be volatile, the compiler doesn't know that it can't be changed by external subroutines during any step in the for loop, so it executes them all just to be sure:

```
volatile uint8_t i;
for (i = 0; i < 200; i++){ ; }
```

works just fine as a 200-CPU-tick (plus a couple more for setting up the for loop) delay.

On the other hand, if you write:

```
uint8_t i;
for (i = 0; i < 200; i++){
```

```
    _delay_ms(100);
  }
```

it will work fine because the compiler thinks it needs to call that _delay_ms() function 200 times.

 Volatile and ISRs: The Bottom Line

If you share a global variable between a function (including main()) and an ISR, you must declare that variable as volatile.

If you don't, the compiler will not realize that the variable can change within the scope of the function because it never sees the ISR being called directly, and it will likely substitute a constant for your variable. Your code will compile just fine, but your ISR won't do anything and you'll scratch your head for 10 minutes until you remember reading this warning. I hope.

Debugging the Circuit

If you haven't already, flash the program in, connect the serial port to your computer, and run the Python *serialScope.py* program. (You may have to tweak the PORT definition to match your serial port.) Now touch the sensor and you'll see the current cycle count. You'll want to play around with the defined SENSE_TIME and THRESHOLD. If you aren't getting at least 5,000 counts when you are not touching the sensor plate, try increasing the SENSE_TIME until you do. Now touch the plate a few times. You want to set the THRESHOLD somewhere in between the untouched reading and what it reads when you put your finger on the plate.

Setting the THRESHOLD too close to the no-press value can make the circuit sensitive to small changes in the intrinsic capacitance of the circuit with weather or people walking by. On the other hand, if you set the THRESHOLD too low, you might need to press down with two fingers or more. You just have to explore a bit until you get it working like you'd like, but that's half the fun.

Capacitive touch sensors are tricky beasts to troubleshoot. One reason is that the extra capacitance you're trying to detect is around the same magnitude as what's normally called "stray capacitance"; that is, the capacitance from having wires next to each other, or running your alligator clips too close to a grounded metal surface.

The other reason these sensors can be finicky is that the capacitance of the sensor itself depends on what you make it out of, what kind of environment it's in, the humidity, and other factors. We've got a lot of parameters that are variable in this system: sensor geometry and capacitance, sampling time (controlled by the delay), and the count threshold to detect a touch.

So where to begin? If you've built the sensor as described, with a 100k ohm resistor, you should be already in the right ballpark. You can substitute a variable resistor or potentiometer in for the 100k resistor, and sweep the value around, which will vary the discharge rate. If you find that you have to use very long sampling times just to get a reasonable number of cycles counted, you might try changing the resistor value.

On the other hand, if you're getting too many counts per period, you might even be running into overflow problems. Remember that a 16-bit counting variable can only get up to 65,535 before it loops back around to zero. Try running a shorter SENSE_TIME at first, and increase it until you get into a reasonable ballpark, especially if you see the sensor value decrease down to, and through, zero when you move your finger slowly onto the sensor.

Once you get the sensor working reliably, experiment with different materials and configurations. Plants? That's been done. What's the strangest capacitive sensor you can come up with?

Introduction to the Timer/
Counter Hardware

9

AM Radio Transmitter and Reaction Timer

In this chapter, we'll test our reaction time, refine our old organ routines, and transmit AM radio directly from the AVR. What do these projects have in common? They're all made possible by the internal timer-counter hardware. Previously, we've marked the passing of time by holding up the CPU in counting delay loops. No more! The AVRs have dedicated hardware that'll do that for us.

In all of these cases, you'll find that using the hardware timers costs a little bit in initial setup, but makes your resulting code significantly simpler, the timing significantly more accurate, and frees up the CPU for useful work.

What You Need

In addition to the basic kit, you will need:

- A speaker and DC-blocking capacitor.

- A pushbutton to test your reaction time.

- A long length of wire for an AM antenna.

- A USB-Serial adapter to display your times.

Timer/Counters: Why and How?

Looking back at the serial-port organ code, the function that made the music (such as it was) was called playNote(). It worked by turning the speaker pin on and waiting, and then turning the speaker pin off and waiting. To refresh your memory, see Example 9-1.

Example 9-1. Old playNote() listing

```
void playNote(uint16_t wavelength, uint16_t duration) {
  uint16_t elapsed;

  uint16_t i;
  for (elapsed = 0; elapsed < duration; elapsed += wavelength) {
                    /* For loop with variable delay selects the pitch */
    for (i = 0; i < wavelength; i++) {
      _delay_us(1);
    }
    SPEAKER_PORT ^= (1 << SPEAKER);
  }
}
```

This code works just fine, but if you'd like the CPU to do anything else at the same time, you're out of luck—it's all tied up doing the important task of waiting for a precise amount of time. We run into a similar situation with our LED blinking code where we invoke the _delay_ms() function. All of our processor power is momentarily tied up just spinning around in a fruitless loop that simply counts up until it's done.

What we need instead is a clock that we can use as a timebase and a counter that'll count up a certain number of clock ticks for us before it acts. This is, of course, what the internal timer/counter hardware peripheral does. Before we get down to applications, let's take a quick tour of the hardware to see how it works. It'll give you a better feel for the possibilities.

Essentially, the timer/counter hardware works as summarized in Figure 9-1. Input arrives from either the system clock or an external source connected up to an input pin (T0 for counter 0). In this way, the same hardware can be used as a timer (counting ticks of the system clock) or a generic counter (counting voltage change events on the dedicated input pin). The current count is stored in an internal timer/counter register (TCNTn).

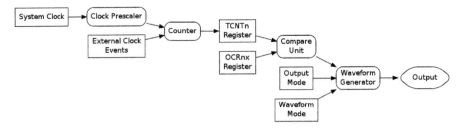

Figure 9-1. *Timer/counter hardware*

Your code can read the count from TCNT registers at any time, yielding the current count value. You can also write to it, and you'll often do so in order to reset the count to zero. With just reading and writing to the timer register, you can make the equivalent of a stopwatch—set the timer value to zero, do something, and then check the value again to see how much time has elapsed.

If instead of a stopwatch, you'd like an alarm clock, you can put the Timer Compare Unit to work for you. Its job is to let you know when a certain count value is reached. You store this compare value in the Output Compare Register (OCRn). This way, you can store the value you'd like for an elapsed time, a frequency or a duty cycle in the OCRn, and then forget about it—the timer hardware will do the rest for you, freeing up the CPU to do more interesting things.

So the counter is counting, and the compare unit is comparing the count value to a value that you set. What happens when the compare value is reached? A compare event triggers the Waveform Generator, and what it does depends on a pair of important configuration options: the waveform mode and output mode. In brief, the Waveform Generator unit can be configured to generate three main types of output depending on the waveform mode: counter, timer, or (in Chapter 10) PWM. Whether you want pins set, cleared, or toggled is determined by the output modes. The timer/counters can also trigger interrupts, which is useful when you want to periodically update variables or run code; you've seen a bunch of interrupt examples in Chapter 8. In this chapter, we'll be focusing on counter and timer waveform modes, and direct-to-pin output.

And if one timer/counter weren't enough, the ATmega series of AVR chips have three timers, two with 8-bit (256 step) resolution and one with 16-bit (65,356 step) resolution. That way, you can have one timer/counter generating a frequency for you, another keeping track of wall-clock time, and the third timing short-duration events. They're very useful once you've learned how to use them.

As you can see, there's a lot of flexibility and utility built into the timer/counter hardware. If you want to count button presses, you can simply hook up your (hardware-debounced) switch directly to the appropriate counter input pin. Or imagine that you want to get the time in between button presses. Then you can set your code to zero the TCNT register at the beginning, connect the counter up to the system clock, and then when the button is pressed, simply read out the value in TCNT. The count will be the number of system clock ticks that have elapsed, which you can then manipulate any way you want. And because all of this is taken care of by the timer/counter hardware, the CPU is free to listen to serial ports or crunch numbers at the same time.

Basic Waveform Generation Modes

When you're configuring the timer/counter hardware, the first thing you'll need to decide is what mode of operation you want the timer/counter operating in. The AVR datasheet includes fairly good descriptions of each of these modes, and also a table that describes the bits you need to set to put the timers in each mode. Because we'll be covering the PWM modes in Chapter 10, here's a summary of the two basic timer/counter modes:

Normal Mode
In this mode, the counter counts up until it overflows at 255 or 65,535. You use this mode most when you're counting clicks, timing an event, or clearing and reading TCNT from your code. We'll be using Normal Mode for the reaction timer.

CTC Mode
In Clear Timer on Compare Match mode, the counter resets itself automatically when it reaches the value that's stored in the OCRnA register instead of waiting until it hits 255 or 65,535. So by writing to the output compare register, we control the *frequency* of the cycles. Configuring a pin to toggle, set, or clear when a match occurs is a very common choice. Use this mode when you want an adjustable frequency or timebase. We'll be using CTC mode for audio frequency generation in the revised organ code and for the (somewhat tuneable) carrier frequency of our AM transmitter. By triggering an interrupt when the counter resets, we can also execute arbitrary ISR code in a strictly timed fashion. This more advanced use of timers with interrupts will be the basis of a real-time clock and all sorts of scheduling systems.

Test Your Reaction Time

I've used milliseconds or microseconds to describe lengths of time quite a lot, but do you really know how long a millisecond is? Or 100 milliseconds? To the CPU, a millisecond is an eternity—at 8 MHz, it can run eight thousand computations in that time—but for humans, 100 milliseconds is fast. When we were debouncing switches, I mentioned that human reaction time was on the order of tens to hundreds of milliseconds. Here's your chance to test it out.

Flash in the *reactionTimer.c* code here, and then open up a serial terminal window at 9,600 baud to communicate with the AVR. The program will wait for any key from your computer keyboard, then wait a slightly random delay time between 1 and 3.5 seconds, and then light all the LEDs. When that happens, your job is to press the button attached to pin PD2 as quickly as you can. Your time, in seconds, is sent over the USART for display. Have a quick skim through the code in Example 9-2 and see if you can figure it out.

Example 9-2. reactionTimer.c listing

```
/*
   Press the button as quickly as you can after the LEDs light up.
   Your time is printed out over the serial port.
*/
```

```c
// ------- Preamble -------- //
#include <avr/io.h>
#include <util/delay.h>
#include <avr/interrupt.h>
#include "pinDefines.h"
#include "USART.h"

#include "support.h"

static inline void initTimer1(void) {
                                /* Normal mode (default), just counting */
  TCCR1B |= (1 << CS11) | (1 << CS10);
  /* Clock speed: 1 MHz / 64,
     each tick is 64 microseconds ~= 15.6 per ms   */
                                /* No special output modes */
}

int main(void) {
  char byte;
  uint16_t timerValue;

  // -------- Inits --------- //

  initUSART();
  initTimer1();
  LED_DDR = 0xff;                          /* all LEDs for output */
  BUTTON_PORT |= (1 << BUTTON);            /* enable internal pull-up */

  printString("\r\nReaction Timer:\r\n");
  printString("---------------\r\n");
  printString("Press any key to start.\r\n");

  // ------ Event loop ------ //
  while (1) {

    byte = receiveByte();                       /* press any key */
    printString("\r\nGet ready...");
    randomDelay();

    printString("\r\nGo!\r\n");
    LED_PORT = 0xff;                            /* light LEDs */
    TCNT1 = 0;                                  /* reset counter */

    if (bit_is_clear(BUTTON_PIN, BUTTON)) {
            /* Button pressed _exactly_ as LEDs light up.  Suspicious. */
      printString("You're only cheating yourself.\r\n");
    }
    else {
      // Wait until button pressed, save timer value.
      loop_until_bit_is_clear(BUTTON_PIN, BUTTON);
      timerValue = TCNT1 >> 4;
      /* each tick is approx 1/16 milliseconds, so we bit-shift divide */
```

```
        printMilliseconds(timerValue);
        printComments(timerValue);
    }

    // Clear LEDs and start again.
    LED_PORT = 0x00;
    printString("Press any key to try again.\r\n");

  }                                                /* End event loop */
  return (0);                            /* This line is never reached */
}
```

I've shifted the pretty-printing functions off to another pair of *support.c* and *support.h* files. If you look at the makefile, you'll see that it includes them in addition to the USART files. All of this is to keep the main *reactionTimer.c* code tight and keep you focused on the timers. So for now, just assume that randomDelay(), printMilliseconds(), and printComments() do what their names imply.

The initialization section is pretty standard for our applications, and we'll get to initTimer1() soon, so skip on down to the event loop, which starts off by waiting for a byte (any byte) across the USART. After a random delay, all the LEDs light up, "Go!" is transmitted on the USART, and we have the first timer-specific bit of code.

As described in the timer/counter overview, the current timer count value is kept in a hardware register called TCNT1 for Timer 1. (Not surprisingly, the counter register for Timer 0 is called TCNT0, and TCNT2 for Timer 2.) In this example, we're using the timer/counter to simply count up at a fixed rate, starting out from zero. Later, when we read the TCNT1 register, we'll know how many timer ticks have elapsed. And because people can have widely varying reaction times, I've chosen to use the 16-bit Timer 1 to allow us to easily count values from one sixteenth of a millisecond up to just over four seconds

So after the random delay, the LEDs are turned on, and the counter hardware register is reset to zero. The next thing the code does is to check if you're already pressing the button and issues an admonishment. (Not that I don't trust you or anything, but you know how the temptation is…) If you weren't found to be cheating, the code continues on.

Next, the code goes into an endless loop until you press the button by using the loop_until_bit_is_clear macro function. But wait, if the CPU is looping around waiting, who's doing the timing in the meantime? That's right, the timer/counter module. When the button is finally pressed (after an eternity in CPU time), all that's left to do is read the TCNT1 value out of the register and convert it to (approximate) milliseconds, print it out, and rate your time.

How do we know how long a timer tick lasts? That's a function of the CPU clock speed and CPU prescaler, so let's have a look at the initialization routine. In fact, when you get there, you'll see that *all* the init routine does is set the clock speed. Looking at Table 15-5 in the "Register Description" section for Timer 1 in the datasheet, you'll see the list of possible clock speeds and the necessary bits to set to get each of them. Some prescaler modes can be set with just one bit, while others require two or three, like "CPU/64," which we use here.

Alternative Representations for Setting Bits

You do remember your bit-shifting logic from Chapter 4, right? You'll frequently need it when reading other people's code, and may want to use it in your own sometimes.

For instance, the initialization code for setting the timer's clock-speed prescaler that we wrote as:

```
TCCR1B |= (1 << CS10) | (1 << CS11);
```

could be written, using the built-in _BV() macros, as:

```
TCCR1B |= _BV(CS10) | _BV(CS11);
```

or using a set_bit style macro as:

```
#define set_bit(register, bit) \
    (register |= (1<<bit))

set_bit(TCCR1B, CS10);
set_bit(TCCR1B, CS12);
```

or (yuck!) as:

```
TCCR1B |= 5;
```

if they're total jerks.

There's no reason to ever write nonreadable code like that last example. To figure out if "5" is setting the waveform generation bits or the clock speed, you'll have to open up the datasheet and do a decimal-to-binary conversion. And all the one-liners compile to the same machine code anyway, so there's nothing at all gained by using the difficult-to-read notation.

The two-line, set_bit macro version ends up taking twice as many instructions in machine code as `TCCR1B |= (1 << CS10) | (1 << CS12);`, and after you're used to the explicit bit shifts, they're just about as readable. If you're writing timing-sensitive code, or setting multiple bits in a single register over and over again, the one-liner versions are better.

How did I figure out these timings? I typed make dis asm and then read the resulting *.lst* file to see how the code converts into the machine language that gets flashed into the chip. You can disassemble the machine code by hand with the avr-objdump command. Looking over the quasi-assembler can help demystify compilation process and is informative even if you don't know a word of assembler yet.

The rest of the reaction timer code is just pretty-printing the results to the serial output and the nice trick used to make a "random" delay. (Using the least significant bits of a fast-updating counter isn't random by any means, but it's good enough to make an unpredictable delay, as long as the counter value depends on human input.) These miscellaneous functions are listed in *support.h* and *support.c*, and should be fairly readable.

So let's quickly recap the timer-relevant details of this project before we move on to something more complex. First, once the timer/counter is initialized, it just runs on its own, counting up until it reaches its maximum value and starts again from zero. In this example, I wanted more than 255 possible values for the reaction times, so I used the 16-bit Timer 1, which can count up to 65,535 before rolling over. The speed at which the timer/counter counts depends on the system CPU speed and the CPU prescaler that we pick when we're initializing the timer. In this case, using an 1 MHz CPU clock and a divide-by-64 prescaler value, each timer tick takes 64 microseconds, which is close enough to 1/16th of a millisecond that we can calculate the timing with a bit-shift divide for convenience.

The initialization of the timer/counter was particularly simple here because we were already using Normal Mode, which is the default, so we didn't need to set any of the waveform generation mode bits. Additionally, we weren't using the output of the timer in any way except to read it straight out of the count hardware register, so we didn't need to set up any of the output-mode bits. All we had to do was set up the clock source/prescaler and off it went.

The rest of this chapter introduces more nuanced ways to use the timer/counter hardware, with just-slightly more complicated initialization routines. Banzai!

Using Timer 0 for a Better 8-Bit Organ

Before we get on to something complicated and slightly hackish like making an AVR into an AM radio transmitter, let's refine our playNote() code from the seri alOrgan project by using the timer/counter in CTC mode. Remember in "Basic Waveform Generation Modes" on page 180, I mentioned that CTC mode is most often used when we want to set the timer/counter to repeat at a given frequency? Well, it turns out that's exactly what we need to set the pitches on our 8-bit Organ.

To get zero-CPU-use audio out of the AVR, we're going to use one of the timer/counter's output modes to toggle our speaker out pin for us each time it goes around a cycle, and then we'll use the CTC mode's adjustable compare value to vary the pitch. We want all of this to run within the audio range, so we'll need to divide down the 1 MHz CPU clock frequency into something more manageable. We'll use Timer 0 here for simplicity and variety, but there's no reason we couldn't use Timer 1 if we wanted higher pitch accuracy or a wider frequency range.

Flash in timerAudio into your AVR and let's dissect the code listing in Example 9-3. As usual, the initialization section calls initialization functions and then the event loop calls our playNote() function and waits. playNote() is fairly straightforward as well. The speaker output is enabled in its data-direction register, and then the values that correspond to our musical pitches are loaded into the output compare register.

Example 9-3. timerAudio.c listing

```
/*

Quick audio demo using Timer 0 to generate audio frequencies directly.

*/
```

```
// ------- Preamble -------- //
#include <avr/io.h>                          /* Defines pins, ports, etc */
#include <util/delay.h>                      /* Functions to waste time */
#include "pinDefines.h"
#include "scale8.h"                               /* 8-bit scale */

static inline void initTimer(void) {
  TCCR0A |= (1 << WGM01);                              /* CTC mode */
  TCCR0A |= (1 << COM0A0);              /* Toggles pin each cycle through */
  TCCR0B |= (1 << CS00) | (1 << CS01);             /* CPU clock / 64 */
}

static inline void playNote(uint8_t wavelength, uint16_t duration) {

  OCR0A = wavelength;                                 /* set pitch */
  SPEAKER_DDR |= (1 << SPEAKER);          /* enable output on speaker */

  while (duration) {                             /* Variable delay */
    _delay_ms(1);
    duration--;
  }
  SPEAKER_DDR &= ~(1 << SPEAKER);           /* turn speaker off */
}

int main(void) {
  // -------- Inits --------- //
  initTimer();
  // ------ Event loop ------ //
  while (1) {
                                               /* Play some notes */
    playNote(C2, 200);
    playNote(E2, 200);
    playNote(G2, 200);
    playNote(C3, 400);

    _delay_ms(1000);
    _delay_ms(1000);
    _delay_ms(1000);

  }                                            /* End event loop */
  return (0);                    /* This line is never reached */
}
```

For making a sound, that's all there is to it—the timer unit takes care of the timing and pin toggling for us. The rest of the function just waits for the specified duration, while the speaker is being driven by the timer, and then turns the speaker off by disabling output on the SPEAKER pin.

Notice what's different here. In Chapter 5, when we wanted to make sound, we toggled the speaker output bit on and off ourselves, and the timing of this toggling was pretty critical. We had to lock up our CPU in cycles of exactly the right length to keep the frequency consistent. Using the hardware timer to do the bit toggling, we only have to worry about waiting for the duration of the note, and that's considerably less critical. Humans hear differences between pitches very well, but you might have trouble discriminating between durations that differ as much as a few tens of milliseconds.

So let's look at the initialization code in initTimer() in the context of our timer hardware flowchart in Figure 9-1, working backward from the desired output. First we can see that we need to configure the waveform generation unit, and it needs to know the desired waveform mode and output mode. Here's a good place to read along with the datasheet. Open up the datasheet to the section on Timer/Counter 0, "Register Description," and follow along. (If you're using a PDF reader that supports indexes, it's a snap to jump to this section.)

For waveform mode, as previously mentioned, you need to think about what you're doing with the timer. In this case, you'll be making a variable frequency output, and CTC mode is perfect. Remember, CTC mode simply counts upward for every tick of its input clock, and then when the value in the counter reaches the value in the compare register (OCR0A), the count is cleared and starts again at zero. In CTC mode, the timer is reset every OCR0A+1 clock ticks (+1 because it starts counting at zero), and so with a fixed-frequency input clock, you can change the output frequency by changing the value in OCR0A.

Unlike the timer example, which used the default Normal Mode, we'll need to set some configuration bits to enable CTC mode. So looking at the table for configuring the Waveform Generation Mode for Timer 0 in the datasheet, Table 14-8 in my copy, we see that we need to set Waveform Generation Mode bit 1 in TCCR0A. TCCR0A | = (1<<WGM01) sets the timer/counter to CTC waveform mode.

Next, we want to set the output mode, so we scroll up a couple pages in the datasheet to Table 14-2, Compare Output Mode, non-PWM. There we find that if we set the COM0A0 bit in TCCR0A, the hardware timer will toggle our OC0A pin for us when the counter reaches our compare match value. Note also that we have to set the DDR as usual to enable the pin for output—this is useful for turning the pin toggling (and our sound) on and off without stopping and starting the counter.

We've set the output mode and the waveform mode. All that's left is to set up the clock prescaler for the counter as we did in "Test Your Reaction Time" on page 180. (Do not forget this step! If you don't set a clock prescaler, the default is for the timer to be stopped.) Because we want audio frequencies in the range of 100–800 Hz, and the CPU clock starts out at one million Hz, we're clearly going to have to divide it down before use.

In Table 9-1, I've worked out some examples of frequencies generated from the internal CPU clock, assuming that your output is a square wave toggled by the timer in CTC mode. (Note that because we're toggling the speaker pin, each audio cycle is actually two trips through the counter, and the highest frequency is 1/2 of what you might expect.)

Table 9-1. Clock prescaler calculations: CTC mode

CPU clock	Prescale	CSx2, CSx1, CSx0 bits	Clock tick time	Highest frequency	Lowest frequency (8-bit timer)	Lowest frequency (16-bit timer)
1 MHz	1	0,0,1	1 microsecond	500 kHz	1.95 kHz (0.5 millisec)	7.6 Hz (0.13 sec)
1 MHz	8	0,1,0	8 microseconds	62.5 kHz	244 Hz (4.1 millisec)	0.96 Hz (1.05 sec)
1 MHz	64	0,1,1	64 microseconds	7.8 kHz	30.5 Hz (32 millisec)	0.12 Hz (8.4 sec)
1 MHz	256	1,0,0	2.56 milliseconds	1.95 kHz	7.6 Hz (130 millisec)	0.03 Hz (33.5 sec)
1 MHz	1024	1,0,1	1.024 milliseconds	488 Hz	1.9 Hz (0.5 sec)	0.007 Hz (134 sec)
8 MHz	1	0,0,1	1/8 microsecond	4 MHz	15.6 kHz (64 microsec)	61 Hz (16 millisec)
8 MHz	8	0,1,0	1 microsecond	500 kHz	1.95 kHz (0.5 millisec)	7.6 Hz (0.13 sec)
8 MHz	64	0,1,1	8 microseconds	62.5 kHz	244 Hz (4.1 millisec)	0.96 Hz (1.05 sec)
8 MHz	256	1,0,0	32 microseconds	15.6 kHz	61 Hz (16 millisec)	0.24 Hz (4.2 sec)
8 MHz	1024	1,0,1	128 microseconds	3.91 kHz	15 Hz (65 millisec)	0.06 Hz (16.8 sec)

Looking over Table 9-1, and sticking to our 1 MHz default clock speed for the moment, we can see that prescale values of 64 or 256 will work for generating our desired 100–800 Hz range. Picking the faster of these two, prescale by 64, gives us a little bit more accuracy in the pitches at the higher-frequency end of the scale, so that's my choice. If we didn't want notes lower than 244 Hz, we would be even better off using the prescale-by-eight option. (And if you *really* care about pitch accuracy, you're better off using 8 MHz, no prescaling, and Timer 1, which has 16-bit resolution. That'll give you most of the range of human hearing with very decent accuracy, although if the music you're playing is bass centric, the divide-by-eight prescaler may be a better choice.)

Before we leave this example, let's recap what's new in this section. When we used the default timer mode, all we needed to set was the clock prescaler. Because we want an adjustable frequency, here we set the timer/counter module for CTC waveform generation mode so that it counts from zero to the value that we've stored in the related Output Compare Register, in our case OCR0A. We generate different audio frequencies by toggling a pin connected to a speaker every time the counter reaches OCR0A and clears back to zero.

To sum up, the new AVR organ works like this:

1. Set the Waveform Generation Mode bits to CTC mode.

2. Set the Compare Output Match Mode bits to toggle the pin with our speaker on it.

3. Set the Clock Select bits to take a prescaled CPU clock as input.

4. Write the value to `OCR0A` that corresponds to the right frequency and then enabling output on the pin in the `DDR`.

Any time that you've got a frequency-generation or variable-timebase task in the future, you can feel free to use this bit of code as a template.

AM Radio

Amplitude-modulated (AM) radio was the first broadcast radio mode to become popular, and is certainly the most accessible for us. A signal is broadcast at a constant radio frequency (the *carrier* frequency); to hear it, you tune your radio to recieve that same frequency. The strength, or amplitude, of this signal is varied over time to mimic the sound wave you'd like to transmit—essentially, the audio sound wave is riding on the carrier wave's amplitude. I plotted out the carrier and signal waves over time in Figure 9-2.

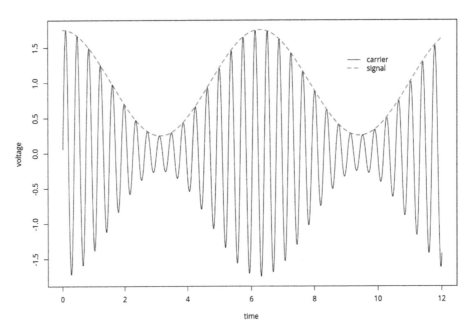

Figure 9-2. *AM modulation*

AM radio allows for a particularly simple receiver. When you tune the radio to the correct frequency, the antenna receives a time-varying voltage signal that looks like the solid line in Figure 9-2--the carrier modulated by the signal. To get rid of the carrier, you simply run the received voltage through a diode, so that you get only the positive voltages. Now you've got a signal that varies from roughly zero to 1.6 V, which you can output directly to a speaker with a capacitor, just as we did in the audio demos.

Indeed, the simplest versions of AM radio receivers are *crystal radios*, which really only have four parts: an inductor and tuning capacitor to select the right carrier frequency, a diode to separate the signal from the carrier, and a high-impedance earpiece that doesn't require amplification (and has the blocking capacitor built in). If you're interested, you can find crystal radio kits that'll allow you to build an unpowered receiver for less than the cost of a nice dinner out. Or, for even less money, you can pick up any cheap powered radio receiver and some batteries.

OK, so you've got an AM radio receiver ready. How do you make the AVR into an AM radio transmitter? The first step is to create the carrier frequency, and for this we're going to use the built-in timer/counter hardware to generate a square wave at just under 1 MHz, right in the middle of the AM radio frequencies.

 1 MHz?

Try as you might, you are not going to find 1 MHz on your AM radio dial. That's because the medium-wave band where AM radio normally lives is usually measured in kiloHertz and runs from around 500 kHz to around 1600 kHz.

Set your radio to 1000 kHz to listen to this AVR project.

Once we've got that set up, we'll modulate the amplitude of the carrier wave by turning on and off the output to the "antenna" pin at our audio frequency—this is the same thing as modulating the carrier with another square wave (at audio frequency). Because both our carrier wave and modulation waves are both square waves, the resulting radio signal will look something like Figure 9-3.

Note that this signal is what's called 100% modulated. When the audio signal is at its maximum, the carrier is fully on, and when it's at its minimum, the carrier is fully off. (Compare with the sine wave in Figure 9-2, which was sketched with 75% modulation.) We'll output this signal directly to an antenna, and send it across the room.

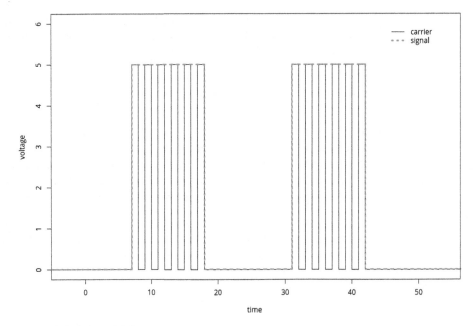

Figure 9-3. *AM modulation: square-wave version*

The Circuit

How much of a radio you'd like to construct is up to you. Because this project is mostly for fun (and to amaze your nongeek friends), I recommend going all-out minimalist. You can broadcast this signal within a room with just a wire hooked up to pin PD5 / 0C0B. A longer wire will broadcast farther and louder, so if you have 10 feet or more of any type of wire just sitting around, that'll do. If you have a wire that's long enough to make a loop around the room you're in, you'll get phenomenal reception when you're inside the loop.

Another super-simplistic broadcast antenna option is just to touch pin PD5 with your finger. You'd be surprised how good an AM antenna your body will make! Just as in with adding more wire, you can increase the signal by holding hands with a friend while you touch the antenna pin.

On the Legality of Broadcasting Low-Power AM Radio

You might be wondering if broadcasting your own bleepy-bloopy AM radio signal is legal. The answer depends on where you live, and what kind of power you're transmitting. In the USA, for instance, it's legal to broadcast on the AM bands if you use less than 100 milliwatts. It's very unlikely that you'll be putting anywhere near that much power with an AVR unless you've got a very long wire, so don't worry about it.

Power limits aside, we're making such a lousy AM transmitter that it's almost surely the case that you won't interfere with anyone else's reception. When I did this experiment, I could only receive the signal within the room I was broadcasting in. And because I was only running the "station" for a few minutes, I didn't worry about it, but I wouldn't leave this circuit powered and running for too long out of consideration for others. If you'd like to be broadcasting for a long period of time, you should probably get yourself an amateur radio license and move over to a frequency that's reserved for radio experimentation—then you can use (almost) all the power you need.

CPU Speed

Thus far, we've been running code that we needed to slow down to a human time-scale, so we were never all that concerned with how fast the AVR was able to run. Generating a radio signal at 1 MHz provides us the opposite problem—we need the chip running as fast as it can—without resorting to an external crystal.

The internal CPU clock in all of the ATmegaxx8 chips (like our 168s) run at 8 MHz, so we should have no real problem making our 1 MHz signal. But all of the ATmegaxx8 chips come from the factory with a 1/8th prescaler between the CPU clock and the CPU. That's right—your chip comes fresh out of the box running at 1/8th of its possible speed. The reason is that, as we've seen here, most of the time the extra CPU speed isn't necessary and just wastes power. But when you need speed, as here, it's nice to be able to put the chip into overdrive.

There are two ways to turn off the prescaler on the ATmega 168 series chips. The first is permanent, and involves changing a so-called *fuse* in the AVR. The "fuses" are actually a bunch of programmable flash memory locations, just like we store our program in, only they directly control the behavior of the chip and are kept separate from the main program space so that we don't mess anything up.

The advantage to setting the CPU speed by setting a fuse is that once you've set the chip up to run at full speed, you won't have to remember to do it again. When you flash in another program, the AVR's CPU clock will still run at 8 MHz as long as you haven't reset the fuse in the meantime. The disadvantage is that sometimes, for power-reduction reasons, you might like to control the CPU speed on the fly from within your code. And this leads us to the second method of modifying the CPU clock prescaler—through software using the *avr/power.h* library functions.

The newer ATmega chips, including all of the xx8 series that we're using here (and most of the new generation of ATtiny chips as well) have the ability to change the CPU prescaler from within software, and to many more possible values than simply 1 MHz or 8 MHz. I'll go over switching the CPU speed both ways, fuses and from software, because you'll still see a lot of code out there where people tell you to set the "fast fuse." But note that you can just as easily add a couple lines to your code and control the speed in firmware.

Setting fuse bits

If you look up in the datasheet, or online, the fuse we're interested in resetting is called the DIV8 clock fuse bit. If you're interested in the nitty-gritty details of setting fuses, and you may need to set some of the AVR's other fuses someday, read "Burning Fuses: Enabling the High-Speed CPU Clock" on page 192. If you'd just like to get the fuse set, and you're using my makefiles, you can simply type make set_fast_fuse.

And I should mention that you don't really need to do any of this for the purposes of the code in this book. I'll be setting the clock to fast-mode in software as needed.

Setting CPU speed in code

The modern way to change CPU speed is through code. Note that this won't work if your chip doesn't support it, and the compiler should throw an error. In that case, you'll need to use the fuse-bit method to enable the chip's full potential. But for the entire ATmegaxx8 line of chips, you'll be able to control the speed dynamically through code. Here's how.

Finally, before we leave the section where I introduced the *avr/power.h* library, I should mention that there are all sorts of other macros available that allow you to shut down parts of the AVR hardware in order to minimize power usage. For instance, if you're not using the analog-to-digital converter (ADC) hardware, you might as well turn it off to save a little power:

```
power_adc_disable();
```

See the avr-libc homepage (*http://www.nongnu.org/avr-libc/user-manual/modules.html*) for the complete listing of all the parts of the chip that you can turn off to save power.

AM Radio: The Code

This code section really gets to show off what timers can do, and we even get to combine a timer with interrupts. Hold on tight!

In the radio code, we'll be using Timer 0 in CTC mode as we did earlier to generate audio in the improved organ code. That is, we have the counter count up to a value

Burning Fuses: Enabling the High-Speed CPU Clock

Believe it or not, most of the AVR chips come from the factory set to divide the system CPU clock by eight. That's right, they're running slowed down 8x by default. Why would Atmel do this to you? Well, for a large majority of projects, the speed just isn't necessary, and you save a lot on power drain by under-clocking. But here, we're pushing the limits of what's reasonable—using the hardware clock to directly produce a radio-frequency signal. We're going to need all the speed we can get.

Changing up the clock speed turns out to be a matter of burning fuses. The AVR chips have two or three bytes of special memory locations that they call *fuse bits*. Because they fundamentally alter the way the chip behaves, the fuse bits are kept separate from the main program flash memory, but otherwise they function similarly. You can read and write them with a flash programmer and AVRDUDE just like programming any other flash memory in the chip.

Because the fuse bits alter the way the chips interact with the world, it pays to be a little cautious with the flash memory because there are a two main dangers.

The worst thing you can do is change the SPI-programming bit, which disables your ability to further program the chip using your flash programmer. Why would you want to do this? Because you might want to use the RESET pin for something other than a dedicated reset line, I guess. But if you do so, the programmer can't signal to the chip that it should enter programming mode without extreme measures. Of course, you *can* unlock the chip again, using a high-voltage parallel programmer circuit, but this is more work than you're going to want to get into just for an extra pin of digital I/O. So until you know better, and are prepared for a high-voltage rescue, don't change the SPIEN-enable fuse bit!

The next worst thing that you can do with fuses is to select the CPU clock to be connected to an external crystal clock source when you haven't got one installed. The CPU will just sit there waiting for an external clock pulse that never comes. Your code won't run, and you won't be able to reprogram the chip (or the fuses) until you provide an external clock source.

This situation really isn't so bad, though. If you've got a crystal lying around, you can just plug in and then reset the fuses to the internal CPU clock as before. And even if you don't have an oscillator crystal on hand, you can set up another AVR chip to create a (say) 1 MHz signal and hook that up to the "dead" AVR's clock input. Then you can reflash the fuse bit to enable the internal clock and you're back in business.

These two warnings aside, what can you do with the fuse bits that's useful? In this chapter, we'll be clearing the default CLKDIV8 fuse that divides the internal CPU clock by eight. Configuring the CPU clock to be driven by an external crystal is also quite common. There are fuse bits that set up how a *bootloader* (program in the chip itself that will flash the chip—often using a serial connection to replace your flash programmer) will operate.

The most convenient way I know to calculate what the AVR fuse bits should be is using an online fuse bit calculator (*http://www.engbedded.com/fusecalc*) program that has all the chip data pre-entered. This fuse calculator even goes so far as to provide you the AVRDUDE flags that you'd need to enter on the command line.

For the ATmega48, 88, 168, and 328 series, the default fuse values are:

- lfuse = 0x62
- hfuse = 0xDF
- efuse = 0x01

and you only need to change the lfuse to 0xE2 to enable high-speed mode. The AVRDUDE flag to set the full-speed clock looks like -U lfuse:w:0xE2:m, which tells AVRDUDE to do a flash memory operation, on lfuse, writing the byte 0xE2 immediately (m, as opposed to reading the data from a file). On a Linux or Mac system, type **man avrdude** or search the Internet for "avrdude man page" to see what all of the command-line arguments do in detail.

Or, using my included makefile, you can simply type **make set_fast_fuse** or **make set_default_fuses** to switch back and forth between full-speed (8 MHz) and low-speed (1 MHz) mode.

Software CPU Clock Speed Control

If you look through the AVR datasheet, in the section on the System Clock and the Register Description, you'll find the "Clock Prescale Register," CLKPR. The lowest four bits of this register (CLKPS3..CLKPS0) allow you to control the clock division by all powers of two from 1 to 256. So even if the main system clock is running at 8 MHz by default, you can run the CPU clock from 8 MHz all the way down to 8/256 MHz, or 31.25 kHz if you'd really like to save power and don't need the extra speed.

Because monkeying around with the CPU speed is not something you'd want to do by accident, there is additionally a "Clock Prescaler Change Enable" bit that has to be set no more than four CPU clock cycles before the prescaler bits are able to be written. Because all of this timing is tight, the avr-libc library provides functions that make it trivial to change the speed. The CPU prescaler macro functions are included in the *avr/power.h* library. The advantage of setting them through the prebuilt libraries is that you don't have to worry about any of the timing details and that nicely named convenience macros are defined for all of the speed grades.

So to set the chip to run at 8 MHz, full speed, you only need to add the following two lines to your code:

```
#include <avr/power.h>
/* and then in the main() function... */
clock_prescale_set(clock_div_1);
```

Or if you'd like to run the chip at 1/2 MHz to save power:

```
clock_prescale_set(clock_div_16);
```

Notice here that setting the clock speed in software essentially ignores the fuse setting. That is, if you have the fuse set to run the chip at 1 MHz (the default), you can either speed it up or slow it down from software.

You can think of the fuse setting as a default speed that the software setting is able to override.

If you set the CPU speed too slow, you should be warned that your flash programmer may be trying to talk too fast for your chip. If this is the case—you've slowed the chip way down and you find that your programmer no longer works—you'll need to slow the programmer down to match. In AVRDUDE, you use the -B flag to reset the bit-clock to a larger (slower) value. If you're running the chip particularly slowly, you may need to add as much as -B 200 to program the chip if you've got it set to clock_div_256.

Also note that everything runs slower (or faster) if you're changing the CPU speed on the fly from within your code. Functions like _delay_ms(100) may not take as much time as you'd expect, and none of the serial communication routines will work either. These functions use the #define F_CPU macro to figure out how fast they have to run. If you're changing the CPU speed in your code on the fly, delays and serial routines won't work unless the currently set speed matches the F_CPU definition in the makefile (or in your code, if you've decided to define it there instead).

But for everything we'll do in this book, we set the CPU speed once in the init section and leave it alone. The corresponding makefile should have the matching F_CPU definition as well, so you won't need to worry about that. It's only if you're mixing and matching that you'll need to think about the CPU speed. If you need to use the serial port, for instance, at a CPU speed other than that defined in F_CPU, you'll need to redo the device initialization stuff to match the new CPU speed. (Or just avoid switching CPU speeds on the fly entirely.)

that determines its frequency, and then clear the counter and start over at zero. Every time it resets, it will toggle a pin. Only this time, it's toggling the pin at roughly 1 MHz and emitting radio waves rather than audio. This is the carrier frequency.

To modulate the carrier, we're going to use another timer, Timer 1. Timer 1 is also run in CTC mode to generate variable frequencies. Only instead of toggling a pin directly, it calls an interrupt service routine every time it resets. Inside the ISR, we simply turn on and off the carrier signal to modulate it, generating the audio on top.

All that's left to do is set the pitch in Timer 1's OCR1A, and let it run for a given amount of time to sound the note. Let's see how it goes in detail in Example 9-4.

Example 9-4. amRadio.c listing

```c
/*
Plays a simple tune, broadcasts it in the AM radio band.
*/

// ------- Preamble -------- //
#include <avr/io.h>                      /* Defines pins, ports, etc */
#include <util/delay.h>                   /* Functions to waste time */
#include <avr/power.h>
#include <avr/interrupt.h>
#include "pinDefines.h"
#include "scale16.h"

#define COUNTER_VALUE   3                /* determines carrier frequency */

// From f = f_cpu / ( 2* N* (1 + OCRnx) )
// Good values for the AM band from 2 to 6: pick one that's clear
// Divide by two b/c we're toggling on or off each loop;
//   a full cycle of the carrier takes two loops.
// 8Mhz / (2 * 1 * (1+2)) = 1333 kHz
// 8Mhz / (2 * 1 * (1+3)) = 1000 kHz
// 8Mhz / (2 * 1 * (1+4)) = 800 kHz
// 8Mhz / (2 * 1 * (1+5)) = 670 kHz
// 8Mhz / (2 * 1 * (1+6)) = 570 kHz
// 8Mhz / (2 * 1 * (1+7)) = 500 kHz

static inline void initTimer0(void) {
  TCCR0A |= (1 << WGM01);                          /* CTC mode */
  TCCR0A |= (1 << COM0B0);          /* Toggles pin each time through */
  TCCR0B |= (1 << CS00);           /* Clock at CPU frequency, ~8MHz */
  OCR0A = COUNTER_VALUE;                    /* carrier frequency */
}

static inline void initTimer1(void) {
  TCCR1B |= (1 << WGM12);                          /* CTC mode */
  TCCR1B |= (1 << CS11);          /* Clock at CPU/8 frequency, ~1MHz */
  TIMSK1 |= (1 << OCIE1A);         /* enable output compare interrupt */
}

ISR(TIMER1_COMPA_vect) {                 /* ISR for audio-rate Timer 1 */
  ANTENNA_DDR ^= (1 << ANTENNA);         /* toggle carrier on and off */
}

static inline void transmitBeep(uint16_t pitch, uint16_t duration) {
  OCR1A = pitch;                           /* set pitch for timer1 */
```

```
  sei();                                         /* turn on interrupts */
  do {
    _delay_ms(1);                                /* delay for pitch cycles */
    duration--;
  } while (duration > 0);
  cli();                          /* and disable ISR so that it stops toggling */
  ANTENNA_DDR |= (1 << ANTENNA);                 /* back on full carrier */
}

int main(void) {
  // -------- Inits --------- //

  clock_prescale_set(clock_div_1);               /* CPU clock 8 MHz */
  initTimer0();
  initTimer1();

  // ------ Event loop ------ //
  while (1) {

    transmitBeep(E3, 200);
    _delay_ms(100);
    transmitBeep(E3, 200);
    _delay_ms(200);
    transmitBeep(E3, 200);
    _delay_ms(200);
    transmitBeep(C3, 200);
    transmitBeep(E3, 200);
    _delay_ms(200);
    transmitBeep(G3, 400);
    _delay_ms(500);
    transmitBeep(G2, 400);

    _delay_ms(2500);

  }                                              /* End event loop */
  return (0);                       /* This line is never reached */
}
```

Skipping straight down to the main() function, you can see that it plays a bunch of beeps overlaid on our AM carrier frequency, to play a simple song. All of the work of generating the radio and audio tones are done by timers. Let's take a look at them.

initTimer0() is actually very very simple. We want a variable frequency (so that we can tune to different stations), so we set the timer in CTC mode. We want the hardware to toggle a pin, so we set the COM0B0 flag. Notice that we haven't set the pin's DDR to output yet—we'll get nothing out until we do. The initialization function then sets the clock directly to the CPU clock, with "/1" prescaling, because we need all the speed we can get. Finally, we tune our broadcast station (very roughly) by selecting the output-compare value that we'll be counting up to. As noted in the comments, this gives us five frequencies that we can tune to in the AM band. You can transmit on other frequencies of course, but your radio may not be designed to pick them up.

initTimer1() has a little more detail to it. Again, we select CTC mode. But notice that the Waveform Generation Mode bits we need to set are different. Timer 1, a 16-bit timer, has many more options than the 8-bit equivalents, and it has four WGM bits that you can set instead of only three. Table 16-4 in the datasheet goes through all of them. I just looked down until I found the CTC mode with a variable TOP value and used that. In order to get the audio pitches in the right range for the values I'd computed, I ended up dividing the CPU clock by eight for Timer 1 and setting the CS11 bit to do it.

Finally, there is one new bit in configuring this timer that we haven't seen before. The Timer Interrupt Mask (TIMSK) registers allow us to configure all of the different ways to trigger interrupts from the timer/counter. The three options include triggering when the counter hits compare values A or B, or alternatively when the counter overflows.

Because we're running the timer in CTC mode, it will essentially never overflow. Remember that when the timer hits a compare value, it is reset, right? So unless that compare value is equal to the maximum value (65,535 for the 16-bit timer), it will never overflow. Instead, the overflow interrupts are more useful when the timer is used in PWM mode, which we'll discuss in Chapter 10.

Anyway, because we wanted to be able to control the pitch of the audio by modifying the compare-and-reset value OCR1A, we enable the interrupt by setting the bit for Output Compare Interrupt Enable 1A (OCIE1A).

The ISR for Timer 1's compare interrupt A, called TIMER1_COMPA_vect, does our 100% modulation of the carrier for us. That is to say, it toggles the antenna output on and off. And that's it. A short and sweet interrupt service routine!

Now the two timers are configured and doing their things, right? Timer 0 is looping through very quickly from zero to three, toggling a pin every time it resets. Timer 1 is looping through at audio rates, triggering an ISR every time it resets, right? Well not quite yet. We haven't enabled the global interrupt bit yet.

That's where the function transmitBeep() comes in. This function sets the pitch in the OCR1A register and then enables interrupts. *Now* the ISR toggles the antenna on and off, creating the audio signal over our carrier. There's a simple _de lay_ms() loop to allow for the duration of the note, and then interrupts are turned off again and the carrier is returned to being full on.

If you're not familiar with radio broadcasting, it might seem strange to leave the carrier on full and claim that it's not making any noise. But look back at the diagrams of how amplitude modulation works. It's the *change* in the carrier wave—the modulation—that carries the pitch. If you just leave the carrier on full, without modulating its volume, that corresponds to a flat line in its outer volume envelope, and a flat line makes no noise. It's only when we start wiggling the volume envelope at a particular frequency (by reenabling the ISR) that we get a pitch back out.

And that's it, really. Our AM radio is a tiny bit of a hardware hack (if you consider hooking up a long wire to an AVR pin as a hardware hack) and the rest is done in software. For the audio, we reuse the concept for generating audio from our improved organ program, only instead we turn on and off the transmitter through an ISR instead of directly driving a speaker. The transmitter is just another CTC-timer generating a really high-frequency square wave toggling our antenna pin. It's not the cleanest radio station in the world, and certainly not professional, but you can play yourself bleepy music across the room.

Summary

In this chapter, we started in on our first of a two-part series on the timer/counter hardware. We used Normal mode to time short-duration events in the reaction timer. Then, we revisited our original organ program, offloading the job of toggling the speaker pin to a variable-frequency CTC-mode timer/counter with the output pins enabled.

Then finally, we shifted the timer into high gear, enabling the AVR's full-speed mode through the *power.h* libraries, and used two timers to make a fully modulated AM radio signal. One timer ran at radio frequencies to create the carrier that you tune your radio to, and the other employed an ISR to turn this carrier on and off at given frequencies to make music.

When configuring timer/counters, so far, the important points to remember are:

- Set the waveform mode to either Normal mode (the default) or to CTC mode by setting the appropriate waveform mode bits.
- Select the clock prescaler speed. You *must* set these bits, because the default value leaves the timer/counter prescaler unconnected, and thus not running.
- Optionally select an output mode if you'd like to set, clear, or toggle output pins from your timer/counter. (And don't forget to set the corresponding DDR bits.)
- If, instead of toggling pins directly, you'd like to have some code executed, you can enable an interrupt to trigger on compare match. (And don't forget to enable interrupts globally with sei().)

In Chapter 10 we'll see how to create "analog" voltage output by using pulse-width modulation. The PWM mode of timer/counter modules will come in handy there. We'll also use timers to control motors in Chapter 11, Chapter 14, and Chapter 15.

We'll use timers plus interrupts again and again, both for making real-time clocks and in conjunction with PWM to make a direct-digital audio synthesizer and even (in Chapter 18) to play back your own voice samples.

In short, this chapter on timers and the preceding chapter on interrupts are the foundation for all of the advanced techniques in the rest of this book. So if it feels like a lot to take in all at once, don't worry. You'll get more examples of using both coming right up!

Pulse-Width Modulation | 10

Fading LEDs and "Analog" Output

So far, everything's been either on or off in our AVR world—strictly digital. LEDs have been either on or off. Speaker cones have been either pulled fully back or pushed fully forward. Electrons have been pushed this way or that through antennas without particular finesse. On and off is fun, but sometimes you want an LED to fade instead of blink, or a motor to run at half speed instead of being always on or off. Or you'd like to make some audio waveforms other than just the square wave, and you'd like them to have volume control.

To do that, we'll need to figure out a way to make intermediate voltages from the AVR's logical high and low, and one of the most common ways of doing so is *pulse-width modulation* (PWM). In brief, PWM toggles the logic output on and off very fast, so quickly that whatever is attached to the output can't react fully. The result is that the output sees a voltage that is proportional to the average percent of the time that the AVR spends with its output on. (If that sounds strange right now, it'll seem perfectly normal by the end of this chapter.)

In Chapter 13, we'll use PWM to play back audio synthesizer waveforms. In Chapter 14 and Chapter 15, we'll use PWM to drive motors at different speeds and even backward. Finally, in Chapter 18, timer/counter PWM will help us build a talking voltmeter that reads out voltages to you *in your own voice*. In sum, we'll be using PWM in a lot of the upcoming projects, so please excuse me for this chapter if we simply pulse some LEDs.

PWM is such a common method of creating analog voltages from digital devices that almost all microcontrollers, including the AVR, have dedicated internal peripheral hardware that takes care of this high-speed bit toggling for you, and I recommend using this feature whenever you can. In this chapter, we'll also step through a completely manual PWM routine that's useful for helping build up your intuition about what's going on, and I've added in another method of using the timer/counter peripheral and its interrupts to output PWM waveforms on any pin that's capable of output. So let's get down to the business at hand—flipping bits, fast.

What You Need

In addition to the basic kit, you will need:

- LEDs and current-limiting resistors hooked up as in previous chapters.

- A USB-Serial adapter.

Bright and Dim LEDs: PWM

PWM is perhaps the easiest technique for us to implement that'll give us a partly-on, analog effect. As mentioned earlier, we'll need to switch a digital output high and low fast enough that whatever device we're driving can't react to the individual on-off pulses, but instead only to the *average value*. We then regularly repeat these pulses and control the average value by varying the percentage of the time in a cycle that the output is held high. The resulting voltages are plotted in Figure 10-1.

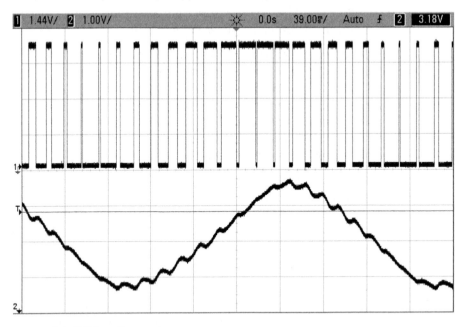

Figure 10-1. *PWM oscilloscope traces*

In Figure 10-1, the top line is the direct-from-the-AVR PWM trace. You can see how the percentage of time that the AVR output is high changes from low to high, and back down to low again. The lower line is the result of passing the PWM signal through a resistor-capacitor filter, like the one I will suggest for use with an amplifier in Chapter 13. This filter provides the slowed response that turns the PWM signal into an averaged-out analog voltage—when the PWM signal spends more of its time at 5 V, the analog output is higher, and vice versa. While the PWM signal is truly digital—it's either high or low—the resulting (filtered) average voltage can take on values in between.

There are two parameters that we need to specify in order to use PWM. This percentage of the cycle time that is spent in the on state is called the *duty cycle*, and the frequency with which we go through a single cycle is usually called PWM frequency. The duty cycle will usually be our control parameter. That is, we vary the duty cycle frequently, possibly even continually, in order to control the "analog" average voltage, just as in Figure 10-1.

For most applications, we'll choose the PWM frequency just once, at the beginning. As I hinted earlier, what's crucial with the PWM frequency is that it's fast enough that whatever system we are controlling doesn't have time to react to each pulse, but rather only the average value. How fast is fast enough? That depends on the application and our tolerance for *ripple*, or the little remaining bits of the PWM pulse train that inevitably sneak through. Because I chose the PWM frequency to be so close to the output waveform's frequency in Figure 10-1, you can see quite a bit of ripple in the output. If I used a much higher PWM frequency, the ripple would be a lot smaller (but it wouldn't make as good an example).

How high your PWM frequency needs to be for a given amount of ripple depends on how slowly your driven device or filter responds to changes in input. For instance, motors are often only able to adjust their speed relatively slowly due to inertia of the arm or wheel or robot or train that they're driving. For most motors, PWM frequencies as low as the 50–500 Hz range are probably optimal. Or they would be, except that they're right in the middle of the range of human hearing, and people like their motors not to sing.

Many modern motor-control circuits use PWM frequencies slightly above 20 kHz (roughly the top frequency of human hearing) to save us the noise of squealing motor windings whenever they can. On the other hand, there are exceptions. Most subway cars have quite audible PWM frequencies, and you can listen to the motors wind up and down—the engineers seem to have been more concerned with driving the train efficiently than the little bit of motor whine.

Creating accurate analog audio for humans, as we will do in Chapter 13, requires even higher PWM frequencies on the order of two times the highest desired frequency, so you often see PWM frequencies higher than 40 kHz. (In our example, for 8-bit audio with the built-in 8 MHz CPU clock, we're limited to 32.5 kHz. Good enough.)

The human eye, unlike the ear, falls in the slow response category. We saw this in the POV toy example, where we used pulses on the order of 2 milliseconds (500 Hz). It turns out that we don't need a frequency anywhere near this high to avoid flickering—for me a period of around 18 milliseconds (just under 60 Hz) doesn't seem to flicker. Remember that here I'm talking about the response time of the human eye, not the LEDs—those can pulse on and off in the megahertz range but we wouldn't notice it. Here, the human optical system is the slowly adjusting mechanism that we're using to average out the pulses.

Brute-Force PWM Demo

But don't take my word for it. Example 10-1 is a fully adjustable, manual PWM routine to play around with. Flash in the program *pwm.c* and experiment with where your own flicker-fusion frequency lies by changing the delay time defined at the top. Then, let's look at the event loop and see how it works.

Example 10-1. pwm.c listing

```
                                        /* Quick and dirty PWM Demo */


// ------- Preamble -------- //
#include <avr/io.h>                     /* Defines pins, ports, etc */
#include <util/delay.h>                 /* Functions to waste time */
#include "pinDefines.h"

#define LED_DELAY  20                            /* microseconds */

void pwmAllPins(uint8_t brightness) {
  uint8_t i;
  LED_PORT = 0xff;                                /* turn on */
  for (i = 0; i < 255; i++) {
    if (i >= brightness) {          /* once it's been on long enough */
      LED_PORT = 0;                                /* turn off */
    }
    _delay_us(LED_DELAY);
  }
}

int main(void) {

  uint8_t brightness = 0;
  int8_t direction = 1;

  // -------- Inits --------- //

  // Init all LEDs
  LED_DDR = 0xff;
  // ------ Event loop ------ //
  while (1) {
    // Brighten and dim
```

```
  if (brightness == 0) {
    direction = 1;
  }
  if (brightness == 255) {
    direction = -1;
  }
  brightness += direction;
  pwmAllPins(brightness);


}                                                    /* End event loop */
  return (0);                              /* This line is never reached */
}
```

This code is split up into two distinct parts. The function pwmAllPins() takes care of implementing PWM. The remaining code in the event loop increases and decreases a brightness variable. Calling pwmAllPins() with the increasing and decreasing brightness makes the LEDs pulse in and out.

In pwmAllPins(), we have a loop over i, which takes exactly 255 steps each time. Inside the i loop, we compare a variable brightness to i and turn on the LEDs if i is smaller. This has the effect of turning on the LEDs at the beginning of each set of 256 and then turning them off as soon as i reaches the value brightness, so for higher values of brightness the LEDs stay on for a greater percentage of the 256 steps. PWM! (But notice that we've locked up the entire CPU just brightening and dimming.)

Now, you can modify the per-step delay time and figure out where you just start to notice the flickering. (Or better still, hook up a potentiometer and adjust the delay time by turning the knob.) You'll soon find your personal flicker-fusion rate. Notice when you move your head that you'll see the persistence-of-vision trailer effects as well.

When you're playing around with the delay, remember that you're taking 256 steps per cycle, so if you delay 20 microseconds per step, that's 5,120 microseconds, or 5.12 milliseconds per cycle. Because there are 1,000 milliseconds in a second, this gives a PWM frequency of 1,000 / 5.12, or around around 195 Hz.

The main() portion of the code sets up a direction variable (as a signed integer) that lets us add to or subtract from the current brightness. Finally, when the brightness hits either limit, direction reverses sign. The result is a brighter-and-dimmer pulsing fade.

When you're playing with the LED demo, you may also notice that the human eye doesn't respond to equal changes in brightness equally. In our simple fade, it looks like the LEDs go through the dark portion of their fade-in and fade-out faster than the light part, even though we know that the duty cycle is changing by +/– 1 delay period each step through the for loop.

The human eye is much better at telling the difference between low levels of light than higher ones. That is, the human eye's response to light is nonlinear. Many LEDs are driven in PWM mode to exploit this fact—if you notice LED traffic lights flickering when you turn your head past them suddenly, that's PWM. The reason that PWM-driven LEDs are so prevalent is that your eyes can't really tell the difference between 90% and 100% duty cycles, so the city can run the traffic lights at 90% and pocket the 10% energy savings.

Timers PWM Demo

If you don't believe me about your eye's nonlinear response to brightness, let's do the experiment. Example 10-2, *pwmTimer.c*, uses the serial port to take in characters you type and convert them to numeric PWM values. And along the way, you'll learn about the best way to implement PWM—letting the hardware take care of it.

Flash in the firmware and then type in 10, 20, and 30 in a random order and see if you can tell which is the brightest. Now type in 210, 220, and 230 and repeat. Much easier to tell the dimmer ones apart, right? Your eye's response to brightness is much closer to reacting to the percent changes in brightness than to the absolute changes. Just something to think about when you're trying to make LED art—equally spaced PWM values won't appear evenly spaced in brightness.

You might be wondering why we're only lighting up three LEDs using the hardware PWM, and the sad reason is that the AVR's dedicated PWM pins are limited to two per timer, for a total of six: four pins at an 8-bit PWM depth, and two at 16 bits. So the software lights up three LEDs in a row with the PWM values you've typed, shifting the new value in, the current values over, and the oldest value out. Now let's see how it's done in Example 10-2.

*Example 10-2. **pwmTimers.c** Listing*

```
                    /* PWM Demo with serial control over three LEDs */

// ------- Preamble -------- //
#include <avr/io.h>                    /* Defines pins, ports, etc */
#include <util/delay.h>                /* Functions to waste time */
#include "pinDefines.h"
#include "USART.h"

static inline void initTimers(void) {
  // Timer 1 A,B
  TCCR1A |= (1 << WGM10);              /* Fast PWM mode, 8-bit */
  TCCR1B |= (1 << WGM12);              /* Fast PWM mode, pt.2 */
  TCCR1B |= (1 << CS11);              /* PWM Freq = F_CPU/8/256 */
  TCCR1A |= (1 << COM1A1);            /* PWM output on OCR1A */
```

```
    TCCR1A |= (1 << COM1B1);                        /* PWM output on OCR1B */

    // Timer 2
    TCCR2A |= (1 << WGM20);                            /* Fast PWM mode */
    TCCR2A |= (1 << WGM21);                         /* Fast PWM mode, pt.2 */
    TCCR2B |= (1 << CS21);                       /* PWM Freq = F_CPU/8/256 */
    TCCR2A |= (1 << COM2A1);                        /* PWM output on OCR2A */
}

int main(void) {

    uint8_t brightness;

    // -------- Inits --------- //

    initTimers();
    initUSART();
    printString("-- LED PWM Demo --\r\n");

                     /* enable output on LED pins, triggered by PWM hardware */
    LED_DDR |= (1 << LED1);
    LED_DDR |= (1 << LED2);
    LED_DDR |= (1 << LED3);

    // ------- Event loop ------ //
    while (1) {

        printString("\r\nEnter (0-255) for PWM duty cycle: ");
        brightness = getNumber();
        OCR2A = OCR1B;
        OCR1B = OCR1A;
        OCR1A = brightness;

    }                                                  /* End event loop */
    return (0);                             /* This line is never reached */
}
```

As with the rest of the timer/counter-based code demos so far, the event loop is quite sparse. It gets a value from the serial port and then shifts the values up a chain, corresponding to the output compare registers of LED1, LED2, and LED3. Note how we don't need to use any more variables to store the "previous" values that we received over the serial line—they're stored in the OCRnx registers just as if they were normal variables.

Writing those three variables takes just a couple microseconds even at 1 MHz. The rest of the CPU time is spent waiting for and processing our serial input. Note how we couldn't do this at all with the software-based PWM approach in *pwm.c*; if we waited for serial input, the LEDs would stop blinking. Even if we just checked if the serial port had new data, it would throw off our PWM timings. Here, all our code has to do to keep the LEDs blinking at their appropriate duty cycle is write values to the appropriate OCRnx registers. The hardware takes care of the rest—counting, comparing, turning on and off pins. In this example, that leaves us free to use the CPU to talk to us over the serial port.

Initializing Timers for PWM Mode

Configuring PWM by timer is a lot like using the hardware timer/counter in Chapter 9 except that we're selecting a PWM waveform generation mode instead of Normal or CTC modes.

Turn your attention to the initTimers() function, and you'll see something similar to what we did in Chapter 9. We set up the timers' waveform modes, set the clock input prescaler, and then set the compare output bits to enable direct output on the OCR1A, OCR1B, and OCR2A pins. Voila.

 Fast PWM Mode

Fast PWM mode is probably the most-used PWM mode, as well as the most straightforward. The counter loops around from zero to its maximum value (255 or 65,535 or another value stored in the OCRxA register, depending on the particular timer and mode) continuously at the speed defined by the prescaler. Along the way, the counter is compared with the contents of the Output Compare (OCRnx) registers. When a match happens, the PWM output pins can be set or cleared and interrupts can be fired.

*Fast PWM mode is fundamentally a hardware version of the **pwm.c** demo code, which continuously looped around from 0 to 255 and compared the counter value to a duty cycle variable. But using the hardware PWM mode can be much faster than doing the same thing in code and uses no CPU cycles.*

Calculating the PWM frequency for fast PWM mode is easy. Take the CPU clock frequency, divide it by a prescaler value if applicable, and then divide by the number of steps per cycle. For example, I've set the prescaler at 8, using an 8-bit timer with 256 steps, and a 1 MHz CPU clock; therefore, the fast PWM frequency is 1,000,000 Hz / 8 / 256 = 488 Hz.

Have a look through the datasheet and make sure you understand at least where to find the bits that are being set in the initialization routine. You'll notice that Timer 1 is more complicated because it's a 16-bit timer—the AVR gives us modes to operate it in 8-bit, 10-bit, or full-resolution modes. We'll use its full resolution later on to drive servo motors in Chapter 11, but for now, notice that we have it set up in an 8-bit PWM mode that uses 255 as its maximum value so that it's consistent with the other LED on Timer 2.

Setting the compare output mode with the COM bits is also a little bit different here than in the CTC case. For one thing, there are different tables for what the bits mean in the CTC, fast PWM and phase-correct PWM cases, so make sure you're looking at the right COM tables. In our case, setting COM1A1, COM1B1, and COM2A1 correspond to the "noninverting" mode—that is, the PWM turns the pin on when it overflows from 255 to 0, and turns it off when it reaches the compare value. This is just what we did in the brute-force PWM example that lead this chapter, and results in higher PWM values corresponding to higher duty cycles and thus brighter LEDs.

Setting up the clock speed prescaler is just the same as it was in the CTC examples, so there's not much that's interesting here. When we configured the prescaler in CTC mode, we were interested in the frequency for its own sake, but here it's not super critical. With the PWM frequency, it's only important that the PWM cycles are fast enough that our system responds to the average value. Play around with the different prescaler settings to get a feel for what range of frequencies are good for driving PWM'ed LEDs. Or take an engineering approach and see "Fast PWM Mode" on page 208 on how to calculate the PWM frequency.

Before we leave the initialization section, note that we enable output for the three LEDs using the DDR registers. By now you might have noticed that even if you hit Return or type "0," the dimmest the LEDs go is still not off. Why is that? When you set the OCR to zero, it doesn't actually turn the pins off. Instead, the pins get turned on as soon as the hardware counter flips over from 255 to zero, and then turned off after the compare match unit compares a zero. That is, each pin is on for 1/256th (0.4%) of the time and this produces visible brightness on the LED.

So what can you do if you want the LED off, like really off-off? The easiest way is to disconnect the pin by putting it in input mode by clearing its corresponding bit in the bank's DDR register. In some cases, you'll want to send an actual ground-voltage, low signal; for instance, if you want to turn off a FET that's attached to the pin. To get a constant logic low voltage, you need to clear the COM bit in the timer's configuration register to decouple the pin from the timer, and make sure the DDR is set for output and the PORT bit is clear as you normally would.

The good news here is that there's no such precaution necessary for the case when you want the LED always on. Setting the OCR to 255 *does* result in output that's always high. It's only when you want the pin entirely off that you need to override the hardware PWM.

And with this example under your belt, you should be able to set up and use hardware PWM anywhere in your code. Notice how little your main code actually needs to do to set or change the PWM average-value output once it's configured. All that's left for your code is to write a value to the output-compare register, and the hardware takes care of the rest. This makes using PWM conceptually very simple: if you want to output a voltage halfway between 5 V and 0 V, write OCR1A = 127 and you're done. It's like you were setting the output's "analog" voltage directly from your code.

"Analog" Output on the Arduino

If you've used the Arduino platform, you're probably wondering why we don't just use the Analog Out pins. Here's the deal—there *are* no Analog Out pins. By opening this book, you've taken the Red Pill, and you're going to find out how deep this rabbit hole goes, right? The Arduino folks have been lying to you! It's all a giant conspiracy to keep you from learning about PWM. Now you know the truth!

OK, more seriously, the Arduino platform aims to abstract away a lot of the nitty-gritty details, and so they don't bother you with the difference between "analog" and PWM output, or require you to know which pins are connected to which timers. Have a look at the analogWrite() function in the Arduino source code file *wiring_analog.c* in the *arduino-1.0/hardware/arduino/cores/arduino* directory. (Change to match your version number.) You'll see that we're all doing the same thing after all.

analogWrite() first checks to see if the value you're writing is 0 or 255, always off or always on. Then it figures out which timer (digitalPinToTimer(pin)) you need to configure for the pin you specified, and then sets the relevant COM bits and finally the OCR register value. Just like we've been doing here! (The Arduino library version sets the COM bits every time you change the duty cycle, which is redundant but makes sure that it's set.)

The price paid for the Arduino pin/timer abstraction is that what we do in one or two lines of code, and two or three cycles of CPU time, the Arduino does in 50+ clock cycles. It tests if you want the pin fully on or off, and it uses a whole switch() expression and memory lookup to figure out which timer registers to write to—and all of this just so that you don't have to look up the pin in the datasheet.

If you're calling analogWrite() infrequently in your code, this will probably work OK, and you'll never notice the speed penalty. If you're setting the OCR bits frequently, as we will be in Chapter 13, this extra code overhead means the difference between the possible and impossible. If you're coming from the Arduino world, you'll probably be annoyed by how much detail about the chip you're required to learn, but once you learn how to actually use the hardware peripherals as they're intended, you'll be surprised by how much more is possible. And once you know how the internal peripherals work, it's not much harder to configure them yourself.

PWM on Any Pin

So far we've seen two ways to implement PWM in our AVR code. One method implements PWM entirely in code by looping and directly setting the pins on and off using the CPU. The "normal" hardware PWM method works significantly faster, but only on six designated pins, two for each timer.

If we want to implement PWM on an arbitrary pin, there *is* a trick, but it's a little bit of hack. Instead of using the built-in pin-toggling function of the timer/counter, we'll instead use the interrupts to trigger our own code, and turn on and off pins from within ISRs. We don't have to tie up the CPU with counting and waiting, as we did in the brute-force PWM example. Rather, we can use a timer/counter in Normal mode to do the counting for us.

Then we trigger interrupts at the beginning of the cycle to turn the PWM pins on and use the output-compare values to trigger another interrupt to turn the pins back off. So this method is a little bit like a hybrid of the brute force and fully hardware PWM methods: the counter and ISRs make it take less than the full CPU time just for the PWM, but because the ISRs take *some* CPU time, it's not as fast or rock solid as fully hardware PWM.

Because we're using ISRs to turn on and off the pins in question, we have to be a little bit careful that the PWM values are long enough that the ISRs have time to execute. Imagine that we set the PWM duty cycle to some small number like 6, and the counter's CPU clock divider to its fastest mode. We then only have six CPU cycles to execute the ISR that turns the LED on at the beginning of the cycle, and this won't work—most ISRs take at least 10 cycles just in program overhead. (We can further hack around this limitation, but at some point it's not worth it.)

So the trick to making this any-pin PWM work is making sure that we've set up the clock prescaler to at least divide by 64. Then we'll have plenty of time for our interrupts, and all is well.

PWM on Any Pin Demo

To recap, the PWM-on-any-pin code works by setting up a timer/counter in Normal mode—counting up from 0 to 255 continuously—and interrupts are set to trigger off the timer. First, the overflow interrupt triggers when the timer rolls over back to 0. In this ISR, we turn the pins on. An output-compare ISR then turns the pin back off once the counter reaches the values stored in the output-compare register. That way, a larger value in the OCR registers mean that the pin is on for more of the cycle. PWM! See Example 10-3 for the code listing.

Example 10-3. pwmOnAnyPin.c listing

```c
// Quick and dirty demo of how to get PWM on any pin with interrupts
// ------- Preamble -------- //
#include <avr/io.h>
#include <util/delay.h>
#include <avr/interrupt.h>
#include "pinDefines.h"

#define DELAY 3

volatile uint8_t brightnessA;
volatile uint8_t brightnessB;

// -------- Functions --------- //
static inline void initTimer0(void) {
                           /* must be /64 or more for ISR timing */
  TCCR0B |= (1 << CS01) | (1 << CS00);
                              /* both output compare interrupts */
  TIMSK0 |= ((1 << OCIE0A) | (1 << OCIE1B));
  TIMSK0 |= (1 << TOIE0);          /* overflow interrupt enable */
  sei();
}
```

```
ISR(TIMER0_OVF_vect) {
  LED_PORT = 0xff;
  OCR0A = brightnessA;
  OCR0B = brightnessB;
}
ISR(TIMER0_COMPA_vect) {
  LED_PORT &= 0b11110000;                     /* turn off low four LEDs */
}
ISR(TIMER0_COMPB_vect) {
  LED_PORT &= 0b00001111;                     /* turn off high four LEDs */
}

int main(void) {
  // -------- Inits --------- //

  uint8_t i;
  LED_DDR = 0xff;
  initTimer0();

  // ------- Event loop ------ //
  while (1) {

    for (i = 0; i < 255; i++) {
      _delay_ms(DELAY);
      brightnessA = i;
      brightnessB = 255 - i;
    }

    for (i = 254; i > 0; i--) {
      _delay_ms(DELAY);
      brightnessA = i;
      brightnessB = 255 - i;
    }

  }                                       /* End event loop */
  return (0);                      /* This line is never reached */
}
```

There are also a couple of details to clean up. First, notice that there are two global variables defined, brightnessA and brightnessB, that will be used to load up the output-compare registers at the beginning of every cycle. Why not write to OCR0A and OCR0B directly? Depending on the timing of exactly when the variable is written and its value, the PWM can glitch for one cycle. A way around that is to always set the output-compare registers at a predictable point in the cycle—inside the overflow ISR. These two global variables can be set by our code in main() whenever, but they're only loaded into the OCR0 registers from inside the overflow ISR. It's a simple buffer.

Triggering three different interrupts from one timing source is surprisingly easy. In the initTimer0 code, we can see that it basically amounts to setting three different bits in the TIMSK (timer interrupt mask) register. As mentioned previously, the clock source for the timer has to be significantly slower than the CPU clock to allow the ISRs time to run, so I've use a divide-by-64 clock setting. Finally, as with all situations when you're using an interrupt, don't forget to enable the global interrupt bit using the sei() function.

The rest of the code is straightforward. The ISRs should be kept as short as possible because they're being called quite frequently. Here, the compare interrupts have only one task. Finally, the main() function demonstrates how to use the any-pin PWM functionality. We simply set the global variable to the desired level whenever it suits us, and the timer and interrupts take care of the rest.

Closing: Alternatives to PWM and a Timer Checklist

In this chapter, I've introduced you to three different methods of producing "analog" output by toggling a digital pin quickly. First, we coded everything up from scratch, using the full CPU time just to create PWM output. Next, we handed all of the duties off to the timer/counter PWM. This is by far the most common and powerful method of creating PWM output, but it's limited to two designated hardware-PWM pins per timer. Bear these restrictions in mind when you're laying out your own circuits, and the hardware PWM facilities will serve you well.

Finally, as a bit of a hack, I demonstrated a method to get PWM output on any pin by using a timer/counter and its automatically triggered interrupts to toggle any pin or pins for you. The costs here are a little more CPU overhead than the direct hardware method, reduced maximum speed due to the time needed to run the ISRs, and the need to use a couple of global variables to avoid glitches when setting up the output compare registers. On the other hand, when you *really* need PWM on a nonstandard pin or pins and you've got a free timer, using the timer in Normal mode coupled to fire off interrupts is a totally valid option.

So with three options in this chapter, we've pretty much exhausted PWM. In closing, though, I'd like to mention a few other options for getting analog output from the AVRs. If you're in need of higher performance, either in terms of reduced digital noise or higher frequency output, there are other options you should know about.

Digital-to-analog converters (DACs):

Simple voltage divider
> If you only need to produce four discrete voltage levels, you can connect both the high end and low end of a resistive voltage divider to two AVR output pins. When both are driven high, the output will be VCC. When both are driven low, the output will read 0 V. When only one of the two outputs is driven high, the output of the voltage divider will be between the two extremes.

Imagine creating a voltage divider with twice as much resistance in one leg as in the other—creating a 1/3 voltage divider. Driving one pin high will output 1/3 × 5 V and driving the other pin high will output 2/3 × 5 V.

If you only need one intermediate analog value but you need it to be accurate, you can hand-pick the voltage divider resistors to get exactly the voltage you need. You could even use a potentiometer to make it tunable.

DIY R-2R DAC

Expanding on the logic of the simple voltage divider, you can make a multi-input nested voltage divider using a lot more resistors that'll let you write out a binary value to the voltage-divider ladder and get the corresponding voltage out. The trick is to pick the resistance values to generate the right intermediate voltages.

For instance, to make an 8-bit R-2R DAC, you hook up all eight pins of PORTB to resistors of value 2R, and connect these together with resistors of value R, with another of 2R to ground at the least-significant bit. (Look up a schematic on the Web if you'd like to make one.) The end result is that each pin on the AVR contributes to the output voltage in a binary-weighted fashion so that you can simply write out the voltage you'd like to the AVR's port. Writing 63 to PORTB produces 5 V/4 with a 5 V VCC, for instance.

Building an R-2R DAC is easy enough, and you can get enough accuracy for eight bits using 1% tolerance resistors for all the values. You can do even better by using the same resistors all around, but using two in parallel to make the R values. If you look up plans on the Web, don't forget that almost all of them require an amplifier following the output, or else you risk loading down the output of the R-2R network with your speakers, for instance.

In addition to simplicity, the advantage of an R-2R-style DAC is that the bits are loaded, and the voltage generated, in parallel—you can change the output voltage almost as fast as you can write a new value to the port that's driving it, which enables you to create signals with frequencies up into the megahertz range. There is also no ripple at a fixed output level, and the transitions between output voltage levels is usually well behaved. The disadvantage, of course, is that the DAC takes up eight pins that you might want to use for something else.

External DAC chips

Although the DIY R-2R DAC might work for 8-bit output, you have to match resistors carefully to get 10-bit resolution, and much more than 12-bit is nearly impossible. So for high-quality audio output, you'll want to use a ready-made chip DAC. Some of these are just factory-trimmed R-2R DACs on the inside, whereas others have some digital logic that do high-frequency digital conversion for you.

Because they're quite frequently used in consumer audio products, you'll find DACs that are well-suited to generating stereo audio signals (16-bit to 24-bit, 44.1 to 96 kHz) for just a few dollars. These modern audio DACs mostly take their input data through SPI or I2C serial data lines, and you'll learn about these protocols in Chapter 16 and Chapter 17.

When shopping for a DAC chip, it's important to consider your desired conversion speed and need for DC accuracy in addition to the resolution in number of bits, because if you try to have everything, you'll end up with a very expensive chip! That said, DACs for audio use aren't very sensitive to absolute accuracy, and the maximum frequency is not difficult to attain, so they're nice and cheap. It's only when you need a DAC that's microvolt accurate or operating into the megahertz range that you'll need to compromise.

Finally, to round out the last couple chapters, which have centered around different uses of the timer/counter hardware, here's a checklist of all the configuration demands to make use of them. This is not meant to substitute for the "Register Description" pages in the datasheet, but should help to guide you through them.

Timer configuration checklist:

1. First, decide on which timer to use. This will mostly depend on how many bits of resolution you need. If the answer is "8-bit is fine," then use Timers 0 or 2. If you need 16-bit resolution, or just aren't using it for anything else anyway, take Timer 1.

2. Next, decide which mode you need: set WGMn0 and WGMn1 bits in TCCRnA and WGMn2 in TCCRnB. See the table "Waveform Generation Mode Bit Description" in the datasheet.

   a. Counting or timing events? You'll want Normal mode. (No configuration bits necessary.)

   b. Are you using the timer as a timebase or frequency generator? That's easiest in CTC mode. Set the WGMn1 bit in TCCRnA.

   c. Are you using the timer for PWM? Usually I use fast PWM mode. Set the WGMn0 and WGMn1 bits in TCCRnA if you don't need adjustable PWM frequency, and additionally set WGMn2 in TCCRnB if you do.

3. Want direct output to the pins? Set COMxA and COMxB bits in TCCRnA accordingly.

4. Determine which clock speed divisor you need and set it with the CSnx bits in TCCRnB.

5. If you're using a compare value, it's nice to set a default value in OCRnA and/or OCRnB. Don't forget to set the corresponding DDR to output mode when you want the pins to output the PWM signal.

6. Using interrupts with your timers?

a. Enable counter overflow interrupt if using Normal mode with bit `TOIEn` in `TIMSKn`.

b. Enable output compare interrupts if using PWM or CTC modes with bits `OCIEnA` and `OCIEnB` in `TIMSKn`.

c. Don't forget to enable global interrupts via `sei()`; and write your interrupt service routines.

Driving Servo Motors

11

Real-Time Clocks and a Laser "Sundial"

Servos are an essential part of any small robot, and they're literally tailor-made for running with logic-level signals. They're so easy to drive with the AVR that they make the perfect introduction to microcontroller-driven movement. Figure 11-1 is a family portrait of a few servo motors that I had lying around.

Figure 11-1. *Some servo motors*

In this chapter, we'll use the servo's reasonably accurate positioning to make a laser sundial—a laser dot that moves around your room that you can use to tell the time.

Along the way, we'll work on calibrating the AVR's internal CPU clock well enough that you can use it as a standalone real-time clock that will keep time to within about a second per day. And that's pretty useful even if you already have a decent clock in your office.

What You Need

In addition to the basic kit, you will need:

- A servo. Any old hobby servo will do.

- (Optionally, but a good idea) a separate power supply for the servo. I used 4xAA batteries. This helps keep the AVR's power supply clean of motor-generated voltage noise.

- A laser pointer that you're willing to take apart. Use a cheapie. I used a cat toy that was given to me.

- A 2N7000 MOSFET to turn the laser on and off.

- A USB-Serial adapter to set and calibrate your clock in combination with your desktop or laptop computer.

Servos

Servos are *positioning* motors with a built-in feedback circuit, and it's this internal circuitry that makes them so simple to use. As positioning motors, they don't spin around and around like traditional motors. Instead, they only rotate through 180 degrees or so, and they can move to the desired position to roughly the nearest degree on command. This makes them ideal for pulling up the landing gear on a model airplane, or for moving robot arms. (Your elbow doesn't spin continuously; why should your robot's?)

You send position controls to a servo with a signal pulse that ranges nominally from 1 ms to 2 ms. When you send a 1 ms pulse, the motor turns to its most-counterclockwise position, and when you send a 2 ms pulse, it turns the shaft to its most clockwise. If you send a pulse of 1.5 ms, the motor turns the shaft to the center, and so on. These are "nominal" values—you'll find that they vary a little bit from servo to servo, but assuming that 1.5 milliseconds is somewhere in the middle is a good starting point.

The circuitry inside the servo is expecting a pulse like this every 10–20 ms, and as long as it receives a pulse, it tries to turn the motor shaft to the right position. When no pulse is seen for a while, the servo disengages and can be turned more or less freely. From our perspective, this means that we need to be able to send a short voltage pulse signal of fairly precise duration that controls the position of the servo, and to send these pulses every 20 milliseconds or so.

Why do I say that servos are a perfect match for microcontrollers? First, because outputting this kind of simple control pulse is a job that's basically tailor-made for the hardware timer circuitry. But most importantly, the AVR doesn't need to supply any of the driving power for the servo, just the control signal. The servo's internal circuitry takes care of driving the motor for us. This is in contrast to DC and stepper motors that we'll see in Chapter 15, where we need all sorts of intermediary circuitry to get a motor to turn. With a servo, we plug it in to power, connect one signal line up to the AVR, and we're running.

The Secret Life of Servos

If you're wondering how servos convert the periodic pulses into motor positions, you'll have to crack open the casing and peek inside. The feedback circuit inside a servo is based on comparing two voltages: one that's proportional to the control signal that you've sent, and one that's proportional to the motor shaft's pointing direction. Every time the servo circuit receives a pulse, it turns its motor for a little while in the right direction to make the two voltages more equal.

The shaft-position voltage is simple enough to generate. A potentiometer is connected to the output shaft of the motor inside the servo's black box. Just like we did in Chapter 7, the potentiometer is wired up as a voltage divider, and the voltage read off the middle terminal is controlled by turning the potentiometer, which is connected to the motor.

(For completeness, I should mention that the drivetrain inside the servo has a set of gears that connects the quick-but-weak motion of a tiny little motor into the stronger-but-slower turning of the output shaft. The geared-down output shaft, not the motor, is connected to the position-sensing potentiometer. The small motor actually turns many times for one half turn of the output shaft. But don't let that confuse the issue; the practical effect is that the stepper motor's shaft is connected to a potentiometer.)

Now let's look at the control signal. When we send a control pulse, the integrator circuit starts to charge a capacitor with a fixed current. As soon as the control pulse drops low, the integrator circuit turns off the current. The result is that the voltage in the capacitor depends on how long it has been charged.

The motor potentiometer voltage and the integrated control pulse voltage are then fed into a *comparator*, which is just about what it sounds like: a circuit that outputs a high voltage level if the first input voltage is higher than the second, and a low voltage level otherwise. This high or low digital signal then controls the motor direction.

The other thing that happens at the end of a control pulse is that the motor is turned on, but it's kept on a timer. For instance, for the servo on my desk, the motor runs for 23 ms per signal pulse. This timer is the reason for the 20 ms update rate

—if we keep the control pulses coming in faster than this timer, the motor will always be moving in the right direction. And that's the essence of servo control.

But if this were the end of the story, the motor would be continually running back and forth, oscillating around the control set point. If the position voltage is a tiny bit low, the motor turns clockwise until the position voltage is a tiny bit high and then the motor turns counterclockwise, and so on. It's a noisy waste of battery power to have the motor continually "seeking" like this. The solution is to implement a *dead band* where the internal circuitry decides that it's close enough and turns the motor off.

Because of this dead band, the positioning accuracy of a servo motor isn't infinite —it won't bother to reposition itself for tiny changes in the control pulse width. The width of the dead band will vary from motor to motor, but I've found that trying to get much more than a few hundred distinct positions from a cheap servo is a losing battle. You can test it out yourself with your motor using the code in this section.

And that explains all the mysteries of the servo-motor! The pulse length is critical because it determines the position. The inter-pulse timing is not nearly so critical, but if you'd like the motor to be always holding its position, the pulses need to arrive every 20ms or so. And finally, the dead band limits how finely you can control the position, but also reduces power consumption by preventing the motor from endlessly seeking.

So servos need a pulse between 1 ms and 2 ms long, and they need this pulse repeated regularly roughly every 20 ms. How are we going to do this? With timers! By far the easiest and most accurate way to drive a servo is simply to hook it up to the output from Timer 1, the 16-bit timer, set the timer's period to be 20 ms, and then use the PWM output pins and register to send the pulses. You can do this easily with up to two servo motors, because the timer has two dedicated output compare pins. Let's see how.

The Circuit

Servos have three pins: voltage supply, ground, and signal. We can connect the first two pins directly up to any 4–6 V power supply. The third pin, signal, we'll connect directly to the AVR. On a breadboard, you'll end up with something like what's show in Figure 11-2.

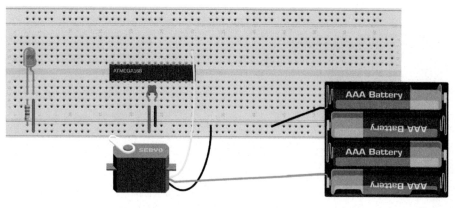

Made with 🟥 **Fritzing.org**

Figure 11-2. *Simple servo hookup*

To take advantage of Timer 1, which has its output compare channels on PB1/OC1A and PB2/OC1B, you may need to disconnect LED1, and connect it to the servo's control pin. Or you might get lucky and they'll work together. It all depends on how much current you're drawing for the LED, which in turn depends on the LED current-limiting resistors you've chosen.

As mentioned earlier, you should also hook the servo up to a supply of 4–6 V. This can be the same power supply that you're using for the AVR, but it's sometimes nice to run your robot's logic and motors on separate circuits so that if your motor stalls out and pulls hard on the battery, it won't subject the AVR to a brownout. If you *are* trying to get by with the same power supply for both the servo and the AVR, note that it'll need to be able to supply at least 500 mA, because a servo can easily draw that much current.

The best practice, though, is to use a separate power supply for the servo. Four AA cells will do the trick nicely. When using a separate power supply for the servo, be sure that the ground for the motor and battery are connected to the ground for the AVR so that they share a common reference voltage level. Otherwise, the AVR and the servo won't be able to agree on what constitutes a voltage pulse on the signal line.

The Code

Physically connecting a servo to the AVR is simplicity itself. Now all we have to do to make it work is set up the AVR's internal timer to create the control pulses. Let's have a look at the code in Example 11-1.

Example 11-1. *servoWorkout.c listing*

```c
                    /* Quick interactive demo running servo with Timer 1 */

// ------- Preamble -------- //
#include <avr/io.h>
#include <util/delay.h>
#include <avr/interrupt.h>

#include "pinDefines.h"
#include "USART.h"

#define PULSE_MIN       1000        /* experiment with these values */
#define PULSE_MAX       2000            /* to match your own servo */
#define PULSE_MID       1500

static inline uint16_t getNumber16(void);

static inline void initTimer1Servo(void) {
                /* Set up Timer1 (16bit) to give a pulse every 20ms */
                        /* Use Fast PWM mode, counter max in ICR1 */
  TCCR1A |= (1 << WGM11);
  TCCR1B |= (1 << WGM12) | (1 << WGM13);
  TCCR1B |= (1 << CS10);  /* /1 prescaling -- counting in microseconds */
  ICR1 = 20000;                              /* TOP value = 20ms */
  TCCR1A |= (1 << COM1A1);             /* Direct output on PB1 / OC1A */
  DDRB |= (1 << PB1);                       /* set pin for output */
}

static inline void showOff(void) {
  printString("Center\r\n");
  OCR1A = PULSE_MID;
  _delay_ms(1500);
  printString("Clockwise Max\r\n");
  OCR1A = PULSE_MIN;
  _delay_ms(1500);
  printString("Counterclockwise Max\r\n");
  OCR1A = PULSE_MAX;
  _delay_ms(1500);
  printString("Center\r\n");
  OCR1A = PULSE_MID;
  _delay_ms(1500);
}

int main(void) {

  // -------- Inits -------- //
  uint16_t servoPulseLength;
  OCR1A = PULSE_MID;                  /* set it to middle position initially */
  initTimer1Servo();
  initUSART();
  printString("\r\nWelcome to the Servo Demo\r\n");
```

```
  showOff();

  // ------ Event loop ------ //
  while (1) {

    printString("\r\nEnter a four-digit pulse length:\r\n");
    servoPulseLength = getNumber16();

    printString("On my way....\r\n");
    OCR1A = servoPulseLength;
    DDRB |= (1 << PB1);                        /* re-enable output pin */

    _delay_ms(1000);
    printString("Releasing...\r\n");
    while (TCNT1 < 3000) {;
    }                              /* delay until pulse part of cycle done */
    DDRB &= ~(1 << PB1);                       /* disable output pin */

  }                                            /* End event loop */
  return (0);                                  /* This line is never reached */
}

static inline uint16_t getNumber16(void) {
  // Gets a PWM value from the serial port.
  // Reads in characters, turns them into a number
  char thousands = '0';
  char hundreds = '0';
  char tens = '0';
  char ones = '0';
  char thisChar = '0';

  do {
    thousands = hundreds;                      /* shift numbers over */
    hundreds = tens;
    tens = ones;
    ones = thisChar;
    thisChar = receiveByte();                  /* get a new character */
    transmitByte(thisChar);                    /* echo */
  } while (thisChar != '\r');

  transmitByte('\n');                          /* newline */
  return (1000 * (thousands - '0') + 100 * (hundreds - '0') +
          10 * (tens - '0') + ones - '0');
}
```

Configuring the timer is the most complicated part of running a servo—after that, the hardware takes care of everything for us. Because we haven't used Timer 1 yet, you might have a look at its chapter in the datasheet. Timer 1 is a 16-bit timer, which gives us enough precision to use it for the 20 ms period and still control the servo control pulse down to microsecond resolution, all without loading the CPU at all. Woot.

For configuration, the most important difference between Timer 1 and the 8-bit timers is that it's got a lot more waveform generation modes. In particular, because 16-bit resolution is often overkill, we can additionally configure Timer 1 in 8-bit, 9-bit, and 10-bit modes as a convenience. (We won't be using those modes here.)

The other main difference is the addition of a separate ICR1 register, which can be used to set the PWM frequency. The details involve how the AVR, an 8-bit machine, deals with 16-bit numbers, but the upshot is that we can use ICR1 to set the frequency for most PWM modes when we're not changing the frequency often, and use OCR1A to set the frequency if we are changing it a lot. (OCR1A and OCR1B are double-buffered, which means they won't get clobbered if, for instance, an ISR gets called in between writing the most significant eight bits and the least significant eight bits.)

OK, so we configure Timer 1 for Fast PWM mode with the top value (which determines the PWM frequency) stored in ICR1. It's convenient, running the chip at 8 MHz, to divide the clock by eight so that each timer tick is 1 microsecond. This lets us set ICR1 to 20,000 microseconds, so that our complete PWM cycle repeats just in time for the servo's nominal update frequency.

 Control Pulse Frequency

The pulse rate of one control pulse per 20 ms is fairly flexible. My servo works anywhere from 10 ms to about 25 ms. Delays shorter than 10ms seem to mess up the deadband circuitry, and because the motor only engages for a maximum of 25 ms per pulse, longer PWM periods allow the motor to disengage a tiny bit before it turns back on, but you might not even notice this in practice. In short, the inter-pulse timing isn't critical.

Finally, the initialization routine sets up the output pin OC1A/PB1 to go high at the end of a PWM cycle, and switch back low as soon as the counter value matches whatever's in register OCR1A. This way, we control the length of the control pulse just by setting a value in a register; the higher we count up, the longer the pulse width.

Jumping down to the main() function, we can see that everything's initialized, some greetings are sent out over the serial line, and then a showOff() routine runs the motor through a preset pattern one time. The event loop asks for a control-pulse length, then sets the output compare register OCR1A to that value. Because the timer is running in microsecond steps, a value of "1400" (for example) will set the pulse length to 1.400 ms, which should be somewhere near the middle of the servo's range. Play around with these values and see where your servo's limits are.

After a couple of seconds, the program stops sending control pulses by setting the data-direction register on PB1 to input, which blocks the timer's automatic output. Now you should be able to turn the servo by hand, though you'll feel some resistance due to the motor's internal gearing. Type in a set value in the serial terminal and compare the resistance when the servo is receiving a command and when it's not. Notice that the servo "fights" you to hold its place as long as it's being sent control pulses. Cool, isn't it? (Alternatively, if you're interested in conserving your batteries, you should note that holding position requires power. If you don't need to hold the motor's position, don't send position pulses.)

As a final experiment with servos for this section, try to figure out your servo's minimum resolution (alternatively, the width of the dead band). Type in "1400" to set it near the middle of its range. Now try "1401" and see if it moves. If not, try "1402" and so on. Mine just twitched noticeably at "1403" or "1404." My servo also has a working range of about 180 degrees from 400 to 2,250, which isn't bad at all. So to control this servo at maximum resolution over the maximum range, we'll need (2,250 − 400) / 3 = 616 steps, which is somewhere between nine and ten bits of information. (Which lines up nicely with the ADC's input range, which makes me think about what I can do with a light-controlled servo. Play around if you've still got the LDR hooked up.)

The final bit of code is a simple modification of the getNumber() routine from the *USART.h* library that we've been using. It takes in a four-digit number via the serial port and converts it into a 16-bit number for use as the servo control pulse length. Notice that we don't check to see whether or not this number is in range. If it's too low, the servo will just seek against its mechanical endstop until the code stops sending pulses. In a real application, once you know how far you want the servo to rotate, you should probably encode limits into your servo routines using #define statements as I do here, so that they're easy to change when you adjust hardware or switch to a different motor.

This little program, in addition to providing a fun way to show off a servo-control technique, can also help you characterize a new servo, especially once it's installed in the final device. With it, you can figure out where the endpoints are, how many degrees it turns per microsecond pulse, how wide the deadband is, etc. So take good notes—we'll use this data later on when we tie all this code together with a clock and a laser driver to make a "sundial."

Servo Sundial

In the days of old, before people worked in offices, the average person could tell the time of day by the position of the sun in the sky. If you put a stake in the ground, it casts shadows. If you then mark out the location of these shadows at known times, you've got something you can use as a clock later on. Real sundials are a bit finicky, changing with the seasons and requiring pointing in a particular direction and all. Plus they need the sunshine as input, which means you'd better have an office with windows. Wouldn't it be a lot easier and more practical to pan a laser around the room with a servo, controlled by a microcontroller, and mark out the time on the wall? Well, there's only one way to find out.

This project could be dead simple—it doesn't require much more than a servo motor and a cheapo laser pointer. I've had one of these up and running in my office for a while now, and it's pretty fun, although there have been complaints about the sticky notes on the ceiling that I use to mark the hours. And once you get it calibrated, it keeps decent time, although it's no atomic clock.

The Build

This is one of the few times where you've got some slight physical construction to do. The first task is to decide how you're going to steer the laser beam with the servo. I've used two different ways to aim the laser using the servo, and you're welcome to choose whichever seems easiest.

The first is to mount the laser directly to one of the plastic "servo horns" that turn with the motor. Hot glue is fantastic for this application, and you're up and running in like 30 seconds. If you're using a lightweight and cheap laser diode from a two-dollar laser pointer cat toy, I wouldn't hesitate to just stick it all directly together. The problem with the direct-mounting method is that the laser (and its wires) end up moving around. Laser diodes can be sensitive to physical vibration, especially when they're active, so the continual jerking around may shorten the life of your laser diode. On the other hand, my cheap laser-pointer laser has worked for a few months now, so it's maybe not a big concern. My version of the direct-glue sundial is show in Figure 11-3.

The other option is to mount a small mirror on the servo horn and bounce the laser off of it. This setup allows you to keep both the motor and the laser fixed, steering the beam around with the mirror. If your laser doesn't like to be shaken around, or is worth more than a few dollars, you should probably at least consider the mirror option. It's the professional way to go. The other advantage is that by adjusting the angle of the mirror, you can adjust the way the beam arcs around the room. Again, I used hot-glue to affix the mirror to the servo horn. The result (with some fog to make the laser beam visible) is demonstrated in Figure 11-4.

Figure 11-3. *Directly mounted servo sundial*

Figure 11-4. *Helium-neon laser servo sundial*

Try turning the servo through its full range, and figure out where on your ceiling or walls it points. Look around for a location with the widest possible angle that you can use to project the sundial on. If you're lucky, you'll be able to use nearly the servo's full range for the sundial without shining the laser in your eye. And if you're truly lucky, there will be the edge of a desk to hot-glue the servo to in just exactly the right spot. Add sticky notes to your ceiling to mark out the time, and you've got the setup in Figure 11-5.

Figure 11-5. *Laser servo sundial*

Using the servo's full range of motion allows you to tell the time more precisely. Remember from the *servoWorkout.c* demo that I figured out that my servo had about 600 usable positions once the width of the dead zone was taken into account? If you're only using half of these, because you're only using half of the servo's total range of motion, you'll have half of the possible time-resolution displayed on your wall.

The other tip to increase resolution is to limit the number of hours that the sweep of the "sundial" represents. If you're only going to be in the office from 9 am to 5 pm, there's no point in displaying times before or after that. If you can use the full servo range, and limit the sundial to displaying 10 hours (600 positions), it'll easily get one-minute resolution.

But don't sweat it too much. If you can locate the laser and servo someplace near to a power outlet (for plugging in a wall-wart to supply your clock with 5 V power) and the range is reasonable, go for it. Even if you're only using half of the range and you need to display a whole day's worth of time, you'll be able to tell the time to the nearest five minutes, which is probably as good as any real sundial, right?

Once you get the software up and running, you can also fine-tune the position of some important times to match the joints in your wall or cracks on your ceiling. By setting the time over the serial port (or with the Python routine), you can test out where the beam falls at various times of the day, and tweak this to your liking. A final tip in this regard: don't screw the servo horn in unless you need to. It's convenient to be able to coarse-adjust the time-locations by pulling the whole attachment off and plugging it back in where you want it.

Or you can do what I did initially, and what our sun-using predecessors did, too, which is to take the position of the beam as granted and just mark off where the beam hits at different times of the day using sticky notes. With a laser sundial, you don't have to correct for the seasons. And you don't have to wait for a full day either; I've included a Python routine that steps the clock through the hours and that makes setting up your sticky notes a piece of cake.

My fantasy is to someday make light-sensitive alarm units (perhaps using the ADC and LDR setup of Chapter 7) and set alarms for myself by physically sticking them on the wall so that the light sensor is in the beam of the laser. When the time comes for the 10 am meeting, the laser hits the sensor, and an alarm is sounded, or a tweet is sent, or an email is dispatched. Rube Goldberg would be proud.

Ready the Lasers!

For this project, you're not going to need a gigantic, multiwatt laser. In fact, the less bright it is, the better from both a power-usage and eye-hazard standpoint. And if you're constantly wiggling the laser diode on the end of a motor, you're not going to want to use anything valuable.

The standard red diode laser that comes in cat toys is perfect and only costs a few dollars, if you're not lucky enough to have one around to scrounge. Most of these diodes come with circuitry that lets them run on three battery cells, or 4.5 V, which is close enough to just plug it straight into a 5 V power supply and hope for the best.

Whether or not you want to leave the laser in its decorative case is up to you. Originally, mine was in a mouse-shaped plastic case. Now I regret having extracted the laser unit, because who doesn't want a servo-controlled laser mouse telling them the time? If you do want to pull out the laser unit, it's as easy as shown in Figure 11-6.

The small "bullet" laser pointers that come in a thin metal casing can be removed only with brutality. I've gotten them loose using a pair of tin-snips and simply cutting through the case. (Do not use regular scissors.) Another option would be to simply buy a bare laser module. Online discount stores like DealExtreme (*https:// dx.com*) have bare laser modules *and* cheap servos.

Many cheap laser pointers come with a switch that you're supposed to press to turn the laser on. We're going to need to take care of that. The easiest way to remove the switch from the circuit is just to solder across it. With a normal pushbutton switch, the two pairs of pins that are on the same side of the button connect to each other when pressed. Soldering a small wire across either pair will completely bypass the switch. You can see where I did this in the first frame of Figure 11-5.

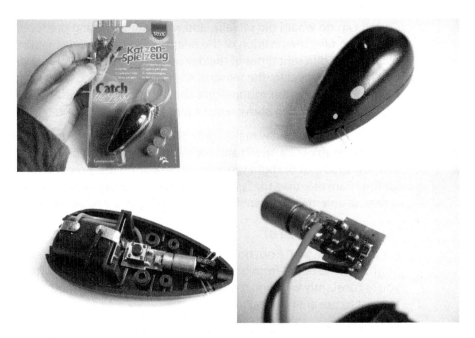

Figure 11-6. *Getting the laser out*

Now all you have to do is figure out how the AVR can turn the laser on and off. In Chapter 15, we'll go over the use of transistor switches in great detail, so you can either look ahead at the description of using low-side MOSFET switches to control small loads, or you can just hook up the circuit in Figure 11-7.

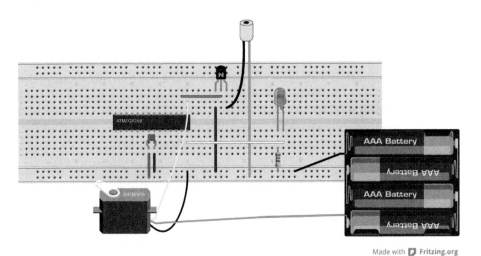

Made with **Fritzing.org**

Figure 11-7. *Breadboarding the laser sundial*

The low-side switch consists of a 2N7000 MOSFET connected between the ground wire of the laser module and the circuit's ground, so connect the ground wire from the laser to pin three of the 2N7000, and then connect pin one of the 2N7000 to our circuit ground. The AVR turns the 2N7000 switch on and off by changing the voltage on pin two of the 2N7000. Finally, because you can power the laser from your breadboard's 5 V rail, simply plug that straight in.

The Code

The code to drive the servo sundial incorporates a bunch of snippets from code that we've seen before, and many of the parts will be familiar, but it's a fair bit of code when it's all put together. So to start, let's sketch out the main sections.

We'll use the 16-bit Timer 1 to drive the servo, and the 8-bit Timer 0 running as fast as possible to provide an accurate timebase for the clock. Because we're mostly interested in displaying the minutes accurately, we're really just keeping the seconds around to count up 60 of them. That is, we don't really care when a second begins or ends as long as they all have the right length in time, and we can count them up. Because seconds aren't tremendously timing-crucial to us, we'll be handling all of the clock functions in the main loop.

The routine will also have to listen to the serial port, because that's how we'll be setting the time. In this case, because we're going through the event loop rather quickly, we can also poll the serial port while we're there. And finally, for fun and for debugging purposes, we'll also be sending the time across the serial line every second.

So that's the overview. This ends up being a large bunch of code, so I'll break it up into a few files so that it's more manageable. The main() routine is found in *servo-Sundial.c*, as are all of the functions to support using the servo. Definitions, function prototypes, and global variables are defined in *servoSundial.h*. Two more utility files are also included from within *servoSundial.c*: one for handling the serial I/O and another for the real-time clock functions. All four of these sections are covered separately here.

Main and the servo

Example 11-2 lists out the code for servoSundial.c.

Example 11-2. servoSundial.c listing

```
                    /* Quasi-realtime-clock with servo sundial. */

// ------- Includes -------- //
#include <avr/io.h>
#include <util/delay.h>
#include <avr/interrupt.h>
#include "pinDefines.h"
#include "USART.h"
```

```c
#include "servoSundial.h"
#include "_servoSerialHelpers.c"
#include "_servoClockFunctions.c"

// -------- Functions --------- //
// Servo setup and utility functions
void initTimer1_Servo(void) {
                      /* Set up Timer1 (16bit) to give a pulse every 20ms */
  TCCR1A |= (1 << WGM11);                       /* Using Fast PWM mode */
  TCCR1B |= (1 << WGM12);                       /* counter max in ICR1 */
  TCCR1B |= (1 << WGM13);
  TCCR1B |= (1 << CS11);            /* /8 prescaling -- microsecond steps */
  TCCR1A |= (1 << COM1A1);        /* set output on PB1 / OC1A for servo */
  ICR1 = 20000;                                 /* TOP value = 20ms */
}

void enableServo(void) {
  while (TCNT1 < PULSE_OVER) {;
  }                             /* delay until pulse part of cycle done */
  SERVO_DDR |= (1 << SERVO);                    /* enable servo pulses */
}

void disableServo(void) {
  while (TCNT1 < PULSE_OVER) {;
  }                             /* delay until pulse part of cycle done */
  SERVO_DDR &= ~(1 << SERVO);                   /* disable servo pulses */
}

void setServoPosition(void) {
  uint32_t elapsedMinutes;
  /* using 32 bits because
     elapsedMinutes * PULSE_RANGE
     will overflow 16 bits */

  elapsedMinutes = (hours - START_TIME) * 60 + minutes;
  OCR1A = PULSE_MIN + elapsedMinutes * PULSE_RANGE / (HOURS_RANGE * 60);
  enableServo();
}

int main(void) {

  // -------- Inits --------- //
  initUSART();
  printString("\r\nWelcome to the Servo Sundial.\r\n");
  printString("Type S to set time.\r\n");

  initTimer0_Clock();
  initTimer1_Servo();
  sei();                                /* set enable interrupt bit */
  LED_DDR |= (1 << LED0);                        /* blinky output */
  LASER_DDR |= (1 << LASER);                 /* enable laser output */

  // ------ Event loop ------ //
  while (1) {
```

```
                                                /* Poll clock routine */
    if (ticks == OVERFLOWS_PER_SECOND) {
      ticks = 0;
      everySecond();
    }

    pollSerial();

  }                                             /* End event loop */
  return (0);                        /* This line is never reached */
}
```

Just as before, we're driving the servo using Timer 1, so the initialization for the servo-driving Timer 1 is almost the same as we used in Example 11-1. I probably cut and paste this same initialization routine every time I use a servo, and then tweak it to fit the particular application.

Up next are a few servo utility functions. When enabling and disabling servo control, it's a good idea to make sure that we're not doing so in the middle of a control pulse—this makes the motor glitch, often all the way down to the minimum end stop. Both enableServo() and disableServo() prevent this glitching by waiting for the Timer 1 counter to be past the longest possible pulse before changing the servo pin's DDR.

setServoPosition() starts off by calculating how many minutes have elapsed since the turn-on time. To get the current control pulse length, we'd like to figure out how many microseconds of extra time to add per elapsed minute. That's the point of PULSE_RANGE/(HOURS_RANGE * 60) in the next line, but depending on your specific values, that'll end up being a number like 1.6—which is unfortunately right in the middle of two small integers. If you round down to one, you'll end up wasting around 30% of the servo's range. If you round up to two, you run up against the servo's endstop before the day is done. For maximum simplicity, you'd do the math using a floating-point math library. Using the AVR's floating-point math library adds an extra 3.5 KB to your program's size, and is generally not a good idea if you can avoid it. Although we've got the space for it here, I thought I'd take the opportunity to show you a workaround.

Rather than use floating-point numbers, we do all the multiplication and division in one line. That way, nothing gets rounded until the end of the calculation. The drawback, though, is that we risk an integer overflow during the calculation. For example, if your clock has been running 12 hours, that's 720 minutes. If the difference between the minimum and maximum servo pulses is 1,000 microseconds, the quantity elapsedMinutes * PULSE_RANGE = 720 * 1,000 = 720,000, which is way too big to fit in a 16-bit integer. The solution is just to use a bigger integer type, so we define elapsedMinutes to be a 32-bit number. Now all of the calculations that involve elapsedMinutes, particularly the risky multiplication, will be done using 32-bit numbers, and we'll get the right answer out. The code here takes less CPU time and less program memory than it would if we had used floating-point numbers, and we get the same answer!

Finally, moving down to main(), we call all the initialization functions, set up outputs, and enable interrupts. The event loop is a super-quick polling loop. If a second has passed, the clock-time handling functions are called via the everySecond() routine. Otherwise, the USART is checked to see if any data came in by calling the function pollSerial() that's defined in the serial helper file.

Before we look into the real-time clock application section, let's quickly get the header file out of the way.

The header
The header file's contents are shown in Example 11-3.

Example 11-3. servoSundial.h listing

```
                        /* Quasi-realtime-clock with servo sundial. */

// ------- Includes -------- //
#include <avr/io.h>

// ------- Defines -------- //
#define PULSE_MIN       1000                /* experiment with these values */
#define PULSE_MAX       2000                /* to match your own servo */
#define PULSE_RANGE     (PULSE_MAX - PULSE_MIN)
#define PULSE_OVER      (PULSE_MAX + 10) /* Must be larger than PULSE_MAX */

#define START_TIME      10                              /* 10 am */
#define STOP_TIME       22                              /* 10 pm */
#define HOURS_RANGE     (STOP_TIME - START_TIME - 1)

#define LASER           PB2
#define LASER_PORT      PORTB
#define LASER_DDR       DDRB

#define SERVO           PB1
#define SERVO_PORT      PORTB
#define SERVO_DDR       DDRB

#define OVERFLOWS_PER_SECOND    31250       /* nominal, should calibrate */

// -------- Global Variables --------- //
volatile uint16_t ticks;
volatile uint8_t hours = 15;                 /* arbitrary default time */
volatile uint8_t minutes = 42;
volatile uint8_t seconds = 57;

// Serial input and output functions
```

```
void pollSerial(void);
void printTime(uint8_t hours, uint8_t minutes, uint8_t seconds);

// Servo setup and utility functions
void initTimer1_Servo(void);
void enableServo(void);
void disableServo(void);
void setServoPosition(void);

// Realtime-clock handling functions
// Use the globals ticks, hours, minutes, seconds
void initTimer0_Clock(void);
void everyHour(void);
void everyMinute(void);
void everySecond(void);
```

At the very top of the code are a bunch of defines that we'll discuss in detail in "Servo Sundial Calibration" on page 238. Particularly, the OVERFLOWS_PER_SECOND variable will let us fine-tune the clock to get reasonably accurate seconds.

The other defines relate to the servo's range of motion and the hours of the day that we'd like the device to run. You should be able to figure out the minimum and maximum for the servo pulse lengths from the *servoWorkout.c* demo code in the previous section.

Finally, before the function prototypes, the four global variables that make the real-time clock tick (tee-hee!) are defined. ticks will be incremented in an ISR, and the other variable names are fairly descriptive. The upshot of defining all of these time variables as global is that we can modify them from within the main() routine or any of the various subroutines that it calls.

The clock

Now let's look at the clock code in Example 11-4.

Example 11-4. _servoClockFunctions.c listing

```
// Realtime-clock handling functions
void initTimer0_Clock(void) {
                /* Normal mode, just used for the overflow interrupt */
  TCCR0B |= (1 << CS00);  /* 8 MHz clock = ~31250 overflows per second */
  TIMSK0 |= (1 << TOIE0);           /* timer overflow interrupt enable */
}

ISR(TIMER0_OVF_vect) {
    /* This is going off very frequently, so we should make it speedy */
  ticks++;
}
void everySecond(void) {
  seconds++;
```

```
   if (seconds > 59) {
     seconds = 0;
     everyMinute();
   }
   LED_PORT ^= (1 << LED0);                                  /* blink */
   printTime(hours, minutes, seconds);                 /* serial output */
          /* Turn off servo motor after three seconds into new minute */
   if (seconds == 3) {
     disableServo();
   }
}
void everyMinute(void) {
  minutes++;
  if (minutes > 59) {
    minutes = 0;
    everyHour();
  }
  // If during business hours, set servo to new minute
  // Otherwise, don't need to move motor when laser is off
  if ((hours >= START_TIME) && (hours < STOP_TIME)) {
    setServoPosition();
    enableServo();
    LASER_PORT |= (1 << LASER);              /* make sure laser is on */
  }
  else {                                     /* make sure laser is off */
    LASER_PORT &= ~(1 << LASER);
  }
}
void everyHour(void) {
  hours++;
  if (hours > 23) {                          /* loop around at end of day */
    hours = 0;
  }
}
```

Between the timer initialization and the servo utility functions in *servoSundial.c*, we've got the servo sorted out. Global defines in *servoSundial.h* lay out the data skeleton for the clock. Now it's time to get the clock up and running. Timer 0 and the associated ISR are the simplest possible clock timebase routine. The combination of the timer running at full speed, and overflowing every 256 steps yields a tick every 31,250th of a second (if the CPU clock runs exactly at 8 MHz).

If you look back at the event loop in main(), it continually checks the ticks variable to see when it hits our defined (and calibrated) OVERFLOWS_PER_SECOND value. When it does, it resets ticks and calls the routine everySecond(). This starts a cascade through the rest of the clock functions—just like the gears in a real mechanical clock.

The basic structure of each of the time-handling functions is the same. For instance, every second, the function increments the seconds variable and then checks to see if enough seconds have added up to warrant calling the everyMinute() function. Once that's done, it handles the rest of the stuff that needs to happen every second. In this case, that's blinking an LED, printing out the time over serial, and disabling the servo motor if it's already been running for three seconds, to save energy.

The everyMinute() routine checks if it should increment the hours, then updates the servo position and turns on the laser if the time is within the device's working hours. Finally, everyHour() increments the hours variable and wraps around to the start of a new day.

This code requires only a few global variables and a small bit of CPU overhead, but provides us with a tunable real-time clock with print-out functions over the serial port and alarm-clock like functions to boot. How can we beat that?

Serial I/O

Finally, wrapping up the firmware code are the two serial support functions in Example 11-5.

Example 11-5. _servoSerialHelpers.c listing

```c
               /* Functions for serial port output formatting and input */

void printTime(uint8_t hours, uint8_t minutes, uint8_t seconds) {
  printByte(hours);
  transmitByte(':');
  printByte(minutes);
  transmitByte(':');
  printByte(seconds);
  transmitByte('\r');
  transmitByte('\n');
}

void pollSerial(void) {
                    /* Poll for serial input -- to set the time. */
  char input;
  if (bit_is_set(UCSR0A, RXC0)) {
    input = UDR0;
    if (input == 'S') {                       /* enter set-time mode */
      printString("Setting time...\r\n");
      printString("Hour: ");
      hours = getNumber();
      printString("\r\nMinutes: ");
      minutes = getNumber();
      printString("\r\nSeconds: ");
      seconds = getNumber();
      printString("\r\n");
      ticks = 0;
      if ((hours >= START_TIME) && (hours < STOP_TIME)) {
        setServoPosition();
      }
    }
  }
```

```
    }
}
```

The printTime function is straightforward enough. As long as we don't mind seeing leading zeros and reading the clock in 24-hour time, all we need to do is reuse our old favorite number-printing function from *USART.c* and spice it up with colons for punctuation.

If you recall the main event loop, it doesn't really do much. It first checks to see if a second has elapsed and triggers the real-time clock functions if it has. Otherwise, it polls the serial line to see if anything has come in. If there has been data on the serial line, it enters the time-setting routine triggers if the character received is "S", and otherwise just ignores anything that comes across the serial line.

The rest of the time-setting routine is implemented as prompt-input pairs until hours, minutes, and seconds have been entered. This interface isn't very sexy, but it allows us (with good timing pressing Return) to get times into the sundial that are accurate down to the second. More importantly, for the calibration routines below, it's very simple to script this time-setting procedure from a Python routine.

But for now, open up a serial terminal, type **S** and enter the current time in 24-hour time format, sit back, and relax. Maybe make marks, put up sticky notes, or even use some removable masking tape to plot out the time on the ceiling. If you're impatient, you can short-circuit this procedure by typing in a time just before the one that you're interested in setting, for instance 10:59:56. Now wait four seconds for 11 o'clock, and the servo will swing into place. Put your sticky note in place within the next minute, and repeat.

While you're setting up the room to match the clock, you'll probably notice that the servo isn't exactly precise. The dead band is a lot easier to see when it's magnified and projected on your ceiling. (In fact, if you'd like to reflash the servo workout routine, you can learn a lot more about the characteristics of your servo this way.)

In my office, the sundial only advances roughly every two or three minutes, and the direction that you approach the current time matters, too. To help with this, I wrote a small Python program, *stepHours.py* (included in the demo program's directory), that slowly approaches each hour, and then stops for you to put up a sticky note and press Return before moving slowly on to the next one.

Servo Sundial Calibration

At this point, I do hope that you've got a little red dot creeping around your ceiling (or walls). It should provide you at least a few hours of accurate time-keeping as-is. But a few hours of accuracy is not enough! You want more. After all, you've put all this effort into hot-gluing a servo to the side of your desk, and taping sticky notes all over your ceiling. It's probably worth a little bit of effort to see how accurate you can make the clock.

The reason behind the lousy accuracy is that the AVR's internal CPU clock isn't really meant for time-keeping. It's meant to give you a quick-and-dirty clock pulse so that the chip can run without any external parts. The AVR datasheet suggests that this clock will be in the range of 7.3 to 8.1 MHz, which is nowhere near accurate enough. (If your chip is running at 7.3 MHz when you're expecting 8 MHz, it will keep accurate time for about 12 minutes!) This is not to say that the AVR's CPU clock will swing around across this wide frequency range—an individual chip's CPU clock is pretty stable—but that if you pick a random chip out of a bucket, it could have a clock that runs fast or slow. Clearly, we're going to have to fix this if our sundial clock is going to keep time.

The engineering (brute-force? proper?) solution to the problem is to use an external crystal instead of the internal clock source. After all, it's easy enough to get a crystal that's accurate to 20 parts per million, giving us a drift of around two seconds per day straight from the factory. Plug in a crystal, toss in a couple of capacitors, and then flash the AVR's fuse bits to use the new clock source, and presto.

The hacker's way is to take whatever we've got coming out of the chip and adjust our timebase to it. In particular, we're counting up 31,250 overflows of the Timer 0 and calling that a second. But if your AVR's internal clock is running fast, it may get 33,234 counts per true second. If we can figure out what this number should be, we'll have a clock that's accurate to roughly one part in 32,000, or 30 parts per million, which is almost as good as the crystal solution, and on the order of a few seconds per day.

As we saw earlier, the interface to the AVR's clock routine was designed to be worked by humans. We type an "S" to enter time-setting mode, and then the hours, minutes, and seconds over the serial port to set it, and it echos the time back over serial every second. To calibrate your sundial, you could set the clock yourself, write down what time it is, and then come back in a while and see how much it has drifted. Then you'll know how fast the clock is running, and you can just scale your counts-per-second define to match.

But doing that yourself is boring. Let's whip up a quick Python routine that we can run on the computer to do the typing and dividing for us. Example 11-6 contains the code that I wrote up to do just that.

Example 11-6. calibrateTime.py listing

```
import time
import serial

def readTime(serialPort):
    '''Reads the time from the AVR over the serial port'''
```

```python
        serialPort.flushInput()
        character = ""
        while(not character == "\n"):        # loop until see end of line
            character = serialPort.read(1)
        ## The time string looks something like '011:045:023\r\n'
        timeString = serialPort.read(13)
        hms = timeString.split(":")
        hms = [int(x) for x in hms] # make hour, minute, second numeric
        return(hms)

def setTime(serialPort, hours, minutes, seconds):
    '''Sends the time over the serial port'''
    serialPort.flushOutput()
    serialPort.write("S")
    time.sleep(0.1)                # delay while AVR sends
    serialPort.write(str(hours) + "\r")
    time.sleep(0.2)                # delay while AVR sends
    serialPort.write(str(minutes) + "\r")
    time.sleep(0.2)                # delay while AVR sends
    serialPort.write(str(seconds) + "\r")

def setTimeNow(serialPort):
    '''Sets the AVR clock to the current time'''
    hours, minutes, seconds = time.localtime()[3:6]
    setTime(serialPort, hours, minutes, seconds)
    return(time.time())

def calculateTimeDelay(serialPort):
    '''Gets AVR time and subtracts off actual (computer) time'''
    avrHMS = readTime(serialPort)
    hms = time.localtime()[3:6]
    hmsDifference = [x - y for x,y in zip(avrHMS, hms)]
    out = "AVR is fast by: {x[0]} hours, {x[1]} minutes, and {x[2]} seconds"
    print out.format(x=hmsDifference)
    return(hmsDifference)

def calculateTimeDrift(serialPort, startTime):
    '''Calculates the ratio to multiply OVERFLOWS_PER_SECOND
    given a start time and current error'''
    h, m, s = calculateTimeDelay(serialPort)
    driftSeconds = 60*60*h + 60*m + s
    elapsed = time.time() - startTime
    print "After {:.0f} seconds, ".format(elapsed)
    return (driftSeconds / elapsed + 1)


if __name__ == "__main__":

    ## Set time automatically, recording start time,
    ##   then periodically calculate multiplication factor
    OVERFLOWS_PER_SECOND = 31250 # set this to equal the value in your code

    SLEEP_TIME = 10
    ratioLog = []
```

```
s = serial.Serial("/dev/ttyUSB0", 9600, timeout=5)
print "Setting time to current time...."
ratio = 0
while not ratio == 1:          # make sure starting time is right on
    startTime = setTimeNow(s)
    ratio = calculateTimeDrift(s, startTime)

## Note: you can either leave this running or
## you can re-run calculateTimeDrift() at any time in the future,
## as long as you don't overwrite the original startTime
while(True):
    ratio = calculateTimeDrift(s, startTime)
    ratioLog.append([time.time()-startTime, ratio])
    newOverflow = int(OVERFLOWS_PER_SECOND * ratio)
    print "OVERFLOWS_PER_SECOND should be {}\n\n".format(newOverflow)
    time.sleep(SLEEP_TIME)

## As you leave this routine running, you should see it bounce
##   around a lot in the beginning and then settle down after
##   running a few hours.  Ironically, it'll converge to a good
##   number faster if it's initially very out of sync.  (If it
##   drifts faster, you can figure out the drift rate sooner.)
## Leave it running for 24 hours and you'll get one-second-per-day
##   accuracy.
```

The Python code includes a bunch of helpful functions that you can use in your own code later on, and illustrates a couple of "tricks" that make interfacing over serial with the AVR easier. The first function, readTime(), takes input from an opened serial port and returns a list of the current hour, minute, and second. Because we're outputting the time in "H:M:S" format from the AVR, we can split this string up on the colons, turn the values to integers, and return them. Done! Almost...

The first additional bit we'll need to do is clear out all the old time messages that the AVR has been sending since we plugged it in. Your operating system has been (helpfully?) storing all of the data coming across the serial port in a buffer for you, which means when you start reading in all the data since you last read from the serial port. This is great when you don't want to lose data in between reads, but it's lousy when you simply want the freshest response, like we do here. The solution is to clear out the receive buffer first, and that's what serialPort.flushInput() does. The code then reads in one character at a time until it sees the newline character (\n) that's sent at the end of every line. Now we know that the next 13 characters to come across will be one time report.

The setTime() routine basically does what we'd do to set the time by hand. It sends an "S" over the line, pauses for a bit, and then sends the hours, minutes, and seconds data. The pausing is a bit of a kludge, in my opinion. What's going on is that the

AVR code echoes what we type back to us as we type it, and it uses the blocking `transmitByte()` routine for simplicity. Unfortunately, that causes the AVR's serial port response to be a little slow, so the Python code compensates for that. It's ugly. We could remove the echoing from the AVR's code, and we wouldn't need the delays in Python, but then we'd be typing blind. These delays are a compromise.

Python Modules

If you write code in Python that's generally useful, you can include it in any of your other programs by simply including ("importing") that module at the top of your code. Then all the functions defined in the imported module will be available under the name of that module.

This makes code reuse super easy. To create a software module, you can just save a bunch of functions in the same file, and import it later to use them. When you write another bit of code that needs one of the functions, just include the module file again. So if you define a function doStuff() in a file called *myModule.py*, you can later use it like this:

```
import myModule
```

```
## And use it
result = myModule.doStuff()
```

And this brings us to the code at the bottom of the module: `if __name__ == "__main__":`. This is a Python trick to make a file both able to run directly *and* be importable as a module. Basically, the code that follows the `if __name__ == "__main__":` statement will only be run if it's the main program being run. If the file is imported from another file, the `if` statement is false, and the code at the bottom gets skipped. This way you can include code that you'd like to test out your module's functionality when it's called directly, but that you don't have to load and run when it's imported as a module. Neat, huh?

If we let this calibration routine run until it's stationary, and use that result, we should get a clock that accurate to within a few seconds per day. Is this acceptable? Well, that's a little more than a minute per month, and it's probably better than the grandfather clock your parents had in the hallway. That should be good enough, right? I mean, the laser only moves perceptibly every couple minutes or so. But still, what if we want more? How accurate can we make this?

Suppose that, even though you've calibrated the seconds as precisely as you can, your sundial still runs fast by one second per day. As long as the clock is consistently fast by one second, you can fix this tiny drift up by adding in a leap second into your code, sometime while you're sleeping. Just test the time with an `if()` statement in your code, and add a `seconds++;` whenever needed to keep the clock in line.

Adding leap seconds like this should make your clock accurate within a handful of seconds per week, and you should really stop here. The limits to how far you can push this exercise are most likely your patience and how stable you can keep the temperature in the room with the AVR—the AVR's internal clock circuitry will run slightly faster as it gets warmer and slower when it gets colder. The AVR's clock also speeds up a little bit as the supply voltage increases, so you'll need to keep that precisely regulated as well. In the end, keeping super-accurate time is best left to government physics labs with large budgets.

And this realization leads us to the absolute *best* way to get a super-accurate AVR clock: get it from the Internet! If you're able to connect to the Net, you'll be able to sync your computer to a national standard clock to within one second. Now just write a Python script that sends the time to your AVR sundial once per day, and you'll never be off by more than a few seconds. Even if you only resync once per month, your clock will be easily as accurate as its displayed resolution. Beats using the sun and shadows!

Analog-to-Digital Conversion II

12

Accurate Voltage Meter and the Footstep Detector

In Chapter 7, you learned the basics of using the ADC to convert continuous analog voltages into digital numbers that you can use in your AVR code. In this chapter, I'll go over some of the extra details that you'll need to work with many real-world devices.

In particular, you'll find that not everything works on the same 0 V to 5 V range that your AVR's ADC wants to use, so we'll have to talk a little bit about input voltage scaling. You may also find that sometimes you want a little bit more accuracy than the AVR's 10-bit ADC can deliver. When this is the case, you can either buy a separate ADC chip or use a software technique known as *oversampling* to get a couple more bits of effective resolution. We'll combine these two ideas to make a surprisingly accurate voltmeter that can read from 0 V to 15 V in hundredths of a volt.

We'll also build up a project that I use in my own home to detect footsteps and turn on a light for the stairs. It detects footsteps using a sensor that's tremendously versatile for detecting sound and vibration—the piezo-electric disk. Because the piezo (for short) produces both positive and negative voltages, we'll look into biasing it so that the voltage always lies in the middle of the range that the AVR likes to see—a technique you'll also want to use for microphones, for instance.

The software tricks in making a very sensitive footstep detector involve ADC data smoothing. In any real-world circuit, there's always some background noise, and the true value that we'd really like to measure often lies buried somewhere within it. When making a very sensitive device, like our piezo vibration sensor, figuring out the difference between this background noise and our desired signal is very important. In this project, we know that the "volume" from the vibrations of a footstep is a fairly short signal, while the background noise is basically constant. We'll use a *moving average* to get a good idea of the sensor's natural bias point as well as the average magnitude of the background noise. Then, when we see a sensor reading that's outside this range, we'll know that it's a footstep.

What You Need

In this chapter, in addition to the basic kit, you will need:

- A battery whose charge you'd like to measure.

- A USB-Serial adapter for voltage display.

- Three resistors of the same value for an input voltage divider.

- A standalone voltmeter to calibrate the AVR voltmeter.

- A piezo disk, preferably with wires attached, for the footstep sensor.

- Two 1M ohm resistors to provide bias voltage for the piezo.

So without further ado, let's get down to it. It's time to learn some pre- and post-ADC signal conditioning.

Voltage Meter

The story of this voltmeter project is that I was building a battery charger that knew when to stop charging a 9 V rechargeable battery. When charging nickel-based rechargeable batteries, the voltage across the battery increases until the battery is full, at which point it levels off and even drops just a little bit. To use this slight voltage drop as a clue that the battery was 100% charged, I needed to read out a voltage into the AVR that was outside of the 0–5 V range and needed enough resolution that I could detect the tiny little dip in charging voltage and not over-charge the battery.

So the design specs are to make a voltmeter that measures a voltage in the range 0–15 V with resolution down to two decimal places—10 mV. "Wait just a minute!" I hear you saying, "The ADC only measures 10-bits or 1,024 steps, which are just about 15 mV each over a 15 V range. How are you going to get more resolution than that? And how are you measuring up to 15 V with just a 5 V power supply?"

Measuring higher voltages is actually easy enough. We simply predivide the voltage down to our 5 V range using a voltage divider. To measure up to 15 V, we only need to divide the input voltage down by a factor of three, which we can do fairly accurately with just three similar resistors. That's the easy part.

To get extra resolution in the measurement, we'll use *oversampling*, which is a tremendously useful technique to have in your repertoire. The idea behind over-sampling is that we take repeated measurements from our ADC and combine them. This almost sounds like averaging, but it's not the same. When we average four numbers, for instance, we add up the four numbers together and divide by four.

When we oversample 4x, on the other hand, we add the four numbers together and divide by *two*, increasing the number of bits in our result by one. To bump up our 10-bit ADC to 12-bit precision, we will use 16x oversampling, adding together 16 samples, dividing by four, and keeping the extra factor of four (two bits) to get us up to 12 bits.

We'll also use an AVR-specific ADC trick to reduce measurement noise. Because the CPU generates electrical noise while it's running, Atmel has provided functionality that shuts down the CPU and lets the ADC run on its own. Using this special "ADC Noise Reduction" sleep mode turns off the CPU and I/O clocks temporarily but leaves the ADC clock running while the ADC conversion takes place, and then wakes the chip back up once the ADC-complete interrupt fires. This reduces noise on the power supply due to either the CPU or any of the other pins switching state, which helps measurement accuracy.

By combining ADC Noise Reduction sleep mode and 16x oversampling, we can actually get just a little more than two decimal places of accuracy in our measurements, but not quite enough to justify reporting the third decimal place. Getting much more precision than that requires a very stable and accurate power supply for the AVR, and a good voltmeter to calibrate it against, so let's call 10 mV good enough and get to it.

The Circuit

Electrically, there's really not much going on here. We want to be able to measure voltages up in excess of AVCC, so we divide the input down with a voltage divider. The voltage divider has twice as much resistance between the battery and the AVR pin as between the AVR and ground, so it's a divide-by-three voltage divider. Using three identical resistors, the circuit will look like Figure 12-1 on a breadboard.

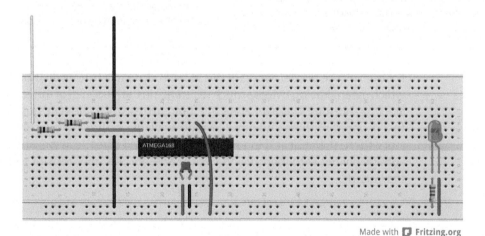

Made with **Fritzing.org**

Figure 12-1. *3x voltage divider*

Oversampling

Oversampling seems like magic. You take a 10-bit sensor, add up 16 observations, and then divide down by four and declare that the result is good to 12 bits. What's going on?

When you take a normal average of a few samples, it has the effect of reducing the variability of the measurement. Intuitively, if one ADC reading happens to be a bit high, the next one might just be a bit low. There are some statistics that I'm sweeping under the carpet (a central limit theorem), but the end result is that the variability of an average drops as the square root of the number of measurements in the average increases. Qualitatively, taking averages of measurements tends to smooth out noise, so if you've got a measurement that's jumping all over the place due to sensor noise, you can take bigger and bigger averages until it's smooth enough for you. When we took moving averages before, we were doing just that.

Adding numbers together (and not averaging) results in a larger number of bits in the sum. If you add two 10-bit numbers, the result can be as large as an 11-bit number. Add up four 10-bit numbers, and the result requires 12 bits. But the last bit isn't any less noisy than the samples that went into the sum. You've got a bigger number for sure, but not a more precise one.

When oversampling, you take many samples to get more bits and then take a (partial) average to smooth the result out so that it's precise enough to justify the extra bits. In our example, we add up 16 samples, enough to end up with a 14-bit number, and then we divide by four (equivalently, drop the least-significant two bits). Now we've got 12 bits that we're pretty sure of.

Anyway, this has all been hand-waving around some fairly serious mathematics. I hope that it gives you a little bit of faith in oversampling—it's a great technique that you should know. To use oversampling, all you have to know is that if you want n more bits of resolution, you take a sum of 2^{2^n} samples and bit shift the result n times to the right (dividing by 2^n).

The main limitation is that you have to take these 2^{2^n} samples before the true input value changes by more than one least significant bit, so oversampling is mainly a technique for slowly varying signals relative to the sampling speed. You can almost always use oversampling for anything that happens on a human time scale, but it's going to slow you down too much for audio. There's a three-way trade-off between speed, precision, and cost. 16x oversampling is 16 times slower than sampling directly, but two-bits more precise and free. If you need faster *and* more precise, you can always pay money for a better ADC!

For more on oversampling and the AVR's ADC converter, see the Atmel application note (*http://www.atmel.com/Images/doc8003.pdf*) "AVR121: Enhancing ADC resolution by oversampling."

For our voltage divider, we want this to be as close to a true 3x division as possible, which means having twice as much resistance in the "top" half of the voltage divider as in the "bottom." Unfortunately, the standard resistor value series jumps from 10k to 22k ohms, so there's no good 2x ratio available without special ordering. Long story short, the easiest thing to do is buy yourself three resistors and make your voltage divider with them, using two in series for the "top" resistor to drop 2/3 of the voltage.

Resistor Tolerance

In the real world, 10k ohm resistors don't really measure exactly 10k ohm, but are rather specified with a tolerance. Common tolerance grades are 1%, 5%, and 10%. One of the cruel realities of economics is that 1% tolerance resistors cost more than 5% resistors, which cost more than 10% resistors, and this means that you'll almost never find a 10% tolerance resistor that's closer to the nominal value than 5%—the manufacturer could sell it as a 5% tolerance resistor for more money.

On the other hand, due to improved manufacturing techniques, 1% resistors are pretty cheap these days, almost to the point that it's not worth it to check. So if you're lucky, you might find that a 5% resistor is accidentally within 1% of the target value, but I wouldn't count on it. Ten years ago, you'd almost never find one.

Voltage scaling in general

Here, were using a voltage divider to predivide down a 0–15 V range to fit the AVR's 5 V maximum. This is a special case of a more general problem: the sensor's range doesn't always match up with the voltage range that works well for the microcontroller.

If your sensor outputs between two and three volts, and you're measuring with an ADC that reads between zero and five volts, you're wasting a lot of the ADC's precision. Using a five-volt ADC reference voltage, and ten bits resolution, we get 5/1024 volts per step, or just under 5 mV per step. Between two and three volts, there are only around 200 of these steps, so in that situation, you've only got around one-fifth of the possible resolution—the sensor will never output high or low enough to make use of 80% of the ADC's range. The point is that you make best use of the ADC's resolution when the voltage range of the ADC matches the voltage range of the sensor.

Basically, we want to rescale and recenter the sensor's signal to match the voltage-measurement range of the AVR. Rather than rescaling the sensor's output, it's often easier to change the ADC's voltage reference. There are two easy things we can do to match the sensor's output voltage range with the ADC's measurement range, and make best use of the 10 bits that we've got.

The AVR chips give us choices in voltage reference, which is *extremely* handy, often meaning that we don't have to use any frontend prescaling circuitry. In our examples, we're using VCC as our voltage reference, which is the simplest solution if your sensors are able to output in that range. If you can easily design your voltage-divider type sensors so that they're between VCC and GND, and use most of the available voltage range, you're done.

Another possibility when the range of the sensor is less than VCC, but the lowest signal is still at ground, is to use a voltage divider on the AREF pin (with a capacitor to stabilize it). This can work very well, with the caveats that cheap resistors are often only accurate to 10% or so, and the values can change with temperature, leaving you with higher or lower absolute voltage measurements depending on the weather. On the other hand, two matched 1% quality resistors in a voltage divider can give you a 2.5 V reference that's just about as accurate as your VCC value —if the resistors have the same resistance, the effects of changing temperature will cancel out.

The AVR chips also have an internal voltage reference, which is nominally 1.1 V, but can range from 1.0 V to 1.2 V across chips. This isn't as bad as it sounds—the voltage level for your particular chip will stay nearly constant over time, temperature, and VCC fluctuations, which is especially handy if you're running a circuit on batteries. If your sensor's output range is between ground and something less than 1 V, the internal reference voltage is the way to go. If the input signal range is higher than 1 V, but you're worried about a changing VCC affecting your measurements, it's often worth it to divide down your input signal and use the internal voltage reference. This is a good trick to use with battery-powered circuits, where VCC changes as the battery drains.

With all these options for the ADC's reference voltage, the hard part of matching the sensor to the AVR is making sure that the minimum voltage stays above ground.

For many sensors, like microphones and the piezo transducer that we use here, the voltage swing is naturally symmetric around ground, guaranteeing that we'll lose half of the signal unless we recenter it to capture the otherwise negative half of the signal. The good news is that with these sources, we don't need the DC level from the sensor. We only care about changes in voltage, say from our voice reaching the microphone or ground tremors reaching our seismograph. In those cases, the simplest circuit to implement is to use a capacitor to block the DC voltage and a voltage-divider circuit to bias the center voltage. We'll use this approach in "The Footstep Detector" on page 254.

When you have a sensor with an extreme range, or if you require biasing, and if the DC level matters, then things are more complicated. With an operational amplifier (op-amp) it's fairly straightforward to build a signal conditioning circuit that'll get your sensor signal just where you want it in terms of bias voltage and range, but that's adding a level of complexity to the circuit that's beyond this book.

The Code

Because we want the voltmeter to be accurate and we're using AVCC as the voltage reference, we're going to have to very accurately measure the AVCC to get the scaling right. This means at least two or three decimal places, which means using a decent voltmeter. *And* we've got the divide-by-not-exactly-three voltage divider in the circuit, which we'll also have to measure and calculate around. While I usually avoid doing much *floating-point* math—math with noninteger numbers—on the AVR, I'll make an exception here because the code is simpler that way. The trade-off is that the floating-point math libraries take up more program space and are much slower to execute than integer math, but for this example, none of the timing is critical, and we have memory to spare. Let's start looking into the code in Example 12-1.

Example 12-1. *voltmeter.c listing*

```c
/* ADC Voltmeter
 * Continuously outputs voltage over the serial line.
 */

// ------- Preamble -------- //
#include <avr/io.h>
#include <util/delay.h>
#include <avr/interrupt.h>
#include <avr/sleep.h>                      /* for ADC sleep mode */
#include <math.h>                        /* for round() and floor() */

#include "pinDefines.h"
#include "USART.h"

/* Note: This voltmeter is only as accurate as your reference voltage.
 * If you want four digits of accuracy, need to measure your AVCC well.
 * Measure either AVCC of the voltage on AREF and enter it here.
 */
#define REF_VCC 5.053
                            /* measured division by voltage divider */
#define VOLTAGE_DIV_FACTOR  3.114


// -------- Functions --------- //
void initADC(void) {
  ADMUX |= (0b00001111 & PC5);                    /* set mux to ADC5 */
  ADMUX |= (1 << REFS0);                  /* reference voltage on AVCC */
  ADCSRA |= (1 << ADPS1) | (1 << ADPS2);   /* ADC clock prescaler /64 */
  ADCSRA |= (1 << ADEN);                         /* enable ADC */
}

void setupADCSleepmode(void) {
  set_sleep_mode(SLEEP_MODE_ADC);            /* defined in avr/sleep.h */
  ADCSRA |= (1 << ADIE);                    /* enable ADC interrupt */
  sei();                              /* enable global interrupts */
}

EMPTY_INTERRUPT(ADC_vect);

uint16_t oversample16x(void) {
  uint16_t oversampledValue = 0;
  uint8_t i;
```

```
    for (i = 0; i < 16; i++) {
      sleep_mode();                     /* chip to sleep, takes ADC sample */
      oversampledValue += ADC;                        /* add them up 16x */
    }
    return (oversampledValue >> 2);         /* divide back down by four */
}

void printFloat(float number) {
  number = round(number * 100) / 100; /* round off to 2 decimal places */
  transmitByte('0' + number / 10);                      /* tens place */
  transmitByte('0' + number - 10 * floor(number / 10));    /* ones */
  transmitByte('.');
  transmitByte('0' + (number * 10) - floor(number) * 10);   /* tenths */
                                            /* hundredths place */
  transmitByte('0' + (number * 100) - floor(number * 10) * 10);
  printString("\r\n");
}

int main(void) {

  float voltage;

  // -------- Inits --------- //
  initUSART();
  printString("\r\nDigital Voltmeter\r\n\r\n");
  initADC();
  setupADCSleepmode();

  // ------ Event loop ------ //

  while (1) {

    voltage = oversample16x() * VOLTAGE_DIV_FACTOR * REF_VCC / 4096;
    printFloat(voltage);
    /*  alternatively, just print it out:
     *  printWord(voltage*100);
     *  but then you have to remember the decimal place
     */
    _delay_ms(500);

  }                                        /* End event loop */
  return (0);                   /* This line is never reached */
}
```

The event loop is straightforward; sample the voltage by calling the oversam ple16x() function, scale it up, and then print it out over the serial port. But in order to run the ADC while the chip is sleeping and incorporate these values in with the oversampling routine, a few things need to be taken care of.

Sleep mode

Making use of the ADC sleep mode is not too hard, once you know how. First, notice that we included *avr/sleep.h* up at the top. This isn't strictly necessary—it defines a few macros that save us from having to look up which bits to set in the datasheet. But then again, as long as it's there, why not use it?

Next, turn to the initialization function `setupADCSleepmode()`. The first line, `set_sleep_mode(SLEEP_MODE_ADC);`, actually just runs `SMCR |= (1<<SM0);` under the hood, but isn't it easier to read with the defines? Whichever way you spell it, a bit is set in the hardware sleep mode register. That bit tells the AVR to enter ADC sleep mode (halt CPU and I/O clocks and start an ADC conversion). When the ADC-complete interrupt fires off, the chip wakes back up and the ISR is called and handled.

Wait a minute—what ISR? We don't really need an ISR because we're sampling on command from a function and sleeping until the ADC is done. But because we've enabled the ADC-complete interrupt to wake up out of sleep mode, the code has to go *somewhere*. The next line, `EMPTY_INTERRUPT(ADC_vect);`, is specific to the GCC compiler and tells it to set up a fake interrupt that just returns to wherever it was in the code. `EMPTY_INTERRUPT()` basically exists just for this purpose—creating a quick, fake ISR that we can trigger when we need to wake the processor up from sleep modes.

Oversampling

All of the work in oversampling is done in the function `oversample16x()`. There's not much to say here, because it's such a straightforward application. One gotcha is that there is a practical limit on how much we can oversample, set by the size of the variable that we collect up the sum of the samples in. Here, I used `uint16_t` `oversampledValue` to keep track of our 16 10-bit samples, and that works out fine. In fact, it's big enough to contain the sum of 64 10-bit values, so if we needed to oversample even more, we could.

The other thing to note while we're here is that we could change the bit-shift division in the last line of `oversample16x()` to divide by 16, and the result would be a regular average of 16 values. This is useful when we'd like to smooth out noise in the sample, and the result will be a 10-bit number that's more stable than any individual ADC reading by itself.

So to sum up the meat of this project, we can get extra resolution by oversampling, and we can reduce noise to the ADC by using the ADC-specific sleep mode to shut down the CPU while sampling. And we can handle higher-than-5 V voltages by simply using a voltage divider before the ADC. Putting all this together with a stable 5 V voltage reference and some careful calibration, we can easily get 12 bits of data from the 10-bit ADC—enough to detect a 10 mV drop on a charging battery.

Sleep Modes

The AVRs have a bunch of different sleep modes that put some of the internal clocks to sleep until some interrupt condition wakes the chip back up. The basic idea is that you can save power by shutting down the hardware that you're not using at any given time, and waking the chip up when an interrupt or timer comes in that it needs to handle.

For instance, you've already seen how you can set up a timer as a system tick that takes care of handling time for you instead of using _delay_ms() routines. If you don't have much else to do with the CPU at the time, you might as well let the CPU doze off a bit to save power. Using the *idle* mode, the lightest sleep mode, is perfect in this case. In idle mode, the CPU clock is shut down, and any interrupt will wake the chip back up. The timer clock, ADC clock, and I/O clocks will all keep running in the background, so you can use idle mode instead of a wait loop and the CPU will wake up with each timer overflow that calls an ISR (like our system ticks). You can even use idle mode if you're transmitting or expecting serial I/O, as long as you're handling your serial input from an interrupt service routine and remember to enable the interrupt.

ADC noise reduction mode is the mode we're using here. It not only shuts down the CPU and I/O clocks, but it also triggers an ADC conversion after the CPU has stopped, and wakes everything back up once the ADC is done, which is exactly what you'd want. How cool is that? (But note that if you're expecting I/O during the ADC sampling time, you'll miss it.)

Power down mode is the other sleep mode that I use a lot. It's the most aggressive of them all—shutting down *all* of the internally generated clocks and peripherals. From a power-usage perspective, you're basically turning the chip off. The AVR will still wake up if it receives any external interrupt like a button being pressed, which is handy if you'd like to implement an on/off button. If you're not using the reset pin for anything else, it makes a nice power-on button to wake the chip back up from power down mode.

You can read up on all of the other sleep modes in the datasheet under the section called "Power Management and Sleep Modes," where it has a very nice table showing you which peripherals get turned off in which modes and what interrupts will wake the chip back up.

The Footstep Detector

In this project, we'll be using the ADC and a sensor to make essentially a DIY accelerometer, but one that's specifically tuned to detect very small vibrations like taps on a tabletop, tiny earthquakes, or in my case, a person walking up the stairs. I'll show you a couple of ways to make the system more or less responsive. I love this project.

The sensor that we'll use to do this can be found for a few bucks or less, and can be scavenged from a whole ton of cheap commercial products: things like musical greeting cards and tiny buzzers. The *piezoelectric disk*, or piezo for short, is a crystal that deforms (slightly) when you apply a voltage to it, or conversely develops an electric voltage when you deform it. The first direction, voltage to deformation, gives you a tinny-sounding speaker, super-precise control over laser deflection mirrors, or inkjet printer heads. The reverse direction, deformation to voltage, lets you build force sensors, high-end acoustic guitar pickups, electronic drum pads, and the vibration-sensor in this chapter, not to mention barbecue grill lighters, where the piezo voltage is high enough to make a spark.

 *Piezos*

Piezoelectricity was discovered in 1880 by Jacques and Pierre Curie. Yes, that Pierre Curie, who also discovered that magnets lose their pull when they are heated to the Curie temperature, and whose discoveries with his wife about radioactivity got them the Nobel Prize, thanks in no small part to a sensitive piezoelectric electrometer. If you asked me to choose between which discovery was more influential, I'd be hard-pressed to answer. The crystal that's providing the high-frequency timebase for nearly every computer and radio device you own? Piezoelectric. Pierre Curie should have gotten two Nobel Prizes.

Almost all piezoelectric substances are crystals or ceramics that have a lattice-like molecular layout, and all the molecules arrange themselves in a somewhat rigid three-dimensional grid. The molecules in the crystal are also polar—they have a positively charged and negatively charged end. When you compress a piezoelectric crystal, these molecules realign and the voltage across the crystal changes. When you let go, the molecules swing back to their original orientation. This makes expansion and contraction of the crystal result in a voltage change, and vice versa.

The kind of piezo disk that we'll be using is actually a thin layer of piezoelectric crystal that's glued to a metal disk on one side and has a conductive layer on the other. The metal disk keeps the fragile crystal from breaking, and the voltage between the conductive layer and the disk varies with compression or bending. Because the crystal is an insulator this two-plate arrangement is basically a capacitor, and the electrical symbol looks like one, but with a box representing the crystal between the plates. But, as I said before, a piezo is special type of capacitor, one that also generates a voltage when bent or squeezed.

What this means for us is that we can put a constant voltage across the piezo and the piezo will charge up to that voltage and just sit there. Then when we bend or compress the piezo, we'll get a temporary positive or negative voltage superimposed on the constant voltage. In the project here, we'll read this changing voltage into the AVR to detect vibrations.

Piezo voltages can be quite large (tens of thousands of volts for the piezos in barbecue igniters) if you really smack the piezo. Because the source of the voltage change is the realignment of molecules in a crystal, a form of static electricity, the total amount of current flowing in or out of the piezo is reasonably small, so you're not going to hurt yourself. Still, we protect the AVR's static-sensitive inputs against possible voltage spikes with the resistor on the input to the AVR's pin PC2 in this section's circuit, and you should probably avoid hitting the disk with a hammer or a drumstick once it's hooked up. We're trying to detect footsteps here.

The Circuit

The first thing you're going to need to do is get your hands on a piezo disk, ideally one that comes with wires already soldered to the disk and conductor. The easiest way to do this is to scrounge one out of a cheap device that was using the piezo to make noise—it'll come already wired up! If you don't have a supply of junked electronic noisemakers handy, most electronics stores will be able to sell you a piezo buzzer for just a few dollars that'll come encased in a black plastic enclosure that serves to make it louder. A few piezo discs are shown in Figure 12-2. Your mission, should you choose to accept it, is to liberate the piezo disk inside by smashing the black plastic without destroying the disk.

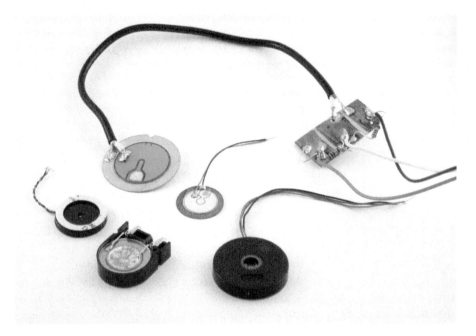

Figure 12-2. *Piezo discs in the wild*

As mentioned in "Piezos" on page 255, piezo sensors will make positive or negative voltages depending on whether it's bent one way or the other. The AVR's ADC, however, only reads from 0 V to VCC, with no range for negative voltages. The workaround is to *bias* the piezo to VCC/2, and to do this we'll use a voltage divider. That way, a small negative voltage on the piezo will add together with the VCC/2 bias voltage to produce an overall voltage just under VCC/2 at the AVR's input pin.

In Figure 12-2, you'll notice that the green piezo element is connected to a piece of circuit board that has the voltage divider biasing circuit already soldered on. This simplifies breadboard connections later on. All you have to do is hook up the red wire to VCC, the black wire to GND, and then the white wire provides the biased sensor value, ready to hook straight into the ADC.

Figure 12-3 demonstrates how this is done. Using high-value resistors for R1 and R2 is important here because you don't want the bias voltage to swamp out small changes in the piezo voltage. Because the voltage divider is always pulling the voltage back to the VCC/2 center point, the smaller the resistance in the voltage divider, the stronger the pull back to center will be because more current is flowing through the divider. For our setup you can easily substitute 10 megohm resistors if you'd like more sensitivity, or drop down to 100k ohm resistors if it's too sensitive. On the other hand, if you make the biasing voltage resistors too large (like 100 megohm resistors or no biasing at all), the biasing at VCC/2 may not work at all, and the voltage will wander away from the fixed bias point.

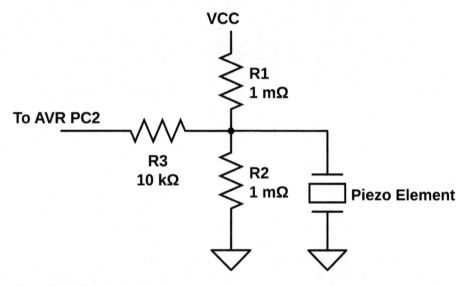

Figure 12-3. *Piezo biasing circuit*

It's worth noting that this circuit actually represents a generally applicable solution to a common problem: any time you have an input signal that can be both positive *and* negative with respect to the AVR's ground, you'll want to provide a pair of bias resistors to pull the "ground" of the sensor up to the middle of the AVR's voltage range so that you can measure both the positive and negative sides of the signal. For instance, if you were connecting a microphone to the AVR, you'd also use a voltage-divider biasing circuit just like this connected to the AVR's input. Additionally, you'd need to add a capacitor between the sensor and the bias circuit/AVR pin in order to keep the microphone from changing the DC level away from this mid-voltage bias point. Here, the piezo's own capacitance serves the same purpose, making adding another capacitor pointless. You should end up with something that looks like Figure 12-4 on your breadboard.

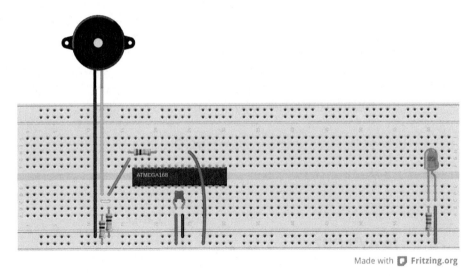

Figure 12-4. *Piezo footstepDetector breadboard*

Finally, the input resistor R3 in Figure 12-3 protects the AVR from the case that we generate a too-high or too-low voltage by really whacking the piezo sensor. The input resistor works like this: inside the AVR, the pins have diodes that prevent too high or low voltages from frying the circuitry, but these diodes can only handle a limited amount of current before the AVR gets burnt out. The input resistor gives us a little bit more assurance that if the external voltage goes too high or too low, not much current will flow. You can increase sensitivity by leaving this resistor out, but you'd better be careful not to hit the piezo sensor hard.

So that's the electronic circuit: three resistors and a piezo disk. The rest of the sensor design is mechanical engineering. For a table-based seismometer with maximum sensitivity, you'll want to do what they do inside commercial accelerometers—put a weight on the end of a beam to magnify the effect of the force and wedge the piezo and the beam together in something solid.

For the beam, anything from a ruler to a piece of scrap two-by-four will do. Tape some coins or something moderately heavy to the far end of the beam, and clamp the near end of the beam to your table, wedging the piezo sensor between the table and beam so that any force applied to the table relative to the weight is magnified by the leverage. (You may need to take precautions against your beam shorting out the conductor and disk sides of the piezo. A piece of electrical tape should work.) With this setup I can detect someone walking up the stairs that lead to my office while the piezo is sitting on my office desk.

I've also gotten pretty good performance just by resting something heavy on the piezo. At the moment, I have the piezo sitting on my desk with a pint glass holding it down as shown in Figure 12-5. As the table is vibrated up and down, the inertia of the pint glass provides the squeezing force that creates a voltage in the piezo. This setup is much simpler and can still detect my footsteps anywhere within the room. It's blinking along with each keystroke even as I type this.

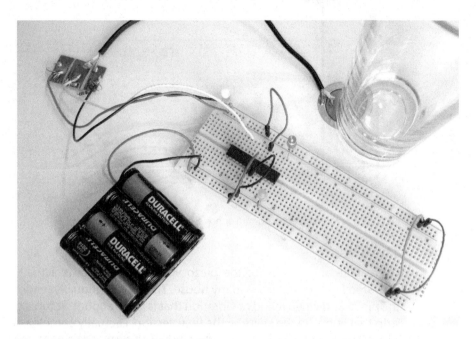

Figure 12-5. *Piezo footstep detector setup*

Once you've got the piezo set up with either a weight or a weight on a beam, you can reduce the sensitivity of the detector in firmware. How loud a signal on the piezo must be in order to count as a footstep is stored in a variable called pad ding. You can optionally hook up a potentiometer to pin PC5, which is also ADC channel 5 to control this parameter directly. We'll read the voltage off the pot, bit shift the value to scale it, and use the result to create a dead band in the center of the ADC's range where the software doesn't react. This is useful if you'd like the accelerometer to detect a hard tap on your desk, but not react to each and every keystroke as you type.

And as long as we're at it, it's nice to have some LEDs for feedback. If you haven't pulled the LEDs off of the PB0-PB7 bank, you've got nothing more to hook up. If you have, attach LEDs to PB0, PB1, and PB7. Your breadboard should now look like Figure 12-6.

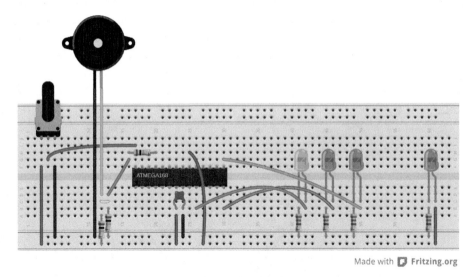

Made with **🅕 Fritzing.org**

Figure 12-6. *Piezo breadboard with optional potentiometer*

The Theory

My real-life application for the piezo vibration detector is actually a footstep-activated light for the stairs in my house. The AVR continually reads the ADC and the piezo, and when it finds a vibration that is large enough, it turns on a LED light strip that lights up the stairs. In the final version, I actually combine an LDR circuit with the vibration sensor here so that it doesn't turn on the lights in the daytime, but let's focus on the vibration sensing part. We'll discuss how to turn on and off light strips (and motors and other electrically large loads) in Chapter 14.

My device turns the light strip on for a few seconds when vibration due to a footstep on the stairs is detected, and goes off automatically after the stairs are still again. In the code, I implement the timeout by restarting a countdown timer every time vibration is sensed.

Because I don't know how hard my footsteps will be, or how much background vibration there is in the house, or how much background electrical noise the sensor sees, I want the sensor to be somewhat auto-calibrating. And because the sensor's rest voltage is determined by a two-resistor voltage divider, I don't want to have to recalibrate the firmware between one version of the device and another in order to account for the variation among resistors. So let's see how we can handle all of these issues in our firmware.

First off, let's tackle the problem of finding the bias voltage of the piezo. While ideal bias resistors provide a midpoint voltage of 2.5000 V, you may have slightly different real-world values for two nominally 1 megohm resistors, and end up with a bias voltage of 2.47 V or so. Deviations from a perfect VCC/2 biasing voltage will manifest as both the minimum and maximum observed ADC values being higher or lower than 511—the midpoint in the ADC's 10-bit range. To make the sensor maximally sensitive, that is, to measure the smallest differences between the ADC value and its midpoint, we need to get this midpoint value measured accurately.

Unfortunately, any time we try to measure the bias voltage, it will have some electrical or physical background noise added on top of it. That is, if we make two ADC readings, they'll probably have different results. On the other hand, the additional noise voltage will be high sometimes and low other times, and if we take an average, the noise will sum up to zero. The strategy is then to take a good long-run average and use that as a measure of the bias value. In order to make the AVR sensor maximally sensitive, it's important to get this average spot on, and this'll give me a chance to show you some important details for implementing exponentially weighted moving averages (EWMA) with integer math. (Hold on to your hats!)

Even with a perfect measure of the central value, there is still a limit to how sensitive we can make the footstep detector. We want to pick a value on either side of the central value and and say that when the ADC reads outside these values, a footstep has been detected. If it weren't for noise in the system, we could pick values just on either side of the middle, bias value. In the real world, we've got some range of (possibly even large) ADC values that we shouldn't treat as footsteps, because they're just the background noise.

The next moving average trick is to track the noise volume so that we can pick our footstep-detection thresholds outside of it. We do this by taking an average of just the positive values (those greater than the midpoint) and a separate average of just the negative values. When there is no external signal present, the difference between these two averages should give a good idea of the average noise volume. This will increase the sensitivity when this noise is relatively quiet, and we can hope to hear fainter footsteps, and to decrease the sensitivity if there's a lot of background noise to avoid "detecting" footsteps when none were present.

Exponentially Weighted Moving Averages

This section is going to go into a little bit of math. It's just a little algebra, but if you're more into programming the dang AVR than thinking about what it all means, feel free to skip on down to "The Code" on page 264. On the other hand, exponentially weighted moving averages (EWMA) are a tremendously flexible and simple-to-use tool once you get used to them, so it's probably worth a bit of your time here understanding what's going on.

Imagine that we have a sensor reading every second. We'll call the raw values x_t where the t labels which second the reading is from. A *time series* of our data is the whole list of x_0, x_1, x_2, ... etc. That is, it's the whole measured history of our sensor value. We'll call our average series y_t. Every time we get in a new sensor value (x_t), we'll update our average value (y_t), so it ends up being another time series.

A regular moving average of our x's just takes, for instance, the last five readings and averages them together. If there's some noise in the readings, it'll hopefully be high in a few of the five readings and low in the others, so that the average value is close to the "true" underlying sensor reading that we're looking for. Every second that we get a new sensor reading, we drop the oldest entry out of the average and add in the new one. That's the "moving" average part—the values that are being averaged together move along with our growing dataset so that we only take an average of, say, five values at a time.

The more terms you choose to average together in your moving average, the better you'll average out the noise signal. If you average 10 values together, for instance, you'll have a better chance at seeing both high and low noise values. On the other hand, you'll be including sensor information from 10 seconds ago into your average value this period. There is always this trade-off between smoothing the values out better and having the average be up to date.

For the AVR to calculate a five-value moving average, we'll need to store five previous values from our sensor. To store 10, we'll need to dedicate even more RAM to the averaging. It's usually not a big deal, but it is possible to use up a lot of memory if you're tracking a few variables with very long moving windows.

My preferred average, the EWMA, only needs two values to work: the current sensor reading and the current average value. Instead of averaging a bunch of values together, in the EWMA, we only need to average two values: the current value and the average value from the last observation. The only complication here is that we don't take an equal average between the two, but a weighted average where we put more weight on the past value (usually) than on the present. For instance, in this chapter's code, we'll average 1/16th of the current value with 15/16ths of the average from last period.

And finally, because what we're after is an accurate value for the bias voltage, we'll want to take some care making sure we calculate everything right. This means avoiding doing division whenever we can, and taking extra care to get the rounding right when we *do* have to divide. Even if we make sure to always divide by a power of two, so that we can use a bit shift, we still lose some information every time we divide. As an example, 7/2 = 3.5, but if we're only using integers, we round up to 4. But 8/2 is also 4, so if we've only got the divided-by-two version, we can't be sure whether it came from a seven or an eight.

Anyway, to the EWMA. In what follows, I'm going to be assuming an EWMA with a 1/16, 15/16 split between the new value and the average. It should be obvious how to generalize this to any other fraction:

$$y_t = \frac{1}{16} x_t + \frac{15}{16} y_{t-1}$$

That is, we calculate this period's EWMA by taking a weighted average of one part this period's sensor value x_t and many parts of the previous EWMA value.

The secret to keeping the EWMA accurate is to put off the dividing-by-m part until we absolutely have to. Multiply both sides by m and we have:

$$16y_t = x_t + 15y_{t-1}$$

and we're almost there. Now we have m times the EWMA on the left side, and no dividing at all. But when we come to next period, we'll need $(m - 1) \times y_t$ on the right side instead of the $m \times y_t$ that we have. Easy enough, we could subtract off one y_t if we knew it. Because we've got $m \times y_t$, we can subtract off $m \times y_t / m$.

But, as I mentioned earlier, when C divides, it just throws away the remainder. There's a trick to making C "round" for us, and it involves adding or subtracting half of the denominator into the numerator before dividing.

 Rounding and Integer Division

C does integer division differently than you or I would. If you were dividing two numbers and wanted an integer result, you'd first figure out what the decimal value was (with integer value and remainder) and then round up or down accordingly. C, on the other hand, figures out the integer part and throws away the remainder. For example, 16/8 = 2, 17/8 = 2, and even 23/8 = 2. (24/8, at least, is 3).

It turns out that we can fool C into rounding by preadding half of the denominator before we divide. In our example of dividing by eight, we need to add four to the number up front before the division: (16 + 4) / 8 = 2, (19 + 4) / 8 = 2, but (20 + 4) / 8 = 3, etc. If you want your integer divisions to be "rounded" to the nearest integer, remember to add or subtract this correction factor of half of the denominator before dividing.

The final equation, minimizing the effects of division and adding in a rounding factor looks like Equation 12-1.

Equation 12-1. Optimized EWMA equation

$$16y_t = x_t + 16y_{t-1} - \frac{(16y_{t-1} - 16/2)}{16}$$

Everything is kept undivided as long as possible, and the average tracks the actual value very well, although we need to remember to divide it back down by 16 before using it.

The only thing that's a little odd about this expression is that the correction factor enters in with a negative sign, but that's because we're subtracting off the whole fractional part. The two negatives cancel out to make a positive and the value that we're using for $15y_t$ is rounded (correctly) up.

The Code

If you've hooked everything up right, you'll have a vibration sensor hooked up to pin PC2 on the AVR. Now let's flash in the code listed in Example 12-2 and use it.

Example 12-2. footstepDetector.c listing

```c
/*
 *          Sensitive footstep-detector and EWMA demo
 */

// ------- Preamble -------- //
#include <avr/io.h>
#include <util/delay.h>
#include <avr/sleep.h>
#include "pinDefines.h"
#include "USART.h"


#define ON_TIME           2000              /* milliseconds */
#define CYCLE_DELAY         10              /* milliseconds */
#define INITIAL_PADDING   16          /* higher is less sensitive */


#define SWITCH            PB7    /* Attach LED or switch relay here */

#define USE_POT            0  /* define to 1 if using potentiometer */
#if USE_POT
#define POT               PC5            /* optional padding pot */
#endif

// -------- Functions --------- //
void initADC(void) {
  ADMUX |= (1 << REFS0);              /* reference voltage to AVCC */
  ADCSRA |= (1 << ADPS1) | (1 << ADPS2);   /* ADC clock prescaler /64 */
  ADCSRA |= (1 << ADEN);                      /* enable ADC */
}

uint16_t readADC(uint8_t channel) {
  ADMUX = (0b11110000 & ADMUX) | channel;
  ADCSRA |= (1 << ADSC);
  loop_until_bit_is_clear(ADCSRA, ADSC);
  return (ADC);
}

int main(void) {
  // -------- Inits --------- //
  uint16_t lightsOutTimer = 0;               /* timer for the switch */
  uint16_t adcValue;
```

```
  uint16_t middleValue = 511;
  uint16_t highValue = 520;
  uint16_t lowValue = 500;
  uint16_t noiseVolume = 0;
  uint8_t padding = INITIAL_PADDING;

  LED_DDR = ((1 << LED0) | (1 << LED1) | (1 << SWITCH));
  initADC();
  initUSART();

  // ------ Event loop ------ //
  while (1) {
    adcValue = readADC(PIEZO);

                       /* moving average -- tracks sensor's bias voltage */
    middleValue = adcValue + middleValue - ((middleValue - 8) >> 4);
         /* moving averages for positive and negative parts of signal */
    if (adcValue > (middleValue >> 4)) {
      highValue = adcValue + highValue - ((highValue - 8) >> 4);
    }
    if (adcValue < (middleValue >> 4)) {
      lowValue = adcValue + lowValue - ((lowValue - 8) >> 4);
    }
            /* "padding" provides a minimum value for the noise volume */
    noiseVolume = highValue - lowValue + padding;

            /* Now check to see if ADC value above or below thresholds */
               /* Comparison with >> 4 b/c EWMA is on different scale */
    if (adcValue < ((middleValue - noiseVolume) >> 4)) {
      LED_PORT = (1 << LED0) | (1 << SWITCH);        /* one LED, switch */
      lightsOutTimer = ON_TIME / CYCLE_DELAY;            /* reset timer */
    }
    else if (adcValue > ((middleValue + noiseVolume) >> 4)) {
      LED_PORT = (1 << LED1) | (1 << SWITCH);      /* other LED, switch */
      lightsOutTimer = ON_TIME / CYCLE_DELAY;            /* reset timer */
    }
    else {                              /* Nothing seen, turn off lights */
      LED_PORT &= ~(1 << LED0);
      LED_PORT &= ~(1 << LED1);                             /* Both off */
      if (lightsOutTimer > 0) {              /* time left on timer */
        lightsOutTimer--;
      }
      else {                                               /* time's up */
        LED_PORT &= ~(1 << SWITCH);              /* turn switch off */
      }
    }
#if USE_POT                              /* optional padding potentiometer */
    padding = readADC(POT) >> 4;            /* scale down to useful range */
#endif
                                          /* Serial output and delay */
          /* ADC is 10-bits, recenter around 127 for display purposes */
    transmitByte(adcValue - 512 + 127);
    transmitByte((lowValue >> 4) - 512 + 127);
    transmitByte((highValue >> 4) - 512 + 127);
```

```
    _delay_ms(CYCLE_DELAY);
  }                                            /* End event loop */
  return (0);                            /* This line is never reached */
}
```

Let's start off with a look through the functions. initADC() and readADC() are general purpose functions that you can quite easily reuse in your code with a simple cut and paste. initADC() sets up the voltage reference, starts the ADC clock, and enables ADC. readADC() takes a channel value as an input, configures the multiplexer register to read from that channel, and then starts a conversion, waits, and returns the result. As you'll see in the main loop, this makes calling multiple channels with the ADC as easy as result = readADC(PIEZO); or result = read ADC(ADC5);.

Rolling down to the main() function, we have the usual declarations for variables, and call the initialization functions, and then run the event loop.

Each cycle through the loop begins with an ADC read from the piezo channel, and then the code updates the middle value, and the high and low averages, respectively. To avoid round-off error, as is done in Equation 12-1, we're not storing the moving-average values, but rather 16 times the moving-average value. Everywhere in the rest of the code where we use both the ADC reading directly and these smoothed versions, we have to remember to finish making the average by dividing by 16.

Notice that we only update the "moving average" for highValue when the measured ADC value is greater than the center value, and only update lowValue when it's below. This way, highValue gives us the average value that's above the middle, and lowValue gives us the average below it. The difference between these two is some measure of how wide the sampled waveform is on average. The value of this difference will track the average volume of background noise when there's no active footsteps. As soon as we tap on the sensor, or step nearby it, the current value of the ADC will go very high or very low, but the average value will track this only slowly, and this is how we tell a real footstep from noise.

On top of this average measure of the background noise, I'll add in an additional bit called padding. If you find that the sensor is triggering too often, or you'd just like it to only trigger on heavy-footed footsteps, you can use this value to add in some extra range in which the sensor won't respond.

I've also left a define in the code (USE_POT) that you can enable if you'd like to hook up a potentiometer to PC5 and control the padding in real time. This makes the circuit easily tunable, and gives you an example of how easy it is to change values within your code via the ADC. When you define USE_POT to 1, the following two extra lines are inserted into the code:

```
#define POT                 PC5         /* optional padding pot */
padding = readADC(POT) >> 4;         /* scale down to useful range */
```

and that's enough to enable you to set the value of the variable padding by turning a knob. Neat, huh? Think back to every bit of code where we've defined a fixed value that you then had to edit, compile, flash, and test out. Why not add in a potentiometer and use an ADC channel to make the parameters adjustable in real time? When you've got the extra ADC channels and the extra processing time, nothing is stopping you.

The rest of the code just takes care of some display LEDs and the timing turning on and off the switch that controls the lights. Each time through the event loop, there's a fixed delay at the very end. The switch only stays on for lightsOutTimer = ON_TIME / CYCLE_DELAY of these cycles after the last detected movement. But the sensor is looking for a new footstep with each cycle through the event loop, so as long as the vibrations continue, the switch's timer variable will continue being reset to its maximum. The switch will turn off only after ON_TIME milliseconds of no activity.

I left these as defines because it's interesting to play with them. If you sample the ADC too slowly (setting CYCLE_DELAY too large), you may miss the loud part of a footstep. If you sample too frequently, the sensitivity to background noise can increase. So you can play around with these values. The CYCLE_DELAY also implicitly sets the maximum time that the switch is on between footsteps; because light sOutTimer is a 16-bit value, you're "limited" to a maximum on-time of 655.36 seconds (about 11 minutes) with a 10 ms CYCLE_DELAY.

The code also takes advantage of the two thresholds, one low and one high, to blink two separate LEDs, providing nice feedback as to how sensitive the circuit is. If only one of the LEDs blinks, your footstep was just above the noise threshold. If both blink and keep blinking back and forth for a second or so, you know that you're detecting the footstep loud and clear.

By increasing the padding variable and making the sensor only react to larger values on the ADC, you could turn this circuit into a knock-detector suitable for detecting secret-knock patterns on a tabletop. For instance, if you want the AVR to do something only when you rap out the classic "shave-and-a-haircut" knock, you could keep track of the timing between detected knocks and only respond if they're in the right approximate ratios.

If you increase the physical sensitivity of the sensor either mechanically by using a long lever arm and heavy weight or electronically by increasing the value of the bias resistors, this application will make a good seismometer. You might, for instance, store the values on a computer and look at them later. Or if you do a little preprocessing in the AVR and only record the values that are extreme, most likely in combination with some external storage, you can make yourself a capable logging seismometer.

Summary

In this chapter, you've learned two important techniques for getting either more accuracy (oversampling) or more stability (moving averaging) out of a digitized analog signal. Along the way, you learned two things about input conditioning: how to divide down a voltage to a manageable level for the AVR's ADC using voltage dividers and how to handle an AC signal that doesn't have a well-defined zero voltage reference.

In all of this, getting as much feedback from your measured system as possible is important. In the case of reasonably slow signals, you can send real-time data to your desktop computer over the serial port for simple diagnostics. For applications with very fast signals, nothing beats being able to hook up an oscilloscope to the circuit in question so that you can simply *see* how the voltages that you're trying to measure are behaving.

The specifics of using any given analog sensor are usually very much application-dependent, so I hope that this chapter gives you enough of a basis to take the next steps yourself. And in the analog world, there's really no substitute for building up your system and testing it out. This includes testing your circuit out in the environment that it'll eventually be used in. No matter how well you think you've specified your sensors and your circuits, you'll occasionally be surprised when they pick up on something in the environment that you hadn't anticipated.

I built a noisemaker with light-dependent resistor light sensors once, wrote all of the firmware, and tested it out thoroughly, I thought. But I had tested it out in a room with strong daylight. As soon as I tried it out in a room with overhead fluorescent lights, there was a warbling noise overlaid on the pitch that I thought it should be playing. It turns out that the light sensors were reacting quickly enough to pick up the relatively quick light pulses that result from driving lights on 60 Hz AC house wiring. This took even longer to debug because it wasn't simply a 60 Hz or 120 Hz pitch overlaid on top, but an interaction of the AVR's sample rate with the 120 Hz bright-dark cycle from the lights. The solution was to take a moving average ADC value that smoothed out the fluorescent bulb's light cycle, and all was well.

Grab yourself a sensor and hook it up to the AVR. See how it behaves, and then start coding up some neat interactions. But don't get caught up in the idea that you can design everything from the specifications. With sensors, sometimes you're going to be surprised by what they pick up, or don't. So you've got to build it first, and then you can get down to puzzling out what's really going on. And in my opinion, that's more than half of the fun. Enjoy!

## PART III

Advanced AVR Topics

Once you've mastered the AVR itself, this last section of the book is dedicated to using modern communications protocols to interface with other devices, building the circuitry you need to drive motors and other electrical devices, and covering a few more of the features of the AVR that you may or may not need every day. The projects here are more involved, and you can read these chapters largely in whatever order you'd like. When you're done with this chapter, you'll be ready to tackle almost any project that you can dream up that needs a microcontroller.

Chapter 13 covers a software and firmware technique that makes good use of what you've learned about PWM. This enables playback of sampled speech, volume control, and mixing of low-fi digital audio signals. You'll end up with a clean sine wave, a nice-sounding abstract droney noisebox, and an improved, serial-port playable "piano."

In Chapter 14 and Chapter 15, I'll show you some simple (and not-so-simple) circuits that you can use to control almost anything that runs on electricity. DC motors, stepper motors, solenoids, and even household appliances can be put under microcontroller control with some additional circuitry. Although the projects in these chapters are basically just about turning motors, I'm hoping that you've got an idea why you'd like motors to turn.

In Chapter 16 and Chapter 17, I cover the two most commonly used modern serial peripheral protocols. This opens up the world of sophisticated digital sensors, high-resolution digital-to-analog converters, and external storage. The demos culminate in integrating a 25LC256 external SPI EEPROM and an LM75 I2C temperature sensor into a long-running temperature logger, but similar techniques let you work with anything that speaks either I2C or SPI.

Chapter 18 and Chapter 19 are all about making the most of the AVR's scarce memory resources, which enables you to do more cool stuff. Thanks to some clever encoding, you can store 10 seconds of sampled low-fi speech data in the read-only flash program memory, enough to make a talking voltmeter that reads out the current voltage to you using your own voice. And though the chip's onboard EEPROM isn't all that fast or abundant, it doesn't disappear when the power goes out and it's writable from within your code. I show off by making an AVR secret encoder/decoder that stores the passwords in EEPROM. If you have two with the same key phrases stored in them, you can pass encrypted messages.

Advanced PWM Tricks | 13

Direct-Digital Synthesis

To create audio that's more interesting than square waves, we're going to use PWM to create rapidly changing intermediate voltages that'll trace out arbitrary waveforms. For now, we'll content ourselves with a few of the traditional synthesizer-type waveforms (sine, sawtooth, and triangle waves), but this project also lays the groundwork for playing back sampled speech. (When we have enough memory at our disposal, in Chapter 18, we'll use the same techniques to make a talking voltmeter.) We'll also be able to change the volume of the sounds and mix multiple sounds together. If you like making spacey, droney sounds or just something more musical than the square wave sounds we've been making so far, this is the chapter for you!

Along the way, we'll really give the PWM hardware a workout. We'll be running the timer/counter with no prescaling (at 8 MHz) and, frankly, we can use all the speed we can get. Generating fancy waveforms in real-time at 31.25 kHz involves enough math that it's tough on the CPU as well, and we'll find that there are just some things we can't do all that easily. But in my opinion, some of the fun of working with small devices like microcontrollers is seeing how much you can do with how little. I hope you'll be pleasantly surprised by what *is* possible.

For starters, we'll make a simple DDS sine wave generator. Unmodulated sine waves are kinda boring, so the next project demonstrates how to mix different DDS oscillators by taking a few (2, 4, 8, or 16) sawtooth waves and mixing them together. To animate the sound, each waveform is slowly shifted a little bit over in time by different amounts, creating a phasing effect that makes a nice drone sound, and is the basis for a lot of 1990's basslines when played rhythmically. Finally, the last project adds dynamic volume control, making your nice AVR into a fairly cheesy sounding "piano." Ah well, beats square waves, right?

Frequencies Within Frequencies

As we work through Direct-digital Synthesis, it's probably a good idea to think of the PWM value you write to OCR0A as being directly translated into a voltage level, because we'll be varying this voltage level over time to make up the desired audio waveform. So when I say "frequency of the waveform," I'm referring to how many times the audio voltage-wave cycles per second.

But of course, we know that deep down, the PWM "voltage level" is itself just another, much faster, train of on-off pulses that repeat at the PWM frequency. These pulses are smoothed out so that they appear to be a nearly constant average voltage at the audio-frequency timescale, and you won't need to worry about them most of the time, as long as your PWM frequency is high enough that your filter does enough smoothing to average them out.

On the other hand, if you've switched output from something slow like a speaker to something that responds a lot faster, like a good amplifier or pair of headphones, you may notice some high-frequency noise that you didn't before. The remedy is to increase the value of the resistor and/or capacitor in your lowpass filter, slowing down its voltage response, so that it damps out the much-higher PWM frequency.

Direct-Digital Synthesis

At the heart of this application is a technique known as direct-digital synthesis (DDS). If you'd like to reproduce, for instance, a sine wave, you start by sampling the voltages along that waveform at regularly spaced intervals in time. Then to play it back, you just output those different voltage levels back over time. You'll store all of the different sample values (voltage levels) for one complete cycle of your waveform in an array in memory, and then play through this sample lookup table at different speeds to create different pitches.

It's easy enough to imagine how to play the fundamental note; you would just step through the lookup table at a fixed speed, storing one value at a time in the PWM compare register to generate that voltage. Now to change the pitch, you'll need to change how quickly you go through the waveform lookup table. The obvious way to do that would be to speed up the playback rate, but there's no good way to do that with the hardware we've got—the system CPU clock runs at a fixed frequency, and to speed up the PWM part, we'd need to also drop down the resolution. There must be a better way.

Instead of changing the clock frequency—how quickly you take each step through the cycle—you change how many steps you take for each clock tick. In order to play a lower note, with a longer wavelength, you play some of the steps for more than a single sample period. To play a higher note, you skip some steps in the waveform table. Either way, the idea is that it takes more or less time to get through one complete trip through the waveform table, resulting in a lower or higher pitch.

There's still a couple more implementation details left, but for starters, imagine that you went through the lookup table, playing each sample for one PWM cycle each. I've written this routine out in pseudocode:

```
uint8_t waveStep;
while(1){
    waveStep++;
    OCR0A = lookupTable[waveStep];
    // (and wait for next PWM cycle)
}
```

Now if you want to play a note that was an octave up, you can go through the same lookup table but skip an entry each time, and the output will cycle through the table twice as fast. In the pseudocode example, that would correspond to incrementing waveStep by two each sample (see Figure 13-1). Here, the basic wavetable has 40 samples. Skipping every other step gives you effectively 20 samples to get through the full wavetable. Alternatively, in the same time it took to play one full sample, you'll get through the wavetable two times by skipping steps. Either way you look at it, the pitch of the output waveform is doubled by skipping steps.

If you wanted to play a note that was an octave down, you'd just need to figure out a way to increment waveStep by 1/2 each time through the loop. This is going to be the secret to DDS. Instead of changing the playback speed of the samples, you change the number of steps you take per PWM cycle.

Original Sampling Rate

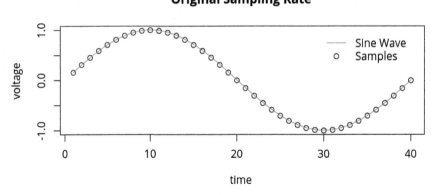

Skipping Every Other Sample

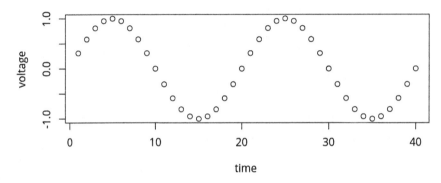

Figure 13-1. *Sampled sine wave*

Playing a note that's up an octave was easy—just advance your counter by two—but the math gets complicated when you want to play at a frequency that isn't an octave. In the 12-tone scale that we're used to, each key on a keyboard differs in frequency from its neighbors by a factor of the twelfth root of two, or about 1.059463. We can't multiply waveStep by 1.06 using only integers. We're going to need to figure out a way to increase our precision.

Getting more precision is actually pretty easy, just use more bits. The secret to getting more precision quickly and efficiently is realizing that it's easy to convert a 16-bit number into an 8-bit one by bit shifting 8 to the right. So we'll do our counting in a 16-bit variable, but stick with a 256-step wavetable. Going from the higher precision number to the lower is just a matter of shifting bits to get the waveStep in the lookup table. In the lingo of DDS, we keep track of our position in the wavetable using a 16-bit *accumulator*, but then we only need to use the most significant eight bits to index the lookup table.

If this seems similar to the trick we used to maintain precision in moving averages in Chapter 12, that's because it is. There, we kept track of our moving average by multiplying and adding together 10-bit ADC values and then waiting until the last minute to do the division.

Another way of saying exactly the same thing is to imagine that for each of the 256 values in our lookup table, we count to 256 before moving on to the next sample. This lets us control the speed that we play through the waveforms down to 1/256th of what we had before. To play the original base pitch, we now need to add 256 to the accumulator for each sample. Playback at an octave down (taking half a step per sample) is as simple as adding 128 to our accumulator each step. Playing a note that's a half-step up means changing our accumulator increment to 271 steps. The result is that we'll advance to the next step most of the time, but sometimes skip one so that the pitch is just a little bit higher. Perfect!

Now our pseudocode looks something like this:

```
uint16_t accumulator;
uint8_t  waveStep;

while(1){
    accumulator += 271;
    waveStep = accumulator >> 8;
    OCR0A = lookupTable[waveStep];
    // (and wait for next PWM cycle)
}
```

Summary: DDS in a Nutshell

You'd like to make a complex analog waveform, and at an arbitrary pitch. How do you do it? The DDS solution is to store a lookup table with the waveform in memory. Every time you need to output a new voltage (in our case using PWM), you advance a certain number of steps through the lookup table and write out the next lookup value to the PWM.

To get more resolution, and thus more tuneability, you keep track of which step in the lookup table you're on using an accumulator with more precision than the lookup table. Then when you want to look up the corresponding sample, for instance in an 8-bit lookup table, you just use the most significant 8 bits, bit shifting away the least significant bits.

For each PWM cycle, you add a relatively large number to your 16-bit accumulator, then bit shift a copy of the accumulator over by 8 bits to get a step number in the 8-bit range of the lookup table. You look up the corresponding step in the lookup table, and the proper duty-cycle is written out to the PWM.

Making a Sine Wave

So let's flash in our first DDS example, *dds.c*. It won't do anything at first, but if you've connected a button and speaker, pressing the button will emit a nice sine wave around 440 Hz. Time to break down the code in Example 13-1.

*Example 13-1. **dds.c listing***

```
                                        /* Direct-digital synthesis */

// ------- Preamble -------- //
#include <avr/io.h>                      /* Defines pins, ports, etc */
#include <util/delay.h>                  /* Functions to waste time */

#include "pinDefines.h"
#include "macros.h"
#include "fullSine.h"

static inline void initTimer0(void) {
  TCCR0A |= (1 << COM0A1);              /* PWM output on OCR0A */
  SPEAKER_DDR |= (1 << SPEAKER);        /* enable output on pin */

  TCCR0A |= (1 << WGM00);                     /* Fast PWM mode */
  TCCR0A |= (1 << WGM01);              /* Fast PWM mode, pt.2 */

  TCCR0B |= (1 << CS00);               /* Clock with /1 prescaler */
}

int main(void) {

  uint16_t accumulator;
  uint16_t accumulatorSteps = 880;            /* approx 440 Hz */
  uint8_t waveStep;
  int8_t pwmValue;

  // -------- Inits --------- //

  initTimer0();
  BUTTON_PORT |= (1 << BUTTON);               /* pullup on button */

  // ------- Event loop ------ //
  while (1) {

    if (bit_is_clear(BUTTON_PIN, BUTTON)) {

      SPEAKER_DDR |= (1 << SPEAKER);               /* enable speaker */
      accumulator += accumulatorSteps;       /* advance accumulator */
      waveStep = accumulator >> 8;        /* which entry in lookup? */
      pwmValue = fullSine[waveStep];          /* lookup voltage */

      loop_until_bit_is_set(TIFR0, TOV0);     /* wait for PWM cycle */
      OCR0A = 128 + pwmValue;                 /* set new PWM value */
```

```
      TIFR0 |= (1 << TOV0);              /* reset PWM overflow bit */
   }
   else {                                /* button not pressed */
      SPEAKER_DDR &= ~(1 << SPEAKER);    /* disable speaker */
   }
 }                                       /* End event loop */
 return (0);                   /* This line is never reached */
}
```

Timer 0 is configured in Fast PWM mode, so for our purposes, think of the value written to the compare register, OCR0A, as representing the average voltage we want to output during that PWM cycle. Note that we're setting the clock input prescaler to a value of 1, that is to say, no prescaling. For sampled audio, we need all the speed we can get.

In the event loop, we check to see if the button is pressed. When it is, the speaker is enabled for output, and the DDS routine inside the if() statement runs. Just as in our earlier pseudocode example, the accumulator is advanced by a number of steps that determine the pitch, then the 16-bit accumulator is divided by 256 (using bit-shift division) yielding the step of the waveform table that we're on. Then the lookup takes place, yielding the (signed) integer pwmValue. I keep this variable signed because it's easier later on when we mix multiple signals together or scale them by volume multipliers, because it's centered on zero.

 Signed Integers

Note here that our wavetables are made up of signed integers. Why? It makes volume control and mixing a lot easier. If the waveforms can vary between –128 and 127 and we divide them in half, we'll get a waveform between –64 and 63, which is still nicely centered, and we can add it together with other waveforms. Only at the last minute, before writing it out to the PWM register, do we convert it to the 0–255 range that we need to fit in the OCR0A register.

Then we load the PWM register, but first we have to wait for the current PWM cycle to finish. This guarantees that we only load up the PWM register with a new value once per cycle, which keeps the sample rate nice and consistent. The OCR is then written to with our signed pwmValue + 128. The number 128 is chosen because the range of signed 8-bit integers goes from –128 to 127, and adding 128 to it maps it nicely into our PWM counter's 0 to 255 range. Finally, the PWM overflow flag bit is reset by writing a one to it, as described in the datasheet, so that we will be able to detect when we've yet again completed a full PWM cycle.

Sample Rate

In this demo, we're using 8-bit PWM to generate a new average-voltage once per PWM cycle. But exactly how frequently are we playing back each voltage-level sample? We'll have to do some math.

Because we're running the AVR off of its internal CPU clock at maximum speed, the CPU clock is 8 MHz. We're using no prescaling, so the effective PWM clock also ticks eight million times per second. Using an 8-

bit PWM, we complete one PWM cycle every 256 clocks, so our resulting PWM frequency is 31,250 Hz.

One of the central theorems of digital signal processing states that you have to sample a sine wave at least twice per period to reproduce it. That is, our current system can reproduce a maximum frequency of 15,625 Hz, which is fairly respectable.

 Lowpass Filter

If you're thinking of amplifying the signal from the AVR synth that we've just made, you might want to put a lowpass filter between your AVR's audio out and your amplifier's audio in. Remember what I said about PWM working to create average voltages when the response of the driven system is slow enough? If you're running the audio out directly into a speaker, the tiny AVR is not going to be able to push the speaker cone back and forth at anywhere near the PWM frequency, and you'll be OK.

On the other hand, if you're plugging the AVR output into an amplifier, the amp may be fast enough to react to the PWM-frequency signals or higher, creating extra noise or even amplifier instability. So let's cut out the higher-frequency components with a lowpass filter.

The simplest lowpass filter is a resistor in series with the AVR out, followed by a capacitor to ground. See Figure 13-2 for an example. The basis of a lowpass filter is the resistor and capacitor, and their product determines the cutoff frequency of the filter—the frequency above which tones get quieter and quieter. With the values here, all frequencies above 1,600 Hz begin to be attenuated, which assures that our 31.25 kHz PWM frequency is nice and quiet.

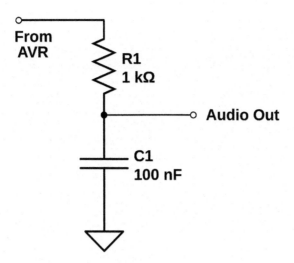

Figure 13-2. *Simplest lowpass filter*

Next Steps: Mixing and Volume

The nice thing about DDS synthesis is that it's incredibly easy to mix two or more waveforms together (add the waveform values), or to make sounds louder or quieter (multiply or divide them). Combining different waveforms with dynamic volume envelopes puts us on the road toward real sound synthesis, and being able to mix a few of these sounds together puts real music within reach.

Toward these ends, I've included two demonstrations. The first mixes two, four, eight, or sixteen sawtooth waves together and then varies their relative phases. It creates a neat, slowly evolving soundscape, and also introduces us to what happens if our event loop is too slow for our sample update frequency—we end up with a lower pitch. The second example demonstrates a simple way to add a dynamic volume envelope to our sounds. Before when we were playing square waves, the speaker was either on or off. There was no idea of volume. But here, with DDS, if we put out a series of voltages that are 1/2 of the PWM value of another series, the resulting sound will be quieter.

Mixing

First off, load up and flash the *fatSaw.c* code and give it a listen. The code is a lot like our DDS sine wave code in Example 13-1, but with the waveform lookup table changed, and multiple sound sources playing at once and mixed together. Then start having a look through the code in Example 13-2.

Example 13-2. fatSaw.c listing

```c
/*
   Direct-digital synthesis
   Phasing saw waves demo

*/

#include "fatSaw.h"

int main(void) {

  uint16_t accumulators[NUMBER_OSCILLATORS];
  uint8_t waveStep;
  int16_t mixer;
  uint8_t i;

  // -------- Inits --------- //

  initTimer0();
  SPEAKER_DDR |= (1<<SPEAKER);                    /* speaker output */
  LED_DDR |= (1<<LED0);

  // Init all to same phase
  for (i = 0; i < NUMBER_OSCILLATORS; i++) {
    accumulators[i] = 0;
  }

  // ------- Event loop ------ //
  while (1) {

                                    /* Load in the PWM value when ready */
    loop_until_bit_is_set(TIFR0, TOV0); /* wait until overflow bit set */
    OCR0A = 128 + mixer;            /* signed-integers need shifting up */
    TIFR0 |= (1<<TOV0);                       /* re-set the overflow bit */

                             /* Update all accumulators, mix together */
    mixer = 0;
    for (i = 0; i < NUMBER_OSCILLATORS; i++) {
      accumulators[i] += BASEPITCH;
      waveStep = accumulators[i] >> 8;

      // Add extra phase increment.
      // Makes shifting overtones when
      // different frequency components add, subtract
      if (waveStep == 0) {                 /* roughly once per cycle */
        accumulators[i] += PHASE_RATE * i;       /* add extra phase */
      }

      mixer += fullSaw15[waveStep];
    }
    mixer = mixer >> OSCILLATOR_SHIFT;
```

```
                                    /* Dividing by bitshift is very fast. */

}                                                        /* End event loop */
  return (0);                              /* This line is never reached */
}
```

The first thing you'll notice is that I've moved the standard preamble, with include files and defines, off to its own *fatSaw.h* file. Many people like to do this to reduce clutter in the main loop. I'm doing it here mainly to save space. In the *fatSaw.h* file are some definitions relating to the number of voices we'd like to produce and even the same initTimer0() function that we used in our first DDS program. (C programmers will argue that putting significant code in an *.h* file is bad practice, because other people aren't expecting it there. I agree, but in the same sense that macro functions are tolerated in *.h* files, I beg your indulgence with a couple bit-twiddling initialization routines.)

Just inside the main() routine, notice that we're defining an *array* of accumulators because we have to keep track of not just one note's location in the wavetable, but up to 16. Moving on to the event loop, the first chunk should look familiar. The routine waits for the current PWM counter loop to complete, then loads the OCR and resets the overflow flag bit.

The mixer chunk is where the interesting action lies. Notice that we've defined a 16-bit signed integer called mixer, in which we'll add up all of the waveform values from the individual digital oscillators. So for each oscillator, we advance its accumulator (here, all by the same amount) and then use a bit shift divide to find out which step in the waveform table we're on. At the end of the mixer code loop, we look up our value from the table and add it to the mixer.

The fun stuff lies in the middle. Here, we advance the accumulator by a few steps in the accumulator's phase each time around the cycle. Each oscillator gets moved forward in its accumulator by a different amount, however, which results in the different versions of the exact same note slipping against each other in time, sometimes peaking all at the same time (when the note sounds lowest) and other times offset from each other (producing overtones). The effect is a slowly changing drone which I find a little hypnotic if it's just left running.

Finally, after we've looped through all of the oscillators and added their values together, the mixer is rescaled to be in the 8-bit range again. But remember that it's a signed 8-bit integer, so we'll have to convert it to an unsigned integer again and add 128 to go from the range –128..127 to 0..255. Here again we use a bit-shift divide. You can try the code out with a regular division, and you'll be able to hear the difference—the pitch will shift down because the AVR isn't able to make its sample updates every 32 microseconds.

Debugging for Speed

There are limits to how much math you can do per cycle at this sampling rate. If you run the PWM as fast as you can, at 31,250 Hz, then there are less than 256 available CPU clock cycles per sample update. This is plenty of time to do some complex operations on a single voice, or simple operations on a few voices, but if you try the fatSaw demo with eight or sixteen voices, you'll end up missing the 31.25 kHz update frequency. The result is that you miss PWM updates and the effective sampling frequency drops to 15,625 Hz and a lower pitch results.

There are two good ways to diagnose these types of high-speed issues in code—look at the generated assembly code or set a pin to toggle at different points in the code, enabling you to look at the timing of individual sections on an oscilloscope.

The avr-gcc suite that we're using includes a reverse-assembler (avr-objdump) that will turn your compiled code into quasi-readable assembly code. With your makefile you can type make disasm and then have a look at the resulting *fatSaw.lst* list file. Though working through AVR assembly is beyond the scope of this book, you can get a rough idea of timings by seeing where your C code translates into long blocks of assembly.

The other useful high-speed debugging method is to blink LEDs and read them on an oscilloscope. For instance, if you're interested in how long the fatSaw routine waits for the PWM overflow flag to clear, you could turn an LED on just before the loop_un til_bit_is_set(TIFR0, TOV0); and turn it off right after. The time spent looping here is equal to the free time you have for code in the event loop, and the period of the waveform will be the 256 cycles * 1/8 microsecond = 32 microseconds that you've got to update the PWM register. If the waveform looks jittery or takes longer than 32 microseconds, it's a warning sign that you're not making your desired sample rate.

So if you really want to do something elaborate with a whole lot of virtual oscillators, you're going to need more processing power. If a factor of two or three in speed will let you do what you'd like, you can clock the AVR's CPU up to 20 MHz by syncing it to an external crystal or oscillator. If you really need much more than that, as one often does for high-quality audio synthesis, the AVR may not be able to keep up, and you may need a dedicated *digital signal processing* (DSP) chip or to offload the sound generation to a real computer and save the AVR for controlling the interaction and interfacing. But before we give up on the good old AVR, let's see if we can't make some interesting musical sounds.

Dynamic Volume Control

Our next step toward getting something that sounds more natural is to put a volume envelope on the sound. When you hit a piano key, a string gets hit by a hammer and goes rather quickly from being still and quiet to vibrating and making sound. This phase is called the *attack*. Then the string settles into its main vibratory modes, with the settling speeds referred to as the *decay* rate and *sustain* level. Then when you let go of the key, the sound dampens out fairly quickly at a speed called the *release rate*. If you wanted to model a piano sound, you'd need to get at least these volume dynamics right. Let's see what we can do.

 **ADSR Envelopes**

This attack-decay-sustain-release volume envelope that we'll be using for our "piano" is pretty much the standard across all sorts of real synthesizers from the 1970s to the present.

Load up the code *adsr.c* and let's get started. If you've never played around with an old synthesizer that has an ADSR volume envelope before, you may want to tweak the defined envelope values in *adsr.h* for a while. Try a long attack, maybe 220, to see how that smooths out the initial sound by more slowly ramping in the initial volume. Try setting the sustain level higher or lower and the sustain time and release rates to play with the default note length.

Once you're done with that, let's dive into the code in Example 13-3.

*Example 13-3. **adsr.c listing***

```
/*
   Direct-digital synthesis
   ADSR Dynamic Volume Envelope Demo
*/

// ------- Preamble -------- //
#include "adsr.h"              /* Defines, includes, and init functions */

int main(void) {

  // -------- Inits --------- //

  uint16_t accumulator = 0;
  uint8_t volume = 0;
  uint16_t noteClock = 0;
  uint16_t tuningWord = C1;

  uint8_t waveStep;
  int16_t mixer;
  uint8_t i;
  char serialInput;

  initTimer0();
  initUSART();
  printString("  Serial Synth\r\n");
  printString("Notes: asdfghjkl;'\r\n");

  SPEAKER_DDR |= (1<<SPEAKER);                     /* speaker output */

  // ------- Event loop ------ //
  while (1) {
```

```
// Set PWM output
loop_until_bit_is_set(TIFR0, TOV0);     /* wait for timer0 overflow */
OCR0A = 128 + (uint8_t) mixer;
TIFR0 |= (1<<TOV0);                          /* reset the overflow bit */

// Update the DDS
accumulator += tuningWord;
waveStep = accumulator >> 8;
mixer = fullTriangle[waveStep] * volume;
mixer = mixer >> 5;

                                   /* Input processed here: check USART */
if (bit_is_set(UCSR0A, RXC0)) {
  serialInput = UDR0;                        /* read in from USART */
  tuningWord = lookupPitch(serialInput);
  noteClock = 1;
}


                                   /* Dynamic Volume stuff here */
if (noteClock) {                   /* if noteClock already running */
  noteClock++;
  if (noteClock < ATTACK_TIME) {                        /* attack */
                      /* wait until time to increase next step */
    if (noteClock > ATTACK_RATE * volume) {
      if (volume < 31) {
        volume++;
      }
    }
  }
  else if (noteClock < DECAY_TIME) {                /* decay */
    if ((noteClock - ATTACK_TIME) >
        (FULL_VOLUME - volume) * DECAY_RATE) {
      if (volume > SUSTAIN_LEVEL) {
        volume--;
      }
    }
  }
  else if (noteClock > RELEASE_TIME) {             /* release */
    if ((noteClock - RELEASE_TIME) >
        (SUSTAIN_LEVEL - volume) * RELEASE_RATE) {
      if (volume > 0) {
        volume--;
      }
      else {
        noteClock = 0;
      }
    }
  }
}


}                                       /* End event loop */
```

```
    return (0);                /* This line is never reached */
}
```

Because this code is a little bit complex, let's start with an overview. The first chunk of code is just the usual DDS routine, waiting for the PWM timer to overflow to set the next value. Then a variable tuningWord gets added to the accumulator, which will result in the desired pitch. Finally, the 16-bit mixer stores the wavetable value scaled up by volume and down by the maximum volume (as a bit-shift division).

Polling USART

Next, the code polls the USART for new data, and sets the tuningWord depending on which key has been pressed. It also sets a noteClock variable, which is incremented to keep track of time for the volume envelope. Finally, a lot of code space (relatively speaking) is spent changing the volume of the note as it evolves over time and the noteClock advances.

The section where we check up on the USART is not particularly difficult to understand, but because it's such a useful technique, I'll expand on it a little bit. In contrast to the last few times we've used the serial port where we wait in an infinite loop for serial data to arrive, in this example, we implement a nonblocking, polled USART input. "Polled" in this sense means that we check to see if new data has come in once every time we go around the event loop. If yes, we process it. If not, we just keep on looping.

Polling for serial data works because the USART raises a "receive complete" (RXC0) flag in the status register (UCSR0A) when it gets a new byte of data in. This flag is automatically cleared whenever the USART data register (UDR0) is read, so we don't have to tell the USART that we're ready for the next byte; it knows automatically.

And because the event loop is running really frequently in this example, at 31.25 kHz, the delay between a received character and playing the note is so short that a human will never know. On the other hand, when you really need *instant* response to incoming serial data, you can always feel free to use an interrupt! You have lots of options.

ADSR Envelope

The other section of the code that still needs explanation is the dynamic ADSR volume envelope calculation bit. An idealized (continuous-volume) version of an ADSR envelope is shown in Figure 13-3. In our implementation, because we can't tell how long the key was pressed, we set a sustain time instead of waiting until the key is released. Otherwise, it's standard.

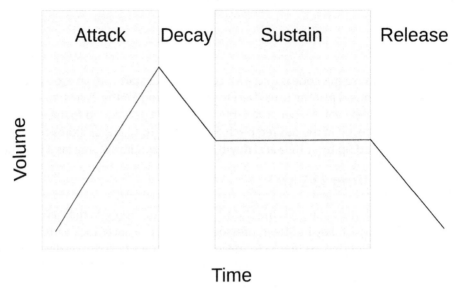

Figure 13-3. *ADSR volume envelope*

The code first determines which phase of the ADSR it's in: attack, decay, sustain, or release. If it's in the attack phase, it increases the volume by one level per AT TACK_RATE ticks of the noteClock. As an example of how this works, consider the clock and volume starting off at zero and an ATTACK_RATE of three. Initially, the clock and volume*ATTACK_RATE are all zero, so no action is required. When the clock ticks over to one, the clock part is larger, and the volume is incremented. Now vol ume*ATTACK_RATE is equal to three, and the volume won't be incremented again until clock tick three, and so forth.

The other stages of the ADSR work the same, only instead of starting from having the clock at zero, e.g. the decay phase starts at the end of the attack phase so the ATTACK_TIME is subtracted off the clock. Because the volume remains constant during the sustain, we just ignore it, and pick back up when it's time to start decreasing the volume again during the release phase.

Auxiliary Files

This program relies on a *lot* of other files to function, and though they're kinda cool from a musical synthesis perspective, they're out of the scope of this book.

The waveform tables are loaded up from header files that store our lookup table in RAM as a 256-byte array. The routines that generate these waveforms are in a Python program that's attached, *generateWavetables.py*. You can also make your own to correspond to whatever timbre you'd like the DDS sounds to take on. However, RAM memory is limited to 1 kB on the ATmega168 chips, and burning a quarter of that memory up for each waveform you'd like to play is dangerous. You'll be fine loading two waveforms into memory, but three is dangerous and loading four will certainly end up with different sections of memory overwriting each other and impossible to debug glitches. You've been warned.

Arrays in Memory

The way that we're storing the waveform tables in memory isn't particularly efficient—we're storing them in the chip's scarce dynamic memory (of which the chip has only 1 kB) even though the values don't change. A much better approach is to store the waveforms in the flash program memory space, where we've got 16 kB of space, and we know for sure that some of it is sitting empty. I'll cover the use of program memory in Chapter 18, so if you need to build a synthesizer with a whole bunch more wavetables, feel free to skip ahead.

Or you can use your head—I'm not exploiting any of the symmetry in the sine waves. Because the second half of the cycle is just the same as the first half but with a negative sign, you could easily cut memory storage in half. You could also cut the storage in half again if you observe that for each sample in the first quarter, the same sample in the second quarter is just 255 minus the first.

I thought the DDS code was complicated enough without this extra optimization, so I left it as simple as possible. This means you can't really use more than three waveforms in the same program without running into trouble.

The scales that are loaded up in *scale.h* are generated by the Python file *generateScale.py*. These accumulator increment values are dependent on the processor speed we choose as well as on using 8-bit PWM. If you're interested in other pitches, or nontraditional pitches, feel free to play around with the scales.

Anyway, DDS synthesis is a great tool. If you're content with a lower bit-depth or a slower sample rate, creating music this way is entirely within the power of an AVR chip, even for multiple voices simultaneously. Indeed, you'll see in Chapter 18 that it's fairly easy to make reasonable-sounding human sampled speech, for instance. And although we're aiming at audio here, bear in mind that similar techniques can be used (with proper buffering for current-handling capability) to smoothly accelerate and decelerate motors, or any other situation where you need time-varying voltage waveforms.

Switches | 14

Driving Simple Loads with Transistors, Relays, and DC Motors

Microcontrollers are great for many things where you need a little bit of computer smarts in a physical system.

One thing they're not suited for is driving big electrical loads. The pins on the AVR are great for driving small things like our LEDs or even a speaker (decoupled with a capacitor so that it doesn't draw too much current). But they just don't put out enough juice to turn a motor—at least not a motor big enough to do anything meaningful!

This is a problem, because everybody needs a robot or two, and robots need motors. The AVR chips (especially the larger ones) make a great small-robot brain. Sure, you can make it flash LEDs and sing through a speaker, but without legs or wheels, your robot is more like a brain in a jar. Your mechanized killer droid is not going to get very far without the ability to turn a motor.

We made a start on this problem in Chapter 11, where you saw how to control servo motors. Servos are designed especially to accept logic-level signals so that the AVR doesn't have to do any heavy lifting. In this chapter, I'll cover a number of circuits that you can use to allow the AVR to run motors that don't have internal interfacing circuitry.

The secret to driving large loads is using transistors between the AVR and a motor. You'll see that's it's easy enough to run a motor forward with just a single transistor used as a switch. You can then add speed control using PWM. If you're not into motors, the same circuits and techniques can control any large DC load. You could drive serious room-lighting LEDs, or power solenoids to latch and unlatch doors.

For the project in this chapter, we'll just be making a motor turn at different speeds. I added a wheel with a white stripe painted on it to make the turning more visible.

But this chapter is much more about enabling you to build something of your own than it is following a particular project.

What You Need

In addition to the basic kit, you will need:

- A DC motor and a power supply. I used a small model-car motor that worked nicely with a 9V battery. Whatever motor you use, make sure you have the right batteries to drive it. (If the toy runs on 4xAA, don't use much more than 6 V.)

- Some transistors for driving the load. I used our old standby 2N7000 because I only needed to drive a small motor. For larger loads, a good choice is something larger like an IRF530 or similar power MOSFET.

- A flyback diode and a smoothing capacitor for the motor. I used a random 1N4007 rectifier diode because I had one on hand. For big loads and high speeds, there are specifically

designed motor flyback diodes. A ceramic capacitor or two in the 10 nF to 1 uF range will work—the value is not critical. Both of these are "optional" in the sense that your motor will probably turn, but you put the transistor at risk of reverse-voltage breakdown when you turn the motor off.

- (Optionally) any other switch-like devices you've got on hand. Relays, SSRs, or Darlington Transistors (TIP120, etc.).

- (Optionally) other DC-powered devices like LED lamps or pumps or fans or solenoids or kids toys or….

- A USB-Serial adapter.

Controlling Big Loads: Switches

As you learned back in Chapter 3, each of the AVR's digital outputs has two transistors—one connected to the VCC supply and one connected to GND. It outputs digital logic by turning one of these two transistors on, making it conduct. The limiting factor for the AVR driving "big" loads is these internal transistors and the fact that they're only tied to VCC. So before we dive into the specifics of motors, let's take a quick overview of our options for circuits that require a higher voltage than the AVR can run at, a higher current than its transistors can handle, or both of the above.

If we can't drive our hypothetical load directly from the AVR like we have been doing with our LEDs or speakers, we'll need to connect the AVR's digital I/O pins up to something else that can act as a switch to drive our motor in its place. All of these switches can be modelled as three-terminal devices that allow some current or voltage to pass through two of their pins depending on the voltage or current at or through the third terminal. We hook up this control terminal to the output of the AVR, and we're set.

High-side Versus Low-side Switches

Even in the simplest case, turning a motor on or off with a switch, there are two choices: putting the switch on the high side (higher voltage, "above" or "upstream" of the motor in the circuit) or putting it on the low side (lower voltage, or "below" the motor). These two cases are illustrated in Figure 14-1.

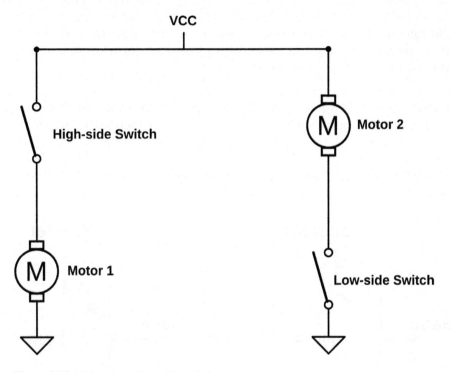

Figure 14-1. *High-side and low-side switches*

If we're talking about a switch that you open and close by pressing a button, the choice is irrelevant—either configuration will stop the flow of electricity when the circuit is opened, so the motor won't run. Notice that "Motor 1" and "Motor 2" both run when their switches are pushed closed, but the high-side circuit works by the switch closing at VCC and the low-side circuit works by the switch closing at GND.

This distinction between high-side and low-side switching will matter a lot when we use electronically operated switches like transistors, which need a voltage difference to turn on. In the low-side switching configuration, the transistor is connected to ground, and the voltage that you use to switch it on or off is thus relative to ground. When you use a high-side switch, the "ground" voltage level that the transistor sees is whatever voltage is present at the high-side of the motor, which is variable and can be tricky to deal with.

The upshot is that it's often a lot easier to use a low-side switch if you've got the choice.

Let's look into the different options for switching larger loads in depth.

Bipolar-Junction Transistors

The first transistors to become popular—the ones that displaced vacuum tubes—were the *bipolar junction* transistors (BJTs). Bipolar transistors can be thought of as a way of taking an input current and using that to allow a much bigger, proportional current to flow between collector and emitter. For most transistors, this current gain is around 100x, which means that if you pass 10 mA through the base, the transistor will allow up to 1 A to flow from collector to emitter. If you reduce the input current to 1 mA, only 100 mA will be able to flow through the transistor. This is the sense in which transistors are amplifiers: small changes in a small current can create big changes in a bigger current.

BJTs are made up of a sandwich of silicon layers that have been positively and negatively charged. Positively doped silicon has ions with a net positive charge mixed in, and vice versa for the negative kind. These are then layered together to make sandwiches with either the negative-doped silicon on the outside (NPN) or the positive on the outside (PNP). Either configuration is a "bipolar junction." When they're left alone, the middle layer prevents electrical conduction from the collector to the emitter:

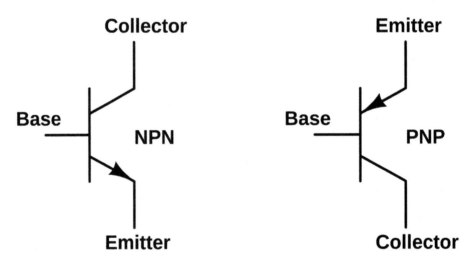

BJTs become interesting under the effects of a control current. Although the middle *base* layer in the silicon sandwich normally insulates the two outside layers from each other, you *can* run a current from the base to the *emitter*, following the little arrow in the circuit symbol. Because of the geometry of the silicon and some quantum mechanics, once your control current introduces free electrons into the base layer, a larger proportional current then flows between the *collector* and *emitter* (also in the same direction as the arrows).

For the NPN transistor, you provide the control current by raising the base voltage up *above* that at the emitter. For the PNP transistor, the control current is created by having the base voltage *lower* than the emitter. Either way, the effect is the same: a small current between base and emitter allows a much larger current to flow between the collector and emitter.

One disadvantage of using BJTs, from the AVR perspective, is that they're current-driven. The AVR's digital outputs are only rated for a few tens of milliamps, so if you are using a transistor with a current gain of 100, the maximum current you can run through the transistor is on the order of one amp. If you need to control more current than that, you either need to buy a transistor with higher current gain or figure out another way to get more drive current. One way to do this is to drive your transistor with another transistor. This is not as crazy as it sounds.

Darlington transistors are just a pair of transistors built together into the same chunk of silicon so that the first one supplies drive current to the second. Because the first transistor amplifies the current that is again amplified by the second transistor, instead of having a gain of around 35–100, Darlingtons have a current gain around 1,000 to 10,000. Now the puny 10 mA that the AVR will put out is able to switch 10–100 A on and off. Hooray!

The other downside of BJTs, and this one is unavoidable, is that they have a voltage drop across the collector/emitter pair—that's wasted from the perspective of your motor, and it heats up the transistor to boot. If you look at the datasheet for a TIP102, one of my favorite power Darlington transistors, you'll see that it has a collector/emitter saturation voltage of around 2 V. This means that if you're driving a motor that's designed for 12 V and 1 A, you'll need a power supply of 14 V, and you'll generate 2 V × 1 A = 2 watts of heat in the transistor. It's gonna get hot and probably need a heatsink.

Finally, in order to control BJT transistors from the AVR, you'll have to convert the digital I/O voltage level into a current for the transistor input. And to do that, you'll use a resistor and Ohm's law.

MOSFETs

The *metal oxide silicon field-effect transistor* (MOSFET for short) is a more recently widespread type of transistor. We're already using a small-signal MOSFET (the 2N7000) in our basic LED-driving setup, and now we'll take a second to talk more about its inner workings.

MOSFETs work by passing current through a channel of silicon that's been positively or negatively doped, just like in the BJT. The difference is that the amount of current that is allowed to pass through the channel depends on an electric field that's imposed on the slice of silicon by putting a voltage on a metal *gate* plate. The gate doesn't actually touch the silicon channel layer. Instead, it's insulated from

Selecting the Base Resistor

If you're using a digital I/O pin from the AVR, you're limited to outputting either 0 V or 5 V (for instance). That's usually too much for a transistor; you'll need to do something to limit the current going into the base. You can calculate the value you need using Ohm's law, with one minor detail: because the negatively and positively doped layers inside the transistor already have a voltage on them, there's a certain minimum voltage between base and emitter (called something like V_{BE}, measuring around 0.7 V for regular transistors, and 1.4 V for Darlingtons) that you have to overcome before *any* current starts flowing. But after that, it's just $V = I \times R$.

As an example, imagine that you've got a 12 V battery and you'd like a current of 500 mA to flow through a motor. Imagine as well that you've got an NPN transistor with a current gain of 100, and you're building the circuit in the low-side drive configuration of "Motor 2" in Figure 14-1. Because you gain is 100, you

want 500 mA/100 = 5 mA to flow from base to emitter. The low-side switch configuration means the emitter is at ground, so you need to add a resistor before the base to make 5 mA from (5 V – 0.7 V), which is the AVR's VCC minus the voltage drop across the inside of the transistor. You have 4.3 V/5 mA = 860 ohms. Putting a resistor around that value between the AVR pin and the base will allow up to 500 mA to flow through the transistor.

If you want to be really sure that the transistor is fully on, in what's known as the saturation region, you'll want to give it a bit more current than it needs, maybe by a factor of two. So pick a base resistor that's smaller by 50% or so. Instead of an 860 ohm resistor, 330 ohms is a standard value that should work. You may need to experiment with this resistance, though, because the transistor's gain is a particularly variable parameter.

the silicon by a thin layer of metal oxide, which explains the mouthful of a name. The electrical symbols for MOSFETs are shown in Figure 14-2.

N-Channel MOSFET

P-Channel MOSFET

Figure 14-2. *MOSFET Symbols*

Applying a voltage to the gate creates an electric field that extends through the insulator and into the channel, which makes a thin "inversion layer" in the channel, which is able to conduct electricity. Here comes the bit you need to remember. With an N-channel MOSFET, a positive voltage from gate to source allows a current to pass from drain to source. With a P-channel MOSFET, a negative voltage from gate to source allows current through, from source to drain. In this sense, the N-channel MOSFET is a bit like the NPN BJT, and vice versa.

Unlike BJTs, MOSFETs are voltage-controlled devices, which means that you don't have to include a base resistor when hooking them up to an AVR I/O pin—just wire up the AVR pin directly to the gate. Even better, small MOSFETs draw very little current when they're switching on or off, and almost none when they're in a steady state, so you don't have to worry about the AVR's current sourcing capabilities. (This is because the gate is insulated from the channel.) Finally, MOSFETs have almost no voltage-drop when they're on: even a small-signal switching MOSFET like our 2N7000 has only a couple of ohms of resistance when switched fully on. This means that less power is wasted heating up the transistor and that the load sees the full driving voltage.

Double Up for Double Current

Another nice feature with MOSFETs, although it's kind of a hack, is that because they only require a little current when turning on, you can easily run a few in parallel off of one AVR pin, especially at low frequencies. So take our 2N7000, for instance, which can handle 200 mA constant or 500 mA pulsed current. If you need to drive 400 mA or up to 1 A peak for a project, you can either go out to the MOSFET store and buy a bigger transistor or you can just use two 2N7000s in parallel, as long as they share the current equally.

And therein lies the secret. Because the on-resistance of a MOSFET increases as it gets hotter, if one of the transistors starts off taking too much of the current through itself, it'll heat up and become more resistive, which will then divert more of the current to the other, cooler MOSFET. In this sense, they're self-balancing.

I say this is a bit of a hack because the 2N7000s were certainly not designed for parallel load-sharing. But the process will definitely work because of the positive temperature/resistance relationship between the transistors (see the datasheet). In fact, many high-power MOSFETs are specifically designed to be operated in parallel; if you look at an industrial forklift, you'll find 20 or so power MOSFETs all in parallel screwed into the same big heatsink.

Anyway, though you're not going to be pushing a locomotive with a handful of 2N7000's, the ability to run a few of them in parallel to batter manage your current load is a handy trick to have up your sleeve.

Switching MOSFETs are designed to turn on and off quickly, with gate voltages that are between two and four volts. As such, they're the perfect "switch" to drive in PWM mode with a microcontroller's pin. Being small and fast, they can't pass a whole lot of current or withstand very high voltages, but our 2N7000 is good for a couple hundred milliamps at 5 V or 100 ms bursts of 50 mA at 60 V—both situations that the AVR alone couldn't handle. In short, switching MOSFETs make the ideal next step when your power or voltage demands are just out of reach of the AVR's digital output drivers.

Power MOSFETs

If you want to power something really beefy, say an electric bike or a heavy robot, you'll want a specifically designed power MOSFET (or several). Modern power MOSFETs are just like their smaller switching MOSFET cousins, only larger and with a geometry that's adapted to deliver more current with less resistance, and thus less wasted heat. The trade-off is that power MOSFETs usually require a higher gate voltage to turn fully on and a little more current as well if you'd like to turn them on and off quickly.

As the MOSFETs get bigger and bigger, the area between the gate and the channel gets bigger. To make the same electric field strength inside the channel of the transistor, more charge is needed. In fact, viewed from the gate and source pins, all MOSFETs behave like a capacitor—a certain charge needs to be pushed onto the gate to create a given electric field between the gate and source, just like a capacitor stores charge in the form of an electric field between its two plates.

With power MOSFETs, this gate capacitance limits how quickly the switch can be turned off and on, which puts limits on how quickly you can PWM the MOSFET switch. Small switching FETs have a small gate capacitance and are easy enough to charge up using just an AVR I/O pin's internal current source, with a gate capacitance in the tens of picofarads, and switching speeds up to 1 MHz. Larger power MOSFETs can have gate capacitances on the order of thousands of picofarads, which means that you've got to charge up effectively a 100 times larger capacitor to get the switch open. This means you'll need more current sourcing capability and probably more voltage to push it through if you want the power FET to switch on at the same speed. The trade-off for the increased gate size is that you get a MOSFET with only 20 milliohms of resistance capable of switching 12 amps at 80 volts.

If you're truly pushing the high-voltage, high-current, high-frequency PWM frontier, you'll want a *gate driver* chip that's tailor-made to supply the fast charging that the biggest power MOSFETs need. If you just want to drive a fairly beefy (5 A at 12 V) small-robot motor at moderate switching speeds (<20 kHz), you can probably drive it directly from the AVR, or at worst through a switching MOSFET as a first stage.

Relays

A lot of people would start out all this discussion of switches with the *relay*. After all, a relay is just a switch that's opened and closed by electromagnet, so they're easiest to understand. Put a current through a coil of wire, and it pulls a piece of metal into contact with another piece of metal and your switch closes. Done.

The reason relays are near the end of my discussion is that they're fairly special-purpose these days. They switch on and off comparatively slowly, going click-clack as they physically open and close. This means that PWM is out of the question as a method of control—you can turn a normal relay on and off a couple of times per second, but not much more. And the coils that make the magnetic field take a lot of current. With the exception of precision (costly and sensitive) relays, most require too much current to be directly driven by the AVR's output pins, so you'll need something like a MOSFET switch just to run the relay.

There's one last thing about relays that's miserable. Being electromagnets on the inside, they build up a magnetic field. When you turn them off, this magnetic field collapses and generates a reverse voltage, which can be quite large. This reverse voltage can, in turn, fry your MOSFET or even the AVR if you don't give the reverse voltage somewhere to go. So relays also need a diode in parallel with them to allow for this "discharge" current, as shown in Figure 14-3.

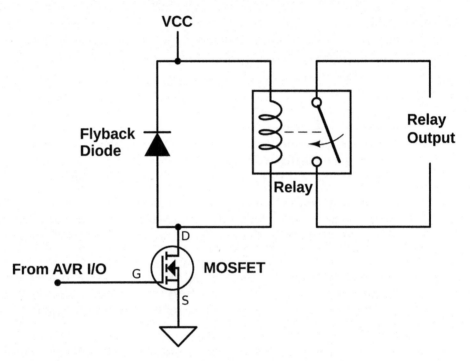

Figure 14-3. *Relay driving circuit*

So relays are a niche switch. Where they really shine is when you can take advantage of the fact that they're physical switches. For instance, if you want to switch a hairdryer or a floodlight on or off, you need to control a lot of (alternating) current at a high voltage. This is a slightly tricky circuit design for solid state, but it's easy enough to find a 5 V or 12 V relay that is rated to switch these kinds of household appliances on or off, wire it up to an electrical socket, and you're done. That's a job for a relay.

Triacs and SSRs

Relays are finnicky, noisy, prone to arcing, not shockproof, and require a bunch of current just to keep them going. You have to build that whole circuit in Figure 14-3 just to drive them. If you really want to get fancy, or if you need to PWM your household appliance, you're going to want something solid state.

The main contenders here are *triacs* and *solid state relays* (SSRs). Triacs are like transistors but used for AC instead of DC. SSRs are basically triacs with some extra circuitry to help isolate the control side from the AC line voltage. Many (most?) SSRs have an LED on the control side and a light-sensitive triac on the AC side, so that turning on or off a washing machine looks to your AVR like blinking an LED; but because there's no direct electrical connection between the AVR side and the wall-voltage side, there is no corresponding electrocution hazard, and that's a darn good thing.

We won't be using either of these in our projects here, but if you ever need to control a wall-voltage device from the AVR, you should look into an SSR. I used one once, along with a temperature sensor, to regulate the heater in an electric coffee roaster.

Switches: Summary

If you want to control real power with the AVR, there's a number of switch-like devices out there that will help you do it. What you need to use will depend on the specifics of the motor or laser or home appliance you want to run.

For providing power to small-robot DC motors, BJTs—particularly Darlington BJT circuits—can work just fine. If you need more current, the advantages of a (more complicated) power MOSFET circuit become more apparent. Keep both of them in mind.

Small switching MOSFETs, like the 2N7000 that we're using, are great for driving small-to-medium loads, even if you have to use a few in parallel. We'll be using a 2N7000 to drive the laser in the laser-sundial application, and for driving power MOSFETs.

Finally, when you need to control house-voltage AC, you've got two main choices. If you're doing low-frequency switching, it's hard to beat the simplicity of a relay driven with a switching FET. If you need to turn the device on and off a lot, you'll want an SSR.

A summary of all of the possible switch choices can be found in Table 14-1.

Table 14-1. Switching: transistors, relays, etc.

Type	Activation	Voltage gain	Current gain	Voltage type	Main use
Bipolar	Current	High	Lower	DC	Amplifying voltage signal
Darlington	Current	Very high	Can be high	DC	Amplifying, sourcing current
FETs	Voltage	Lower	High	DC	Sourcing current
Relay	Current	-	-	AC or DC	Literal switching
SSR	Voltage	-	-	AC	Medium-speed PWM

DC Motors

The simplest motor that we'll deal with is the plain-old DC motor. A DC motor takes a voltage across its two inputs, alternately charges up two internal electromagnets, and uses the resulting magnetic force to spin a shaft. If you reverse the sense of the voltage, the motor spins the other way. If you apply more voltage, it'll turn faster (within limits). DC motors are great for spinning things relatively fast when positioning precision doesn't matter; when they are geared down, they turn more slowly but provide more torque. A geared DC motor is probably what you want to use to drive the wheels of your robot or automatically raise and lower your windowshades.

If DC motors are so simple, there shouldn't be all that much to say about using a microcontroller to drive DC motors, right? Not necessarily! Grab yourself a small motor to play around with, strap on your 2N7000, construct the circuit in Figure 14-4, and let's run some experiments.

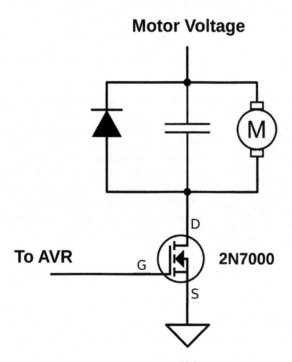

Figure 14-4. *DC Motor with low-side MOSFET switch*

First, look over the circuit in Figure 14-4 and Figure 14-5. You should recognize this as the low-side switch configuration, with a motor in the middle: one side of the motor is connected directly to VCC and the other side to the 2N7000 switch that is connected to ground. The *flyback diode* in Figure 14-4 is important to provide a

Motor as Generator

Why is a DC motor's speed controlled by the voltage we apply across the terminals?

Just as our piezo disk could be viewed as converting vibration to voltage or voltage to vibration, most motors are actually also electrical generators. Generators (intentionally designed ones) work by spinning a permanent magnet inside a series of coils, and the changing magnetic field induces electrical currents in the wires. Motors work in exactly the opposite way: changing electrical currents in the wires create changing magnetic fields inside a series of coils, which spin the magnet and spindle.

For just about any DC motor, if you put voltage into its terminals, you'll create motion in its shaft. If you spin the shaft, you'll find that a voltage develops across the terminals. The faster you spin the motor, the higher the generator voltage.

In a motor, this generator voltage is called *back voltage* or *back EMF* (electro-motive force, which is another word for voltage) and is what limits a motor speed. When a motor starts up because you've applied 5 V to it, the forward voltage is 5 V, and because the motor isn't spinning yet, no back voltage is generated. As the motor speeds up, its effective generator puts out more and more voltage, but in the opposite sense to the applied voltage. When the back voltage just equals the forward voltage, the motor stops speeding up, and it's reached maximum speed. If you increase the applied voltage, the motor speeds up until the generated back voltage just equals the new applied voltage.

You'll see the same thing with the current, too. When you first turn the motor on, and the voltage difference is maximized, current goes rushing through the motor. As the motor comes up to speed, the difference between the applied voltage and the back voltage shrinks, and less and less current is fed through. An ideal motor, driving no load, with no friction and no wire resistance, would stop drawing current once it gets up to speed. In the real world, some current is needed to drive the load and overcome friction, but at cruising speed, the current draw will be minimized if not minimal.

Normal brushed DC motors make kinda crappy generators. The one on my desk measures about half a volt with no load put on it when I spin it as fast as I can. Brushless DC motors or stepper motors, on the other hand, are pretty darn effective. You can demonstrate this by taking a stepper motor and putting an LED across two of the paired coil wires and giving it a spin.

In fact, each pair of pole wires of a stepper motor put out AC when used as a generator, so you can connect two LEDs back to back across the pole wires. When the coil puts out a positive voltage, one LED will light, and when it puts out a negative voltage, the other LED will light. And now do the same thing with the other pole of the motor—add two more LEDs. If you could see fast enough, you'd see that the LEDs light up one at a time in exactly the sequence that we'll end up using to drive the motor.

path for the current that's flowing through the motor to continue on after we've switched the motor off. Finally, the optional capacitor smooths out noise that the DC motor itself makes as the brushes inside switch from one polarity to the other.

If you're using a separate voltage source for the motor, like a battery, be sure to connect the negative pole of the battery to your circuit ground, and the positive end directly to the motor as shown in Figure 14-5. Notice that the battery ground and the MOSFET's ground are both connected to the AVR's circuit ground. This gives the AVR, its power supply, the 2N7000, and the battery the same reference voltage.

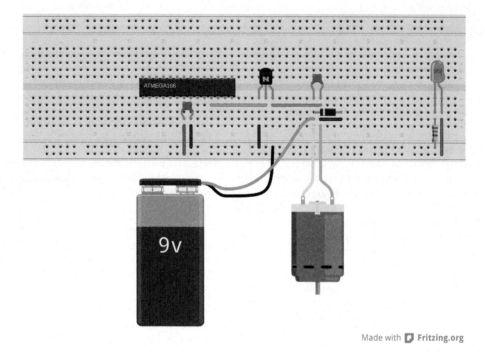

Figure 14-5. *DC Motor on a breadboard with a battery*

As a first experiment, hook up the transisor, motor, diode, and capacitor as in Figure 14-4. If you don't have a battery handy, and your DC motor will run on the breadboard's 5 V, feel free to connect the high side of the motor directly into the power rail. This circuit is temporary anyway, so feel free to use alligator clips to hook it all together wherever you need to.

Now, without any code in the AVR, you can verify that you can control the motor by applying 5 V and 0 V to the gate of the transistor through a wire. Pull out the AVR side of the wire that connects the gate of the MOSFET to the AVR. Tap it alternatively to the 5 V and ground power supply. You should see the motor start to spin when you connect the wire to 5 V, and stop spinning when you connect it to ground. This is exactly what we'll have the AVR doing in a few minutes.

What happens if you just hold the wire in your fingers? MOSFET gates take very little current to turn on and off, and you may be coupling enough voltage from power line radiation to turn it on. If not, try alternately touching your 5 V power supply and then ground with your free hand. You'll find that your body charges and discharges enough to flip the switch.

Now let's put the motor under the AVR's control. Reconnect the gate of the 2N7000 transistor to pin PD5 as in Figure 14-5, and we'll use Timer 0 and the output compare

Flyback

What happens when you turn off a running motor? For a little while, the motor's still spinning, so it's still generating its back voltage. But the motor's generator voltage turns out to be a relatively small effect when if you suddenly turn off the power.

While the motor was running, the motor windings have been passing current through them and have built up these powerful magnetic fields that in turn spin the motor. All of a sudden you shut this current supply off, and the magnetic fields collapse, and as they do so create a voltage in the same direction as the applied voltage was (and opposite the back voltage). The faster the current is shut off, the higher this voltage is. That is, the motor windings act like an *inductor*.

You can think of inductors as being like flywheels for the current—when you try to stop a current suddenly, inductors try to keep the current flowing in the same direction, and this can show up as a high voltage developing across them. With my little motors on my desk, I get roughly 30 V peaks, even though

I'm driving them with a 5 V power supply—it's all in how quickly you shut the driving current off. With bigger motors and higher currents and voltages, the voltage spikes can get into the hundreds of volts.

This is where the flyback diode comes in. It provides a path for the current generated by the "inductive kick" to go, namely through the motor, back up the diode, and through the motor again in a loop. This short-circuit loop continues until the magnetic fields are discharged.

So the energy built up in the coils creates a high voltage across the motor's coils. Where does this energy go? Some of it is cancelled out by the motor's generator voltage, some of it is dissipated in the winding resistance of the motor (heating up the motor), and some of it heats up the flyback diode.

In conclusion, if you'd like to keep high flyback voltages from frying your transistor switches, please remember to add in a flyback diode.

pin functionality to experiment with simple DC motor driving. If you've still got that circuit set up, the transistor is already hooked up in the right place.

Flash in the code and then you can start playing around with your motor. Driving a motor with signal-switching FETs is a little bit sketchy, so you might want to keep a finger on the MOSFET and see if it warms up excessively. It shouldn't get hot unless you're putting the motor under a load, though. Let's look at the code in Example 14-1.

Example 14-1. dcMotorWorkout.c listing

```
                              /* Demos PWM control of a DC motor */

// ------- Preamble -------- //
#include <avr/io.h>
#include <util/delay.h>
#include <avr/interrupt.h>
#include "pinDefines.h"
#include "USART.h"

#define SPEED_STEP_DELAY 2                       /* milliseconds */
```

```
// -------- Functions --------- //
static inline void initTimer0(void) {
  TCCR0A |= (1 << WGM00);                      /* Fast PWM mode */
  TCCR0A |= (1 << WGM01);                   /* Fast PWM mode, pt.2 */
  TCCR0A |= (1 << COM0B1);                   /* output PWM to pin */
  TCCR0B |= (1 << CS02);            /* Clock with /1024 prescaler */
  //TCCR0B |= (1 << CS00);        /* Clock with /1024 prescaler, pt.2 */
}


int main(void) {

  uint8_t updateSpeed;

  // -------- Inits --------- //
  initTimer0();
  OCR0B = 0;

  ANTENNA_DDR |= (1 << ANTENNA);    /* now hooked up to MOSFET, output */
  LED_DDR |= (1 << LED0);
  LED_DDR |= (1 << LED1);

  initUSART();
  printString("DC Motor Workout\r\n");

  // ------ Event loop ------ //
  while (1) {

    updateSpeed = getNumber();

                                    /* Ramp up/down to desired speed */
    if (OCR0B < updateSpeed) {
      LED_PORT |= (1 << LED0);
      while (OCR0B < updateSpeed) {
        OCR0B++;
        _delay_ms(SPEED_STEP_DELAY);
      }
    }
    else {
      LED_PORT |= (1 << LED1);
      while (OCR0B > updateSpeed) {
        OCR0B--;
        _delay_ms(SPEED_STEP_DELAY);
      }
    }
    LED_PORT = 0;                                      /* all off */

  }                                           /* End event loop */
  return (0);                   /* This line is never reached */
}
```

There's nothing particularly new in the code, and I copied a large part of it straight from other examples. I just wanted to write something that you can get a feel for driving motors with. (Once you've gotten a library of working examples for yourself, you'll find that this kind of code reuse is phenomenally handy.) The Timer 0 initialization routine is taken straight from our PWM examples; it sets up the timer to output the PWM waveform on pin PD5. The getNumber() routine takes in a number (as ASCII characters) that's sent over the serial line.

The main event loop waits for you to type in a PWM value over the serial line and then adjusts the OCR0B register smoothly up or down to that value, lighting up LEDs for acceleration or deceleration, respectively. As befits a simple demo program, almost all of the time is spent sitting and waiting for you to type something in.

The real point of the program, though, is to get you familiar with driving small DC motors by PWM, so flash this in and start typing PWM duty-cycle values. Hit Return after each one, and it'll ramp up the motor.

The first thing to notice is that, although the PWM duty cycle will vary the percentage of the time that the motor is powered, that is not the same as controlling the speed. With my different motors, they would start turning only in the 20–60 (out of 255) range, even at their proper working voltages. Motors, and especially gearmotors, have different internal frictions and coil inductances that make them unique.

Next, change the clock prescaler in initTimer0. First, just try commenting out the TCCR0B |= (1<<CS02); line to change from prescaling by 1,024 to 256. At 1,024, the PWM frequency is a fairly low 31.25 Hz. At low duty cycles, you may be able to hear the individual pulses. At a prescaling of 256, you should be able to hear a low hum coming from the motor windings—the PWM frequency is around 125 Hz. Look at the datasheet where it describes the possible clock settings and experiment with them all. As you increase the PWM frequency, you'll notice that the range of duty cycles over which the motor runs will change. How different motors respond to different PWM drive frequencies depends a lot on the winding resistance and inductance, which varies from motor to motor, as well as the driving voltage.

Finally, you can experiment with how quickly your motor changes speed when driven at different duty cycles. The macro definition #define SPEED_STEP_DELAY 10 sets the rate at which the PWM duty cycle changes. If you set this to zero, the PWM will change as soon as you hit Enter and transmit the new value. If you set it higher, the motor will ramp up more slowly. Try to imagine what would happen if you had this motor and a wheel on a robot or vehicle. Think about what kinds of accelerations it can handle. Load the wheel down with your hand. (Or if you've built a bot already, playing around with code like this will let you discover your traction limits.)

 *Motor Specs*

*If you're buying a motor, there are a couple of specifications that you should know about. The first spec is the **rated voltage**. Most DC motors will run +/– 50% of their rated voltage, but you want one that matches your power source, or vice versa. For small bots, look for something in the 3 V to 12 V range to match your batteries.*

*The other spec is **stall current**, which is just the rated voltage divided by the coil winding resistance. Stall current is the maximum current that the motor will draw when it's just starting up (or when it's stalled out) and the back voltage is at 0 V. The transistor that you're running the motor with should be able to deliver at least this much current, if not a little more as a safety margin.*

Gearmotors

The good thing about DC motors is that they spin very fast. The disadvantage, though, is that they don't have much turning force, or *torque*, at lower speeds. As you noticed with the PWM speed control demo, it's easier to stall the motor out when it's turning slowly than when it's at full speed, and if your motors are anything like mine, it wasn't hard to stop even at full speed.

Suppose you've got a motor that turns at 6,000 rpm, and is only able to drive a 10 gram robot. Perhaps you'd rather have the wheels turn 60 times per minute, but push a 1 kg robot. Using gears with your motor will let you make this trade-off. Gears are like a lever—you can push a heavier weight, but it travels less (rotational) distance per unit time.

These days, there are scores of small gearmotors available for small to medium robots, RC cars, etc. Depending on the size of the wheels and the weight of the robot, something in the 100:1 gear reduction ratio tends to be about right. If you want to build something lightweight to play around with code and scoot around the room, it's hard to beat the Tamiya double gearbox kit, which you can find for under $10 and has a nice assortment of matching tires.

Advanced Motors 15

H-Bridges and Stepper Motors

In Chapter 14 we discussed how to use the AVR to drive big loads in the simplest, on-off case. Adding in PWM to the mix allows you to, for instance, vary the speed of a motor. That's great, right? Now your little robot is going forward fast and forward slow. But what do you do when you want to put it in reverse?

In this chapter, I'll introduce you to some useful concepts for more advanced motor-driving. The first step in all this is to build (or buy) a circuit that can reverse a DC motor by applying voltage to it in either polarity. Such a circuit is called an *H-bridge*, and I'll go into detail about how you can build your own if you need to.

If you are only driving small motors, there is very probably a premade solution out there that is cheaper, easier, and more reliable than building your own. For instance, the SN754410 chip provides two full H-bridges in one package.

Finally, we'll dip our toes into driving stepper motors. Steppers are great for fairly accurate positioning coupled with decent speed. Driving one stepper motor is roughly equivalent to driving two DC motors, but we'll see that some coordination (in code) is necessary.

For fun and inspiration, a bunch of motors that I've driven with the AVR code and SN754410 H-bridge chip are shown in Figure 15-1. These include stepper motors on the left, gear motors in the middle, and two small plain DC motors on the bottom right.

Figure 15-1. *Motors, motors, motors*

This chapter doesn't have finished projects so much as demonstrations of the key ideas and circuits necessary for handling these advanced motor modes. What you build them into is entirely up to you!

Going in Reverse: H-Bridges

If you want to run your DC motor backward, and you're hooking things up by hand, all you have to do is reverse the polarity on the motor by swapping the wires around. How are we going to do the same thing electronically? The answer turns out to be a circuit called an *H-bridge*. Unfortunately, there's no such thing as a DIY H-bridge circuit that's simple, powerful, *and* efficient. We'll go through a couple of designs here, starting with simple and inefficient and ending with powerful and efficient but a bit complicated. Of course, you can also go out and buy a wide range of motor-driver and H-bridge chips ready-made that'll do as good a job, or better, than anything you can make yourself.

To reverse a DC motor, you need to be able to drive one side of the motor either high or low, while the other side is driven low or high, respectively. An H-bridge achieves this with two switches, a high-side *and* a low-side switch, for each motor connection. Have a look at the rough sketch in Figure 15-2 and you'll see why they call it an "H" bridge.

What You Need

For this chapter, what you'll need depends on how much you'd like to get out of it.

For experimenting with H-bridges:

- A DC motor and a power supply capable of driving it. Many small model-car motors will run on 4–6 V, or 4xAA batteries.

- MOSFETs for building an H-bridge. I use two IRF9530s, two IRF530s, and two of our standby 2N7000.

- If you don't want to build an H-bridge by yourself but just want experience with using one, you'll need one of either an SN754410 or L293D chip.

- A USB-Serial adapter.

For experimenting with stepper motors:

- A stepper motor and a power supply to drive it. Because we're just experimenting, any old stepper that you can find will work. A junked printer or scanner will probably have a 9–12 V stepper motor inside it if you'd like to take one apart. A 9 V battery is just right in that case.

- A working H-bridge. If you didn't build your own in the first section, an SN754410 or L293D chip is a very good choice.

- A USB-Serial adapter.

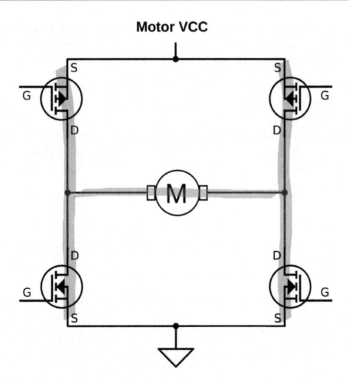

Motor VCC

Figure 15-2. *H-bridge sketch*

Each side of the H-bridge is just a push-pull MOSFET driver, in exactly the same configuration as the circuitry inside the digital I/O pins on the AVR but using higher-wattage components. To understand how it works, first look at one side of the H. When the top P-channel FET is turned on and the lower N-channel FET is off, the side is pulled to the motor-high supply voltage. Turn off the top switch, and turn on the low-side switch, and the voltage is pulled down to ground. This way, you can set either side of the H to high or low voltage. Now if you drive one side to the high voltage while the other is low, current flows and the motor spins. Switching the roles of the two sides reverses the motor. Success!

There are a couple of complications to this circuit, though. The first is how to interface this circuit with the AVR. The low-side FET is easy enough, and it will sink as much as 5 A with a 5 V AVR output with the parts specified. The high-side FET is trouble, though. To turn it on, you just have to pull the line low, which is easy enough. To turn it fully off, though, you need to raise the gate voltage to the same as the source of the FET, which is at the motor supply voltage. If you're running motors that want 9 V or 12 V or even more, you can't close the high-side switch without some intermediate circuitry.

The other danger with this circuit sketch is *shoot-through*. What would happen if you opened both the upper and lower switches on the same side? If each MOSFET has an on resistance of about half an ohm, the total resistance is only 1 ohm, or just about as much as you'd get if you put a screwdriver across the battery terminals: not good! The battery will put out as much current as it can, and something will burn: either the battery, your wiring, or the MOSFETs.

Finally, note that I picked a pair of MOSFETs with similar part numbers. These are designed to be used as a complementary pair and have similar characteristics. This matters a lot for controlling shoot-through and can be a gotcha when you're designing your own circuits. Because the high-side and low-side FETs we use are matched and have similar switch-on times, we can get away with a single signal to open one and close the other. (With random MOSFETs, you'll want some circuitry to control shoot-through.)

So with matched MOSFETs on the high and low side, we can drive them both at the same time. Because they're complementary, one will turn off just about as the other turns on. Now you might be tempted to drive these as is with the AVR's output pins, and that's not a horrible idea for low-voltage applications where the motor voltage is up to 5 V.

Things get more complicated when you want to drive a motor with more voltage than the AVR's VCC. The low-side switch is no problem—many FETs (and our IRF530s) will push a fair amount of current when the gate is held at 5 V with respect to ground. The problem is that you can't shut off the high-side switch completely without a source of 9–12 V, and the AVR's output pins aren't going to cut it any more. So what we're going to do is use transistor switches to drive our transistor switches as shown in Figure 15-3.

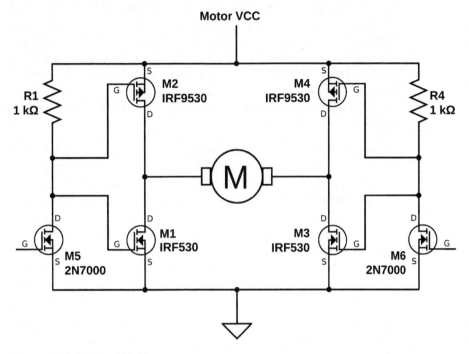

Figure 15-3. *Working H-bridge*

This H-bridge is stable and "smokeproof" (meaning, it's not possible to send it into a short-circuit mode through software). If the bridge is not hooked up to the AVR or if the AVR is sending a logic low, the gate of the 2N7000 is low and the 2N7000 is not conducting. If the 2N7000 is not conducting, the voltage on the power MOS-FETs is pulled up by the 1k ohm resistor to the motor power supply level, which shuts off the high-side MOSFET and fully opens the low side, which essentially grounds this side of the bridge.

When the left side 2N7000 gets a logic high voltage, it conducts and pulls both power MOSFETs' gates to ground. The low-side power MOSFET turns off when grounded, and the high-side MOSFET turns fully on, so the whole side is pulled strongly high. So a high signal to the half-bridge driver sets the output high, and vice versa.

Code: Taking Your H-Bridge Out for a Spin

The drive modes for this bridge are really simple. Because the state of the half-bridges mimics their input, you can just pretend that the AVR digital output is driving the motor, and the bridge will take care of the heavy lifting. This means that if you want the motor to rotate one way, simply set one AVR output pin high and the other low. To reverse, switch the high and low values. Easy!

But what happens when both sides of the bridge are held high or both held low? The motor doesn't know anything about high or low voltages. It only sees the voltage difference across its terminals. So if the motor wasn't moving to begin with, the modes (high, high) and (low, low) don't do anything. Both of these modes are just like connecting a wire across the two terminals of the motor. On the other hand, if the motor was already turning and then you switch to (high, high) the situation gets more interesting—you've just shorted out the terminals of a moving motor.

Look back at Figure 15-3, and think back to the motor-as-generator discussion in "Motor as Generator" on page 299. For concreteness, let's imagine that the motor was being powered (high, low) just before getting turned off to (high, high). Because the motor windings are inductors, they want to keep the current flowing in the same direction as their magnetic fields wind down. So the current will want to flow in a loop from the motor, up the open high-side FET, over to the other high-side FET, and back down into the motor. But because the motor is a generator, as long as it's turning, it's making a voltage that opposes this current. When you short-circuit a running motor, these two opposing voltages act like an electronic brake for the motor and stop it faster than it would if you just disconnected it.

So before we get to controlling *both* speed and direction by applying PWM to the circuit, let's play around with digital logic control of the bridge to get a good feel for how it works in Example 15-1. In the following H-bridge examples, the PD5 and PD6 pins (that we've used for the speaker and antenna previously) are connected to the bridge. If these are still hooked up, it might be time to pull them out or even to start up a new breadboard with another AVR chip.

Example 15-1. hBridgeWorkout.c listing

```
// Simple demo of an h-bridge

// ------- Preamble -------- //
#include <avr/io.h>
#include <util/delay.h>
#include <avr/interrupt.h>
#include "pinDefines.h"

static inline void setBridgeState(uint8_t bridgeA, uint8_t bridgeB) {
  /* Utility function that lights LEDs when it energizes a bridge side */
  if (bridgeA) {
    PORTD |= (1 << PD6);
    LED_PORT |= (1 << LED0);
  }
  else {
    PORTD &= ~(1 << PD6);
```

```
    LED_PORT &= ~(1 << LED0);
  }
  if (bridgeB) {
    PORTD |= (1 << PD5);
    LED_PORT |= (1 << LED1);
  }
  else {
    PORTD &= ~(1 << PD5);
    LED_PORT &= ~(1 << LED1);
  }
}


int main(void) {
  // -------- Inits --------- //

  DDRD |= (1 << PD6);                  /* now hooked up to bridge, input1 */
  DDRD |= (1 << PD5);                  /* now hooked up to bridge, input2 */
  LED_DDR |= (1 << LED0);
  LED_DDR |= (1 << LED1);

  // ------ Event loop ------ //
  while (1) {

    setBridgeState(1, 0);                          /* "forward" */
    _delay_ms(2000);

    setBridgeState(0, 0);                  /* both low stops motor */
    _delay_ms(2000);

    setBridgeState(0, 1);                          /* "reverse" */
    _delay_ms(2000);

    setBridgeState(1, 1);              /* both high also stops motor */
    _delay_ms(2000);

    // For extra-quick braking, energize the motor backwards
    setBridgeState(1, 0);
    _delay_ms(2000);
    setBridgeState(0, 1);
    _delay_ms(75);                  /* tune this time to match your system */
    setBridgeState(0, 0);
    _delay_ms(2000);

  }                                          /* End event loop */
  return (0);
}
```

The code includes one convenience function that takes a pair of values, one for each side of the H-bridge, and sets that output pin and an indicator LED. So if you call setBridgeState(1,0) it will turn on both the first H-bridge side and the first

LED, and turn off the second H-bridge side and second LED. Then the rest of the code enables output by setting the DDR for each and starts demoing the four possible H-bridge drive states.

At the very end, I tried an experiment with reversing the motor while it's still running in an attempt to get it to brake faster. Especially if your motor has a heavy wheel on it, you may be able to notice that using reverse as a brake stops the motor even faster than the two "normal" braking modes. Anyway, it's a handy technique if you find your robot coasting down to a stop too slowly.

Experts-Only H-Bridge

If you're using unmatched P-channel and N-channel FETs, or you're looking for more control, you can also drive the high side and low side separately as shown in Figure 15-4. This comes with the benefit that you can fine-tune the opening and closing times of the upper and lower FETs so that they're as fast as possible without shoot-through even with unmatched parts by tweaking the relative timing of signals in software.

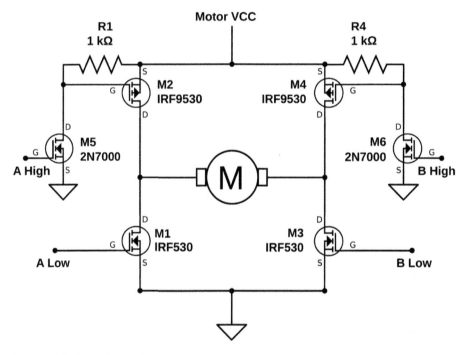

Figure 15-4. *Four-wire H-bridge*

If you hook up an H-bridge as in Figure 15-4, think super hard about the polarity of the control signals. In particular, when the "A High" signal is written high, the 2N7000 conducts, pulling the MOSFET gate low, which makes it conduct. When the "A Low" signal is written logic high, it also conducts. So what you're never going to want to do is have the AVR drive the two pins on the same side high at once.

On the other hand, driving both pins on the same side *low* at once opens both the upper and lower MOSFET switches, which leaves the motor to spin mostly freely. This mode is often called "coasting." If all four switches are open, it's like the motor isn't connected to anything at all and is free to turn.

There are also four other modes where only one transistor conducts, which end up being like coasting except that one leg of the current passes through a flywheel diode and one through a transistor. These modes are interesting for high-speed PWM, because you can alternate between driving and not driving by simply toggling one switch.

But let me repeat my warning that you should be extra careful with this circuit. Never close both the top and bottom MOSFETs on either side at the same time. Nobody likes burnt MOSFETs.

PWM and the H-Bridge

Being able to move a motor forward and backward is great, but for a real-world robot, you're going to want to have forward and backward with speed control. And the way to do this with digital outputs from your microcontroller is, of course, our old friend PWM. Because we're dealing with more current and external switches, not to mention a motor with inductance, things get a tiny bit more complicated. Here, I'll step you through what you need to know. We'll be using *both* our home-made H-bridge and an SN754410 (or the similar, but lower current, L293D) H-bridge chip to demonstrate the two main PWM modes that are commonly used to control motor speed. Table 15-1 summarizes the four drive states available to us with a standard H-bridge circuit.

Table 15-1. Our H-bridge's drive states

Left input	Right input	Current path	Result
0	0	Motor shorted, low side	Braking
0	1	Right to left	"Forward"
1	0	Left to right	"Backward"
1	1	Motor shorted, high side	Braking

With our H-bridge, we have three choices for driving the motor: forward, backward, and brake. This gives us basically two choices for PWM—alternating between forward and braking or between forward and backward. The first choice is called "sign-magnitude" drive, and the second is "locked-antiphase." Each PWM drive mode has its advantages and disadvantages, both for our code and for the driving circuit, so let's look at them briefly.

Drive Modes: Sign-Magnitude

Sign-magnitude drive is usually implemented in hardware motor drivers with two wires: one controls the direction of rotation (the "sign") and the other is PWM-ed to control how fast it goes (the "magnitude"), as summarized in Table 15-2.

Table 15-2. Sign-magnitude drive

Sign	Magnitude duty cycle	Result
1	100%	"Forward" full speed ahead
1	50%	"Forward" half speed
1	0%	Dynamic braking
0	0%	Dynamic braking
0	50%	"Backward" half speed
0	100%	"Backward" full speed

Sign-magnitude drive modes are usually implemented in a motor driver's discrete IC logic circuitry, but we can do the same in code. When we're going forward, we'll leave one side permanently on high and assign the other side to PWM control so that it toggles between high and low to alternate between driving and dynamic braking with both high. Going backward just means switching which side stays permanently high (and reinterpreting the PWM).

Note that we're using all three possibilities here—forward, reverse, and dynamic braking—although we're not using all four possible bridge states. We never use the (low, low) braking state, but that's OK because it's the same as the (high, high) state for all intents and purposes.

Drive Modes: Locked Anti-phase

In locked anti-phase mode, you only use two of the H-bridge's possible drives, forward and backward. The halves are "locked" to be out of phase with each other: when one is high, the other is always low. This simplification means that you could potentially control the bridge with just one wire, with both direction *and* speed controlled by the PWM duty cycle as summarized in Table 15-3.

Table 15-3. Locked anti-phase drive

PWM duty cycle	Result
100%	"Forward" full speed ahead
75%	"Forward" half speed
50%	Stopped
25%	"Backward" half speed
0%	Backward"" full speed

If you'd like to modify the H-bridge circuit for explicit locked anti-phase drive, you can add (yet another) 2N7000 and a pull-up resistor to invert the AVR's signal as shown in Figure 15-5.

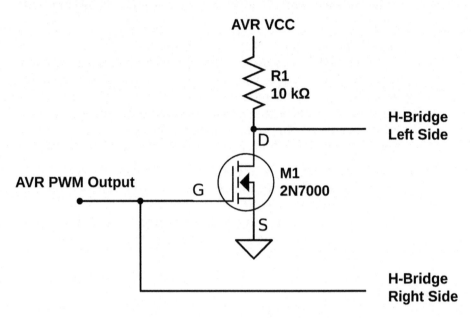

Figure 15-5. *Locked anti-phase circuit*

This circuit is a simple digital inverter—when the AVR's output is low, the direct signal passed to the H-bridge's right side is low. The voltage on the 2N7000 is also low, so it doesn't conduct, so the wire leading to the H-bridge's left side is pulled high. When the AVR pin is high, the 2N7000 conducts, pulling the left side low while the right side gets the direct high voltage.

The simplest way to control a locked anti-phase driver PWM bridge in code is to hook it up to a hardware-togglable pin and let the timer/counter module handle the rest for you. Your main code merely has to write the PWM value to the correct output-compare register.

Drive Modes: Comparison

Which of the possible drive modes is better? Well, as with everything, there are pluses and minuses to each. Locked anti-phase is simpler in that it only requires one wire between AVR and H-bridge, and that one timer/counter hardware PWM can handle everything for you.

The main problem with locked anti-phase drive is that, on startup, the motor is running at full speed in one direction or another until the AVR has gotten its PWM routine up and running to slow it down. This startup glitch is usually trivially short, but if your initialization routines take a long time to run, you might consider moving the motor-driver initializations to the top of your code. Similarly, if you accidently disable the timers, or you zap the AVR, or if the control signal wire comes unplugged, the motors run full speed ahead, which is definitely not what you want when something goes wrong. (Big robots *must* have kill switches attached to their power supplies.)

Secondarily, locked anti-phase mode keeps the H-bridge active and switching even while stopped, so it uses a little more power than sign-magnitude. It turns out not to be nearly as much as you might think, though. If you run the PWM at a high enough frequency, the motor windings end up building and collapsing magnetic fields and very little actual current flows; the motor doesn't turn, and little power is lost. (A little bit of power is lost to the flyback diodes and FETs because of the unequal and not-exactly-instantaneous switching speeds of the FETs.)

One thing in sign-magnitude's favor is that sometimes it's conceptually natural to think of "shifting" into forward or backward first and then controlling the speed. If something goes wrong, the sign-magnitude drive style will usually end up with the motors stopped, which is a bonus. Finally, if your motors spend a lot of time stopped, sign-magnitude is a slightly better choice for power use.

 Coasting

*Our H-bridge in **Figure 15-3** is a compromise design. In order to avoid the situation where both switches in a side are closed at the same time (which causes long-run shoot-through and catastrophic failure), we tied the P-channel and N-channel FET controls together. As a result, one (and only one) of the FETs on a side is conducting at any given time.*

Though we need the one-FET-closed states, and it's mandatory to avoid the both-FETs-closed state, the fourth state, both-FETs-open, is actually useful. When both of the switches on a side are open and not conducting, the motor can spin freely and coast. Access to a coasting mode allows another type of PWM, similar to our sign-magnitude drive, that alternates between drive and coast.

Because of this, most of the IC bridge chips offer an "enable" or "brake" line that will allow you to use both the braking mode we use here and the coasting mode where none of the FET switches are closed and you're relatively free to push the motor around.

*You **can** modify this circuit to enable coasting, but at the cost of another transistor or two, or other complexities. For a neat idea of how to do this with a quad opto-isolator instead of our 2N7000, see **BJT H-Bridge** (http://www.mcmanis.com/chuck/robotics/tutorial/h-bridge/bjt-circuit.html).*

H-Bridge Chips I Have Known and Loved

One problem I have with recommending motor driver parts is that they're in very active technological development at the moment. What was the best H-bridge driver three years ago isn't the best H-bridge driver today, although some classics remain popular. Here's a quick rundown of some available H-bridge silicon.

In the old days, for small loads up to 1 A, I would have recommended either the SN754410 or the L293D parts. I still have a soft spot in my heart for the SN754410, which builds four half-H bridges into one DIP part and has built-in flyback diodes. If you're nearing the 1 A current limit, I recommended you take some of the heat load off the chip by providing your own diodes externally and/or paying attention to heat-sinking. The big drawback with the SN754410 and L293D is that they use Darlington transistors internally, so you have to count on losing 1–2 V on the high side *and* the low side at higher currents. Because of this voltage drop, you'll want to run your application with a higher-voltage motor and battery for efficiency's sake. With that one drawback, the SN754410 is a complete two-motor solution for around a US dollar in a handy chip format. You should have a couple of these in your parts drawer. I'll use this chip to drive stepper motors in "Stepper Motors" on page 320.

Competing with the SN754410 on the low-voltage, lower-amperage side of the market are a bunch of MOSFET-based surface-mount devices that are intended for driving toys or other small motors. The DRV883x family from TI and the A3959 and A495x series from Allegro Micro all offer 1–2 A MOSFET designs in tiny, tiny little packages. Because of their small size, these are not necessarily easy to solder together, but you can do it with practice. Or you can buy motor-driver breakout boards from hobbyist-friendly shops like Sparkfun or Pololu.

For medium-sized motor loads, the next step up on current-handling is another old classic—the L298 driver. The L298 is good for a max of 3 A, at a cost of around $5. This is one of the most popular motor drivers of all time, and is also a Darlington-based design, with all the accordant drawbacks. They have a strange pinout but are very easy to mount to a heatsink, which you'll need if you're going to use them above 2 A. The L298 is such a classic that I can't fail to mention it, but I would rather spend a little more money on a modern chip.

Above 5 A or so, you're going to want a MOSFET design. Because DC motors are used in cars to adjust seats and drive fans and so on, there's a variety of motor drivers that drive tens of amps at 12 V. The VNH2SP30 from ST is surface-mount, but not tiny, and includes all the bells and whistles you could want from a motor driver. The BTN7960 from Infineon is a similar half-bridge, so you'll need to buy one chip for each side of the H-bridge, but they come in larger packages and may be easier for you to work with. If you're pushing either of these drivers anywhere near their limit of 30 A, you will need a small fan for cooling in addition to a heatsink. You'll probably also want to use thick wire.

At really high current levels, you'll want to build your own H-bridge. Because N-channel FETs switch faster and have lower losses than their P-channel cousins, high-current bridges are almost exclusively built from N-channel MOSFETs, even on the high side. This means generating a control voltage for the high-side FETs that is higher than the battery supply by 5 to 10 volts. Because this quickly becomes a design hassle, there are dedicated MOSFET driver chips that provide voltage-doubled, high-side switch drivers and prevent shoot-through and limit maximum current, all in one IC. With one of these chips plus two N-channel MOSFETs, you've got one half of a bridge. Duplicate the circuit again, and you've built a full bridge with all the bells and whistles of an integrated solution, but without any of the power limitations. Now you can build that autonomous electronic forklift you've been thinking about.

Stepper Motors

Stepper motors can provide high positioning accuracy like a servo, while being able to rotate continuously like a normal DC motor. Stepper motors are found inside things like printers and scanners, where it's important to be able to repeatedly move a very precise distance (say, 1,200 dots per inch). Stepper motors have two distinct sets of coils inside them and get the name "steppers" because they rotate a fixed number of degrees each time the magnetic fields reverse in the coils.

Brushed (regular) DC motors have a pair of flexible conductive brushes that make and break connections for the two coil windings inside as they turn, constantly reversing the polarity of the magnetic field induced in the coils. The connections are precisely aligned; just as the electromagnets have pulled themselves close to the permanent magnets in the shell, the electromagnets' polarity is switched and they repel themselves away from the same permanent magnet. Getting this timing/positioning just right makes the motor spin on its own even with DC applied to the motor's two terminals. You apply DC voltage, but the brushes periodically reverse the direction that this current flows through the internal electromagnets, making the motor turn.

Stepper motors have no brushes. You're expected to know when to switch the current one way or the other through the coils. The great advantage of stepper motors is that you can control when it takes a step, and how many it takes, by controlling these coil currents. This means that your microcontroller can count up how many steps the motor has taken and know exactly where the motor shaft is currently pointed.

But if you thought it was a pain to have to use an H-bridge in the previous section, you're not going to like the fact that most steppers require *two* H-bridges to drive: one for each coil winding. If you're building a system with a bunch of stepper motors in it, each with two H-bridges to drive it, you'll get tired of hand-tuning H-bridges pretty quickly. In this chapter, I'll use a common dual H-bridge driver chip, the SN754410.

Even using a dual H-bridge chip is taking a fairly low-level approach these days. There are a few dedicated stepper-motor driver chips out there that do all sorts of useful and complicated things for you, not the least of which is enabling you to take even smaller, smoother steps than we'll be able to here. These chips take a load off of your microprocessor by incorporating some of the driving logic and the two H-bridges in one. On the other hand, you can do a lot with a simple dual-H driver chip, and you'll get a better feel for what's really going on.

Kinds of Stepper Motors

There's quite a variety of different stepper motors out there, but I'll be focusing on the most common type that you're most likely to see and use: a hybrid stepper with 200 steps per revolution, driven in bipolar mode.

Hybrid stepper motors have both permanent magnets and electromagnets on the rotating core. This gives the stepper motor a bit of a pull toward fixed detent positions when no current is applied, but with enough current, the motor can rotate itself out of one detent state into the next. These detents make it much more likely that the motor will take one and only one step when driven in full-stepping mode; plus they give the motors some holding torque when all electrical power is turned off.

Bipolar stepper motors rely on you driving the poles of the electromagnets one way and the other via something like an H-bridge. We're going to drive current back and forth through the whole coil—bipolar style.

Finally, most steppers have 200 steps per revolution, though you'll find that especially cheaper and smaller ones sometimes have fewer steps per revolution. You can also buy 400-step steppers if you want to. If you need more resolution or smoother rotation, you can use *microstepping*, a PWM-like technique, to drive the motor between steps. We'll discuss microstepping in detail in "Microstepping" on page 336.

Figure 15-6 is a diagram of a four-step-per-rotation stepper motor's insides. The central core is a permanent magnet attached to the shaft, with its north pole pointing in the direction of the arrow. Around the outside are four coils, arranged in two pairs. When current flows from 2A to 2B, for instance, the two coils become electromagnets with their north poles pointing to the left, in the direction of the arrows. Because the north pole of the magnet on the shaft is attracted to the south poles and repelled by the north poles of the surrounding electromagnets, it will turn until the shaft's north pole is halfway between the two south coil poles.

In a stepper motor with 200 steps per rotation, the permanent magnet attached to the rotating shaft and the coil magnets on the outside of the case both have many teeth that are slightly offset from one another. Instead of the motor shaft turning 90 degrees to align up between the nearest coil magnets, it only turns 1.8 degrees. The principle is the same, however, and I find the simpler four-step analogy more useful.

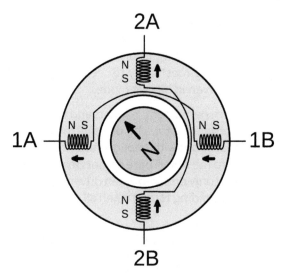

Figure 15-6. *Stepper motor inside*

Full Stepping and Half Stepping

Now that we know how a stepper motor is built and what makes it rotate, let's look in detail at how we can drive it.

The simplest way to drive a stepper motor is in *full steps*. In full stepping, both of the coils are energized all the time, so both electromagnetic fields are pulling all the time on the permanent magnets attached to the motor shaft. If you change the coil-driving voltages around in the right way, you can get the motor to spin. See Figure 15-7.

Looking at the diagram, starting from the upper left and going clockwise, you can see the pattern of coil voltages required to spin the motor shaft clockwise. Going from the top-left state to the top-right state requires reversing the voltage on the horizontal coil pair. Then to take the next step, you reverse the voltages on the vertical pair. Following this cycle, changing the polarity of one coil first, then the other, will make the stepper motor rotate.

Also note that if you start off by changing the voltages on the vertical pair first, you move down to the lower-left motor state. Turning the stepper motor counter-clockwise is simply a matter of moving through the same pattern of driving voltages the other way around.

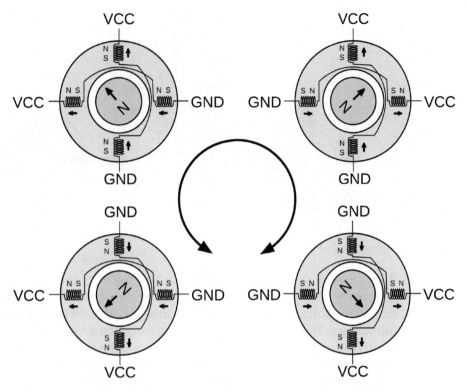

Figure 15-7. *Full steps*

Half stepping is a simple variation on full stepping. Instead of having all coils ener-gized all the time, half of the time one coil pair is turned off, causing the rotating magnet to point directly at the coil that it's most attracted to. This way, you get eight steps per cycle instead of four, or 400 steps per rotation instead of 200.

To see how half stepping works, we'll insert a step between the upper-left and upper-right full-stepping states. See Figure 15-8.

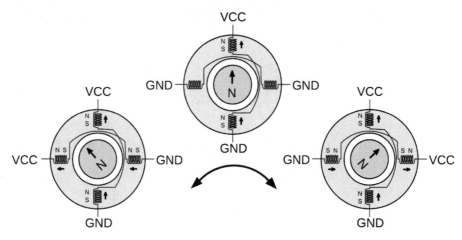

Figure 15-8. *Half steps*

If we were full stepping, the first step to turn the motor clockwise would be to reverse the polarity on the horizontal coil pair. To take a half step, we first simply turn off the horizontal coil pair, either by driving both ends of the coil at the VCC or GND voltages. The north pole of the rotating magnet then points straight up, at the south pole of the still-energized vertical pair, and the motor's shaft has turned 45 degrees counterclockwise. The next half step, then, is to reenergize the horizontal coil pair, but in the opposite polarity of the initial state.

In summary, to go from full steps to half steps, instead of simply reversing each coil's current, you take an intermediate step where you turn off that coil first. See Table 15-4 if you'd like to see that written out in a table. (And notice that you can get the full-stepping pattern simply by skipping the odd-numbered phases.)

Table 15-4. *Half-stepping coil currents*

Phases	Coil 1	Coil 2	Degrees rotation, 4-step motor	Degrees rotation, 200-step motor
0	+	+	0	0.0
1		+	45	0.9
2	-	+	90	1.8
3	-		135	2.7
4	-	-	180	3.6
5		-	225	4.5
6	+	-	270	5.4
7	+		315	6.3
0	+	+	360	7.2

Identification of Stepper Motor Wires

The stepper essentially has two electromagnet coils inside it, and if you've got a bipolar stepper motor, you're probably looking at four wires sticking out. Two of these wires are the ends of one coil, and two are the ends of the other. Now you need to figure out which is which. I'll show you three ways, and there are probably more.

The first is to simply hook up an ohmmeter to two wires arbitrarily. If you get wire-ends from two different coils, they should be not connected. When you get a pair from the same coil, you will be able to read off the coil resistance in ohms. Write this down somewhere. And while you're at it, write down which colors are common to a coil.

If you already know the coil resistance, one neat way to figure out the pairing scheme is to connect an LED across two wires, spin the motor shaft, and see if the LED lights up. If it does, you've found a coil pair and demonstrated that a stepper motor can be used as a generator. The spinning magnets inside the stepper make an alternating current in the coil as the north and south poles on the rotor swing past.

The final way to figure out the coil pairing is to connect the wires together pair-wise. For instance, connect wire one with wire two, and separately connect wire three to wire four. If it is hard to turn the motor, you've got the pairings right. If you switch the connections (one to three, two to four) you should be able to turn the motor freely. What's happening is that when you short out the coils, the generated electricity creates a magentic field inside the motor that opposes your turning it. Remember with DC motors how the speed was limited by the generator voltage equalling the driving voltage? When you try to turn a shorted stepper motor, you're fighting this generator voltage.

Anyway, if you've done any or all of the three experiments, you'll have a good feeling for some of the internal physics of stepper motors *and* you'll know which wires form the two coil pairs.

Too Many Wires!

If you've got a motor with five, six, or eight wires coming out of it, don't fret. Consult Figure 15-9 to see what's going on inside the motor.

If your motor has five or six wires, you can use an ohmmeter to find the pair ends. Looking at Figure 15-9, you'll notice that the coil resistance between a center tap and any of the coil ends will be half of the resistance across two coil ends. For instance, a six-wire motor on my desk has roughly 5 ohms of resistance per coil, so the end-to-end resistance between the end wires is 10 ohms. Once you've found the two pairs with 10 ohms resistance between them, you're done. You can ignore the extra two center taps.

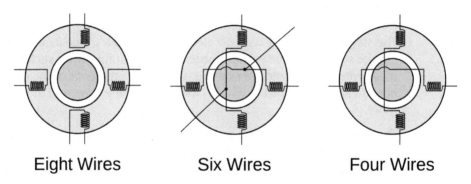

Figure 15-9. *Possible stepper motor wiring patterns*

Most five-wire steppers are essentially the same as six-wire motors, except the two center tap wires are connected together inside the motor body. Just as with six-wire motors, the center tap will show half of the resistance to other wires on an ohmmeter. Ignore it and you're done.

 Center Taps, Unipolar Motors

In the case of five- or six-wire steppers, the extra wires tapped off between the coil pairs enable you to drive the motor without using an H-bridge by supplying a high voltage to the center tap and alternately grounding either end of the coil pair to activate it. This style of motor and drive are both referred to as unipolar, because each individual coil is only ever being driven with one polarity: high voltage in the center and ground on the coil end.

Because you can choose to ignore the center taps, a unipolar stepper can always be driven as if it were a bipolar motor. The reverse isn't true, of course.

If you've got a stepper with eight wires, a *bifilar* stepper motor, you've got your work cut out for you! It's fairly easy to figure out which four pairs of wires are connected together with an ohmmeter, and in principle you can just connect up the four wire ends together in pairs to mimic the wiring of the four-wire, bipolar, stepper motor. But now you face two problems: you don't know which coils are on opposite sides of the motor, and then you don't know which wires to connect to get the two opposite coils in the same polarity. If you're really determined to drive a bifilar stepper motor, there are 12 ways to connect the wires up, and two of them will work. Grab a cup of patience and take good notes.

Dual H-Bridge Chips: The SN754410

So you've just figured out which two pairs of wires correspond to the inner coils that spin your stepper motor. Now we need to hook each coil up to an H-bridge circuit so that we can charge up the coils in either polarity; applying a positive driving voltage on one side and then on the other, just like we did with the DC motor earlier.

The chip we're using for this project actually consists of four half-H-bridges. That means that each side of the "H" can be driven to the high or low voltage independently, just like our demo H-bridge could. We'll control the four half-H sides with four wires from the AVR. Each one sets an "H" side to high or low drive voltage, respectively. Once we've hooked up the stepper motor's two coils to the four H-halves, we'll be able to run current one way through the coil by setting one AVR pin high and the other low, and then reverse the current flow (and the sense of the electromagnetic field) by setting the first pin low and then the other high.

Each half-H is "smokeless" in the sense that when it sees a logic high voltage, it connects only its high-side switch internally, and vice versa for logic low. If we set both sides of the same coil (and the same "H") high or low, no current flows through the coil unless the motor is being turned externally. It's like the previous example where we shorted the two coil ends together.

Let's have a look at the SN754410 chip's pinout in Figure 15-10 and make sure that we understand how everything works. If you'd like to read along in the chip's datasheet, go right ahead.

The pins labelled "1 Out" and "2 Out" are the left and right halves of a complete H-bridge. The corresponding "In"s control the voltage on the "Out"s. There's additionally a "1,2 Enable" line which, when held at the logic high voltage, enables the driving transistors on the "1,2" side. Disabling the H-bridge means that all of the driving switches are open, and it's as if the motor were entirely unconnected. Whenever the H-bridge is enabled, the two outputs are pulled either high or low through the bridge's transistors.

You'll notice that there are also two VCC voltage supply pins. One is for the logic-level voltage that you connect to the AVR, and the other is for the high voltage level that you'd like to use to drive your motor. In the case of the SN754410 you can use up to 36 V, depending on your stepper motor.

SN754410

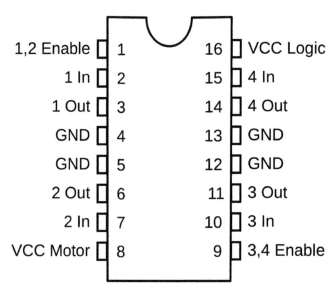

1,2 Enable	1	16	VCC Logic
1 In	2	15	4 In
1 Out	3	14	4 Out
GND	4	13	GND
GND	5	12	GND
2 Out	6	11	3 Out
2 In	7	10	3 In
VCC Motor	8	9	3,4 Enable

Figure 15-10. *SN754410 pinout*

Finally, you'll notice that there are four ground pins. They are all connected together internally, and are additionally connected to the chip's internal heat sink. The idea is that, if you're making your own printed circuit board, you can connect the ground to a large piece of copper on your PCB, which will act as a radiator to help cool off the chip. Without this additional heat-sinking, the chip's maximum current rating of 1 A continuous is a bit ambitious, and you'll note that the chip can get hot to the touch in use. If it gets too hot (burning-your-finger hot) you should be ready to disconnect the motor VCC as quickly as possible—you *can* burn these chips out if you're drawing too much current.

Now let's hook up the AVR, the SN754410 motor driver, and the stepper motor all together. See Figure 15-11 for an example.

My stepper motor is rated for 11 V DC, it says, so a 9 V battery gets it in the right ballpark. If your stepper is rated for any other voltage, connect this supply up to pin 8 as in the diagram. Note that if you connect the stepper to the same power supply as the AVR, the stepper motor might draw enough current to drop the voltage down on the AVR, causing it to be unstable. That's why these motor drivers come with separate power supplies for the logic and motor sections.

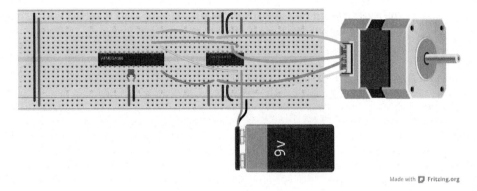

Figure 15-11. *Stepper motor and H-bridge*

Hook up the two wires that are common to one coil to one side of the SN754410 so that they're connected to the same H-bridge. In my example, the blue and yellow wires form one coil and the orange and green wires form the other. Which one of the two wires you designate as "1" or "2" is irrelevant. You can swap them around once you get the software running, and getting it "wrong" just means the motor will rotate counterclockwise where you think it should be clockwise. Now connect the other pair to the other side—outputs "3" and "4."

Connect the logic power and the two enable lines to the AVR's breadboard VCC rail (and notice that I jumpered it across to make the wiring simpler). Connect up the grounds to ground. At least one of these *must* be connected. The others are optional.

Now run wires to the AVR's pins PB0, PB1, PB2, and PB3. If you've still got your LEDs hooked up to these pins, feel free to leave them in. They won't interfere with the logic levels for the motor driver chip, and they'll give you some nice visual feedback about which coil phases are currently energized.

Make sure that PB0 and PB1 go to one side of the chip (the same H-bridge) and that PB2 and PB3 go to the other side. If you swap PB0 for PB1, the motor will run the other direction, but if you swap PB0 with PB2, the motor won't run.

Once you've got the stepper motor and driver connected, you're ready to run some code.

The Code

To drive the stepper motor forward, say, we'll need to energize and deenergize the coils in the motor in a given pattern at a given rate. This suggests that we store the stepping pattern in an array and then just step through it with an indexing variable. To take steps at a regular speed, we can use a timer/counter set in compare-match mode to handle the variable timing and an interrupt to do the work of setting up the AVR's output pins. And then once that framework is set up, we can do something elaborate with it. We'll start off with the code in Example 15-2.

Example 15-2. Partial stepperWorkout.c listing

```c
                            /* Stepper Motor Demo with Accelerated Moves */

// ------- Preamble -------- //
#include <avr/io.h>
#include <util/delay.h>
#include <avr/interrupt.h>
#include "USART.h"

        /* Set these to +/- 1 for half-stepping, +/- 2 for full-stepping */
#define FORWARD     1
#define BACKWARD    -1
#define TURN        400         /* steps per rotation,
                                   depends on stepping & motor */

        /* These parameters will depend on your motor, what it's driving */
#define MAX_DELAY    255                /* determines min startup speed */
#define MIN_DELAY     8                 /* determines max cruise speed */
#define ACCELERATION  16        /* lower = smoother but slower accel */

#define RAMP_STEPS   ((MAX_DELAY - MIN_DELAY) / ACCELERATION)

// -------- Global Variables --------- //
const uint8_t motorPhases[] = {
  (1 << PB0) | (1 << PB2),                              /* full */
  (1 << PB0),                                           /* half */
  (1 << PB0) | (1 << PB3),                              /* full */
  (1 << PB3),                                           /* half */
  (1 << PB1) | (1 << PB3),                              /* etc. */
  (1 << PB1),
  (1 << PB1) | (1 << PB2),
  (1 << PB2)
};

volatile uint8_t stepPhase = 0;
volatile int8_t direction = FORWARD;
volatile uint16_t stepCounter = 0;

// -------- Functions --------- //
void initTimer(void) {
  TCCR0A |= (1 << WGM01);                               /* CTC mode */
  TCCR0B |= (1 << CS00) | (1 << CS02);
  OCR0A = MAX_DELAY;                    /* set default speed as slowest */
  sei();                                /* enable global interrupts */
          /* Notice we haven't set the timer0 interrupt flag yet. */
}

ISR(TIMER0_COMPA_vect) {
  stepPhase += direction;               /* take step in right direction */
```

```
  stepPhase &= 0b00000111;              /* keep phase in range 0-7 */
  PORTB = motorPhases[stepPhase];       /* write phase out to motor */
  stepCounter++;                            /* count step taken */
}

void takeSteps(uint16_t howManySteps, uint8_t delay) {
  UDR0 = delay;            /* send speed/delay over serial, non-blocking */
  OCR0A = delay;                   /* delay in counter compare register */
  stepCounter = 0;              /* initialize to zero steps taken so far */
  TIMSK0 |= (1 << OCIE0A);              /* turn on interrupts, stepping */
  while (!(stepCounter == howManySteps)) {;
  }                                              /* wait */
  TIMSK0 &= ~(1 << OCIE0A);                  /* turn back off */
}

int main(void) {
  // --------- Inits --------- //
  initUSART();
  _delay_ms(1000);
  initTimer();
  DDRB = (1 << PB0) | (1 << PB1) | (1 << PB2) | (1 << PB3);

  // ------ Event loop ------ //
  while (1) {

    direction = FORWARD;
    takeSteps(TURN / 2, MIN_DELAY * 2);
    _delay_ms(1000);

    direction = BACKWARD;
    takeSteps(TURN, MIN_DELAY);
    _delay_ms(1000);

    direction = FORWARD;
    takeSteps(TURN / 16, MAX_DELAY);
    direction = BACKWARD;
    takeSteps(TURN / 8, MAX_DELAY / 2);
    direction = FORWARD;
    takeSteps(TURN / 16, MAX_DELAY);
    _delay_ms(1000);

  }                                      /* End event loop */
  return (0);                   /* This line is never reached */
}
```

As I suggested earlier, most of the heavy lifting in this example is done with a timer/
counter and some global variables, so that's a good place to start our analysis. The
constant array motorPhases[] contains the bit values that we need to energize the
motor coil windings and is arranged in the right order to make the motor turn one
direction. For concreteness, let's say that the horizontal coil in the motor is connected through the H-bridge to the AVR pins PB0 and PB1. When you set PB0 high

and PB1 low, the coil is energized with one polarity, and when PB1 is high and PB0 is low, the other polarity.

The current position in the motor phase table is stored in the global stepPhase. There is code inside the ISR to keep stepPhase within the range of the motorPha ses[] table. The direction that the motor should turn is stored in direction and an overall counter of how many steps have been taken is stored in stepCounter.

The ISR that uses these global variables is short and sweet. First the stepPhase is incremented or decremented depending on the value of direction. stepPhase &= 0b00000111; makes sure that we're keeping the steps in the range zero to seven so that it never overflows the motorPhases[] lookup table. Finally, the ISR sets up the output on PORTB according to the current stepping phase and increments the step counter. If we let the counter and ISR free-run, the motor would turn at a speed determined by the frequency of compare-match interrupts coming from the timer.

And speaking of timer initialization, it's is a totally standard "clear timer on compare match" (CTC) setup, where the delay between steps is set using the OCR0A register that the timer counts up to. The only thing noteworthy here is that, although we set up the global interrupt enable bit, the code *doesn't* enable the specific compare-match interrupt just yet. As soon as the interrupt is enabled, the ISR code will run and the motor will start spinning. We're not ready for that yet.

Next, let's look at the takeSteps() function that'll actually do something for us. Basically, it simply uses this timer/counter and ISR framework that we've just set up. We specify how many steps we'd like the motor to take and the delay between steps that determines the rotation speed, and the routine makes it happen.

For fun, and for your intuition about what's going on, the takeSteps() function starts off by sending the current delay value out over the serial line. Later, when we implement complex movements that speed up and slow down, you can watch this output change on your computer using something like our *serialScope.py* application.

The rest of the code does the real work. The delay value is written to the output-compare register for Timer 0, the stepCounter is reset, and then the output compare interrupt enable bit (OCIE0A) is set. At this point, the ISR will start firing and the motor will start turning at the specified speed. Because the ISR increments the stepCounter with every step, all that remains is for us to wait until it reaches the desired value, and then turn off the compare interrupt to shut the motor off.

That's all you need for simple stepper motor control. If you're interested in seeing what you can do with just the basics, flash in the code example with the shortened version in Example 15-2. (make flash MAIN=stepperWorkout_short.c should work.)

Acceleration Control

The problem with our naïve demo based simply on the takeSteps() routine is that we're telling the motor to start up at full speed, take a bunch of steps, and then stop instantaneously. If the stepper motor is strong enough and your load light enough, you can get away with these jerky, start-stop movements. But it's equivalent to driving by flooring either the gas or brake pedal. This style may be OK for Formula One races, but it's tough on the car, the environment, and the passengers. And with stepper motors, this can lead to missing steps.

To see how steps get missed, it's worthwhile to think of the stepper motor shaft and motor coils as two distinct parts of your motor system. Under light loads and at low speeds, the motor shaft catches up almost instantly when you advance the phase of the driver and the coils. As you speed up the driver or increase the inertia of the motor's load, the motor shaft phase can start to lag behind the coil phase. If you try to spin the motor faster and faster, eventually you'll get to the point where the shaft phase gets more than one step behind the driver and coils. (Try it! Add takeSteps(TURN, 2); to the code and see what happens.)

Look again at the single-stepping diagram in Figure 15-7. If the motor's shaft lags more than one step behind the driver when you are full-stepping, the coil ends up pulling it in the direction that's exactly opposite of the direction you'd like it to be turning. This can cause missed steps, a nasty grinding noise, and all of a sudden your AVR chip doesn't know where the motor is pointing any more because it thinks it has taken steps but the motor didn't turn.

A better idea is to ramp up the speed, from slowly moving to full speed ahead. Taking a little more time per step at the beginning gives the motor shaft more time to catch up to the driver's phase, and helps to prevent missed steps. Once your heavy load has started to turn, you can speed the motor up. And of course you'll want to ramp the speed back down again in anticipation of stopping. Ramping the speed up and down like this allows you to run the motor at a higher cruising speed than you would otherwise be able to start the motor off with, and it makes for smoother motion control and less stress on moving parts. It's a win all around.

In the demo code, I implement an acceleration profile that's particularly easy to code up and understand, yet performs pretty well in the real world. Motion control turns out to be a deep subject, and if you know a lot about the geometry and masses of your particular setup, you can probably optimize this code for your situation. This is particularly true if you're planning a complicated path where you don't necessarily want to stop the motor fully between movements. Still, try this code snippet first for generic situations.

We assume that the motor is initially stopped and that we'd like it to be stopped again but having rotated through a given number of steps as fast as possible. We'll model the movement in three stages: an acceleration stage, a cruising stage where the motor runs at maximum speed, and a deceleration stage. If the number of steps is too few to reach maximum speed and decelerate back down in time, we speed up as much as possible and then immediately start ramping back down. Let's see how that works in Example 15-3.

 Trapezoid Speed Profile

I'm calling this speed profile "trapezoid" because the speed per step increases linearly up to the maximum speed, holds steady, and then decreases linearly per step until it's stopped. Thus, the velocity is a linear function of the number of steps—the position.

But because each step takes less time than the previous one, the velocity is not a linear function of time, so this isn't a constant acceleration curve—the acceleration is also an increasing function of time during the ramp-up stage.

Example 15-3. *stepperWorkout.c trapezoidMove() listing*

```c
void trapezoidMove(int16_t howManySteps) {
  uint8_t delay = MAX_DELAY;
  uint16_t stepsTaken = 0;

                                /* set direction, make howManySteps > 0 */
  if (howManySteps > 0) {
    direction = FORWARD;
  }
  else {
    direction = BACKWARD;
    howManySteps = -howManySteps;
  }

  if (howManySteps > (RAMP_STEPS * 2)) {
                      /* Have enough steps for a full trapezoid */
                                               /* Accelerate */
    while (stepsTaken < RAMP_STEPS) {
      takeSteps(1, delay);
      delay -= ACCELERATION;
      stepsTaken++;
    }
                                                   /* Cruise */
    delay = MIN_DELAY;
    takeSteps((howManySteps - 2 * RAMP_STEPS), delay);
    stepsTaken += (howManySteps - 2 * RAMP_STEPS);
                                               /* Decelerate */
    while (stepsTaken < howManySteps) {
      takeSteps(1, delay);
      delay += ACCELERATION;
      stepsTaken++;
    }
```

```
    }
    else {
                                              /* Partial ramp up/down */
        while (stepsTaken <= howManySteps / 2) {
            takeSteps(1, delay);
            delay -= ACCELERATION;
            stepsTaken++;
        }
        delay += ACCELERATION;
        while (stepsTaken < howManySteps) {
            takeSteps(1, delay);
            delay += ACCELERATION;
            stepsTaken++;
        }
    }
}
```

Because we want the motion profile to be the same whether we're spinning the motor clockwise or counterclockwise, we can set the direction global variable at the beginning of the routine and convert the number of steps into a positive number.

The minimum and maximum delays, which are the inverse of the speed, are set in define statements at the top of the program, as is the acceleration, how much to reduce the delay per step. This means that the number of steps needed to complete an acceleration or deceleration ramp is fixed and can also be computed in a define (RAMP_STEPS).

Because everything is precomputed, the trapezoidMove() routine just has to figure out if it has enough steps to spend some time cruising at the maximum speed—if the number of steps to take is longer than two ramps—or whether it should go straight from acceleration to deceleration. In the first case, the routine loops through a series of single steps at increasingly small delays and counts the steps taken as it goes along. The cruising stage is implemented with a single call to takeSteps() at the maximum speed: setting the delay to the defined MIN_DELAY. Finally, the deceleration phase is a single-step loop that's the mirror image of the acceleration stage.

When there are not enough steps desired to reach maximum speed, and thus cruise, the routine is even simpler. The acceleration stage lasts for half of the steps, and takes single steps more and more quickly. At the halfway point, it's time to start decelerating again, and the deceleration routine just adds to the delay with each step until it's done.

Microstepping

Compared to taking full steps through the motor's rotation, taking half steps gains us higher spatial resolution and helps to smooth out the discrete steps, which can cause jerkiness at low speeds and excess noise at high speeds. You might be wondering if it's possible to take this further. Of course it is! But it's not easy.

Microstepping lets you drive a stepper motor to intermediate positions between the half steps by controlling the ratio of coil currents in the two coil pairs. You can control the coil currents by using PWM, changing the driving voltage, or using other current-limiting circuits, but the basic idea is that by varying the magnetic pull on the rotor coming from the two coils you should be able to make the motor move to any angular position you'd like. Figure 15-12 shows an example of the voltages you'd use to get quarter-step microstepping. Perhaps it's easiest to think of controlling the average driving voltages by using something like PWM, and you can certainly do just that.

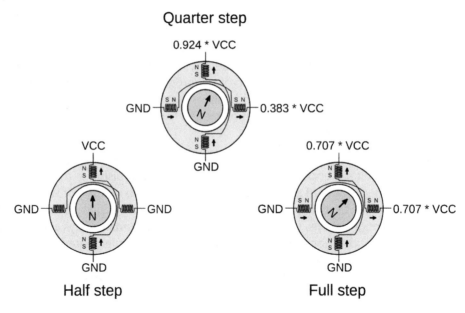

Figure 15-12. *Equal power microstepping example*

We already know that when only the vertical pole is full on, the rotor will align so that its magnet's north pole points straight up. We also know that when both of the coils are equally on, the rotor points to the 45 degree position. If we slightly increase the duty cycle for one coil pair and slightly decrease the duty cycle of the other, the rotor should turn a tiny bit and end up somewhere between the half-step and quarter-step positions.

Equal Power Microstepping

The mathematics isn't pretty, but it's not really more than a little physics and some trigonometry. We want to figure out how much power we need from each coil pair for a given angle, holding the total power constant around the circle.

Power is a function of voltage (or duty cycle) squared, so adding up the duty cycles from the two coils is like adding up lengths of legs of triangles. That means the duty cycles that we'd need to use are sine and cosine functions of the desired rotation angle. Easy, right?

In contrast, when we implemented half stepping we were *not* keeping the power constant as we rotated the motor around the circle. In fact, the motor pulled 1.414 times stronger when both coils were on than it did with just one on. We'd need to throttle the two phases back by a factor of sin(pi/4) or 0.707 when they're both on to maintain equal power around the cycle.

Whether or not this is a good thing depends on your application. The slightly uneven power cycle of regular half stepping makes it a little bit noisier than it would be under equal-power half stepping, but when both coils are fully engaged, the motor has roughly 40% more torque. Most microstepping chips will aim for equal power, so you'll be losing some of your possible motor torque. The way we implemented half stepping is both the easiest and gets the maximum performance out of a given voltage source, at the expense of being a little "jerkier."

Now, it would be possible to calculate all of the sines and cosines ahead of time, store them in a table in memory, and then use the built-in PWM hardware (conveniently, there are two compare values per timer!) to implement microstepping on your own with our SN754410 H-bridge. If you'd like a challenge after this chapter, I recommend it as a good learning experience.

On the other hand, if you'd like to simply *use* microstepping and stepper motors rather than learning something, I honestly have to recommend buying an integrated indexer and driver chip. Chips like the Allegro A4988 or TI's DRV8825 take care of a bunch of current-limiting and power-handling details that you can't reasonably mimic yourself.

Most importantly, the dedicated driver chips allow you to use a higher supply voltage with your motor than you would otherwise. The extra voltage can give the motor an extra kick as it transitions between steps, but would burn the motor out if you applied this higher voltage constantly. The chips take care of the current limiting for you, while providing the motor with extra power bursts. Because chips like the Allegro or TI drivers implement this current control in a way that actually improves the performance of your stepper motor, I recommend buying a slightly lower voltage stepper than your power supply, maybe by a factor of two, to give the IC the headroom it needs. (For details, the datasheets from Allegro go into good depth.)

With a dedicated stepper-driver IC, all you have to do is provide a high or low signal on a *direction* pin to set which way it's going to rotate, and a rising-edge on a *step* pin to make it move. The controller chip takes care of the rest. Your AVR code then just has to supply a positive-going pulse every time that you'd like the motor to turn one step. Whether you do this purely in code or make use of the timer/counter hardware is up to you. Using a stepper-driver IC is a lot like driving a simple DC motor in sign-magnitude mode, only you have some assurance that with each toggling of the PWM pin, the motor has turned a precise, known amount.

In fact, the dedicated indexer/driver chips make life so simple, that there's almost nothing I can say about them here! You buy one, follow the circuit diagrams to set the maximum currents to match your motor, and then pulse it from the AVR. If that's too much work for you, you can even buy them already preintegrated into a circuit board from many hobbyist supply shops including Sparkfun, Adafruit, and Pololu, to name a few. The bare chips only cost a few dollars, and the preassembled boards aren't too bad. You've got no excuse not to go out and buy a couple. When you want the motor to turn five steps, you just pulse a control line five times.

 The Limits of Microstepping

As you try to subdivide the motor's phase circle into finer and finer pie slices, you end up having to vary the voltage applied to the coils by smaller and smaller amounts. This places real demands on your current-control circuitry, or in our case the PWM accuracy. Friction inside the motor and the presence of the permanent magnet in hybrid stepper motors further complicate issues. When you're relying on tiny differences in applied current to turn the motor a tiny fraction of a degree, you can't expect to get much torque between the two steps.

Because of these factors, there's a real limit to how many microsteps you can expect per cycle, even with the best-designed dedicated chip drivers. Exactly how many microsteps are practical is a topic of hot industry debate and depends on why you're using microstepping in the first place, but the value almost certainly lies between 8x and 16x. Reconfiguring a driver chip between 4x, 8x, and 16x is usually quite simple, though, so test them all out!

SPI | 18

Interfacing with External Memory

So far, when we've been talking serial, we've really meant the kind of old-school asynchronous serial protocol that's based on RS-232, which is how computers used to talk to printers in the 1970s. But there are other serial data transfer modes out there, more or less appropriate in different situations.

In this chapter and the next, we'll look at two modern serial protocols. This chapter deals with the serial peripheral interface (SPI), which is blindingly fast and better suited for a small number of devices. The other protocol, I2C ("inter integrated circuit"), has an addressing scheme and is easily extended to a network of up to 128 devices using only two wires (and ground), but is a lot slower than SPI.

From a user's perspective, however, most of the time you've got a cool new device and you just want to talk to it. The peripheral devices that need speed will speak SPI and those that play well with others will speak the I2C protocols, so you're going to need to learn to use both of them. Fortunately, because these protocols are so widespread, our AVR microcontrollers have internal hardware that makes coding for them a breeze once you know how. That's what this chapter and the next are all about.

This chapter gets your AVR chip talking SPI serial with an external EEPROM chip. We're building up toward a standalone data logger application by the end of Chapter 17, and we're going to need a bunch of nonvolatile memory to store the data in. External EEPROMs and other flash-memory devices provide a cheap and easy way to keep lots of data around even when the power goes out, so they're worth knowing about in their own right. But if you're not so interested in the particular application, just think of the EEPROM as a generic SPI device and you'll still learn something useful.

What You Need

In addition to the basic kit, you will need:

- An SPI device to talk to. Here, I'm using a 25LC256 32K SPI EEPROM chip because they're cheap and similar to many other off-board memory devices.

- A USB-Serial adapter.

How SPI Works

I love the SPI (serial peripheral interface) bus protocol. It's like a shark, brutally efficient at what it does, and essentially stripped of all frills. When you want to move a lot of data really fast between a few devices, it's hard to beat SPI.

One reason that SPI is so fast is that, unlike our old friend UART, it's a clocked, or *synchronous*, protocol. With UART, we were always worried about a baud rate, the rate at which to transmit and expect data. The transmitting and receiving devices have to be precisely in sync, agreeing on when to set and read the voltage levels on the transmit and receive lines. And this means that UART serial can only transmit data as quickly as the two devices can agree on the timing, which limits the speed to a few hundred thousand bits per second at best. (We've been running at 9,600 baud, which is a little conservative; it's about 1/10th of the fastest UART speed.)

With SPI, in addition to the transmitting and receiving lines, there's a third wire that's used as a clock line that synchronizes the two communicating devices. This way, both can agree that they'll read and write data on the positive voltage transition, for instance. This means that the bit rate can be as fast as the two devices can agree on a rising voltage edge. SPI speeds usually start at 1 megahertz, and 10 megahertz is pretty much standard. That's a hundred times faster than the fastest asynchronous serial setups, and a thousand times faster than what we're using for UART. And these days it's not uncommon to have SPI buses in consumer electronics devices running as fast as 50–100 MHz. That's really, really fast.

The other reason that SPI can be so fast is that there's almost no overhead, and thus no extra work for the CPU to do to make use of the data as it comes across. Our old serial protocol relied on a start bit and a stop bit to keep synchronized and to delimit the bytes one from the next. This means that for every 8 bits of data, 10 signals need to be sent, which further slows it down. This *data framing*--knowing where one byte starts and the previous one ends—is handled by yet another wire in SPI.

So if you've been following along so far, you've got the picture that SPI is fast, but you've probably also counted at least four wires necessary for SPI: a clock line, two data lines (one for each direction), and a fourth line that's used to signal the start and end of a transaction. That's the design trade-off with SPI; it's a simple protocol that's brutally fast, but requires a lot of wires. It's time for some diagrams and definitions.

The most common type of SPI bus setup looks something like Figure 16-1. A *master* device is responsible for generating the clock signal (SCK) that all of the *slave* devices receive. Both master and slave devices use the clock signal to synchronize their voltage signals on the MOSI, or "master-out-slave-in," and MISO, or "master-in-slave-out," data lines. The data direction on the two lines should be obvious, which is another reason to love SPI, but just to be sure, the master sets the voltage on MOSI, and the slave sets the voltage level on MISO. (I also drew little arrows for you.)

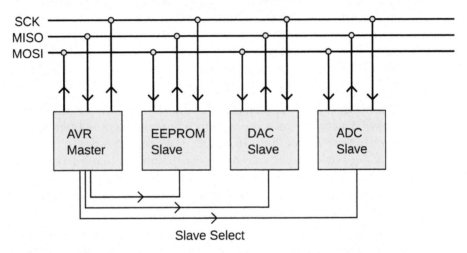

Figure 16-1. *The SPI bus*

Rounding out the signal lines, the slave-select (or chip-select) lines control which slave device is currently active. Note that there is one slave-select line per slave device. On an SPI bus, all the chips can be connected to the same SCK, MISO, and MOSI wires, but each target chip also has to have its own chip select line. This requirement of one extra wire per device is what keeps SPI basically limited to small networks, or forces you to use trickery like port expanders to address all of the devices.

If you're writing your own SPI from scratch, and not using the AVR's dedicated hardware SPI, you should also know that the slave-select lines use inverse logic. That is, the slave-select lines are normally held at the high voltage level and are dropped down to ground to signal who's turn it is to speak.

Now, the SPI bus protocol is strange in one way, and understanding this strangeness is key to writing code that'll eventually use SPI, so pay extra close attention right now. Despite the rather dramatic naming choice for the two devices, both "master" and "slave" devices do exactly the same thing—on one edge of the timing clock, they set up one bit for output, and on the next edge of the timing clock, they read one bit in as input. It's just that the master, as noted previously, is responsible for generating the clock signal and deciding which slave to speak to.

Let me say that again, because it's the key to understanding SPI. With every clock tick, *both* the master and the slave transmit *and* receive a bit of data on their respective lines. Consequently, there's no real concept of separate "send" and "receive" actions in SPI—both are sending and receiving all the time. I like to think of it as "bit trading."

Bit Trading Example

As an example, imagine that you're communicating with a device that that takes in an 8-bit command and returns 16 bits of response data. If the AVR is the master device, it needs to set up its data line and clock out 8 bits of data in a row. At the same time, it's just received an 8-bit byte from the slave device, but because the slave hadn't received the command yet, the byte probably isn't meaningful. The AVR can probably throw it away.

After clocking out the 8-bit command string, the AVR needs to clock out 16 more bits of data to the slave, during which time the slave will send its 16-bit response back to the AVR. For these 16 bits, the slave probably doesn't care what the AVR is sending, but it needs to receive the clock signal so that it can transmit its bits. This is bit trading; the AVR needs to send out 16 bits to get 16 bits back. It probably doesn't matter what bits the AVR sends, though it's customary to send all zeros when you're just waiting for a response.

I say "probably" because there are some slave devices that are smart enough to receive the next command while still sending the response to the previous one, effectively doubling the data throughput. When this is the case, it can be tricky to keep the timing of command and response straight. This is why it can help to bear in mind the simultaneous bit-for-bit trading nature of SPI.

The other time that the SPI bus can seem strange is when you're dealing with sensors. Some devices, like temperature sensors, for instance, don't really take any input and are designed as slave devices. Because of the way SPI works, the AVR master has to *send* data—any data—to the sensor in order to get data back. The sensor ignores this data and is just using it for the clock source; but from the perspective of the AVR, it may seem odd to send data to your sensor. Keep in mind the way SPI works under the hood, that you're really bit trading, and this won't seem so strange.

Shift Registers

If you'd like to take a deeper look into the SPI bus, you'll need to understand *shift registers*, because shift registers are what let the devices on an SPI bus convert data between *serial* data (one bit at a time) and *parallel* data (all eight bits at once).

The AVR's CPU—and whatever the CPU is connected to—wants to work with bytes. Rather than connecting them together with eight wires (which we'd probably call a "parallel data cable") and simultaneously transmitting a bit on each wire, it's physically simpler to send the bytes one bit at a time (in serial) over just one or two wires, and then reassemble the received bits into our 8-bit byte after they've all arrived. The circuit that does this serial-to-parallel and parallel-to-serial conversion is a shift register, which is basically eight clocked one-bit memories arranged in a row. When the clock ticks, each memory cell takes on logic value that the cell to the left of it had. How does this work?

Imagine eight people standing in a line, and a ninth person who's handing them red or blue rocks. When a clock ticks, everyone passes their rock to the right down the line. After eight clock ticks, each of the eight people will have rocks whose color depends on the sequence of rocks that were fed in one at a time. Now you can read out the data that came in one bit at a time, but all together as an 8-bit byte—a serial-to-parallel conversion.

In Figure 16-2, the serial sequence "1,0,1,0,0,0,0,0" was clocked in one bit at a time. After eight clock ticks, you can read the parallel value out (in mirror-image).

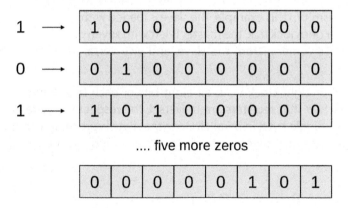

Figure 16-2. *A shift register*

Some shift registers also operate the other way around: parallel in, and serial out. You can load up all eight memory cells at once and then read out the value of the rightmost memory cell as you advance the clock. The output is then a serialized version of the same pattern of bits that you loaded in. "Universal" shift registers let you both read and write to the register in parallel, making them serial-to-parallel or parallel-to-serial converters.

And this is why I love the SPI protocol: it's just two of these universal shift registers linked together in a loop. Both the master and slave have a shift register, and the input of each is connected to the output of the other through the MOSI and MISO lines so that they form a ring. See Figure 16-3.

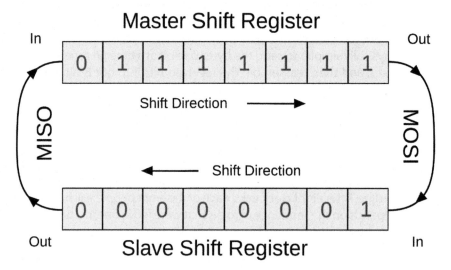

Figure 16-3. *SPI is shift registers*

Both devices' shift registers start out parallel-loaded with the data that they're going to transmit. In this example, the slave is loaded with all zeros, and the master all ones. After one clock tick, the master is left with seven of its original bits and the first one that's come in from the slave, and vice versa, because it's completely symmetric.

After a total of eight clock ticks, all eight bits of each byte have traded places. Because the two shift registers are universal, the respective processors can read them out as a single byte, in parallel. Once that byte is processed, the registers are reloaded, and the next bytes are ready to move around the circle.

 Shift Registers Driving Shift Registers

Here's where it gets meta! Remember that we had an issue with a proliferation of slave-select lines in a big SPI network? You can solve this by using a shift register connected to the slave-select lines, and addressing the shift register with the AVR SPI hardware. This is not for the faint of heart, but it's an elegant solution to a common problem.

To select a slave device, you first slave-select the shift register and send it the right byte to drop the desired device's slave-select line. When you latch in this address byte and deselect the shift register, the SPI bus is set up to talk to your slave device. This trick lets you easily address eight devices on your SPI bus with nothing more than the normal four AVR SPI pins and a shift register.

Other Uses of Shift Registers

Shift registers are good for more than SPI and serializing data streams. In fact, given that input and output pins on AVR microcontrollers are often scarce in my designs, shift registers are an essential part of my electronics-design toolkit.

First, let's think about how a shift register could be used as an output-pin multiplier. With two pins, you can shift eight bits of data into a shift register one at a time. If it's important that none of the outputs change until they have the full data, there are shift registers that have additional *enable* lines that only latch the data into an output register once all eight (or however many) bits have been clocked in.

So say you need to light up 16 LEDs in particular patterns. One way to do this is with one AVR output pin per LED, but that uses up almost all of the pins on the AVR. Using shift registers, you can be a lot more clever. If you use one 8-bit shift register, you only need two pins, data and clock, to control all eight bits of output from the register. Naively, you could just hook up another two pins to another shift register, and you've got all 16 LEDs under control with only four AVR pins.

But you can do better. If you can shift the bits in fast enough that the blinking isn't noticeable on the output, you can chain the two shift registers together, wiring up the output of the eigth bit of the first register to the input of the second. This way you're driving all 16 outputs with just the same two pins. And if you need simultaneous change on all 16 outputs, you can use shift registers with an output register, for the cost of only one more AVR pin to toggle their enable pins.

Now if that's not good enough, remember that the AVR's hardware SPI peripheral is built to take in eight bits and clock them out to a shift register in the receiving peripheral. Usually, we're thinking of a memory chip, sensor, DAC, or other "real" peripherals. But we can also use the SPI to talk to plain-old shift registers, for pin-multiplying purposes.

When you want to load up a particular pattern of eight bits on a generic shift register using the SPI hardware, all you have to do is connect the MOSI to the shift register's input, write the byte to the SPDR data register, and watch it go. And remember, the hardware SPI is *very* fast—transmitting the bits at megahertz rather than mere kilohertz.

The 74HC595 is a very common 8-bit serial-in, parallel-out shift register with built-in a storage register. They sell for 15–20 US cents each, and half of that in bulk. You can cascade as many of these as you need to multiply your AVR pins' output capabilities. In many applications, you'll find that the AVR's output pins are scarce. When this is the case, combined with the AVR's dedicated SPI hardware, a shift register can be your very best friend.

And of course, there's a parallel-to-serial equivalent shift register, the 74HC165 chip, that you can use to effectively multiply the number of digital inputs the AVR can have. As previously, you can use the SPI hardware to read in bytes from the shift registers, taking in parallel data when latched, shifting it into the AVR's SPI register one bit at a time, and then reading the full byte out in your code. It's essentially the same trick, just in reverse. If you find yourself needing a parallel-to-serial input expander, the 74HC165 chip is a good bet.

EEPROM External Memory

Because the SPI bus is fast, you'll find that it's mostly used by devices that need speed: ADCs and DACs for audio or much faster signals, output expanders, and memory. In this section, we'll work on a demonstration of the AVR's SPI capabilities using an offboard SPI EEPROM memory chip that'll let us store 32 KB of data. (OK, that's not a lot, but similar principles take you up into the gigabytes because SD/MMC flash memory cards have an SPI interface.)

External Memory

When you need to store more data than you've got space for inside the AVR chip, it's time to look to external memory. There are two main types of external memory: volatile types that rely on constant power to remember their data, and nonvolatile memory that is slower and more expensive but retains its data even when the lights go out.

Volatile memory (SRAM, DRAM, etc.)

There are all sorts of electronic tricks for storing bits of information as voltages. Static random access memory (SRAM) and dynamic random access memory (DRAM) take two different approaches to storing your bits. SRAM uses a network of transistors that hold the last voltage level that was imposed on them —as long as the power stays connected.

DRAM, on the other hand, charges or discharges one tiny capacitor per bit to store the logical one or zero. This means that dynamic RAM's many capacitors need periodic reading and recharging, a cycle called a "memory refresh," which static RAM doesn't.

Both rely on power to retain data—cut the power, and poof! The data stored in memory is gone. These two types of memory can be quite cheap per megabyte, and read and write quickly—SRAM has a slight speed advantage.

Dynamic RAM is a lot cheaper for large memories, but the necessary refresh circuitry makes it impractical for small microcontroller designs. For use with a microcontroller, static RAM is the easiest way to go when you need a lot of fast storage but don't mind losing it when the power is off. In particular, Microchip makes a range of 23Kxxx SPI serial SRAM chips that can be used just like the EEPROM in this chapter, but they run on lower voltage, which complicates the power supply.

EEPROM

EEPROM (electrically erasable programmable read-only memory) is probably the most flexible type of external memory, although it's not particularly cheap or fast. The advantage that it does have, though, it that EEPROM is nonvolatile (doesn't go away when the power is turned off) and there are plenty of chips available that run on 5 V supplies without level conversion. EEPROM, like the one we're using in this chapter, can hold its memory for a very long time with no power—Microchip's datasheets specify longer than 200 years!

Flash

Flash memory is a newer type of EEPROM that is significantly cheaper and offers faster write times, but at the expense of *only* being able to write a page of memory at a time. While with generic EEPROM, you can change one byte without modifying its neighbors, with flash memory, the bytes are arranged in pages of multiple (often 512) bytes that must all be written together. So to change one byte, you read all 512 into your microcontroller's memory, change one byte, and then send them all back out to flash storage.

Because this procedure is power consuming, time consuming, and no fun, there are also flash memory chips that have a small embedded controller inside that takes care of all this for you. When you need more memory that you're able to get from a plain-vanilla EEPROM, something like Atmel's AT45 series of flash memories are fantastic. They have onboard SRAM buffers so that you can access one while the other is writing to flash. You can get them with a 66 MHz SPI bus and 2 MB of memory for under $1.50, though you'll have to supply them with 3.6 V instead of 5 V.

SD cards

Finally, you should know about SD/MMC cards. Under the hood, they've got a small processor and a bunch of flash memory. Most SD cards also allow you to read/write to them with SPI. One catch is that, as with the higher-storage Atmel chips, they also need to be run at a lower voltage, usually between 3.0 and 3.6 volts. The other disadvantage is that, being flash chips inside, you have to read and write in 512-byte pages.

On the plus side, the SPI protocol for running SD cards is well documented, and it's hard to beat 2 GB of storage for only a few bucks. You'll find tutorials on the Web for how to use SD cards with an AVR, and even how to incorporate a FAT filesystem so that you can easily transfer files to and from your desktop computer.

The memory chip I've chosen is one of a family of very common EEPROM chips, the 25LC256 from Microchip. Why? Because it has a decent amount of nonvolatile memory for making a logger, it works on a wide 3.5–5.5 volt range, it's available as a DIP part for breadboarding, and it's basically cheap. It's also part of a family of SPI EEPROMs with memory ranging from 512 bytes to 128 kB. Small(ish) EEPROMS like this are usually used for storing configuration data, but even with just 32 KB, sampling the temperature once every five minutes, we'll get over three month's of runtime. Or if we sample temperature every 10 seconds, it'll run for three and a half days. Thirty-two thousand samples is more than you'd think.

If you look at the datasheet for the 25LC256 chip, it supports exactly six commands: read, write, write-enable, write-disable, read status, and write status. When you'd like to read from the chip's memory, you first pass it the read command, then the memory start address, and then just keep clocking in/out bytes until you've had enough. To write, you first have to send a write-enable command. Then, send the write command, the start address, and then up to 64 bytes of data. When you're done writing, the AVR raises the voltage of the slave-select line, and the EEPROM flashes the bytes into memory.

There are a couple of complications, which are common to about every memory type out there, so I'll go into some detail for you. First, writing the received data into memory takes a bit of time. With the 25LC256, it's guaranteed that a write won't take more than 5 ms, but that's quite a long time in microprocessor-land. This is why the EEPROM chip also has a status register and a bit in that register that tells you that it's busy writing. After you (or the AVR) write a block of data to memory, it's customary to check up on the status register until the "write-in-process" bit is clear if you need to use the EEPROM again within a short period of time, as is frequently the case when you're saving a bunch of data.

The other complication is that the memory inside the EEPROM is internally arranged in "pages" of 64 bytes each. Other memory devices, like flash cards or SD cards, will have a similar layout but with different numbers of bytes per page. Because writing to memory is relatively slow, it makes sense to do as much of it at once as possible, but this means that you have to have some internal temporary storage inside the EEPROM device, and that the places it's going to store the data are simultaneously accessible. Hence, memory pages.

The gotcha with paged memories is that you have to send less than one page of data, or else it wraps around. For example, say we're going to save eight bytes of data starting at memory location 60. The first four bytes will fit within the page easily, going into locations 60, 61, 62, and 63. The next four bytes, however, will wrap around and get written into memory locations 0, 1, 2, and 3, rather than 64, 65, 66, and 67, because memory locations 64, 65, 66 and 67 don't exist on that page. Yoiks!

There are a few ways to work with paged memory. The first, and by far the slowest, is to always write one byte at a time. If you can live with (in our case) 5 ms per byte, this is just fine. If you find that you need speed, the fastest method is to accumulate 64 bytes of data together in an array in the AVR and then send them all directly to the same page in EEPROM, only incurring the 5 ms write delay at the end. You can see that this about 64 times faster. All you have to do is make absolutely sure that you start each block at an even multiple of 64 in the EEPROM's memory address space.

I once built an accelerometer logger that had to write into a memory that had a 512-byte page structure. But I didn't want to keep all 512 bytes in the AVR's RAM at once, because it would use up half of what I had available. As a compromise, I always used multiple-of-512 start addresses and sent the bytes over to the flash memory chip as they came, but kept count of how many I'd sent. Once I'd gotten 512 bytes across, the AVR closed the connection with the memory chip, and the flash memory flashed. While the flash wrote the block of 512 bytes into its memory, the AVR had to buffer up a few more data inputs until the flash signalled that it was ready again.

I mention this more complicated example because it's a common problem with interfacing between integrated circuits (or any kind of production line, or even cooking with friends). If some processes run at different speeds, you often need to have some ability to buffer up data, test when the downstream chips are ready, and then send it as soon as possible.

SPI Demo Hookup

Figure 16-4 demonstrates how to hook up an SPI EEPROM chip on your breadboard.

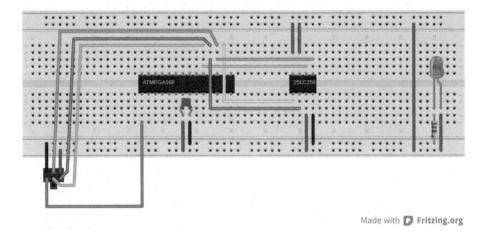

Made with ⬛ Fritzing.org

Figure 16-4. *SPI EEPROM demo hookup*

In order to hook up the 25LC256 EEPROM, you're going to need to connect power to the chip, naturally. VCC and GND are pins 8 and 4, respectively. There are also two different ways to prevent the chip from working, a write-protect line and a hold line, both of which are active low. So we'll tie both of these pins (3 and 7) to VCC. Notice that I snuck the VCC rail around to the other side of the chip to make this easier.

Finally, we'll connect the SPI interface. Pin 1 is the slave select pin (labelled "chip select" in the 25LC256 datasheet), and we'll connect that to the AVR's PB2, using the yellow wire in the diagram. SCK is pin 6 on the 25LC256, and goes to AVR PB5, the green wire. MISO (labelled "SO" on the 25LC256 datasheet) is pin 2 and connects to AVR PB4, which is the gray wire. Finally, pin 5 is MOSI ("SI") and connects to AVR pin PB3 using the orange wire.

You've doubtless noticed that we've reused the AVR's programming lines. This is no mistake. The AVR's self-flashing routines use the SPI bus just as the EEPROM does, only the AVR's equivalent of a slave-select line is its reset line. And of course, we don't have to worry about the 25LC256 interfering with the AVR during programming, because its slave-select line will not be pulled low by the AVR.

Pull-up Resistors on RESET

If you're having trouble programming the AVR after installing the chip, double-check your connections, and then consider adding a 10k or 100k ohm pull-up resistor between the 25LC256's pin 1 (slave select) and VCC. This will make sure that the memory chip's slave select pin doesn't accidentally get dragged low by the AVR when you're loading a new program.

Adding a pull-up resistor on a reset or slave-select line is often cheap insurance against startup glitches and other transients. In fact, the Atmel Application Note AVR042 recommends using an external pull-up resistor of greater than 10k ohms on the reset pin in addition to the built-in one. I've never had problems related to spurious resets, but if you're designing a high-reliability application, it's probably a good idea.

SPI Demo Code

Because I'd like to reuse almost all of the EEPROM memory code in this chapter's final temperature-logger project, when I worked on the demo project I tried to keep much of the EEPROM-specific code separate from the demo code. What I did was to open up the main *spiEEPROMDemo.c* file in one window, and the *25LC256.c* and *25LC256.h* files in another. I had thought about halfway through what functions I'd need—writing, reading bytes to and from the EEPROM, plus whatever was necessary to get that done. By the end, I realized that I wanted a bulk-erase and two-byte read and write facilities. Although I don't use all of the functions in the demo code, you'll see how they could be useful later on.

Let's first take a look at the demo code in Example 16-1. When you're reading through, notice that almost none of the nitty-gritty of handling the EEPROM memory is present—it's all handled in the library functions.

Example 16-1. **spiEEPROMDemo.c listing**

```
                              /* SPI EEPROM 25LC256 Demo */

// ------- Preamble -------- //
#include <avr/io.h>
#include <util/delay.h>

#include "pinDefines.h"
#include "macros.h"
#include "USART.h"
#include "25LC256.h"

int main(void) {
  uint8_t i;
  uint8_t address;
```

```
// --------- Inits --------- //
initSPI();
initUSART();

// ------ Event loop ------ //
while (1) {
  printString("\r\n====  EEPROM Memory Playground ====\r\n");
  printString("Address  Value\r\n");

  for (i = 0; i < 10; i++) {  /* print out first ten bytes of memory */
    printString("  ");
    printByte(i);
    printString("      ");
    printByte(EEPROM_readByte(i));
    printString("\r\n");
  }
  printString(" [e] to erase all memory\r\n");
  printString(" [w] to write byte to memory\r\n\r\n");

  switch (receiveByte()) {                          /* take input */
  case 'e':
    printString("Clearing EEPROM, this could take a few seconds.\r\n");
    EEPROM_clearAll();
    break;
  case 'w':
    printString("Which memory slot would you like to write to?\r\n");
    address = getNumber();
    printString("\r\nWhat number would you like to store there?\r\n");
    i = getNumber();
    EEPROM_writeByte(address, i);
    printString("\r\n");
    break;
  default:
    printString("What??\r\n");
  }


}                                        /* End event loop */
  return (0);                    /* This line is never reached */
}
```

First off, you'll note that we include the *25LC256.h* header in the includes section. Just as with the *USART.h* library that we usually include, we also have to have the 25LC256 code linked in by adding it to the EXTRA_SOURCES list in the makefile.

The first half of the event loop is just printing out over UART. In addition to printing out a menu, a for loop prints out the first 10 memory locations for you to play around with. The remainder of the demo is a switch statement that handles keyboard input, clearing memory, or storing an input into memory. The only EEPROM-specific commands here are EEPROM_readByte and EEPROM_writeByte, and

EEPROM_clearAll from the library. And that's just as it should be: after all, the whole point of writing an EEPROM library is so that I'll never have to open up the datasheet again!

SPI EEPROM Library Header

So let's turn to the EEPROM library code. After all, this is where all of the fun SPI stuff happens. Let's start out with the *25LC256.h* file in Example 16-2.

Example 16-2. **25LC256.h Listing**

```
                                    /* SPI EEPROM 25LC256 Library */
#include <avr/io.h>
#include "pinDefines.h"


                            /* Which pin selects EEPROM as slave? */
#define SLAVE_SELECT    SPI_SS_PORT &= ~(1<<SPI_SS);
#define SLAVE_DESELECT  SPI_SS_PORT |= (1<<SPI_SS)

// Instruction Set -- from data sheet
#define EEPROM_READ        0b00000011              /* read memory */
#define EEPROM_WRITE       0b00000010          /* write to memory */

#define EEPROM_WRDI        0b00000100            /* write disable */
#define EEPROM_WREN        0b00000110             /* write enable */

#define EEPROM_RDSR        0b00000101      /* read status register */
#define EEPROM_WRSR        0b00000001     /* write status register */

// EEPROM Status Register Bits -- from data sheet
// Use these to parse status register
#define EEPROM_WRITE_IN_PROGRESS     0
#define EEPROM_WRITE_ENABLE_LATCH    1
#define EEPROM_BLOCK_PROTECT_0       2
#define EEPROM_BLOCK_PROTECT_1       3

#define EEPROM_BYTES_PER_PAGE        64
#define EEPROM_BYTES_MAX             0x7FFF

// Functions

void initSPI(void);
                /* Init SPI to run EEPROM with phase, polarity = 0,0 */

void SPI_tradeByte(uint8_t byte);
                /* Generic.  Just loads up HW SPI register and waits */

void EEPROM_send16BitAddress(uint16_t address);
                    /* splits 16-bit address into 2 bytes, sends both */

uint8_t EEPROM_readStatus(void);
                            /* reads the EEPROM status register */
```

```
void EEPROM_writeEnable(void);
                            /* helper: sets EEPROM write enable */

uint8_t EEPROM_readByte(uint16_t address);
                        /* gets a byte from a given memory location */

uint16_t EEPROM_readWord(uint16_t address);
                        /* gets two bytes from a given memory location */

void EEPROM_writeByte(uint16_t address, uint8_t byte);
                        /* writes a byte to a given memory location */

void EEPROM_writeWord(uint16_t address, uint16_t word);
                        /* gets two bytes to a given memory location */

void EEPROM_clearAll(void);
                        /* sets every byte in memory to zero */
```

Remember, the idea in C is to store definitions in the header files and keep your code in .c files. In *25LC256.h*, I define all of the macros that we'll be needing to work with the chips.

First, I define SLAVE_SELECT and SLAVE_DESELECT macros. The point here is that if you wanted to hook up your memory chips to use a different chip-select pin in the AVR, you could do so just by changing these two lines, and the rest of the code would work as planned. Next, I make nice mnemonic names for the commands that the SPI memory chip understands. I took these straight out of the memory's datasheet. I did the same thing with the bit names from the memory's status register so that I didn't have to remember which bit is flipped when there's a write in progress, or the chip is write-protected. Finally, because we'll be doing page-by-page writes and complete chip erases, I needed to note down the number of bytes per page and the maximum size of the memory.

As you can see, writing a header file like this for new hardware is mainly an exercise in going through the hardware's datasheet, understanding what it needs, and then making a bunch of definitions that'll make your life easier when doing the actual programming. And after you've done that, you can start to think about what kinds of functions you need to talk to the thing.

Finally, the include file gets to the function prototypes—essentially predefining what all the functions do, what arguments they take, and what type of data they return. Having all the function prototypes in the header file like this is a little bit redundant, but writing them all out is a good exercise for thinking your problem completely through, and having them all written down (and well-commented) is a good resource for later. In principle, you only have to read through the .h file to know how to use the library. (In practice, you'll almost always have to or want to dive into the code.)

SPI EEPROM Library C Code

Finally, we get to the meat of the code—the C source code that actually talks SPI to the EEPROM. Without further ado, let's learn some SPI! Follow along with Example 16-3.

Example 16-3. **25LC256.c** *listing*

```c
#include "25LC256.h"

void initSPI(void) {
  SPI_SS_DDR |= (1 << SPI_SS);                     /* set SS output */
  SPI_SS_PORT |= (1 << SLAVE_DESELECT);    /* start not selected (high) */

  SPI_MOSI_DDR |= (1 << SPI_MOSI);                  /* output on MOSI */
  SPI_MISO_PORT |= (1 << SPI_MISO);                 /* pullup on MISO */
  SPI_SCK_DDR |= (1 << SPI_SCK);                    /* output on SCK */

  /* Don't have to set phase, polarity b/c
   * default works with 25LCxxx chips */
  SPCR |= (1 << SPR1);             /* div 64, safer for breadboards */
  SPCR |= (1 << MSTR);                              /* clockmaster */
  SPCR |= (1 << SPE);                                 /* enable */
}

void SPI_tradeByte(uint8_t byte) {
  SPDR = byte;                    /* SPI starts sending immediately */
  loop_until_bit_is_set(SPSR, SPIF);            /* wait until done */
                            /* SPDR now contains the received byte */
}

void EEPROM_send16BitAddress(uint16_t address) {
  SPI_tradeByte((uint8_t) (address >> 8));   /* most significant byte */
  SPI_tradeByte((uint8_t) address);          /* least significant byte */
}

uint8_t EEPROM_readStatus(void) {
  SLAVE_SELECT;
  SPI_tradeByte(EEPROM_RDSR);
  SPI_tradeByte(0);                          /* clock out eight bits */
  SLAVE_DESELECT;
  return (SPDR);                             /* return the result */
}

void EEPROM_writeEnable(void) {
  SLAVE_SELECT;
  SPI_tradeByte(EEPROM_WREN);
  SLAVE_DESELECT;
}

uint8_t EEPROM_readByte(uint16_t address) {
  SLAVE_SELECT;
  SPI_tradeByte(EEPROM_READ);
```

```
    EEPROM_send16BitAddress(address);
    SPI_tradeByte(0);
    SLAVE_DESELECT;
    return (SPDR);
}

uint16_t EEPROM_readWord(uint16_t address) {
    uint16_t eepromWord;
    SLAVE_SELECT;
    SPI_tradeByte(EEPROM_READ);
    EEPROM_send16BitAddress(address);
    SPI_tradeByte(0);
    eepromWord = SPDR;
    eepromWord = (eepromWord << 8);                 /* most-sig bit */
    SPI_tradeByte(0);
    eepromWord += SPDR;                              /* least-sig bit */
    SLAVE_DESELECT;
    return (eepromWord);
}

void EEPROM_writeByte(uint16_t address, uint8_t byte) {
    EEPROM_writeEnable();
    SLAVE_SELECT;
    SPI_tradeByte(EEPROM_WRITE);
    EEPROM_send16BitAddress(address);
    SPI_tradeByte(byte);
    SLAVE_DESELECT;
    while (EEPROM_readStatus() & _BV(EEPROM_WRITE_IN_PROGRESS)) {;
    }
}

void EEPROM_writeWord(uint16_t address, uint16_t word) {
    EEPROM_writeEnable();
    SLAVE_SELECT;
    SPI_tradeByte(EEPROM_WRITE);
    EEPROM_send16BitAddress(address);
    SPI_tradeByte((uint8_t) (word >> 8));
    SPI_tradeByte((uint8_t) word);
    SLAVE_DESELECT;
    while (EEPROM_readStatus() & _BV(EEPROM_WRITE_IN_PROGRESS)) {;
    }
}

void EEPROM_clearAll(void) {
    uint8_t i;
    uint16_t pageAddress = 0;
    while (pageAddress < EEPROM_BYTES_MAX) {
        EEPROM_writeEnable();
        SLAVE_SELECT;
        SPI_tradeByte(EEPROM_WRITE);
        EEPROM_send16BitAddress(pageAddress);
        for (i = 0; i < EEPROM_BYTES_PER_PAGE; i++) {
            SPI_tradeByte(0);
        }
```

```
    SLAVE_DESELECT;
    pageAddress += EEPROM_BYTES_PER_PAGE;
    while (EEPROM_readStatus() & _BV(EEPROM_WRITE_IN_PROGRESS)) {;
    }
  }
}
```

initSPI

The first function is initSPI, which initializes the SPI mode. In this case, it's terribly simple. We configure all of the pins we're using for input and output, and then set the clock, master or slave mode, and SPI enable bits in the SPI Control Register, SPCR.

 SPI and Output Pins

Notice in this code that we first set up the data-direction registers for the pins that we're using for SPI, and then enable the SPI-specific hardware. This ordering turns out to be crucial, and the source of a very subtle bug that's caught me twice now.

When the SPI is in master mode, it's got a provision for deferring to other SPI masters in a multimaster setup. If the AVR has its slave-select pin configured as input (which is the boot-up default) and the pin is toggled low, it goes into a passive SPI mode in order to not interfere with the other masters on the bus. So as long as the slave-select pin is low in master mode, it won't send out a clock signal.

Because of this, you should enable the pullup on the slave-select pin, even if you're not using the pin as an output, before you enable SPI mode. Otherwise, you risk random electrical fluctuations shutting down your SPI. In our case, I'm using the SS pin as an output, so I set it as output and set it high before enabling SPI.

One possible complication with other devices is that you'll have to set up the phase and polarity of the SPI bus lines. In our case, the EEPROM is already configured for operation in the so-called Mode 0, which is the boot-up default for the AVR. Otherwise, you'd have to set up the polarity using the CPOL and CPHA bits. If you find yourself needing to change the SPI data mode, there's a handy table in the AVR datasheet, Table 18-2, SPI Modes that summarizes it all, along with nice timing diagrams in Tables 18-3 and 18-4. Or read "Phases and Polarities" on page 357.

Setting the clock division bits (SPR1 in our example) is largely unnecessary. After all, we're running the AVR at 1 MHz, and most SPI devices handle 10 MHz or higher data rates. On the other hand, at higher and higher frequencies, wires become effectively antennas and circuits that should work if designed with short connections on a printed circuit board can fail entirely when you're using long wires and assembling stuff on a breadboard. So in this example, I'm running the SPI bus at a

1/64th multiplier, or 15.6 kHz. That's still plenty fast for transferring memory in and out of our EEPROM, but you should know that we could be running even faster if we needed to.

Did I mention that I love SPI?

Phases and Polarities

If there's one complication to the SPI protocol that's kind of miserable, that's the question of clock *phase* and *polarity*.

The polarity in question just refers to whether the clock signal is normally high and transitions to a low voltage represent the start of a clock tick, or whether the clock signal is normally low, and it's an rising voltage that signals the start. This isn't so hard to figure out, and it's usually just a matter of looking at the device's datasheet.

Phase is it a little more confusing. Regardless of polarity, clock pulse has two transitions: a leading edge and a trailing edge. The issue of phase is whether to set up the data on the leading edge (and sample on the trailing edge) or to set up the data on the slave-select transition (and be ready to sample by the first leading edge). Phase zero means that the devices *sample* on the leading clock edge, and phase one means that devices *set up* on the leading edge.

Combining phase and polarity means that there are *four* possible SPI "data modes," and unfortunately you'll probably see all of them eventually. So here's my cheat sheet for setting the AVR's phase and polarity bits, CPHA and CPOL:

1. Figure out the polarity. This is easy to read from the timing diagrams in your device's datasheet. If the clock idles low, CPOL=0, and if it idles high, CPOL=1.

2. Now look to see when the data is *sampled*. If it's sampled on a rising edge, the phase equals the polarity, and you're in (CPOL, CPHA) = (0,0) or (1,1). If the data is instead set up on a rising edge and sampled on a falling edge, you're in one of the mixed modes: (CPOL, CPHA) = (0,1) or (1,0).

3. Combine the info from steps 1 and 2, and you should know where you stand.

Alternatively, you may find that the datasheet for your device lists its SPI "data mode." Mode 0 is (CPOL, CPHA) = (0,0), mode 1 is (0,1), mode 2 is (1,0), and mode 3 is (1,1). The EEPROM we're using in this example can talk mode 0 or mode 3, and mode 0 is the AVR default, so no configuration is necessary. Score!

Anyway, if you're at all unsure about the data mode of your SPI devices, try communicating with it. Many devices will send back a status register or device ID string or something that you can use to double-check that you've got it right.

SPI_tradeByte

The SPI_tradeByte function takes care of communicating over SPI at the lowest level. Remember that SPI works by clocking two shift registers that are linked together in a loop? Once the SPI is enabled and set to master mode, all that's necessary to get our byte transferred out, and a new one read in, is to load it into the SPI Data Register SPDR. Now, the AVR's SPI hardware takes over.

If we want to read the output from the slave device that was sent to us, our code needs to wait for the transaction to finish and then read the SPDR data register, where the outgoing data used to be and the incoming data now resides. All the SPI_tradeByte code does is wait for the transmission to be complete. Reading out the new byte (if you want to) is left for the calling code.

Convenience Functions

The rest of the *25LC256.c* file defines a bunch of convenience functions. All of these basically just code up what the EEPROM's datasheet said to do to talk to it, so I won't go into all of them in too much detail. However, the basic flavor of an SPI transaction runs through all of them, so it's worth taking a quick peek.

Look at the function EEPROM_readByte, for example. As with all SPI devices, the EEPROM needs to know when it's being spoken to, and this is done by sending a digital low voltage over it's slave-select (or chip-select, depending on the datasheet) line. Then the AVR sends the command to read out memory from the EE-PROM, which is defined in the *.h* file. (Remember, at the same time, the EEPROM is loading up the SPDR with a byte, but we don't really care what it is.) Next the AVR sends the 16-bit address of where to start reading memory from. Because we do this so often, I wrote a convenience function that breaks up a 16-bit number into two 8-bit bytes and sends them separately.

Having sent the read command and the address, all that remains is to read out some bytes. In this case, the function reads just one and then returns. Note again that the AVR is sending a byte worth of zeros—it had to have something to trade for the EEPROM's byte. If we wanted to read more bytes, the AVR could keep trading bytes with the EEPROM, and because the EEPROM is in read mode, it would send the next byte out of its memory. In this case, though, we're happy with one byte, so the function deselects the slave-select line (raising it to a logic high voltage level), and returns the value of SPDR, which has the last value read out from the memory.

The EEPROM_writeByte command is only a bit more complicated. In order to prevent EEPROM memory corruption, you have to first send a write-enable command before issuing the write command. This is done in the usual way—drop the slave-select line, load a byte across to the EEPROM with the write-enable command, and then reraise slave select. Now the EEPROM is ready for writing, and the procedure is similar to reading.

Finally, because writing to an EEPROM can take a few milliseconds, the last line in the write command continually reads the EEPROM's status byte: dropping the slave line, sending the "read status" command, sending a byte to receive the response, and then reraising slave line at the end. Each time through this cycle, the code checks to see if the write-in-progress bit is set and keeps looping until it isn't.

Because the EEPROM is structured in 8-bit bytes, like the AVR, it takes a little bit more work to read and write 16-bit numbers, so I wrote convenience functions for these. If you look at EEPROM_readWord for instance, you'll notice that it's just about

the same as EEPROM_readByte except that there are two calls to SPI_trade
Byte(0) after the address is sent, and the return value is a 16-bit data word that's
been reconstituted from the two bytes that get read in.

Finally, there's a function that erases the entire EEPROM. The fastest way to do this
is to start on a page boundary (multiple of 64 in the address space) and load up 64
bytes of zeros, and then write it permanently to memory. Repeating this for every
page of 64 bytes in the EEPROM blanks the whole device in minimum time. This
function is a good example of the page-by-page style of writing that gets the fastest
speed out of EEPROMs.

Summary

Using the AVR's built-in SPI hardware is easy and is definitely the fastest way to get
data in and out of the microcontroller. In terms of configuration, it's not hard at all;
in terms of use it is even easier—just write your byte to a register. Here's a summary:

1. Set up the SCK and MOSI pins (PB5 and PB3, respectively) for output.

2. Set up the MISO pin (PB4) for input, with pullup enabled.

3. If the AVR is the clock master, set the pullup on SS (PB2) if you're not using the
   pin as output.

4. Make sure the SPI clock speed is low enough to work with your intended device,
   and set a speed divider if it's not, or even if you just don't need the extra speed.

5. Set the AVR into clock master mode and enable SPI.

6. When you start communicating with a given slave device, begin by flipping its
   slave-select line low.

7. Now when you want to send a byte to that slave, write it to SPDR, wait for the
   transaction to end, and read the response back again from SPDR.

8. Finish up a transaction by setting the slave's slave-select line high again. When
   you want to talk to another device on the SPI line, simply drop its slave-select
   line low to start, and away you go.

9. The rest of the details are application-specific. Most devices have their own
   command sets, address spaces, etc. All of them will be based around sending
   a series of 8-bit bytes, and all of these should be laid out in their datasheets.

Still, communication between devices *can* be tricky. When you're looking at a new
peripheral chip, be prepared to sit down with the datasheet for an hour or so. The
first step is to turn all of the useful chip-specific commands into nice, readable
definitions, and store them in a header file. Then write down all of the transaction
types you'll need, look them up in the datasheet, and start coding and testing.

Logging Digital Thermometer

I2C is a tremendously popular protocol for interfacing microcontrollers with small sensors and these days even with devices that require more speed. Its main advantage is that you can talk to a large number of devices with just a couple of wires, which makes it much more like a network than the SPI bus. When you find yourself wanting to talk with I2C devices, this chapter will get you a head start!

We'll be continuing on from Chapter 16 toward building a logging I2C thermometer. If you use the SPI EEPROM chip from last chapter, the logger will be capable of recording the temperature at a variable frequency for at least a few days on AA batteries. Then, when you want to read the data back out, the AVR code will dump it over the USB-Serial port back to your desktop computer for graphing and analysis.

And even if you don't need a logging thermometer, you should be able to modify this code reasonably easily to work with other I2C devices. Indeed, I wrote most of the code in this chapter for a logging accelerometer that our hackerspace sent up into near-space with a helium balloon. There are I2C sensors available for almost any quantity you'd like to measure, all you have to do is look around.

In the previous chapter, I extolled the main virtues of the SPI bus: it's fast and simple. At least as long as you're only communicating with a few devices. When you're dealing with more than a few peripherals, the requirement to have one slave-select line per device on the network can get out of hand. (Imagine if the Internet worked like SPI! Each computer would need a physical wire to every other computer in the world just to tell the other that you're ready to talk to it.)

Instead, we can give each device an address and require the master to send this address as a data prefix that the slave devices will listen for. That would drop SPI's requirement of four wires (plus one more for each additional device) down to three.

What You Need

In addition to the basic kit, you will need:

- An I2C device to talk to—my example uses the very common LM75 temperature sensor.

- For the LM75 temperature sensor, you'll also need a surface-mount to DIP adapter.

- Two 10k ohm resistors to use as pull-ups for the I2C data line.

- SPI EEPROM Memory chip from the previous chapter for logging data.

- A USB-Serial adapter.

And because most of the time we're only sending meaningful data one way or the other, maybe we don't need truly bidirectional, full-duplex communications like SPI provides. Maybe we could run everything half duplex, drop yet one more wire, and use only two? And if we could, we'd call the two wires by the more generic names "serial clock" and "serial data." Hmmm....

Welcome to the beginnings of the I2C protocol. In contrast to SPI, it's designed to use a minimum number of wires (two, plus ground) and yet handle a large network of devices (up to 128 with "standard" I2C). The trade-off is that I2C is a bit more complex from a user's standpoint, and not capable of the same extreme speeds. However, when you need to connect your AVR to an LCD screen, a few buttons, some sensors, and a dozen networked multicolor blinky lights, I2C is the way to go. (Of course, nothing stops you from using both SPI and I2C peripherals at the same time—the AVR's hardware peripherals are independent of each other.)

What's in a Name? (TWI, I2C, and I²C)

"I^2C" was once a trademark of Philips Electronics and is now owned by the spin-off IC company, NXP. While there's absolutely no licensing issues surrounding *using* the "I^2C" protocol, you'll have to pay NXP money if you'd like to use the name "I^2C" with your hardware.

Because of this, Atmel uses what they call a "Two-wire interface" (TWI) protocol that happens to be 100% compatible with "I^2C," but by calling it something else, they sidestep the trademark issue. So when you're reading through Atmel documentation, feel free to read "I^2C" anywhere you see "TWI."

There are also a handful of "I^2C"-like protocols, most of which are tiny variations (SMBus, PMBbus, etc.) or which are largely interoperable. So when I write "I2C," I don't mean "I^2C," but instead the whole family of "I^2C"-like protocols that all work together. (And besides, typing superscripts all the time gets old.)

How I2C Works

Let's start our discussion of I2C from the ground up. That is, we'll start with some wires, then talk about the signals that run on the wires, and then finally the protocol that interprets these signals. The two wires that the I2C protocol uses are called SCL, for "serial clock," and SDA, for "serial data." The functions of these two lines won't be particularly surprising.

Like SPI, I2C is a synchronous protocol, so there is a clock master that's controlling the communication by sending out the timing signal. Unlike SPI, there's a very strict convention about phase and polarity, thank goodness. With two exceptions, the I2C data line can change between high and low states only while the clock line is low, and data is to be read only while the clock line is high.

The two exceptions are made for the *start* and *stop* signals, respectively. A start signal is a falling edge while the clock line is held high, and a stop signal is a rising edge with the clock high. When the clock is low, anything can happen on the data line, but as soon as the clock line is pulled high, the only two allowed changes signal the beginning and end of a transmission, respectively. (See the timing diagram in Figure 17-1.)

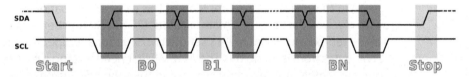

Figure 17-1. *I2C data timing*

So an I2C conversation starts by pulling the SDA line low before the clock is started up. This is the start signal. Next, the master starts the clock with a low pulse. Data is then set up on the low clock phase and read out on the high clock phase until the transaction is over. In the end, the clock is stopped, and the master sends the stop signal by releasing the SDA line.

The I2C protocol doesn't stop there, though. In order to allow multiple devices to share the same two lines, each slave device needs to know when it's being spoken to. As hinted at earlier, this is done with an addressing scheme. In the original, and still most common, version of the I2C standard, each device has a specific seven-bit address, and every communication between the bus master and that device must start with the address.

But wait a minute…seven bits? The eighth bit is reserved for a read/write direction bit that determines whether the master or slave is going to send data over the data line next. A one/high-level direction bit means that the master expects to read data off the line, and a zero/low-level direction bit means that the master is going to write data to the SDA line.

So if the AVR sends a start, then the address of a slave device, and then a zero, the slave device knows that it's going to receive a byte from the AVR (that is, the master is going to write a byte) immediately afterward. If the last bit after the address is a one, then the slave is responsible for sending data; the master reads data off the bus.

There's one final complication that you need to know about. The device that's receiving the data, whether it's the master or slave, is responsible for acknowledging that it has received the byte. To do this, a ninth bit is sent after every 8-bit byte. A zero or low ("ACK") indicates that the byte is acknowledged and signals that the sender should continue sending. A high bit ("NACK") indicates that there was an error or that the transmitter should stop sending or that the whole communication is about to end, depending on the circumstances.

Note that the "ACK" or "NACK" bit is sent by the *receiver* rather than the transmitter. This makes it possible to detect if there's been an error in the transmission, which can be handy if you're operating in an electrically noisy environment. (And this is in contrast to SPI, where everything's just assumed to work.)

Later on in this chapter, you'll implement this exact conversation in code, but for now, to give you the flavor of a "complicated" I2C transaction between the AVR and an LM75 temperature sensor, let's set the LM75 up for a temperature reading and get two bytes from it. To do this, the AVR will first need to send a byte to the LM75, to put it in temperature-reading mode, and then the AVR will need to receive two bytes (the temperature) from the LM75. The oscilloscope trace from this conversation can be seen in Figure 17-2.

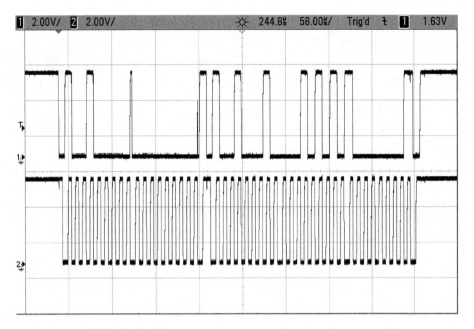

Figure 17-2. *AVR talking I2C with LM75*

To read the scope trace, it helps to keep three things in mind. First, I2C bytes are nine bits long—there's always the ACK/NACK at the end. Second, if you look carefully at the clock line (the lower line), you can see how there are five slightly wider lows and one wide high. These occur at the start or end of every full byte. And finally, data is read out during the high clock period and changed during the lows. If you focus on the clock line, find a high, and then look up to the data line and read the value off, you can decode this. (You'll notice that the LM75 is pretty quick about noticing a low clock and setting up its next bit as soon as it can.)

First, the AVR sends a start signal, changing the data line while the clock line is still high. Then the AVR sends the LM75's address (1001000), followed by another zero to signal write mode, and the LM75 acknowledges. That thin upward spike in the scope trace during a clock low comes right after the slave's ACK bit (the final zero) and the master picking up again to send the zero that starts off the next byte.

The second byte sent by the AVR is all zeros, which represents the temperature-register and tells the LM75 that a temperature read is coming next. The LM75 acknowledges again—a ninth zero. Now, because the AVR will be issuing a new command, the AVR briefly halts the clock signal while it's high and sends another start command. That's the downward transition in the data line during the long clock high period.

Next the AVR sends the address again, but this time followed by a one (10010001), indicating that the LM75 should speak. The LM75 acknowledges by holding the data line low, and then sends the most significant byte of data. In my office, it was apparently 21 degrees (00010101).

The AVR now acknowledges this byte with a zero, and the LM75 sends the least-significant byte, which in the case of the LM75 is the decimal place. For the cheap LM75s only the first bit counts, and it stands for half a degree. Here, the LM75 sent 10000000, so the full temperature reading is 21.5 degrees. Fancier LM75s can read down to the eighth of a Celsius degree, so there may be meaningful data in the first three of these bits.

And then finally, because it's the end of the communication, the AVR sends a NACK (a one) and the stop signal by holding the clock line high and raising the data line.

I2C Protocol Summary

So to recap:

1. The SDA data line and SCL clock lines are both held normally high by pull-up resistors. Data is signalled as a zero by pulling the line low, or as a one by allowing the line to float back up high.

2. Communication starts with a start signal: pulling the data line low before the clock has started up.

3. Data is then set up during the clock low periods, and read out when the clock is high.

4. The first byte after a start is always the seven-bit address of the slave, followed by a direction bit indicating whether master or slave will be sending data on the SDA line next.

5. After each byte sent, the receiving device sends either an ACK bit (a low voltage, or zero) or a NACK bit (high, or one) depending on whether the communication is to continue.

6. If the master needs to change the direction of communication in the middle, it can send another start signal, followed by the address and new direction bit.

7. Finally, after the last transmitted byte, the master stops the clock and then releases the data line, sending a stop signal.

 *I2C Wiring*

Both of these lines are normally held high when nobody is transmitting. In fact, electrically, the two I2C lines are held high by a pull-up resistor, and to send a zero on the data line, the devices connected to them pull the lines low with low-side transistor switches and just let the lines "float" back up to their high state.

A practical speed limit on how fast the I2C bus can run is how quickly this pull-up resistor can drag the whole wire back up to the high voltage level. For long I2C connections, the capacitance between the signal wires and ground can slow this transition down even further. If you're having trouble with noise on a long (many inches) I2C line, that's a good first place to start looking; try slowing down the data rate and see if that fixes the problem.

If you need the line to run faster, you can try to fine-tune the pull-up resistors on the line, but you may need to reroute the I2C lines to reduce inter-wire capacitance.

I2C Demo Hookup

It's time to hook up the I2C thermometer to your breadboard. Don't unplug the SPI EEPROM when adding in the LM75 temperature sensor, because we're going to be using both together to make the temperature logger by the end of the chapter.

The LM75 is only available these days as a surface-mount component, so we're going to have to do a little bit of adapting to get it to fit into the breadboard. The easiest way to go is to purchase a pre-made SOIC-to-DIP 8 pin adapter. The usual suspects for hobbyist electronics prototyping supplies will have these for a couple of dollars, but you may be able to get them cheaper from online auction sites.

Solder the LM75 into the adapter and then plug the adapter into the breadboard and you're all set. If the adapter were in fact a DIP chip, you would have something like Figure 17-3.

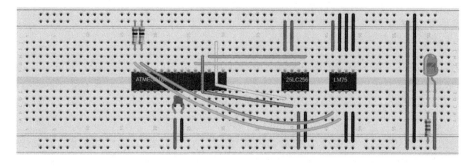

Made with **Fritzing.org**

Figure 17-3. *I2C/LM75 demo hookup*

As with the 25LC256, the LM75 needs power and ground connected to its pins 8 and 4, respectively. In addition, the LM75 has three address pins that I've decided to set all to zero by grounding—they're pins 5, 6, and 7 next to the VCC pin. Additionally, because I'm not using the external switch pin, pin 3, I ground it.

That leaves pins 1 and 2, SDA and SCL, which hook up to the AVR's TWI pins, PC5/SDA and PC4/SCL. Last but not least, connect up the I2C protocol's required pull-up resistors. They can be connected at either the AVR side or the LM75 side—whichever is convenient. That's all that's necessary for the circuit: basically two wires and two resistors. Too easy!

I2C Demo Library

If you just read my description of all that goes on in an I2C transaction, you'll agree that it's a lot of work to go through just to send a byte and get two back. (And if you read through the detailed description in the AVR datasheet, you'll realize that I was giving you the short version!)

But because the protocol is so detailed, you can leave most of the details to hardware. The AVR's "TWI" hardware, like the SPI and USART modules, has a register that is used to store data to be sent out across the I2C lines and stores the received byte after a successful receipt. All of the clocking and timing is taken care of by the AVR.

The TWI hardware helps you out with much more, however. If you'd like the AVR to act as an I2C slave, TWAR holds its address, and TWEA ("enable acknowledge") automatically handles the generation of acknowledge bits when the AVR is receiving. There is an interrupt flag that signals, in slave mode, that the AVR is being addressed. The rest you need to handle in your code.

If you want the AVR to behave as bus master, it needs to send start and stop signals, and you can send them by setting TWSTA and TWSTO bits, respectively. The AVR takes care of the timing, not sending its own start signal until after the line is clear. Then you send the address of the device you're talking to, and then data, with or without acknowledge bits as configured.

If you thought I was a genius for being able to transmit the signal in Figure 17-2, you'll be surprised how easy the AVR hardware makes it all. And for this demo, I basically just reused an old I2C library of mine that I had lying around, and frankly I encourage you to do the same whenever possible.

Because the AVR hardware takes care of so much of the low-level detail, the individual functions that read and write to the I2C bus are fairly straightforward and quite short. First, have a read through the header file in Example 17-1, and then we'll dig into the code.

*Example 17-1. **i2c.h** listing*

```
// Functions for i2c communication
#include <avr/io.h>
#include "pinDefines.h"

void initI2C(void);
    /* Sets pullups and initializes bus speed to 100kHz (at FCPU=8MHz) */

void i2cWaitForComplete(void);
                    /* Waits until the hardware sets the TWINT flag */

void i2cStart(void);
                    /* Sends a start condition (sets TWSTA) */
void i2cStop(void);
                    /* Sends a stop condition (sets TWSTO) */

void i2cSend(uint8_t data);
                /* Loads data, sends it out, waiting for completion */

uint8_t i2cReadAck(void);
            /* Read in from slave, sending ACK when done (sets TWEA) */
uint8_t i2cReadNoAck(void);
            /* Read in from slave, sending NOACK when done (no TWEA) */
```

By now, you're not surprised to see an initI2C function that sets up the necessaries for using hardware TWI. Because I'm not using interrupt-driven code, i2cWaitFor Complete sits in a loop until an already-in-progress I2C byte is sent.

If you look back on the description of I2C in "How I2C Works" on page 363, you'll see that we're basically doing three things: sending data (and waiting for it to be acknowledged) or reading in data either with or without an acknowledge at the end. Of course, as the master, the AVR is also responsible for bracketing the conversation with start and stop conditions.

Let's turn now to the `i2c.c` listing in Example 17-2. The actual code itself is not much longer than the words typed to describe it!

*Example 17-2. **i2c.c listing***

```
#include "i2c.h"

void initI2C(void) {
  TWBR = 32;                                      /* set bit rate, see p. 242 */
                                   /* 8MHz / (16+2*TWBR*1) ~= 100kHz */
  TWCR |= (1 << TWEN);                                        /* enable */
}

void i2cWaitForComplete(void) {
  loop_until_bit_is_set(TWCR, TWINT);
}

void i2cStart(void) {
  TWCR = (_BV(TWINT) | _BV(TWEN) | _BV(TWSTA));
  i2cWaitForComplete();
}

void i2cStop(void) {
  TWCR = (_BV(TWINT) | _BV(TWEN) | _BV(TWSTO));
}

uint8_t i2cReadAck(void) {
  TWCR = (_BV(TWINT) | _BV(TWEN) | _BV(TWEA));
  i2cWaitForComplete();
  return (TWDR);
}

uint8_t i2cReadNoAck(void) {
  TWCR = (_BV(TWINT) | _BV(TWEN));
  i2cWaitForComplete();
  return (TWDR);
}

void i2cSend(uint8_t data) {
  TWDR = data;
  TWCR = (_BV(TWINT) | _BV(TWEN));                    /* init and enable */
  i2cWaitForComplete();
}
```

Initialization is just a matter of configuring the SDA and SCL pins for output, selecting the bit rate, and hitting the enable button in the TWI configuration register, TWCR. If you want to run the I2C bus very slowly, that's also fine, and there are also two prescaler bits in the TWI status register, TWSR, that you can use to divide the base rate by 1 (default), 4, 16, or 64.

I2C Bus Speeds

A word or two on the bit rate, while we're here. The oldest I2C standard specified 100 kHz for the maximum bit-rate, and then came 400 kHz "Fast-mode" and 1 MHz "Fast-mode Plus" and recently 3.4 MHz "High-speed mode" and 5 MHz "Ultra Fast-mode." My guess is that before the English language runs out of superlatives to go with "fast," there will be a few more I2C speed grades as well.

In practical situations, the speed over the bus line is limited by how quickly the pull-up resistors can reraise the line's voltage, and this in turn is limited by the intrinsic capacitance in the line. As you get up into higher and higher frequencies, the lines behave more like transmission lines than instantaneous signals, and you have to start worrying about termination and internal reflections and stuff like that.

If none of the above makes any sense, or it does and you just don't feel like working these design issues into your circuit board, stick with the lower-speed 100 kHz or 400 kHz modes.

The function i2cWaitForComplete is the equivalent of the blocking-wait that we did in the UART code. When the byte in progress has been transferred across the I2C line, the TWINT flag is set. Here, we just loop until the transfer's done. Unlike the UART code, where it can take a long time to get a byte in, especially if we're waiting for a human to type it, here the wait is usually short enough that the cost of a blocking wait is not a problem.

The rest of the code simply gives readable names to the process of setting the bits we need to set in the TWI control register in order to send or receive data and includes the i2cWaitForComplete command where necessary. In particular, each of the other commands set the TWINT and TWEN bits, which has the effect of resetting the interrupt flag and making sure that the TWI interface stays enabled. The additional bits in the TWCR that are either set or not determine the type of transaction: a start or stop signal; sending or receiving data; and with or without an ACK.

 I2C Error Codes

If you wanted to be very careful about things, you could check up on the codes returned in the TWI status register after every transmission and make sure that there's nothing strange going on. The AVR datasheet has five or six brutal pages going through all of the error codes and their causes. The util/twi.h standard library includes mnemonic macros for each of the I2C transaction status codes for your convenience.

Honestly, I've only had use for them once, and that was when I was trying to troubleshoot a problem that turned out to be of my own making—not sending a NACK at the end of a final byte caused the I2C data flash chip I was using to lock up every other conversation. You may get more out of the result codes than I did, however, so feel free to read through that section of the AVR datasheet when the time arises.

I2C Thermometer Demo

With I2C, just as with SPI, getting the AVR's hardware to speak the protocol and shuttle data across is only half of the battle. The rest is in the specifics of communicating with a specific target chip. In the case here, it's a cheap digital thermometer that sends the temperature over I2C. If you'd like to follow along as I work through the code in Example 17-3, go download the datasheet for your version of the LM75. (It's a mostly standardized chip produced by multiple manufacturers, but with little difference across them. The datasheets should all be similar, too. For what it's worth, I've looked at the ones from NXP and from National Semiconductor.)

Example 17-3. *i2cThermometer.c listing*

```
                   /* Reads LM75 Thermometer and Prints Value over Serial */

// ------- Preamble -------- //
#include <avr/io.h>
#include <util/delay.h>
#include <avr/power.h>

#include "pinDefines.h"
#include "USART.h"
#include "i2c.h"

// -------- Defines -------- //

#define LM75_ADDRESS_W          0b10010000
#define LM75_ADDRESS_R          0b10010001
#define LM75_TEMP_REGISTER      0b00000000
#define LM75_CONFIG_REGISTER    0b00000001
#define LM75_THYST_REGISTER     0b00000010
#define LM75_TOS_REGISTER       0b00000011
// -------- Functions --------- //

int main(void) {

  uint8_t tempHighByte, tempLowByte;

  // -------- Inits --------- //
  clock_prescale_set(clock_div_1);                          /* 8MHz */
  initUSART();
  printString("\r\n====  i2c Thermometer  ====\r\n");
  initI2C();

  // ------- Event loop ------ //
  while (1) {
                   /* To set register, address LM75 in write mode */
    i2cStart();
    i2cSend(LM75_ADDRESS_W);
    i2cSend(LM75_TEMP_REGISTER);
    i2cStart();                      /* restart, just send start again */
```

```
                              /* Setup and send address, with read bit */
    i2cSend(LM75_ADDRESS_R);
                              /* Now receive two bytes of temperature */
    tempHighByte = i2cReadAck();
    tempLowByte = i2cReadNoAck();
    i2cStop();

    // Print it out nicely over serial for now...
    printByte(tempHighByte);
    if (tempLowByte & _BV(7)) {
      printString(".5\r\n");
    }
    else {
      printString(".0\r\n");
    }

                                    /* Once per second */
    _delay_ms(1000);

  }                                 /* End event loop */
  return (0);               /* This line is never reached */
}
```

Find the section in the LM75 datasheet devoted to I2C, and we'll work through the AVR code. The first thing I always do with I2C devices is create a definition for the slave's 7-bit address with a zero and a one tacked on the end, so that I can remember which one is write mode and read mode.

Now if you read the datasheet, you'll see that the last three bits of the address for a LM75 is "hardware programmable" by wiring up three pins of the chip to either VCC or GND where they take on values of one or zero, respectively.

I've wired up my LM75 with all three address pins to ground, so the address is 1001000. When we want to send data *to* the LM75, we'll use 10010000 in the address field, and when we want to read data *from* the LM75, we'll send 10010001, so I've defined LM75_ADDRESS_W and LM75_ADDRESS_R accordingly. I've also defined the four possible register pointer values from the datasheet, although we'll only use one here. These allow you to set trigger temperature points in the LM75's memory so that you can use it as a standalone thermostat or temperature controller, turning on an off an appliance when the temperature gets too hot or too cold.

Inside the event loop, the routine simply reads the temperature from the LM75, converts it from the two-byte format that it natively comes in, and transmits the value over the UART serial line. Let's work quickly through the I2C communication section, though. To see why the code does what it does, have a look at the I2C timing diagrams located somewhere near halfway through the datasheet.

The LM75 comes in power-up default ready to read out its temperature data, but just so that we're sure it's giving us a temperature reading (and to demonstrate sending a restart signal), let's set the temperature pointer just to be sure. Find the section in the LM75 datasheet where it describes something like "Read Temperature register including pointer byte (2-byte data)" or similar. Because the AVR hardware will take care of a bunch of the low-level detail for you, what you're looking for in these diagrams are things like start and stop conditions, what bytes need to be sent in what order, and where ACK and NACKs are expected of the AVR when receiving data.

Communication with the thermometer starts off, naturally, with a start command. To set the pointer byte, we need to write to the LM75, so the AVR will send the LM75's address plus the write flag and expect an ACK to be sure everything is OK. After the ACK, the AVR sends the temperature register command, which happens to be all zeros, and expects another ACK.

Now the AVR wants to read from the LM75, so it has to change the data direction. To do this, the AVR sends a restart and then the LM75's address byte plus the read flag this time, and expects an ACK. Next, the LM75 should transmit a single byte, followed by an ACK, and then another byte, this time followed with a NACK to mark the end of the transmission. Finally, the AVR sends a stop signal to free up the I2C bus line for other communication. See how that translates fairly cleanly into code?

SPI and I2C Data Logger

Now let's put all that we know about SPI and I2C together with a USART serial user interface. That's right, three serial communication modes in one little project!

Combine an AVR, the EEPROM memory, and the LM75 thermometer and four AA batteries, and you've got a portable temperature logger that will run for days. And because the data is stored in the EEPROM, you can unplug the device at any time and pick up from wherever you left off. And when you connect it to your desktop computer's serial port, you can dump all of the data and do whatever you'd like with it.

You should also note that, although this is a thermometer application, it could be anything. Data loggers are all very similar, and not particularly difficult to write once you've figured out how to communicate with the devices in question. For instance, if you wanted to build a GPS location-logger, you'll be stoked to know that GPS modules almost all speak UART serial, and that parsing their report strings isn't all that hard at all. Or maybe you're interested in building a logging accelerometer. For instance, most accelerometers speak I2C and are even easier to integrate into a data logger. Heck, I don't know what it is that you're interested in logging, but here's a simple framework to do it.

You've already seen the basics of how to work with both the SPI EEPROM and the I2C data from the LM75 temperature sensor. And because I wrote these functions into standalone libraries, reusing the functions is as easy as including the header files in the code and linking to their code in the makefile.

The main new bit in this project is a simple UART-serial based menu system that only activates if you type "m" within a few seconds of resetting the AVR chip. The goal was to build a device that's both free-standing and can be controlled when plugged into your desktop computer. Implementing the menu is actually quite simple—you simply configure the serial port, wait for a few seconds, and then test if the desired character came across in the meantime. If yes, enter a menu loop that repeats until you type "s" to start logging. If "m" wasn't received over the serial port during the delay time, jump straight into the event loop.

Let's see how it all comes together in Example 17-4.

Example 17-4. *loggingThermometer.c listing*

```c
// ------- Preamble -------- //
#include <avr/io.h>
#include <util/delay.h>
#include <avr/interrupt.h>
#include <avr/power.h>

#include "pinDefines.h"
#include "USART.h"

#include "i2c.h"                             /* for i2c functions */
#include "25LC256.h"                         /* for EEPROM specific */

// -------- Defines --------- //

#define LM75_ADDRESS_W 0b10010000
#define LM75_ADDRESS_R 0b10010001
#define LM75_TEMP_REGISTER          0b00000000
#define LM75_CONFIG_REGISTER        0b00000001
#define LM75_THYST_REGISTER         0b00000010
#define LM75_TOS_REGISTER           0b00000011

#define CURRENT_LOCATION_POINTER  0
          /* where to store a pointer to the current reading in EEPROM */
#define SECONDS_POINTER           2
                              /* store seconds-delay value here */
#define MEMORY_START              4
              /* where to start logging temperature values */
#define MENU_DELAY                5
              /* seconds to wait before bypassing main menu */

// -------- Functions --------- //

static inline void printTemperature(uint8_t tempReading) {
```

```
                                      /* temperature stored as 2x Celcius */
  printByte((tempReading >> 1));
  if (tempReading & 1) {
    printString(".5\r\n");
  }
  else {
    printString(".0\r\n");
  }
}

int main(void) {
  uint16_t secondsDelay;          /* how long to wait between readings */
  uint16_t currentMemoryLocation;          /* where are we in EEPROM? */
  uint16_t i;                      /* used to count memory locations */
  uint8_t tempHighByte, tempLowByte, temperatureByte;    /* from LM75 */
  uint8_t enterMenu;                              /* logical flag */

  // -------- Inits --------- //
  clock_prescale_set(clock_div_1);                      /* 8 MHz */
  initSPI();
  initI2C();
  initUSART();
  LED_DDR |= (1 << LED0);

                            /* Load up last values from EEPROM */
  secondsDelay = EEPROM_readWord(SECONDS_POINTER);

                      /* Delay to allow input to enter main menu */
  printString("*** Press [m] within ");
  printByte(MENU_DELAY);
  printString(" seconds to enter menu. ***\r\n ");

  for (i = 0; i < MENU_DELAY; i++) {
    _delay_ms(1000);
  }

  if (bit_is_set(UCSR0A, RXC0) && (UDR0 == 'm')) {
    enterMenu = 1;
  }
  else {
    enterMenu = 0;
  }

  while (enterMenu) {
    printString("\r\n====[  Logging Thermometer ]====\r\n  ");
    currentMemoryLocation = EEPROM_readWord(CURRENT_LOCATION_POINTER);
    printWord(currentMemoryLocation - MEMORY_START);
    printString(" readings in log.\r\n  ");
    printWord(secondsDelay);
    printString(" seconds between readings.\r\n");
    printString(" [<] to shorten sample delay time\r\n");
    printString(" [>] to increase sample delay time\r\n");
    printString(" [?] to reset delay time to 60 sec\r\n");
    printString(" [d] to print out log over serial\r\n");
```

```
    printString(" [e] to erase memory\r\n");
    printString(" [s] to start logging\r\n\r\n");

    switch (receiveByte()) {
    case 'd':
      SLAVE_SELECT;
      SPI_tradeByte(EEPROM_READ);
      EEPROM_send16BitAddress(MEMORY_START);
      for (i = MEMORY_START; i < currentMemoryLocation; i++) {
        SPI_tradeByte(0);
        printTemperature(SPDR);
      }
      SLAVE_DESELECT;
      break;
    case '<':
      if (secondsDelay >= 10) {
        secondsDelay -= 5;
        EEPROM_writeWord(SECONDS_POINTER, secondsDelay);
      }
      break;
    case '>':
      if (secondsDelay < 65000) {
        secondsDelay += 5;
        EEPROM_writeWord(SECONDS_POINTER, secondsDelay);
      }
      break;
    case '?':
      secondsDelay = 60;
      EEPROM_writeWord(SECONDS_POINTER, secondsDelay);
      break;
    case 'e':
      printString("Clearing EEPROM, this could take a few seconds.\r\n");
      EEPROM_clearAll();
      EEPROM_writeWord(CURRENT_LOCATION_POINTER, MEMORY_START);
      EEPROM_writeWord(SECONDS_POINTER, secondsDelay);
      break;
    case 's':
      printString("OK, logging...\r\n");
      enterMenu = 0;
      break;
    default:
      printString("Sorry, didn't understand that.\r\n");
    }
  }

  // ------ Event loop ------ //
  while (1) {

    currentMemoryLocation = EEPROM_readWord(CURRENT_LOCATION_POINTER);

                              /* Make sure in temperature mode */
    i2cStart();
    i2cSend(LM75_ADDRESS_W);
    i2cSend(LM75_TEMP_REGISTER);
```

```
                                          /* Get Temp from thermometer */
  i2cStart();                     /* Setup and send address, with read bit */
  i2cSend(LM75_ADDRESS_R);
  tempHighByte = i2cReadAck();             /* two bytes of temperature */
  tempLowByte = i2cReadNoAck();
  i2cStop();
  temperatureByte = (tempHighByte << 1) | (tempLowByte >> 7);
        /* temperatureByte now contains 2x the temperature in Celcius */
  printTemperature(temperatureByte);             /* serial output */


                               /* Save the new temperature value */
  EEPROM_writeByte(currentMemoryLocation, temperatureByte);

  /* move on to next location and record new position
     if not already at the end of memory */
  if (currentMemoryLocation < EEPROM_BYTES_MAX) {
    currentMemoryLocation++;
    EEPROM_writeWord(CURRENT_LOCATION_POINTER, currentMemoryLocation);
  }

                                               /* delay */
  for (i = 0; i < secondsDelay; i++) {
    _delay_ms(1000);
    LED_PORT ^= (1 << LED0);            /* blink to show working */
  }

}                                         /* End event loop */
  return (0);                    /* This line is never reached */
}
```

Pointers in EEPROM

First off, I just copied the definitions for the LM75's I2C address into the top of the code to make reading and writing just as easy as it was in the demo program. What follows next, though, is a little bit interesting. I define three EEPROM memory locations.

The first defined memory location is the one in which I plan to store the memory location where the current temperature reading should go. (If you've never been through pointers in C, reread that sentence until it makes sense.) The idea is that if the AVR is reset, we don't want to start writing again at the beginning of memory, because then we'd overwrite whatever data we have in memory. So instead, we keep track of where we should be writing next. But we can't keep track of it in RAM, because we lose that when the battery goes dead, so we write the current EEPROM memory location itself into EEPROM. CURRENT_LOCATION_POINTER is the memory location where the current memory location value is stored.

Next, I wanted the device to be menu-configurable in terms of how many seconds to sleep between data readings, rather than have the value hardcoded into a #define or something. But this also means that whatever value is last decided on needs to be stored somewhere nonvolatile—on our SPI EEPROM. `SECONDS_LOCA TION` is the location in EEPROM where the number of seconds per update is stored.

Jumping briefly down to the `main()` body, you can see that just after the various serial initialization functions are called, the code initializes a variable `secondsDe lay` from the EEPROM location defined earlier. Because the code uses this value frequently, it's probably worthwhile to keep it in RAM like this. If RAM is tight, though, you could simply reread the value from EEPROM every time you needed it.

 Configuration Parameters and Internal EEPROM

Storing nonvolatile configuration parameters like this is very common in small embeddded devices, and to help with that, the AVRs actually have a very small amount of built-in EEPROM so that you can do the same trick as here, but without needing external memory.

*Unfortunately, internal EEPROM is measured in bytes rather than kilobytes, so it's not very good for data-logging purposes, but we'll see in **Chapter 18** how to use internal EEPROM to store configuration parameters and other user data.*

Both of the memory pointer and the delay value are 16-bit numbers, so note that I'm allocating two bytes for each in choosing the locations. Finally, `MEMORY_START` is a useful definition to have around. This way, we'll know where to start recording again after a complete memory erase.

The UART Serial Menu

We saw a simple UART-serial menu system in a few examples so far. This one's the most elaborate. In this menu, there are options for setting the delay, printing out all the data from the EEPROM over the serial line, erasing the SPI EEPROM, and simply leaving the menu and entering logging mode. First, let's talk about how to get into menu mode, and then we'll look at the menu code itself.

When the chip first wakes up from a reset, it prompts over the UART serial line to to press "m" within a few seconds to enter the menu. This is followed by a completely normal delay, and then the serial receive flag is checked. If anything came through, it's checked to be equal to "m" or not. If it is, a flag variable, `enterMenu`, is set, and otherwise, not.

Now the menu loop can easily be constructed as a `while(enterMenu)` loop around a `switch()` statement that reads from the serial input, so that any of the commands in the menu can be run, and as long as they don't change the value of `enterMenu`, we loop around for the next command. Then, if the serial input "s" is received, the enterMenu variable is set to zero and the while() is no longer true, and execution moves on to the event loop.

This pattern of a while() loop with a switch() inside, where one or more of the options invalidate the while(), is a common pattern for things like menus and multiple-choice routines.

From the perspective of this chapter, the other interesting detail in the menu section is the way that dumping all of the logged memory is handled. Here, we use the feature of the EEPROM that it will continue spitting out its memory contents one at a time as long as it receives an SPI clock. Because the last-stored memory location is in the variable currentMemoryLocation, we can run through all of the logged memory by starting at the defined MEMORY_START and reading out currentMemoryLocation-MEMORY_START values and printing them out over the UART serial port.

Accessing all of the logged EEPROM memory in one SPI transaction like this is by far the fastest way to dump all of the EEPROM, but it won't actually have any real effect on overall speed, because the SPI bus is so much faster than the UART printout. Oh well.

The Logger's Event Loop

Finally, whether the user has hit "s" to escape from the menu loop or never entered the menu to begin with, we enter the event loop, and the next chunk of code sets the LM75 temperature pointer and reads out the temperature just as we did in the temperature sensor demo.

The nine-bit temperature value is trimmed down to eight bits so that it fits more easily in memory, the memory location is updated if it's still within the range of the EEPROM's maximum number of bytes, and the data is stored. The memory address pointer in EEPROM is then updated and the AVR delays.

In my personal version of this code, I also added in a slow timer to provide a system tick so that you can put the AVR and LM75 to sleep, using the timer and an interrupt to wake everything back up. Dig into the LM75's sleep mode in its datasheet if you're interested. With both the AVR and the LM75 asleep (and the EEPROM drawing no power), the power drain is less than a battery's self-discharge rate. If you only take a temperature reading once every fifteen minutes, you could leave it running for a year! Not bad for around $5 in parts.

Using Flash Program Memory

18

Talking Voltmeter Project

The project for this chapter pulls off something pretty cool: storing enough sampled sound data in your limited 16 KB of memory so that you can build a voltmeter that talks to you using your own voice. It's not easy or even particularly sensible, but it gives me a good excuse to demonstrate how to use data stored in program memory.

Storing nonprogram data in flash program memory space is also very useful for any kind of constant data that you'd like to use in your programs—waveforms, menu strings, lists of birthdays, or any other sort of data that doesn't need to change.

What You Need

In addition to the basic kit, you will need:

- A speaker and blocking capacitor for audio output.

- A USB-Serial adapter for debugging.

- Some voltage in the 0–5 V range that you'd like to test (or a potentiometer hooked up as a voltage divider).

Using Flash Program Memory

If we had tried to use more than one or two waveforms in "Direct-Digital Synthesis" on page 272, we would have run out of memory. Not flash program memory —the ATmega168 has 16 K of that, and we were only using 1 or 2 K—but RAM. The irony of this is that we were storing entirely static data (a lookup table for a sine wave) in our scarce dynamic memory while the difficult-to-change flash memory section was largely empty.

We're doing the same thing when we print out a fixed string over the USART. Every time we write something like printString("hello world!");, the compiler actually sticks the string "hello world!" into RAM somewhere just so that it can print the string back out later. But there was no reason for that string to be in RAM other than that our printString function requires it. We don't change the string data at all, so it's just sitting there and taking up RAM. In this chapter, you'll learn how to rewrite a printString routine so that it can use strings stored in program memory and save up on RAM when necessary.

This becomes more important if you want to implement a menu system, where you'll want a large number of strings to serve as prompts for the user. For every character you include in your menu, that's one byte taken away from your program logic. Indeed, if you want to make an application menu that uses more than 1,000 characters or so, you're *forced* to start putting some of them into flash program memory, or else you won't have any RAM for your program to use.

And that's doubly the case in this chapter; we're going to be building a low-fi talking voltmeter. Reproducing audio, unless you're synthesizing it yourself in real time, requires a lot of data just to get only moderate quality. Even with clever encoding, this project will end up storing 14 kB of data in flash program memory to use for voice playback. That's 14 times the amount of RAM we have.

If you want high-fidelity speech out of an AVR, there are actually a bunch of ways to go about it, but all involve an external DAC chip and a store of megabytes of external memory. (If you're into that sort of thing, you'll also need to brush up on your SPI protocol, because most of the parts use SPI to communicate. See Chapter 16.)

Instead, with a little ingenuity, and by taking full advantage of the 16 kB of memory in program space, we can whip up a decent speech-playback routine. As we did in Chapter 10, we'll be using a PWM output pin to drive a speaker with a fast enough signal to make decent audio output. Getting a few seconds of voice-quality audio into approximately 14 kB is quite a feat, but we'll manage by using a two-bit differential pulse-code modulation (DPCM) encoding and playback scheme.

But before we get too much into the speech-playback side of things, you'll need to learn some fundamentals of AVR memory use, more C language facilities, and about using the *avr/pgmspace.h* library.

The *avr/pgmspace.h* library allows you to write (constant) data into flash memory and access it from your code. The overview is that using the pgmspace library's PROGMEM macro stores your data in program flash memory, and then pgm_read_byte will read a byte out of program memory for you, if you tell it where to look. Modifying our existing code to take advantage of data stored in flash memory isn't entirely straightforward, but by the end of this chapter, you'll have learned most of the tricks.

Memory Addresses

C has been hiding some of the cruel realities of the world from you. When you wrote myNumber=7; the chip stored away the number seven somewhere in memory, in a location that it was calling "myNumber" as a mnemonic shorthand. At the silicon-and-transistors level, that "somewhere in memory" corresponds to a physical location inside the chip, and that's what the AVR needs to know when it retrieves or modifies data. The number of the physical memory location where your data sits is called its *address*; an analogy with the address of your house on your street.

Think of 1600 Pennsylvania Avenue NW, Washington, DC. We call this address "The White House" because it's easier to remember than the full address, so it's like the variable name. But if you want to see who's inside the White House, you've inevitably got to walk down Pennsylvania Avenue until you hit #1600, and look inside. And just like a number stored in a variable's memory address, the inhabitant of the White House changes from time to time as well.

When you first declare a variable, the compiler figures out which RAM slots it still has open, allocates an appropriate number of slots for the type of variable you've chosen, and associates that address with the variable name. Then when your code uses that variable, the compiler looks up the corresponding address and writes that number into the AVR machine code. So when you write uint8_t myNumber; the compiler picks a memory address for you, say RAM slot #1452, and associates "myNumber" with #1452. The compiler also notes the variable type—that is, that you're storing a single-byte, unsigned integer in that location. Later, when you read and write to the variable myNumber, the compiler again looks up the name, finds the corresponding address, and reads or writes the correct number of bytes to or from that memory location.

When you declare a variable, the compiler associates that variable with a location in RAM. But what if you want to associate a "variable" name with a location in program memory where you'd like to store some nonchanging data? This is what the PROGMEM macro does for you—it stores your constant data in program memory and then associates the name and variable type that you give it with a variable name for your convenience.

Just as uint8_t myNumber; creates a reference to a memory address for when you type "myNumber" in your code, const uint8_t myFlashNum PROGMEM = 17; creates a reference from "myFlashNum" to the location in program memory space where it's just written the data "17." In short, adding the PROGMEM macro allocates the variable in question in program flash memory instead of in RAM.

Now when you want to access the data stored in flash, you call the pgm_read_byte() command and pass it the memory address in flash where your data has been stored. The only thing that's missing is a way to go from the name of a variable ("myNumber" or "myFlashNum") to the corresponding memory address in order to use the pgm_read_byte command.

The Address-Of Operator: &

Getting the address of a variable turns out to be very easy. C has an operator &, called the *address-of* operator, that returns the address that's associated with a variable name. To get the address of a variable, you use the address-of operator like so: &myNumber, which returns the address of the previously defined variable myNumber. For example, take this code sample:

```
uint8_t myNumber = 150;
printByte(myNumber);
printWord(&myNumber);
```

When you print out myNumber you'll get back 150. When you print out &myNumber, you'll get something like 1260, which is the physical address of the eight bits in RAM where your number is being stored. (C returns the address as a special type of number, called a *pointer*, but I'll get to that soon.)

To use program-space flash memory, you start out with the PROGMEM macro, which writes your constant data into the flash memory at programming time. Next, use pgm_read_byte(), which requires the address of memory as an argument and fetches whatever value is in that location in memory. And to get the memory address, you use the address-of operator &, which gives you the memory address where your data is stored. Time for some example code!

We'll start off by storing a very long string in program memory, and then printing it out over the serial line one byte at a time (with a pause per character for dramatic effect). There are some important details along the way, so let's dig in to Example 18-1.

Example 18-1. progmemDemo1.c listing

```
                         /* First steps into using program memory */

#include <avr/io.h>
#include <util/delay.h>
#include <avr/pgmspace.h>
#include "USART.h"

const char myVeryLongString[] PROGMEM = "\r\nHi there, \
this is an example of a long string.\r\n\
The kind that you wouldn't want to store in RAM.\r\n";
const uint16_t sixteenBits PROGMEM = 12345;

int main(void) {
  initUSART();
  char oneLetter;
  uint8_t i;
```

```
while (1) {
    for (i = 0; i < sizeof(myVeryLongString); i++) {
        oneLetter = pgm_read_byte(&(myVeryLongString[i]));
        transmitByte(oneLetter);
        _delay_ms(100);      /* slow it down to simulate typing effect :) */
    }
    _delay_ms(1000);

    printWord(&sixteenBits);      /* this throws a compiler warning... */
    transmitByte('\r');
    transmitByte('\n');
    printWord(pgm_read_word(&sixteenBits));
}                                       /* End event loop */
return (0);                      /* This line is never reached */
}
```

 Note

The empty backslashes at the end of the string's lines just serve to continue the text on the next line. I did that mostly so that it would print in this book. Normally, I just let my long lines run long.

First, look at the PROGMEM declaration lines. The way the *pgmspace.h* library is written, we can append the PROGMEM macro to any variable type, and it'll find some free space in flash memory and write our variable there instead of RAM. It only really makes sense, though, to do so with long strings or arrays, but I store a 16-bit integer here just for fun and to give us practice working with 16-bit "words" in addition to just bytes.

Skip down inside the event loop. The first command is a for loop that loops over every character in our very long string and prints each one out to the serial port, one at a time. There are a couple of interesting things here. First is the sizeof() command, which returns the size in bytes of myVeryLongString. We'll discuss this a little more later.

Continuing in the for loop, we use the pgm_read_byte() command to get a byte out of program-space memory. Which byte? If myVeryLongString[i] is the ith character in the myVeryLongString array, then &(myVeryLongString[i]) is the address of the ith character. (The parentheses are optional, but they make it clearer that we're after the address of the ith byte of the string.)

The rest of the loop sends data over serial, then delays. The meat of this example is the storage and retrieval of program-space data. And to make sure that you have a good grasp on the difference between addresses and variables, the last few lines play around with the address of the 16-bit number that's also stored in program space.

What should `printWord(&sixteenBits);` print out? And what should `printWord(pgm_read_word(&sixteenBits));` print? Answer these questions yourself before you read on.

The first print statement takes the address in memory of `sixteenBits` and just prints it out. When I run it on my AVR, I get flash-memory address 205, but you may get something else around there depending on your compiler version and options. Then the code calls `pgm_read_word(&sixteenBits)` and actually fetches the data out of the memory address in question. Lo and behold, it's our 12345!

OK, let's quickly recap before we dive off the deep end. You can store data in program memory with the `PROGMEM` macro and read it back with `pgm_read_byte()` and `pgm_read_word()`, respectively, as long as you know the address. You can get the address with `&`, and if you're interested in the address of a byte within a string or array, you can get its address by using the address-of operator around the individual character element in the string that you're interested in: `&myString[4]`. These simple operations will get you halfway to mastery of using `PROGMEM` and addresses; you can now use `PROGMEM` from the main loop. But if you'd like to use `PROGMEM` strings in functions or ISRs, you'll have to learn how to store addresses in variables and pass them off to functions. And this requires *pointers*.

PROGMEM Variables: Constant and Global

Because `PROGMEM` data is burned into flash memory along with the program itself, the `PROGMEM` data is not variable and is available from any subroutine in the program. This has two important consequences for declaring program-space "variables" in C.

First off, because you can't ever change a `PROGMEM` "variable," you should probably preface the declaration with the keyword `const`, which tells the compiler to throw an error if you try to change the contents of this memory location later on. The most recent version of `avr-gcc` actually *requires* you to declare your `PROGMEM` as `const`, whereas prior versions only recommended it. It's probably a good idea either way.

Secondly, because your `PROGMEM` is nonvolatile and sitting there in program memory, it is available from within any subroutine. It is thus a global variable and should be declared in the global namespace. That is, `PROGMEM` variables should be declared outside of any function definitions so that C knows that it's not limited in scope to any specific function, and that any function can access the data stored there.

For myself, I find it easiest to define all of my `PROGMEM` data in a separate header file. That way, the data is defined as global by being included at the top of the main .c file, and it's easy to open the file and make sure that each entry is declared `const` by just looking down the first row of text.

Pointers

Have a close look at the compiler output when you ran make on the preceding example. (Or run make clean then make again to force it to recompile.) You'll notice that you got some warnings back from the compiler. In particular, I get something like:

```
warning: assignment makes integer from pointer without a cast
warning: passing argument 1 of 'printWord' makes
         integer from pointer without a cast
note: expected 'uint16_t' but argument is of type 'uint8_t *'
```

What's going on? The code *works*, right? Yes, the code does work. But it's missing a subtlety of the C language, one that will help keep you out of a lot of trouble in the future. It's what the compiler is warning you about with its "making an integer from a pointer" business. So let's take a diversion to talk a little bit about pointers.

Make Size (and avr-size)

When you're interested in knowing how large your code is or how much RAM it's using, there's a utility program for that, and it's called avr-size. (The standard GCC size routine is called, shockingly, size.) To save you from typing filenames, I've included a "size" target in the makefile that comes with the book's code.

Take a minute now to type in **make size**. You'll see two lines, one for "Program" memory and one for "Data" memory. The former is program-space data flash memory usage. This is where your code (and now PROGMEM data) is stored. With an ATmega168, you've got 16 kB of program memory.

The "Data" line is how much of the available RAM your program uses. Because there's no operating system, you have no real way of knowing when your AVR program runs out of memory except to check the value here. If you ever find the chip behaving super-strangely, and you suspect that you may have run the AVR out of RAM, this is the easiest way to diagnose the problem for sure.

I also ran make size on progmemDemo1 just to make sure that all of the data that should be stored in program space is actually stored in program space. If you run make size after compiling progmemDemo1, you should see all your variables in program memory, and zero bytes of data memory (RAM) used.

The other time I use make size is in the next chapter, when tweaking audio samples in the talking voltmeter example. Naturally, I wanted to get as much speaking time crammed into the chip as possible. Checking make size after adding a sample into memory lets me know how close I am to the 16 kB limit.

Pointers in Brief

The *pointer* is a special variable type that should be used specifically for storing memory addresses. For the AVR, as I mentioned earlier, a pointer is a 16-bit number. But it's a special 16-bit number. In addition to being big enough to store a memory address, pointers additionally keep track of the *type* of the variable they point at.

Pointers are declared with a "*" between the type definition and the declared variable name: uint8_t* myPointer;. (I'll clarify the type declaration part shortly.)

Remember, an address is the location of a byte in memory. If I just give you the raw address as a 16-bit number, you have no way of knowing what type of data the stored byte represents. Is the byte at our address the first letter in a string? Is it a single byte number or letter (uint8_t or char)? Is it the most significant byte of a two-byte number (uint16_t)? You don't really know unless you keep track somehow, and that's the extra magic that's in a pointer. A pointer is an address with a type: it contains the numerical address of the memory referred to and also informs the compiler what type of data it will find there.

The pointer keeps track of the type of variable it points to by being declared to be a pointer *to a type*. When you initialize a pointer as uint8_t* myPointer, you've declared that the pointer will be used *only* to point to 8-bit unsigned integers. char* myString[] is a pointer to a character array (or a string). You use uint16_t* muchData[] to point to an array in memory where each entry is a 16-bit unsigned type. The typing helps make sure that you're interpreting the stored data correctly.

When the compiler warns you that you're mismatching types, especially with pointers, pay attention! If you end up pointing your pointer to the wrong type of data in memory, you stand a good chance of interpreting that data incorrectly.

Now that we've got a variable type to store memory addresses in, let's see how to work with them in Example 18-2.

Example 18-2. **progmemDemo2.c listing**

```
                    /* Second steps into using program memory */
                       /* Storing the addresses in pointers */

#include <avr/io.h>
#include <util/delay.h>
#include <avr/pgmspace.h>
#include "USART.h"

const char myVeryLongString[] PROGMEM = "\r\nHi there, \
this is an example of a long string.\r\n\
The kind that you wouldn't want to store in RAM.\r\n";
const uint16_t sixteenBits PROGMEM = 12345;

int main(void) {
  initUSART();

  const char *stringPointer;
  const uint16_t *wordPointer;
  uint8_t i;
  char oneLetter;

  stringPointer = &myVeryLongString[0];      /* address of first char */
  // stringPointer = myVeryLongString;             /* same as above */
  wordPointer = &sixteenBits;                /* address of first byte */
```

```
while (1) {
  for (i = 0; i < sizeof(myVeryLongString); i++) {
    oneLetter = pgm_read_byte(stringPointer + i);
    transmitByte(oneLetter);
    _delay_ms(100);     /* slow it down to simulate typing effect :) */
  }
  _delay_ms(1000);

  printWord(pgm_read_word(wordPointer));
}                                           /* End event loop */
  return (0);                       /* This line is never reached */
}
```

The essential difference between this code and *progmemDemo1.c* is that we're reading the bytes with pgm_read_byte(stringPointer+i) instead of pgm_read_byte(&(myVeryLongString[i])). That is, we store the address of our PROGMEM data in a pointer, stringPointer, and then simply add i to that address to reach successive letters in the string. Note that there's no address-of operator here, because pointers are *already* addresses.

Let's look at how we assign the addresses to our pointers. First, you'll see that the pointers are declared as const char* stringPointer and const uint16_t* word Pointer, in order to match the string and uint16_t word, respectively. Now look down to where we assign the addresses to the pointers. There's no secret about the line wordPointer = &sixteenBits—it stores the address of the variable six teenBits in the pointer wordPointer. (The compiler verifies that the types match for us.)

When you want to define the address of an array, you've got a little bit of a problem. Imagine an array of 10 bytes in memory. You've got 10 addresses! Which one do you pick to be the "address of the array"? In C, you always pick the address of the first (zeroth) element. So we can assign the address of our PROGMEM string to the pointer like so: stringPointer = &myVeryLongString[0].

Some time long ago, someone invented a "clever" shorthand for referencing the address of the first element of a string or array in memory: stringPointer = my VeryLongString. What's confusing about this is that it doesn't look like an address assignment, but it is. This statement is in every way identical to the one earlier, which explicitly gets the address of the array's first element. Whichever you'd like to use in your code is fine by me, and seasoned C programmers have it drilled into their heads that "arrays used on the right side of an equation decompose to a pointer to their first element." (Get that tattooed on your forearm!) You'll see this again when we pass arrays to functions.

Arrays and Pointers

In C, arrays are special, in an awkward way. When you use an array on the right side of an assignment, or pass it as an argument to a function, what you actually get is a pointer to the array's first element.

Because of this, you can either get the address of the first element explicitly:

```
char* stringP = &myString[0];
```

or you can take advantage of the decomposition rule:

```
char* stringP = myString;
```

The latter doesn't look like it's setting the address of a pointer, but that's exactly what it does.

As a result of the decomposing-to-pointer rule ("arrays used on the right side of an equation decompose to a pointer to their first element"), the one way that you shouldn't assign the address of an array is the one that might at first glance look most reasonable:

```
char* brokenP = &myString; (Don't do this!)
```

This results in a warning: assignment from incompatible pointer type warning. (It may work anyway, or it may not, depending on your compiler. Do you feel lucky?) This is a warning because myString on the right side is already a pointer to the first element of myString, and so &myString is the address of the pointer, and not the address of a char as required.

I'll keep saying this over and over, because it's important: pointers store addresses. We need addresses to use the pgm_read_byte() and pgm_read_word() commands to get our fixed data out of flash memory. As demonstrated in Example 18-2, a pointer is a convenient way to store the address because we can add to it just like a normal number. Because it's an address, adding to it allows us to move on to the next entry in memory. And because the pointer tells the compiler the size of our data type, the compiler knows how many more bytes it needs to increment in memory to get to the next entry.

Pointers as Arguments to Functions

The last piece of the pointer puzzle that we'll need for working with program-space memory is how to work with arrays and pointers to arrays when they're passed as arguments to functions. It's very common to call a function that runs on static data that's stored in program memory, and to do this, we need to pass the address of the data to the function.

As a practical example, let's write a function that prints out strings from flash program memory that we can use to replace our old printString() function. Because we will eventually need to call `pgm_read_byte`, we'll need the addresses of the strings. And passing addresses means passing pointers to the strings. See Example 18-3 for an example of how this works.

Example 18-3. **progmemDemo3.c listing**

```
                         /* Third step into using program memory */
                            /* Passing pointers to functions */

#include <avr/io.h>
#include <util/delay.h>
#include <avr/pgmspace.h>
#include "USART.h"

const char myVeryLongString1[] PROGMEM = "\r\nHi there, \
this is an example of a long string.\r\n\
The kind that you wouldn't want to store in RAM.\r\n";
const char myVeryLongString2[] PROGMEM = "All work and no play \
makes Jack something something.\r\n";

void printString_Progmem(const char *stringP) {
  char oneLetter;
  while ((oneLetter = pgm_read_byte(stringP))) {
    transmitByte(oneLetter);
    stringP++;
    _delay_ms(100);                          /* only b/c it's cute */
  }
}

int main(void) {
  initUSART();
  while (1) {
    printString_Progmem(&myVeryLongString1[0]);
    printString_Progmem(&myVeryLongString1[50]);
    printString_Progmem(myVeryLongString2);
    _delay_ms(1000);
  }                                          /* End event loop */
  return (0);                     /* This line is never reached */
}
```

Let's look at the `printString_Progmem` function. It is our first function that takes an explicit pointer as an argument; specifically, a `const char*`. The const is there because we're pointing to a memory location that's in PROGMEM, remember?

For comparison, here's the version of `printString` from our USART library:

```
void printString(const char myString[]){
  uint8_t i=0;
  while(myString[i]){
    transmitByte(myString[i]);
    i++;
```

```
    }
  }
```

If you compare the two versions, you'll find that they have a few important differences. The RAM version of printString passes the array of characters as an array. The PROGMEM version passes the array as a pointer to the memory location of the array in PROGMEM. In the PROGMEM version, the function stores each letter temporarily in a variable in RAM (oneLetter) in order to avoid making two calls to pgm_read_byte, which is slower than reading the data straight out of RAM. (This is probably a bit of overoptimization for a printing routine where the USART routine is the slowest part, but the principle is sound.)

And now that we understand the PROGMEM version of the printString function, have a look down in the while(1) loop where we've been calling it. Just as when we were assigning addresses to pointers in Example 18-2, we pass a pointer as an argument to a function by getting the address of the variable we'd like to pass. In that sense, our function printString_Progmem works exactly like pgm_read_word does—it expects an address, stored as a pointer, as an argument. So you have your choice of calling it with the two different ways of getting the address of an array: &myVeryLongString1[0] or myVeryLongString1. Both pass the address of the first element of the array.

Finally, if you have a data array that's *not* a string, you can't count on a zero being a signal for the end of the array (for example, what if you needed to store a bunch of zeros?) In this case, you have to use some other mechanism for signalling the end of the array. By far the most common method is to pass the pointer to the beginning of the array, and the number of entries in the array. If your numbers are correct, the function will not run over the end of the array data. Example 18-4 presents an example of a typical data-array function call with pointers.

Example 18-4. **progmemDemo4.c listing**

```c
                        /* Fourth step into using program memory */
                    /* Passing data array pointers to functions */
#include <avr/io.h>
#include <util/delay.h>
#include <avr/pgmspace.h>
#include "USART.h"

const uint16_t myData[] PROGMEM =
    { 1111, 2222, 3333, 4444, 5555, 6666, 7777, 8888, 9999, 10000 };
const uint16_t myData2[] PROGMEM = { 123, 456, 789, 012, 345, 678, 999 };

void printData_Progmem(const uint16_t * dataPointer, uint8_t length) {
  while (length) {
    printWord((uint16_t) dataPointer);            /* print out address */
    printString(": ");
    printWord(pgm_read_word(dataPointer));          /* print out data */
    printString("\r\n");
    dataPointer++;                             /* move to next uint16_t */
    length--;                                /* one less element to go */
    _delay_ms(100);
  }
}

int main(void) {
  initUSART();
  while (1) {
    printData_Progmem(myData, sizeof(myData) / 2);
    printString("\r\n");
    _delay_ms(1000);
    printData_Progmem(myData2, sizeof(myData2) / sizeof(myData2[0]));
    printString("\r\n");
    _delay_ms(1000);
  }                                              /* End event loop */
  return (0);                          /* This line is never reached */
}
```

As advertised, the printData_Progmem() function takes the array pointer and its length as explicit arguments. It loops through the data by incrementing dataPointer, adding two bytes to the address every time dataPointer increases by one. Wait, *two bytes*? Yup. Run the code and check out the memory addresses it's reading from, if you don't believe me.

Because the pointer is declared as a pointer to uint16_t types, it changes the address it points to by two bytes' worth for every time it's incremented. This makes iterating over different types of data with pointers very easy—just make sure that you've got the pointer's type declaration right and you can iterate through memory by address just as you would with an array by index.

But it also imposes a little extra burden on how you call the function. Namely, you have to know how many entries you've got in the data array and pass that number to the function when you call it. Unfortunately, C's built-in sizeof() command returns the length *in bytes* of the array. So if you've got an array of 16-bit integers, you'll have to divide the result of sizeof() by two somehow.

sizeof

sizeof() returns the size in *bytes* in the array (or other variable) in question. When you pass an array to a function, you need to know the number of entries in the array. For instance, when you store an array of 16-bit integers, sizeof() returns the length in bytes, which is twice as big as the number of 16-bit words that you've stored.

The easiest way to deal with this is just to pass sizeof(mySixteenBitArray)/2 to the function, and this works fine as long as you always remember to do it and always get the size of the array variable type right.

On the other hand, because this problem arises so often there's a common idiom for dealing with the bytes-to-entries conversion problem. Because each entry in an array has to be of the same type, you can divide the total length of the array by the length of one element, say the first one, to get the total number of elements. The example code I provided does this. Some people even go so far as to define this into a macro when they end up using it a lot (a cute trick, no?):

```
#define \
SIZE_OF_ARRAY(a) (sizeof(a) / sizeof(a[0]))
```

Summary

This section started out as a simple exercise in storing data in flash program memory and then reading it back out again. How could it all get so complicated?

To store data in program memory, we use the PROGMEM macro when defining our constant data. What otherwise looks like a normal global variable assignment winds up as a variable whose address points off into nonvolatile flash program memory instead of RAM. Reading the values out of this memory isn't so complicated, but the two functions we've got, pgm_read_byte and pgm_read_word, both require the *address* in memory where the data is stored.

Addresses are easily obtainable with the "address-of" operator, &, and using this you can call pgm_read_byte to get your data back out. If all you ever do is use PROGMEM from within the main() function, this is all you'll ever need.

But in order to use PROGMEM data from within your own functions, you'll need to be able to pass the address as a variable. The specific type of variable that stores addresses is called a *pointer*. This stores the memory location (a 16-bit number for the AVRs) of your variable and is declared in a way that indicates the type of the data that it points *to* so the compiler at least knows what kind of data you're pointing at and can fetch it easily. Using a pointer also allows you to increment memory locations by the appropriate number of bytes and use the type-checking system to make sure that you're not making any gross mistakes.

Finally, if the data in question is a *string*, an array of characters that finishes with a zero, your function can use the final zero to find the end of the data. On the other hand, if your data is an array, you'll need to pass its number of elements to the called function as well because you can't tell how large the array is from the pointer.

If you've never seen pointers before, that was probably quite a whirlwind tour. And if you're a hard-boiled pointer fan, you'll probably notice that I haven't mentioned a few of your favorite applications, like pointers to functions. With what we've covered here, you've got everything you need to use GCC's PROGMEM facilities. For a quick introduction to the last class of Pointers 101, feel free to read up on dereferencing pointers in the next section. Otherwise, it's time to get down to business of programming AVRs.

Optional: Dereferencing Pointers

Pointers store memory addresses where you've got data stored. We've been using pointers coupled with the pgm_read_byte() function to get data out of program flash memory locations. What if you'd like to store references to RAM memory locations? After all, that's what the rest of the world does with pointers. When the data is in RAM, you can read and write that data as if the pointer were a normal variable by *dereferencing* the pointer like so: *myPointer = 7;.

In C, the dereferencing operator * skips over the reference to the memory address that the pointer actually stores and goes straight to the memory location that's addressed. Among other things, this lets you treat the pointer exactly as you would any other variable, except that by changing the address stored in the pointer, you can change which variable the pointer is behaving like.

In fact, to keep this from getting too metaphysical, I find that the best way to get your head around dereferenced pointers is to think of them as *being* the variable who's address they currently point to. In the following comments, I've noted the effect of the command, and in parentheses how you can think about what's going on as a shortcut:

```
uint8_t a = 7;
uint8_t b = 2;
uint8_t myArray[] = {10,11,12};
uint8_t c;
uint8_t*  p;

p = &a;          /* p stores address of a */
c = *p;          /* c = 7 (c = a) */

*p = 5;          /* 5 into memory at p (a = 5) */
c = a;           /* c = 5 */

p = &b;          /* p stores address of b */
*p = 12;         /* 12 into memory at p (b = 12) */
c = b;           /* c = 12 */
```

```
p = &myArray[0];    /* p stores address myArray */
c = *(p+2);         /* c = 12 (c = myArray[2]) */
*(p+1) = 25;        /* 25 into memory at p+1
                       (myArray[1] = 25) */
```

The last example shows how you can use pointers to read from and write to arrays, and this is how one usually deals with arrays in RAM. In fact, the only real difference in writing code for dealing with RAM-based arrays and those written into nonvolatile program memory space is that you use *(pointer+i) to access the memory stored at the RAM location and pgm_read_byte(pointer+i) or pgm_read_word(pointer+i) to get the values out of flash. The important disctinction is that with RAM-based arrays, you can also write to the dereferenced pointer, whereas flash memory is nonvolatile.

Even if you only ever use PROGMEM variables in your AVR programming, I hope that this discussion of dereferenced pointers helps reinforce the way pointers work—they are addresses with a type—and if you want to access values stored therein, you have to dereference it one way or the other, * or pgm_read_byte().

Talking Voltmeter

If you're at all like most people, getting your head around pointers is serious work. If that's the case, you might want to take a break from reading code for a minute. Hook up a speaker to your AVR, flash in the talking voltmeter code, and think about how sweet it would be to have your own talking voltmeter programmed with your own voice. If that doesn't give you the motivation to carry on, you're not half as geeky as I am.

The main project for this chapter is certainly the most ambitious out of the whole book, and it combines a lot of aspects from previous projects into one, as well as making use of 14 kB of program-space flash memory. We'll take the bird's-eye view first and then dive in to the details one by one.

In order to create the audio output, we use the fast PWM output of Timer 0, direct to the output-compare pin, as we did in Chapter 10. PWM using Timer 0 is set at a fixed frequency of around 31.25 kHz, as before, so what we hear is the changes in average voltage due to the duty cycle changing over time.

Timer 2 is configured in CTC mode and counts up until a fixed value and then triggers and interrupt. I've set the frequency of Timer 2's cycle to be around 8 kHz to match the sample rate of the audio input files. (You can play with this to speed up or slow down sample playback.) Each time Timer 2's ISR is called, it loads a new sample value into Timer 0's output compare register.

The Timer 2 ISR is a busy place. Because the data is packed into PROGMEM in 8-bit bytes but we only use two bits per sample, once every four times the ISR is called, it reads a new byte and unpacks it into four values. Then the ISR undoes the DPCM encoding, which involves reading the two-bit number, picking the corresponding value from a table, and then adding that value to last period's sample value. (See "Generating the Audio Data" on page 406 for details on the DPCM encoding and decoding.)

The Timer 2 ISR also tests to see if the end of the sample data table has been reached, and if so it turns itself off and sends no new samples to the Timer 1's PWM register until it's restarted from the event loop. Because the ISR loads in new values to Timer 1, when Timer 2 isn't running, the output PWM is constant and no signal is produced.

The code is split among three files: *talkingVoltmeter.h*, *talkingVoltmeter.c*, and *allDigits.h*. The first header file lays out all of the data structures and initializations for *talkingVoltmeter.c*, which does all the work. The other header file, *allDigits.h*, contains the DPCM data for the speech samples. I'll hold of on discussing this data file until "Generating the Audio Data" on page 406.

PROGMEM Data Structures and the Header File

Let's start our discussion of the speech-generation part of the code with the data and the functions that use it, in Example 18-5.

Example 18-5. talkingVoltmeter.h listing

```
                              /* Include file with DPCM data in it */
#include "allDigits.h"
#include <avr/pgmspace.h>

// Now define sample-table names used in digits file
// From here on, no matter what you call the samples,
//   you can refer to them as "ONE_TABLE", etc.
#define ONE_TABLE     DPCM_one_8000
#define TWO_TABLE     DPCM_two_8000
#define THREE_TABLE   DPCM_three_8000
#define FOUR_TABLE    DPCM_four_8000
#define FIVE_TABLE    DPCM_five_8000
#define SIX_TABLE     DPCM_six_8000
#define SEVEN_TABLE   DPCM_seven_8000
#define EIGHT_TABLE   DPCM_eight_8000
#define NINE_TABLE    DPCM_nine_8000
#define ZERO_TABLE    DPCM_zero_8000
#define POINT_TABLE   DPCM_point_8000
#define VOLTS_TABLE   DPCM_volts_8000
#define INTRO_TABLE   DPCM_talkingvoltmeter_8000

#define SPEECH_DELAY  2000                            /* milliseconds */

          /* -------------- Globals used by the ISR -------------- */
volatile uint8_t *thisTableP;    /* points at the current speech table */
volatile uint16_t thisTableLength;   /* length of current speech table */
```

```c
volatile uint16_t sampleNumber; // sample index
volatile int8_t out, lastout;   // output values
volatile uint8_t differentials[4] = { 0, 0, 0, 0 };
const int8_t dpcmWeights[4] = { -12, -3, 3, 12 };


    /* These arrays let us choose a table (and its length) numerically */
const uint16_t tableLengths[] = {
  sizeof(ZERO_TABLE), sizeof(ONE_TABLE), sizeof(TWO_TABLE),
  sizeof(THREE_TABLE), sizeof(FOUR_TABLE), sizeof(FIVE_TABLE),
  sizeof(SIX_TABLE), sizeof(SEVEN_TABLE), sizeof(EIGHT_TABLE),
  sizeof(NINE_TABLE), sizeof(POINT_TABLE), sizeof(VOLTS_TABLE),
  sizeof(INTRO_TABLE)
};

// Create an indexing table of all of the start addresses for
// each spoken digit.  And then store this index in PROGMEM.
const uint8_t *const tablePointers[] PROGMEM = {
  ZERO_TABLE, ONE_TABLE, TWO_TABLE, THREE_TABLE, FOUR_TABLE,
  FIVE_TABLE, SIX_TABLE, SEVEN_TABLE, EIGHT_TABLE, NINE_TABLE,
  POINT_TABLE, VOLTS_TABLE, INTRO_TABLE
};

void selectTable(uint8_t whichTable) {
                         /* Set up global table pointer, lengths */
  uint16_t pointerAddress;
  thisTableLength = tableLengths[whichTable];
  pointerAddress = (uint16_t) & tablePointers[whichTable];
  thisTableP = (uint8_t *) pgm_read_word(pointerAddress);
}


                     /* Extra defines for the non-numeric values */
#define    POINT  10
#define    VOLTS  11
#define    INTRO  12


///----------------    Init functions    ------------------///

void initTimer0(void) {
  // Timer 0 Configured for free-running PWM Audio Output
  TCCR0A |= (1 << WGM00) | (1 << WGM01);              /* fast PWM mode */
  TCCR0A |= (1 << COM0A0) | (1 << COM0A1);     /* output on PD6/OC0A */
  TCCR0B = (1 << CS00);                             /* fastest clock */
  OCR0A = 128;                                 /* initialize mid-value */
  SPEAKER_DDR |= (1 << SPEAKER);                  /* output PD6 / OC0A */
}


void initTimer2(void) {
  // Timer 2 loads OCR0A, provides sampling frequency
  TCCR2A = (1 << WGM21);                        /* CTC, count to OCR2A */
  TIMSK2 = (1 << OCIE2A);               /* turn on compare interrupt */
  OCR2A = 128;                    /* controls sample playback frequency */
```

```
                  /* note: no clock source selected yet, so won't start up */
}

void initADC(void) {
  // ADC for Voltmeter function
  ADMUX |= (0b00001111 & PC5);                      /* set mux to ADC5 */
  DIDR0 |= _BV(ADC5D);                 /* turn off digital circuitry on PC5 */
  ADMUX |= (1 << REFS0);                    /* reference voltage is AVCC, 5V */
  ADCSRA |= (1 << ADPS1) | (1 << ADPS2);    /* ADC clock prescaler /64 */
  ADCSRA |= (1 << ADEN);                               /* enable ADC */
}
```

The very first line of *talkingVoltmeter.h* includes a single data header file that includes the DPCM-encoded sample values for all of the spoken-out digits. If you look at *allDigits.h*, you'll see that it looks like this:

```
const uint8_t DPCM_one_8000[] PROGMEM = {
  153,
  90,
  106,
  150,
  ...
}
const uint8_t DPCM_two_8000[] PROGMEM = {
  250,
  ...
}
```

Next, a series of twelve #define statements take the names of the samples in the *allDigits.h* datafile and maps them to defined names and numbers that are used in the rest of this code. I did this so that you could easily add your own audio data, and would only have to change these 12 top-level definitions. So if your datafile has tables called "one" and "two" instead of "DPCM_one_8000" and "DPCM_two_8000," modify these defines and everything else should work fine.

Next, I define some global variables. The first two are used to select which sample should be playing. The pointer, uint8_t* thisTableP, is used to point to an address of the uint8_t speech data arrays that we just included. When it points to DPCM_one_8000[ ], for instance, the chip will speak the word "one"; when it points to DPCM_two_8000[ ], the chip says "two," and so on. The other variable contains the length of the selected data array, so that the playback function knows when to stop.

The next three global variables keep track of exactly which sample is playing and what the previous and current PWM output values are.

Then there are two arrays defined in RAM that will hold the four two-bit differentials (differentials), and the vector of the step sizes that the decoder will take when reconstructing the audio.

Indexing arrays: arrays of pointers in PROGMEM

To use the speech data that's stored in PROGMEM, we're going to need both it's starting address and the length of each array of spoken samples. And we'll do it in a way that makes accessing the data easy, storing the sound for "one" in position one of the arrays.

Getting the lengths and storing them in tableLengths[] is a breeze—we simply store the lengths of the indexed speech-sample arrays in RAM using sizeof() because we know that we're using single-byte integers to do the encoding. When the time comes to select which table we're using, the function selectTable() sets a global length variable equal to the selected size: thisTableLength = table Lengths[whichTable]. When we call selectTable(1), it looks up the length from this table that's in slot one and stores it in the global variable thisTableLength that the ISR can access.

The next array is an array of pointers to the speech data. That is, each entry in tablePointers is a pointer that contains the starting address of one spoken digit. As with the lengths table, the pointers are arranged in numerical order so that tablePointers[1] contains the pointer that points to the data array that speaks out the number "one." (That's the convenient part.)

In this sense, tablePointers is like an index. If you want to know where the speech data for the number "four" is stored, you can look it up in tablePointers[4]. If you want the number i, you just fetch the data from the location stored in tablePoint ers[i]. This is much simpler than the alternative, which is to write a bunch of if statements like this:

```
if (i == 4){
  address = FOUR_TABLE;
}
else if (i == 5){
  address = FIVE_TABLE;
}
// ... etc for each digit
```

(Don't forget that when we reference an array of data like like FIVE_TABLE, C actually returns a pointer to the first entry of the array.)

But there's one twist here: I stored the tablePointers indexing array itself in PROG MEM! And why not? It's an array of pointers that contains addresses of data that's stored in flash memory. Those addresses surely aren't going to change, so this lookup table that contains those addresses won't change either. This pattern is surprisingly useful, and when you have many arrays to index (more than just the

12 we use here), it becomes increasingly important to store both the individual arrays *and* their address pointers in PROGMEM.

The cost of storing our indexing array in PROGMEM is that we've now got pointers to our data in PROGMEM that are themselves stored in PROGMEM. So to get our data table, we have to do two reads from program memory: once to get the address of our data table, and then to start accessing the data table itself. Once you've got that, conceptually, it's not so bad. See Figure 18-1.

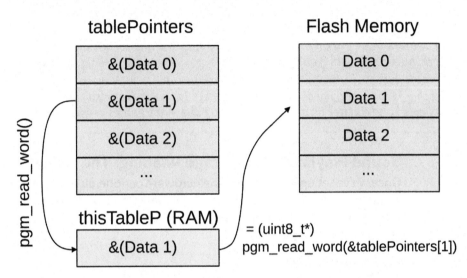

Figure 18-1. *Table of flash memory pointers in flash memory*

The relevant line in the selectTable(uint8_t whichTable) function is:

```
thisTableP =  (uint8_t*) pgm_read_word(&tablePointers[whichTable]);
```

Here, we're looking up a pointer in the tablePointers array by its index. Because the pointer is stored in PROGMEM, we take the address and call pgm_read_word to get the address data. Finally, because the data is just a 16-bit address (pgm_read_word doesn't know what type of data we've stored in the address we pass it) we have to recast it as a pointer to a uint8_t. Now that we have a RAM copy of the pointer to the data (it's address) and the size of the data, the selectTa ble() function simply writes the pointer and size out to global variables that the ISR uses to read its sample data.

The rest of the *talkingVoltmeter.h* file consists of routine initialization routines. Timer 0 is configured at full speed, fast PWM mode, and set to output directly to the speaker pin. Timer 2 is a simple "system-tick" style timer: it counts up to a certain value and runs its ISR that loads a new sample into Timer 0's PWM register. It's clock-speed is set to run four times slower than Timer 0, at about 8 kHz to match our sampled audio data. Finally, the ADC is initialized for full-range 5 V measurements on PC5, but you can change this easily enough.

 Yo Dawg. I Heard You Like PROGMEM

This general pattern, storing pointers to other memory locations in an index, is very useful. You'd do the same thing if you were storing text for menu items, for example. If you stored a menu prompt in menuString0[] and another in menuString1[] in PROGMEM, you can create a second array of pointers to each one that lets you reference them by merely selecting the index of the pointer array. If you don't choose to store the pointer array in PROGMEM, you can get a pointer to your string data like this: char* p = stringPointers[i]. If you do decide to store the pointers in PROGMEM as well, you can retrieve the pointers you want like this: char* p = (char*) pgm_get_word(&stringPointers[i]), which really isn't all that much more complicated and can free up a lot of RAM if you have many entries in your menu.

Sound Playback and Voltage Reading: The .c File

Once we've set up the data and the hardware peripherals are configured, it's time to sample voltages on the ADC and generate some audio. This means working through the code in Example 18-6.

Example 18-6. talkingVoltmeter.c listing

```c
// Talking Voltmeter Example

#include <inttypes.h>
#include <avr/io.h>
#include <avr/interrupt.h>
#include <util/delay.h>
#include <avr/pgmspace.h>
#include <avr/power.h>
#include "pinDefines.h"
#include "USART.h"

#include "talkingVoltmeter.h"

void startSampleTimer(void) {
  sampleNumber = 0;                      /* back to start of sample table */
  TCCR2B = (1 << CS21);                         /* turn on timer clock */
               /* Two clock options above end up ~8kHz on 8MHz system */
}
void stopSampleTimer(void) {
  TCCR2B = 0;                        /* disable sample-playback clock */
  OCR0A = 128;                        /* idle PWM at mid-voltage */
  lastout = 0;                        /* start at 0 next time */
}
void speak(void) {
```

```
  startSampleTimer();
  loop_until_bit_is_clear(TCCR2B, CS21);              /* Wait until done */
}

void updatePWMAudio(void) {
  OCR0A = out + 128;                       /* re-center for 0-255 PWM */
  lastout = out;                                   /* update last value */
  sampleNumber++;                                  /* on to next sample */
}
void unpackByte(uint8_t dataByte) {
                             /* Select pairs of bits from byte, save out */
  differentials[0] = (dataByte >> 6) & 0b00000011;
  differentials[1] = (dataByte >> 4) & 0b00000011;
  differentials[2] = (dataByte >> 2) & 0b00000011;
  differentials[3] = (dataByte & 0b00000011);
}


/* Timer 2 controls sampling speed.
   ISR reads new data, loads PWM values into OCR0A */
ISR(TIMER2_COMPA_vect) {
  /* Since we can decode 4 2-bit values at once, need to know where
     we are in the 4-step mini-cycle. */
  uint8_t cycle = sampleNumber & 0b00000011;       /* keep last 2 bits */
  uint16_t tableEntry;
  uint8_t packedData;

  if (cycle == 0) {                       /* at first sample, re-load */
    tableEntry = sampleNumber >> 2;            /* where we are in table */
    if (tableEntry < thisTableLength) {
                        /* read the next byte from the selected table */
      packedData = pgm_read_byte(&thisTableP[tableEntry]);
      unpackByte(packedData);    /* split up byte into differentials[] */
    }
    else {                                  /* at end of table, done. */
      stopSampleTimer();
    }
  }
        /* Decode the differences: current value = last + difference */
  out = lastout + dpcmWeights[differentials[cycle]] - (lastout >> 4);
  updatePWMAudio();
}                              // end  ISR (TIMER2_COMPA_vect)

void printString_Progmem(const char *stringP) {
  char oneLetter;
  while ((oneLetter = pgm_read_byte(stringP))) {
    transmitByte(oneLetter);
    stringP++;
  }
}


int main(void) {
  uint16_t voltage;
  uint8_t volts;
```

```
uint8_t tenths;
uint8_t vcc = 51;                                      /* 10x VCC, in volts */

clock_prescale_set(clock_div_1);                              /* 8 MHz */
initTimer0();
initTimer2();
sei();                                             /* for timer2 ISR */
initADC();
initUSART();

printString_Progmem(PSTR("\r\n--=( Talking Voltmeter )=--\r\n"));

selectTable(INTRO);
speak();

while (1) {

  ADCSRA |= (1 << ADSC);                                 /* start ADC */
  loop_until_bit_is_clear(ADCSRA, ADSC);

  voltage = ADC * vcc + vcc / 2;      /* vcc/2 to make rounding work */
  voltage = voltage >> 10;               /* divide by 10-bits for ADC */
               /* "voltage" is now actually 10x real-world voltage */
  volts = voltage / 10;
  tenths = voltage % 10;

  transmitByte('0' + volts);               /* serial output as well */
  selectTable(volts);                /* 0 points to ZERO_TABLE, etc */
  speak();

  transmitByte('.');
  selectTable(POINT);
  speak();

  transmitByte('0' + tenths);
  selectTable(tenths);
  speak();

  printString_Progmem(PSTR("  volts\r\n"));
  selectTable(VOLTS);
  speak();

  _delay_ms(SPEECH_DELAY);

}                                                 /* end while */
  return (0);
}
```

The ISR

Because the bulk of the work of decoding and playing the speech samples takes place in Timer 2's ISR, let's start there first. The general overview is that, because our two-bit samples are stored four to a byte, for every fourth sample, we need to load up another byte and break it up into the four parts.

The first line defines a local variable, cycle, that takes on a value of zero, one, two, or three depending on which sample is currently running. The fastest way to do this is just to mask off the lowest two bits, and interpret them as an integer. Next, if we're at the first sample of a cycle, we need to figure out which byte of the speech data array to unpack next, or if we're at the end, to stop. To do this, we divide the sample number by four using a bit-shift by two, which gives us the current byte number, tableEntry. Because we're at the first position in a byte, the routine calls unpackByte to unpack an 8-bit number into four two-bit parts.

Look up at unpackByte() for a second. It sets all four values of the differentials array by shifting the passed data sample byte over by six bits, four bits, two bits, and zero bits (i.e., not shifting at all), and then masking that byte so that only the lowest two bits remain. Shifting to the right by six leaves only the top two bits, so those are obvious. Shifting to the right by four leaves the top four bits, and the masking selects out only the lower two of those, and so on. At the end of this process of shifting and masking, each element of differentials[] contains a two-bit number from zero to three.

Jumping back down to the ISR, if the cycle is anywhere but the first position, nothing happens and we go on to decompress the data and update the PWM output. Because this is "differential" PCM, the data stored is the (quantized) differences between the last sample value and the next one. The decoding step consists of adding this difference value to the old output.

We also subtract a sixteenth of the previous value to make the decoding stable. The reason that we need to do this is that there's a slight chance that approximation errors in our sampling routine add up in a row long enough to max out the volume on playback. Subtracting off a small fraction each time shrinks the sample value a little bit toward zero and prevents these random errors from accumulating. If you don't believe me, try flashing the code without this term, and you'll probably hear that it distorts.

Finally, the ISR calls updatePWMAudio(), which adds 128 to the signed integer value to center it between zero and 255, and then writes the new volume level to Timer 0's output-compare register and controls the PWM duty cycle, outputting an average voltage level to the speaker.

main()

The main function starts off with some variable definitions. Of them, the most interesting is setting the calibrated vcc variable. Remember, the ADC's absolute accuracy is only as good as the VCC level, and the vcc variable should contain the calibrated voltage of your VCC times 10. On my system, for instance, I get 5.08 V, which is 50.8, so I round up to 51 and that's the vcc.

Just after all the usual initialization routines, the code prints out a long string that's stored in flash memory, partly to verify our serial connections, but mostly as a demonstration of how simple it can be to use PROGMEM strings directly in your code.

The last part of the initialization section speaks out a prerecorded introduction to the talking voltmeter. If you can't hear this, something's wrong. This demo also shows you how the speech playback system works. Remember that to pass the desired data to the ISR, we saved its start location and length in two separate global variables. The function selectTable() uses the PROGMEM index of pointers to the data to get the starting position from memory. selectTable() also looks up the length of the chosen speech data from the length array tableLengths.

Once the data is pointed to, all that remains is to call the speak() function, which resets the sample counter to zero and starts up Timer 2, then waits for the sample table to reach the end, and shut down Timer 2 again. Note that I'm implicitly using the Timer 2 clock-select bit as a status flag for whether or not there is currently a sample playing.

Finally, now that you understand how the system plays back a spoken digit by setting up pointers to the current sample and letting the timer hardware take care of the rest, the event loop should be an easy read. An ADC sample is taken, the value scaled up by the VCC value times 10 and then back down by 1,024, to yield an eventual value that should be 10 times the actual measured voltage. The remainder of the event loop simply prints out the values on the serial line and simultaneously speaks them out through the speaker.

Now, if you're interested in the nitty-gritty of how I got my seven seconds of my sampled voice into 14 kB of data talking to you, or to make your own samples, read on to the next section.

Generating the Audio Data

Eight-bit audio, even at a minimum data rate for speech, requires a *lot* of data. Human speech has a highest frequency of around 4 kHz, which means we'd need an 8 kHz sample rate to reproduce it. (Read up on "Nyquist Frequency" online if you'd like to know more.) That's around 8 kB per second, and if it takes about 1/2 a second to read out a digit, we'll need 48 kB just to sample 10 digits plus "point" and "volts." That's not going to work for us at all. We'll need to figure out a way to divide that by four and still retain intelligibility. We'll use Differential Pulse-Code Modulation (DPCM), which is an audio compression method developed for compressing speech over phone lines in the 1950s.

Differential Pulse-Code Modulation
First off, pulse-code modulation is actually just the fancy name for what we've been using to play "analog" audio all along. Basically, the "pulse codes" are what

old-timey engineers called our digital samples. Pulse-code modulation is just producing audio by changing the binary data that you feed into a digital-to-analog converter over time—just exactly what we were doing in Chapter 10, using filtered PWM output to do the digital-to-analog conversion.

The "differential" in DPCM means that instead of using the voltage level values, we store the *changes* the voltage levels. For smooth signals, like audio signals tend to be, the difference between two samples is drastically smaller than the maximum range from quietest to loudest. If you're using eight bits for output, you can often encode the same data with just two or three bits per sample. That's a dramatic reduction in the amount of data required.

As mentioned, for the talking voltmeter, we'd need roughly 48 kB of raw uncompressed PCM output. But if we use two-bit DPCM, we can shrink our data requirements to 12 kB, which will fit in the ATmega168's flash memory with room to spare. The sound quality *will* be reduced somewhat, but you'll be surprised how intelligible it is.

Cornell University Microcontroller Class Webpages

If you're at all interested in video, speech, or audio generation, the final projects and lab exercises from Cornell University's ECE 4760: Designing with Microcontrollers class (*http://people.ece.cornell.edu/land/courses/ece4760/FinalProjects/*) is a great resource. Professor Land has even posted his lectures to YouTube. It's a great resource both for ideas and even working code snippets.

Indeed, I got the basis for the talking voltmeter code from Cornell University's ECE 4760 Speech Generation page (*http://people.ece.cornell.edu/land/courses/ece4760/Speech/index644.html*). In the end, I rewrote some sections, fixed (IMO) a bug, and adapted the code to function with multiple speech tables, but the basic framework is theirs. While I rewrote the encoder in Python, it's basically a copy of similar code from that website that's written for Matlab.

If you're using the Cornell code, note that the ATmega644 that they use has a different pinout from the ATmegaxx8 series, so you may have to move some pins around for everything to work. For instance, the direct-PWM-output (OCR0A) pins are in different locations across the two chip series; PB3 on the 644 is equivalent to PD6 on our series of chips. But once I changed those around, the code worked just fine.

Encoding Two-bit DPCM

To start our discussion of DPCM, imagine that we have a series of sample values like [..., 200, 201, 204, 208, 206, 203, 200, 198, ...]. (From the way the values rise and fall, they could be the top of a sine wave, or something similar.) The first step in DPCM is to take the differences between successive sample values: [..., 1, 3, 4, -2, -3, -3, -2, ...]. Notice how nice and small these difference values are? Heck, we could represent those precisely with three bits, as opposed to the eight bits in our original sample, and we'd be done.

One-bit DPCM consists of deciding whether the samples change upward or downward—we've only got two choices with one bit. If we encode an positive difference as a one, and a negative difference as a zero, the preceding differences string looks like [..., 1, 1, 1, 0, 0, 0, 0, ...]. Now to reconstruct the data back into eight bits, all we know is that it went up for three periods and down for four. We'll have to decide on how big each step up or down is going to be.

Picking that step size is actually a little tricky, because we're trading off how quickly the DPCM can respond to big changes against how smooth our output can be for small changes. Just from looking at our data, we'd pick something like plus or minus two, because the increases and decreases are about two-ish on average.

Let's assume that we start off with the correct sample value of 200. The decoded version of our one-bit DCPM with step size of two would give us the following sequence: [..., 200, 202, 204, 206, 204, 202, 200, 198, ...], which really isn't that bad an approximation of our original data. The peak at 208 isn't as high, and the slope of the change is always constant, but it could work.

Two-bit DPCM improves on the one-bit version by allowing for two different rates of increase and two different rates of decrease. That is, instead of just choosing up or down in the encoding stage, we get to choose between a large step up and a small step up, a large step down and a small step down. For our example, we might decide that any change smaller than 2.5 is a small step, and larger than 2.5 is a big step:

STEP TABLE	UP	DOWN
BIG	3	0
LITTLE	2	1

Using two-bit numbers, we map these steps (big down step, small down step, small up step, big up step) to (0,1,2,3). Encoding like this, we get [..., 2,3,3,1,0,0,1,...] for the difference sequence.

In the one-bit scenario, we had to pick a step size in order to reconstruct the data. To play back our two-bit DPCM series, we need to choose twice as many values— a size for our small steps and a size for the big steps. Let's use 1 for the small steps and 3 for the big steps, giving us the mapping (0,1,2,3) to (-3, -1, 1, 3). Now our reconstructed series would look like [..., 200, 201, 204, 207, 206, 203, 200, 197]. Because we could pick two levels for the differences, the encoding can accommodate both slow changes and faster changes. We don't lose as much on the peak at 208 as we did with the one-bit version, and the slow-changing parts are more accurately represented as well.

See Figure 18-2 where I've plotted them. The two-bit DPCM line overlaps the actual values most of the time, while the one-bit DPCM misses a lot, but is right much of the time. The one-bit DPCM, having only the choice of two slopes, up or down, makes waveforms that look like triangles, while the two-bit DPCM starts to look a little more rounded and natural.

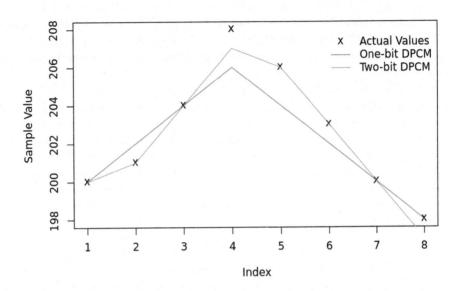

Figure 18-2. *Graph of one- and two-bit DPCM example*

To do the encoding into two-bit DPCM, we needed to pick a positive-going and negative-going threshold to distinguish between big and small steps, and when we reconstructed the original signal, we needed to pick two more values—the sizes of the big and small steps in either direction. Picking these values is a compromise between speed of response and smoothness, and the choices are interdependent. If you chose the threshold to be large in the encoding step, you should probably have a fairly large difference for the big step when you're decoding.

For any given signal, there is a best choice for each of these values, but that's getting way beyond our needs. In fact, the next level of cleverness in sample encoding, Adaptive DPCM, is simply an encoding method where the different step sizes are changed on the fly to best match the audio sample. So when the audio is slowly changing, the thresholds and reconstruction differentials are smaller, and when there's a lot of movement in the waveform, both thresholds and differentials are increased to match. The algorithms for doing ADPCM are yet more complicated, but the general idea is simple once you've got the DPCM concept.

Anyway, *do* feel free to play around with both the thresholds and the reconstruction differential values. When encoding, the thresholds are stored in the *wave2DPCM.py* file as `TWO_BIT_THRESHOLDS = [-0.05, 0, 0.05]`. In the encoder, I've normalized the samples to a maximum and minimum values of 1 and –1, respectively, so the thresholds are effectively in percentages. Any change that's bigger than 5% of the maximum value is a big change. The reconstruction differentials are stored in *talkingVoltmeter.h* in `reconstruction_differentials`. These are on our usual 8-bit scale of –128 to 127, so the big step is scaled to be bigger than 5% of 128—at 12, it's around 10%—and the small step is about 2.5%, or 3. Within reasonable ranges, you may find that you get better or worse reproduction. If you change the numbers around drastically, you'll get horrible digital-sounding squawky noises. Enjoy!

Encoding DPCM: wave2DPCM.py

Everything you need to load up your own *.wav* files into the AVR is included in this Python file. The short version of the procedure is that you record files of yourself (or you can use an online speech synthesizer like AT&T Natural Voices Text-to-Speech Demo (*http://www2.research.att.com/~ttsweb/tts/demo.php*)) saying the words "zero" through "nine," "point," "volts," and anything else you want the volt-meter to repeat for you. Then save these files as 8,000 Hz, mono *.wav* files with names like *one.wav*, etc. (See the bottom of Example 18-7 for a list of the digits used.)

Running the *wave2DPCM.py* program in a directory with all the correctly named files gives you a header file that'll plug right in to the `talkingVoltmeter` project. (Or you can download some of my extra sample voices from links on this book's website.) If you make your own samples, you'll need to keep them short to fit into memory. If you need more room, feel free to remove the introductory `talking voltmeter` prompt from the project to make more space. To do so, you'll need to remove it from the Python file, the *talkingVoltmeter.h* file that includes it, and in the initialization part of the `main()` function in *talkingVoltmeter.c* where the function to play the file is called.

In case you'd like to customize the code, let's get at least a good overview understanding of what's going on in *wave2DPCM.py*, listed in Example 18-7.

Example 18-7. wave2DPCM.py listing

```
## Functions to convert mono, 8kHz .wav files to differential PCM

## If you've got 'sox' installed on your computer, this code calls
##   'sox' and re-codes the files for you.  If not, you've got to do it.

## Finally, given a bunch of wav files with names like one.wav, two.wav
##  this writes the DPCM data out to a header file for including in AVR C

from struct import unpack
import wave
import os
import sys
```

```
def unpackMono(waveFile):
    w = wave.Wave_read(waveFile)
    data = []
    for i in range(w.getnframes()):
        data.append(unpack("h", w.readframes(1))[0])
    return(data)

def scaleData(data):
    scale = max(max(data), abs(min(data))) * 1.0
    return([x/scale for x in data])

def getDifferences(data):
    differences = []
    for i in range(len(data)-1):
        differences.append(data[i+1]-data[i])
    return(differences)

def quantize(data, thresholds):
    quantized = []
    n = len(thresholds)
    thresholdRange = range(n)
    for d in data:
        categorized = False
        for i in thresholdRange:
            if d <= thresholds[i]:
                quantized.append(i)
                categorized = True
                break
        if not categorized:
            quantized.append(n)
    return(quantized)

def pack4(data):                       # for 2-bit data
    packedData = []
    for i in range(len(data) / 4):
        thisByte = 0
        thisByte += 2**6 * data[4*i]
        thisByte += 2**4 * data[4*i+1]
        thisByte += 2**2 * data[4*i+2]
        thisByte += data[4*i+3]
        packedData.append(thisByte)
    return(packedData)

def packTwoBitDPCM(filename):
    data = unpackMono(filename)
    data = scaleData(data)
    differences = getDifferences(data)
    quantized = quantize(differences, TWO_BIT_THRESHOLDS)
    packed = pack4(quantized)
    return(packed)

def createHeader(filename, packedData):
    baseFilename = filename[:-4]
```

```python
    outfile = open("DPCM_" + baseFilename + ".h", "w")
    outfile.write('uint8_t DPCM_{}[] PROGMEM = {{\n'.format(baseFilename))
    for byte in packedData:
        outfile.write('  {:d},\n'.format(byte))
    outfile.write('};\n')
    outfile.close()


def fixWaveFile(filename):
    w = wave.Wave_read(filename)
    bitrate = w.getframerate()
    channels = w.getnchannels()
    bits = w.getsampwidth()*8
    if not bitrate==8000 or not channels==1 or not bits==16:
        newFilename = filename[:-4] + "_8000.wav"
        returnValue = os.system(SOXCOMMAND.format(filename, newFilename))
        if returnValue:
            raise(SOX_Exception("""Something went wrong calling sox:
SOXCOMMAND.format(filename, newFilename
Is sox installed?  If not, just make sure that you've saved 8kHz mono wav files."""))
        filename = newFilename
    return(filename)


class SOX_Exception(Exception):
    pass


if __name__ == "__main__":

    ## Default is to convert all wav files in the current directory.

    TWO_BIT_THRESHOLDS = [-0.05, 0, 0.05]

    SOXCOMMAND = "sox {} -r 8000 -c 1 -b 16 {}" # for converting wave file
    ## install sox, or use itunes or audacity to convert
    ## wavefile to 8kHz, 16-bit, one-channel

    wavefiles = [x for x in os.walk(".").next()[2] if x.endswith(".wav")]
    for filename in wavefiles:
        filename = fixWaveFile(filename) # converts if needed, returns new filename
        packedData = packTwoBitDPCM(filename)
        createHeader(filename, packedData)

    ## And create a digits sample set for talkingVoltmeter.h:
    digits = ["one", "two", "three", "four", "five", "six",
              "seven", "eight", "nine", "zero",
              "point", "volts", "talkingvoltmeter"]
    allDigits = open("allDigits.h", "w")
    for digit in digits:
        filename = "DPCM_" + digit + "_8000.h"
        print filename
        allDigits.write(open(filename).read())
    allDigits.close()
```

Let's start at the top. unpackMono(waveFile) converts the specified 16-bit mono *.wav* audio file into it's corresponding numeric data. The result is a list of numbers ranging from −32,768 to 32,767. scaleData(data) changes the range to (-1,1), and then getDifferences(data) subtracts each sample from the one before it. This is the first step in DPCM encoding.

The function quantize(data, thresholds) does the DPCM encoding. For each difference value, it figures out where it falls relative to the thresholds and gives it a corresponding numeric value. The last stage of the algorithm part is to then pack these two-bit values into eight-bit numbers to load into the AVR. pack4(data) does the packing.

The next function, packTwoBitDPCM(filename) just wraps up all of the preceding steps into one function for convenience. The input is a filename, and the output is packed two-bit DPCM data. Now all that's left is to write the data out into an *.h* file to include with your AVR code, which is handled by createHeader(). Finally, I've included a convenience function that double-checks your *.wav* file's bitrate, number of channels, and bit-depth, and runs the command-line utility sox to convert the file if it's not right. If you don't have sox installed on your system, go get it! It's an awesome audio tool—the rightly nicknamed Swiss army knife of audio files. If you don't want to install sox, just make sure that you're saving your audio samples as 16-bit, 8,000 Hz, mono *.wav* files, and you'll be OK.

After if __name__ == "__main__", we get to actually calling these functions and doing the work. The bit thresholds are defined here, as is the command-line call to sox if you need it. After that, the code loops through all the *.wav* files in the directory, encodes them in DPCM, and writes out an individual header file for each. The last loop just combines all of the listed names into a single header file, *allDigits.h*, that you can include in the *talkingVoltmeter.h* project without any further modification.

EEPROM 19

AVR Secret Decoder Ring

In Chapter 16 we used external EEPROM (electrically erasable and programmable ROM) for nonvolatile external data storage. For making a data logger it was just right: EEPROM provides low-power, long-term storage of fairly large amounts of data. But if all you want is a little bit of data to survive a chip reset, adding an extra chip and tying up the SPI or I2C lines just for a few bytes of configuration data seems overkill. That's why the Atmel chip designers put a small amount of EEPROM on each of the ATmega chips for you to use.

In this chapter, we'll turn the AVR into a Vigenère Cipher encoder and decoder, storing the encryption key strings in nonvolatile EEPROM memory so that you don't have to remember them yourself. Because the keys are stored on the AVR, you can make them fairly long and fairly complicated, making even a trivial example encryption scheme like this unbreakable for short enough messages. And because you can also preload key strings into the EEPROM, you can set up two AVR Secret Decoder Rings with the identical memory contents. Give one to a friend, and you'll have a marvellous high-tech/low-tech encryption system.

Of course, if you encrypt important information using the AVR Secret Decoder Ring, you'll want you be sure that you never reflash the chip or let it out of your possession.

What You Need

In this chapter, in addition to the basic kit, you will need:
- A USB-Serial adapter.

The AVR's internal EEPROM is full of trade-offs. There's not a whole lot of it and it's a little bit slow to erase or write to—taking 1.8 ms for a write or 3.4 ms for an erase and write combo. In practice, if you're writing an application that runs on a human timescale or only needs to save configuration information periodically, the speed isn't an issue. You've still only got 512 bytes, but whether that's a lot or a little depends on your application.

The final limitation of EEPROM is that each memory cell has a given number of erase and write cycles that it can go through before it becomes unreliable. On the other hand, reads are unlimited, your data won't be forgotten when the power goes off, and the EEPROM is specified for 100,000 writes.

In short, unlike the timer/counter modules, the ADCs, any of the serial communications hardware, or the interrupt system, the AVR's internal EEPROM is a niche utility. It's not fast enough to use as buffer memory or large enough to store tons of data, and you don't want to write to it all the time. But when you *do* need a small amount of nonvolatile memory to save the AVR's state when the power goes off, the built-in EEPROM is terribly convenient. Working with the EEPROM is also a great excuse for us to use all that we've just learned about pointers and memory addresses, so let's get to it.

Using EEPROM

The AVR's hardware-level EEPROM functions are fairly straightforward but a little bit cumbersome to use. For instance, to write a byte to a memory location, you need to first check that the EEPROM is ready to use, then write the data to one register, write the address where you'd like to save the data to another register, then set an enable bit, and then within four cycles set the write bit and optionally wait for it to finish. Pshwew!

If you have multiple bytes to read and write, all of this can get annoying, so it should be no surprise that the *avr/eeprom.h* library has a bunch of utility functions that streamline using EEPROM. Using these functions, combined with what we now know about pointers, makes working with the EEPROM easy.

Storing in Memory

First off, there are two types of functions in the *avr/eeprom.h* library that store a variable: eeprom_write_byte() and eeprom_update_byte(). The difference is that the "write" commands just write to EEPROM, whereas the "update" commands first verify that the data has actually changed before performing a write operation. The extra read from EEPROM only adds a few microseconds, as opposed to milliseconds for the write command, and it can possibly save you time if the EEPROM value hasn't changed. But more importantly, using eeprom_update_byte() avoids unnecessary writes to EEPROM, which is a good idea because EEPROM, although rewriteable, isn't rewriteable indefinitely. We'll be using the "update" family of functions exclusively. Forget about "write."

EEPROM Life Span

Rewriting EEPROM causes electrical wear-and-tear on the insulating semiconductor layer that is responsible for retaining the data. The AVR datasheet says that the internal EEPROM is good for around 100,000 write and erase cycles. That's quite a few, right? Well, maybe. If you write to the EEPROM once per hour, then you have an expected 11 years of useful EEPROM life. At one write per minute, 100,000 writes is only 69.5 days. If you write to EEPROM once per second, you're looking at just under 28 hours of expected lifetime before data may start getting lost.

There are small improvements possible around the margins, like writing to different memory addresses instead of reusing the same memory cells every time—called **wear leveling.** *But in the end, if you need to save your data very frequently, maybe EEPROM isn't the right choice.*

In the *avr/eeprom.h* library, EEPROM read and update commands come in a few different types, tailored for reading and writing different types of data. If you read through the include file *avr/eeprom.h*, you'll find that the EEPROM update functions are specified as follows:

```
void    eeprom_update_byte (uint8_t *__p, uint8_t __value)
void    eeprom_update_word (uint16_t *__p, uint16_t __value)
void    eeprom_update_dword (uint32_t *__p, uint32_t __value)
void    eeprom_update_float (float *__p, float __value)
void    eeprom_update_block (const void *__src, void *__dst, size_t __n)
```

With the exception of the *block* update command, the functions take two arguments: an address to store the data (passed as a pointer of the correct type) and the value to store in memory. These avr-libc functions take care all the low-level details: checking that the EEPROM is ready for a write, enabling the EEPROM write bits, loading up the necessary registers, and so on.

Floats

I've been avoiding using float *type variables. Floats are 32-bit floating-point representations that let you represent numbers with decimal places. The floating-point–compatible math libraries end up taking up a bunch of memory and are slow. In my experience, there's almost always a way to rephrase your problem that can avoid using floating-point numbers; for instance the way we dealt with fractional frequency steps in the direct-digital synthesis method in* **Chapter 13.** *But just in case you've been secretly using* floats *all along, now you know how to store them in EEPROM.*

The eeprom_update_block command is a little bit more complicated, but it makes nice use of pointers and memory addresses. The three arguments, in order, are: the address of the first element of a source array of data, the address in EEPROM where you want to start writing, and the size of the array in bytes. Internally, the function starts at the first byte of the RAM array and the specified location in EEPROM, and takes one step at a time, writing one byte to EEPROM before moving on to the next.

Let me walk you through some quick example usages of all the different update commands in Example 19-1.

Example 19-1. *quickDemo.c listing*

```
#include <avr/io.h>
#include <avr/eeprom.h>

int main(void) {

  // Store the 8-bit value 5 in EEPROM slot 0
  uint8_t *address = (uint8_t *) 0;
  eeprom_update_byte(address, 5);

  // Store the 16-bit value 12345 in EEPROM slots 5 and 6:
  eeprom_update_word((uint16_t *) 5, 12345);

  // Store a character array (string) in EEPROM slots 16-28:
  char *stringPointer = (char *) 16;
  char myString[] = "hello world.";
  eeprom_update_block(myString, stringPointer, sizeof(myString));

  return (0);
}
```

The first example is the most straightforward: we create a pointer to the EEPROM's memory address 0 with the type uint8_t* so that we're set up for storing a uint8_t variable. Then, using eeprom_update_byte(), we write the number five into EE-PROM. If you wanted to store another byte of data in the next memory slot in EEPROM, you could simply add one to the pointer and go on: eeprom_update_byte(address+1, 17);.

In the next example, we store the 16-bit value 12345 into EEPROM memory locations five and six. Instead of creating a uint16_t* pointer variable just to encode the number five as an address, we convert the type of the Memory Address 1 to a pointer on the fly. You *could* just write a simple numeric "5" here and it will work because this is a trivial demo example, but the compiler would complain that eeprom_update_word expects a pointer to an unsigned 16-bit integer. If we *were* using a pointer, and you wanted to store another 16-bit integer, you'd be able to simply add one to the pointer and it would know to skip forward to memory slot seven because the pointer is declared to be 16-bits wide. That's one reason that using pointers, which join an address with a type, is handy.

The third example writes a string into EEPROM using the `eeprom_block_up` `date()` function. The first thing to remember about strings is that they're really arrays of characters that are terminated with a numeric zero. Thus the length of my string is the 12 characters that you probably counted out, plus the trailing zero. That's how I figured out that I'd be writing from address 16 to address 28 (inclusive). But I didn't have to figure out the length of the string myself; using `sizeof(my String)` takes care of the counting for me.

Just about now, if you've got a whole lot of different variable types that you'd like to store into EEPROM, you're probably starting to worry about how you're going to keep their starting and ending locations straight. If you make a mental mistake on any of the addresses, you can overwrite data or read from the wrong bits. The good news is that you can let the compiler handle all of that for you, and you'll see how in "Organizing Data in EEPROM" on page 425. Before I show you how to read out EEPROM values in code, though, let's take a peek at the chip's memory using AVRDUDE.

AVRDUDE and EEPROM

Not only can AVRDUDE read and write to the flash program memory in the AVR chips, but it can also read and write to EEPROM if your programmer supports it. A fun way to have a look at the EEPROM in your chip is to use AVRDUDE's terminal mode.

If you've been using the makefile that I've included with the *AVR-Programming-Library* library included with the book, all you have to do is type **make avrdude_ter minal** and you're in. All that does is add the -nt flags to your usual AVRDUDE command line ("t" is for terminal mode) but it's easier to run from the makefile, no?

Once you're in terminal mode, you're talking directly with the AVR chip itself. You can type **help** and get a list of options. In our case, to see what's stored in EEPROM, type **dump eeprom**.

If you haven't flashed any code that uses the EEPROM into your chip yet, you'll find that each byte in memory is set to 255, or 0xff, which is what EEPROMs (including flash memory and similar) default to when they're reset. If you'd flashed and run the little *quickDemo.c* code snippet, this is what you'd get after it has run once and written to EEPROM:

```
avrdude -c usbasp -p atmega168  -nt

Reading | ################################################# | 100% 0.00s

avrdude: Device signature = 0x1e9406
avrdude> dump eeprom
>>> dump eeprom
```

```
0000   05 ff ff ff ff 39 30 ff   ff ff ff ff ff ff ff ff   |.....90.........|
0010   68 65 6c 6c 6f 20 77 6f   72 6c 64 2e 00 ff ff ff   |hello world.....|
0020   ff ff ff ff ff ff ff ff   ff ff ff ff ff ff ff ff   |................|
0030   ff ff ff ff ff ff ff ff   ff ff ff ff ff ff ff ff   |................|

avrdude> quit
```

If you've never seen a memory dump before, this code can be helpful for visualizing what's going on. On the far left are memory addresses of the beginning of the row, in hexadecimal. The middle two sections are blocks of eight bytes each, again represented in hexadecimal. This is literally, byte for byte, the memory that's sitting in your chip's EEPROM. The far right is the representation of the data in ASCII, which is good for finding strings (nonprinting characters are printed as periods).

Let's see what we can learn from this. Well, we wrote a uint8_t 5 to position zero, and there it is. It doesn't show up on the ASCII side because five isn't in the range of printable characters. Next, we wrote a 16-bit 12345 (in decimal) at position 5. 12345 is 0x3039 in hexadecimal, but we've got 39 30 in our memory dump. Storing 16-bit numbers with the least-significant byte first is called *little-endian* storage, and it's an arbitrary choice. The *avr/eeprom.h* library functions handle the data consistently, loading up the LSB register first, then the MSB so you won't have to be concerned with the byte ordering unless you end up editing EEPROM memory dumps directly.

Finally, we come along to the string. Note that it starts at location 0x0010, or 16 in decimal just as it was supposed to. I defined the string's array to be just the right size for the string (using char myString[]) so it's stored in the minimum amount of space in memory. And there it is, trailing 00 byte and all. Then the rest of the memory space is still unused, all 0xff. By default AVRDUDE only shows you the first 64 bytes, so if you'd like to see the rest of the EEPROM in your chip, type **dump eeprom 0 512**.

 Waiting for an EEPROM Write to Finish

Before we leave the section on writing EEPROM, I should mention that the avr/eeprom.h library also includes a couple of helper functions to test if the EEPROM is ready for access again after a write command. Remember, a write and erase command to EEPROM takes 3.6 ms. To that end, eeprom_is_ready() checks the EEPE bit in the EEPROM control register for you, and eeprom_busy_wait() just loops around until that bit is clear.

You won't need to use the eeprom_is_ready() command for reading or writing to EEPROM, though; the library's read and write commands already check for you. The only use I've ever had for these functions is double-checking that an EEPROM is done before entering sleep mode.

Data Types

Numbers represented in binary have a necessarily limited number of distinct values they can take on. For instance, if you've only got one bit, all you can represent are the numbers zero and one. Two bits gets you zero, one, two, and three. Three bits covers the range zero to seven inclusive, and so on. Each additional bit doubles the number of possible values that binary digit can have.

If you want to represent negative numbers as well as positive numbers, you can use one bit as a positive/negative sign. This cuts the maximum value that's representable in half, but then adds an equal number of possible negative values (plus one). The numbers are stored internally in *two's-complement* order, but this is an implementation detail that you can ignore or look up on Wikipedia if you're interested.

I strongly prefer the fixed-width variable type names that got introduced with ISO standard C99 for microcontroller work, because you know at a glance how many bits you're dealing with. With a big computer, where resources aren't critically allocated, I'm entirely happy to use 64 bits to represent the number five, but on our AVRs, large data types take up an unnecessary amount of memory and usually take significantly more CPU time to process. It's a good idea to use the smallest data type you can.

Before C99, there were a few integer types, but the size of each wasn't guaranteed at all and could vary across computer architectures:

char
    Meant to represent ASCII character data, the char type is almost always an unsigned 8-bit integer. On the AVR, it's identical to uint8_t, but I tend to use char when I mean to represent ASCII data and uint8_t when I'm thinking about the numerical value.

int
    "Integers" in standard C are at least 16 bits. On the AVR, an int is usually 16 bits. There's an avr-gcc compiler flag to redefine int as 8 bits, but you're asking for trouble if you enable it. (See why I like uint16_t now?)

long
    "Long integers" are 32 bits on the AVR.

long long
    Double long integers are 64 bits on the AVR.

word
    "Word" isn't really a defined C type, but people commonly use it as they would int. Here, what we call a "word" is a 16-bit integer.

The AVR ATmega chips have an 8-bit architecture, meaning that they're built to work with data that comes in 8-bit *bytes*. A byte gets you a range of integers, for instance, between zero and 255. When you need more numbers, the next step up is to string two bytes together, giving you a 16-bit *word* that can range, for unsigned integers, from 0 to 65,535, or from −32,768 to 32,767. Early Macintoshes and PC-ATs used 24-bit addressing, but that seems to have died out. The next commonly used integer is the 32-bit "long" integer, which covers the range from 0 to 4,294,967,295 when you need it.

Reading from Memory

Once you've got data stored in EEPROM, it's simple enough to read it back out. Just like the update commands that we used for writing, there are corresponding read commands: uint8_t eeprom_read_byte(), uint16_t eeprom_read_word(), and uint32_t eeprom_read_dword(). Using these functions is straightforward: Pass them a memory address, and you get the data out. For reading stored strings or other array data, we'll want to use the block read mode, eeprom_read_block(), which is worth a demonstration. See Example 19-2.

Example 19-2. favoriteColor.c listing

```
#include <avr/io.h>
#include <avr/eeprom.h>
#include <USART.h>

#define STRING_MAXLEN        0x20              /* 32 characters */
#define STRING_ADDRESS       0x20
#define COUNTER_ADDRESS      0x10


int main(void) {

  char myString[STRING_MAXLEN];
  char *eepromAddress = (char *) STRING_ADDRESS;
  uint16_t counter;

  initUSART();

  while (1) {
    // Read from EEPROM and print out
    eeprom_read_block(myString, eepromAddress, STRING_MAXLEN);
    counter = eeprom_read_word((uint16_t *) COUNTER_ADDRESS);
    printString("\r\nYour old favorite color is: ");
    printString(myString);

    // Take input, store in EEPROM
    printString("\r\n\r\n Type your new favorite color.  ");
    readString(myString, sizeof(myString));
             /* pass by address, function will change its values */
    eeprom_update_block(myString, eepromAddress, STRING_MAXLEN);
    counter++;
    printString("Thanks! \r\nYou've answered the same question ");
    printWord(counter);
    printString(" times.  \r\n");
    eeprom_update_word((uint16_t *) COUNTER_ADDRESS, counter);
  }

  return (0);
}
```

This demonstration code reads a string out of EEPROM, prints it out for you, and then asks you for a new string and stores it in the same place. Run it once and put in your favorite color. Then use AVRDUDE in terminal mode and dump the EEPROM to see the contents. Quit AVRDUDE and reopen a terminal to change the color again. See how it goes?

And now that we've had an introduction to pointers, we can discuss a little bit of the magic that's going on here when we're passing the variable myString from one function to another. Let's start with the first eeprom_read_block() statement. If you look up the function in the AVR libc function reference, you'll find the function prototype reads void eeprom_read_block (void *__dst, const void *__src, size_t __n). Phswew! Taking that apart, you'll see that the function returns nothing. So how is it reading the data? Where does it go?

The answer lies in the arguments. The first argument is the pointer to a destination string where we want the data stored after it's read out. The benefit of passing our function a pointer to a string is that the function doesn't have to worry about assigning any variables in memory because we've already done that in the main() routine. We've defined the array myString[32], and then passed the address of myString to eeprom_read_block(), which fills it up.

Remember that when an array is passed to a function, what's really passed is just a pointer to its first element. When we pass myString as an argument, it is the same as passing &myString[0]: the memory address where it should start storing the data it gets out of EEPROM. When the eeprom_read_block() function reads its first byte in, it stores it in the memory address that is pointed to by myString. Then it increments the pointer and stores the next byte, and so on, until it's done.

How does the function know when it's done? The third argument of the function is the length that we'd like read. We need to be careful here! If the compiler only allocated space in memory for 32 bytes, for instance, but we pass the ee prom_read_block() function a length that's greater than 32, it'll just keep writing as if nothing had happened. There's no telling what is stored in the next region of memory, and we might end up corrupting other variables. (Writing over the end of an array, and its close cousin the buffer overflow, are *the* classic sources of crashes and exploitable bugs in C code. If you pass a string or array to another function, make *sure* that you know how long it is.)

All that remains now is the second argument, a pointer to the starting EEPROM address. If you're going to read from EEPROM memory, of course you have to tell it where to start and how many bytes to read at a time. The type of pointer you pass to the read functions should also reflect the size of the data you're going to read out. So if you are reading a byte, you pass a uint8_t*, and if you're reading a word, you pass a uint16_t*.

But what kind of pointer should you pass if you'd like to read out a block of some number of bytes? eeprom_read_block() expects a memory address in the form of a void*, a void pointer. A void pointer should probably actually be called a "generic" pointer—it's a pointer without a type. It's what you define when you just don't care what type of data you're pointing at. On the AVR platform, if you increment a void pointer, it increases by a byte, so it's essentially a basic bytewise pointer.

The one virtue that a void* has is that it matches anything. So if you, the programmer, know that the data you've got stored in EEPROM is character data, you can pass the eeprom_read_block() a character pointer and you won't have to convert the type of the pointer just to match the type of the function argument. Or said another way, if you write your function with a void pointer as an argument, you're simply saying that all you care about is the address and not the type at all. The eeprom_read_block() function can get away with that because in the third argument, you have to tell it how many bytes of data you want to read.

I've also included a counter that shows how many times you've suffered through the favorite color routine. It's a simple (and probably optimistic) uint16_t counter, stored at a fixed location in EEPROM, that gets updated and resaved each time you run the program. If you want to test the 100,000 write cycles for the EEPROM, just keep typing in colors! (Are there 100,000 words for colors?)

Saving and Loading EEPROM

The most valuable (and fun) thing about EEPROM is that it's nonvolatile. You can power down your chip completely, and the data in EEPROM will still be there when you turn the chip back on, even thirty years later. (Can you say the same for your hard drive?) But what if you want to send that data to a printer? Or save the EEPROM values to your desktop computer so that you can upload them again later? Or preload the EEPROM with data from some other source entirely?

Naturally, we'll use AVRDUDE. We already saw how we could dump the EEPROM data to the screen from within terminal mode. If you'd like a more permanent record, you can save all of the EEPROM to a quasi-readable file using a command like `avrdude -c usbasp -p atmega168 -U eeprom:r:myEEPROM.hex:i` (where you'll need to substitute your own programmer's options).

The *myEEPROM.hex* file is stored in Intel hex dump format. This format uses the first eight digits for the memory address, followed by the data, and the last two digits as a checksum. Because of the checksum, editing the *.hex* files directly is a little bit awkward, but having the checksums around guards against data corruption. Use this if you just want to store, copy, and reupload EEPROM data.

If you'd like to edit the data, the easiest way is to dump the data in raw binary mode. With my setup, `avrdude -c usbasp -p atmega168 -U eeprom:r:myEE PROM.raw:r` creates a binary file with the data in it. You'll want to use a hex editor to edit this file. There are about a thousand freeware hex editors out there, so you can just pick one.

Alternatively, you can open up the file in a Python interactive session, edit the data, and write it back out:

```
>> eeprom = file("myEEPROM.raw").read()   ## Reads in as a string
>> eeprom[15:28]
'hello world.\x00'
>>> eepromList = list(eeprom)   ## Converts to list so can edit elements
>>> eepromList[15] = "j"
>>> eeprom = "".join(eepromList)   ## Back to string
>>> eeprom[15:28]
```

```
'jello world.\x00'
>>> file("newEEPROM.raw", "w").write(eeprom)
```

Now if you want to reupload either the hex or raw format EEPROM memories to the AVR, you issue a command like **avrdude -c usbasp -p atmega168 -U ee prom:w:myEEPROM.raw:r**, where the only thing I changed was eeprom:r: for read to eeprom:w: for write. Using this strategy, you can load whatever values into the EEPROM that you'd want to, even programmatically. This is handy if you're flashing a bunch of devices but would like each one to have a unique serial number, for instance. A single Python routine can take care of flashing the program memory by calling AVRDUDE, creating an EEPROM image with the serial number in it, and then flashing that across as well.

The dumpEEPROM-edit-and-reflash procedure is good for a quick, one-time edit, and although you *can* write routines to generate EEPROM data that are separate from your C code, it turns out that you don't have to. What do you do if you want to preload EEPROM value into the AVR but don't want to have to keep track of all the memory locations yourself? The answer is the EEMEM macro—the topic of the next section.

Organizing Data in EEPROM

By now, you should be able to do anything you want to with EEPROM using just the read and write commands, if you conscientiously keep track of what data is in which memory locations. Heck, you can even preload values into EEPROM by saving them to a file and uploading them with AVRDUDE as you just saw. On the other hand, keeping track of memory locations is a drag, and hand-editing EEPROM dump files isn't much fun either.

When you're saving variables in "normal" RAM, you don't have to worry about keeping track of the addresses by yourself—you leave that to the compiler. You just type in a=7; and the compiler figures out where to stash the number, and goes looking in the right place when you ask it to print out the value a again.

In this section, you'll see how to use C's built-in variable handling and (pointer) addressing scheme to handle the EEPROM memory management chores for you automatically, and additionally how to initialize data in EEPROM the easy way. Along the way, you will learn a bit more about how you actually *use* pointers for storing and recalling memory addresses. All of this is made possible by the EEMEM macro. I'll demonstrate how this works in Example 19-3.

Example 19-3. eememDemo.c listing

```
#include <avr/io.h>
#include <avr/eeprom.h>
#include <USART.h>

#define STRING_LEN    80
```

```
// Define EEMEM variables
uint8_t eepromCounter EEMEM = 0;
char eepromString[STRING_LEN] EEMEM = "Welcome to the EEMEM Demo.\r\n";
uint16_t eepromWord EEMEM = 12345;

int main(void) {

  initUSART();
  char ramString[STRING_LEN];
  uint8_t counter;

  while (1) {
    printString("\r\n-----------------\r\n");
    eeprom_read_block(ramString, eepromString, STRING_LEN);
    printString(ramString);

    printString("\r\nThe counter reads: ");
    counter = eeprom_read_byte(&eepromCounter);
    printByte(counter);

    printString("\r\nMy uint16_t value is: ");
    printWord(eeprom_read_word(&eepromWord));

    printString("\r\n   Enter a new introduction string below:\r\n");
    readString(ramString, STRING_LEN);
    eeprom_update_block(ramString, eepromString, STRING_LEN);
    counter++;
    eeprom_update_byte(&eepromCounter, counter);
  }
  return (0);
}
```

Designating variables to be stored in EEPROM memory is easy enough; see the first three (global) definitions for usage. All you need to do is add the EEMEM qualifier to the variable declaration. C will then go ahead and allocate addresses in EEPROM to store those variables. In your code, you can get those addresses back using the & "address-of" operator whenever you need to.

Notice how much easier this is than generating an EEPROM file by hand, having to remember where all the addresses are, and copying them into your C code. Here, the preloaded EEPROM is stored *in* your code, and its address is available to you.

As we move down through the main() function, you'll see how it's used. Because our printString function needs a copy of the string in RAM to work, we had to declare a big enough character array to handle the string stored in EEPROM. And then before we can print it out, we use the eeprom_read_block() function to copy the string out of EEPROM memory and into our RAM character array, ramString.

Don't forget that eepromString is an array, so that passing it as an argument to a function is really passing the address of the first element.

The next few lines demonstrate how to read byte (8-bit) and word (16-bit) values out of EEPROM. It's easy when the EEMEM macro keeps track of the variable addresses for us. To get the data stored as eepromCounter, we need to pass its address to eeprom_read_byte(). If we allocated this memory manually, we'd have to remember that the counter data was stored at EEPROM memory slot whatever. But here, we simply use the "address-of" operator on the EEMEM-defined variable, and we're all set. Compare read_byte with read_block—we have to explicitly use the & operator here because we wanted the address of an integer. We didn't need to use the & operator in the earlier example because in that case we wanted the address of an array.

If you dump the EEPROM using the AVRDUDE terminal, you'll find that the 16-bit number is stored at memory location 81. You could have figured that out yourself (one byte for the counter plus 80 bytes for the welcome string), but it's a lot easier to let gcc take care of it all for you. Much more importantly, if you change your code, adding a variable or two stored in EEPROM, or changing a string's length, all the addresses get updated automatically when you recompile.

The last half of the demo takes input from you, stores it as the next welcome string, increments the counter, and stores that away in EEPROM, too.

Initializing EEPROM

But if we just flash this program into our chip, the program will just print out a bunch of garbage because although we've changed the program, we haven't updated the EEPROM yet. (Try it!) Where did our predefined EEPROM data go?

When the EEMEM statement allocates the variables in EEPROM, it writes them into our compiled .elf file, so in principle the variables are usable by the rest of the code. But AVRDUDE doesn't flash the EEPROM without our permission. This means that we can reflash the program memory or the EEPROM memory or both, which is very handy if we've got some values in EEPROM that we'd like to keep. The upshot of this is that in order to preload the EEPROM data, we need to split it out into an EEPROM file and burn that into the AVR in a separate step, just as we were doing in "Saving and Loading EEPROM" on page 424.

Where you normally type **make flash** to compile and load the program into the AVR, you can type **make flash_eeprom** to generate the EEPROM file and flash it into EEPROM. And if you type just **make eeprom**, you'll end up with a copy of the Intel hex file that it uses. Feel free to open it up in a hex editor and have a look. This time, though, you won't need to edit the EEPROM memory dump file, because it's generated from your C code.

If you haven't already, set the EESAVE fuse bit and play around with this two-stage program and EEPROM cycle. Change some of the 'EEMEM' variables' initial values in your code, and type `make flash` to reprogram the chip. You'll notice that the values stored in EEPROM didn't change. Now `make flash_eeprom` and they will be updated. If you edit the code and reflash that in and none of the memory addresses have changed, you'll find the variables preserved in whatever state you last left them.

The one thing to be careful of is moving or adding new EEMEM definitions. EEMEM is allocated in the same order it's defined in your file. If you switch the order of the variables around, between the string and the `uint16_t` variable for instance, the variables will get assigned different addresses in EEPROM, and things will get scrambled up. If you do change the ordering of EEMEM variables, or even just want to be on the safe side, reflash *both* the program memory and the EEPROM. To be on the super safe side, you can first run run `make clean`, which will remove all of the compiled files—machine code and EEPROM. Then use `make flash flash_ee prom` to remake your entire project from scratch and flash both program and EE-PROM memories.

The EESAVE Fuse Bit

Naturally, there's a catch. ATmega168 chips come from the factory with a fuse setting that automatically invokes an EEPROM erase every time you program the chip. This can be handy if you want all of the chip's memory to be in a known state and don't want data from previous incarnations lying around in EEPROM. Just remember that your EEPROM will be blank unless you reload it each time after a programming cycle.

On the other hand, sometimes you want to flash one program over another without losing the EEPROM values—if, for instance, you've found a bug in the code that doesn't impact the addresses or content of EEPROM. Or maybe you've got user data stored in EEPROM that you don't want to forget. (Though actually, the safest thing to do in that case is to save the EEPROM to a file.)

If you'd like the EEPROM to *not* be erased automatically when you flash in a new program, you'll have to set the EESAVE bit in the high fuse byte. Starting from a stock mega168 chip, you'd pass AVRDUDE an argument like `-U hfuse:w:0xd7:m`. Or if you're using m makefile, just type `make set_eeprom_save_fuse`. You can reset the EESAVE fuse by writing a 0xd9 to hfuse or by invoking `make clear_ee prom_save_fuse`.

If you haven't set the EESAVE fuse bit, make sure that you're flashing the EEPROM initialization values *after* you've flashed in your program. The order is important because each time you reprogram the chip, it will reinitialize the EEPROM.

Project: Vigenère Cipher Encoder/Decoder

I've already walked you through a bunch of the good uses for EEPROM and how you'd implement it. In my projects, I've never used more than a few bytes of EEPROM —for serial numbers or for storing a couple configuration parameters. Nonvolatile storage in small amounts like this is invaluable when you need it, but you never really need all that much.

For instance, in a logging accelerometer I made, I used five bytes of EEPROM—one for a sensitivity setting (2 g / 8 g) and four for the location of the last page write on the SD card that was used for storing the data. This enabled it to restart in the right place in case it lost power or had a brownout. That's not an ideal use of EEPROM because the logger ended up saving its state every three minutes or so, but it only had to run for four hours anyway, and it was only four bytes, so if it burned them out, I'd just switch to another location.

In this project, however, I'm going hog-wild. The program itself is a menu-driven Vigenère cipher encoder and decoder that stores its code phrases in EEPROM. I'm also storing the strings that are used as menu prompts in EEPROM, just because I can. (Flash program memory is a better place for storing static data, but that's the topic of Chapter 18.)

A *Vigenère cipher* is an old encryption method, based on the Caesar cipher. In the Caesar cipher, every letter of the message is replaced with a letter that's been shifted by the same number of letters in the alphabet. If the shifted result runs off the end of the alphabet, you start over at "a" again. So if the message is "hello" and the shift is one, the encrypted message is "ifmmp." Julius Caesar is reported to have used the secret key "c," which shifts all characters over by three and isn't really all that clever: "C" for Caesar. It might have worked in Emperor Caesar's time, but it's easily crackable these days.

On the other hand, two changes can make the encryption unbreakable. The first is to shift each letter by a different amount, depending on their position in the message. The most common way to do this, called a Vigenère cipher, is to have a key phrase that's easy to remember and then shift each letter in the message by a number of letters that corresponds to the key phrase. So if your key phrase is "abdc" and the message is "hello," you'd encrypt as follows: "h" is shifted over by one because of the "a," to become "i." "e" is shifted over two letters because of "b," and becomes a "g." The AVR version here updates the Vigenère cipher to use the full range of printable ASCII characters, but the operation is the same. To decrypt, you just apply the same idea in reverse—subtracting the letter value of each letter in the key phrase.

For short key phrases, the Vigenère cipher is good enough to challenge a novice cryptanalyst. If you use a five-letter key phrase, for instance, cracking the code is like solving five simultaneous Caesar ciphers, which is hard, but possible if the plaintext message is long enough. If you want truly unbreakable encryption, you can make the key phrase truly random and as long as the message—a "one-time pad." Using a medium-length memorable key phrase gives you encryption that's somewhere between these extremes of simple to decrypt and unbreakable.

So flash the code example and play around. If everything looks like garbage after you've flashed the code in, don't forget to reinitialize the EEPROM. **make clean flash flash_eeprom** should get you set up. Enter a sample message, and either use a precompiled code phrase or enter your own. What's fun about Vigenère ciphers is that they're symmetric—if you encrypt twice with the same code phrase, then decrypt twice, you still get back to your original message.

Now let's see what makes the program tick. I've split the code up into two sections to make it more manageable. Let's have a look at the header first in Example 19-4.

Example 19-4. vigenereCipher.h listing

```
#include <avr/io.h>
#include <avr/eeprom.h>
#include "USART.h"

#define MAX_TEXT_LENGTH  256
#define CODE_LEN         64

// -------- Global Variables -------- //
char EEMEM code0[CODE_LEN] = "ettubrute";
char EEMEM code1[CODE_LEN] = "attackatdawn";
char EEMEM code2[CODE_LEN] = "theraininspainfallsmainlyontheplain";
char EEMEM code3[CODE_LEN] = "ablewasiereisawelba";
char *codePointers[] = { code0, code1, code2, code3 };

// Menu strings.  Why not store them in EEPROM?
char EEMEM welcomeString[] = "\r\n--== Vigenere Cipher  ==--\r\n";
char EEMEM menuEncode[] = " [e] to encode text\r\n";
char EEMEM menuDecode[] = " [d] to decode text\r\n\r\n";
char EEMEM menuEnterText[] = " [n] to enter new text\r\n";
char EEMEM menuCodeText[] = " [c] to select your code phrase\r\n";
char EEMEM menuChangeCode[] = " [x] to modify code phrases\r\n";
char EEMEM promptCode[] = "code: ";
char EEMEM promptText[] = "\r\ntext: ";

char EEMEM promptSelectCode[] = "Select codephrase:\r\n\r\n";
char EEMEM promptTypeText[] = "Type your text: ";

// Given the address of an EEPROM string, prints it out
// Used for menu items
void printFromEEPROM(char *eepromString);

// Takes input from serial, stores it in the text array
void enterText(char text[]);

// Reads code phrases out of EEPROM and prints them.
// Uses the codeBuffer for temporary storage
void displayCodes(void);

// Changes a code phrase, both in EEPROM and the current code
void changeCode(char codeBuffer[]);
```

```
// Pick a code phrase from EEPROM
void selectCode(char code[]);

// Encodes the passed text string, in place
void encodeVigenere(char text[], char code[]);

// Decodes the passed text string, in place
void decodeVigenere(char text[], char code[]);
```

You can see that I'm going to be letting the compiler allocate the EEPROM memory using the EEMEM keyword—there are tons of EEMEM declarations in the global-variable section of the file. Other than those defines, I'd like to draw your attention to the array of character pointers that's defined to point to the four code phrase strings: codePointers.

codePointers is really just an index. To find the address of the second key phrase, for instance, you first look up the address of the desired code string in EEPROM from the array codePointers[], and then you're ready to fetch the string itself out via printFromEEPROM() or eeprom_read_byte(), or whatever.

Almost every time I have a bunch of related strings stored in memory, EEPROM, program flash, or even RAM, I'll create this kind of pointer-array for indexing purposes. It's much easier to type code like:

```
char* codePointers[] = {code0, code1, code2, code3};
stringAddress = codePointers[i];
printFromEEPROM(stringAddress);
```

than it is to explicitly handle each case:

```
if (i==0){
  printFromEEPROM(code0);
}
else if (i==1){
  printFromEEPROM(code1);
}
else if (...){
  // etc. for each possible code
}
```

Next we come to a bunch of strings that we're going to use for prompts and menu items later on. Why am I doing this? When we print out a string using print String("hi");, for instance, the compiler allocates memory to encode the phrase "hi" *both* in the program memory, and as a variable in RAM, because our print String() command takes a normal RAM array as an argument. Here, we stash the strings in EEPROM instead and read the characters out from EEPROM one by one, which saves on RAM. A better place to store nonchanging prompt strings is in program memory, as we saw in Chapter 18, but I had the extra storage space in EEPROM, so why not?

Finally, we have the function prototypes. When we write free-standing libraries in C, we almost always have a header (.h) file and a code (.c) file. In these cases, it's mandatory to prototype your functions in the header file, so that the compiler knows what functions your main code has available to it just by including the header file. Here it's not strictly necessary because all of my functions are defined in the main file, but it's still nice for style. Looking through all the function proto-types like this can give you a good overview of what the code does.

From the prototypes, we can see that there are functions for printing strings stored in EEPROM to serial output, for entering text into strings, for displaying the code phrases, for changing the code phrases, for picking an active code phrase, and for encoding and decoding. The main() routine basically ties all these together and gives us a fairly sophisticated program.

Most of these functions use a trick that's made possible by pointers. You'll notice that they all have return type void, meaning they don't return anything. But then how can a function like enterText(), which takes in text and "updates" a text string variable, actually work? The answer is that the argument, a text string (a character array with a zero at the end), is passed into this function by its address: the pointer to its first memory element. Everything the function does with this "array," it's ac-tually doing in the memory location that is passed by the pointer. So the function doesn't need to return anything at all; all the changes to the variable are done within the function itself.

When we call enterText(char text[]) from the main() routine, we pass a string that's defined in main() somewhere, let's say that it's called textBuffer in main(). This data, the letters that make up the string, are stored somewhere in RAM. When we pass the array to the enterText() function, remember that what's being passed is actually the address of the first character in RAM. When the enterText() function stores a letter in text[0], it's actually storing the letter in the memory address that was passed to it—the same memory slot that's pointed at by the first character of textBuffer in main().

The upshot of passing arrays by pointers like this is that the called function can write directly to the same memory that's been allocated in main(). This in turn means that there's no reason for our enterText() function to pass anything back to main() as a return value—it can just edit the underlying variable memory di-rectly, and then when the function returns, main() will have the new character data already sitting in textBuffer.

In order to see how this all works in practice, and to play around some with reading and writing to EEPROM memory using pointers, let's dig into the C code now. Because the listing is so long, I'll break it up into an outline first in Example 19-5, and then we'll fill in the details as we work through it.

Example 19-5. *vigenereCipher_outline.c listing*

```c
/*
Vigenere Cipher encoder / decoder demo
And an excuse to play around with EEPROM memory
 */

#include "vigenereCipher.h"

// -------- Functions --------- //

void printFromEEPROM(char *eepromString);
void enterText(char text[]);
void displayCodes(void);
void changeCode(char codeBuffer[]);
void selectCode(char code[]);
void encodeVigenere(char text[], char code[]);
void decodeVigenere(char text[], char code[]);

int main(void) {
  // -------- Inits --------- //

  char textBuffer[MAX_TEXT_LENGTH];
  char codeString[CODE_LEN];
  char input;
  initUSART();

  // ------ Event loop ------ //
  while (1) {

    // Menu
    printFromEEPROM(welcomeString);
    // .... more fany menu printing
    printFromEEPROM(menuDecode);
    input = receiveByte();

    switch (input) {
    case 'e':                 // encode
      encodeVigenere(textBuffer, codeString);
      break;
    case 'd':                 // decode
      decodeVigenere(textBuffer, codeString);
      break;
    case 'n':                 // new text
      printFromEEPROM(promptTypeText);
      enterText(textBuffer);
      break;
    case 'c':                 // choose code
      selectCode(codeString);
      break;
```

```
    case 'x':                    // change code
      changeCode(codeString);
      break;
  }
}                                        /* End event loop */
return (0);                          /* This line is never reached */
}
```

Before we get lost in the trees, let's have a look at the whole forest—let's start with the `main()` routine. First off, RAM storage for two strings (character arrays) are allocated—`MAX_TEXT_LENGTH` for the `textBuffer` and `CODE_LEN` for the `codeString`. We'll store the encrypted and decrypted text in the former, and the code phrase in the latter.

At the top of the event loop, you'll see a lot of printing statements that are responsible for creating the menu that you first see when you run the program. I've shortened them because they are a little bit repetitive. Most of the printing action takes place from EEPROM. We'll definitely want to see how that's done in the `printFromEEPROM()` function.

The rest of the event loop is a simple event dispatcher. We type in a menu item, and then the `switch` / `case` statement calls the right function. All of these functions change one or the other of the two character arrays in RAM declared within the scope of `main()`: `textBuffer` and `codeString`. And because both the text and the code phrase are printed out just above in the menu, any updates to either that occur in these functions are immediately displayed to the user.

All the rest of the action is in the individual function definitions, so let's have a look at those now:

```
void printFromEEPROM(char* eepromString){
  uint8_t letter;
  do {
    letter = eeprom_read_byte((uint8_t*) eepromString);
    transmitByte(letter);
    eepromString++;
  } while(letter);
}
```

First off, `printFromEEPROM()` makes good use of the EEMEM macro. Remember that what EEMEM did for us was to assign a variable name to a location in EEPROM, so that we could use it by taking the address of that "variable." That's what makes `printFromEEPROM(char* eepromString)` tick. Notice that the argument is a pointer to characters stored in memory—in this case, the address in EEPROM.

`printFromEEPROM()` then takes the pointer to a memory address, reads a byte out of memory, transmits it across the serial line, and then moves on to the next byte in memory by incrementing the pointer. It does this as long as the letter it read out is anything other than a zero, which marks the end of the string. The only other catch is the typecasting of the type `char*` to `uint8_t*`, which is essentially meaningless because both types refer to a byte of data, but *we* know we've stored characters, while the function `eeprom_read_byte()` expects to have stored numerical data. (If you omit the typecast, the compiler throws a warning about it, but everything works just fine.)

The next function, `enterText()`, is basically `printFromEEPROM` in reverse, with the result stored in RAM:

```
void enterText(char text[]){
  uint8_t i=0;
  char letter;
  do{
    letter = receiveByte();
    transmitByte(letter);        /* echo */
    text[i] = letter;
    i++;
  } while(!(letter == '\r') && (i < (MAX_TEXT_LENGTH-1)));
  text[i-1] = 0;
}
```

For every letter that you type in over the serial line, another character is stored in the RAM character array `text[]`. This ends when you either send a carriage return (\r) or the maximum length of the text buffer is reached, and then a zero is added to designate the end of the string. Again, when you're looking at this function, remember that it's all done with pointers; inside this function, the character array `text[]` is actually an address in RAM of some variable that's defined in `main()`. So when a letter is stored in `text[]` inside this function, it's actually stored in the RAM locations that go with whatever variable in `main()` was passed to the function.

Previously, we took input from the serial port and stored it in variables, so why do we need pointers and addresses here? In the other examples, everything was taking place from the context of a `main()` function. Here, only the variables defined inside the function `enterText()` and the arguments passed to it (and globals and defines) are available inside that function. The point of passing the string variable `text[]` by its address is that the function can write to memory starting at that address and it will be as if the function wrote directly into the RAM string variable in `main()` that we passed as an argument to this function:

```
void displayCodes(void){
  uint8_t i;
  for (i=0; i<4; i++){
    transmitByte(' ');
    transmitByte('0'+i);
    printString(": ");
    printFromEEPROM(codePointers[i]);
    printString("\r\n");
  }
}
```

displayCodes() is a convenience function that loops over all of the code phrases and prints them out along with their index number. It calls the already-defined printFromEEPROM function to do most of the work involved with actually printing out the strings. But remember in the header when I said to remember that RAM array of pointers to our EEPROM code phrases? Well, this is where it comes in handy.

Each entry in the global array codePointers[] points to the corresponding memory location in EEPROM where the codes are stored, and as a result we get to write slick code like printFromEEPROM(codePointers[i]);. Each entry in codePointers is a pointer to EEPROM—the address of the start of the string in EEPROM memory. So by picking the second codePointer, we get the starting address of the second code string, which we then pass to printFromEEPROM, which then steps through the whole string address by address, byte by byte.

This same array-of-pointers trick also comes in handy in the functions select Code(char code[]) and changeCode(char codeBuffer[]). Because they work very similarly, let's look at selectCode(). Here, the function prints out all the code phrases for us to select from, takes input from us as to which we want to use, and returns the corresponding code string. Only instead of returning the string directly, the main() function passes it the address of a string to selectCode(), and then it's modified in place:

```
void selectCode(char code[]){
  char input;
  char* codeAddress;
  printFromEEPROM(promptSelectCode);
  do{
    displayCodes();
    input = receiveByte();
  } while((input < '0') || (input > '3'));
  codeAddress = codePointers[input-'0'];
  eeprom_read_block(code, codeAddress, CODE_LEN);
}

void changeCode(char codeBuffer[]){
  char input;
  char* codeAddress;
  printString(" -- Choose code phrase to replace:\r\n");
  do{
    displayCodes();
    input = receiveByte();
  } while((input < '0') || (input > '3'));
  codeAddress = codePointers[input-'0'];
  printString(" -- Enter new code: ");
  enterText(codeBuffer);
  eeprom_update_block(codeBuffer, codeAddress, CODE_LEN);
}
```

Remember that the character string in RAM, code[], is passed to the function by the address of its first element. When the line eeprom_read_block(code, codeAddress, CODE_LEN); is run at the end of the function, it is going to pull a string from EEPROM and write it into the RAM *address* &code[0]—the memory address of the RAM string that's available in main().

The pointer array codePointers[] is responsible for getting the right location in EEPROM to copy the data from. Here's how it works. Imagine that we've just typed in the character "2" because we want code phrase number two. input - '0' subtracts the ASCII character values for "2" and "0," resulting in a numeric two. Now the codePointers array stores the memory locations of our four code strings in EEPROM, so codeAddress = codePointers[2] gets the address of code phrase number two.

Now we've got the starting address of a string in RAM memory that was passed as an argument, the starting address of the code string in EEPROM, and the defined macro that says how many bytes to copy. The last line simply block-reads this code phrase data into RAM memory—starting at the address pointed to that was passed as an argument to the function. Because we called this function from main() as selectCode(codeString);, our variable codeString now contains the copied value from EEPROM. I love it when a plan comes together.

The other thing that's cute about this function is the way that the do{}/while{} loop makes sure that we type a valid code number by re-asking us for input until the value lies between 0 and 3. This is important because otherwise we'd accidentally type in a number that's bigger than three, the function would go looking for an EEPROM memory pointer where there aren't any stored, and who knows what would happen!

```c
void encodeVigenere(char text[], char code[]){
  uint8_t codePosition = 0;
  uint8_t textPosition = 0;
  do{
    if (code[codePosition] == 0){   /* loop when at end of code phrase */
      codePosition = 0;
    }
    text[textPosition] += code[codePosition] - 32;
    if (text[textPosition] > 126){
      text[textPosition] -= 95;
    }                          /* keeps within printing characters */
    codePosition++;                       /* and move on to the next */
    textPosition++;
  } while(text[textPosition]);  /* until zero at the end of string */
}

void decodeVigenere(char text[], char code[]){
  uint8_t codePosition = 0;
  uint8_t textPosition = 0;
  do{
```

```
        if (code[codePosition] == 0){
          codePosition = 0;
        }
        if (code[codePosition] > text[textPosition]){
          text[textPosition] += 95;
        }                       /* keeps within printing characters */
        text[textPosition] -= code[codePosition] - 32;
        codePosition++;
        textPosition++;
    } while(text[textPosition]);
}
```

In comparison, the functions encodeVigenere and decodeVigenere are almost boringly straightforward. As mentioned earlier, Vigenère ciphers work by adding the numerical values of a letter in the code phrase to the plaintext to encrypt it, and subtracting the same code phrase from the encrypted text to get the plaintext back. Doing this in C is made easy by the equivalence of numbers and letters in ASCII. The first printable character is "space" at ASCII 32, and the last printable character is "~" at 126—that's 95 printable characters in all. When you add the difference between the code phrase's character and 32 to the text character, wrapping around to the beginning if the sum is too large, you've just Vigenère-ciphered. Decoding is the subtraction version of the same procedure, with bounds-checking to make sure the subtracted characters stay in the printable range.

Conclusion, Parting Words, and Encouragement

20

Learning AVR: The Missing Chapters

That was quite a lot of material! Surely there is nothing left to learn about working with the AVR microcontroller or any of its peripherals, right? Wrong!

By now you should have the base knowledge to read the datasheet or scour around the interwebs to find what you need. In that spirit, here is a list of all the topics that I didn't have room for, but that I feel like you should know about anyway.

The Watchdog Timer

The watchdog system is a very slow timer that can be configured to run from 16 milliseconds all the way up to 8 seconds. It is special in that when it reaches the end of its time, it can fire an interrupt or reset the chip. Why would you want to reset the chip every second?

The primary use of the watchdog timer is as a safeguard against runaway code. If your event loop normally takes, say, 20 milliseconds, you can configure the watchdog timer for 40 milliseconds. At the bottom of your event loop, you zero the watchdog timer out again. When your code is running normally, the watchdog timer will never fire.

But if anything goes horribly wrong and your chip freezes up—say you're doing a blocking wait for peripheral input that never arrives—the watchdog will reset your AVR at least once in a while. You can very cleverly structure your code to take advantage of this and provide nearly foolproof functionality of the first part of your routine.

Another use of the watchdog is as a source of sleep-mode interrupts. If you are putting the chip to sleep for long periods of time, and you configure the watchdog to use a normal interrupt rather than the system reset, it can be a handy wakeup source because it runs so slowly. You can put your chip to sleep for up to eight seconds at a time.

For more on the watchdog system, see the chapter in the datasheet on "System Control and Reset."

Power Savings

I hardly scratched the surface of power saving and sleep modes. You saw how to enter sleep mode and vary the CPU prescaler, but there's even more you can do. For instance, if you really need to minimize power use, you can turn off all of the peripherals that you don't need. Read up on these in the "Power Management" section of the datasheet, but then go straight to the avr/power.h library for implementation because it's much more readable in your code.

My first choice for lowering power consumption is just to stay in sleep mode as much as possible. Following that, I'll shut down whatever peripherals I can, but this gets tricky if you're actually using some of them. A no-code-change method to reduce your power usage is just to use a lower voltage for VCC—all of the A series chips run on 3.3–3.6 V just fine.

Crystals and Alternate Clock Sources

Here, we always used the internal calibrated RC oscillator as a timebase, but you can also supply an external crystal and set some fuses to use it. This gives you the advantage of a super-accurate timebase. I've only really needed a crystal for high-speed USART serial communications and USB emulation. Other people swear by them.

Another option, if you've got an accurate external timebase, is to calibrate the internal oscillator to the external source by varying the byte in the OSCCAL register to change the speed. The problem is that the OSCCAL register is a normal, volatile, register and gets lost on reset.

A solution, once you've found a good value, is to write the calibration byte to a safe place in EEPROM and then read the value back out and store it back in the OS CCAL register as part of your initialization routine at the top of main().

Bootloaders

With a number of the ATmega chips, notably the mega88 and mega168, you have the option to reserve some space at the end of the program memory for a bootloader program that gets automatically called on reset, if the right fuses are enabled. This bootloader code is able to write to program flash memory, so that you can program the chip with only a serial cable. The old-school Arduinos used to do this, for instance.

I'm not a big fan of bootloaders because the serial port depends so much on the CPU speed that it can get messed up if you play around with the CPU speed fuse settings. That said, you can't set the fuses from within a bootloader either, so it makes for a nice safe playground. You should have an ISP on hand as a fallback.

Analog Comparator

The AVR not only has an ADC, but also an analog comparator built in. In short, it can trigger interrupts when the analog voltage on one pin (AIN0) exceeds that on another pin (AIN1). With a fixed voltage threshold, you could just use the ADC and compare it to a number in code. But the ADC allows you to figure out the *difference* between two signals.

The comparator can also share the ADC multiplexer, so you can use same ADC pins in place of AIN1. You *do* have to turn off the ADC to use its multiplexer for the comparator, however.

Debugging

If there's anything I like about microcontrollers, it's putting together a project quickly and having it work. Of course, it's sometimes fun and sometimes frustrating to debug the darn thing for a few hours, but I usually learn something along the way.

Advice on debugging is usually the same old chestnuts, and I'm afraid I'm going to dish them up as well:

- Is it powered?
- Is the reset line pulled low?
- Have you declared variables used in your ISRs as volatile?
- Have you actually called those initialization subroutines that you just defined? (How many times do I write a timer init, and then forget to call the darn function!)
- When all else fails, reduce or simplify to the closest known working state.
- Toss a 0.1 uF decoupling capacitor on the power pins of any or all ICs.
- Never assume anything. Or at least test or verify your assumptions.
- Put LEDs on everything. (Within reason.) Do you see the problem?
- Put oscilloscope probes on everything you can't use an LED for. Are the voltage levels what you expect? Why or why not?
- Buy all critical parts in pairs, and don't hesitate to swap one out if you think it may be buggy. Even if it's a low probability of being the problem, it's a quick fix.

Put This Book Down and Build!

Now get out there and build stuff! Take photos, post project writeups, and post your code for all to see.

Index

Symbols

25LC256.h listing, 352
_BV() macro, 68

A

acceleration control, 333
ADC sleep mode, 253
   (see also noise reduction)
address-of operator, 384
adsr.c listing, 283
AM radio project
   amRadio.c listing, 195
   carrier frequency, 188
   circuit for, 190
   code for, 192
   CPU speed and, 191
   power limits for, 191
   receiver for, 189
   square-wave modulation, 189

American Standard Code for Information Interchange (ASCII), 88
analog comparator, 441
analog outputs (on Arduino), 9
analog sensors, 128, 268
analog-to-digital converters (ADCs)
   accuracy /stability in, 268
   basics of, 127
   exponentially weighted moving averages, 261
   footstep detector project, 254
   hardware overview, 128
   initialization of, 139
   integer division in, 263
   internal voltage reference, 249
   light meter project, 131
   minimum configuration, 131
   night light project, 147

noise reduction in, 247, 253
oscilloscope project, 142
oversampling and, 245, 247, 253
piezoelectric disks and, 254
prescaler options, 139
project supplies, 128, 246
successive approximation and, 130
troubleshooting, 141
uses for, 141
voltage meter project, 246
voltage pre-scaling for, 249
voltage sensors, 128
analogWrite() function, 210
AND operator, 72, 112
Arduino
   analog output in, 9, 210
   AVR programming with, 27
   benefits of, 21
   breadboard connections, 32
   diagram of flash wiring, 28

drawbacks of, xii, 22
flashing as a target, 26
hardware programming in, 29
pin diagram, 23
portpins.h bug, 27
programming toolchain, 20
terminal emulator software, 86
vs. other IDEs, 25
writing C in, 25
arrays, 390
Atmel AVRISP mkII flash programmer, 30
attack-decay-sustain-release (ADSR) volume envelopes, 282, 286
ATtiny44/45, 12
attributions, xvii
averaging vs. oversampling, 248
AVR ATmega microcontrollers
benefits of, xi
built-in pull-up resistor, 109
built-in USART device, 82
C code structure in, 47
configuring serial communication in, 83
driving large loads with, 289
hardware overview, 8
hardware registers in, 49
interfacing over serial, 241
internal clock speed, 191
internal EEPROM on, 416
limited memory in, 4
naming conventions, 12
pin overview, 5
programming in Arduino, 28
(see also programming)
selection of, 12
timer/counters in, 179
voltage reference in, 250
avr-gcc code compiler, 15, 282
avr-size utility program, 387

avr/eeprom.h library, 416, 420
avr/io.h file , 93
AVRDUDE
common configurations, 40
error messages, 38
fuse-bit settings, 193, 428
options for, 38
programmers supported, 16
reading/writing to EEPROM, 419
saving/loading EEPROM, 424
starting, 37
avrMusicBox.c listing, 119

B

back voltage, 300
base resistance, 294
battery power, 59, 250
(see also DC motors)
baud rate, definition of, 80
bipolar-junction transistors (BJTs), 292
bit trading in SPI, 342
bit twiddling
advanced application of, 66
bit shifting, 64, 183
bit-shift roll, 66
bitwise logical operators, 67
clearing bits with AND/NOT, 72
Cylon eyes project, 61, 66
overview of, 77
pin numbering and, 65
project supplies, 62
setting bits with OR, 70
toggling bits with XOR, 71
usefulness of, 61, 74
_BV() macro, 68
bitmasks, 70, 73, 112
bitwise logical operations, 61
blinkenlights, 52

blocking capacitors, 98, 99
Boss Button project
bossButton.c listing, 125
bossButton.py listing, 123
button bounce, 115
buttons, 108, 158
(see also digital input)
(see also interrupt programming)

C

C language
arrays in, 390
ASCII and, 88
AVR code structure, 47
benefits of, xii
bit shifting instructions, 65
code reuse with modules, 96, 242
coding in Arduino IDE, 25
compiler errors, 42
dereferencing operator, 395
functions in, 58
integer division in, 263
memory addresses, 383
naming conventions, 85
zero-indexing in, 65, 104
C99 integer types, ISO standard for, 421
cadmium-sulfide light-dependent resistor (LDR), 131, 142
calibrateTime.py listing, 239
capacitive sensors
circuit for, 168
code for, 170
debugging, 175
global variables and, 172
principle behind, 166
sensor for, 167
timing of, 166
capacitors, 98
capSense.c listing, 170
Central Limit Theorem, 248

central processing unit (CPU)
basics of, 8
CPU clock, 8, 191, 193, 239
noise reduction, 247, 253
setting speed in code, 192
character-to-ASCII converter,
89
clearing bits, 72
cli() function, 163
CLKPR (Clock Prescale Register), 194
clocks
accuracy of, 239, 243
alternate sources for, 440
as timebase, 178
double-speed mode, 94
enabling high-speed, 193
noise reduction and, 247,
253
prescalers for, 8, 139, 187,
191
types of, 8
code editors, 14
code examples, permission to
use, xvii
comparators, 219, 441
compare events, 179
compiler errors, 42, 48, 388
computer-side scripting, 123
configuration registers, input-
output, 50
const keyword, 386
constants, human-friendly
synonyms for, 64
control pulse frequency, 224
cross-platform compatibility,
16, 86
crystal radios, 189
crystals, 440
CTC waveform mode, 180, 186
Cylon eyes project, 61, 66

D

Darlington transistors, 293

data
organization in EEPROM,
425
serial vs. parallel, 342
types of, 421
data framing, 340
data logging, 374, 380
data smoothing, 246
data-direction register (DDR),
49
Data-Direction Register (DDR),
110
datasheets
accessing, 7
External Interrupts section,
163
macro definitions, 92
Power Management and
Sleep Modes, 254
Power Management section, 440
Register Description section, 94
System Control and Reset
section, 440
UCSR0B functions, 92
DC motors
back voltage in, 300
basics of, 299
dcMotorWorkout.c listing,
302
diagram of beadboard, 300
diagram of circuit, 299
flyback diode in, 302
running in reverse, 307
specification for, 305
torque in, 305
vs. stepper motors, 320
DDRx (see data-direction register)
dead band in servo motor, 220
debouncer.c listing, 117
debouncing, 115
debugging
ADC code, 139, 147
ADC output, 141

basic steps to, 441
button press interpretation,
114
capacitive sensors, 175
EEPROM chip installation,
350
global variables, 175
hardware registers, 51, 93
I2C initialization, 371
pin output, 51
pointer initialization, 388
portpins.h bug, 27
programmer-to-AVR communication, 54
sampling frequency, 282
serial port loopback testing,
88
with USART, 97
decomposing-to-pointer rule,
390
define statements, 64, 379
dependencies, keeping track
of, 20
dereferencing operator, 395
desktop-side scripting, 123
differential pulse-code modulation (DPCM)
basics of, 407
encoding two-bit data, 407
wave2DPCM.py encoding,
410
digital input
Boss Button project, 121
button presses, 112
configuration of, 110
debouncing, 115
music box project, 119
project supplies, 107
pushbutton checklist, 122
pushbuttons/switches, 108
state change indicators,
114
digital output
AVR C code structure, 47
blinking LED project, 46, 51
configuration of, 50

hardware registers, 48
POV pattern generator, 45
POV toy, 51
project supplies, 45
digital signal processing (DSP) chip, 282
digital thermometer project, 363, 372
(see also I2C protocol)
digital-to-analog converters (DACs), 129, 213
direct digital synthesis (DDS)
accumulators, 275
ADSR envelopes, 286
auxiliary files for, 286
basics of, 272
code for, 276
debugging for speed, 282
digital signal processing chip and, 282
dynamic volume control, 282
fatSaw.c listing, 279
lowpass filter and, 278
mixing, 279
project overview, 271
project supplies, 271
pseudocode for, 273
PWM frequency and, 272
sample rate and, 278
sine wave creation, 276
summary of, 275
DRAM (dynamic random access memory), 346
drive modes, h-bridge
coasting, 318
comparison of, 317
locked anti-phase, 316
sign-magnitude, 316
states available, 315
drivers, for Windows, 37
duty cycles, 203
dynamic volume control, 282

E

EEPROM (electrically erasable programmable read-only memory)
automatic erase settings, 428
AVRDUDE terminal mode, 419
benefits of external, 346
block update command, 417
convenience functions, 358
data organization in, 425
defining memory locations, 378
detecting a write completion, 420
float type variables and, 417
hookup of external, 349
initialization of, 427
initSPI function, 356
internal size limits, 379, 416
lifespan of, 417
quickDemo.c listing, 418
reading from, 421
saving and loading, 424
utility functions for, 416
write cycle limits, 416
electro-motive force (EMF), 300
encryption/decryption project
encryption used in, 429
vigenereCipher.h listing, 430
vigenereCipher_outline.c listing, 433
errors
AVRDUDE errors, 38
compiler errors, 42, 388
I2C error codes, 371
PB1 undeclared, 27
programming errors, 42
(see also debugging)

event loops, 48, 58, 156, 380, 439
exponentially weighted moving averages (EWMA), 261

F

fatSaw.c listing, 279
fixed-width variable type names, 421
flash memory
basics of, 347
determining file size, 387
memory addresses, 383
overview of, 394
pointers and, 386
PROGMEM variables, 386
progmemDemo1.c listing, 384
talking voltmeter project, 396
flash programmers, 16, 27, 30
floating-point math, 251, 417
flyback diodes, 302
footstep detector project
bias voltage in, 261
circuit for, 256
code for, 264
components used, 254
exponentially weighted moving averages and, 261
integer division in, 263
overview of, 268
theory behind, 260
for() loops, 76, 174
free-running ADC mode, 138, 145
frequency
control pulse frequency, 224
cutoff frequency, 278
PWM voltage level and, 272
sampling frequency, 282
selection of in PWM, 203

FTDI cables, pinout summary, 85

functions
 in C language, 58
 naming conventions for, 85
 pointers as arguments to, 390
 prototyping of, 96
 scope of, 58

fuse bits, 192, 428

G

GCC code compiler, 15, 48, 112
gearmotors, 305
gedit text editor, 14
global variables, 172

H

H-bridges
 alternatives to, 326
 avoiding shoot-through in, 310, 318
 avoiding short-circuit mode, 311, 318
 chip for dual, 327
 chip selection, 319
 coasting mode, 318
 diagrams of, 310, 311, 314
 digital logic control in, 312
 DIY vs. ready-made, 308
 drive state comparison, 317
 drive states available, 315
 four-wire control of, 314
 hBridgeWorout.c listing, 312
 locked anti-phase drive mode, 316
 project supplies, 308
 sign-magnitude drive mode, 316
 stepper motors and, 320

hardware flash programmers
 Arduino, 29
 Atmel AVRISP mkII, 30
 LadyAda's USBTinyISP, 31
 Parallel Port, 30
 USBTiny/USBasp, 31

hardware peripherals
 analog/digital converters (ADCs), 10
 benefits of, xiii, 5
 clocks for, 8
 configuration of, 91
 interrupt service routines, 10
 interrupt system, 155
 power saving and, 440
 serial communication with, 9
 timer/counters, 11, 177

hardware registers, 48, 50, 64, 65, 93

helloInterrupt.c listing, 159

human-readable code, 64, 85, 183

I

I/O registers, 7

I2C protocol
 addressing scheme in, 363
 benefits of, 361
 bus speeds in, 371
 byte acknowledgement, 364
 code for, 369
 data logging in, 374
 data timing in, 363
 demo hookup, 367
 demo library, 368
 EEPROM configuration, 378
 error codes in, 371
 event loops in, 380
 function of, 363
 initialization of, 370
 overview of, 366

 project supplies, 361
 speed limits in, 367
 thermometer project, 372
 UART serial menu and, 379
 vs. two-wire interface, 362

initI2C function, 369
initInterrupt0() function, 160
initSPI function, 356
initTimers() function, 208
initUSART() function, 84, 90

input-output configuration registers, 50

inputs, 9
 (see also digital input)

INT0/INT1 external interrupts, 158

integers
 division in C language, 263
 floating-point math, 251, 417
 pre-C99 types, 421
 signed, 277
 unsigned, 76
 using 32-bit, 4

internally triggered interrupts, 157

interrupt programming
 AVR pinouts/PCINT names, 165
 capacitive sensors, 166
 externally triggered, 157
 function of, 161
 INT0/INT1 external interrupts, 158
 internally triggered, 157
 interrupt vector names, 161
 ISR() function, 160, 253
 pin-change interrupts, 163
 polling-style programming, 156
 real-time response, 158
 sleep-mode interrupts, 440
 turning interrupts on/off, 163
 usefulness of, 155, 157

Interrupt Service Routines (ISRs), 10, 157, 253
interrupt vector names, 161, 162
ISP headers, 35
ISR() function, 160, 172, 253

L

LadyAda's USBTinyISP flash programmer, 31
LDR (see cadmium-sulfide light-dependent resistor)
LEDs
  connection of, 33
  current-limiting resistors for, 52
  dimming with PWM, 202
  naming with zero-indexing, 65
less-than-or-equal-to construction, 104
light meter project
  ADC initialization, 139
  ADC power pins, 135
  circuit for, 131
  code for, 137
  potentiometer, 136
  uses for, 131, 141
lightSensor.c listing, 137
Linux
  AVRDUDE errors, 40
  programming toolchain, 16
  Python installation, 123
  terminal emulator software, 86
locked anti-phase drive mode, 316
logging digital thermometer project, 363, 372
lowpass filters, 278

M

Mac OS
  programming toolchain, 20
  Python installation, 123
  terminal emulator software, 86
macros
  datasheet definitions of, 92
  GCC convenience macros, 112
  power minimizing with, 192
  PROGMEM macro, 383
  _BV() macro, 68
main loop, 48
main() function, 47, 58
make/makefiles
  configuration of, 40
  dependency tracking, 20
  determining file size, 387
  function of, 16
master SPI device, 341
math coprocessors, 4
memory
  chip selection and, 12
  flash memory, 381
  interfacing with external, 339
  memory addresses, 383
  types of, 8
  types of external, 346
  waveform storage and, 287
microcontroller projects
  AM radio, 188
  basic kit for, xiv
  blinking LEDs, 31, 46, 51
  Boss Button, 121
  capacitive sensor, 166
  Cylon eyes, 61
  footstep detector, 254
  light meter, 131
  logging accelerometer, 158
  logging digital thermometer, 363
  loopbacks, 83

music box, 119
night light, 147
oscilloscope project, 142
permission for code use, xvii
servo sundial, 226
software vs. hardware approach to, xii
square-wave organ, 97, 184
talking voltmeter, 396
Vigenère cipher encoder/decoder, 429
voltage meter, 246
microcontroller-controlled resistance, 142
microcontroller-specific library routines, 63
microcontrollers
  basics of, 3
  built-in peripherals for, 5
  function of, xi, 5
  interfacing with desktop computer, 79, 126
  limitations on, 4
  similarities among brands, xii, xiii
  user interaction with, 108
  uses for, xi, 5
microstepping, 336
mixing digital audio, 279
modules, 96, 242
MOSFETs (metal oxide silicon field-effect) transistors
  2N7000, 55, 293
  gate charge, 297
  gate driver chips, 296
motion detector (see footstep detector project)
motors
  back voltage in, 300
  DC motors, 299
  H-bridges for, 307
  project supplies, 308
  stepper motors, 307, 320
  unipolar, 326

moving averages
EWMA implementation, 261
usefulness of, 246
multiplexing
analog comparator and, 441
multiplexer (mux) switch, 130
nightlight project and, 147
setting mux bits, 148
music (see direct digital synthesis; music box project; square-wave organ project)
music box project, 119

N

negative numbers, 421
night light project
circuit for, 150
code for, 150
multiplexing and, 147
noise reduction, 247, 253, 254
NOT operator, 72
Notepad text editor, 14

O

OCRn (Output Compare Register), 179
OR operator, 70
oscilloscope project
AVR code for, 143
desktop code for, 145
synergies and, 147
uses for, 142
outputs, 8
(see also digital output)
oversampling
basics of, 247
practical limit on, 253
usefulness of, 245
vs. averaging, 248

P

Parallel Port flash programmer, 30
PCINT (pin-change interrupts), 163
persistence-of-vision (POV) toy
basis of, 51
building the circuit, 52
code for, 56
creating patterns, 58
POVDisplay function, 57
simplest version of, 53
switch for, 55
persistence-of-vision (POV), pattern generation with, 45
phase, SPI protocol, 357
photocells/photoresistors, 132
piezoelectric disks, 254
pinout diagram, 6
pins
accessing with I/O registers, 7
ADC power pins, 135
analog output from, 210
arrangement of, 6
dedicated to PWM, 206
default state of, 50
define statements for, 64
diagram of, 5
diagram of Arduino labels, 23
diagram of ISP connectors, 32
diagram of PCINT names, 165
diagram of SN754410, 327
digital inputs of, 9, 110
digital outputs of, 8, 48
FTD cable pinout summary, 85
function of, 5
naming conventions, 6, 87
pin masks, 163

pin-change interrupts, 163
RESET pin, 55
serial pin connection, 87
zero-indexing and, 65
PINx hardware register, 50
playNote() function, 100, 119, 177
pointers
address storage in, 390
address-of operator, 384
arrays and, 390
as arguments to functions, 390
basics of, 387
dereferencing operator, 395
progmemDemo2.c listing, 388
polarity, SPI protocol, 357
polling-style program, 156, 285
port x data registers, 50
port x input pins address, 50
portpins.h bug, 27
potentiometers (pots), 136, 142
POVDisplay function, 57
power down mode, 254
power management, 440
power supply
ADC power pins, 135
battery power, 59, 250
connection of, 32
LED indicator for, 33
minimizing use with macros, 192
printBinaryByte() function, 89, 95
printByte() function, 95
printString() function, 84, 95
PROGMEM macro
data structures, 397
data variables, 386
function of, 383
pointer arrays, 400
progmemDemo1.c listing, 384

program memory, size limitations on, 4
  (see also flash memory)
Programmer's Notepad, 14
programming
  Arduino environment, 21
  basic steps of, 16
  basic supplies needed, 14
  checking installation with
    AVRDUDE, 37
  flashing, 42
  hookup, 31
  ISP headers, 35
  overview of, 13
  software toolchain, 16
  toolchain overview, 14
  troubleshooting, 42
pull-up resistors, 109, 350
pulse-code modulation, 407
pulse-width modulation
  (PWM)
  advanced techniques using
    (see direct digital synthesis)
  alternatives to, 213
  average value control, 202
  basics of, 201
  differential pulse-code
    modulation, 407
  duty cycle specification,
    203
  fast mode, 208
  frequency selection, 203
  H-bridges and, 315
  LED dimming with, 202
  manual routine for, 204
  on non-dedicated pins, 210
  overview of, 213
  project supplies, 201
  pwm.c listing, 204
  pwmOnAnyPin.c listing,
    211
  pwmTimers.c listing, 206
  ripple tolerance, 203
  timer initialization, 208
  timers demo, 206

Vactrols and, 142
pushbuttons, 107, 122, 158
  (see also digital input)
  (see also interrupt programming)
Python
  benefits of, 104
  code modules, 242
  debugging with serial-
    Scope.py, 139, 332
  DPCM encoding with, 410
  installation of, 123
  pyserial library, 146
  readTime() function, 241
  terminal emulator software,
    86
  wavetable pre-calculation
    with, 287

Q

quickDemo.c listing, 418

R

RAM
  limitations on, 4
  single-bit memory networks in, 49
random toggling, 76
rated voltage, 305
RC oscillators, 440
reactance, 134
reaction time, testing, 180
readTime() function, 241
real-time responses, 158
receiveByte() function, 84
Register Description section,
  93
relays, 296
RESET pin, 55
resistance, microcontroller-
  controlled, 142
resistor tolerance, 249

return(0), 48
ripple voltage, 203
RX-TX hookup, 87

S

sample and hold circuit, 130
sample rate, 278
scope, of variables in C language, 58
SD/MMC cards, 347
sei() function, 163
sensors
  analog, 128
  capacitive touch, 166
  voltage, 128
serial communication
  AVR configuration, 83
  built-in peripherals for, 9
  computer setup, 85
  implementation of, 83
  local echo, 88
  loopback testing, 88
  project supplies, 79
  servo motor I/O, 237
  SPI protocol for, 339
  square-wave organ project,
    97
  synchronous vs. asynchronous, 83, 340, 363
  terminal emulator software,
    86
  troubleshooting, 89
  USART basics, 80
  USART overview, 105
  USB-serial adapter, 85
serial communications
  USART polling, 285
serial library, installation of,
  123
serial pins, connection of, 87
serial protocols, 80
serial-to-TCP/IP bridge, 126
serialLoopback.c listing, 84
serialOrgan.c listing, 101

serialScope.py listing, 145
servo motors
    code for, 221
    connecting to AVR, 220
    control pulse frequency, 224
    control signal in, 219
    function of, 219
    position controls in, 218
    project supplies, 218
    servoWorkout.c listing, 221
    sundial project, 226
    uses for, 218
servoClockFunctions.c listing, 235
servoSerialHelpers.c listing, 237
servoSundial.c listing, 231
servoSundial.h listing, 234
setting bits, 80
shift registers, 342
shoot-through, in H-bridges, 310, 318
sign-magnitude H-bridge drive mode, 316
simpleButton.c listing, 113
sine waves, using DDS (direct-digital synthesis), 276
single-conversion triggering, 138
sizeof(), 394
slave devices, in SPI protocol, 341
slave-select pin, in SPI protocol, 356
sleep mode, 253, 440
    (see also noise reduction)
slowscope, 142
slowScope.c listing, 143
SN754410 dual H-bridge chips, 327
software toolchain
    Arduino setup, 20
    Linux setup, 16
    Mac setup, 20
    make/makefiles, 20

Windows setup, 18
solid state relays (SSRs), 298
sound (see direct digital synthesis) (see square-wave organ project) (see talking voltmeter project)
speech playback (see talking voltmeter project)
speed
    debugging high-speed issues, 282
    limitations on, 4
    setting in code, 192
    speed profiles, 334
SPI (serial peripheral interface)
    benefits of, 339
    bit trading in, 342
    bus setup, 341
    clock phase/polarity, 357
    configuration overview, 359
    convenience functions, 358
    data framing in, 340
    data logging in, 374
    EEPROM hookup, 349
    EEPROM library C code, 354
    EEPROM memory chip and, 346
    function of, 340
    initSPI function, 356
    output pins and, 356
    shift registers in, 342
    SPI demo code, 350
    SPI library header, 352
    SPI_tradeByte function, 357
square-wave organ project
    additional files for, 104
    amplification for, 99
    code for, 101
    keyboard for, 97
    keypress conversion, 104
    library for, 100
    speaker capacitor, 98
    timer/counters and, 184
SRAM (static random access memory), 346
stall current, 305

start bits, UART serial, 80
state change, testing for, 114
stepper motors
    acceleration control, 333
    basics of, 320
    bifilar stepper motors, 326
    code for, 330
    diagrams of, 321, 325, 336
    dual H-bridge chip, 327
    full/half stepping, 322
    H-bridges for, 320
    half-stepping coil currents, 324
    kinds of, 321
    microstepping, 336
    project supplies, 308
    trapezoid speed profile, 334
    usefulness of, 307
    vs. brushed DC motors, 320
    wire identification, 325
stop bits, USART serial, 80
successive approximation DAC, 130
sundial project
    calibrateTime.py listing, 239
    calibration, 239
    circuit for, 230
    clock for, 235
    code for, 231
    laser attachment, 226
    laser preparation, 229
    positioning, 228
    range of motion for, 228
    serial I/O for, 237
    servoClockFunctions.c listing, 235
    servoSerialHelpers.c listing, 237
    servoSundial.c listing, 231
    servoSundial.h listing, 234

T

talking voltmeter project
    audio data generation, 406

diagram of flash memory pointers, 401
differential pulse-code modulation, 407
ISR() function, 405
main() function, 405
overview of, 396
pointer arrays, 400
sound playback, 402
speech generation for, 397
talkingVoltmeter.c listing, 402
talkingVoltmeter.h listing, 397
TCNTn (timer/counter register), 178
terminal emulator software, 85, 86
text editors, 14
TextMate, 14
thermometer project, 363, 372
timebases, 440
timer/counters
    AM radio project, 188
    basics of, 11
    block diagram, 178
    clock prescaler settings, 187
    configuration checklist, 215
    overview of, 198
    project supplies, 177
    PWM demo, 206
    PWM initialization, 208
    reaction time testing, 180
    servo motor configuration, 223
    square-wave organ, 184
    timerAudio.c listing, 184
    types included, 179
    usefulness of, 177
    watchdog timer, 439
    waveform generation modes, 180
toggleButton.c listing, 114
toggling bits, 71
torque, 305
touch sensors, 166

transistor switches
    bipolar-junction transistors, 292
    Darlington transistors, 293
    driving large loads with, 290
    high- vs. low-side, 291
    metal oxide silicon field-effect transistors (MOSFETs), 293
    overview of, 298
    project supplies, 290
    relays, 296
    summary of, 298
    triacs/SSRs, 298
transistors
    bipolar-junction transistors, 292
    Darlington transistors, 293
    driving large loads with, 289
    selecting base resistor, 294
transmitByte() function, 84
trapezoid speed profile, 334
triacs, 298
troubleshooting, 42, 89
    (see also debugging)
    (see also errors)
TWI (two-wire interface) protocol, 362
two's complement order, 421

U

UART/USART serial
    additional uses for, 97
    configuration of, 83, 90
    data logging with, 374
    difference between, 83
    I2C protocol, 379
    overview of, 105
    polled serial input, 285
    synchronous vs. asynchronous communication, 340

transmitting/receiving with, 94
    UART serial basics, 80
    UART.c file, 90
UCSR0B register, 92
UDRE0 (USART0 Data Register Empty), 94
USB-serial adapter, setup of, 85
USBTiny/USBasp flash programmers, 31

V

Vactrols, 142
variables
    definition of, 58
    float-type, 417
    global variables, 172
    naming conventions, 85
    pointers and, 387
    PROGMEM variables, 386
    variable types, 383
Vigenère cipher, 429
volatile keyword, 173
voltage dividers, 131, 213, 247
voltage meter project
    circuit for, 247
    code for, 251
    design specifications, 246
    oversampling in, 247
    overview of, 268
    resistor tolerance, 249
    sleep modes, 253
    supplies needed, 246
    voltage scaling in, 249
voltage sensors, 128
voltmeter.c listing, 251
volume control, 282

W

watchdog timer, 439
wave2DPCM.py program, 410

waveform modes, PWM hardware, 179, 208, 287
wear leveling, 417
while() loops, 48, 67
Windows
 drivers for, 37
 programming toolchain, 18

Python installation, 123
terminal emulator software, 86

X

XOR operator, 71

zero-indexing, 65, 104

About the Author

Elliot Williams is a Ph.D. in economics, a former government statistician, and a lifelong electronics hacker. He was among the founding members of HacDC, Washington DC's hackerspace, and served as president and vice president for three years. He now lives in Munich, Germany, where he works for an embedded hardware development firm that has, to date, exactly one employee (and CEO). This book came out of his experiences teaching AVR programming workshops at HacDC.

Colophon

The cover and body font is BentonSans, the heading font is Serifa, and the code font is Bitstreams Vera Sans Mono.

CPSIA information can be obtained at www.ICGtesting.com
Printed in the USA
BVOW10s1452181115

427638BV00005B/17/P